The Olmec World

RITUAL AND RULERSHIP

The Olmec World

RITUAL AND RULERSHIP

with essays by

Michael D. Coe, Richard A. Diehl, David A. Freidel, Peter T. Furst,

F. Kent Reilly, III, Linda Schele, Carolyn E. Tate, Karl A. Taube

Principal Photographers

John Bigelow Taylor

Justin Kerr and Bruce M. White

THE ART MUSEUM, PRINCETON UNIVERSITY

in association with Harry N. Abrams, Inc.

This book was published on the occasion of the exhibition "The Olmec World: Ritual and Rulership," organized by The Art Museum, Princeton University.

The Art Museum, Princeton University
December 16, 1995–February 25, 1996

The Museum of Fine Arts, Houston
April 14–June 9, 1996

The exhibition and publication of this book were made possible in part by Leonard H. Bernheim, Jr., '59, and Stephanie Bernheim; The Brown Foundation, Inc., Houston; The Frelinghuysen Foundation; the Friends of The Art Museum, Princeton University; The Henfield Foundation; the Jay I. Kislak Philanthropic Fund; Alastair B. Martin, '38; The Curtis W. McGraw Foundation; The Andrew W. Mellon Foundation; the National Endowment for the Arts; Neutrogena Corporation through Lloyd E. Cotsen, '50; the New Jersey State Council on the Arts/Department of State; Gillian T. Sackler; and D. J. and Jane Sibley.

Paper and cloth editions published by The Art Museum, Princeton University, Princeton, New Jersey 08544-1018

Cloth edition distributed in 1996 by Harry N. Abrams, Incorporated, New York
A Times Mirror Company

Managing Editor: Jill Guthrie
Project Coordinator: Matthew H. Robb
Consulting Editor: Elizabeth P. Benson
Copy Editor: Brenda Gilchrist
Designer: Bruce Campbell
Typesetter: Paul Baker Typography, Inc.
Printer: Arnoldo Mondadori Editore
Map Design: American Custom Maps, Albuquerque, New Mexico
Principal Photographers: John Bigelow Taylor, Justin Kerr, Bruce M. White

Cover illustration: *Shaman in Transformation Pose*, 800–600 B.C., Veracruz. Polished gray stone with traces of cinnabar, h. 17.5 cm.; w. 15.5 cm.; d. 9 cm. The Art Museum, Princeton University, Museum purchase, gift of Mrs. Gerard B. Lambert by exchange (cat. no. 42). Frontispiece: *Standing Figure Holding Supernatural Effigy*, 800–500 B.C., Mexico. Jade, h. 21.9 cm.; w. 8.1 cm.; d. 4.1 cm. The collection of Robin B. Martin, currently on loan to The Brooklyn Museum (cat. no. 35). Catalogue Frontispiece: *Supernatural Riding a Jaguar*, 900–600 B.C., Río Pesquero, Veracruz. Gray-green jadeite, h. 8.9 cm.; w. 3.1 cm.; d. 5 cm. Private collection (cat. no. 63).

Library of Congress Catalog Card Number 95-78295
ISBN 0-943012-19-8 (paper) / ISBN 0-8109-6311-6 (cloth)

Printed in Italy

For Gillett G. Griffin
genius locus of pre-Columbian Art
who brought the wonders of the arts of the Americas
to Princeton and taught us to understand and appreciate
the artistic legacy and the nobility and humanity
of these great indigenous civilizations.

Contents

Foreword and Acknowledgments

A major exhibition of Olmec art is long overdue and much awaited. Of the great Mesoamerican civilizations, the Maya and the Aztec have received the most public attention, particularly the former because of the advances in the decipherment of hieroglyphs. In contrast and perhaps because of a lack of comparable linguistic tools, the Olmec have received relatively scant attention despite the grandeur of the monuments, the extraordinary beauty, power, and technical brilliance of the portable objects, and their seminal importance to the development of later Mesoamerican civilizations. With the exception of one monumental work and the head of a life-size statue, the exhibition is comprised of over 250 superb, small-scale objects in ceramic, jade, and stone, many never publicly exhibited or published. The decision to limit the exhibition to objects from the United States was a practical one, but it has demonstrated the great wealth of material in this country, with which we have been able to bring the themes of the exhibition and catalogue to life.

In the selection of the objects for the exhibition, we have tried to observe the date of their entry into the United States as carefully as possible. The majority of objects are recorded in this country before 1972, although in some instances that information was accepted on faith. Whether or not an object entered the country before or after 1972 does not mitigate or compensate for the loss of archaeological context. It is impossible to turn one's back on these works of art and important cultural artifacts, however, and they have been selected and presented in an attempt to understand them within the ideological, ritual, and political context for which they were created. It was very moving to read in a letter from Mariano Audelino Péréz Péréz and Antonio de la Torre López, president and secretary of the Board of Trustees of the Ik'al Ojov Cultural Center, authorizing the loan of objects to the exhibition from the National Museum of the American Indian: "We look forward to contributing to the knowledge about the cultures from whom we originate...." We are most grateful to all the lenders, public and private, who have been so forthcoming and hope that the exhibition and catalogue will in some measure repay their generosity.

The distinguished scholars who have contributed the essays have brought the breadth and depth of their knowledge of ancient Mesoamerica to bear on the Olmec. The essay by David A. Freidel, Department of Anthropology, Southern Methodist University, situates the Olmec within the perspective of Mesoamerican civilization. Richard A. Diehl, Department of Anthropology, University of Alabama at Tuscaloosa, and Michael D. Coe, professor emeritus, Department of Anthropology, Yale University, provide a comprehensive account of the history and current state of Olmec archaeology, and Carolyn E. Tate, assistant professor, Department of Art, Texas Tech University, defines and discusses the Olmec art style. Peter T. Furst, adjunct professor, Department of Anthropology, University of Pennsylvania; F. Kent Reilly, III, assistant professor, Department of Anthropology, Southwest Texas State University; Linda Schele, John D. Murchison Regents Professor of Art, University of Texas at Austin; and Karl A. Taube, associate professor, Department of Anthropology, University of California at Riverside, interpret the ideological and ritual functions and political implications of Olmec objects, further explored in the catalogue entries. We are most grateful to George E. Harlow, Graduate School Class of 1977, curator of Minerals and Gems, Department of Earth and Planetary Sciences, American Museum of Natural History, for precise mineralogical identifications and descriptions of many of the lithic objects in the exhibition.

Mention must be made of those by now historical figures, the generation of archaeologists, art historians, anthropologists, curators, artists, and collectors who were the first to recognize the significance of the Olmec and their great legacy, and who built the foundation on which this catalogue ultimately rests: Ignacio Bernal, Robert Woods Bliss, Alfonso Caso, Miguel Covarrubias, Gordon F. Ekholm, who studied and authenticated the majority of objects in this exhibition and catalogue, Marshall H. Saville, Matthew W. Stirling, and George C. Vaillant.

While it is our hope the catalogue will provide a useful approach to the study of Olmec art and new information and interpretations that will stimulate debate and research in the field, it has been organized and written as a narrative with a general audience in mind. The thematic structure of the exhibition and catalogue of the objects was a collaborative effort based on the material and interpretations of Carolyn E. Tate and F. Kent Reilly, III, with contributions by Gillett G. Griffin, Matthew H. Robb, and Karl A. Taube. Elizabeth P. Benson, consulting editor, vetted the catalogue of gratuitous errors, and Brenda Gilchrist, copy editor, polished our grammar and style. The index is by Peter Rooney, whose reputation is well-deserved. The quality of the illustrations is due to the three principal, outstanding photographers, John Bigelow Taylor, Justin Kerr, and Bruce M. White. We also are indebted to many photographers across the country, both private and those in museums, for their excellent work.

We would not have entrusted this catalogue to any designer but Bruce Campbell, who has been assisted by Anandaroop Roy. Many of the excellent drawings are by James A. Campbell, Bruce's son, and Princeton University graduate student Tina Najbjerg. Bruce Daniel of American Custom Maps designed the maps of Mesoamerica. We are extremely grateful to the staff of Paul Baker Typography and to Peter Garlid and Stefano Marescotti of

Arnoldo Mondadori Editore for their excellent work in typesetting and printing the catalogue, and to Paul Gottlieb of Harry N. Abrams, Inc., for his enthusiasm and interest in the project.

A special word must be said about Matthew H. Robb as his title, project coordinator, does not truly reflect his contribution to the scholarly apparatus, content, writing, and realization of the catalogue. He is Princeton Class of 1994, a student of Gillett G. Griffin, and received the Grace May Tilton Senior Thesis Prize for his thesis on the Olmec. He joined the project as a research assistant and quickly exceeded all expectations in his command and critical judgment of the material, and his ability to get the job done.

Jill Guthrie, managing editor, willed the catalogue into being. This catalogue has been the most demanding of her considerable professional skills as an editor and production manager, and I am sure the authors and all associated with the catalogue will attest to her formidable ability to motivate and persuade others to the exacting standards she brings to all the Museum's publications. Our debt to her is immeasurable.

A great many people must be thanked for their moral and practical support. Dr. E. Wyllys Andrews, The Middle American Research Institute, Tulane University; Brent R. Benjamin, Museum of Fine Arts, Boston; Jeffrey Blomster, Anthropology Department, Yale University; Kimberly A. Bush and Carol Robbins, Dallas Museum of Art; Diane Dubler; Diana Fane, The Brooklyn Museum; Virginia M. Fields, Los Angeles County Museum; Genevieve Fisher, Peabody Museum of Archaeology and Ethnology, Harvard University; Claudia Giancola and John Menser, Ancient Art of the New World; Sidney M. Goldstein, Saint Louis Art Museum; Stacey Goodman, Sotheby's; Julie Jones, who in addition to her help with loans from The Metropolitan Museum of Art, was a most appreciated listener; Peter David Joralemon, who is credited throughout the catalogue for his pioneering and fundamental work on Olmec iconography; Barbara Kerr; Mary Jane Lenz, Ramiro Matos, and Mary T. Nooney, National Museum of the American Indian, Smithsonian Institution; Patrick McCaughey, Wadsworth Atheneum; Gordon McEwan and Becky Smith, Denver Art Museum; Vivian Merrin; Sandra Noble, The Foundation for the Advancement of Mesoamerican Studies; Eve Nolan, National Geographic Image Collection; Ronald D. Normandeau, Anthropos; Diane Pelrine, Indiana University Art Museum; Linda Schildkraut, the Merrin Gallery, was endlessly patient with faxes and phone calls and always helpful; Paul Schweizer, Munson-Williams-Proctor Institute Museum of Art; Jane M. Walsh, National Museum of Natural History, Smithsonian Institution; Stephen L. Worthington, Hudson Museum, University of Maine; Margaret Young-Sánchez, The Cleveland Museum of Art. At the University, David Blinder, director, and Sue Hartshorn, associate director, of the Development Office; Kevin R. Perry, Interactive Computer Graphics Laboratory, Office of Computing and Information Technology; Janice J. Powell and the staff of Marquand Library; and Lorraine A. Sciarra, University counsel, were very supportive of the project.

Edward and Samuel Merrin were of inestimable help persuading collectors to lend key objects and expediting photographs. Judith Small Nash very kindly interceded with collectors on our behalf, and Alphonse Jax and John A. Stokes, Jr., shared their first-hand knowledge of many of the works of art.

The regulations of another institution prevent me from naming the designer of the installation of the exhibition. In addition to his professional credentials, he also is a serious student of the Olmec. His knowledge and sympathy for the material have intelligently informed the presentation of the objects. David and Mair Digges La Touche and Shelly Uhlir of Benchmark executed the elegant and unobtrusive mounts, and Gene Clarici as always did a superb job with the silk screening.

Everyone in the Museum has contributed in some way to the exhibition and catalogue, and all have to be thanked for being patient with the director, who was distracted from so many other duties by this project. Several members of the staff must be singled out for their direct involvement and contributions. Charles K. Steiner, associate director, was tireless and effective in coordinating the fundraising campaign and preparing contracts, and was ably assisted by Mary Anne Randall, business manager. Maureen McCormick, registrar, and Ann V. Gunn, associate registrar, carried out the complicated logistics required for over 250 widely dispersed loans with their usual professional thoroughness and care. Karen Richter, assistant, registrar's office, especially is to be thanked for her assistance with photography. Alison Speckman has done a superb job of printing many of the black-and-white photographs. Nicola Knipe, Cara Reichel '96, and Carla Zimowsk provided invaluable assistance to Jill Guthrie. Craig Hoppock, building superintendent, supervised the construction for the installation and the cases. Also to be thanked are Evan Scheele and Michael Hall, preparators, and Hal Jones and the staff of Atelier Art Services for preparing the exhibition for travel to Houston.

Financial support for the exhibition came from many sources, all of whom are most gratefully acknowledged: Leonard H. Bernheim, Jr., '59, and Stephanie Bernheim; The Brown Foundation, Inc., Houston; The Frelinghuysen Foundation; the Friends of The Art Museum, Princeton University; The Henfield Foundation; the Jay I. Kislak Philanthropic Fund; Alastair B. Martin, '38; The Curtis W. McGraw Foundation; The Andrew W. Mellon Foundation; the National Endowment for the Arts;

Neutrogena Corporation through Lloyd E. Cotsen, '50; the New Jersey State Council on the Arts/Department of State; Gillian T. Sackler; and D. J. and Jane Sibley.

The last major public exhibition devoted to the Olmec, "The Olmec Tradition," was organized by The Museum of Fine Arts, Houston, in 1963. It is especially appropriate, therefore, that the exhibition will be shown at Houston. The immediate and enthusiastic response to the exhibition by Anne Schaffer, curator, African Art and Art of Oceania and the Americas at Houston, supported by the director, Peter C. Marzio, is very much appreciated.

An exhibition on the Olmec has long been the dream of Gillett G. Griffin, research curator of pre-Columbian and Native American Art at the Museum, and one of the most passionate and stalwart champions of Olmec art. In his writings he has signaled Guerrero as an important source of Olmec objects and added to the canon of monuments through his discoveries of Monument 10 at Chalcatzingo and, with Carlo T. E. Gay, the murals at Juxtlahuaca, Guerrero. We hope the dedication of this catalogue expresses, in some measure, Princeton's great debt to him.

Allen Rosenbaum
Director
The Art Museum, Princeton University

Lenders to the Exhibition

The Art Museum, Princeton University

Leonard and Stephanie Bernheim

The Brooklyn Museum

Landon T. Clay

The Cleveland Museum of Art

Claudia Stokes Cooney

Dallas Museum of Art

Denver Art Museum

John B. Elliott

The Foundation for the Advancement of Mesoamerican Studies

Gillett G. Griffin

Sandy Gross and Anne Conaway

Hudson Museum, University of Maine

Indiana University Art Museum

The Jay I. Kislak Foundation

Herbert L. Lucas

Los Angeles County Museum of Art

Louis and Dena Marienthal

Christopher B. Martin

Dana B. Martin

Robin Martin

Jan and Frederick Mayer

Samuel Merrin

Vivian and Edward Merrin

The Metropolitan Museum of Art

The Middle American Research Institute, Tulane University, New Orleans

National Museum of the American Indian, Smithsonian Institution

Munson-Williams-Proctor Institute, Museum of Art, Utica, New York

Museum of Fine Arts, Boston

Peabody Museum of Archaeology and Ethnology, Harvard University

Private Collections

The Saint Louis Art Museum

Elena Austen Stokes

John A. Stokes, Jr.

Marisol Hernandez de Stokes

Rebecca Herrero Stokes

Wadsworth Atheneum, Hartford

Mr. and Mrs. Raymond Wielgus

Mr. and Mrs. William B. Ziff

Dr. and Mrs. Wally Zollman

The Olmec World

RITUAL AND RULERSHIP

MESOAMERICA

Gulf of Mexico

Gulf Coast

Yucatan
Peninsula

Highlands

Itzaccihuatl
Popocatepetl

Balsas River

Nexapa River

Tepecuacuilco
River

Amatzinac
River

Balsas River

MEXICO

Lake Catemaco
Tuxtla Mts   Chacalapa River
Cerro Cintepec   Coatzalcalcos River
Río Bari
Chiquito
River   Tonala
Heartland   River
Laguna
Manatí
Uspanapa   Grijalva
Coatzalcalcos   River   River
River   Coachapa
Isthmus   River
of
Tehuantepec

Usumacinta
River

Usumacinta
River

BELIZE

Gulf
of
Tehuantepec

GUATEMALA

Motagua
River

HONDURAS

Pacific Ocean

EL
SALVADOR

NICARAGUA

COSTA
RICA

Figure 1. Map of Mesoamerica.

0   25   50   75   100
miles

0   25   50   75   100
kilometers

N

Figure 1.

Preparing the Way

DAVID A. FREIDEL

The art of the Olmec civilization—now more broadly termed the Middle Formative Ceremonial Complex of Mesoamerica[1]—continues to astound and inspire us after fifty years of intense study. We still can't quite believe that this convergence of brilliant conception and superb craft occurred at the very beginning of Mesoamerica's civilization. That fact is no longer in serious dispute, however, and we are left to wonder what there might be about this part of the Americas' geographical place and natural environment that encouraged the sudden flowering of this great artistic tradition (fig. 1).[2] We also have to ponder the enduring beliefs of the people who wandered into and eventually settled Mesoamerica over millennia. We need to anticipate the spectacular consensus their descendants forged across languages and distances in a vision of their shared world as an ordered and comprehensible totality. Despite the eons of slowly accumulated skills and experience behind them, civilized worlds' mentalities are ultimately invented. They are conjured out of immediate political necessities, combined with special cultural opportunities, in the work of sages.[3]

Once invented, however, worldly visions are locally reinvented repeatedly over time, reflecting the particular histories of regional societies within the broader civilization. The result is a mosaic of cultures that, while different and distinct, shares elements of a common intellectual heritage. The Olmec crystallization of ideas influenced later Mesoamerican religions and cosmologies in ways we are still learning to appreciate.

People migrated into Mesoamerica at least ten thousand years before the Olmec civilization.[4] For thousands of years they lived in small groups of families, hunting animals and gathering wild plant foods. Gradually, some of these plants responded to human use by becoming domesticated. The people, in turn, adjusted their plans for living in certain places for certain periods of time to the life cycles of important food sources, especially plants undergoing domestication. Archaeologists spend a lot of time, both in the field and in the laboratory, tracing out exactly how the Mesoamericans evolved a village farming life from this slow dance of animals, plants, and people.[5] On the face of it, none of this has much to do with art. But for later Mesoamericans, and I think for the Olmec, art was very much the face of ordinary people's reality. To paraphrase the anthropologist Claude Lévi-Strauss, plants and animals are not only good to eat, but good to think. It is hardly surprising that animals and plants along with other important everyday things like water and fire, birth and death, and infancy and old age are the stuff of which Olmec art is made.[6]

The burst of creative energy reflected in Olmec art, however, was also inspired by, in addition to thinking, public communicating—storytelling, singing, dancing, questing beyond the local area— over a hundred generations or more. Long before the first visible art in Mesoamerica, interesting archaeological patterns occur by which the Archaic bands drifted into becoming Formative villages. Richard S. MacNeish, who in the 1960s directed the research in the Tehuacan Valley of southern Mexico, details some of these patterns. Tehuacan Valley provides especially powerful evidence since it straddles ancient trails leading from highland to lowland country and its sites exhibit remarkable preservation of perishable artifacts and food remains from the Archaic period. For example, by the fifth millennium B.C., during the Coxcatlan phase in this high, arid valley, evidence exists that three patterns had begun to coincide: (1) ritual human sacrifice (in Coxcatlan Cave, roughly 5200–4800 B.C., actually at the end of the El Riego phase), (2) trade in obsidian and other exotic commodities, and (3) hybridization of domesticates.[7]

The first pattern confirms what we might suspect, namely, that broadly shared religious conventions of later Mesoamerica, such as human sacrifice and penitential bloodletting, were probably deeply rooted in Archaic society. Sacrifice is the key expression of the covenant between the living and the dead, human beings and gods. MacNeish identifies the sacrificial burials in Coxcatlan Cave as proof of strong shamanic leadership in El Riego phase society.[8]

The second pattern in Tehuacan Valley is potentially related to the first. From the beginning of the record, outside materials like volcanic stone trickled into the valley. But after 5000 B.C., trade routes suggest trips to source areas, not simply visits with neighbors. Trade in both imperishables, like stone, and perishables, like crop seeds, marks this trend of expanded exchange networks. Obsidian, which is usually black or gray, although sometimes green or reddish brown, is natural volcanic glass. Similar to other stones lacking clear crystalline structure, it lends itself, through judicious chipping, to being shaped into sharp-edged tools. The ancient people of Mesoamerica used a variety of stones to fashion chipped tools, axes, planes, drills, knives, spear points, scrapers—objects used in everyday work and in special activities such as war, sacrifice, and bloodletting.

A curious fact about obsidian's early occurrence in Mesoamerica's archaeological record is that, away from the areas of abundance, it is normally found in the form of chips and flakes useful for precision-cutting tasks.[9] Later, during the the time of the Olmec, flake technology gave way generally to carefully prepared, small, thin blades. During the sixteenth century, Spanish eyewitnesses noted that Mesoamericans made weapons and sacrificial instruments from obsidian blades. I suspect this is very ancient practice, and that the incipient Archaic trade in obsidian chips and blades, and cores for making them, had to do with an emerging consensus across Mesoamerica concerning bloodletting.

Most archaeologists think obsidian was employed for ordinary tasks, and I don't doubt this was part of its use.[10] The problem is that traded imperishable materials might have served a variety of ceremonial and ordinary functions; indeed, this will eventually be the crux of my argument about Olmec art. By the time of Olmec civilization, trade in obsidian blades was extensive and complicated.[11] Among the Classic Maya, the blade fragment came to stand for the act of sacrificing, metaphorically denoted in the glyph as "harvesting."[12]

Harvesting may be what the ancient ancestors had in mind when they embarked on sacrifice and bloodletting. After 5000 B.C. the people of Tehuacan, and those in encampments elsewhere in Mesoamerica, increasingly relied upon plant foods they not only harvested, but also helped to grow. Helping plants to grow can be a canny business, requiring knowledge about how plants reproduce and how hybrids can be created for different, desirable qualities. It is no accident that maize—the plant that came to be the great Mesoamerican staple—can only reproduce with human intervention, midwifery, we might say, in light of the probability that women were the gardeners in the Archaic. Speculation aside, certainly the trend toward agricultural lifeways was fostered by the deliberate exchange of stock for hybridization across Mesoamerica.

If we focus on the mere fact of hybridization, we can marvel at the ingenuity that produced it, but not appreciate the patterned web of ideas that sustained it. The Archaic Mesoamericans, who could not have anticipated they were embarked on a path toward agriculture, engaged their knowledge and visions of the world in the daily practice of living. One aspect

of that world was the journeying among places and the communities that settled into them. Journeying requires rules relating people to each other in peaceful ways: protocols, rituals, languages, and models of the world. The web of ideas sustaining gardening, which could never have been based just on local knowledge, must always have bound Mesoamerica's communities scattered through the mountain valleys and tropical forests. It connected them in a fundamental, common understanding of the cycle of plants—through death and life—to the rhythms in people, animals, the weather, the heavens, in nature writ large.[13] Shaman is the general term for a person knowledgeable in nature and the supernatural, and I think shamans were the ones who did the journeying. Being connected, Mesoamericans were open to strangeness, to innovation, to the absorption of different technologies and concomitant interpretations of the material world. Hybridization of cultures accompanied the hybridization of plants; Mesoamerica thus emerged from the Archaic united in its reliance upon these hybridizations and understanding of them as metaphor.

INVENTING POLITICS THROUGH ART IN THE FORMATIVE

This seminal period in the Archaic is as distant in the past from the Olmec as the Olmec are from us today. During the three thousand years leading up to the Olmec, Mesoamericans, sharing local knowledge, gradually redefined themselves as farmers and craftspeople. They invented, diffused, and perfected technologies like the firing of clay vessels and objects and the shaping, grinding, and polishing of tools and ornaments from stone and shell. The work in wood, largely perished, no doubt paralleled these trends. Materials like cactus fiber, alien to our experience, were central to theirs. Mesoamericans were expert net-, rope-, and basket-makers. We can only imagine the qualities of their work in weaving from the textiles adorning the clay figurines that burst into view in the second millennium B.C. These slow generational improvements in technology occurred in stable villages that often stayed in one location for hundreds of years.

We envision the transformation to village life in Mesoamerica, with its recasting of social roles and changes in material culture.[14] But there was a direction to this change, given by the combination of regional exchange and domestication, that encouraged social and technical innovation, and consequent problems, to accumulate. Just as the continental plates under Mesoamerica grind slowly against each other over eons only to erupt periodically in spectacular volcanic mountain-building, so the slow accumulation of changes in late Archaic and Early Formative times gave way to the sudden self-reflection and synthesis of the Olmec.

In retrospect, pressures building in the lifeways of these incipient farmers and craftspeople can be seen to make radical culture change among a few of them, including the creation of sublime art, a means to survival. Some of these pressures may have been straightforward enough. Reliance on agriculture is risky. All the hard work and ingenuity in the world of gardeners and farmers will fail if the right natural conditions in water, temperature, and soil do not prevail. In the early stages of gardening in Mesoamerica, failure in harvest might have been offset by continued, adequate dependence on natural foods. As commitment set in, however, it would have become increasingly difficult—at least in terms of social arrangements—to revert to hunter-gathering. Reliance on the network of travelers linking communities effectively conjoined reliance on domesticates, since through such networks food could flow in times of crop failure. Pilgrims walking the paths of Mesoamerica thus came to be more than shamans and their companions questing for knowledge and spiritual power. They took on the roles of trading partners and the social elite in a regional economy.

The imperishables exchanged among the villages of the Early Formative period (1500–900 B.C.) are not obviously valuable in our notions of economy: obsidian for flakes and blades, iron ore mirrors, seashells, stingray spines, and, rarely, greenstone ornaments. They are the kinds of materials used in later Mesoamerica for the manipulation of supernatural forces. Primary among the goals of this sacred work was, and remains, the bringing of rain and good crops. What Mesoamericans considered worth exchanging over long distances were things that induced magical results directly tied to sustenance. But the materials deemed magical by wandering shamans were also used by the Olmec and later peoples as insignia of political and social authority—"luxury status markers," archaeologists sometimes describe them. Moreover, by the time of the European encounter, greenstone and red shell—along with cacao, cotton cloth, metal axes, and other things—were employed as currencies in ordinary transactions.[15]

There is a certain logic to equating materials capable of conveying prosperity magically with materials acting as tokens of material wealth and status. Things that appear from the outside world, like the beans in our own folktale, Jack and the Beanstalk, easily symbolize the drawing of extra-ordinary power into the core rhythms of daily survival. Things that come into being through painstaking craftwork require a revelation of their true nature from within a prosaic form or material. The conjuring of spirits by shamans had to manifest materially to be potent and impressive—and here were material means. As the rains bring natural growth, visitors from the outside world could bring magic-invoking prosperity through trade and exchange. Like plants nurtured from the earth by gardeners, art could be elicited from the ground by craftsfolk; and this art brings the visitors. Perhaps the most magical of all the crafts is pottery-making, which turns earth itself into useful and wonder-ful, enduring shapes. Property and prosperity are derived only on the surface from hard work and determination. The deeper sources are magical and supernatural.

Life in a Mesoamerican village now revolves around small things; and small differences can be important—in agricultural success, craft compe-tence, the social graces, physical health. As often as not, manifest differences in material prosperity provoke gossip about supernatural powers. Social inequality at the outset of village life may have worked similarly. With the emergence of the Early Formative villages, the expectable stresses of differ-ential success in food production, crafts, and the work yielding property could have translated into assertions of differential success in soliciting super-natural help, for good and for evil.

Figure 2. Crouching Hollow Figure, 1200–900 B.C., Las Bocas, Puebla. Clay with white to ivory slip, h. 30.1 cm.; w. 40.2 cm.; d. 23.8 cm. Private collection.

With the wisdom of hindsight, I think Early Formative community leaders, shamans and sages among them, discovered a strategy for coping with the increasingly complicated and stressful world of agriculture and craft production. Through art, they impressed upon the material forms of prosperity an increasingly elaborate and coherent symbolism conveying the message that worldly wealth affirmed, and served, the reciprocal relation-ship between the community and the cosmos. Along with the privileges of using this wealth and prosperity, those most adept at generating them took on the burden of maintaining them on behalf of all.[16] The health of the community, and its capacity to reproduce itself, could be measured in its material prosperity. Nowadays, shamans are sometimes reluctant to receive their calling. They must be recruited by the gods and ancestors, who threaten or hurl personal afflictions on them, forcing them to cure themselves and thus to prac-tice their work. Perhaps the Early Formative leaders were prevailed upon, through their knowledge of the creative forces, to cure and nurture their communities. Their political descendants in some Mesoamerican societies, particularly the Maya, demonstrably took on this shamanic responsibility forever afterward.

RULERS AS CREATORS

The Olmec shaman-kings emerged from the Early Formative elites in a time of social discord and promise. They evidently understood their mission to act as nurturers: parents of the present and midwives to the future—mother-fathers, as some Mesoamericans say today. They gathered the energies of their people, including artisans, and focused them on the process of creation as an iteration of the primordial moment that brought this version of the world into being. The details of their saga of the creation are, and will probably remain, unknown. We can infer its broad pattern, which must have been clear and transcendent to those who heard it.

An essential metaphor of the Olmec cosmos was the human life cycle. The natural cycles of weather and crops, the cyclical transfer of wisdom and authority through generations, were probably keyed to the human journey. The many Early Formative hollow ceramic infants reveal the Olmec fascination with infancy (fig. 2; cat. no. 1). Surely more than ornaments, these images functioned as receptacles for procreative power, for the soul, as did the doll-sized images of the later Maya civilization.[17] It is a physical fact of life that males cannot bear children and a political likelihood that Olmec rulers were primarily male. Metaphysically, Mesoamerican male adepts engender life through ritual and sacrifice, and so it was for the Olmec. Perhaps unsurprisingly, numerous small stone carvings of Olmec lords lack genitalia altogether and thus sidestep the issue of gender (fig. 3; cat. no. 12).

In Olmec art, old women midwives hold babies (fig. 4; cat. no. 5), but old men also experience birth. A small Middle Formative black stone figure (fig. 5; cat. no. 215) depicts the conundrum of a bearded male sage as mother-father. His wizened visage grimaces as his tense, lean torso arches into the contractions of birth. He squats, drawing his knees up to reveal the heart-shaped birth aperture, female

Figure 3. Kneeling Bearded Figure, 900–400 B.C., Puebla. Dark greenish gray serpentine, h. 29.3 cm.; w. 18 cm.; d. 16 cm. Private collection.

genitalia, from which emerges an exclamation-point-shaped, circumcised penis. On his buttocks are incised two circles, that, together with his scrotum, mark the triangular hearth of heaven: the three-stone place at the center of the universe where god as maize was reborn after the destruction of the last world. More than the symbol of virility, that which he-she gives birth to is also the Olmec symbol of raindrops, and the squatting birth position is the pose of men letting blood from their

Figure 4. Old Woman Holding Infant in Lap, 1200–900 B.C., Las Bocas, Puebla. Clay with traces of red and black pigment, h. 7.6 cm.; w. 4.2 cm.; d. 7.2 cm. Private collection.

Figure 5. Crouching Male Figure, 900–500 B.C., Puebla. Steatite, h. 7.2 cm.; w. 4.6 cm.; d. 5.1 cm. Dallas Museum of Art, gift of Mr. and Mrs. Eugene McDermott, the McDermott Foundation, and Mr. and Mrs. Algur H. Meadows and the Meadows Foundation.

penises in later Maya art. Precious stone was thus rendered into a jewel of insight into an essential mandate of worldly power: to give birth and sustain life, men must give genital blood.

Lending credence to this interpretation of this figure is evidence discerned by F. Kent Reilly, III, in rebus-writing etched into Olmec carved and polished stone celts and plaques (fig. 6; cat. no. 216).[18] An Olmec creation plaque (fig. 7; cat. no. 131) shows the three stones of creation at the base of a mountain, from which emerges a cross-shaped plant. This vision of creation foreshadows the Classic Maya creation myth. The cross-shaped plant is similar to the maize plant incarnation of the Classic Maya First Father in his resurrection scene. After entering the sky, First Father consecrated its eightfold order—four sides and four corners. First Father then established the sky-house of the world. On the Olmec creation plaque, four seeds surround the maize plant. The incised borders define four Y-shaped corners, matching the eightfold order of the Maya myth. Above the cross-shaped tree hovers the sky-house of the Olmec, a rectangle marked with crossed-bands and edged with thirteen leaves or feathers. At the base of the stack of images is the triadic female hearth-birth place; at the top is the quadratic male ordered house-field-world place. Flying over Mesoamerica today, we cannot help but be struck by the quilt pattern of rectangular fields blanketing the mountains and forests wherever there are farmers. The Early Preclassic farmers and the Olmec sages after them really did decorate their world with the symbol of their ordered cosmos.

So, by analogy with later Maya mythology and imagery, the Olmec vision layered the cycle of maize, the cycle of human life, and the patterns of the wheeling stars upon each other in a dense description of elemental cause and effect. Gardening as cosmology may strike us as strange. But like an army, a civilization travels on its stomach. The Olmec sages never lost sight of agriculture as the basic prosperity upon which everything else depended. To be sure, they undoubtedly wished to maintain effective communication with their constituencies and thus anchored into the experience of farmers. Nevertheless, I think they believed in their insight into the connected order of things and in the efficacy of their magical craft to maintain

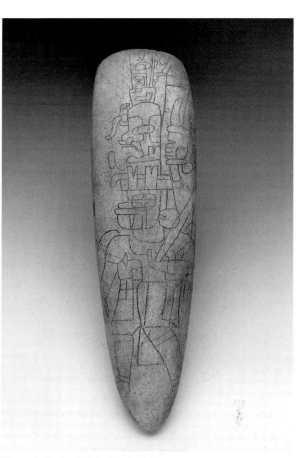

Figure 6. Incised Celt: Masked Figure, 900–500 B.C., Guerrero? Jadeite, h. 27.9 cm.; w. 7.9 cm.; d. 3.9 cm. Dallas Museum of Art, Dallas Art Association Purchase.

Figure 7. Tablet with Incised Glyphic Inscription, 900–500 B.C., Ahuelican, Guerrero. Greenstone, h. 8.8 cm.; w. 8.8 cm.; d. 1.8 cm. Dallas Museum of Art, Dallas Art Association Purchase.

Figure 8. Seated Ruler in Ritual Pose, 900–500 B.C., San Martin Texmelucan, Puebla. Dark green serpentine with traces of cinnabar, h. 18 cm.; w. 13.6 cm.; d. 7.8 cm. Dallas Museum of Art, gift of Mrs. Eugene McDermott, the Roberta Coke Camp Fund, and the Art Museum League Fund.

this order through their bodies and their power objects, which we deem their art.

Some Olmec power objects—the monolithic sculptures, greenstone pavements, vast clay edifices—harnessed enormous amounts of human labor to create and install. As Reilly observes, the great ceremonial centers were models of the creation of the cosmos.[19] There, the original gods and ancestors could be reborn and nurtured, the flow of sustenance from the otherworld to this world assured. These central projects surely demanded complicated political and economic arrangements. The sheer logistics of feeding the participants must have been daunting. To launch such work, rulers needed to command the resources of many people, either voluntarily or through coercion, which is the path to state organization. The rationales for the successful production of large public monuments and the patient grinding of a single, small, stone diadem jewel by a homebound artist may well have been the same: the enhancement of power to bring prosperity to the people. Once established, the principle that some individuals were responsible for

materially generating the magic necessary to community survival led to grand-scale endeavors.

The Olmec thought of creation in terms of the performance of individual creators, as in the images of the lord lifting the world tree incised on celts and sculpted in the round. The small-scale sculptures may show conventional features, but, like the grand monolithic heads and figures, they can also portray distinctive personalities, as in the magnificent seated lord (fig. 8; cat. no. 15). In light of the general goals of Olmec art, the intention of portraiture was perhaps not so much to commemorate or exalt individuals as to extend their soul force into material forms that amplified their life-sustaining powers. The realistic stone portrait masks (fig. 9a, b; cat. nos. 187, 188) are a case in point. We think of masks as a means of changing our perceptions of what a person looks or is like. Olmec stone portrait masks, however, reveal, rather than obscure, the wearer's true nature in an enduring medium.

Seeing the stone Olmec faces, we can imagine that these people regarded themselves as immortalized through their objects. But if the metaphor of the planting and sprouting of maize and other

domesticates informed the Olmec cosmos, as it did the later Maya, true immortality lay in the capacity for people to be "sown in death and dawned back into life"—to use the modern Maya words for the great cycle, elucidated by Dennis Tedlock.[20]

The practical problems facing Olmec leaders—the orderly transfer of political power from generation to generation and the effective maintenance of order facilitating reproduction of society—found a compelling solution in what could be dubbed the conservation of soul force through recycling. Just as maize crops provide meal for the present and seed for the future, so great Olmec leaders nourished the gods and their people in life and became the seeds of future leaders in death. The exquisite jewels, masks, and other powerful objects now in museums no doubt accompanied the bundled remains of the dead on their journeys. In my opinion, they were not placed there to console the dead in the afterlife, but to sustain the soul so that it might find its way back to this world and rebirth—they were planted with the bones to insure their sprouting in future generations. Masks and figurines reminded the Olmec what they should look like, and where their

Figure 9a. Mask, 900–500 B.C., Río Pesquero, Veracruz. White and gray jadeite, h. 18 cm.; w. 16.7 cm.; d. 10 cm. Dallas Museum of Art, gift of Mr. and Mrs. Eugene McDermott, the McDermott Foundation, and Mr. and Mrs. Algur H. Meadows and the Meadows Foundation.

Figure 9b. Mask, 900–600 B.C., Río Pesquero, Veracruz. Serpentine, h. 17.8 cm.; w. 13.9 cm.; d. 10.2 cm. Private collection.

souls should abide: in human form. When we think of the Olmec burying all that treasure, we should think of farmers preparing their fields, not miserly lords trying to take wealth with them into death. The elaborate arrangements of figurines and talismans in cached offerings, like those described by Carolyn E. Tate in this volume, display the Olmec intentions to plant performed power that would endure and nurture from below as the rains did from above.

The Path of Life

The Olmec left a rich legacy to their immediate intellectual and cultural descendants in Mesoamerica. They midwifed the successful birth of Meso-american civilization, which, in purely practical terms, relied upon a convergence of conditions: plants that effectively responded to human intervention and became staple domesticates, a diverse and dramatic landscape that encouraged regional exchange of desirable resources, and a healthy and growing population. The effective reproduction of families, communities, and societies—the central dynamic in this history—required coherent visions of the world. Passed on as knowledge, the practical facts of daily life had to be integrated in narratives and performances transferred across generations. In Olmec life, worldly visions took on transcendent, universal, and standardized dimensions, joining societies across Mesoamerica into a civilization. Olmec art is our best window into those visions.

Many of the specifics of the Olmec cosmos alluded to here come from our more detailed knowledge of the legacy of the Maya and other later Mesoamerican civilizations. The papers in this volume evince a common belief in Mesoamerica as a long-term cultural tradition with many roots in the Olmec experience, affirming the assertions of our own scholarly forebears Miguel Covarrubias, Matthew Stirling, Philip Drucker, Michael D. Coe, and others.[21] It is a tricky business back-streaming from later cultures into the past. We are always in danger of imposing without adequate reason later meanings on early examples of symbols or forms. Some forms, especially in great visions, have enduring meaning—the world tree of Mesoamerica, discussed by Linda Schele in this volume, is a case in point. In the end, we who work to understand the past must take some chances with our backward push into seminal conceptions and judge our efforts by whether they continue to expand our knowledge or are discarded in favor of better ideas. Generally, I think we are well past the danger of overestimating the role of the Olmec sages as midwives to Mesoamerica. The objects in this exhibition, and the papers in this volume, amply confirm the Olmec legacy.

Notes

1. F. Kent Reilly, III, "Visions to Another World: Art, Shamanism, and Political Power in Middle Formative Mesoamerica," Ph.D. diss., University of Texas at Austin, 1994, uses this term as a more neutral reference than Olmec civilization, with its connotations of a cultural heartland in the Gulf Coast region.

2. Olmec origins are a perennial subject of discussion in Mesoamerican studies. For recent articles on the subject, see Robert J. Sharer and David C. Grove, ed., *Regional Perspectives on the Olmec* (Cambridge, 1989), and for a summary, David C. Grove and Susan D. Gillespie, "Ideology and Evolution at the Pre-State Level, Formative Period Mesoamerica," in *Ideology and Pre-Columbian Civilizations*, ed. Arthur A. Demarest and Geoffrey W. Conrad (Santa Fe, 1992), 15–36.

3. Reilly (as in note 1) documents this process of invention.

4. The documented occurrence of Paleo-Indian occupation at Monte Verde, Chile (Thomas D. Dillehay, *Monte Verde: A Late Pleistocene Settlement in Chile* [Washington, D.C., 1989]) twelve thousand years ago requires that overland migration through Central America preceded that occupation by a significant period of time. See David J. Meltzer, "Coming to America," *Discover* 14 (1993), 90–97, for an explicit review of this complex issue. We still have no clear picture of the period of Paleo-Indian entry into Mesoamerica.

5. See Barbara L. Stark, "The Rise of Sedentary Life," in *Supplement to the Handbook of Middle American Indians*, vol. 2, *Archaeology*, ed. Jeremy A. Sabloff, assisted by Patricia A. Andrews (Austin, Tex., 1981), 345–72, for a summary of Paleo-Indian and Archaic archaeology in Mesoamerica; idem, "Origins of Food Production in the New World," in *American Archaeology, Past and Future, A Celebration of the Society for American Archaeology 1935–1985*, ed. David J. Meltzer, Don D. Fowler, and Jeremey A. Sabloff (Washington, D.C., 1986), 277–321, for a theoretical discussion of the complicated arguments surrounding domestication in the Americas.

6. See, for example, Virginia M. Fields, "The Iconographic Heritage of the Maya Jester God," in *Sixth Palenque Round Table, 1986*, ed. Virginia M. Fields (Norman, Okla., 1990), 167–74, for her discussion of the representation of the Olmec, and later Maya, Jester God's royal diadem jewel in the image of a maize sprout. See also Mathew G. Looper,

"Observations on the Morphology of Sprouts in Olmec Art," *Notes on Precolumbian Art, Writing and Culture,* no. 58 (Austin, Tex., 1994), for his evaluation of Olmec royal jewels as various sprouting plants.

7. Richard S. MacNeish directed the exemplary archaeological research in Tehuacan Valley, Mexico. I draw much of this discussion from volume 5 on excavation and reconnaissance in the monographic series on this work: Richard S. MacNeish et al., *The Prehistory of the Tehuacan Valley , vol. 5, Excavations and Reconnaissance* (Austin, Tex., 1972).

8. See Richard S. MacNeish "Tehuacan's Accomplishments," in *Supplement*, ed. Sabloff (as in note 5), 31–41.

9. See Kenneth G. Hirth, ed., *Trade and Exchange in Early Mesoamerica* (Albuquerque, New Mexico, 1984).

10. See, for example, Robert S. Santley, "Obsidian Trade and Teotihuacan Influence in Mesoamerica," in *Highland-Lowland Interaction in Mesoamerica: Interdisciplinary Approaches*, ed. Arthur G. Miller (Washington, D.C., 1983), 69–124, for a discussion of Classic period trade in obsidian between highland Mexico and Maya country.

11. Robert H. Cobean et al., "Obsidian Trade at San Lorenzo Tenochtitlán," *Science* 174 (1971), 666–71.

12. Linda Schele, David Stuart, and Nikolai Grube, "A Commentary on the Inscriptions of Structure 10L-22A at Copán," *Copán Note 98* (Honduras, 1991).

13. See F. Kent Reilly, III, "The Ecological Origins of Olmec Symbols of Rulership," Master's thesis, University of Texas at Austin, 1987, for an analysis of Olmec art and architecture from this perspective.

14. See Kent V. Flannery, ed., *The Early Mesoamerican Village* (New York, 1976), for a set of professional papers on the early Mesoamerican village.

15. See David A. Freidel, "Terminal Classic Lowland Maya: Successes, Failures, and Aftermaths," in *Late Lowland Maya Civilization: Classic to Postclassic*, ed. Jeremy A. Sabloff and E. Wyllys Andrews, V (Albuquerque, 1986), 409–30, for a general discussion of Mesoamerican currencies.

16. Mary Helms has written extensively and eloquently on the relationship between trade, craft production, and rulership. See Mary W. Helms, *Craft and the Kingly Ideal: Art, Trade and Power* (Austin, Tex., 1993).

17. See David Freidel, Linda Schele, and Joy Parker, *Maya Cosmos: Three Thousand Years on the Shaman's Path* (New York, 1993), chap. 4.

18. See Reilly (as in note 1).

19. See Kent F. Reilly, III, "Enclosed Ritual Space and the Watery Underworld in Formative Period Architecture: New Observations on the Function of La Venta Complex A," in *Seventh Palenque Round Table, 1989* (in press); idem, "Olmec Iconographic Influences on the Symbols of Maya Rulership: An Examination of Possible Sources," in *Sixth Palenque Round Table,* ed. Fields (as in note 6), 151–74.

20. See Dennis Tedlock, *Popol Vuh: The Definitive Edition of the Mayan Book of the Dawn of Life and the Glories of God and Kings* (New York, 1985), for a masterful English translation of the Popol Vuh and his elaboration of these interpretations.

21. See Michael D. Coe, "The Iconology of Olmec Art," in *The Iconography of Middle American Sculpture* (New York, 1973), 1–12, for a concise review of the Olmec as an anchoring tradition in Mesoamerica.

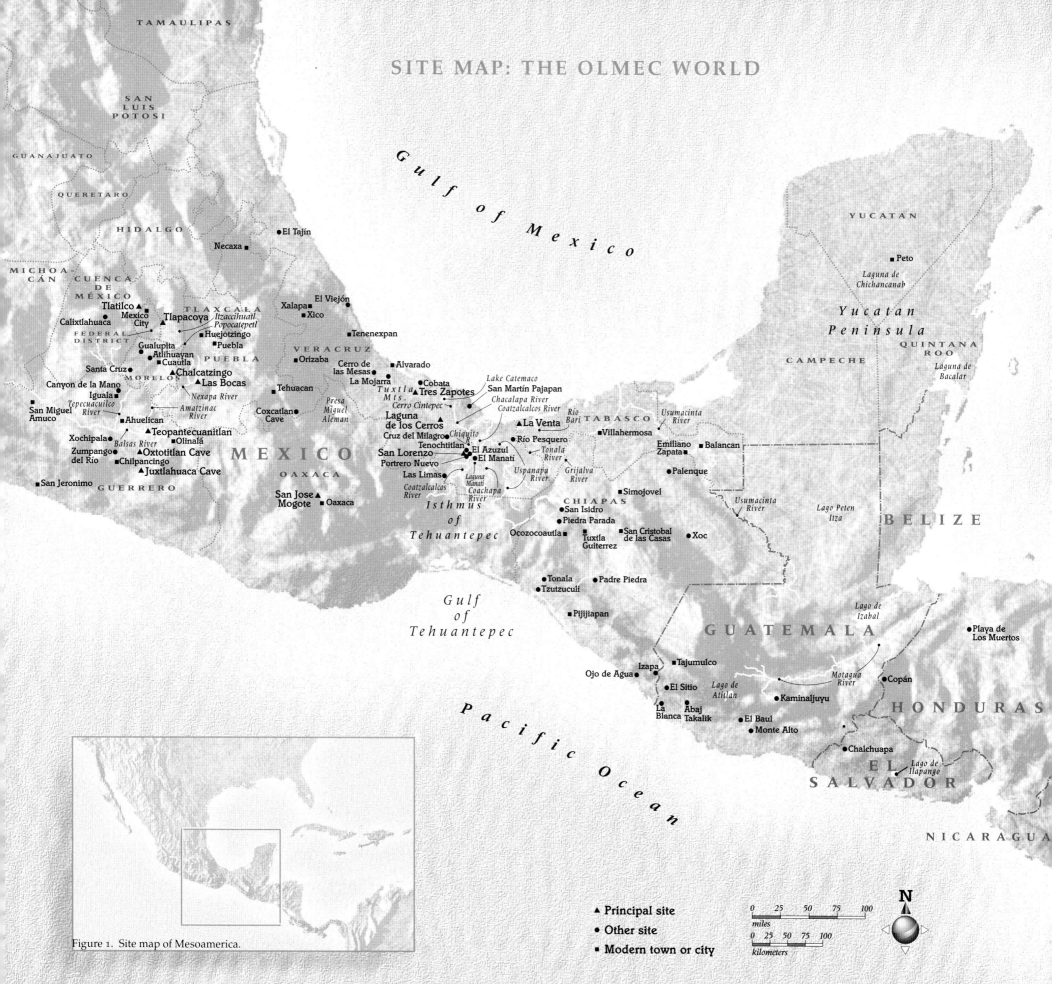

SITE MAP: THE OLMEC WORLD

TAMAULIPAS

SAN LUIS POTOSI

GUANAJUATO

QUERETARO

Gulf of Mexico

MICHOA-CÁN

HIDALGO

■ El Tajín
Necaxa ■

CUENCA DE MÉXICO

TLAXCALA

Xalapa ■
El Viejón •

■ Tlatilco ▲
Calixtlahuaca •
Mexico City •
▲ Tlapacoya
Itzaccihuatl
Popocatepetl
■ Huejotzingo

Tenenexpan ■

Gulf of Mexico

YUCATAN

Peto ■

Laguna de Chichancanab

Yucatan Peninsula

QUINTANA ROO

CAMPECHE

Laguna de Bacalar

FEDERAL DISTRICT

Gualupita •
Atlihuayan •
Cuautla •

■ Puebla

PUEBLA

VERACRUZ

Orizaba •

Cerro de las Mesas •
La Mojarra •

Cobata •
San Martín Pajapan •

Lake Catemaco

Santa Cruz •
Canyon de la Mano •
Iguala •

MORELOS
▲ Chalcatzingo
▲ Las Bocas

Nexapa River

Tehuacan ■

Tuxtla Mts.

▲ Tres Zapotes
Cerro Cintepec ▲

Chacalapa River
Coatzalcalcos River

Alvarado •

Río Barí

Usumacinta River

TABASCO

San Miguel Amuco •

Tepecuacuilco River

Amatzinac River

Ahuelican ▲

▲ Teopantecuanitlan

Coxcatlan Cave •

Presa Miguel Aleman

Laguna de los Cerros ▲

Cruz del Milagro •
Chiquito R.
San Lorenzo ▲
Tenochtitlan •
Portrero Nuevo •

▲ La Venta

El Azuzul •
El Manatí •

Río Pesquero •

Villahermosa •

Emiliano Zapata •
■ Balancan

Xochipala •
Zumpango del Río •

Balsas River

▲ Oxtotitlan Cave
Olinalá •
Chilpancingo •

MEXICO

OAXACA

▲ Juxtlahuaca Cave

Las Limas •

Coatzalcalcos River

Laguna Manati
Coachapa River

Tonala River

Uspanapa River

Grijalva River

Palenque •

Lago Peten Itza

BELIZE

San Jeronimo •

GUERRERO

San Jose Mogote ▲
Oaxaca •

Isthmus of Tehuantepec

Simojovel •

CHIAPAS

San Isidro •
Piedra Parada •

Usumacinta River

Ocozocoautla •
Tuxtla Guiterrez ■

■ San Cristobal de las Casas
Xoc •

Gulf of Tehuantepec

Tonala •
Tzutzuculi •

Padre Piedra •

Pijijiapan •

GUATEMALA

Lago de Izabal

Playa de Los Muertos •

Pacific Ocean

Ojo de Agua •
Izapa •
Tajumulco ▲

El Sitio •

La Blanca •
Abaj Takalik •

Lago de Atitlan

Motagua River

Copán •

Kaminaljuyu •

HONDURAS

El Baul •
Monte Alto •

Chalchuapa •

EL SALVADOR

Lago de Ilapango

NICARAGUA

Figure 1. Site map of Mesoamerica.

▲ Principal site
• Other site
■ Modern town or city

0   25   50   75   100
miles

0 25 50 75 100
kilometers

N

Figure 1.

Olmec Archaeology

RICHARD A. DIEHL AND MICHAEL D. COE

Of all the ancient civilizations known, none is more intriguing than the Olmec in Mesoamerica. Despite the three thousand years separating us from them, Olmec works trigger strong emotional responses in modern viewers. Thus it is not surprising that scholars have puzzled over the Olmec and the role they played in pre-Columbian Mesoamerica ever since 1862 when José Melgar y Serrano reported the Colossal Head of Hueyapan, Veracruz, the first Olmec work known to the modern world. What is surprising is the lack of a consensus on even the most basic facts about Olmec life and culture after decades of archaeological research and study. Every time the fundamental facts about the Olmec appear to be settled, skeptics raise new challenges. Despite new discoveries and the growing accumulation of information, Olmec studies seem to resemble a Mesoamerican cycle of time, inexorably returning to its starting point. At times we have asked ourselves, why is this so? Things are not supposed to be this way in normal science and scholarship. Research is supposed to answer existing questions and open the way for new ones. Are Olmec studies really so different and if so, why? What is the Olmec Problem? Why is it so difficult to resolve? Our ideas and opinions about these topics are the subject of this essay, but they will surely not be the last word.

THE OLMEC PROBLEM

The Olmec Problem concerns the true nature of Olmec society and history. It arises from two very different visions of the Olmec and the entire Mesoamerican world during the Early and Middle Formative periods (1500–400 B.C.). One can be labeled the *Olmec-centric school* while the other has been called the *Primus inter Pares school*.[1] Olmec-centric scholars hold that the Olmec created Mesoamerica's first true civilization—that is, a complex, hierarchical society dominated by a small elite with political territories, long-distance trade in exotica, and Mesoamerica's oldest known art style and symbol system. According to this view, Olmec cultures in southern Veracruz and Tabasco evolved earlier and faster than their neighbors, to whom they transmitted many elements of their culture and art style. The survival of these elements in Classic and Postclassic cultures constituted an Olmec heritage to later Mesoamerican civilizations and is the basis for calling the Olmec Mesoamerica's Mother Culture. This Olmec-centric reconstruction incorporates the research and ideas of many scholars, including Ignacio Bernal, Alfonso Caso, John Clark, Miguel Covarrubias, Beatriz de la Fuente, Matthew W. Stirling, Paul Tolstoy, and George C. Vaillant, and is the one we espouse.[2]

The *Primus inter Pares* school denies the Olmec priority and considers them just one of many similar Formative period societies in central and southern Mesoamerica, certainly no more advanced than any other and contributing little if anything to later civilizations. Its adherents claim that many culture traits commonly called Olmec either originated outside the southern Gulf Coast Olmec heartland or were so widely distributed that they cannot be considered Olmec. Like the Olmec-centric school, this line of reasoning is as old as Olmec studies; J. Eric S. Thompson can be considered its founder and more recent proponents include William R. Coe, Arthur Demarest, Kent B. Flannery, John Graham, David C. Grove, Norman Hammond, Joyce Marcus, and Robert Stuckenrath, Jr.[3]

In this essay we reaffirm the bona fides of Olmec culture by establishing its coherence in time and space, confirming the existence of the Olmec art style, showing how the Olmec differed from their neighbors, and examining their contributions to later Mesoamerican civilization. Specifically, we will address the following major issues: (1) Who were the Olmec? (2) When did Olmec culture flourish? (3) What did the Olmec landscape look like? (4) Did the Olmec have a unique art style? (5) What relationships did they maintain with other Mesoamerican societies? and (6) Were they Mesoamerica's Mother Culture?

WHO WERE THE OLMEC?

The Olmec lived in southern Veracruz and western Tabasco, Mexico, from 1500 to 600 B.C. and penetrated virtually every region of Mesoamerica (fig. 1). By the end of the period their influence had left its mark at Chalcatzingo, Morelos; Teopantecuanitlan and San Miguel Amuco, Guerrero; Tlatilco, Las Bocas, and Tlapacoya in central Mexico; the Valley of Oaxaca; and numerous centers in the Pacific piedmont and coastal zones of Chiapas and Guatemala. We do not know what they called themselves, indeed, they almost certainly did not consider themselves a unified ethnic group. Modern scholars mistakenly applied *Olmeca*, the Aztec name for the region's inhabitants, to the much older culture we are considering and, like a bad penny, the misnomer has refused to go away. Biologically, the Olmec were Native Americans whose Ice Age ancestors entered the New World from northern Asia via the Bering Strait land bridge. This may come as a surprise to readers familiar with recent sensationalistic claims that the Olmec were Egyptians, Phoenicians, West Africans, Chinese, or even refugees from sunken continents. Scholars rightly dismiss such ideas as

General Periods[1]	EARLY FORMATIVE		MIDDLE FORMATIVE		LATE FORMATIVE
	Pre-Olmec	Initial Olmec	Intermediate Olmec	Terminal Olmec	Epi-Olmec
Estimated dates B.C.[2] (1800 · 1500 · 1200 · 900 · 600 · 300 · 0)					
San Lorenzo Phases	Bajío Ojochí Chicharras	San Lorenzo	Nacaste	Palangana	Remplás
La Venta Phases	Early Barí Middle Barí	Late Barí	Early La Venta A&B	Late La Venta	Early San Miguel	Late San Miguel

1. Idealized 300-year segments.   2. Based upon Lowe (4) and Rust III and Leyden (6)

Figure 2. Chronology chart for the Olmec heartland.

outlandish fairy tales and will continue to do so until archaeologists uncover at least one Old World artifact or human skeleton in an Olmec archaeological site. A verified archaeological find of this sort would be truly revolutionary, but none has appeared and it is unlikely any will.

Culturally, the Olmec were farmers who cultivated maize, beans, squash, cacao, and other plants and also consumed the wild plants, game, and fish abundant in their environment. Their predecessors prior to 1500 B.C. lived in egalitarian societies that lacked differences in social status and wealth. After that date Olmec societies, as they evolved into much more complex, hierarchically arranged social groups anthropologists call chiefdoms, lost these egalitarian qualities. Most of the population continued to live in small villages and hamlets strung along the river levees and other low rises overlooking the sluggish, meandering rivers and back swamps lacing the Olmec heartland.

The leaders of these chiefdoms lived in towns considerably larger and more impressive than the hinterland settlements. These towns, represented today by San Lorenzo, La Venta, Laguna de los Cerros, and other large archaeological sites, housed hundreds and even thousands of people. They contained many specialized buildings and constructions not found in the smaller communities, including mounds, platforms and artificial ridges constructed of earth; and large palaces; open plazas, ball courts, and artificial lagoons or reservoirs, and elaborate, carved stone drain systems. Stone monuments portraying human rulers and supernaturals symbolized the earthly power and divine favor enjoyed by the rulers. Staggering quantities of axes, celts, figurines, and other objects made from jade and other semiprecious stones were used in daily life and deliberately buried beneath the mounds and plazas, presumably as offerings to the denizens of the supernatural world.

WHEN DID OLMEC CULTURE FLOURISH?

Olmec culture rose and fell during what archaeologists call the Early and Middle Formative or Preclassic periods. Gareth Lowe divided Olmec history into five periods based on radiocarbon determinations and changes in the styles of pottery and other artifacts: Pre-Olmec (1500–1200 B.C.), Initial Olmec (1200–900 B.C.), Intermediate Olmec (900–600 B.C.), Terminal Olmec (600–300 B.C.), and Epi-Olmec (300 B.C.–A.D. 1) (fig. 2).[4] Pre-Olmec and Initial Olmec equate with the Early Formative period in the general Mesoamerican chronology, Intermediate and Terminal Olmec with the Middle Formative, and Epi-Olmec with the Late Formative.

PRE-OLMEC (1500–1200 B.C.)

The earliest evidence of human occupation in the Olmec heartland is found on the natural levees of the Río Barí, an old, silted-in stream near La Venta,

Tabasco, where farmers settled as early as 2200 B.C.[5] Similar villages occurred along all the river valleys of the Olmec heartland in the following centuries. Although they appear to lack the monumental art and architecture, social hierarchies, and complex institutions that characterize Olmec culture, these villages clearly provided the local population base for later Olmec expansion.[6] By the end of the Pre-Olmec period, San Lorenzo and La Venta were growing faster than other communities and fragments of basalt monuments in some of the deepest levels at San Lorenzo suggest that the Olmec sculptural tradition existed prior to 1200 B.C.[7]

INITIAL OLMEC PERIOD (1200–900 B.C.)

The large Olmec capital of San Lorenzo flourished and collapsed during the Initial Olmec period.[8] San Lorenzo's hinterland included small villages and hamlets, smaller satellite elite centers, and special-purpose shrines. La Venta, Laguna de los Cerros, and perhaps Tres Zapotes were inhabited at this time, as well, but little is known about these early occupations. For reasons still unclear, San Lorenzo entered a period of decline and abandonment prior to 900 B.C.

INTERMEDIATE OLMEC PERIOD (900–600 B.C.)

During the Intermediate Olmec period, La Venta achieved a prominence that may have surpassed San Lorenzo's in earlier times. La Venta's internal site chronology is divided into four phases (I–IV) based on excavations in Complex A, north of the Great Pyramid.[9] Each phase lasted approximately a century but conflicting radiocarbon dates complicate the picture. The first published dates placed the occupation at 800–400 B.C., whereas more recent (and presumably more accurate) radiocarbon determinations push each phase back about two hundred years.[10] Other sites of this period include Río Pesquero, a reoccupied San Lorenzo during its brief Nacaste phase, and the San Martín Pajapan shrine atop the volcano of the same name in the Tuxtla Mountains.[11]

TERMINAL OLMEC AND EPI-OLMEC PERIODS (600 B.C.–A.D. 1)

The Terminal Olmec and Epi-Olmec periods are poorly understood. La Venta's prominence may have lasted as late as 400 or 300 B.C.; Complex A witnessed considerable construction activity during La Venta's last two centuries and the stylistic characteristics of several stone monuments would place them a few centuries before the birth of Christ. San Lorenzo was reoccupied at the beginning of the Terminal Olmec period, but no sculptures can be dated to this time and it was definitively abandoned by about 400 B.C. True Olmec culture drew to a close by 300 B.C., but a derived, epigonal culture survived north of the Tuxtla Mountains at Tres Zapotes and perhaps elsewhere. Ironically, although Tres Zapotes was the first Olmec site known, the nature of its Olmec occupation remains an unresolved mystery.[12] Most of the sculptures and pottery appear to date to Terminal and Epi-Olmec times. Stela C, a stone slab with an Epi-Olmec figure carved on one side and *7.16.6.16.18, 6 Etz'nab, 3 Uo* (31 B.C.), the oldest known date in the Mesoamerican Long Count Calendar, on the other, surely belongs to this period, as do many other monuments.[13] However, the two Tres Zapotes colossal heads and the gigantic head from nearby La Cobata appear to be considerably older. The Epi-Olmec period was an especially important time in the history of Mesoamerican writing systems because numerous early inscriptions occur in the western half of the Olmec heartland. In addition to Tres Zapotes Stela C, they include the enigmatic Tuxtla statuette and La Mojarra Stela 1, a large stone sculpture with one of the oldest and longest known texts on any Mesoamerican monument.[14]

THE OLMEC CULTURAL LANDSCAPE

The pace of discovery in Olmec archaeology has increased so dramatically in recent years that our current view of the Olmec world is quite different from even ten years ago. A brief overview of the Olmec cultural landscape as we understand it today will highlight some of these recent discoveries and illustrate the rich complexity of Olmec life and culture. This landscape was dotted with many kinds of

settlements, including large towns, smaller villages, tiny hamlets, specialized workshops where artisans produced monuments and other elite products, and shrines at special sacred places. These settlements were organized into realms, loosely delimited territories controlled by leaders who lived in the capitals. In the following pages we will describe the two realms about which we know the most, those of San Lorenzo and La Venta.

SAN LORENZO'S REALM

San Lorenzo covers the top and sides of a plateau overlooking the Río Chiquito, an arm of the Coatzacoalcos River. In its heyday it must have controlled most of the Coatzacoalcos River valley and perhaps the adjacent hinterland as well. This vast territory is virtual archaeological terra incognita except for San Lorenzo itself, but recent research at El Azuzul, a natural hill the Olmec turned

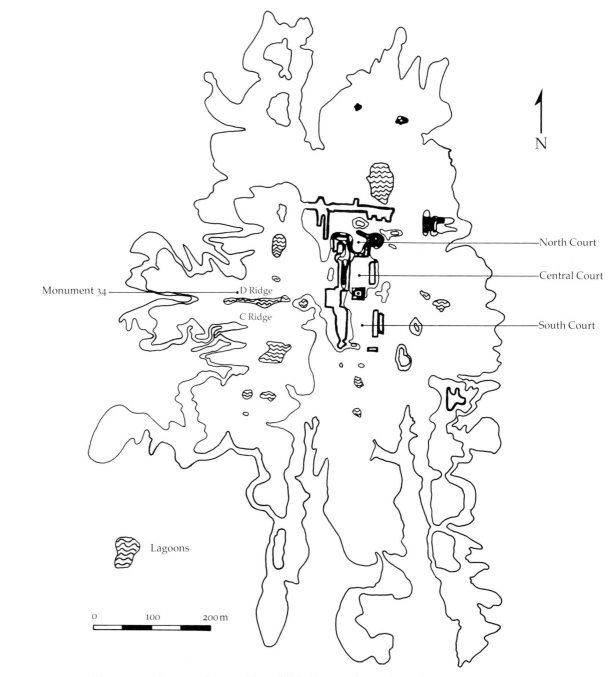

Figure 3. San Lorenzo plateau with artificial ridges on the north, south, and west sides.

Figure 4. San Lorenzo Monument 61. A colossal head of a San Lorenzo ruler of the Initial (Early Formative) period.

Figure 6. San Lorenzo Monument 34. A kneeling figure missing its head and articulated arms.

Figure 5. San Lorenzo Monument 14. This giant rectangular sculpture once functioned as an Olmec ruler's throne.

into an artificial acropolis through the construction of terraces, and El Manatí, a spring where they deposited offerings of wooden sculptures and other precious objects, provides fascinating insights into Olmec ritual life.

San Lorenzo's inhabitants modified the natural shape of their plateau by constructing six outwardly projecting, artificial ridges on the north, south, and west sides (fig. 3.).[15] To date, only the Group D ridge, on the western edge of the plateau, has been excavated extensively. However, these excavations reveal the magnitude of Olmec construction projects: human carriers transported an estimated 67,000 cubic meters of soil in baskets to create a platform approximately 200 meters long, 50 meters wide, and 6.5 meters high![16] The function of these ridges has been debated since they were first identified in 1967; Michael D. Coe believes they were designed to turn the entire site into a gigantic bird effigy, which was never completed. This hypothesis has not met universal acceptance. Another explanation, which does not conflict with the bird-effigy

Figure 7. San Lorenzo Monument 52. A seated water deity.

proposal, is that they served as the foundations for "palaces" or elite precincts. Numerous battered and broken basalt monuments were found resting on a hard, red sand floor that originally served as the Group D ridge surface. Once thought to be remnants of the violent events accompanying San Lorenzo's abandonment, they now appear to belong to a workshop where discarded monuments were recarved into smaller sculptures.[17] Furthermore, Ann Cyphers Guillén's recent investigations indicate that together with the adjacent natural plateau, the Group D and Group C ridges formed a locus of elite activity, perhaps even a ruler's palace.[18] Evidence for this intriguing suggestion includes the tremendous effort that went into constructing the ridges; the colossal heads and basalt thrones symbolic of rulership; the palacelike structure with red earth walls and floors and large, basalt-column roof supports; the artificial lagoons or reservoirs excavated into the ridge surface; the two-hundred-meter-long drain system with troughs and covers laboriously carved from basalt; and the numerous

stone sculptures depicting themes related to water and the supernatural. Only large-scale investigations of this and the other artificial ridges can prove this hypothesis.

San Lorenzo has yielded more than seventy stone monuments, among them some of the finest sculptures ever created in Mesoamerica.[19] The known inventory includes ten colossal heads, three table-top altars, or thrones, and a bewildering array of human and animal portrayals sculpted in the round (figs. 4–7).

El Azuzul occupies a natural ridge called the Loma del Zapote, located three kilometers south of San Lorenzo, above the juncture of two ancient river courses, an ideal strategic location from which San Lorenzo's rulers could have controlled river traffic. A serendipitous accident of the kind so common in archaeology occurred when a local farmer struck a buried Olmec monument in 1987.[20] The monument and three others in the immediate area were found resting on a red clay floor where the Olmec left them when they abandoned El Azuzul in

about 900 B.C. The first set of Olmec sculptures to appear in their original setting, they illustrate the Olmec practice of arranging sculptures in multi-monument scenes. Two kneeling young men are so similar in posture, dress, and facial features they almost certainly represent identical twins (fig. 8). Two seated felines, one recarved from an earlier, larger monument, and slightly smaller than the other, face the young men and are so similar they also may depict twins. The arrangement and subject matter of these sculptures recall the later pan-Mesoamerican belief in twins as culture heroes who wrested the essentials of life from the malevolent supernaturals, who denied them to mortal humans. If this is the message of the El Azuzul tableau, it is the oldest known example of this basic Meso-american belief.

Prominently displayed on one of the terraces cut into the hillside, the sculptures would have been visible to everyone approaching from the rivers at the base of the hill. How many other monuments remain buried beneath the soil that has eroded down the slopes of El Azuzul over the past three thousand years? How frequently did the Olmec move these (and other) monuments to create different scenes according to the ritual being observed? Only future archaeological investigations can answer these questions.

Most Olmec archaeological sites are communities where people lived out their daily lives. However, the Olmec also had isolated shrines where they conducted rituals. These sacred spots, thought to be inhabited by supernaturals, include springs, mountaintops, and caves. El Manatí, a perpetually wet bog fed by a spring at the base of a hill twenty kilometers from San Lorenzo, was one such sacred place. Since 1988 Ponciano Ortiz, María del Cármen Rodríguez, and their colleagues have uncovered at least forty life-size, carved wooden human busts along with a host of other objects in the muck surrounding the spring (fig. 9).[21] The facial features of the busts are quintessentially Olmec in style and appear to portray real individuals. They seem to have been manufactured on the spot prior to interment, and some, at least, were painted red and carefully wrapped in plant leaves before being ritually deposited in the organically inactive bog soil, where

Figure 8. Stone sculptures from El Azuzul.

haps additional territory as well. Rebecca González Lauck has recently published the first complete site plan of La Venta. It shows numerous earth mounds and plazas, many oriented eight degrees west of north (an alignment that had special significance to the La Venta Olmec), covering the entire ridge.[22] Earlier fears that the site was destined to be obliterated by modern buildings have proved unfounded. The Tabasco state government recently reclaimed the site by removing the modern buildings and creating an attractive, protected archaeological park complete with a visitors center and replicas of many monuments in their original locations.

The best-known features of La Venta are the one-hundred-foot-high Great Pyramid and Complex A, a mound and plaza group located to its north (fig. 10).[23] Unfortunately for archaeologists who must reconstruct entire cultures on the slimmest

they were preserved for more than three thousand years. One deposit contained three busts—two females and one male—arranged in a semicircular tableau or scene. Other objects placed as offerings included a wooden scepter tipped with a shark's tooth, sacrificial stone knives with wooden handles, knotted cords, rubber balls, handfuls of plant leaves, animal bones impregnated with hematite, greenstone beads, and almost one hundred jade and serpentine axes. A more grisly aspect of Olmec ritual is presented by the bones of children sacrificed as ritual offerings. Ortiz and Rodríguez believe that Olmec worshipers performed rituals to a water deity during a period of one or two centuries and perhaps had a notion that organic materials would not perish in the eternally saturated muck.

LA VENTA'S REALM

Although modern La Venta is an "island" of high ground surrounded by marshes, the Olmec capital occupied a ridge overlooking the then-active Río Palma River. During the Intermediate Olmec period, La Venta probably controlled the region between the Mezcalapa and Coatzacoalcos rivers and per-

Figure 9. El Manatí wooden busts.

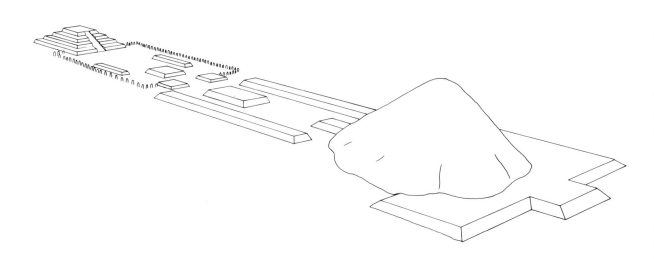

Figure 10. Perspective drawing of La Venta's Great Pyramid and Complex A.

threads of evidence, both constructions include many unique features not found anywhere else in the Mesoamerican world. These features, especially Complex A's spectacular buried offerings and architecture, make the La Venta Olmec appear so strikingly different from other Mesoamerican societies that a false impression is created. It is as if future archaeologists tried to reconstruct twentieth-century America based on a few excavations at Disneyland, resulting in a hopelessly confused picture.

Before the Great Pyramid was cleared of the dense forest covering it, archaeologists assumed it was a typical rectangular Mesoamerican pyramid. When the vegetation was removed, the mound surface emerged as a conical structure with vertical troughs and ridges, giving it the appearance of a volcano or cupcake mold (fig. 11). Robert Heizer

Figure 11. Aerial view of La Venta's Great Pyramid.

Figure 12. Massive Offering at La Venta during excavation.

suggested that this closely approximates its original shape and that the builders intended to erect an "artificial mountain" modeled on a sacred mountain in the Tuxtlas, the source of basalt for their monuments. Other scholars attribute its rounded shape to twenty-five hundred years of erosion. González's recent excavations at the Great Pyramid's south edge indicate the base was more square than round, perhaps signaling a return to the older interpretation of its form. Her 1995 excavations may resolve this issue, just as future excavations may uncover the tomb many archaeologists believe remains buried inside the mound.

Although Complex A covers only a tiny portion of La Venta, it was until recently the only part of the site investigated. Complex A was erected during four construction phases over a period of four centuries. Beneath the mounds and plazas the Olmec placed a wealth of offerings and caches, including polished jade celts, at times placed in cruciform patterns; lustrous, polished concave mirrors ground from magnetite, ilmenite and other iron ores; a courtly tableau constructed of twenty-two jade and serpentine figurines and celts; and four large mask-like mosaic pavements created from hundreds of serpentine blocks placed in a yellow and orange sand matrix. The most unusual buried features are

Figure 13. La Venta Tomb A as reconstructed above ground.

Figure 14. Objects of jadeite found in Tomb A at La Venta.

three Massive Offerings, large pits (one measuring seventy-seven feet on each side and thirteen feet deep) filled with hundreds of tons of serpentine blocks (fig. 12). Late in the history of Complex A, several richly appointed burials were placed along the north-south axis line bisecting it. One skeleton, which had occupied a clay-filled sandstone sarcophagus, had completely disintegrated in the highly acidic soil, but the red pigment covering the body, the paper-thin jade earspools, a serpentine figurine, and a jade bloodletter were still in place. A nearby tomb constructed with giant basalt columns in the form of a subterranean "log house" (fig. 13) contained the red-pigment-impregnated remnants of two infants accompanied by a rich offering of jade figurines and jewelry (fig. 14).

RÍO PESQUERO

Despite the scores of exquisite Olmec jade and serpentine objects known to come from the Río Pesquero site near Las Choapas, Veracruz, this site has never received serious archaeological study.[24] Archaeologists from the University of Veracruz's Institute of Anthropological Investigations salvaged a few masks, axes, and other ritual implements from the river bottom where local fishermen discovered a large cache, but hundreds of pieces ended up on the international art market. The lavish use of greenstone combined with the iconography on certain objects suggest Río Pesquero had close ties to La Venta. Unfortunately, we do not know whether the site was an Olmec settlement under La Venta's control, an independent entity, or a shrine to a water deity like El Manatí.

SAN MARTÍN PAJAPAN

Mountains were also sacred places for ancient Mesoamericans. Rain deities resided in their cloud-covered peaks, while ancestors and earth deities occupied the underworld within. Caves, common in mountainous country, were believed to be portals to the underworld, transition zones between the "real" world of the flesh and the world of the mind and spirit. The Olmec were the first Mesoamericans to express these beliefs in art and ritual forms that

Figure 15. Stone sculpture found at the summit of San Martín Pajapan.

19

Figure 16. Painting 1-d, Oxtotitlan Cave, Guerrero.

rero, contain wall paintings in clear Olmec style.[26] In Juxtlahuaca Cave, the paintings occur deep within the bowels of the earth, more than a mile from the entrance, while in Oxtotitlan Cave they are found at the entrance. The polychrome Juxtlahuaca paintings show a large male in Olmec regalia standing over a smaller crouching figure, perhaps a captive. Oxtotitlan contains both large polychrome murals and smaller designs executed in black. Oxtotitlan Mural 1, the most spectacular Olmec painting extant, depicts a man in an elaborate bird costume seated on what appears to be a stone "altar," or throne, similar to Altar 4 from La Venta. Painting 1, a four-part composition located in a separate grotto, includes the only known representation of what is thought to be a very basic component of Olmec myth: a human male engaging in sexual intercourse with a jaguar (fig. 16). The mere act of painting these murals and compositions must have been a ritual in itself, but whatever other ceremonies were performed in the caves remain unknown. The relationship between those among the Olmec who visited these cave shrines and those whose influence appears in the architecture and sculpture of nearby centers, such as Chalcatzingo, San Miguel Amuco, and Teopantecuanitlan, is a major unresolved mystery of Olmec history.

THE OLMEC ART STYLE

Is there a definable Olmec art style or is it merely, as some maintain, a miscellany of motifs spread hither, thither, and yon in Formative Mesoamerica? We believe there IS an Olmec art style; in fact, its recognition preceded a definition of Olmec culture. A bit of history is in order. Credit for recognition of the Olmec civilization must go to a handful of archaeologists and students of art, above all to Stirling (the man who really put the Olmec on the archaeological map) and to Covarrubias, Caso, and Vaillant. Olmec was known as an art style, albeit a strange one, distinct from Aztec, Maya, and Zapotec, and without a real context, before Olmec culture was defined. It all began in 1900 when Marshall H. Saville described a remarkable jade object now known as the Kunz Axe (fig. 17). He compared it to other objects all in an unknown, unnamed style.[27] In 1927, in a review of

have survived the ravages of time. La Venta's Great Pyramid, if indeed it functioned as a surrogate mountain, may be one such expression. The shrine site at the summit of San Martín Pajapan is another. Here the Olmec placed a large, carved stone sculpture of a kneeling man, who leans forward grasping a bar or staff of office with both hands (fig. 15).[25] His elaborate headdress bears a striking resemblance to both La Venta's Monument 44 and a small diopside figurine possibly from Río Pesquero. Why did the Olmec place this sculpture on such an isolated mountaintop? Did it function as part of a shrine? What herculean efforts were needed to move the stone uphill over treacherous terrain? We may never know the answers to these questions,

since the monument was moved in the nineteenth century, before archaeologists could record its setting and context. However, Alfonso Medellin Zenil, who transported the sculpture to Xalapa, reported evidence for later pre-Columbian and even modern offerings around it.

JUXTLAHUACA AND OXTOTITLAN CAVES

Caves are the third kind of isolated locality with special sacred significance for the Olmec. The alluvial valleys and volcanic mountains of the Olmec heartland are not good cave country, indeed, no caves are reported in the region. Two caves, however, Juxtlahuaca and Oxtotitlan, in distant Guer-

Tribes and Temples by Frans Blom and Oliver La Farge, Hermann Beyer called attention to the sculpture found on the summit of San Martín Pajapan and noted that it was in the same style, which he christened Olmec.[28] Although Blom and La Farge had visited La Venta, they described its sculptures as Maya; Saville and Beyer were far keener observers.

Vaillant and his wife, Suzannah, were the first to excavate Olmec objects in an archaeological context, as part of their long-term research on the Preclassic occupation (which they called the Middle Cultures) in the Valley of Mexico and elsewhere in the central highlands. In 1932 they unearthed two hollow Olmec ceramic "babies" in Preclassic strata at the site of Gualupita, Morelos.[29] From this time on Vaillant remained a consistent advocate of the priority of Olmec among the complex cultures of Mesoamerica. Even more significant was a program begun by Matthew and Marion Stirling among the Olmec sites of the Gulf Coast, lasting from 1939 (when they began work at Tres Zapotes) through 1946.[30] This campaign marked the effective discovery of the Olmec civilization in what was soon recognized as its heartland. Unfortunately, it proved to be difficult to build stratigraphic sequences at the three great Olmec centers where they dug: Tres Zapotes, La Venta, and San Lorenzo. First, very little was then known of Preclassic culture history in the rest of Mesoamerica, let alone the Gulf Coast; the only intensive excavations carried out by then, namely the Vaillants's work in the Valley of Mexico, were deficient in many ways and radiocarbon dating had not yet been invented.[31] Second, preservation of ceramics is extremely poor in the acidic soils of the Gulf Coast. And third, Stirling's assistants, Clarence Weiant and Philip Drucker, were not well trained in stratigraphy and ceramic analysis. The net result was that the Olmec occupation in the heartland was almost impossible to fix within the total culture history of Mesoamerica; Drucker, for instance, placed La Venta Olmec on the same level as Early Classic Tzakol culture in the Maya lowlands (he was only off by thirteen hundred years!).

Notwithstanding these problems, the Gualupita discovery and the Olmec figurines and ceramics beginning to appear at the largely looted site of Tlatilco in the Valley of Mexico convinced Stirling, Caso, Covarrubias, and Vaillant that the Olmec phenomenon was earlier than the Classic civilizations of Mesoamerica, including the Maya. However in 1941, Thompson, the mighty antagonist to the thesis of Olmec priority over Classic Maya, published an influential but mistaken attempt to refute Stirling's claim that Stela C at Tres Zapotes, with its Olmec were-jaguar face, was dated in the Maya Long Count system, and that it predated the oldest known Maya inscription.[32] Thompson consistently argued thereafter, until radiocarbon dating proved him wrong in 1957, that Olmec culture was a product of the Early Postclassic and related to the Toltec phenomenon.

To address and hopefully resolve these issues, the Sociedad Mexicana de Antropología held a round table on the subject of "Mayas y Olmecas" in May 1942 in Tuxtla Gutiérrez, Chiapas. This conference marked the beginning of the recognition of Olmec as not just an art style, but an important civilization, based on Stirling's great discoveries.

Figure 17. Kunz Axe, 900–500 B.C., provenance unknown. Jade, h. 28 cm. Courtesy Department of Library Services, American Museum of Natural History.

Caso laid out the main conclusions of the conference: "Olmec culture is in no sense primitive. It ought rather be called a *classical* culture, of great refinement, implying centuries of preparation and development, and which significantly influenced later cultures." And, in what was to become the rallying point of both proponents and opponents of Olmec antiquity: "This great culture, which we have encountered in ancient levels, is without a doubt the mother of other cultures, such as the Maya, the Teotihuacan, the Zapotec, that of El Tajín, and others. To reconstruct this mother culture, we need to follow a methodology similar to that used by linguists for the reconstruction of mother languages: starting from resemblances among different cultures, to finally arrive at the original trait from which the resemblances are derived."[33] So, the Mother Culture idea of Olmec, anathematized by Mayanists and others in subsequent decades, was born.

At the same time, Covarrubias, who was greatly influenced by Olmec objects then appearing in Guerrero and the Valley of Mexico, laid the foundation for our understanding of the Olmec art style. A short synopsis of his ideas appears in the *Mayas y Olmecas* conference volume, followed by fuller treatments in articles in *DYN* and *Cuadernos Americanos*.[34] He presented his ideas in final form in his post-humously published book, *Indian Art of Mexico and Central America*, where he states:

> "Olmec" art is the very antithesis of the formalized and rigid art of the highlands or the flamboyant baroque of the lowlands of the Classic period, both overburdened with religious symbolism and ceremonial functionalism. On the other hand, its aesthetic ideology is in the spirit of the early cultures: simplicity and sensual realism of form, vigorous and original conceptions. The "Olmec" artists were mainly concerned with the representation of a peculiar type of human being made up of solid, ample masses, powerful and squat, quite in accord with the physical build of some Indians in southern Mexico. They handled those forms with architectural discipline and sensitivity. They delighted in the smooth, highly polished surfaces of their jades, broken occasionally by fine incised lines to indicate such supplementary elements as tattooing, details of dress, ornaments, and glyphs. These lines are sharp and precise, soft curves

and angular shapes with rounded corners, curiously reminiscent, all at the same time, of the decorative style of Maya glyphs, of the lines of early Chinese art, of the Peruvian Chavín culture and of the art of the Indians of the American Northwest Coast.[35]

Although hundreds of Olmec objects have appeared since Covarrubias first published the Spanish version of this text in 1946 and scholars have made great strides in understanding the meanings behind Olmec art, nothing we have learned contradicts his classic formulation of the art style. It thus seems strange that a few modern scholars maintain that there is no such thing as an Olmec style and hypothesize that the St. Andrew's cross, the hand-paw-wing, and other "so-called 'Olmec motifs'" neither originate on the Gulf Coast nor belong to a coherent style.[36]

The refutation of this hypothesis lies not so much in the art as in the archaeological context in which this art is found and in which it spread. In the matter of style per se, there have been numerous descriptions, but few attempts at comprehensive formal analysis, apart from de la Fuente's thesis of the use of the Golden Mean by Olmec sculptors. On the other hand, the *content* of Olmec religious art is beginning to be understood, above all in Peter David Joralemon's studies of Olmec iconography, stimulated by the figures incised on the Las Limas greenstone statue.[37]

Iconographic research on the Olmec has taken two paths. One path was pioneered by Peter T. Furst, who demonstrated the strongly shamanic undercurrent in much Olmec imagery, with particular emphasis on figures exhibiting powerful individuals in the act of transforming from humans to jaguars and vice versa.[38] The other path was taken by Joralemon, who in several studies has shown the presence among the Olmec of a highly codified and differentiated pantheon, as complex and well defined as the supernatural systems of the later Classic civilizations of Mesoamerica.[39] This pantheon, which includes many creatures combining the features of powerful tropical animals (like the jaguar, crocodile, and harpy eagle) with those of humans, is already present in fully developed form at the very beginning of Initial Olmec and con-

tinues through the demise of Olmec culture. Moreover, exactly the same religious system is found everywhere in Mesoamerica where Olmec objects—whether monumental or portable—have been discovered. The Olmec supernatural system may be represented in the form not only of discrete images, but also (especially on pottery) of a *pars pro toto* shorthand repertory of signs indicating specific deities to the beholder; thus, a bowl carved with so-called flame eyebrows (actually, the crest of a harpy eagle), upper jaw, and crossed-bands stands for a dragonlike creator and earth god.[40]

All of this indicates some kind of powerful, all-pervasive, and almost certainly centralized theological control over large parts of Mesoamerica during the Early and Middle Formative, directly contradicting assertions that the iconographic elements taken as characteristic of the Olmec style are randomly distributed in time and space.

THE OLMEC AND THEIR NEIGHBORS

Were the Olmec truly Mesoamerica's most advanced societies before 600 B.C., and, if so, did they have any impact on their contemporaries in other parts of Mesoamerica? We answer both questions affirmatively because two sets of archaeological data strongly support our positions and we know of none that refute them. First, it is clear that southern Gulf Coast Olmec created many new basic cultural characteristics and elaborated others far beyond the achievements of their neighbors. Second, the Olmec were the driving force behind two horizons, episodes of contact in which they passed their art style, ideology, and culture on to receiver groups throughout Mesoamerica.

What are these basic culture traits for which we claim Olmec priority? Below we list eleven fundamental characteristics of Mesoamerican political life, ritual, cosmology, and belief that appeared first among the Gulf Coast Olmec. We could expand the list but these are sufficient to establish our two basic points: (1) the Olmec were Mesoamerica's most complex society prior to 600 B.C. and (2) their influence on later Mesoamerican civilizations was so great that they deserve to be called Mesoamerica's Mother Culture.

1. Complex settlement systems. Recent investigations in both the San Lorenzo and La Venta realms reveal multitiered, hierarchical settlement systems that integrated towns, smaller villages, tiny hamlets, craft workshops, and special ritual locales into unified social, political, and economic units.[41] Settlement patterns of this sort are characteristic of highly developed chiefdoms and occurred nowhere else in Mesoamerica until centuries later.

2. Cosmological town plans. San Lorenzo and La Venta were laid out in cosmograms, patterns reflecting Olmec visions of the cosmos. Although we cannot yet decipher the meanings of these cosmograms, we know they incorporated mounds, plazas, reservoirs, artificial ridges, drain systems, and other surface features as well as buried offerings and caches into complex symbolic representations. That these representations were never visible in their entirety to human observers was irrelevant since their encoded messages were intended for the supernatural world. Such patterns did not occur anywhere else in Mesoamerica before 600 B.C.

3. Large politically integrated territories. We lack precise data on the size of Olmec polities, but the spacing of Olmec centers suggests their subordinate territories were significantly larger than those of their contemporaries in central Mexico, the Valley of Oaxaca, and southern Mesoamerica prior to 600 B.C.[43]

4. A highly sophisticated symbol system expressed in a coherent art style. The Olmec art style is Mesoamerica's oldest, fully elaborated system of conventionalized symbols and symbol complexes.

5. Stone sculpture. Monumental stone carving was a defining characteristic of every Mesoamerican civilization. The Olmec not only invented this mode of expression but took it to a height rarely equaled in later times. Even after their neighbors adopted the concept of sculpting stone monuments, the Olmec remained unsurpassed in the quantity and quality of their sculptures.

6. Portraits of rulers. Colossal heads, seated and kneeling individuals, "altars," and stelae depicted living or recently deceased individuals. The same appears to be true of the wooden busts found at El Manatí. In addition to establishing the tradition of ruler portraits, which became integral to Maya and other later cultures in southern Mesoamerica, Olmec sculptors provided some of the best evidence for the existence of exalted rulers in their society. When similar lifelike portraits in stone first appeared elsewhere in terminal Preclassic and Early Classic times, their inspiration clearly derived from Olmec practices.

7. Special sacred ritual locales. The spring, cave, and mountaintop sites described above are the earliest such sites in Mesoamerica. The belief practices they represent were established by the Olmec, continued in vogue throughout the pre-Columbian period, and even survive in many regions today.

8. The ballgame. The oldest known evidence for the Mesoamerican ballgame is found in Olmec deposits. San Lorenzo's Palangana mound complex is the first known, purposefully constructed ballcourt. San Lorenzo also has figurines of men in characteristic ballplayer costumes and El Manatí has yielded the earliest known rubber balls.[44]

9. The ritual use of rubber. El Manatí provides the oldest examples of the ritual use of latex, a practice followed by all later Mesoamerican cultures.

10. Infant sacrifice in water-related rituals. The remains of sacrificed infants at El Manatí are the oldest proof of what remained an important cult activity during the next twenty-five hundred years. According to the excavators, the skeletons clearly show that the children were sacrificed prior to being placed in the bog. Parenthetically, a much earlier instance of apparent child sacrifice in the Tehuacan Valley's Coxcatlan Cave contains no evidence connecting it to water ritual.[45]

11. Extensive trade networks. Although all early Mesoamericans acquired goods and raw materials from beyond their local area, the Olmec moved a greater quantity and more different kinds of goods than any of their predecessors or contemporaries. Obsidian, basalt, greenstone, shell, iron ore, and a large array of perishables entered Olmec centers from as far away as central and western Mexico and the Pacific coast of southern Mesoamerica. Probable Olmec exports included rubber, cacao, pottery, figurines, caiman skins, jaguar pelts, and the services of painters, sculptors, and other master artisans. The Olmec defined the precious nature of these valued commodities, which retained their high values throughout the remainder of pre-Columbian time.

A dynamic, growing culture like the Olmec surely exerted a profound impact on its neighbors. In fact, Olmec influence was so widespread and pervasive archaeologists call it a horizon. Horizons are relatively short periods during which art styles or some of their elements, along with the associated belief systems, spread far beyond their homeland. Two distinct Olmec horizons have been identified; Olmec A and B, sometimes called the San Lorenzo and La Venta horizons, respectively.[46] Evidence for these horizons can be detected everywhere in central and southern Mesoamerica except for the Maya lowlands, a region so lightly populated at this time that it failed to attract Olmec attention.

The inspiration for Olmec Horizon A is traced to San Lorenzo. The horizon markers include monumental, three-dimensional stone sculpture; hollow whiteware figurines depicting babies; and Calzadas Carved pottery. These traits are indigenous in San Lorenzo's Initial Olmec period culture and appear as intrusive elements at San Jose Mogote in the Valley of Oaxaca; Tlatilco, Tlapacoya, and Las Bocas in central Mexico; several sites in Guerrero; and Abaj Takalik, La Blanca, and the Mazatán region in the Pacific coastal region of Chiapas and Guatemala.

La Venta served as the epicenter for the even more widespread Olmec Horizon B, characterized by blue-green jade carvings and a preponderance of narrative relief over sculpture-in-the-round. By this time carved ceramics and hollow baby figurines had disappeared from the Olmec cultural repertory. Olmec B's geographical extent included the Río Balsas region (a possible source for the famous Olmec blue-green jade) and Teopantecuanitlan in Guerrero; Chalcatzingo, Morelos; Pijijiapan, Chiapas; Monte Alto on Guatemala's Pacific piedmont; Chalchuapa, El Salvador; and Costa Rica's Nicoya region.

How did the Olmec manage to influence so many societies? Archaeologists, who have wrestled with this problem for many years, still do not agree on the mechanisms involved. Military conquest and mass religious proselyzation can be ruled out, but trade and commerce for exotic goods played a major role in the equation. The specific chains of events differed from one region to another, depending upon a host of local factors and Olmec interests. The Mazatán area of coastal Chiapas, one of the best-known regions of Formative Mesoamerica, provides an instructive example. John Clark and

Michael Blake have reconstructed what they call the Olmecization of the local Mokaya culture during Olmec Horizon A.[47] Prior to 1200 B.C., when egalitarian societies were the rule everywhere else in Mesoamerica, the precocious Mokaya underwent rapid cultural evolution. Mazatán's rich natural resources fostered the growth of simple chiefdoms, societies in which social status differences had begun to emerge but were not yet fully institutionalized. Clark and Blake feel these early Mokaya chiefdoms significantly influenced Pre-Olmec populations in Veracruz and Tabasco and were later influenced in turn by the Olmec.

As Clark and Blake have reconstructed the process, Gulf Coast Olmec initiated relationships with local Mokaya leaders via the easily traveled Isthmus of Tehuantepec before 1200 B.C., perhaps in order to exchange their own pottery and obsidian acquired elsewhere for exotic goods and raw materials. The enduring relationships that grew out of these contacts triggered significant changes in Mokaya societies. Clark and Blake have identified a three-step acculturation process reflected in the ceramics of the two areas: (1) Mokaya importation of Olmec pottery for elite use in feasting and public ceremonies; (2) Mokaya imitation of Olmec pottery and figurines by the elite; and (3) adoption of the entire Olmec ceramic complex, utilitarian vessels as well as elite wares, by Mokaya commoners and elites. By 900 B.C. the formerly numerous small Mokaya chiefdoms had consolidated into one large unit ruled by a single regional capital. Paramount Mokaya leaders living in this center controlled access to Olmec goods, erected their own stone monuments, and commissioned portraits in Olmec-style ceramic figurines.

We do not know how the Olmec actually accomplished this result. Olmec leaders or merchants may have forced these changes on Mokaya chiefs or worked behind the scenes to promote the ascent of individuals sympathetic to their goals. It is possible the Olmec did not actively encourage the changes, but instead local leaders were inspired by Olmec examples. In any case, Mokaya leaders adopted Olmec symbols and at least some of the beliefs they represented. They also instituted changes in Mokaya life that affected everybody, regardless of

social position. Mokaya society became more hierarchical, complex, and centralized. New ideas, religious beliefs, and patterns of living modeled on the Olmec replaced the old. These changes were not limited or ephemeral: they restructured Mokaya society and continued in force long after Olmec contact ceased. The Mokaya never reverted to their older, more egalitarian lifeways, and Olmec patterns remained firmly implanted in Mazatán and elsewhere in Mesoamerica. A few centuries later the Izapa culture, southern Mesoamerica's second cultural florescence, flowered in the old Mokaya homeland. Epi-Olmec period Izapa culture was a vigorous amalgam of new traits and Olmec root stock. Its distinctive art style diffused south along the Pacific coast and into the Guatemala highlands, ultimately penetrating the Maya lowlands to the north where it formed the base for Classic Maya art. At the same time it moved north and west across the Isthmus of Tehuantepec, penetrating the former Olmec homeland.

Thus the cycle of cultural contacts came full circle: Pre-Olmec to Mokaya, Olmec to Mokaya, transformed Mokaya to Epi-Olmec. The Olmec provided the essential advance to the level of civilization, however, and left an indelible imprint on all subsequent Mesoamerican cultures. That is our justification for recognizing the Olmec as Mesoamerica's Mother Culture.

Notes

1. See David C. Grove, "Olmec: What's in a Name?" and Paul Tolstoy, "Western Mesoamerica and the Olmec" in *Regional Perspectives on the Olmec,* ed. Robert J. Sharer and David C. Grove (Cambridge, 1989), 8–14, 275–302, for two recent examinations of the controversy.

2. Ignacio Bernal, *The Olmec World,* trans. Doris Heyden and Fernando Horcasitas (Berkeley, 1969), 186–93; Alfonso Caso, "Definición y extensión del complejo 'Olmeca,'" in *Mayas y Olmecas: Segunda Reunión de Mesa Redonda sobre Problemas Antropológicos de México y Centro America* (Mexico, D.F., 1942), 43–46; John E. Clark and Michael Blake, "El Origen de la Civilización en Mesoamerica: Los Olmecas y Mokaya del Soconusco de Chiapas, México," in *El Preclasico o Formativo: Avances y Perspectivas,* ed. Martha Carmona Macías (Mexico, D.F., 1989), 385–403; Miguel Covarrubias, *Indian Art of Mexico and Central America* (New York, 1957), 50–83; Beatriz de la Fuente, *Los Hombres de Piedra: Escultura Olmeca* (Mexico, D.F., 1977); idem, "Order and Nature in Olmec Art," *The Ancient*

Americas: Art from Sacred Landscapes, ed. Richard F. Townsend (Chicago, 1992), 121–33; Matthew W. Stirling, "Monumental Sculpture of Southern Veracruz and Tabasco," in *Handbook of Middle American Indians: Archaeology of Southern Mesoamerica*, vol. 3, ed. Gordon R. Willey (Austin,Tex., 1965), 716–38; Tolstoy (as in note 1); George C. Vaillant, "A Pre-Columbian Jade," *Natural History* 32 (1932): 512–20, 556–58.

3. William R. Coe and Robert Stuckenrath, Jr., "A Review of La Venta, Tabasco and Its Relevance to the Olmec Problem," *Kroeber Anthropological Society Papers*, vol. 31 (Berkeley, 1964), 1–43; Arthur Demarest, "The Olmec and the Rise of Civilization in Eastern Mesoamerica," in *Regional Perspectives*, ed. Sharer and Grove (as in note 1), 303–44; Kent V. Flannery and Joyce Marcus, *Early Formative Pottery of the Valley of Oaxaca* (Ann Arbor, 1994), 385–94; John A. Graham, "Olmec Diffusion: A Sculptural View from Pacific Guatemala," in ibid., 227–46; Grove (as in note 1); Norman Hammond, "Cultura Hermana: Reappraising the Olmec," *Quarterly Review of Archaeology* 9 (1991),1–4; J. Eric S. Thompson, "Dating of Certain Inscriptions of Non-Maya Origin," *Carnegie Institution of Washington: Theoretical Approaches to Problems*, vol. 1 (Washington, D.C.,1941).

4. Gareth W. Lowe, "The Heartland Olmec: Evolution of Material Culture," in *Regional Perspectives*, ed. Sharer and Grove (as in note 1), 33–67. Lowe's chronology is based on uncalibrated radiocarbon determinations.

5. William F. Rust, III, "New Ceremonial and Settlement Evidence at La Venta, and Its Relation to Preclassic Maya Cultures," in *New Theories on the Ancient Maya*, ed. Elin C. Danien and Robert J. Sharer (Philadelphia, 1992), 123–29; William F. Rust, III, and Robert J. Sharer, "Olmec Settlement Data from La Venta, Tabasco, Mexico," *Science* 242 (1988):102–4.

6. William F. Rust, III, and Barbara Leyden, "Evidence of Maize Use at Early and Middle Preclassic La Venta Olmec Sites," *Corn and Culture in the Prehistoric New World*, ed. Sissel Johannessen and Christine A. Hastorf (Boulder, Col., 1992), 181–201.

7. Michael D. Coe and Richard A. Diehl, *In the Land of the Olmec: The Archaeology of San Lorenzo Tenochtitlán*, vol. 1 (Austin, Tex., 1980), 294.

8. Ibid.

9. Philip Drucker, "La Venta, Tabasco: A Study of Olmec Ceramics and Art," *Bureau of American Ethnology*, Bulletin 153 (1952); Philip Drucker, Robert F. Heizer, and Robert J. Squier, "Excavations at La Venta, Tabasco, 1955," *Bureau of American Ethnology*, Bulletin 170 (1959).

10. Robert F. Heizer, John A. Graham, and Lewis K.Napton, "The 1968 Investigations at La Venta," *Contributions of the University of California Archaeological Research Facility*, no. 5 (Berkeley, 1968), 127–54.

11. Coe and Diehl (as in note 7),188–99; Peter David Joralemon, in Lee A. Parsons, John B.Carlson, and Peter David Joralemon, *The Face of Ancient America: The Wally and Brenda Zollman Collection of Precolumbian Art* (Indianapolis, 1988), 40; Alfonso Medellín Zenil, "El Dios Jaguar de San Martín," *Boletín del Instituto Nacional de Antropología e Historia* 33 (1968): 9–16.

12. Michael D. Coe, "Archaeological Synthesis of Southern Veracruz and Tabasco," in *Handbook*, ed. Willey (as in note 2), 679–715; Philip Drucker, "Ceramic Sequences at Tres Zapotes, Veracruz, Mexico," *Bureau of American Ethnology*, Bulletin 140 (1943); Ponciano Ortiz Ceballos, "La cerámica de los Tuxtlas," professional thesis, University of Veracruz, 1975; Matthew W. Stirling, "Stone Monuments of Southern Mexico," *Bureau of American Ethnology*, Bulletin 138 (1943); C. W. Weiant, "An Introduction to the Ceramics of Tres Zapotes, Veracruz, Mexico," *Bureau of American Ethnology*, Bulletin 139 (1943).

13. Matthew W. Stirling, "An Initial Series from Tres Zapotes, Vera Cruz, Mexico," *National Geographic Society Contributed Technical Papers*, no. 1 (Washington, D.C.,1940).

14. Fernando Winfield Capitaine, "La Estela 1 de La Mojarra, Veracruz, México," *Research Reports on Ancient Maya Writing* 16 (Washington, D.C., 1988); idem, *La Estela 1 de La Mojarra* (Mexico, D. F., 1990); John S. Justeson and Terrence Kaufman, "A Decipherment of Epi-Olmec Writing," *Science* 259 (1993): 1703–11.

15. Coe and Diehl (as in note 7), 387.

16. Richard A. Diehl, "Olmec Architecture: A Comparison of San Lorenzo and La Venta," in *The Olmec and Their Neighbors: Essays in Memory of Matthew W. Stirling*, ed. Elizabeth P. Benson (Washington, D.C., 1981), 69–82.

17. Ann Cyphers Guillén, "Investigaciones Arqueológicas Recientes en San Lorenzo Tenochtitlán, Veracruz: 1990–1992," *Anales de Antropología*, Instituto del Investigaciones Antropológicas, Universidad Nacional Autónoma de México (forthcoming); idem, "From Stone to Symbols: Olmec Art in Social Context at San Lorenzo Tenochtitlán" (paper delivered at Dumbarton Oaks, Washington, D.C., October 10, 1993).

18. Guillén (as in both references in note 17).

19. Matthew W. Stirling, "Stone Monuments of the Río Chiquito, Veracruz, Mexico," *Bureau of American Ethnology*, Bulletin 157 (1955): 1–23; Coe and Diehl (as in note 7), chap. 6.

20. Anton Schnell, "An Olmec Group of Sculptures at El Azuzul," *Mexicon* 11 (1989): 106–7; Ann Cyphers Guillén, "Three New Olmec Sculptures from Southern Veracruz," *Mexicon* 16 (1994): 30–32.

21. Ponciano Ortiz, María del Cármen Rodríguez, and Paul Schmidt, "El Proyecto Manatí, Temporada 1988: Informe Preliminar," *Arqueología* 3 (1988): 141–54; Ponciano Ortiz and María del Cármen Rodríguez, "Proyecto Manatí 1989," *Arqueología* 1 (segunda época 1989): 23–52.

22. Rebecca González Lauck, "Proyecto Arqueológico La Venta," *Arqueología* 4 (1988): 121–65; idem, "Recientes Investigaciones en La Venta, Tabasco," in Carmona Macías (as in note 2), 81–90.

23. Drucker (as in note 9); Drucker, Heizer, and Squier (as in note 9); Heizer, Graham, and Napton (as in note 10).

24. Joralemon (as in note 11).

25. Frans Blom and Oliver La Farge, *Tribes and Temples: A Record of the Expedition to Middle America Conducted by The Tulane University of Louisiana in 1925*, 2 vols. (New Orleans, 1926); Alfonso Medellín Zenil (as in note 11).

26. Carlo T. E. Gay, "Oldest Paintings in the New World," *Natural History* 76 (1967): 28–35; David C. Grove, "The Olmec Paintings of Oxtotitlan Cave, Guerrero, Mexico," *Studies in Pre-Columbian Art and Archaeology*, no. 6 (Washington, D.C., 1970).

27. Marshall H. Saville, "A Votive Axe of Jadeite from Mexico," *Monumental Records* 1 (1900): 138–40.

28. Hermann Beyer, "Nota bibliográfica sobre 'Tribes and Temples' de F. Blom y O. La Farge," *El México Antiguo* 2 (1927): 305–13.

29. Susannah B. Vaillant and George C. Vaillant, "Excavations at Gualupita," *Anthropological Papers of the American Museum of Natural History*, vol. 35, pt.1 (New York, 1934).

30. Marion Stirling Pugh, "An Intimate View of Archaeological Exploration," in *The Olmec*, ed. Benson (as in note 16), 1–15.

31. Douglas E. Bradley and Peter David Joralemon, *The Lords of Life: The Iconography of Power and Fertility in Preclassic Mesoamerica* (Notre Dame, Ind., 1992).

32. Thompson (as in note 3).

33. Caso (as in note 2), 43–46.

34. Miguel Covarrubias, "Origen y Desarrollo del Estilo Artístico 'Olmeca'," in *Mayas y Olmecas* (as in note 2), 46–49; idem, "Tlatilco, Archaic Mexican Art and Culture," *DYN* 4–5 (1943): 40–46; idem, "El Arte 'Olmeca' o de La Venta," *Cuadernos Americanos* 28 (1946): 153–79.

35. Covarrubias (as in note 2), 50–83.

36. David C. Grove (as in note 1), 10.

37. Michael D. Coe, "The Olmec Style and Its Distribution," in *Handbook*, ed. Willey (as in note 2), 739–75; Philip Drucker (as in note 9); Beatriz de la Fuente, "Order and Nature" (as in note 2); Peter David Joralemon, "A Study of Olmec Iconography," in *Studies in Pre-Columbian Art and Archaeology*, no. 7 (Washington, DC, 1971); idem, "The Olmec Dragon: A Study in Pre-Columbian Iconography," in *Origins of Religious Art and Iconography in Preclassic Mesoamerica*, ed. Henry B. Nicholson (Los Angeles, 1976), 27–71; Anatole Pohorilenko, "The Olmec Style and Costa Rican Archaeology," in *The Olmec*, ed. Benson (as in note 16), 309–27.

38. Peter T. Furst, "The Olmec Were-Jaguar Motif in the Light of Ethnographic Reality," in *Dumbarton Oaks Conference on the Olmec*, ed. Elizabeth P. Benson (Washington, D.C., 1968), 143–74; idem, "Jaguar Baby or Toad Mother: A New Look at an Old Problem in Olmec Iconography," in *The Olmec*, ed. Benson (as in note 16), 149–62.

39. Joralemon (as in both in note 37).

40. Michael D. Coe, "The Olmec Heartland: Evolution of Ideology," in *Regional Perspectives*, ed. Sharer and Grove (as in note 1), 68–82.

41. Stacey Symonds on the San Lorenzo realm, personal communication to Diehl, 1994; Rust and Sharer (as in note 5); Rust and Leyden (as in note 6).

42. David C. Grove, " 'Olmec' Horizons in Formative Period Mesoamerica: Diffusion or Social Evolution?" in *Latin American Horizons*, ed. Don Stephen Rice (Washington, D.C., 1993), 83–111.

43. Hernando Gómez Rueda, "Nuevas Exploraciones en la Region Olmeca; Una Aproximación a los Patrones de Asentamiento," in Carmona Macías (as in note 2), 91–100; idem, "Territorios y asentamientos en la Region Olmeca: hacia un modelo de distribución de población," *Trace* 20 (1991): 60–67.

44. Coe and Diehl (as in note 7), 62–70; Ortiz and Rodríguez (as in note 21).

45. Ortiz and Rodríguez (as in note 21); James E. Anderson, "The Human Skeletons," *The Prehistory of the Tehuacan Valley: Environment and Subsistence*, vol. 1, ed. Douglas S. Byers (Austin, Tex., 1967), 94.

46. Lowe (as in note 4); Tolstoy (as in note 1); see Grove (as in note 42) for a contrary opinion.

47. John E. Clark, "Olmecas, olmequismo, y olmequización en Mesoamérica," *Arqueología* 3 (1990): 49–54; Clark and Blake (as in note 2).

Art, Ritual, and Rulership in the Olmec World

F. KENT REILLY, III

When Mesoamerican scholars discuss the origin of civilized life in Mexico, they always begin with references to Olmec culture. In the ongoing debates that accompany such discussions, however, different researchers use the term *Olmec* in different ways. Moreover, the definition of Olmec has changed as new artifacts of uncertain provenance have been added as data to the debate. Confusion has resulted from scholars' various emphases, biases, and points of view. Thus, Olmec has come to mean many different things. In the most commonly applied definition, Olmec refers both to an archaeological culture centered in the Mexican Gulf Coast and an early, geographically dispersed pre-Columbian art style that shares features with the material remains of the archaeological Olmec culture, especially in Guerrero.

Despite the lack of consensus on what the term Olmec embraces, scholars agree that Olmec was the dominant cultural expression of the Early and Middle Formative periods in Mesoamerica (1500–300 B.C.). Because some current definitions of Olmec have been based partially on material evidence supplied by Olmec-style objects of unknown provenance, however, many researchers have been reluctant to enter the definition debate. Nevertheless, these objects, while unaligned in any archaeological context—and many of unparalleled beauty—have been pivotal in determining the current stylistic and iconographic identification of Olmec art. Therefore, hard evidence in the form of archaeological data, when available, both in and

outside of the Olmec heartland, has become an even more critical resource.

The Olmec Gulf Coast archaeological culture is now firmly dated at 1200–600 B.C. The seven-hundred-year life span of the Gulf Coast Olmec is generally divided into two archaeological temporal periods, or horizons: the San Lorenzo Horizon 1200–900 B.C. and the La Venta Horizon 900–600 B.C. Within the Gulf Coast heartland, Olmec subsistence patterns were a mixture of swidden, river levee, and horticultural systems.[1] Material evidence also suggests that the heartland Olmec were connected to other Mesoamerican cultures through long-distance trade. Recent ethnographic and linguistic research strongly suggests that the Gulf Coast archaeological Olmec spoke a language belonging to the Mixe-Zoque linguistic family.[2] On Olmec sociopolitical organization, archaeological evidence is much more tenuous.[3] Hypotheses define the Olmec as an empire, theocracy, chiefdom, early state, or fully developed state. Current research favors a protostate or at least a paramount chiefdom level of political organization within the Olmec heartland.[4]

In contrast to the geographic limits of the heartland-centered *Olmec archaeological culture*, objects created in the *Olmec art style* are found throughout Mesoamerica. The many symbolic elements and motifs that have been important factors in defining the Olmec style can be seen on small-scale objects created in wood, clay, and stone as well as on monumental sculpture found both in the heartland and far beyond. While the majority of Olmec-style art objects are small and easily carried, the hallmarks of

the archaeological Olmec heartland culture are the enormous earthen platforms; colossal basalt heads; table-top altars; and representations in sculpture of individuals, executed with such realism they approach modern concepts of portraiture.

Few scholars question the hypothesis that the Mesoamerican monolithic sculpture tradition originated in the Olmec heartland. This tradition also began to spread beyond the heartland in the La Venta Horizon. Investigations at Abaj Takalik, in Guatemala, and at Chalcatzingo, Morelos; Teopantecuanitlan, Guerrero; and other areas of highland Mexico show those sites erecting free-standing examples of monolithic sculpture after 900 B.C.[5]

Proof of an Olmec presence outside the Gulf Coast heartland, however, has never been determined solely by the presence of monolithic sculpture, but rather by the presence of objects executed in the Olmec style. This usually means objects incised or painted with elements of the Olmec symbol system or, if a human or zoomorphic supernatural depiction, carrying the stylistic, classically Olmec attributes of the drooping were-jaguar mouth and the cleft forehead.

The Olmec of the Gulf Coast were not, however, the only Formative period culture producing specialized categories of artifacts. Graves dating to the Early Formative period have yielded a treasure trove of distinctive ceramic artifacts several of which were unknown in the Olmec heartland. In the Valley of Mexico, at Tlatilco and Tlapacoya, artisans working in clay produced stirrup-necked bottles, large hollow figurines, solid female figurines, and exquisite zoomorphic vessels shaped

Frontispiece. La Venta Altar 4.

in the form of fish, ducks, and other aquatic animals native to the lake that covered a large part of the valley floor. The inhabitants of ancient Tlatilco placed these distinctive ceramics in the tombs of their honored dead, but they also included ceramic vessels marked with Olmec-style symbols. The existence of Olmec-style material in the graves of a non-Olmec people is currently interpreted by most observers as evidence of Olmec influence in the Valley of Mexico. However, as we shall see, a few scholars believe that the appearance of Olmec symbols in Tlatilco graves proves that it was not the Olmec alone who were responsible for many of the symbols and artifacts now attributed to them.

In a large riverine valley on the border of the modern Mexican states of Morelos and Puebla, the graves of a number of Early Formative villages, collectively known as Las Bocas, have yielded ceramic objects rivaling and, in some instances, surpassing those of Tlatilco and Tlapacoya. As at Tlatilco, the graves at Las Bocas yielded two types of objects—those distinctive to the site and village culture and those carrying Olmec symbols and motifs (fig. 1a,b; cat. nos. 246a, 109). The Olmec zoomorphic ceramics share with the vessels of Tlatilco the theme of the fauna of the natural world, and the large Olmec kaolin hollow figures are finer than any others. However, Las Bocas also produced a large number of stylized ivory-slipped ceramic figurines that seemingly depict the activities of the elite inhabitants of this early central Mexican village. These expressive, mostly solid figures show the Las Bocas villagers in various shapes and sizes. Some of them have Olmec symbols incorporated into their coiffures (fig. 2; cat. no. 236). The figurines are often in indolent or lecherous postures (fig. 3; cat. no. 240). A few small figurines are hollow and have Olmec-style symbols cut into their bodies (fig. 4; cat. no. 237). The fact that these figures carry symbols of Olmec ideology identifies them as more than just representations of village life. The recovery of many of them from graves strongly suggests they are portrayals of the dead in the supernatural otherworld.

Over the years, arguments have persisted about the origins of the Olmec symbols and style and the realistic human forms commonly thought to be an Olmec trait. The continuing doubts concerning

Figure 1a. Plate, 1200–900 B.C., Las Bocas, Puebla. Blackware with traces of cinnabar, h. 3.2 cm.; diam. 14.5 cm. Anonymous loan to The Art Museum, Princeton University.

Figure 1b. Carved Bottle, 1200–900 B.C., Las Bocas, Puebla. Blackware with traces of red pigment, h. 21 cm.; diam. 14 cm. Private collection.

what makes an object "Olmec" have caused some researchers to challenge the generally accepted heartland origin of the Olmec style and symbol system.[6] David Grove, the most recent excavator of the highland site of Chalcatzingo, has questioned whether artifacts known to originate from highland and Pacific Coast Formative period sites and bearing "Olmec-style" symbols and motifs are Olmec at all.[7] But if all the objects created in the Olmec style and carrying Olmec symbols did not originate in the Olmec heartland, from where did they come? Explanations of the extensive presence of Olmec-style objects throughout Formative period Mesoamerica currently range from conquest, to colonization, to missionary activity. The precise mechanisms by which these objects and symbols spread throughout Mesoamerica are still a topic of debate.

A plausible theory, supported by archaeological evidence, favors the long-distance trade and interaction sphere hypothesis, in which lowland coastal products—including marine shells, tropical birds' feathers, and, possibly, cotton and cacao beans—were exchanged for highland serpentine, obsidian, and other stones.[8] Yet, economics alone fails to explain the wide distribution of the Olmec art style and the many stylistic and thematic variations within that style. Economics together with ideology provide a more satisfactory account.

The proven antiquity of the Olmec style in the Gulf Coast heartland, and the recognizable stylistic and motif variations within the large corpus of Olmec-style objects recovered outside that heartland, have led to extended discussions and, sometimes, controversy about the social and economic mechanisms accounting for the Olmec phenomena.[9] Given the ongoing nature of this controversy, I believe a reexamination of Olmec definitions and, if necessary, the development of a new and dynamic template explaining the stylistic and thematic variations in the Olmec art style, without denigrating the formidable achievements of the Gulf Coast heartland Olmec, are required. In pursuit of this template, I have proposed that many of the Olmec-style artifacts created between 900 and 500 B.C. would be better classified as ritual objects that functioned in a geographically dispersed *Middle Formative Period Ceremonial Complex*.[10] This hypoth-

Figure 2. Seated Figure, 1200–900 B.C., Las Bocas, Puebla. Clay with traces of red pigment, h. 6.2 cm.; w. 5.1 cm.; d. 4.2 cm. Private collection.

Figure 3. Man and Woman Embracing, 1200–900 B.C., Las Bocas, Puebla. Clay with ivory slip and traces of red pigment, h. 9 cm.; w. 5 cm.; d. 6 cm. Private collection.

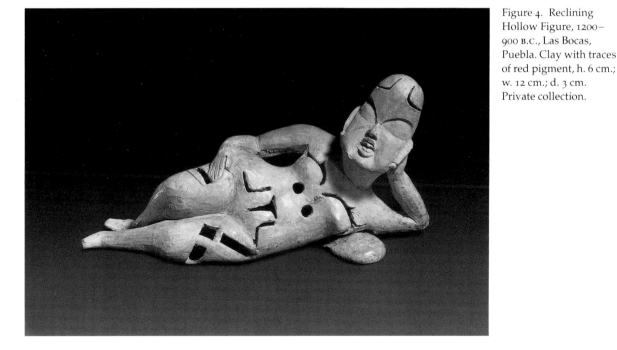

Figure 4. Reclining Hollow Figure, 1200–900 B.C., Las Bocas, Puebla. Clay with traces of red pigment, h. 6 cm.; w. 12 cm.; d. 3 cm. Private collection.

THE MIDDLE FORMATIVE CEREMONIAL COMPLEX MODEL

Simply stated, the Middle Formative Ceremonial Complex consists of the physical evidence—artifacts, symbols, motifs, and architectural groupings—for the rituals practiced by, and the ideology and political structures of, the numerous ethnic groups forming the demographic and cultural landscape of Middle Formative period Mesoamerica. The methodology used to recover the underlying ideology visualized by Olmec objects is the structural analysis of Olmec-style iconography.[11] When this is combined with an ethnohistorical approach, the political ideology can be recovered as well. The inhabitants of the Olmec heartland were the primary source for this ceremonial complex, but other contemporary Mesoamerican ethnic groups contributed, too.[12]

Ceremonial complexes are no more rare in the Americas than in the Old World.[13] The Formative period was not the only time in which ceremonial complexes flourished in Mesoamerica. The presence of Teotihuacan war imagery among the Classic period Maya (A.D. 200–900) represents a Mesoamerica-wide Classic Period Ceremonial Complex. The combination of Classic period Teotihuacan and Maya iconography at such Epiclassic sites as Xochicalco, Morelos and Cacaxtla, Tlaxcala indicates an Epiclassic Ceremonial Complex in these highland areas. The forced adoption of Aztec ideology and rituals by non-Aztec elite groups in Late Postclassic Mesoamerica can also be discussed in terms of an Aztec Ceremonial Complex.

The Mesoamerican Middle Formative period was an era of increasing political complexity and enormous artistic output. Monumental sculpture, until then restricted to the Olmec Gulf Coast heartland, began to be created at centers both in the Mexican highlands and along the Pacific coast state of Guerrero. Many symbols and motifs that in the Early Formative period may have been restricted mostly to the easily accessible medium of clay, in the Middle Formative are found over a wide area on small-scale ritual objects carved in the Olmec style from jade and other forms of greenstone.[14] These easily transportable, greenstone objects can

esis explains the stylistic and material evidence far better than conquest, missionaries, or even long-distance trade. Based on what is known now, there can be little argument that within the broad geographical limits of this ceremonial complex throughout both the Early and Middle Formative

periods, the Olmec heartland held the most concentrated remains of these ritual objects. However, many of the other ethnic groups participating in the ceremonial complex must have contributed a large portion of the symbols, motifs, and artifacts that are hallmarks of Middle Formative ceremonial life.

be classified in four categories: celts or hand axes; seated and standing human figures; zoomorphic supernaturals; and ritual objects such as masks, bloodletting instruments, and divinatory apparatus.[15] The function of these objects was twofold: to act as props in shamanic rituals and to provide, through the symbolic information they bore, visual validation for the political authority of the rulers who manipulated them in these rituals. In order to understand the interrelatedness of these two essentially ideological functions, it is important to know the role art played in shamanic rituals and the meaning, as well as ritual function, of Olmec-style motifs and symbols.

SHAMANISM

An ancient, but living worldwide religious tradition, shamanism is based on the belief that the spirits of ancestors and the controlling forces of the natural world, or gods, can be contacted by religious specialists in altered states of consciousness.[16] Fundamental to shamanism is the conviction that the cosmos and everything in it are imbued with a life force or soul and are interconnected. Shamanism centers on techniques of ecstasy used by a religious practitioner called a shaman in rituals of supernatural communication. Individuals may become shamans by being chosen directly by the spirits of the supernatural or inheriting shamanic power from an ancestor or apprenticing to a practicing shaman.

In shamanic rituals the shaman achieves the trance state. In this trance, the shaman is understood to travel to the supernatural otherworld and upon his return to communicate his revelations to the community. The trance state itself is often described as the act of flying between different planes of reality. It can be brought on by a variety of ecstatic techniques, such as meditation, drumming, dance, pain, sensory deprivation, and the taking of hallucinogens. In the shamanic view, these techniques, since they open the portals between the natural and the supernatural realms, are held sacred. Thus, "the pre-eminently shamanic technique is the passage from one cosmic region to another—from earth to sky or from earth to the underworld. The shaman knows the mystery of the break-through in plane."[17]

SHAMANIC ORGANIZATION

The internal organization of shamanism and the shaman's sociopolitical function vary greatly from culture to culture. In many shamanic societies the shaman's role may overlap with the priest's, medicinal curer's, and sorcerer's. Shamanic religious organization may be individualistic, collective, or institutional. Individualistic shamanism is traditional shamanism: a single individual (the shaman) has access to the supernatural in trance and relates the experience to the community. Collective shamanism allows a number of individuals to participate in the shamanic trance journey. Institutional shamanism exists in "state"-level cultures where political leaders validate their power through the ritual medium of the trance journey.

Shamanistic trance is rarely the basis for political authority in societies that are more complex than a tribe or, perhaps, a chiefdom. Recent hieroglyphic discoveries demonstrate conclusively, however, that Classic period Maya kings validated their right to royal power by publicly proclaiming their ability to perform the shamanic trance journey and transform into power animals.[18] Linda Schele's and David Freidel's iconographic and epigraphic discoveries successfully show how shamanism's ideology was the foundation of Classic period Maya political validation.[19]

Formative period Mesoamerica was not alone in validating political authority through shamanic authority. In the Old World, Shang Dynasty China (1726–1122 B.C.),[20] early Yamato period Japan (ca. A.D. 50–300),[21] and Silla Dynasty Korea (A.D. 668–935)[22] are prime examples of state-level political authority based on shamanism. Presently, controversy surrounds the origins of institutionalized shamanism. However, as we shall see, investigation of Olmec-style artifacts should help to define the origins of political structures based on institutional shamanism in Mesoamerica and, perhaps, other areas of the world.

SHAMANIC HUMAN-ANIMAL TRANSFORMATION

Trance and the trance-induced journey are the focus of shamanic worship. Shamans worldwide are often aided in their trance journey or shamanic flight by *nagualo,* animal spirit companions. These spirit companions can either carry the shaman into the supernatural otherworld or guard against malevolent spirits who might harm or even kill him. They take the form of both deceased shamans and power animals, such as the jaguar, eagle, or bear. In the trance state some shamans achieve animal-human transformation. "On these occasions the shaman projects his consciousness into an animal form on an imaginal level and it is in this 'body' that he or she goes forth on the spirit journey."[23] In the otherworld, shamans, in the forms of their power animals, are known to have spirit battles with other shamans. Such battles can result in the death of one or both of the opponents, in which case the shaman's human body also dies.

THE SHAMANIC RITUAL COSTUME

Few shamanic ritual objects play a greater role in the visualization of the shamanic trance journey and the shaman's spirit companions than the shamanic costume. It is central, researchers have shown, to the public acceptance and thus legitimization of the shaman. Though much of the shamanic experience is interior and personal, the shaman's success depends on his tribe's or group's acceptance and sanction. However, "the mode of expression whereby the shaman relates to the social system is not standardized or ritually fixed."[24] Ritual and "the shaman's accessories provide a dramatic means by which the tribal audience can affirm and participate in the shaman's visionary experience."[25] "The shaman's costume itself constitutes a religious hierophany and cosmography; it discloses not only sacred presence but also cosmic symbols and metaphysic itineraries. Properly studied, it reveals the system of shamanism as clearly as do the shamanic myths and techniques."[26] In effect, the shamanic costume is a symbolic map of the cosmological structure in which the shaman travels to the supernatural otherworld.

Many details of the shamanic costume are closely related to the concept of the ecstatic journey or shaman's flight, taking the form of avian symbols attached as single feathers dangling from the shirt, small wings affixed to the shoulders of the costume, or collars of feathers worn around the neck. The species from which the feathers come vary, but the most prominent are owls and eagles. Many groups believe the eagle is the ancestral, first shaman. Furthermore, the eagle plays a central role not only in many shamanic initiations, but also in a symbolic complex focusing on the cosmological function of the world tree as the *axis mundi* and the mechanism of ascent in the shaman's ecstatic journey.[27]

Shamanic Cosmology

The cosmos described by the shaman's costume and other ritual accouterments is a multitiered configuration centered on the *axis mundi.* The number of tiers, or planes, in the shamanic cosmos varies from culture to culture, but generally there are three, consisting of sky, earth, and underworld. The underworld and sky realms are also perceived as supernatural otherworld locations. For some Meso-american peoples the underworld was understood to rotate up at sunset from under the earthly realm to become the night sky. The stars and other celestial bodies were thus perceived as inhabitants of the supernatural otherworld.[28] Like all other shamanic cosmological models, the center point in the Maya earthly grid was the *axis mundi.* In Mesoamerican and other cultures, the *axis mundi* was conceived as a great tree or mountain linking all three levels of the cosmos. This world tree or mountain connected the human world to the realm of the supernatural.[29] Shamanic vision quests are sometimes described as ascensions to the otherworld via the *axis mundi.*

Analyzing Shamanic Art

Discussions of shamanic costumes and the art objects integral to these costumes often focus on whether they are the origins of art itself.[30] Esther Pasztory, however, pointed out that "visual art is not essential to shamanism" and that "shamanism

is primarily linked with aural traditions and only secondarily with the visual." Nevertheless, she concludes that "when art objects are used by shamans, they acquire characteristics that fit in with shamanic values . . . [that] much of the emphasis in shamanic art is directed toward the visualization of the shamanic trance journey. . . [and that when] art objects in shamanism are made to help communicate certain ideas, more emphasis is placed on the subjects they represent than on their formal appearance."[31]

Pasztory divided shamanic art into four thematic categories: "human figures, animals, animal-human contact, and cosmic charts." She suggests that human or anthropomorphic figures may represent the "shaman, or a mythical first shaman, as a human individual with magical powers." This shamanic control of magical powers is artfully conveyed by anthropomorphic figures in frontal poses with orant gestures. Anthropomorphic figures also function as the shaman's helping spirits or as specific deities. Magical powers manipulated by the shaman in trance and in trance rituals are often transmitted through objects carved to portray parts of the human and animal body (hearts, skeletons, horns, etc.) and, most strikingly, transformation masks. The power of shamanic masks to transport the wearer from the natural to the supernatural plane and to reveal supernaturals encountered in trance states is common in shamanic rituals. Pasztory cautioned, however, "without ethnographic information, it is often impossible to tell shamans, spirits, and deities apart: all partake of similar power attributes and have interchangeable iconographic traits."[32]

Pasztory is convinced that, like the anthropomorphic, the animals category is ambiguous: "The animals represented include the hunted animals . . . as well as power animals. The power animals may be animal versions of the supernatural deity who controls the animals, the helping spirit of the shaman, or the shaman in animal disguise."[33] Power animals and animal spirit companions are often depicted as fabulous, composite, zoomorphic supernaturals, whose combined body parts create visual metaphors for creatures that cross different levels of reality.

Pasztory's final thematic category is cosmology: "A three-dimensional representation of the cosmos is often an integral part of the shamanic performance."[34] This three-dimensional cosmic model is frequently the ceremonial space in which the shamanic ritual is conducted, although two-dimensional cosmic models are not unknown.

Analyzing Olmec-Style Art

Generally, the term *style*, when applied to objects identified as works of art, refers to the "formal qualities" linking the specific object to other works of art. With works of art produced by a prehistoric people, the definition of style can encompass a larger meaning. For archaeologists and prehistorians, style can be central to any attempt to understand the belief system of a prehistoric people. The anthropologist Robert Layton broadened the definition of style to include the efforts of prehistoric people to communicate *ideas* through art.[35] In this context, Layton defined style as: "one of the necessary components of visual communication but . . . it acquires special qualities when it becomes part of art—qualities which express the artist's sensitivity to form and significance. Because of this, it is possible to study how a culture fills the world around it with meaning."[36]

In any discussion of Formative period art, Layton's definition of style provides a methodology for the recovery of meaning. In an anthropological approach to the Olmec style, style itself becomes a term implying the ability of an object to communicate messages from the past. Objects are billboards and framing devices that provide structure for the iconographic information incised on their surfaces. Using this approach to style, Olmec objects are both prehistoric data and communication devices. In the context of a specific theoretical approach, Olmec-style objects can be understood as a symbolic system for the visualization of ideology.

Much of the difficulty in formulating a successful definition of the Olmec style is compounded by the seven-hundred-year period during which it was produced. We must contend not only with the style's regional differences, but with its long-term evolution and change.[37] The archaeological record makes clear, however, that Olmec art can be traced largely to the Gulf Coast Olmec heartland.

Miguel Covarrubias was the first scholar and artist to use a systematic approach in defining the formal qualities of the Olmec style.[38] Objects created in the Olmec style first came to his notice on excursions in Guerrero. Searching for local folk art, he dropped in at *pulquerias* and traded drinks with the local *campesinos* in exchange for "small idols of fat personages of extraordinary mongoloid traits and with thick unpleasant-looking mouths."[39] Stunned by the power and integrity of these objects, Covarrubias was impressed with the consummate skill of the carvings and the dark greenstone and blue jade from which they were made.

Using an ethnographic and physiographic approach, Covarrubias compared Olmec-style human depictions with contemporary Mexican ethnic groups. He found the humans depicted on the ancient objects "made up of solid ample masses, powerful and squat, quite in accord with the physical build of some Indians of Southern Mexico."[40] His most useful tool in the interpretation of Olmec-style art was his own artistic insights. Covarrubias interpreted Olmec art as a style centered on human beings depicted as "short and fat, with wide jaws, a prominent chin, short and flat noses with the septum perforated, mongoloid eyes with swollen eyelids, and with artificially deformed heads in the shape of a pear."[41] He thought the most important characteristic of these grotesque human depictions was the drooping, downturned, often toothless mouth. This trapezoidal-shaped mouth with its thickened upper lip, Covarrubias believed, gave the figures a "fierce and evil-looking appearance, with a bold protruding upper lip like that of a prowling jaguar" (fig. 5; cat. no. 36).[42]

In Covarrubias's eyes, the Olmec style stood apart from the rest of ancient Mexican art because its artists chose to represent "almost exclusively man, that is to say, themselves, or at least their esthetic ideal."[43] Other ancient Mexican art was "generally subordinated to religious ideas and frequently limited by its traditional stylizations."[44]

He linked the extraordinary Olmec stone carvings, many from Guerrero, with the equally accom-

Figure 5. Supernatural Effigy Plaque, 900–400 B.C., Cuautla, Morelos. Greenstone, h. 14.9 cm.; w. 6.7 cm.; d. 2 cm. William P. Palmer III Collection, Hudson Museum, University of Maine.

plished ceramic arts of the Formative period. In his view, the "'Olmecs' modeled clay with the same masterly sensitivity with which they carved jade."[45] The skill of these ancient stone carvers captivated him: "'Olmec' artists dominated the material to impose the form required, carving it with the same realistic looseness with which they modeled clay. So advanced a lapidary technique employed all imaginable methods: cutting the stone, abrading, crumbling by percussion, and an unknown manner of obtaining the splendid polish of the pieces. The 'Olmec' lapidaries were able to make the most amazing perforations in jade objects—holes in thin plaques and tubular beads several inches long, some so minute that it is difficult to string them."[46]

Michael D. Coe has pointed out that identifying meaning in an art style based on a different concept of reality than our own is difficult. But an important iconographic clue to interpreting Olmec art is provided by the metaphoric functions of zoomorphic supernaturals in Formative period cosmology.[47] The primary zoomorphic supernatural, the Olmec Dragon, has been isolated by Peter David Joralemon.[48] He demonstrated that the Olmec Dragon dominates much of the thematic content of Olmec art and that Olmec artists used four general methods to convey the symbolic elements defining this ubiquitous supernatural in either a full-figured, *pars pro toto*, frontally faced, or profile variant.[49]

Joralemon's Olmec Dragon is a composite beast whose several body parts derive from natural animals (fig. 6). In identifying an Olmec zoomorph as a supernatural hybrid the locomotive body parts are decisive. Thus, a single motif—i.e., the hand-paw-wing, a composite of a human's hand, animal's paw, and bird's wing—on the body of an avian- or saurian-derived zoomorph alerts the viewer to the fact that it is able to move among several cosmic realms.

Another recent insight into the formal qualities of the Olmec style is the principle of multiple perspective, or multiple horizons. Many incised compositions are best understood when their distinct elements are placed in relative spatial position.[50] This principle creates visual fields in which a four-by-four orientation, as in a courtyard, is shown top view, while objects within the field are in profile. The use of multiple points of view, which in Olmec art resembles the sections of a paper castle before it is cut out, folded, and assembled, is not restricted in Mesoamerica to Middle Formative artists.

This cut-out and fold-up concept was also used by Maya artists in drawings accompanying hiero-

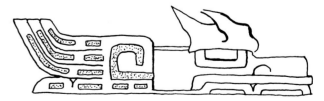

Figure 6. A *pars pro toto* Olmec Dragon.

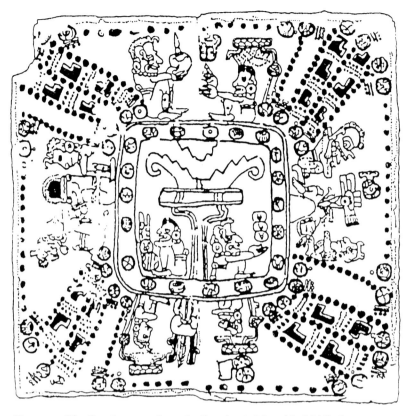

Figure 7a. The Creation page from the Postclassic Maya Madrid Codex.

Figure 7b. The Creation page from the Postclassic Maya Madrid Codex, reinterpreted within European spatial convention.

glyphic texts in the four surviving Postclassic codices. A cosmic diagram in the Madrid Codex is a four-by-four orientation of the cosmic directions conflated into a single, one-dimensional plane (fig. 7a). The deities and the world tree within that plane are rendered in profile. When European spatial convention is applied to this illustration, the central world tree and its flanking deities stand in the middle of a flat plane (fig. 7b). The corners of this cosmic model are marked by the cardinal and intercardinal directions. The continued use of the principle of multiple perspective, or multiple points of view by later cultures is further proof that the templates of Mesoamerican art, political structure, and religion were first created in a permanent medium by the Olmec and other Formative period cultures.

IDENTIFYING THE SHAMANIC CONTENT OF MIDDLE FORMATIVE OLMEC ART

Linking archaeological artifacts with shamanic ideology is a difficult task. Connecting certain Olmec-style motifs, symbolic elements, and stylistic variations with political validation is even more difficult. Any such attempts should be made within the prescribed boundaries of what is known about the function of shamanic art in general and Mesoamerican art in particular. But if my model is correct—i.e., that a ranked or stratified social order is the product of economic and political power gained through institutionalized shamanic ritual performance—supporting evidence must be provided by the artifacts manipulated by elites. The ritual functions of these artifacts must then be identified by placing them in Pasztory's categories of

shamanic art. In search of such evidence, I shall now examine Middle Formative costume details and ritual artifacts and show how they are examples of the shamanic trance journey, cosmological diagram, or human-animal transformation.

OLMEC AND MIDDLE FORMATIVE COSMOLOGY

Olmec and Middle Formative cosmology is fueled by shamanic magic. The Olmec and other Middle Formative peoples perceived their universe as multileveled, containing natural and supernatural oppositions. An axis described iconographically as maize or a cosmic mountain connected the levels. These ancient Mesoamericans did not view the cosmic levels as separate and distinct constructions, but as a living and interconnected universe.

Figure 8. Bas-relief from Chalcatzingo Monument 2, which appears to depict a ritual human sacrifice.

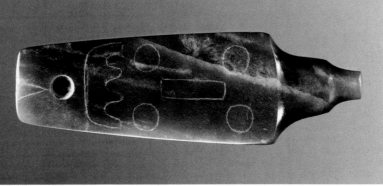

Figure 10. Perforator Handle, 900–600 B.C., Guerrero. Blue-green jade, h. 1.2 cm.; w. 7.2 cm.; d. 2.5 cm. Anonymous loan to The Art Museum, Princeton University.

Figure 11. Incisions on the underside of fig. 10.

Figure 9. Perforator, 900–600 B.C., Río Pesquero. Gray-green jadeite, h. 8.9 cm.; w. 3.1 cm.; d. 5 cm. Private collection.

Close study of Olmec iconography reveals that Middle Formative cosmology was almost certainly a blend of myth and natural phenomena. The growth cycle of maize, habits of particular species of animals, meteorological events, and motion of astral bodies generated symbolic metaphors for describing the cosmic order. The metaphors took the form of zoomorphic supernaturals or dragons who possessed the ability to cross cosmic boundaries.[51] Individual elements on the dragons' chimerical bodies identified their cosmological realms.[52]

Bloodletting played a significant role in the cosmology of Olmec and Middle Formative ceremonies, as it continued to do in later Mesoamerican cultures.[53] Blood was a magical substance opening the portal between the natural and supernatural cosmic divisions. Though scenes of bloodletting are not as numerous in Olmec art as they seem to be in the art of the Classic Maya, strong evidence for bloodletting and human sacrifice exists in Middle Formative period art. Chalcatzingo Monument 2 appears to depict a ritual human sacrifice in which two masked performers dispatch a bound and seated captive with paddle-shaped clubs, while a third elevates a bundle of vegetation (fig. 8).

Among the Olmec-style artifacts is a category of objects shaped like ice picks identified as bloodletters. Peter T. Furst pointed out that this category may be too all encompassing and that many of these objects may, in fact, be weaving picks.[54] Two, however, are unquestionably ritual bloodletters. The first has a blade carved to represent a stingray spine (fig. 9; cat. no. 77), a preferred bloodletting instrument since it came from the underwater otherworld. The second, beautifully carved from dark green jade, lost its pointed end sometime in antiquity (fig. 10; cat. no. 78). An incised line for a beak and the ubiquitous "flame eyebrows" identify the handle as an avian zoomorph. The handle carries secondary, incised information about the ideological function of blood in Olmec religion. The underside is incised with a four-dots-and-bar motif, an abstract symbol of the terrestrial Olmec Dragon—the earth (fig. 11; cat. no. 78)[55]. The now broken point of this bloodletter drew forth the magical fluid—blood—that opened a path of communication between the two cosmic realms.

THE EARTHLY REALM

Iconographic investigations reveal that the Olmec Dragon, like later Mesoamerican primordial monsters, floated on the surface of the waters of creation.[56] In some titanic struggle in the mythic past, the body of this great leviathan was broken apart to form the earth and sky realms.[57] The terrestrial aspect of this saurian supernatural—represented as a full-figure in monumental sculpture, and in abstract form on Early Formative ceramics—is a dominant theme in Middle Formative sculpture and ceramics.[58]

The largest full-figured sculptural depiction of the Olmec Dragon is La Venta Monument 6, a sandstone sarcophagus (length 2.8 meters, width 0.96 meters, height approximately 0.86 meters) carved sometime around 400 B.C. in the form of the Olmec terrestrial dragon (fig. 12).[59] Shown floating on the primordial waters of creation, split-stemmed vegetation emerges from its back. The La Venta ruler buried in this sarcophagus was literally interred within the body of the Olmec Dragon itself.

While not all Olmec dragons are equipped with distinct physical attributes, many have ones occurring with enough frequency they can be considered definitive. Among these are backward L-shaped eyes on dragons viewed in profile, trough-shaped eyes on dragons viewed frontally, and eyes topped with flame eyebrows. The dragons' locomotion is supplied by the hand-paw-wing motif (fig. 13). Olmec dragons have few teeth and gumlines with downturning brackets.

Inturning gum brackets, except when descending fangs are explicitly depicted, are standard equipment on zoomorphic earth monsters. Gum brackets are also prominent in the *pars pro toto* representations of the Olmec Dragon. A line of gum brackets came to represent the surface of the earth itself in Middle Formative Olmec-style sculptural compositions, for example, the rock carving from the site of San Isidro Piedra Parada, El Salvador (fig. 14). Ultimately, a single inturning gum bracket symbolized the surface of the earth, as on both an incised tablet and incised vessel (fig. 15; cat. nos. 131, 198).

The great, gaping maw, a feature of most frontal Olmec dragons, could function as the portal between the natural and supernatural divisions of the Olmec cosmos.[60] Supernatural gateways thus served as paths of access to and communication with supernatural power. In the highland areas of Middle Formative Mesoamerica, the gaping maw was frequently quatrefoil-shaped. Monument 9 from Chalcatzingo is a superb illustration of the frontal view of this gaping maw (fig. 16; cat. no. 37).

THE SKY REALM

For Mesoamericans, the celestial realm was closely related to the underworld/otherworld, which they also conceived of as an underwater domain. The exquisite renderings of fish, ducks, turtles, and other aquatic creatures, hallmarks of Early Formative ceramics, are almost certainly metaphors of this underwater/otherworld (cat. nos. 52–56, 60).

Figure 14. Carved relief at San Isidro Piedra Parada, El Salvador.

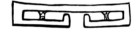

Figure 15. Details of an Incised Tablet (bottom) and Vessel (top).

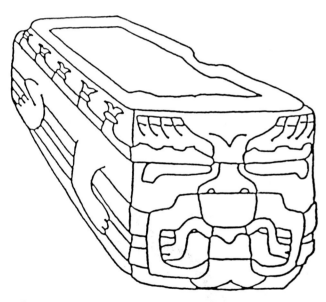

Figure 12. La Venta Monument 6 in the form of the Olmec terrestrial dragon.

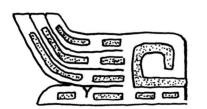

Figure 13. Hand-paw-wing motif from a ceramic vessel from Tlatilco.

Figure 16. Chalcatzingo Monument 9, 700–500 B.C.?, Chalcatzingo, Morelos. Granodorite, h. 183 cm.; w. 142 cm.; d. 15.2 cm. Munson-Williams-Proctor Institute Museum of Art, Utica, New York.

The presence of these zoomorphic vessels in tombs at the sites of Tlatilco and Las Bocas in the Mexico-Puebla highlands indicates that the tombs and their contents were regarded as gateways to the underwater/otherworld.[61] I believe future research will show that the dwarfs, fetuslike creatures, and hunchbacks who inhabited this otherworld had their counterparts in the celestial realm as well.[62]

The celestial/otherworld domain was also symbolized by a zoomorphic supernatural, the celestial dragon, which, like its terrestrial counterpart, was artistically rendered in either a full-figured, abstract, or *pars pro toto* representation. Occasionally both of these zoomorphic supernaturals are shown together: a ceramic vessel from the Valley of Mexico Formative period site of Tlapacoya has carvings of the Olmec Dragon in both its sky and its earth manifestations (fig. 17). The frontal and profile views of the Olmec dragons on the Tlapacoya vessel are similar in several respects. Most details in the frontal view can be matched with those in the profile view. They share crested eye ridges, gum bracket markings in their mouths, and nostril configuration. The frontal image has trough-shaped eyes and the profile, backward L-shaped eyes. One interesting problem was how to render the prominent cleft between the eyes on the frontal view in the profile view. This was solved by disengaging the cleft from the profile image and rotating it behind the head as a separate element.

The crossed-bands motif, present only in the mouth of the frontal image on the Tlapacoya vessel, is noticeable on many Olmec dragons with strong sky realm associations. In the Classic Maya iconographic system, the crossed-bands, if not the hieroglyph for the sky itself, symbolizes a celestial location. In a remark made to Coe, Charles Smiley suggested that the crossed-bands is a symbolic replication of the crossing point of the ecliptic and the Milky Way.[63] If true, the crossed-bands would symbolize the center of the sky.

The crossed-bands appears most frequently in Olmec-style art on pectorals and on the front pieces of belts worn by both humans and anthropomorphic supernaturals (fig. 18; cat. no. 143). It also often occurs as a body marking associated with Olmec celestial dragons. On the Tlapacoya ceramic vessel,

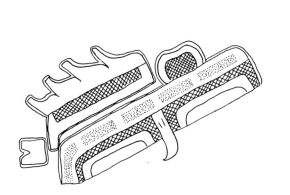
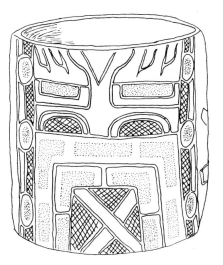

Figure 17. Ceramic vessel from Tlapacoya with frontal and profile view of the Olmec Dragon.

the crossed-bands on the frontal but not the profile Olmec Dragon indicates more than a stylistic variation. Furthermore, some Early Formative abstract dragons have the crossed-bands and others do not. Because of its strong celestial associations, the crossed-bands in the mouth of the frontal dragon on the Tlapacoya vessel most likely suggests that this creature is a sky beast.[64] Chalcatzingo Monument 5 is certainly a full-figured Olmec sky dragon: it is not only marked with the crossed-bands, but floats above a motif (the Lazy-S) recently shown to be the symbol of a celestial location (fig. 19).[65]

The placement of the celestial monster in paired opposition with the profile image on the Tlapacoya vessel probably can be read as a cosmic diagram of the earth and sky. Since the crossed-bands is a specific sky location or celestial marker, the Olmec Dragon is either two separate creatures or a single monster with both terrestrial and celestial aspects.[66]

Another celestial motif on the Olmec Dragon is the diamond-shaped symbol named and identified by Coe in its Formative period context as a star glyph, the ancestor of the Maya Venus/Lamat hieroglyph (fig. 20a).[67] A potsherd from Tlapacoya dramatically illustrates this association of the celestial symbol with the Olmec Dragon (fig. 20b). The incised frontal supernatural image, with its almond-shaped eyes surrounded by trough eyes and flame eyebrows, has, in the middle of its face, a symbol identical to the Maya Lamat glyph instead of a

Figure 18. Standing Figure Holding Crossed-Bands, 900–600 B.C., Guerrero. Light green serpentine, h. 7.8 cm.; w. 4 cm.; d. 3.5 cm. Private collection.

Figure 19. Chalcatzingo Monument 5, the Olmec sky dragon.

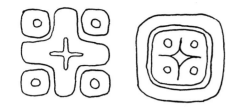

Figure 20a. Maya Venus/Lamat hieroglyph.

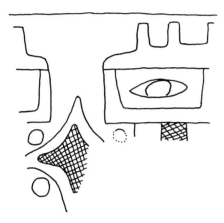

Figure 20b. Incised frontal image of Olmec celestial dragon from a potsherd from Tlapacoya.

mouth and nose. More recently, Coe's astral interpretation of this diamond-shaped star symbol has been dramatically confirmed by a ceramic bottle from the Middle Formative region of Puebla (Las Bocas) on which six diamond-shaped elements marking the sinuous body of a bicephalic supernatural prove to be ancestral to the double-headed serpent ecliptic monsters of Classic Maya cosmology (cat no. 107).

In its *pars pro toto* representation, the Olmec celestial realm can appear as a sky band, with repeated inward-angled horizontal bands derived from the frontal Olmec Dragon's V-shaped cleft (fig. 21a). Just as for the earth the symbol can be a single row of gum brackets, so for the sky it can be a series of V-shaped clefts.

On La Venta Stela 1 (fig. 21b) the Olmec Dragon's abstracted open mouth has become a portal in which a single figure stands. The cleft in the top register of this composition is a single pair of inward-angled horizontal bands. A striking example of the fusion of the full-figured Olmec celestial dragon and the horizontal bands sky

symbol is seen incised on an enormous jade bead (cat. no. 211). Here, the Olmec celestial dragon carries the bands sky symbol on its back in much the same way the later Classic Maya sky dragon carries celestial symbols.

By the Late Formative period (300 B.C.–A.D. 1) the bands sky motif is used to identify the location of celestial events, for example, on the monuments of Izapa. On Izapa Stela 23 from Izapa Stela Group 1, a figure falls from a sky band (fig. 22a). From this sky band a bicephalic ecliptic monster is hung. On Stela 2 from Izapa Stela Group 5, a celestial bird

Figure 21a. Incised vase from Tlapacoya showing Olmec Dragon with V-shaped cleft.

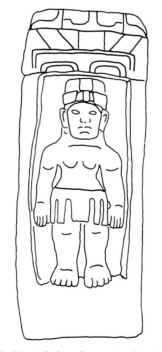

Figure 21b. La Venta Stela 1, figure standing in the open mouth of the Olmec Dragon.

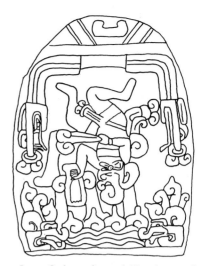

Figure 22a. Izapa Stela 23, figure falling from a sky band.

Figure 22b. Izapa Stela 2, celestial bird falling from an identical sky band.

Figure 22c. Izapa Stela 60, celestial bird kneeling on top of sky band.

falls from an identical sky band (fig. 22b). However, on Stela 60 from the same group, the sky band has migrated to the bottom of the composition and the celestial bird kneels on top of it (fig. 22c).[68] Undoubtedly, the action should be understood as taking place in the sky realm.

THE *AXIS MUNDI* AS THE WORLD TREE

All shamanic cosmologies have an *axis mundi* linking the celestial, terrestrial, and underworld realms. In the New World, the concept of the world tree as *axis mundi* is not limited to the pre-Columbian populations of Mesoamerica. Many Native American groups, including modern Maya populations and Zoque communities in Chiapas, still possess a cosmology in which the world tree

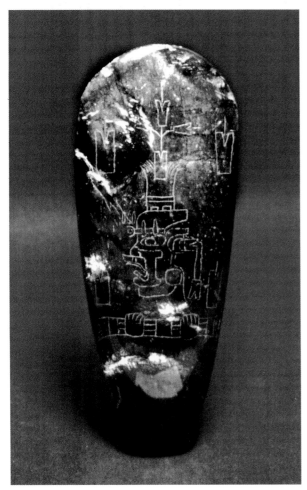

Figure 23. Incised Celt, 900–600 B.C., Río Pesquero. Jade, h. 24.8 cm.; w. 10.2 cm. Private collection.

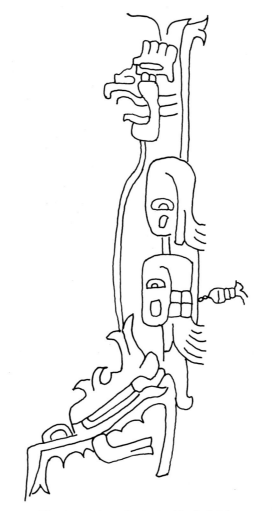

Figure 24. The upended saurian incised in the left leg of the Young Lord.

Figure 25. Incised jade celt from Río Pesquero.

functions prominently.[69] The *axis mundi* is no less fundamental to Olmec and Middle Formative cosmology and political validation. The world tree is rendered either as an upended saurian supernatural whose tail or upper body sprouts vegetation or, more naturalistically, as a sprouting maize plant. In *pars pro toto* representations, the world tree is reduced to a trefoil worn in the headdresses of Middle Formative supernaturals and rulers (fig. 23). The wearers are thus identified as occupants of the cosmic center and the interface of the natural and supernatural oppositions in nature. The saurian world tree must have emerged from constant recombinations of the symbols of the Olmec Dragon. An upended saurian appears as the world tree on a Middle Formative serpentine statue referred to as the "Young Lord" (fig. 24; cat. no. 193).

FUSING THE IMAGES OF THE RULER AND THE WORLD TREE

Middle Formative political validation was obtained by ritually defining the political leader as the world tree. In Olmec cosmograms where the world tree/ruler is central, the other four points are identified as sprouting maize seeds.[70] An example of this five-point cosmogram/political validation is incised on a Middle Formative jade celt from the heartland site of Río Pesquero (fig. 25). The central point of this cosmogram is a human figure wearing a buccal mask and a headdress topped by a bifurcated fringe, perhaps feathers, from which trefoil vegetation emerges.[71] Virginia M. Fields researched the origins of this trefoil in the center of the Classic Maya royal headband, determining that its real-life source is maize. She also suggested that the two pairs of sprouts flanking the central trefoil of the Maya headband are maize seeds.[72]

More recently, Schele has hypothesized that two types of vegetation are the sources for the symbols in the royal headdress.[73] Working from a suggestion by Matthew Looper, Schele believes that the trefoil is derived from a dicot, specifically, beans or squash, and that the four flanking elements, as Fields suggested, are a sprouting monocot—in this case, maize.[74] Building on a proposal of Freidel, Schele concluded that the vegetative elements "not only encompass the major components of the food production system—that is, corn as monocot, beans and squash as dicots, and cuttings of fruit and nut bearing trees—but they also are associated with the major methods by which plants are hybridized in the process of domestication. These are cross-fertilization and grafting."[75] Another of Freidel's observations adds an important shamanic aspect to this pattern of rulership and vegetative symbolism, Schele further stated: "In the archaic hunter-gatherer societies that preceded the Olmec, the individuals that were responsible eventually for the domestication of plants were shamans and *curanderos*. They were the ones who kept track of plant lore and who regularly planted and harvested those plants important to their craft." Freidel set forth that the shamans' and *curanderos'* domestication of plants resulted in the special role of sprouts and plant husbandry in the symbolism of Olmec rulership and later royal symbolism.[76]

As we have seen, the world tree has reptilian as well as maize associations. The connection between the standing figure on the Río Pesquero celt and the upended saurian world tree is made clear on examining the lower part of the standing figure's body closely. This reveals that his legs are inset with the flame eyebrows, backward L-shaped eyes, protruding nostril, and gum brackets identified with the upended Olmec dragon in his role as the upended crocodilian world tree. Thus, the body of this ruler is incorporated into the upended crocodilian world tree itself.

To demonstrate that this ruler occupies the center of the five-point cosmogram, it is necessary to reinterpret the incised image by European con-

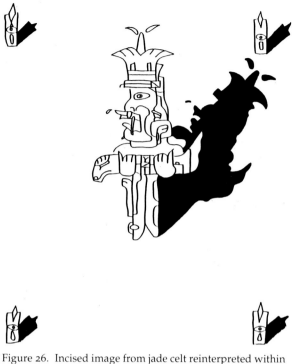

Figure 26. Incised image from jade celt reinterpreted within European spatial convention.

ventions of spatial illusion. Shadows give the incised images real dimensions, making the central position of the ruler obvious; the corners marked by the cleft and sprouting maize seeds become the other four directions (fig. 26). The legs of the standing figure also form the mouth of the upended crocodilian world tree, offering further proof that the standing figure is the interface between the natural and supernatural.

Among depictions of the world tree in the iconography of Middle Formative cosmology and rulership, the saurian, while important, is not the dominant form. The world tree is most often rendered as cruciform-shaped vegetation, sprouting from the heads of anthropomorphic figures on the surface of celts or appearing in cruciform-shaped arrangements of celts. At La Venta, celts in this cruciform shape were buried as caches beneath ritual space. These deposits marked the cosmic stage on which the Olmec ruler performed the rituals of both the *axis mundi* and the shamanic trance journey into the otherworld.

THE SHAMANIC TRANCE-JOURNEY (OR FLIGHT) COSTUME

The elaborate clothing worn by an enthroned individual in Mural 1 on a cliff face above the north grotto at Oxtotitlan Cave identifies the painting's subject: a specific moment in a shamanic flight or cosmic travel ceremony (fig. 27). Large (width 3.8 meters by height 2.5 meters) and remarkably well-preserved (considering it has been exposed to the elements for some twenty-seven hundred years), the Oxtotitlan mural is located with other paintings in a series of shallow grottos near the city of Chilpancingo, Guerrero.[77] The Oxtotitlan murals join those of Juxtlahuaca Cave, also in Guerrero, as the only known examples of large-scale Formative period polychrome paintings.[78]

Enough of Oxtotitlan Mural 1 has survived to allow an excellent reconstruction by the Mexican artist Felipe Dávalos. The enthroned figure's most striking article of costume is his complex bird helmet or mask, which was once physically connected to a feather cape and backrack. The resemblance of the bird helmet's features to an owl's is too striking to go unmentioned. The iris of the hollowed-out, large round eye, Grove suggested, "once held

Figure 27. Drawing of the polychrome mural above the grotto at Oxtotitlan Cave, Guerrero.

Figure 28. Monument 22, throne in sunken patio of Chalcatzingo, Morelos.

an object such as a piece of jade or a polished magnetite mirror." This owl mask is cut away in shamanic X-ray style to provide a view of the human face under the mask, leaving no doubt in the mind of the beholder that this is a human in ritual costume, not a zoomorphic supernatural.[79]

The rest of the costume reiterates the avian theme. A feathered cape suspended from the arms replicates the wings of a bird. Both the down-pointing right hand and arm and the uplifted left arm are hung with what are almost certainly jade bracelets, with bands to which the feathered cape is attached. When the arms are outstretched, these allow the cape to spread like the wings of a bird. Behind the seated individual is a backrack with an intricate feathered-tail assemblage. Around his waist is an apron or loincloth hanging over a brown, possibly hide, skirt, which is painted with two hand-paw-wing motifs, each containing an in-turning spiral. The association between the hand-paw-wing motif and the inturning spiral and avian themes serves to identify this figure as a cosmic flier, which is further supported by the crossed-bands pectoral on the chest.

The throne on which this cosmic flier sits is made up of three zoomorphic faces. The eyes of the upper, frontal face, which is the best preserved, are marked with the crossed-bands, a strong indica-

Figure 29. Incised bowl, 900–600 B.C., Xochipala, Guerrero. Stone, h. 6.4 cm.; diam. 15.5 cm. Private collection.

tion this zoomorph is a variant of the Olmec sky dragon, and are framed by eyebrows identical to those on the throne, Monument 22, in the sunken patio at Chalcatzingo (fig. 28).[80] From the upper jaw, two downturned fangs descend. Between the two fangs runs a striped, horizontal band, undoubtedly a sky band. At Oxtotitlan and on La Venta Altar 4, the horizontal band motif identifies the seats as sky thrones. Though the incised motifs on the upper register, or ledge, of Chalcatzingo Monument 22 are badly damaged, some form of banding, though not horizontal, also appears to have existed on this monument. However, in the case of the Chalcat-zingo throne zoomorph, the eyes are not marked with the crossed-bands, which suggests that it is the Olmec earth dragon. The features of the other two zoomorph faces, which form the "legs" of the Oxtotitlan throne, have been obscured by the ravages of time, but in each case at least an eye and a blunt fang are visible. Overall, the Oxtotitlan throne is strikingly similar to a supernatural image incised on a stone bowl from Xochipala (fig. 29). The Oxtotitlan throne may well originally have had a fourth face like the image on the Xochipala bowl, but the mural is too badly damaged in its lower section to allow such a reconstruction.

The mouth of the tricephalic throne monster in Oxtotitlan Mural 1 is actually formed by the grotto beneath. Grove reports that "in times past the cave contained lagoons of water during the rainy season; on occasion this water would overflow the mouth

Figure 30. Front of La Venta Altar 4.

of the cave and cascade into the fields below."[81] The enthroned figure's legs dangle over the edge of the throne in what Anne-Louise Schaffer identified, in reference to the Maya, as the "posture of royal ease."[82] The figure at Oxtotitlan is depicted at the precise moment before he will lift off and fly through the thin membrane of the cosmic portal into another reality.

La Venta Altar 4 and the Olmec Heartland Shamanic Flight Costume

Sky thrones, like the one in Oxtotitlan Mural 1, played a critical role in Middle Formative iconography and the ritual accouterments of shamanic flight. No single throne exemplifies this concept more than La Venta Altar 4, a truly monumental example of heartland sculpture (height 160 centimeters, width 319 centimeters, depth 190 centimeters), first identified as a royal seat or throne by Grove (fig. 30).[83] Now that Olmec altars are recognized as the seats or thrones of Olmec rulers, it makes sense that they would also be used to convey the iconography of rulership, which would support a heartland origin for much of the Olmec-style symbol system.

The central image on the front of La Venta Altar 4 is a life-size human figure seated cross-legged in a niche surrounded by a ropelike element, attached to which are four symbols that have been interpreted as plants. This interpretation may be correct—the four symbols are positioned similarly to the four elements of sprouting vegetation at the corners of Chalcatzingo Monument 9—but the symbols could also be plates with smoking jars or incense burners placed in them. A pattern has been established associating such plates with elite burials at both La Venta and Chalcatzingo.[84]

The La Venta Altar 4 figure, like his Oxtotitlan counterpart, wears an intricate, raptorial avian helmet or headdress. Whereas the Oxtotitlan helmet covers the wearer's face completely and uses the X-ray style to reveal the human face beneath the mask, La Venta Altar 4's avian helmet is tied to the wearer's head with a strap but it does not have a mask. The human features are thus visible beneath what would have been the avian beak. Grove is convinced, and I concur, that the elaborate crest on the back of the bird helmet pinpoints the species as the harpy eagle (*Harpia haryja*).[85]

In Postclassic Mesoamerican iconography, the harpy eagle is affiliated with the sun and human sacrifice.[86] Owls, on the other hand, are nocturnal birds, messengers between the supernatural realm and human beings.[87] Considering the day and night associations of these two avians incorporated into the shamanic flying costumes at two Middle Formative sites—the owl at Oxtotitlan and the harpy eagle at La Venta—an opposition between day and night at these sites may have been incorporated into the shamanic flight costumes of the rulers.

La Venta Altar 4's niche figure holds the end of a rope in his right hand; the end of another rope passes under his left knee. The rope held in his right hand goes around the side of the altar where it ends tied around the wrist of a seated human figure, whose facial features have been recarved in modern times (fig. 31). The left side of the altar is too extensively damaged to determine whether there was a counterpart to the figure on the right side. Grove argues that the rope symbolizes kinship and ancestral or lineage relationships.[88] However, the fact that the rope is tied around the seated figure's wrist and not held in his hand and that his other hand is held across his chest in a posture of submission leads me to conclude that he is a captive whose blood will open the supernatural ritual in which the central figure participates.

The altar's ledge, which overhangs the seated

Figure 31. Right side of La Venta Altar 4.

Figure 32. Top of La Venta Altar 4.

central figure, is incised with five identifiable symbols: a double merlon motif at each corner; a sky band; an earth band; and, overlapping both the sky and earth bands, the head of a feline, perhaps a jaguar, who holds the crossed-bands in his open mouth. The ledge as a whole is a one-dimensional cosmic model. Within this, the function of the sky and earth bands is self-evident, but what of the double merlon, jaguar, and crossed-bands motifs?

The double merlon motif can mark the entrance or portal to the supernatural otherworld as well as the Olmec sacred mountain and the otherworld contained within.[89] The double merlons on the corners of this ledge in effect mark those corners and perhaps Altar 4 itself as the location of portals. The jaguar with the crossed-bands in his mouth is best understood if we keep in mind that Altar 4, like its Oxtotitlan and Chalcatzingo counterparts, is a throne. In Oxtotitlan Mural 1, the zoomorphic throne is shown with its occupant. In order to view

La Venta Altar 4 in the same light, we can imagine the life-size central figure from the niche seated atop Altar 4, directly above the frontal jaguar (fig. 32).

La Venta Altar 4 is thus both a throne and a cosmological model. The throne visualizes the Olmec ruler as the interface between the natural and supernatural realms. The feline/jaguar, the ruler's animal spirit companion, is his means of locomotion in his trance journey into the otherworld. Peter T. Furst, in his article first identifying the shamanic content of Olmec art and ideology, discussed several South American myths in which jaguars are the instrument of human travel to the otherworld.[90] He observed that the seat or stool on which a Yecuana shaman sits while performing nocturnal curing rituals is carved in the shape of a jaguar. The felines on Altar 4 and La Venta Monument 59, which I discuss below, can also be interpreted as jaguar-shaped shaman's stools.

Figure 34. Supernatural Riding a Jaguar, 900–600 B.C., Río Pesquero, Veracruz. Gray-green jadeite with a milky patina and a vein of a softer mineral, h. 8.9 cm.; w. 3.1 cm.; d. 5 cm. Private collection.

Figure 33. La Venta Monument 59.

Figure 35. Bloodletter handle, 900–600 B.C., Mexico. Greenstone. Private collection.

On Altar 4, the fact that the feline image overlaps both the sky and earth bands and holds the crossed-bands motif in his mouth underscores his role in supernatural travel.

Without a more explicit example of a jaguar throne, my conjecture would remain simply that. Happily for my argument, such a throne exists: La Venta Monument 59 (height 95 centimeters, width 65 centimeters, length 113 centimeters), a three-dimensional, snarling supernatural jaguar with a ledge on its back (fig. 33). Undoubtedly, Monument 59 is a three-dimensional depiction of the jaguar carved on the ledge of Altar 4.

My interpretation of Altar 4's symbolic function is further confirmed by a small carved jade showing a supernatural being transported on the back of a sinuous feline (fig. 34; cat. no. 63).[91] In this case, the supernatural rides his feline transporter, holding onto its tail for dear life. The round shape of this feline's ears is identical to that of the feline's on the ledge of Altar 4.

Another carved jade, the handle of a jade blood-letter, has a thematically similar scene (fig. 35). Here, the transporter is marked with what appear to be dragon more than feline characteristics. The human figure stretched out on his stomach along the supernatural's back clings to its head to keep from being thrown off. On each of these two carved jades, a supernatural aids in the action of cosmic flight.

Returning to the throne in Oxtotitlan Mural 1, I am convinced the three zoomorphs with their crossed-bands eyes are supernatural transporters and portals. Since La Venta Altar 4 is the same as the kind of throne depicted at Oxtotitlan, it was probably also a supernatural aid to cosmic flight. The flying costumes worn by Olmec rulers and other Middle Formative ritual practitioners under-score the importance of shamanic ideology to Middle Formative political validation.

The trance journey remains at the heart of sha-manic ideology. The existence of diverse images such as the depictions of rulers wearing the sha-manic flier and world tree costume suggests the possibility of regional and perhaps ethnic variations within the larger body of Middle Formative Olmec-style objects. The wide geographical range and the overarching theme of access to supernatural power and political validation conveyed by these objects reinforces my hypothesis that behind this tradition lay the Middle Formative Ceremonial Complex. Olmec-style objects first appeared in the Gulf Coast heartland of the archaelogical Olmec, indicating that the complex originated with that people. With our knowledge of the iconographic content of Olmec-style art, we may soon be able to test a given geographical and linguistic area to see whether ideology and political structure were indeed based on this complex.

Notes

1. Richard A. Diehl, "Olmec Archaeology: What We Know and What We Wish We Knew," in *Regional Perspectives on the Olmec*, ed. Robert J. Sharer and David C. Grove (Cambridge, 1989), 23–26.

2. For a discussion of the Olmec/Mixe-Zoque connection, see Lyle R. Campbell and Terrence S. Kaufman, "A Linguistic Look at the Olmec," *American Antiquity* 41 (1976): 80–89.

3. Ibid., 26–31.

4. For a discussion of Olmec political organization, see Coe and Diehl, this volume; and Philip Drucker, "On the Nature of the Olmec Polity," in *The Olmec and Their Neighbors: Essays in Memory of Matthew W. Stirling*, ed. Elizabeth P. Benson (Washington, D.C., 1981), 29–48.

5. For a discussion of the spread of monumental sculpture throughout large areas of Middle Formative Mesoamerica, see David C. Grove, "'Olmec' Horizons in Formative Period Mesoamerica: Diffusion or Social Evolution?," in *Latin American Horizons*, ed. Donald S. Rice (Washington, D.C., 1993), 83–112.

6. Miguel Covarrubias argued early on for a Guerrero or Mixteca Alta genesis for the Olmec in *Indian Art of Mexico and Central America* (New York, 1957). Covarrubias's conclusions have been supported by Gillett G. Griffin of The Art Museum, Princeton University, and the Olmec scholar Carlo T. E. Gay.

7. David C. Grove, "Olmec: What's in a Name?" in *Regional Perspectives on the Olmec*, ed. Sharer and Grove (as in note 1), 8–14.

8. For the original proposal for the interaction sphere model, see Kent V. Flannery, "The Olmec and the Valley of Oaxaca: A Model For Inter-regional Interaction in Formative Times," in *Dumbarton Oaks Conference on the Olmec*, ed. Elizabeth P. Benson (Washington, D.C., 1968), 79–110.

9. In an attempt to resolve this controversy, David Grove and Robert Sharer organized a symposium entitled "Regional Perspectives on the Olmec," at the School of American Research, Santa Fe, 1984, which ultimately led to the volume of essays by the same name (as in note 1), xix–xxiv.

10. For the original proposal for a Middle Formative Ceremonial Complex, see F. Kent Reilly, III, "Cosmos and Rulership: The Function of Olmec-Style Symbols in Formative Period Mesoamerica," *Visible Language* 24 (1990): 12–37. The term Middle Formative Period Ceremonial Complex arose from investigations to discover an archaeo-logical model that would best describe what I believe happened in Formative period Mesoamerica. This model proved to be the Southeastern Ceremonial Complex, a label used to define the art style and ritual activity associated with it produced by the cultures of the eastern United States during the Mississippian period (A.D. 900–1600).

11. A technique developed primarily within the discipline of linguistics, structural analysis is fundamentally the identification of substitution sets. Because writing is absent from the cultures of the Middle Formative period, I propose a principle of iconographic substitution equivalent to the structural analysis used in linguistics. This principle argues that if two or more symbolic elements substitute for each other in a similar iconographic context, they probably carry similar—if not exactly the same—meanings.

12. For a discussion of the role of other ethnic groups within my proposed ceremonial complex model, see Joyce Marcus, "Zapotec Chiefdoms and the Nature of Formative Religions," in *Regional Perspectives on the Olmec*, ed. Sharer and Grove (as in note 1), 148–97.

13. Other unified, yet ethnically diverse, cultural or ideological expressions are those of the Hellenistic Levant, Christian Medieval Europe, and the spread of Islam and Buddhism across wide areas of Asia.

14. For the archaeological evidence for this change, see Grove (as in note 5).

15. See Tate, this volume.

16. See Furst, this volume.

17. Mircea Eliade, *Shamanism: Archaic Techniques of Ecstasy*, trans. Willard R. Trask, Bollingen Series 76 (Princeton, N.J., 1970), 259.

18. Stephen Houston and David Stuart, "The *Way* Glyph: Evidence for 'Co-Essences' among the Classic Maya," in *Research Reports on Ancient Maya Writing*, no. 30 (Washington, D.C., 1989).

19. Linda Schele and David Freidel, *A Forest of Kings: The Untold Story of the Ancient Maya* (New York, 1990); Linda Schele, David Freidel, and Joy Parker, *Maya Cosmos: Three Thousand Years on the Shaman's Path* (New York, 1993).

20. K. C. Chang, *Art, Myth, and Ritual: The Path to Political Authority in Ancient China* (Cambridge, Mass., 1983), 44–55. A leading scholar on ancient China, Chang gives conclusive evidence in his chapter on "Shamanism and Politics" that Shang Dynasty Chinese rulers acted as chief shamans. According to Chang, the imperial ancestors spoke through the medium of the oracle bones, but the Shang emperor was the one who interpreted the symbols.

21. Joseph W. Kitagawa, *Religion in Japanese History* (New York, 1966), 3–45.

22. K. C. Chang, "An Introduction to Korean Shamanism," in *Shamanism: The Spirit World of Korea*, ed. Chai-shin Yu and Richard W.I. Guisso (Berkeley, 1988), 30–51.

23. Nevill Drury, *The Elements of Shamanism* (Longmead, England, 1989), 28–29.

24. John A. Grim, *The Shaman: Patterns of Religious Healing*

among the Ojibway Indians (Norman, Okla., 1983), 41.

25. Ibid.

26. Eliade (as in note 17), 145.

27. Ibid., 156–58.

28. Schele, Freidel, and Parker (as in note 19), 75–107.

29. J. Eric S. Thompson, *Maya History and Religion* (Norman, Okla., 1970), 195.

30. For a more in-depth examination of the origins of shamanic art, see Andreas Lommel, *Shamanism, the Beginnings of Art* (New York, 1967); and Ann T. Brodzky, Rose Daneswich, and Nick Johnson, "Stones, Bones and Skin: Ritual and Shamanic Art," *Artscanada* (Toronto, 1977).

31. Esther Pasztory, "Shamanism and North American Indian Art," in *Native North American Art History: Selected Readings*, ed. Zena P. Mathews and Aldona Jonaitis (Palo Alto, Cal., 1982), 9.

32. Ibid.

33. Ibid.

34. Ibid., 17.

35. Robert Layton, *The Anthropology of Art* (New York, 1981).

36. Ibid., 170–71.

37. For a discussion of the chronology of Olmec sculpture, see Susan Milbrath, "A Study of Olmec Sculptural Chronology," *Studies in Pre-Columbian Art and Archaeology*, no. 23 (Washington, D.C., 1979).

38. Miguel Covarrubias, "El arte 'Olmeca' o de La Venta," *Cuadernos Americanos* 28, no. 4 (1946): 153–79; and idem (as in note 6), 13–83.

39. Miguel Covarrubias, "Olmec Art or the Art of La Venta," trans. Robert Thomas Pirazzini, in *Pre-Columbian Art History: Selected Readings*, ed. Alana Cordy-Collins and Jean Stern (Palo Alto, Cal.), 1.

40. Covarrubias, *Indian Art* (as in note 6), 54.

41. Covarrubias, "Olmec Art or the Art of La Venta," (as in note 39), 4.

42. Ibid., 5.

43. Ibid., 4.

44. Ibid.

45. Covarrubias, *Indian Art* (as in note 6), 55.

46. Ibid.

47. Reilly (as in note 10), 12–37.

48. Peter David Joralemon, "The Olmec Dragon: A Study in Pre-Columbian Iconography," in *Origins of Religious Art and Iconography in Preclassic Mesoamerica*, ed. Henry B. Nicholson (Los Angeles, 1976), 27–71.

49. Ibid., 37–40.

50. Reilly (as in note 10), 30–34. This conflation of the cosmological divisions is not unknown in Mesoamerican art. It was a technique also used by the Classic period Maya (A.D. 200–900), the most striking example of which is the composition carved along the front edge of a bench discovered by David Webster at the site of Copan. Within this horizontal space, the Maya artist executed a cosmic model consisting of motifs and symbols representing the divisions of the cosmos into realms of sky, earth, and underworld. What the viewer has to understand is that the edge of the bench is carved to represent a vertically stacked model of sky over earth and earth over underworld. What the viewer actually sees are the symbols and motifs of the three cosmic realms laid out in a horizontal composition.

51. Joralemon (as in note 48), 37–40; F. Kent Reilly, III, "Visions to Another World: Art, Shamanism, and Political Power in Middle Formative Mesoamerica," Ph.D. diss., University of Texas at Austin, 1994.

52. For a full definition of the Olmec Dragon, see Joralemon (as in note 48).

53. For a discussion of bloodletting among the ancient Maya, see Linda Schele and Mary E. Miller, *The Blood of Kings: Dynasty and Ritual in Maya Art* (Fort Worth, Tex., 1986); David Stuart, "Blood Symbolism in Maya Iconography," in *Maya Iconography*, ed. Gillett G. Griffin and Elizabeth P. Benson (Princeton, N.J., 1988), 175–221.

54. Peter T. Furst, personal communication, April 1994.

55. For the linkage of the four-dots-and-bar motif with the Olmec Dragon, see Joralemon (as in note 48), 47.

56. Reilly (as in note 10), 12–37.

57. In Aztec mythology the primordial dragon was identified as Cipactli. While floating on the surface of the primordial sea, Cipactli is torn apart by Quetzalcoatl and Tezcatlipoca. These two deities create the earth from the lower part of Cipactli's body, the sky from the upper part. For a brief account of this myth, see B. C. Bundage, *The Fifth Sun: Aztec Gods, Aztec World* (Austin, Tex., 1979), 31–32.

58. Peter David Joralemon, "A Study of Olmec Iconography," *Studies in Pre-Columbian Art and Archaeology*, no. 7 (Washington, D.C., 1971), 35.

59. For a full account of the excavation of La Venta Monument 6, see Matthew W. Stirling and Marion Stirling, "Finding Jewels of Jade in a Mexican Swamp," *National Geographic Magazine* 82 (1942): 635–61.

60. David C. Grove, "The Olmec Paintings of Oxtotitlan Cave, Guerrero, Mexico," *Studies in Pre-Columbian Art and Archaeology*, no. 6 (Washington, D.C, 1970), 11, 32; Joralemon (as in note 48), 37–40.

61. In a personal communication (1992), Muriel Porter Weaver, who excavated at Tlatilco, informed me of the presence of several unfired examples of these aquatic, zoomorphic ceramic vessels in the tombs. She stated that their condition supports my interpretation that this category of ceramics was intended for tomb, not daily, use.

62. See Tate, this volume.

63. Charles Smiley in Michael D. Coe, "Olmec and Maya: A Study in Relationships," in *The Origins of Maya Civilization*, ed. Richard E. W. Adams (Albuquerque, N.M., 1977), 189.

64. In Classic Maya art the sky was often depicted as a great, crocodilian-derived, zoomorphic supernatural. The Classic Maya cosmic monster is often marked with the crossed-bands motif as well as other celestial symbols. For a description of the Maya cosmic monster, see Schele and Freidel (as in note 19), 66.

65. Iconographic analysis of the recently discovered Monument 31 from the highland site of Chalcatzingo demonstrates for the first time that at least by the Middle Formative period, the Lazy-S motif, like its Classic Maya counterpart, was associated with clouds, bloodletting, and a celestial location. Although the Lazy-S motif figures prominently in the iconographic corpus at Chalcatzingo, until the analysis of Monument 31 no context existed for its meanings. For a more complete analysis of the Lazy-S, see F. Kent Reilly, III, "The Lazy-S: Evidence for a

Formative Period Iconographic Loan to Maya Hieroglyphic Writing," in S*eventh Palenque Round Table, 1989*, ed. Merle Green Robertson (in press).

66. Joralemon summarizes the ideological implications of the dual nature of the Olmec dragon in "The Olmec Dragon" (as in note 48), 37–47.

67. Coe (as in note 63), 189.

68. The Izapan origin of the celestial bird iconographic complex is fully developed by Constance Cortez, "The Principal Bird Deity in Preclassic and Early Classic Maya Art," Master's thesis, University of Texas at Austin, 1986. Current investigations of the ideological function of the celestial bird (see Schele, Freidel, and Parker [as in note 19]) have determined that this supernatural is the avatar of Itzam-Na, the Classic Maya primordial shaman deity. The image of the celestial bird—Itzam-Ye—on any man-made or supernatural object symbolizes that the object is animated and magical.

69. Susana Villasana Benitez, "La Organización social de los Zoques de Tapalap, Chiapas," in *Estudios Recientes en el Area Zoque* (Chiapas, 1988).

70. Throughout much of Mesoamerican cosmological thought was a perception of not one, but five world trees corresponding to the five world directions of east, west, north, south, and center. These five directional world trees served as conduits for the movement of supernatural power from one cosmic realm to another.

71. My current research leads me to believe that if the incised image on this celt is a human figure, then he wears the costume of the Middle Formative maize lord in his Milky Way manifestation.

72. In 1984 Virginia M. Fields was the first to link the Formative period three-pronged motif, or trefoil, to the Maya jester god headdress. The story of her discovery is told in two pivotal works in which she developed her hypothesis: "The Origins of Kingship among the Lowland Classic Maya," Ph.D. diss., University of Texas at Austin, 1989, and "The Iconographic Heritage of the Maya Jester God," in *Sixth Palenque Round Table, 1986* , ed. Virginia M. Fields (Norman, Okla., 1991), 167–74.

73. Linda Schele, "Sprouts and the Early Symbolism of Rulers in Mesoamerica," paper delivered at the Conference on Early Symbolism in the Writing of the Maya, Hildesheim, Germany, 1993; and this volume.

74. Ibid.

75. Ibid.

76. Ibid.

77. David C. Grove was the first researcher to bring the Oxtotitlan murals to public attention in "The Olmec Paintings of Oxtotitlan Cave" (as in note 60).

78. The Juxtlahuaca Cave paintings and their identification as Olmec-style works of art was first proposed by Carlo T. E. Gay, "Oldest Paintings in the New World," *Natural History* 76 (1967): 28–35.

79. For a full discussion of the function of the "X-ray style" in shamanic art forms, see Lommel (as in note 30), 129–33.

80. William Fash, "The Altar and Associated Features," in *Ancient Chalcatzingo*, ed. David C. Grove (Austin, Tex., 1987), 82–94.

81. Grove (as in note 60), 31.

82. Anne-Louise Schaffer, "The Maya 'Posture of Royal Ease,'" in *Sixth Palenque Round Table*, ed. Fields (as in note 72), 203–16.

83. David C. Grove, "Olmec Altars and Myths," *Archaeology* 26 (1973):128–35.

84. For a more complete discussion of the relationship between Middle Formative grave goods at Chalcatzingo and the burial practices at La Venta, see David C. Grove, *Chalcatzingo: Excavations on the Olmec Frontier* (New York, 1984), 75; Marcia Merry de Morales, "Chalcatzingo Burials as Indicators of Social Ranking," in *Ancient Chalcatzingo* (as in note 80), 95–114.

85. Grove (as in note 83): 130.

86. Joralemon (as in note 48), 52–58.

87. Mary Ellen Miller and Karl A. Taube, *The Gods and Symbols of Ancient Mexico and the Maya: An Illustrated Dictionary of Mesoamerican Religion* (New York, 1993), 128.

88. Grove (as in note 83): 130–34.

89. For a more complete discussion of the origin and function of the "double merlon" motif, see Elizabeth P. Benson, "An Olmec Figure at Dumbarton Oaks," *Studies in Pre-Columbian Art and Archaeology*, no. 8 (Washington, D.C., 1971), 10 n. 2; F. Kent Reilly, III, "Olmec Iconographic Influences on the Symbols of Maya Rulership: An Examination of Possible Sources," in *Sixth Palenque Round Table*, ed. Fields (as in note 72), 151–66.

90. Peter T. Furst, "The Olmec Were-Jaguar Motif in the Light of Ethnographic Reality," in *Dumbarton Oaks Conference on the Olmec*, ed. Elizabeth P. Benson (Washington, D.C., 1968), 151.

Art in Olmec Culture

CAROLYN E. TATE

Art (along with other aesthetic activities, such as oral tradition, ritual performance, divination, costuming, hunting, warfare, and city planning) reveals a culture's predilections, myths and world view, ideals of human behavior, and most feared elements of existence. An informed view of the Olmec art style is thus important, especially since art is the major document we have of the ancestral civilization of Mesoamerica. Olmec art challenges us to relate it to a social matrix for which nearly no direct evidence exists. We have only what we have found of their art and their cities to guide us. In this consideration of the enigmatic Olmec art style, which has attracted interest more for its fantastic were-jaguar creatures and the power perceived in its forms than for any ideals it may reflect, I shall discuss the material, visual, and psychological aspects of the art, hoping to reveal some of the beliefs, ideals, and rituals of Olmec civilization.

For decades Mesoamerican specialists have grappled with the issues of what defines Olmec art and culture, how far an object can stray from the definitions and still represent the ideas and presence of Olmec culture, and whether Olmec ideology prevailed wherever Olmec-style objects are found. In an article published in the *Handbook of Middle American Indians* thirty years ago, Michael D. Coe defined the Olmec art style on the basis of formal qualities, iconography, symbols, and the representation of costume, weapons, and paraphernalia.[1] He moved from a discussion of the range of objects on which the art style appears to a definition of the art style, concluding with an examination of its spatial and temporal distribution. While he said

Figure 1. Standing Figure with Sack, 900–600 B.C., Guerrero. Jade, h. 8.3 cm.; w. 3.8 cm.; d. 3.5 cm. Anonymous loan to The Metropolitan Museum of Art.

his definition of the style is based on "climax-region" (southern Veracruz and northern Tabasco, commonly referred to as the heartland) objects, in fact, he used examples from all parts of Meso-america of such things as war clubs, cleft heads, and torches. This contradiction occurred because canonically correct objects, which are the richest iconographically and seem best suited for an iconographic study, are not from the climax area. Coe's lasting contributions in the article are his naming of most of the sculptural formats used by the Olmec, clear discussion of the elements creating the sense of monumentality in Olmec art, identification of the avian serpent (a topic developed in this volume by Karl A. Taube), recapitulation of many of the previously identified symbols incised on Olmec objects, and a diagram designating Olmec art as the basis for all known major art styles of lowland Mesoamerica. Beatriz de la Fuente later argued in her 1981 article in *The Olmec and Their Neighbors*, that Coe, along with Hermann Beyer, Miguel Covarrubias, George Kubler, and Marshall Saville overemphasized the presence of the jaguar as the basic motif of Olmec art.[2]

Here, de la Fuente divided Olmec monumental art into three categories: human, animal, and composite. She pointed out that in her catalogue of Olmec monumental sculpture, consisting of 206 pieces, over half (that is, 110) represent human beings.[3] She broke down the human representations into three "themes": lords under supernatural protection, mediators, and allegorical portraits. In the present volume, these themes are termed "subjects" and additional ones are identified, but de la Fuente's insistence that Olmec art is centered on the human figure reminds scholars that the supernatural and cosmological iconography revolves around

a human fulcrum. Furthermore, de la Fuente proposed that an "internal rhythm" governs the composition of the forms in Olmec monuments. She applied the Greek Golden Mean, a measure of harmonic proportion, to several Olmec sculptures, including Monuments 4 and 10 from San Lorenzo, concluding that the details and features of the monuments correspond to the geometric junctions of the Greek ideal order. The Olmec artists attempted to visualize harmonic proportion in their sculpture and to create an allegory of cosmic order. This observation recognizes that the Olmec artists and patrons skillfully and subtly manipulated form to convey the character of the ideal ruler and society.

For the purposes of this discussion, Formative period objects embodying the themes, formats, subjects, and formal qualities associated with the dominant form of shamanic kingship, not only from the Gulf Coast but also from other areas in Meso-america, will be called "Olmec." Most of the objects in the exhibition probably date to the Middle Formative and are part of a widespread ceremonial complex, as discussed by F. Kent Reilly, III, in this volume. If we assume that the high culture area (the Gulf Coast Olmec) lacked a standing army of sufficient size to patrol many distant outposts in the western and southern areas of Mesoamerica, then the expansion of the ideology that informs Olmec style objects was not a matter of miliary might. There is no evidence that conquest or war forced peoples to participate in this belief system. Connections among distant Mesoamerican peoples may first have been made in the course of exploration to gather knowledge about the world. The resulting interactions probably included trade of knowledge and spiritual concepts as well as culturally desirable materials. The institution of hierarchical rulership appealed to certain groups, who would have already possessed a shamanic worldview brought from Asia. They adopted and contributed to the concepts and rituals of shamanic kingship: creating sacred landscapes and art and structuring their societies in ways that expressed the premises of the Olmec ideological system. Each society transformed their situation to a different degree, modifying the prevailing sense of human identity and the structure of the cosmos with certain aspects of the new mode of government by shamanic rulers. This begins to resolve the question of why a hallmark of Olmec art, the Kunz Axe, came from an area not purely Olmec, specifically, Oaxaca, and why so many other hallmarks were found in the Balsas River Basin (fig. 1; cat. no. 119). In the Gulf Coast, the closest analogy to the ceremonial axe are the buried mosaic pavements at La Venta. No ceremonial axes have been found at Gulf Coast sites, but the Kunz Axe could have been made as a portable export to convey the concept and presence of the patron of fertility, rain, and water. The axe could also have originated in the Guerrero region, where a tradition of stone carving existed and major axes have been found that perhaps employed the similar Teopantecuanitlan monoliths as models. In any case, using only Gulf Coast objects to define the Olmec art style (unless the definition is limited to monumental sculpture, which would omit nearly all the objects in this catalogue and much of what we have come to think of as Olmec) is not satisfactory. When more excavation data from individual areas are available, relations among the separate cities and theirs to the whole will be better understood.

ART IN THE MAGIC-COSMIC WORLD VIEW

In assigning cultural meaning to art forms and ritual activities, I shall rely here on recent scholarly recognition that ancient American civilizations grew out of an obvious substrata of shamanic ideology. I shall propose interpretations of Olmec culture based on inference from the system of shamanic beliefs common to many traditional, nonindustrial societies and indigenous to ancient Mesoamerica. The Olmec lived in a "magic-cosmic" world that sees stones, trees, rain, animals, and humans infused with power, and where, according to Jonathon Haas, as summarized by Alan Roland, there is "a nonrational, noncausal monistic relationship between planetary and other celestial bodies with past lives on one hand, and with everyday relationships and events on the other, through correspondences, identities, and emanations that are metonymically understood. Philosophically, this is based on the idea that human beings constitute a microcosm with a number of inner correspondences and identities with the forces of the macrocosm or cosmos."[4] It is reasonably safe to assume that like most other nonindustrial, traditional societies, and as witnessed throughout Mesoamerica, the Olmec operated under some variation of the magic-cosmic world view.

The energy that animates humans also suffuses the rest of nature. Individuals thus tend to see themselves as similar to rather than separate from or better than the diversity of forms in the world. This energy also imbues other natural phenomena, including time and space. Through intense exchanges of energy in ritual and individual transformational processes, humans and natural phenomena influence each other, creating correspondences between the visible world and the unseen. As Roland put it, "Objective causality does not exist in this world, but rather only juxtapositions, identities, and synchronicities."[5]

The concept that objects are animate applies to the Olmec works in this catalogue. As I discuss their materials and manufacture, it will become apparent they are more than just art objects, but are links with primordial power. This is not the power sought by individuals in Western society to feel superior to or to control others (often linked with money, intellectual or physical might, or superior weaponry), but power as it might be defined in ancient China. Here, as K. C. Chang observed, the seizing of political power was a combination of luck (birth into the proper clan and lineage), strategy (marriage to the right person and adroit political maneuvering), good actions (winning popular support), and "access to ancestral wisdom and foresight" (obtained through the ability to manipulate and control art objects and the symbols inscribed upon them).[6] I believe that any consideration of Olmec power must take seriously the reality of the spiritual experience, the appeal of shamanic ecstasy, and the unusual powers that spiritual practitioners can obtain. Whether or not modern scholarship is open to alternate realities, the Olmec subscribed to such a one. In defining the role of art objects in the formulation of Olmec political power, the ancient view of spiritual power should be considered.

In his article "The Idea of Power in Javanese Culture," Benedict Anderson nearly expressed my own understanding about the ancient Olmec concept of power: "Power exists independent of its possible users. It is not a theoretical postulate but an existential reality. Power is that intangible, mysterious, and divine energy which animates the universe. It is manifested in every aspect of the natural world, in stones, trees, clouds, and fire, but is expressed quintessentially in the central mystery of life, the process of generation and regeneration."[7] I would add that the Olmec appear to have practiced specific bodily and mental disciplines to hone their awareness and ability to access this power. The process of transformation is also inherent in the "central mystery of life," which itself is fueled by a combination of power and self-effort. A caterpillar weaves a cocoon and through the power inherent in the cosmos transforms into a moth. Humans practice ascetic disciplines like bloodletting, fasting, chanting, or meditation to become vessels for cosmic forces, enabling them to transform into animal spirit companions. Depending on their effort and intentions, the practitioners' access to power may sharpen the intellect, provide a favorable outlook on the course of events, or heighten the awareness of events, information, and other people's feelings and thoughts. Such abilities have been attributed to naguals in the literature on Mesoamerica. In the sixteenth century many native political and spiritual leaders professed to have such powers. These beliefs, however, were regarded as superstitions by the Spanish, and were not sympathetically investigated.

The case for Olmec sculpture as a visible statement of the supernatural power of the shaman-king has been argued since Peter T. Furst's 1968 article on human-jaguar transformation brought to light the fact that the Olmec, like many other societies, believed they could shed the limitations of the human condition through transformation into animal spirits and through this "death" of human consciousness make contact with beings of the spiritual realm.[8] More recently, F. Kent Reilly, III, in an article on a figure in this catalogue, the Shaman in Transformation Pose (cat no. 42), emphasized the political function of Olmec shamanic imagery, which formed a "visible charter for rulership in the heartland and in those areas of Mesoamerica that participated in the Formative Period Ceremonial Complex."[9]

Western scholarship generally does not accept inference or direct perception as evidence. Therefore, we are confronted with the conundrum of trying to understand through written texts and intellectual scientific and art-historical analysis how the Olmec accomplished, for example, the often depicted human-animal transformation, or what spiritual state they achieved when standing in meditation like the figures of La Venta Offering 4. It seems that the Olmec contacted the power flowing through the avian serpents and earth monsters, rain-making shamans, shaman-kings, transformation figures, dwarfs, fetus figures, hunchbacks, contortionists and meditating figures that form the corpus of Olmec art.

COMPONENTS OF THE OLMEC ART STYLE

The Olmec art style is the material expression of the concerns and beliefs of a local society interpreted through the mandates of its political leaders, the artist's individual predilection, and the Olmec ideological system. This definition includes not only the appearance of the art object, but also the acquisition of materials, selection and sources of the subject, format, and theme, the processes of manufacture, and the uses and functions of the object in ritual and in the society.

THE CHALLENGES OF BASALT AND JADE

Books on Olmec art frequently mention that the art style of the Gulf Coast Olmec uses materials that do not naturally occur at the ceremonial centers: basalt, jade and other greenstones, hematite, quartz, onyx, and other stones. The Gulf Coast Olmec not only employed the readily available river clays, vegetal materials, and other local commodities, but also sought, under challenging circumstances, the rare materials for their ceremonial cities, which, when built, demonstrated their ingenuity, skill, teamwork, and administrative ability. The cities also expressed the efficacy of their world view and, above all, the veracity of their rulers' divine origin and power. The hallmarks of Gulf Coast Olmec ceremonial cities are the basalt colossal heads and thrones. They demonstrate the successful resolution of a seemingly impossible task achieved under the guidance of a powerful ruler. These carved basalt boulders, thunderingly quiet statements that loomed in the ceremonial cities, identified the rulers with the terrible, metamorphic powers of the earth.

The Gulf Coast Olmec sought enormous boulders that had been spit out of a volcano. Formed during a distant era, these stones, metamorphosed and brought into the present by a violent, fiery birth, came from an unknowable part of the cosmos: the belly of the earth. What could better symbolize majesty, the forces of transformation, and the ancient and terrible power of the earth than this material? The people, who thus chose this substance for its significance, selected boulders weighing up to forty metric tons to prove their superiority in manipulating and possessing it. The San Lorenzo people dragged boulders some forty to fifty kilometers from the flanks of Cerro Cintepec to the low-lying areas of Río Chacalapa, where they may have loaded them on balsa rafts and floated them for more than ten kilometers to a laguna. From there, they transported the boulders two and a half kilometers over a course rising fifty meters in elevation.[10]

Apparently following the example of the San Lorenzo people, the La Venta artists also conquered and possessed basalt boulders, which they carved into images of their rulers' heads and incorporated

into their shamanic rituals. To this feat they added others, including the acquisition and crafting of serpentines and tough green jadeites from distant shores of the known world. This attachment of value to greenstone was a concept imported by the Gulf Coast Olmec from Chiapas (where the earliest documented use of greenstone is as beads placed in the mouths of human burials about 1500 B.C.[11]) or Oaxaca (where, between 1150 and 850 B.C., at San Jose Mogote, most burials include a jade bead in the mouth[12]), or possibly Guerrero. This greenstone, which demands phenomenal effort to shape, drill, and polish, signifies rulership and perhaps water, represented by rain and the generative power of the primordial sea (shown by the La Venta Massive Offerings of serpentine blocks under the ceremonial court).[13] Adopted by most later Mesoamerican civilizations, these ideas may not have originated with the Gulf Coast Olmec but perhaps in the periphery of Mesoamerica, which suggests that Olmec culture did not evolve as a monolithic whole but gradually through the stimulation of intellectual and technical exchange of knowledge, ideas, and materials with distant, strange peoples.

Travel and exploration during the period in which Mesoamerica's first civilization was in the process of defining itself would have required exceptional individuals brave enough to surmount psychic and physical dangers. These heroes integrated the periphery with the center of each city's cosmos. In many societies, they obtained some of the qualities of the archetypal travelers, the sun and moon,[14] and since the principal exchange in the Formative period was between the eastern and western shores of the known world, we could expect this to be true of the Olmec as well.

So far the only positively identified source of Mesoamerican jade is the suture zone of the Caribbean tectonic plate, which forms the Motagua River Valley in Guatemala. The ancients probably did not quarry jade but used alluvial boulders. This is true of Guerrero, where river cobbles of jade, including the prized blue-green jade of the standing figures, have been found.[15] This translucent blue, diopside jadeite and the emerald green jade were the most striking materials carved by the Olmec, although stones of other composition and color

Figure 2. Standing Figure, 900–600 B.C., Guerrero. Blue-green serpentine, h. 25 cm.; w. 9 cm.; d. 4 cm. Private collection.

were often used, especially in Guerrero where the ancient lithic tradition manifests most often in local stones (fig. 2; cat. no. 26).

Somehow the first people to use jade (apparently those of coastal Chiapas in 1500 B.C.) found a source and developed the technology to work it. The acts of obtaining and working these valuable stones related to the shamanic journey. This involved traveling through the landscape and communicating with the spirits and people encountered, then transforming the resistant material into three-dimensional spheres placed in the mouths of those whose spirits had departed on other journeys.

About 1000 B.C., when jades and massive quantities of greenstones were brought to La Venta, both the material and the concept of using it were endowed with the values of distant time and space. These acquisitions may have declared, as Mary Helms explained, "the successful (ideal) attainment of knowledge and ritual efficacy as well as the personal state of spiritual purity necessary to elicit the supernatural aid required to obtain wealth."[16] Burying the greenstones under the ceremonial court of La Venta symbolized the primordial, underworld sea, as Reilly proposes in this volume, and was evidence of wealth and contact with the distant, uncivilized powers dwelling at the periphery of time and space. The buried caches of stones recreated the cosmos on the horizontal as well as the vertical plane.

Fine craftsmanship and lapidary skills are acknowledged aspects of Olmec art. As a participant in the creation of the ceremonial city, the Olmec artist's task was to instill into tangible objects that which engendered the human race and established civilized life, conveying this information to both distant and civilized individuals. In the process, the artist manipulated the powers inherent in the materials, the ritual for which the object was prepared, and the subject. Helms made the point that these powers were perceived as outside the individual and as distant and supernatural "energetics," which the artist must draw into the object and the situation. Skilled crafting compressed into contemporary forms the original transformative act of the creators, kept alive through oral literature.[17]

A principal theme in Olmec art, transformation is also the essence of making figures from tough stones. The working of basalt, jade, and serpentine is perhaps less dramatic than, for instance, the smithing of gold, but probably more laborious. According to Gerardo Reichel-Dolmatoff, "The goldsmith, like the shaman, is one who makes transformations, for by working the gold and giving it a culturally significant form he makes the material pass from a profane to a sacred state."[18] While the varieties of technical skills in stone-working may be fewer, the difficulty and time involved are greater. The visualizing, planning, and roughing out of the image and, in the case of jade, the repetitive tasks of drilling, grinding, and polishing with the available abrasives (nothing harder than quartz, which is not much harder than jade) require many hours of persistent effort and concentration to produce noticeable results. During the fabrication of ritual objects, the artists likely withdrew from society and underwent austerities, probably including meditative communication with spiritual energies; chanting, drumming, or dancing; and possibly bloodletting.[19] Like the transporting of the basalt boulders and the burying of the serpentine blocks at La Venta, the finding, acquiring, and shaping of valuable stones were enormous challenges, whose success proved the artist's supernatural capability to exercise spiritual discipline and communicate with unpredictable powers for long periods of time.

MODELING CLAY

The stones the Olmec used, whether from nearby or distant sources, are igneous or metamorphic. They were formed in fire, the element that allows humans to handle godlike forces of destruction and creation. Of course, fire is hot, like the sun, and many of the descendants of the Olmec culture, such as the Maya, called their priests Ah K'in, He of the Sun, and associated their male rulers with celestial bodies such as the sun and planets. Olmec basalt and jade-type stones are incompressible, invulnerable, and, as we have seen, very tough to carve.

Clay, on the other hand, is slowly and gently deposited in beds of soft layers in standing bodies of water, which are considered feminine by the Maya. It is dug from the feminine earth in locations near a village or ceremonial center and worked on the ground. To work with clay, the artist kneads it and adds other minerals to make it the desired consistency. It is shaped, dried, and decorated, and finally subjected to a male element, fire, which makes the object more durable and infuses it with the strength of both feminine and masculine

Figure 3. "Pretty Lady," 1200–900 B.C., Tlatilco, Mexico. Clay with traces of red and black paint, h. 11.5 cm.; w. 5 cm. Anonymous loan to The Art Museum, Princeton University.

Figure 4. Figure Arranging Hair, 1200–900 B.C., Las Bocas, Puebla. Clay with traces of red pigment, h. 13.4 cm.; w. 5.5 cm.; d. 2.5 cm. Private collection.

of female figures was largely supplanted by the male-oriented institution of shamanic kingship. Perhaps ceramic figures were largely fashioned by women, who took great care with such details as hair, adornment, and character.

Portrayals of both men and women in the ceramic traditions of the Early Formative are far more personal and varied in expression than sculptural representations of either sex in the Middle and Late Formative (fig. 4; cat. no. 239h). Most of the ceramics were found in household debris or tombs, suggesting that clay figures commemorated family members in their ordinary lives, and that these lives included a strong ritual component. Whether or not modeling clay was a gender-specific, feminine activity, the artists of the highlands who made the hollow and small solid figures were skilled in observation, wit, and dexterity and created some of the masterpieces of Formative period art.

SCULPTURAL FORMAT

Most previous discussions of the Olmec art style include lists of the kind of objects that bear Olmec subject matter.[21] I believe what is meant by the Olmec art style will be clarified if we distinguish between the sculpture's format—or its general plan and shape related to its function—and its themes and subjects. In monumental sculpture, the Gulf Coast Olmec produced a fairly wide variety of formats. Sculptures fully in-the-round, with no subsidiary low-relief or incised imagery—emulating the way the actual subjects would occupy real space—are rare. The majority of sculptures are worked all the way around, but usually with a flatness in the overall form or details that is abstract in effect. Thus, while shaped somewhat like actual human heads, some colossal heads have flat backs and most have low-relief features like helmets or ear ornaments. Thrones, themselves three-dimensional, have decoration in high and low relief. Considered the earliest formats in monumental sculpture (1250–1150 B.C.), thrones combine realism and abstraction as well as full round and relief work. Generally speaking, they are the largest Olmec monumental sculptures.

Seated figures, dwarfs, animals, and multifigure

domains. These acts are similar to the fundamental duties of women in Mesoamerica: grinding, mixing, shaping, and baking bread from corn, activities that also take place on the ground.[20]

While few Olmec stone sculptures depict women, ceramic figures of women are common. In fact, female figures, usually referred to as "pretty ladies" (fig. 3), predominate in the Early Formative

village societies of Tlatilco and Chupicuaro. When the changing political climate of the Middle Formative Ceremonial Complex affected Mesoamerican villages, large images of men in stone and infants in hollow ceramic began to be made, with fewer representations of women. Although these observations clearly need further research, it is intriguing to consider that the older tradition

Figure 5. Las Limas Figure, Veracruz. Greenstone, h. 55 cm. Regional Museum of Veracruz.

Figure 6. Monument 1, Teopantecuanitlan, Guerrero.

sculptures from the Gulf Coast are the most fully round Olmec monuments, although they usually have supplementary incised or low-relief imagery (fig. 5). Sculptures in these formats often incorporate negative space in the composition, lending a greater naturalistic effect. Stelae with low relief, columnar objects, and low circular slabs are fundamentally flat shapes with low-relief decoration. Monumental standing figures, which are uncommon, are rendered in high relief, remaining largely attached to the slab for support.

Outside the Gulf Coast, monumental sculpture is scarcer. Formats include seated figures, larger-than-life disembodied heads, circular disks with low relief, the monoliths of Teopantecuanitlan (fig. 6), the carvings of Chalcatzingo, Chalchuapa, and Xoc, and animals, stelae, and, rarely, blocky standing figures. For the most part, all these sculp-

tures are large objects of complex shape with high and low relief.

Smaller-scale portable stone sculptures tend to be more completely in-the-round and dynamic in composition than the monuments. Many formats are found in the Gulf Coast sites, including standing, kneeling, and seated stone figures; various ornaments (low-relief plaques, mirrors, maskettes, pendants, and effigies of animal parts such as stingray spines and jaguar teeth); ritual objects such as "spoons" and perforators; plain and incised ceremonial celts; masks of human faces; and tools such as polishers, knives, axes, and so forth (figs. 7–9; cat. nos. 19, 130, 191). Similar formats have been found in the Mexican central highlands and Guerrero, and as far south as Honduras and Costa Rica. It is notable that large ceremonial axes come from all parts of the Olmec world except the Gulf Coast.

Figure 7. Standing Figure, 900–600 B.C., Southern Veracruz. Fine-grained, blue-green jadeite with white-to-green inclusions and traces of cinnabar, h. 15.9 cm.; w. 6 cm.; d. 2.5 cm. Private collection.

Figure 8. Mirror, 900–600 B.C., Río Pesquero, Veracruz. Ilmanite, h. 10.9 cm.; w. 15.5 cm.; d. 1 cm. Anonymous loan to The Art Museum, Princeton University.

Figure 9. Mask, 900–600 B.C., Veracruz. Light green-to-gray-blue quartzite with inclusions of pyrite and chlorite, h. 15.9 cm.; w. 15.5 cm.; d. 9 cm. Private collection.

Figure 10. Jaguar Effigy Vessel, 1200–900 B.C., Las Bocas, Puebla. Reddish brown clay with brownish black slip, h. 29.3 cm.; w. 21 cm.; d. 34.1 cm. Private collection.

7.

9.

8.

10.

In ceramics, Gulf Coast Olmec objects include plain and decorated simple vessels, effigy vessels, figures, and hollow figures. But the great achievement in Olmec pottery is found in the central highlands of Mexico where Olmec artists, probably female, became adept at creating ceramic hollow figures, incised vessels, and complex zoomorphic vessels (fig. 10; cat. no. 51).

STYLE: REALISM AND ABSTRACTION

In its representation of real people and their actions in contemporary or mythic time, Olmec art seems to have begun as three-dimensional. As we shall see, it focused on human beings and their inner, transformational states, and on the embodiment and exercise of power. The greatest variability in the Olmec art style is where we might expect to find it: in the regional aesthetic canons of form and interpretations of subject matter. Obviously, there were regional styles, but variations in form are often clearer indicators of region than are theme and subject matter.

In describing the Olmec art style, most scholars have termed it "realistic" rather than "abstract." Covarrubias characterized the Olmec aesthetic as simple and sensually realistic.[22] Coe said of Olmec art: "In the sense that it eschews geometric abstraction for curvilinear naturalism, the style is 'realistic'; in fact, it is more 'realistic' than even the Classic Maya, if one takes into account that the Olmec artists were depicting creatures that they believed actually existed, no matter how monstrous or farfetched. . . . This is not to say the treatment of monstrous forms is not grotesque; it is, but it is never reduced to abstraction."[23]

De la Fuente separated subject and theme from form, and divided sculptural themes into categories similar to those in this volume. She found that a "sense of the supernatural is revealed in both human beings and in those of composite appearance through the integration and interplay of animal imagery or abstract or symbolic elements with the human form." Depending on the subject matter, she recognized that both naturalism and abstraction coexisted in the form.[24]

The degree of naturalism (or realism) and ide-

Figure 11. Standing Figure Holding Supernatural Effigy, 800–500 B.C., Mexico. Jade, h. 21.4 cm.; w. 8.1 cm.; d. 4.1 cm. The collection of Robin B. Martin, currently on loan to The Brooklyn Museum.

alism (a type of abstraction) in a form points to what the artist wishes to convey. For Olmec art to be realistic, the objects should be life size, anatomy carefully portrayed, and abstraction absent. Low and high relief should not be combined. If realism is reduced to its most simple definition as "the representation of things according to their appearance in visible nature (without idealization),"[25] then Olmec art to all intents is not realistic, but should be seen as a combination of realism and abstraction.

Consider the standing figure holding a supernatural effigy (fig. 11; cat. no. 35). The image's form, though recognizably human, is abstracted. The head to body ratio of the adult figure is 1:4 rather than a more natural 1:7. If extended, his hands would reach to his knees. Instead of exploring the musculature, the artist renders the limbs with swelling volumes that taper subtly at the joints. The surface is given the abstract polish of a mirror in place of the uneven texture of flesh. Artistic emphasis is not on the external form of the figure but on his state of mind. Perfect symmetry, expression of deep inner equilibrium, and the relaxed, elongated facial features represent an idealized state of being.

Other abstract aspects of Olmec art include the composition of figures, which, as de la Fuente has demonstrated, merges underlying geometric harmonies with meaningful bodily positions. Contrast is achieved by juxtaposing high and low relief, and broad, smoothly curving and detailed, descriptive areas. The stones used for portrayals of people (gray, green) are not natural colors for humans. Their highly polished surfaces, suggestive of the mirrors found in caches and worn as pectorals, indicate that the beings portrayed engaged the supernatural. Limited movement is portrayed, mostly through asymmetry and the rendition of implied inner powers. Many figures seem to swell with life or power, imparting a sense of incipient movement to their quiescent positions. Added to this, the tendency to regularize forms, such as faces, torsos, and limbs, creates an expansive sense of monumentality in even mediocre works of Olmec art.

The recognition that a fundamental feature of the Olmec art style is a combination of abstraction and naturalism points to the fact that the Olmec archetypal mode of thought also combined abstraction and naturalism or rationality. The imagery of Olmec thought employs metaphor and analogy, focusing on concepts and mythical events as opposed to the physical forms of people and things. In Olmec art the emphasis is on inner transformation and its outward signs rather than the human body.

ICONOGRAPHY: THE TWO-DIMENSIONAL MIDDLE FORMATIVE DIAGRAMS FOR RITUAL PRACTICE

The Olmec symbol system has been the subject of intense scrutiny ever since Covarrubias drew some of its motifs in 1946. Peter David Joralemon made an important first step by isolating and enumerating many motifs and motif clusters and proposing a series of gods.[26] Reilly has considered the symbol system in light of shamanic cosmology, the natural environment, and the rise of kingship, and he suggested that it functioned as a cross-linguistic, ideological communication system among shamanic rulerships parallel to that of the Mississippian chiefdoms of the southeastern United States.

Although low-relief and incised carving are present on the earliest Gulf Coast Olmec monumental sculptures, their development into a codified symbol system seems to have occurred during the period of intensified interaction between Mesoamerican regions around 900–700 B.C. In freestanding monumental and cliff sculpture during that period, low-relief imagery often relates events. On La Venta Stela 3 we see an encounter between two important people; on La Venta Monument 29 and Chalcatzingo Monument 21, the images of world-centering primordial acts, such as the raising of the world tree; and Chalcatzingo Monument 1 depicts the rainmaking powers exercised by a shamanic ruler.

Incised imagery generally supplements the meaning of three-dimensional sculptural objects. This imagery represents the spiritual essence of places, the natures of cosmologically important animals and plants propitiated in ritual, and supernatural beings encountered by the shamanic practitioner in the course of manipulating the object or engaging in other ritual practice. Incised images are not events or scenes. Human figures are rarely shown in their entirety unless they embody a supernatural, in which case they wear the latter's regalia or bodily markers.

Coe, and later Joralemon, recognized an important aspect of the two-dimensional symbol system: that "abbreviated symbolic statements. . . are produced by applying the *pars pro toto* principle to complex iconographic images."[27] The incised imagery deals with cosmological concepts, supernatural beings, and ritual acts and objects. With this system, coded concepts could be included, for example, on a celt, a small ceramic figure of a woman wearing a cap with Olmec dragon (cat. no. 236), or a little carved figure such as the fetus figure with avian cape (fig. 12; cat. no. 117).

Regarding two-dimensional imagery, Joralemon noted that it is limited to frontal and profile depictions or a combination of the two.[28] Reilly added that "many incised compositions are best understood when the principle of multiple perspective, or multiple horizons, is applied to them."[29] The shape of the Dallas tablet, for example, represents the horizontal dimension of space (cat. no. 131). Paralleling the edge of the plaque are incised lines that reiterate the concept of the terrestrial plane of existence. Space, shown as it is conceived, reaches to the four directions and thus is square. Optical reality was irrelevant, and so no illusion of it is created through converging lines. Within this cosmic

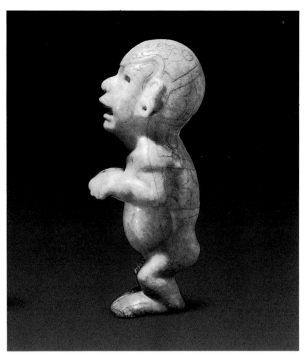

Figure 12. Standing Figure with Incisions, 900–600 B.C., Chiapas. Light grayish green albitite, h. 14 cm.; w. 5.4 cm.; d. 5.8 cm. Private collection.

Figure 13. Juxtlahuaca Cave mural.

framework, symbols indicate the levels of the vertical axis of existence. This kind of spatial indicator was used relatively late in the Olmec era. The symbols on the Dallas tablet and other incised objects, such as the Dallas celt (cat. no. 216) and a small spoon on loan to The Brooklyn Museum (cat. no. 72), are shown in profile or frontal view, whichever is most informative and economical, and from a mid-object viewpoint, with no foreshortening.

The relatively few Olmec objects whose original locations are known demonstrate how ritual space was incorporated in their art. Take, for example, the mural of the standing and kneeling male figures in Juxtlahuaca Cave, Guerrero (fig. 13). Here a towering figure of a man dressed in a jaguar skin and tall headdress decorated with a jade plaque of a cleft-headed supernatural stands over a kneeling man wearing symbols of his rulership: green earspools and ceremonial bar. The kneeling figure seems to have come for supernatural sanction by the jaguar-garbed figure, who bestows it with a kind of wand. Where does the kneeling man find the jaguar-garbed being? In the cave. No painted lines separate the scene from the cave's natural surfaces. In fact, the feet of the figures probably originally rested on a horizontal, crusty mineral ridge corresponding to a water level on the wall. The figures are completely integrated with their surroundings. Similarly, we know the Olmec made ritual environments for their objects, going so far as to create the massive underground "seas" of serpentine blocks at La Venta and placing objects like the cruciform celt-deposit/world tree above them. Portable Olmec objects almost certainly occupied specific places in shrines, caches, or burials—ritual spaces designed as their theaters. The sharks, caimans, harpy eagles, and ospreys incised on these objects signal cosmic environments, and hence are markers of spatial concepts in ceremonial centers that may not all have been as elaborate as La Venta.

Incised signs follow a logical syntax that is based on the correspondence of metaphoric symbols to a cosmic framework. For example, on the Dallas tablet, the three stones on which creation rests are placed at the bottom of the vertical column and the crossed-bands sky, with its thirteen nubs suggesting the number of constellations, is seen at the

top. Signs also appear on the human body, which provides the spatial locative for the incised information. In his study of the Young Lord (cat. no. 193), Reilly proposed that the animals and ritual acts are incised on the body to correspond to cosmological levels. The figure thus becomes a series of sacred locations corresponding to the cosmic levels of sky, earth, underworld. Similar to Aztec thought, the parts of the human body have cosmic significance, and the proper location for ritual activity is determined by the left and right sides of the ruler's body.[30]

FUNCTION

To the Olmec mind, skillfully crafted objects were inseparable from the ritual landscapes in which they functioned. A carved celt carried by a trader spoke of its maker's world and also became part of the trader's ritual journey, which might include prayers made, supernatural forces outwitted, and humans encountered on previous trips. An imported celt, when presented as a gift, embodied the giver's superior power and knowledge.

From basalt boulder heads to hematite dwarfs, the stones from which these Olmec objects were crafted were infused with powers inherent in their roles in the territory of the ancestors and the landscape of sacred forces. The use of these nonlocal stones declared the owner's knowledge of distant places, events, and societies. Handling the portable objects in ritual involved an exchange of creative power between the shaman/chief and the sacred object. Many portable objects were buried in caches in specific locations in the sculptured ceremonial centers, thereby imbuing the earth with webs of knowledge of the mundane and spiritual worlds.

An art object (or an object of skilled crafting) is never the real thing. Even if it serves as a vessel for a supernatural force, it is not the supernatural but a vessel into which the supernatural is ritually installed and from which it can be de-installed, rendering the vessel useless. As images of ritualistic transformation, portable sculptures, which were probably kept hidden and revealed only to those people who were worthy of such esoteric knowledge, are vessels of and primers for shamanic

behavior. As trade items, which they surely were, they must have been valuable repositories of secret knowledge.

THEMES

This catalogue presents the themes of Olmec portable art: supernatural power and heredity, the bases for rulership; rituals of shamanic meditation and transformation; animals and the animating energies they embody; diagrams of cosmic ritual; fertility and mortality. Each theme is expressed by a range of ritual objects for an audience, human and supernatural, elite and common, local and outsider, who benefits from seeing and manipulating them.

If a theme in art represents an overarching cultural concern, the details of a specific art object relate that concern to a specific event, place, supernatural power, thing, or individual. In Olmec art, the two major themes are rulership and shamanism. Rulership is shown by many subjects: colossal heads of rulers, thrones carved to represent shamanic kings emerging from caves in a reenactment of an origin myth, sculptures of human figures seated or standing in meditation or kneeling to indicate the physical movement analogous to the spiritual movement of supernatural transformation, effigies of the faces of shamanic rulers in ecstatic trance, human hollow infants who probably were sacrificed royal offspring or heirs of royal lineages, symbols of power animals and important food plants over which the rulers exercise control, and, of

Figure 14. Oval Spoon with Incisions, 900–600 B.C., Veracruz. Translucent blue-green jadeite, h. 2.7 cm.; w. 6.7 cm.; d. 0.5 cm. Private collection.

Figure 15. Mask, 900–600 B.C., Veracruz. Jade, h. 15.5 cm.; w. 14 cm.; d. 6.9 cm. Private collection.

course, statements of power inherent in the acquisition and craftsmanship of the sacred materials.

Shamanism, the second major theme, has been defined by Mircea Eliade as "ascent to heaven, descent to the underworld to bring back the patient's soul or to escort the dead, evocation and incarnation of the 'spirits' in order to undertake the ecstatic journey, 'mastery over fire,' and so on."[31] These features are all identifiable in Olmec art. Ascent to heaven is seen at La Venta in the symbolism of the world tree in the form of cruciform caches of celts rising from magnetic mirrors placed over enormous deposits of the greenstones representing the underworld seas.[32] The Avian Serpent in Olmec art is a celestial flier who brings rain.[33] An Olmec leader like the Young Lord wore an avian mask, indicating his ability to fly. Cosmic maps of the spiritual realm are written on his body. Also indicative of the journey to celestial or underworld realms and mastery over fire are the "fliers," who appear, for example, on a celt in Offering 4 at La Venta and a spoon in this catalogue (fig. 14; cat. no. 70). Both "fliers" wear short capes and skirts. Stretched out horizontally, they hold their heads up at acute angles to peer through the darkness of

the spiritual realm, which they illuminate with "torches" held in their outstretched hands. The Costa Rican jade celt and pendant in this catalogue also show Olmec flying figures (cat. nos. 169, 68). Descent to the underworld to bring back the soul or escort the dead is the primary theme of the ball-playing Hero Twins' journey in the Maya *Popol Vuh*, and is strongly suggested by the Olmec figures emerging from cavelike niches on La Venta Altar 4 and Chalcatzingo Monument 1. The shaman's ability to identify with animal spirit companions is represented in Olmec art through supernatural masks (fig. 15; cat. no. 182), human-animal transformation figures (cat. nos. 42–50), and such images as Oxtotitlan Painting 1-d. Although we know that this occurred, our Euroamerican rational intellect makes it difficult to fathom how it was accomplished.

The case for the use of hallucinogens to achieve altered (spiritual) consciousness has been suggested, owing to the discovery at San Lorenzo of bones of the toad *Bufo marinus,* whose glands contain, among other powerful substances, hallucinogenic compounds.[34] The Olmec, like most shamanic peoples, also practiced austerities to attain spiritual awareness, probably during the course of initiatory rituals. In Mesoamerica, of course, the most infamous ascetic act is self-inflicted bloodletting. Rosemary Joyce et al. documented a complex of symbols, including knotted cloth, knuckledusters, and shark's teeth, linking blood-letting to rulership.[35] Methods of controlling the mind in order to perceive supernatural realms probably included fasting, for which we have proof among the Maya and Aztec, and seclusion, perhaps in caves, suggested by the murals deep in Juxtlahuaca Cave.

MEDITATIVE TRANCE, MAGICAL BEINGS, AND OTHER SUBJECTS IN OLMEC ART

THE SHAMAN'S STANCE

Standing figures have been found in Costa Rica, El Salvador, Guatemala, Honduras, the states of Chiapas, Guerrero, Mexico, Michoacan, and Puebla,

as well as the Olmec heartland. Pieces have also been excavated at Chalcatzingo, Kaminaljuyu, and, of course, La Venta. These apparently simple figures were important in the formation and maintenance of Olmec ritual. The excavators of La Venta Offering 4, the group of sixteen standing figures and six celt halves, noted that four figures seemed to face toward a fifth, made of particularly bright green jade, but said that "[t]here is nothing about them to indicate whether they are priests who are performing some ritual, or whether they are dancers, or perhaps candidates for some sacrificial rites."[36] I believe the sculptures' forms do reveal much of their significance. The specific pose of the figures from La Venta Offering 4 (fig. 16) is captured to perfection in two examples in this catalogue (cat. nos. 19, 26). These and other examples excavated from La Venta all stand with legs slightly apart and knees flexed, a stance that makes the spine straight and the limbs and muscles relaxed. The arms hang loose by the sides. (In other standing sculptures the hands may meet at the navel or hold a bar, scepter, or Olmec Supernatural.) The eyes focus toward some distant or inner phenomenon. The head always shows evidence of cranial deformation, adding verticality to the figures.

The flexed knees and elongated spine is a position of meditation in Chinese Tai Chi, where it is called Hun-Yuan Kung, or Beginning Posture. The practitioner stands straight, placing the feet parallel and shoulder-width apart. The head is held as if suspended by a string from above, and all other parts of the body relaxed, with the shoulders dropped and the arms hanging naturally. The knees are flexed, never locked. In this position, it is said that the earth is invoked by the rootedness of the feet, the sky by the verticality of the spine, and humanity by the sinking of energy to the Tan T'ien, an energy center below the navel.[37] In the ancient discipline of Hatha-Yoga, this position is called Tadasana, the Mountain Pose. If practiced ardently, it teaches endurance, steadiness, contentment, and enables the person to experience the flow of energy spiraling up from the feet to the top of the head. The spine-aligned standing posture could have been discovered independently by the people of Formative period Mesoamerica to emulate the world tree or cosmic mountain, and thereby aided in developing the mental and physical self-discipline necessary to master the mind and control the spiritual entities inherent in the body. Lama Anagarika Govinda, author of *Foundations of Tibetan Mysticism* and other books on Eastern philosophy, described the relationship between human leaders and sacred mountains in Eastern thought: "There are mountains which are just mountains and there are mountains with personality. . . . Personality consists in the power to influence others, and this power is due to a consistency, harmony, and one-pointedness of character. If these qualities are present in an individual in their highest perfection, he is a fit leader of humanity, be he a ruler, a thinker, or a saint; and we recognize him as a vessel of supra mundane power. If these qualities are present in a mountain, we recognize it as a vessel of cosmic power, and we call it a sacred mountain."[38]

For the Olmec, certain mountains were indubitably sacred, whether they were natural—San Martín Pajapán, at whose summit was the majestic

sculpture of a leader raising the world tree;[39] the twin mountains of Chalcatzingo; the Cerro de León, to the southwest of Teopantecuanitlan—or man-made, for example, Pyramid C-1, the volcano effigy at La Venta. La Venta Offering 4 may represent a gathering of sixteen spiritual practitioners who, having assumed the standing meditative posture, concentrate on the cosmic axis and focus their power on the eastern side of the sunken ceremonial courtyard (representing the surface of the underworld). They meditate next to cosmic axis effigies (the celts) bearing the incised images of a "flier" to the otherworld and the earth monster from whom the world tree grows.

No other standing figures have been found in such large groups. The others excavated in the ceremonial courts at La Venta were on the center line of the site in caches, pseudoburials, and burials, either singly or in groups of twos or threes. When associated with a figure (or pseudoburial, as in Tomb C, where the regalia was placed to correspond in scale and position to a human figure, but with no evi-

dence of bone or tooth remains), they were found in the abdominal or groin area. This was true of the standing figure excavated at Chalcatzingo.[40]

The standing figure excavated at Chalcatzingo dates from the Cantera Phase (ca. 700–500 B.C.), the same period as the major reliefs at that site. It was found in Burial 33, the earlier of the Olmec-style burials at the site, at right angles to and under another Olmec-style burial containing the decapitated head of a monumental, heartland-type seated figure.[41] This suggests that the first local ruler to adopt the Olmec ideological system, whether influenced by Guerrero or the Gulf Coast, possessed this standing figure as an emblem of his power. At his death, it was buried with him. Archaeologists found the figure in the abdominal region, either placed near the groin to suggest fertility or lineage or the cosmic axis or near the navel to suggest, as in Aztec thought, the "conduit for the entire body."[42]

ECSTATIC FACES

Much consideration has been given to the question of portraiture among the Olmec colossal heads; the same consideration is due wearable masks. The Olmec artists who made the Río Pesquero masks had the capacity to fashion their chunks of fine stone into physically recognizable, anatomically correct images. The keenly observed ceramic figures from Las Bocas (cat. nos. 236–239) demonstrate this capability on the part of Formative period artists. However, the Río Pesquero masks are too symmetrical and adhere too closely to the beauty of perfect geometrical shapes to be anything but idealized images.

In Olmec art, likenesses of the human form abound, but the artist's challenge was to represent the soul within the physical form. The sculptors who carved the life-size human masks recreated the yielding texture of flesh in the toughest of stones. To achieve their artistic goal, they must have selected certain details from actual or imagined faces, such as a nose or the shape of a face, then subordinated these details to the whole for the desired effect.

We wonder what delight attracted the intense focus and inspired the incipient smile on a mask

Figure 16. La Venta Offering 4.

Figure 17. Mask with Incisions, 900–600 B.C., Río Pesquero. White and gray jadeite with red pigment, h. 17 cm.; w. 16 cm.; d. 9 cm. Private collection.

Figure 18. Bearded Maskette with Incisions, 900–600 B.C., Tabasco. Green serpentine, h. 7.6 cm.; w. 5.4 cm.; d. 3 cm. Private collection.

from Río Pesquero (fig. 17; cat. no. 186). We sense the intake of breath. But the piece does not unlock clues to a personality. Close inspection reveals the geometry of the composition: a series of inter-locking triangles compose the face. The nose and mouth form a triangle whose apex is low on the forehead, between the eyebrow ridge. A line drawn from the outside edge of the drilled pupils to the center of the chin precisely passes the outside cor-ners of the nostrils, incorporating the eyes into another interlocking triangle. These and other geo-metric distributions of features are softened by the delicately modulated curves that create mounds of apparent flesh below the eyes, where chin meets cheek, and flanking the nostrils. Typical of the ren-dering of Olmec-style faces, the features are con-centrated in the center of the face, leaving broad, contrasting areas of gently curving planes. The appropriate question to ask is what is portrayed in this sensually abstracted manner? The answer, I think, is spiritual ecstasy.

The incised masks and face plaques in Olmec art

seem to be images of both internal and external realms. In this case, we see the archetype of ecstasy, and we also see a reflection of the spiritual realm, of images of the spirit creatures this person encoun-tered. The subject of the mask seems to have been marked by the spirit images as one of their own, as possessing the powers of the underworld predators shark and crocodile.[43] The right eye of the mask is flanked by two double merlons signaling a cleft in the earth or entrance to the underworld, suggesting that the subject looks inward, toward the spiritual components of its being to enter the realm of the powerful creatures. Even if this mask is the ideal-ized portrait of a specific person, it represents a visionary state, rather than memorializing features or personality.

A whole category of face effigies too small to be masks were probably worn as headdress or chest ornaments. They can be described as face plaques; they are all pierced with tiny holes for attachment or suspension. Even smaller are the many face effi-gies representing humans and stylized composite

beings, to which the term "maskette" has been applied. Four maskettes were included in caches at La Venta, which at least provides some clues to their function.

Small—ranging from 7/8 to 1 5/16 of an inch in diameter—the four maskettes were found in three different caches, Offerings 5, 6, and 7, in the north-east platform of the northern ceremonial courtyard. Near Offering 4, they all were deposited in the same construction phase, Phase III. Each of the three offerings was a "pseudoburial," a cache with wear-able objects, such as earspools and beads, arranged as if deposited on a body—but with neither skeletal remains nor sufficient space for a body. The mask-ette in Offering 5, made of dark green translucent jade with many tiny biconical perforations at the top and sides, is the effigy of a human face with a downturned mouth. Offering 5 was marked by eight small pieces of volcanic tuff, four each in two rows running from east to west. Near the western end was a "necklace" of jade beads; near the eastern end, about eight inches from the "necklace," were two jade earspools set five inches apart, parallel to the "necklace." Five inches east (or above) the earspools was the maskette. It is as if a head or a wooden mask and jade regalia had been laid in the pit (accompanied by three pottery vessels) and the maskette attached to it.

The objects in Offerings 6 and 7 were laid out in similar fashion. In Offering 6 two jade maskettes in the form of highly stylized jaguar faces just under an inch in height were placed in such a manner that they could have been on a wooden mask's or imaginary figure's eyes or cheekbone area. Offer-ing 7 held the fewest objects. As in Offering 5, the maskette was placed in such a way that it could have been the central focus of a headband or head-dress, and it was amply perforated for attachment or suspension.[44]

Several pieces in this catalogue were probably worn as regalia or deposited in pseudoburials of regalia. The bearded maskette from Tabasco (fig. 18; cat. no. 153) has a downturned mouth like the mask-ette's in La Venta Offering 5. The 1 3/4-inch maskette from Veracruz (cat. no. 151) is dark green jade with dramatic white veins, its features realized in harsh, trapezoidal geometry relieved by sweeping lines

Figure 19. Standing Figure, 900–600 B.C., Puebla. Dark green serpentine, h. 8 cm.; w. 1.5 cm.; d. 4 cm. Private collection.

Figure 20. Crouching Figure, 900–600 B.C., Alta Verapaz, Guatemala. Polished black stone, h. 25 cm. National Museum of the American Indian, Smithsonian Institution.

Figure 21. Seated Figure of a Man, 900–600 B.C., Mexico. Hematite, h. 11 cm.; w. 8 cm.; d. 6 cm. Wadsworth Atheneum, Hartford, the Henry D. Miller Fund.

around the eyes and a high polish. The jade maskette from Costa Rica (cat. no. 165) was probably recarved to make a generic smiling-weeping face into a more emphatic feline. The larger, 3-inch greenstone human head maskette (cat. no. 227), which has a faint outline around the eyes, indicate that they were once defined by attached pieces of shell. The 2¹/₂-inch blue-green jade jaguar face pendant from Veracruz (cat. no. 167) also recalls the ones in the La Venta pseudoburials. Similar maskettes are worn by figures on monumental sculpture, for example, the were-jaguars on the headdresses of San Martín Pajapán Monument 1 and La Venta Altar 5.

HUNCHBACKS, DWARFS, AND DEFORMED FETUS FIGURES

Hunchback sculptures are easily recognizable and always small-scale. The serpentine standing hunchback, which split and was repolished in ancient times (fig. 19), is an excellent example, having a typical Olmec face, deformed head, and a mere 3¹/₄ inches in height. The hunchback emerging from the mouth of a beast (cat. no. 65) shows us that these characters went on and returned from otherworld journeys. Their powers were imitated, as seen by the bearded hunchback impersonator (cat. no. 213), also about 3¹/₄ inches tall. This fascination with hunchbacks continued with later civilizations. Maya and Aztec rulers kept hunchbacks and dwarfs in their courts to serve as messengers who could cross over the barrier to the otherworld.

Heretofore a wide range of sculptures has been referred to generally as "dwarfs." Elizabeth K. Easby and John F. Scott described the crouching figure in the Museum of the American Indian, New York (fig. 20) as part of a "class of childlike or dwarflike figures distinguished by a crouching pose, raised hands, and, usually, an upturned face."[45] They refer to the bright green, hydrocephalic, short-limbed figure found in Cerro de las Mesas, now in the National Museum of Anthropology, Mexico City, as a "jaguar baby."[46] In this catalogue, a number of important figures of both categories are assembled for the first time, and so we are able to consider a variety of small figures with physical abnormalities and make distinctions between them.

The figures with features of achondroplastic dwarfism, including marked shortening of the extremities and depression of the nasal ridge, are the easiest to isolate. The Cerro de las Mesas "jaguar baby" in the National Museum does not have feline teeth, eyes, ears, or tail, and so probably does not represent a jaguar. It shares the blocky build, extremely abbreviated limbs, and arms raised in front of the torso to shoulder height with the figure in the Wadsworth Athenaeum, Hartford (fig. 21; cat. no. 111), which has an idealized Olmec face with downturned mouth. Probably representing achondroplastic dwarfs, both were carved from extremely prized materials: the latter figure from a rare hematite, the former from a brilliant, deep green jade.

A great deal can be determined about Olmec beliefs regarding dwarfs from the single archaeologically retrieved dwarf in a cache, La Venta Offering 1943-M in Mound A-3. This small, polished stone dwarf was cached with three other figures at La Venta.[47] Two of the figures are smaller examples of the human standing figure, only pudgier in the belly and with heads somewhat large in proportion to the body (La Venta Figurines 8 and 9). The figure I believe is a dwarf was described by Philip Drucker as shorter, squatter, and with a more pronounced bend to the knees than the others—the only "infantile" figure excavated at La Venta to date—and possibly having had eyes inlaid with iron pyrite.[48]

Drucker's drawing of the section through Mound A-3 revealed the large stone cist containing a pseudoburial in the center of the mound (Tomb C had an adult-proportioned standing figure at the abdominal area of the pseudodeceased).[49] Fourteen meters south of Tomb C was the "child's grave" and one meter farther south was the dwarf's cache, near the south end of the mound where Pavement No. 2 commences under the surface of the courtyard. The "child's grave," or Tomb D, was marked by a 30-by-50-centimeter bed of cinnabar from 22 to 25 centimeters thick. Cinnabar streaked another 10 centimeters of the clay in each direction for a total area of 50 by 70 centimeters, large enough for a tiny child of normal stature or a young dwarf. The cinnabar held small jade earspools and ornaments and a clay pot, but no traces of human remains were found, as is usual. In metaphoric terms of the Olmec

sacred landscape, the four figures lay between the "child's grave" and the shores of the underworld sea, possibly serving to identify the deceased as a dwarf rather than a child. The dwarf's burial between the ruler in Tomb C and the underworld sea suggests that it was the ruler's special messenger to the supernatural world. The dwarf exhibits symbolic features that link it to several pieces in the catalogue. Drucker mentioned a slight crest on top of its head, a feature more obvious on two small standing stone figures with large crested heads, bird masks, and forearms projecting forward like the La Venta dwarf's (cat. nos. 117, 118).

Dwarfs were of such importance that at least three heartland monuments depict them. Potrero Nuevo Monument 2, the well-known "altar" in the University of Veracruz Museum of Anthropology (UVMA), Xalapa, shows two dwarfs with their arms above their heads supporting a slab marked with the gum brackets of the earth monster or Taube's Avian Serpent.[50] On another altar from nearby San Lorenzo, dwarfs appear on opposite sides of the stone holding celts (Monument 18).[51] La Venta Monument 5 seems to represent a kneeling dwarf holding a receptacle.[52] The two altars include the dwarfs within the cosmic context of the earth: on the Potrero Nuevo altar, they support the earth's surface, which is also the seat of the ruler; on the San Lorenzo altar, they hold celts, which can form the substance of the cosmic axis (as in La Venta Offering 10, the cruciform arrangement of celts emanating from a mirror, buried above the underworld sea) or be associated with rain or lightning, similar to their Maya and Aztec counterparts. The fact that the dwarfs were in their service may have lent legitimacy to the rulers who occupied the dwarf thrones.

Among Indians of the Western United States is a widespread belief that the dwarf is an individual who "grants power or serves as a guardian spirit."[53] Willard Z. Park wrote there were many tribes who believed that a little green man dwells in the mountains, where he shoots his arrows and is the "guardian spirit of medicine men and those who have become magicians solely through supernatural aid."[54] Among the Maya of Lake Atitlan, dwarfs were considered "experimental" people, counterfeit

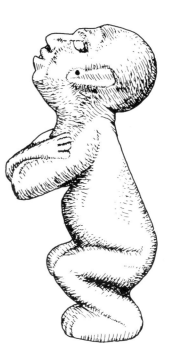

Figure 22. La Venta Figurine 11, h. 11 cm.

Figure 23. Dwarf, National Museum of Anthropology, Mexico City.

forms of humans, from the previous creation.[55] In Maya art, they appear with rulers and water-birds—underworld dwellers—during public bloodletting ceremonies. For example, they can be seen on Period Ending stelae and in underworld scenes such as the central carved panel of Yaxchilan Structure 33 Hieroglyphic Staircase, in which the ruler-to-be, Bird Jaguar IV, descends in the company of two dwarfs marked with Venus signs to the primordial ballcourt where cosmic battles were fought.[56] Such dwarf associations seem to have their roots in Formative period cosmology. The Olmec dwarf thrones demonstrate that dwarfs were the supports of rulers. The La Venta dwarf figurine and the dwarf's grave suggest that the dwarf was the intercessor between the ruler and the vast green underworld sea, and perhaps also the guardian spirit of the ruler's shamanic powers.

The fourth figure in the cache near the La Venta dwarf's burial is described by Drucker as a "dancer" because the head is tilted back, arms are folded across the chest, and knees are strongly flexed (fig. 22).[57] Drucker notes the similarity between this figure's pose and one from Guerrero, then in Covarrubias's collection, now in the National Museum (fig. 23). The latter sculpture exhibits severe malformation of the face in being chinless. These two sculptures introduce a very puzzling group of figures, not usually made of the most precious stones, which has three or four subgroups of imagery. I refer to them as "deformed fetuses."

The eighteen fetus sculptures known to me share five salient features: toothlessness, hairlessness, deeply flexed knees, oversized heads, and an infantile appearance. They take one of three arm positions: forearms crossed over chest (cat. no. 115), arms flexed and held in front of chest (cat. no. 117), or arms grasping the head (cat. nos. 112–114). In addition to the Guerrero dwarf, six are chinless. Three have a version of the typical Olmec down-turned, toothless, "were-jaguar" mouth, but the rest have no were-jaguar features. Although the figures' shared traits all pertain to newborns, none of them are lying down, as newborns must, nursing, or being held, nor do they resemble the older, sitting hollo-figures. Instead, they assume this peculiar crouching position. Two seem to have

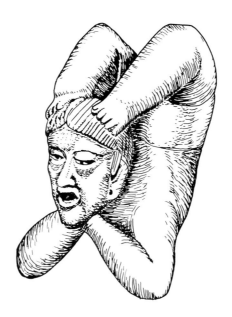

Figure 24. Acrobat, National Museum of Anthropology, Mexico City, h. 22 cm.

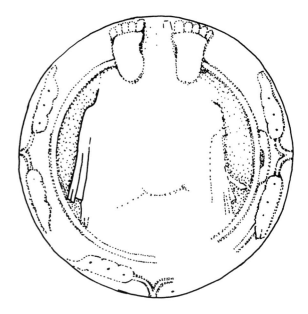

Figure 25. San Lorenzo Monument 16, diam. 185–194 cm.

features obscured by a membrane (cat. nos. 114, 117). These characteristics have led me to call them fetuses, an interpretation confirmed by a group of obstetricians.[58]

Serrated flame eyebrows and incised pelts grace the heads and backs of two of these sculptures (cat. nos. 117, 118). Many scholars believe that the serrated brow in Olmec art represents the prominent, erectile tufts of feathers on the back of the head of the large raptor, the harpy eagle.[59] On the more complete figure two spiny oyster shell designs alternate with three circles on each side of the pelt.[60] The head is cleft by a deep groove that runs from the top of the front of the head to the middle of the shoulder blade area. It seems likely that a crest of feathers was inserted there and affixed with wax. Loving attention was paid to the anatomy of this figure. Its eyes are deeply drilled to accept insets and emphasized by fine lines. Delicate carving carefully describes the fleshy neck, protruding collarbones and the hollow between them, little shoulder muscles, and the ribs. In this sculpture, a very special human fetus transforms into a crested crocodilian,

combining sky, earth, and underworld features and abilities.

Each fetus figure seems to be straining, either to support its head, listen to sounds from a distant world, or communicate in some way, and for this reason the figures are full of pathos. Although not ideally beautiful in any sense, they are haunting and strike a sympathetic chord in the viewer. This disturbing, enigmatic theme in Olmec sculpture underscores the fascination with deformities; babies, dwarfs, and hunchbacks; shamanic transformation; and clairvoyant states induced by trance, yogic and/or epileptic.

SHAMANIC CONTORTIONS

Román Piña Chán called the kaolin ceramic sculpture of a man with his feet resting on his head excavated at Tlatilco an "acrobat" (fig. 24). This piece, now in the National Museum, was found with a stone mirror and the contents of what seems to have been a divining bundle, suggesting the person interred there may have been a shaman.[61]

Figure 26. Río Pesquero Altar, National Museum of Anthropology, Mexico City, diam. 70 cm.

Figure 27. Circular Relief, Centro de Investigaciones de los Olmecas y Mayas, diam. 75 cm.

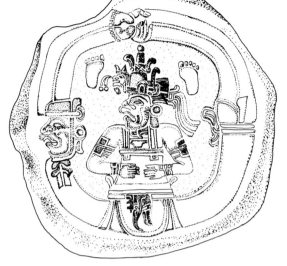

Figure 28. Shook Panel, San Antonio Suchitepequez, Guatemala, diam. 81 cm.

I believe that this figure's extreme contortion signifies that it and several other sculptures in the same position illustrated in this catalogue are in an ecstatic state frequently experienced by temporal lobe epileptics or yogic adepts.[62]

The steatite figure from Guerrero (cat. no. 40) had detailed carving on all four sides. It will stand on any side, but the figure's belly shows ancient wear, suggesting that it was placed on the belly and used thus over a considerable period of time. This figure wears the triangular backflap skirt similar to that of the "fliers" on the La Venta Offering 4 celts. The "flier" figure incised on a spoon in this catalogue (cat. no. 70) also wears a short skirt . These parallels in costume indicate that the figures performed similar rituals related to journeying to a spiritual realm. The small serpentine acrobat (cat. no. 41) assumes the same position, but has a typical Olmec puffy upper lip. Marking its feet are the crossed-bands and circle signs, found on monuments depicting supernaturals, such as Laguna de Los Cerros Monument 1. Joyce et al. related the signs to the complex of bloodletting iconography.[63]

The foot-on-head stance is represented by ceramic figures from Las Bocas (cat no. 39) and ceramic vessels from Tlatilco (cat no. 38).

Identical positions are memorialized on a group of monuments from diverse parts of the Olmec world: San Lorenzo Monument 16 (fig. 25); the Río Pesquero Altar in the National Museum (fig. 26); a very similar circular slab in the Centro de Investigaciones de los Olmecas y Mayas in Villahermosa (CICOM) (fig. 27); La Venta Monument 65; a little-known Maya limestone stela in the CICOM; and the "Shook Panel" from San Antonio Suchitepequez, Guatemala (fig. 28). The positions on the latter object are the most revealing. Along the border of the circular stone is an extremely attenuated figure in profile who arches backward to grasp his ankles with his hands, acting as a human wheel. This figure, who is dressed in the short backflap skirt of the "fliers," encloses the frontal torso and profile head of another figure, who wears a stone "spoon" or bloodletting implement as a pendant and a head-dress with a maskette in front and a sprout emanating from the crossed-bands on top. With his

royal regalia, the enclosed figure seems to be the ruler, and since the soles of his feet appear above his head, he may also be in a backward-arching position. The head of an eagle connects the two figures at their navels, reinforcing the theme of shamanic flight. At least this "acrobat" was linked with rulership, bloodletting, and shamanic flight. Posture was an indicator of meaningful activity in Meso-american art, and so it is unlikely this pose was merely a visual pun. Each of the above figures is clearly human and none exhibits the attributes of monsters or deities. Therefore, we must assume this position had significance.

Most people cannot accomplish it. They must either be double-jointed; have the Ehlers-Danlos syndrome, a variable abnormality featuring hyper-mobility of joints, weakness and bleeding, and extremely elastic, rubberlike skin;[64] have practiced attaining this position for many years; or achieve it involuntarily during an hysterical or epileptic seizure. Epileptics may arch over backward with both head and feet on the floor or, less commonly, lie on the chest with their feet on the head. Ali b.

Rabban al-Tabari, a ninth-century physician, called epilepsy the "diviner's disease because some [epileptics] prophesy and have visions of wonderful things."[65] And in the fifteenth century, the physician Guainerius wrote of a "choleric youth who said that in his paroxysms he always saw wonderful things, which he most ardently desired to set down in writing for he hoped they would most certainly come in the future. Wherefore the ancients called this disease 'divination.'"[66] Dostoyevski described what is possibly his own experience in *The Idiot:* "There are moments, and it is only a matter of five or six seconds, when you feel the presence of the eternal harmony… a terrible thing is the frightful clearness with which it manifests itself and the rapture with which it fills you."[67]

William Gordon Lennox wrote that although illusions and hallucinations are not uncommon among temporal lobe epileptics, ecstatic experiences are rarer. Among his patients, a woman had an ecstatic experience with sound hallucinations accompanied by color. On one occasion she said she "became aware of small hobgoblinish figures floating in the air. They were a sort of translucent blue, a little more solid than smoke. I have had several dreams in which an attack, probably a real one, came from an outside force. Some creature clinging to the window curtains would leap down upon me and shake until I would think that I couldn't endure any more."[68]

Owsei Temkin discussed the epileptic as prophet in his study of epilepsy in history. He concluded that the epileptic might see things hidden to others and reveal them to us if only society acknowledged the existence of prophesy.[69] Epileptic behavior must have offered some benefits to the Olmec community. The visions of extraordinary beatitude; of small hobgoblinish creatures; and of auras, music, voices, or prophecy were most likely respected in shamanic Olmec society. While these experiences would be difficult to depict on monumental sculpture or small stone carvings, the extreme, instantly recognizable posture of a prophet or visionary would signal such a vision. The small-scale "fliers" on monumental sculpture, for example, La Venta Monument 19 and Chalcatzingo Monument 12, seem to illustrate this. Hearing music or voices also brings to mind the "listening" fetus.

Contemporary research on epilepsy enables us to calculate the frequency of epilepsy in populations and to recognize the physical and psychic behavior caused by epilepsy.[70] It also helps us to evaluate the interpretation of epilepsy in Olmec art. Approximately one percent of any population is thought to experience symptoms of epilepsy. This common type, called grand mal epilepsy, consists of recurring physical seizures, occasionally including the severe arching of the back (opisthotonus), for several seconds. Grand mal seizures may be accompanied by loss of consciousness. About five percent of those experiencing epilepsy, or one in five hundred people, have some form of temporal lobe (also called psychomotor) epilepsy.[71] Only temporal lobe epileptics report the ecstatic religious experiences and clairvoyant episodes recounted above. They experience different kinds of seizures that change over their lifetime. The salient characteristic of temporal lobe epilepsy is a dissociative state, which may be ecstatic or fearful. It may also be perceived by the epileptic as demonic possession or split personality.[72] The reactions people have to their epilepsy are largely conditioned by the responses of their families and communities.[73] Some shamanic societies around the world have considered epilepsy a sign of divine election to shamanic practice.[74] After the crisis and resulting spiritual and physical disequilibrium, if the person accepts the suggestion to practice shamanism made by the spiritual entity experienced in the vision, he or she feels cured. "It is not to the fact that he is subject to epileptic attacks that the Eskimo or Indonesian shaman, for example, owes his power and prestige; it is to the fact that he can control his epilepsy."[75]

Assiduous practice of this posture and the posture of the standing figures can play an important role in the quest for the realm beyond rationality and material existence.[76] Within the many systems of yoga, these postures, whose practice and attainment involve physical and psychic discipline, become vehicles for the absolute, divine, ecstatic consciousness. In the words of a modern practitioner, "Mind is the greatest force on this earth. He who has controlled his mind, is full of power."[77] From the yogic standpoint, the practice of

difficult postures is an exercise leading to control of the mind.

A few contemporary scientists have proved that disciplined postures, meditation, and other specific ritual practices stimulate the temporal lobe of the brain. They hypothesize that love and religious, ecstatic, and mystical experiences arise from the temporal lobe. Out-of-body experiences, time distortions, a sense of cosmic communion, and hallucinations all can be evoked by surgical stimulation of the temporal lobe. The temporal lobe has the capacity to generate learned seizures (not the epileptic type, but *normal*, "transient, very focal, electrical displays" within the temporal lobe) at the discretion of the individual.[78] For those of us whose cultures do not value such experiences, this research provides a rational explanation for the visionary states prized by the Olmec and other peoples of Mesoamerica. The crux of the matter is that it is nearly impossible for any human being to attain the position of the Olmec "acrobats." So why did the Olmec show us something so unusual?

If the "acrobat" pose is the result of a specific effort rather than of a neurological disturbance, this discipline, involving the intention to achieve a visionary state, could hardly have avoided stimulation to the temporal lobe; the pose, therefore, along with the standing and kneeling poses, must have led to some sort of religious or mystical state.

Whether an image of a rare type of seizure or a position acquired through mental and physical discipline, the "acrobat" posture in Olmec art seems to signify a person in a visionary or ecstatic psychic state who is integrated into the ritual life of the community. Therefore, the kaolin figure excavated from a "shaman's grave" may have represented the contorted shaman himself. It is noteworthy that the contorted shamans in bas-relief appear on flat, circular stones, a rare format in Olmec art. In Maya art, such stones sometimes show a ruler's important captives in a similar pose. Maya rulers stood on these circular stones to symbolize the appropriation of their captives' political power. We wonder if Olmec rulers placed their feet on the soles of the visionaries' feet in order to tap their psychic powers.

Figure 29. La Venta Altar 5.

INERT INFANTS

The inanimate baby, carved on monuments such as La Venta Altar 5 and San Lorenzo Monuments 20 and 12, as well as the Las Limas Figure, is an important subject of Olmec sculpture. Why would the Olmec memorialize such a lifeless being?

The subject can be explored in light of the foregoing discussion of the temporary loss of consciousness due to temporal lobe epilepsy. Children's physical responses to psychomotor attacks often begin with their rushing in panic to an adult and complaining of the sense of being plagued. They may cling to the adult, screaming fearfully. This description is suggestive of the angry infants on the sides of La Venta Altar 5 (fig. 29). "This initial phase is followed by a loss of contact or communication, a vacant stare, often some tonic stiffening of the body."[79] In both types of epilepsy, grand mal

and temporal lobe, individuals may lose consciousness and fall to the floor, limp, with their eyes shut, remaining unresponsive for several minutes, and appearing to be dead.[80] Possibly the Olmec recognized that this condition in an infant might lead to the ability to prophesy in an adult, who might become a powerful shaman. Perhaps they considered this condition a temporary shamanic death and resurrection, a journey by the young soul to the underworld realm of the spirits, a shamanic election.

CONCLUSION

A complex but finite universe of formats, materials, themes, subjects, symbols, and stylistic emphases exists in what has been called the Olmec art style. Far more than merely a style, however, Olmec art

objects codified and communicated a shamanic reality whose fundamental truths were shared by disparate peoples across Mesoamerica. Each sculptural subject represents an aspect of the interpretation of the external world and the realm of shamanic transformation and served as both a model for ritual action in the local arena and proof of communication between humans and the supernatural beings that pervaded the landscape and cosmos. Taken together, the subjects of Olmec art must present a nearly complete view of the ideological concerns of America's first civilization.

In this essay I discussed the significance of the formal aspects of Olmec art within the framework of the magic-cosmic or shamanic world view. I proposed identifications and interpretations of several subjects, including idealized humans in standing, meditative poses that align the body and spirit with the cosmic axis; contortionists in impossible positions achieved through control of temporal lobe epilepsy or disciplined practice, hoping thereby to govern the mind; and humans in whose deformities were seen indications of close contact with personified forces of nature and shamanic power. These hypotheses suggest that the acquisition and maintenance of shamanic powers were a goal of individuals and polities in the Formative period and a primary impetus in the development of the remarkably consistent ideology referred to as Olmec culture.

Olmec culture as far as we know seems to have had no antecedents; no material models remain for its monumental constructions and sculptures and the ritual acts captured in small objects. The primal power of the art style springs partly from this lack of formal precedent. Sculptural objects were the direct expression of the cultural focus of the Olmec. The themes the Olmec established became their most enduring legacy: the attainment of a spiritually powerful state through meditation, sacrifice, and other austerities; the accomplishment of contact with the reality beyond the physical world; and the realization of supernatural sanction demonstrated by the building of complex ceremonial centers, which reproduced the variety of the natural world and the archetypal movements of the celestial world.

NOTES

Several individuals participated in the interpretations suggested here. My interest in the "acrobat" position was piqued during a visit to the Centro de Investigaciones Olmecas y Mayas (CICOM), Villahermosa, Tabasco, Mexico in the summer of 1993, when Rick Dingus, a colleague at Texas Tech University, Lubbock, pointed out that the pose on a Maya stela was identical to the locust position in Hatha Yoga. Throughout the course of this work, he helped clarify my thoughts on ancient Olmec spirituality. I wish to acknowledge and thank Mimi Crossley, an independent scholar in Houston, for alerting me to the importance of epilepsy as a factor in shamanism and its bearing on the "acrobat" pose. I mentioned to Phoebe Lloyd, also a colleague at Texas Tech, my need to discuss these ideas with a physician, and she introduced me to her collaborator, Gordon Bendersky, professor of Medicine at Hahnemann Hospital, Philadelphia, who is very interested in portrayals of epilepsy in art. Bendersky spoke to neurologists about my theories concerning the frequency of opisthotonus among psychomotor epileptics and to obstetricians about my fetus idea. His comments and suggestions, in addition to the many articles he kindly made available to me, aided me in formulating the arguments presented here. My contribution is merely to knit the pieces together, and of course I am responsible for any misrepresentations of the medical facts or theories of these generous colleagues. I thank all of them for making their insights available.

1. Michael D. Coe, "The Olmec Style and Its Distribution," in *Handbook of Middle American Indians: Archaeology of Southern Mesoamerica*, vol. 3, ed. Gordon R. Willey (Austin, Tex., 1965), 739–75.
2. Beatriz de la Fuente, "Toward a Conception of Monumental Olmec Art," in *The Olmec and Their Neighbors: Essays in Memory of Matthew W. Stirling*, ed. Elizabeth P. Benson (Washington, D.C., 1981).
3. Ibid.
4. Alan Roland, *In Search of Self in India and Japan: Toward a Cross-Cultural Psychology* (Princeton, 1989), 299 n. 14.
5. Ibid., 11.
6. K. C. Chang, *Art, Myth, and Ritual: The Path to Political Authority in Ancient China* (Cambridge, Mass., 1983), 95.
7. Benedict R. O'G. Anderson, "The Idea of Power in Javanese Culture," in *Culture and Politics in Indonesia*, ed. Claire Holt (Ithaca, N.Y., 1972), 1–69.
8. Peter T. Furst, "The Olmec Were-Jaguar Motif in the Light of Ethnographic Reality," in *Dumbarton Oaks Conference on the Olmec*, ed. Elizabeth P. Benson (Washington, D.C., 1968), 143–78. The work of Peter T. Furst, F. Kent Reilly, III, David Freidel, Linda Schele, David Stuart, John Justeson, and Terence Kaufman, among others, has proven that the Olmec and other Mesoamerican societies' world views parallel in broad principles and in many fascinating details the shamanic societies in other parts of the world described by Mircea Eliade, Willard Z. Park, Gerardo Reichel-Dolmatoff, Holger Kalweit, Carmen Blacker, K. C. Chang, and others.
9. F. Kent Reilly, III, "The Shaman in Transformation Pose: A Study of the Theme of Rulership in Olmec Art," *Record of The Art Museum, Princeton University* 48, no. 2 (1989): 6.

10. Michael D. Coe and Richard A. Diehl describe the acquisition, transportation, and carving of the San Lorenzo basalt boulders in greater detail in *In the Land of the Olmec: The Archaeology of San Lorenzo Tenochtitlán*, vol. 1 (Austin, Tex., 1980), 295–96.
11. John E. Clark et al., cited in James F. Garber et al., "Jade Use in Portions of Mexico and Central America— A Summary," in *Precolumbian Jade: New Geological and Cultural Interpretations*, ed. Frederick W. Lange (Salt Lake City, 1987), 211.
12. Ibid.
13. Matthew W. Stirling pointed out that the Chinese name for jade, *yu*, means "ruler of water" and probably had this meaning during the Shang period (later Zhou documents date the term to 2704 B.C.). This parallels the relationship between jade preciousness and water in Mesoamerica. See Stirling, "Aboriginal Jade Use in the New World," in *Proceedings of the 37th International Congress of Americanists*, vol. 4 (Buenos Aires, 1966), 22.
14. Mary W. Helms, *Craft and the Kingly Ideal* (Austin, Tex., 1993), 109–10.
15. Muriel Porter Weaver, *The Aztecs, Maya and Their Predecessors* (New York, 1993), 47–48.
16. Helms (as in note 14), 137.
17. Ibid., 16–17.
18. Gerardo Reichel-Dolmatoff, *Goldwork and Shamanism: An Iconographic Study of the Gold Museum* (Medellín, 1988), 17.
19. Fray Diego de Landa described the ascetic and ritual practices of the Maya artists of Yucatan who carved wood statues, *Diego de Landa's Yucatan Before and After the Conquest*, trans. William Gates (New York, 1937), 76.
20. See Paula Krotser, "Potters in the Land of the Olmec," in Michael D. Coe and Richard A. Diehl, *In The Land of the Olmec: The People of the River*, vol. 2 (Austin, Tex., 1980), for an analysis of womens' role in contemporary pottery making in the villages around San Lorenzo.
21. See Coe (as in note 1); C. William Clewlow, Jr., "A Stylistic and Chronological Study of Olmec Monumental Sculpture," *Contributions of the University of California Archaeological Research Facility*, no. 19 (Berkeley, 1974); Susan Milbrath, "A Study of Olmec Sculptural Chronology," *Studies in Pre-Columbian Art and Archaeology*, no. 23 (Washington, D.C., 1979).
22. Miguel Covarrubias, "El Arte 'Olmeca' o de La Venta," *Cuadernos Americanos* 28 (1946): 153–79.
23. Coe (as in note 1), 747–48.
24. De la Fuente (as in note 2), 85–86; idem, "Order and Nature in Olmec Art," in *The Ancient Americas: Art from Sacred Landscapes*, ed. Richard F. Townsend (Chicago, 1992), 85–86, 121–33.
25. Horst de la Croix, Richard G. Tansey, Diane Kirkpatrick, *Gardner's Art through the Ages*, 9th ed. (New York, 1991), 1104.
26. His deity designations have been debated by Anatole Pohorilenko and others. See Anatole Pohorilenko, "On the Question of Olmec Deities," *Journal of New World Archaeology* 2 (1977): 1–16.
27. First discussed by Coe (as in note 1) and later by Peter David Joralemon, "The Olmec Dragon: A Study in

Pre-Columbian Iconography," in *Origins of Religious Art and Iconography in Preclassic Mesoamerica*, ed. Henry B. Nicholson (Los Angeles, 1976), 37.
28. Joralemon (as in note 27), 27–71.
29. F. Kent Reilly, III, "Olmec Iconographic Influences on the Symbols of Maya Rulership: An Examination of Possible Sources," in *Sixth Palenque Round Table, 1986*, ed. Virginia M. Fields (Norman, Okla., 1991), 151–66.
30. For a stimulating discussion of the body in Aztec ideology, see Alfredo Lopez Austin, *The Human Body and Ideology: Concepts of the Ancient Nahuas* (Salt Lake City, 1988).
31. Mircea Eliade, *Shamanism: Archaic Techniques of Ecstasy*, trans. Willard R. Trask, Bollingen Series 76 (Princeton, N.J., 1970), 376.
32. F. Kent Reilly, III, "Enclosed Ritual Space and the Watery Underworld in Formative Period Architecture: New Observations on the Function of La Venta Complex A," in *Seventh Palenque Round Table, 1989*, ed. Virginia M. Fields (San Francisco, 1994), 125–35. As the title indicates, Reilly proposes that the Massive Offerings of serpentine blocks buried in the Complex A courtyards functioned as effigies of the ocean and, by extension, the watery underworld. The cruciform deposits of jade celts rising from a mirror were placed underground, above the centers of the Massive Offerings, and represented the world tree rising from the underworld seas.
33. See Taube, this volume.
34. At San Lorenzo, they constituted 9.5 percent of total faunal remains. Coe and Diehl, (as in note 10), 378, 383; Peter T. Furst, "Jaguar Baby or Toad Mother: A New Look at an Old Problem in Olmec Iconography," in *The Olmec and Their Neighbors: Essays in Memory of Matthew W. Stirling*, ed. Elizabeth P. Benson (Washington, D.C., 1981), 149–62. For recent research into the viability of the excretions of *B. marinus* as hallucinogenic, see Wade Davis and Andrew T. Weil, "Identity of a New World Psychoactive Toad," *Ancient Mesoamerica* 3 (1992): 51–59.
35. Rosemary Joyce et al., "Olmec Bloodletting: An Iconographic Study," in *Sixth Palenque Round Table, 1986*, ed. Fields (as in note 29), 143–50. For a different interpretation of these motifs, see Schele, this volume.
36. Philip Drucker, Robert Heizer, and Robert J. Squier, "Excavations at La Venta, Tabasco, 1955," *Bureau of American Ethnology*, Bulletin 170 (1959): 156.
37. Tsung Hwa Jou, *The Tao of Tai-Chi Chuan: Way to Rejuvenation* (Warwick, N.Y., 1981), 141–42, 112–13.
38. Quoted in W. Y. Evans-Wentz, *Cuchama and Sacred Mountains*, ed. Frank Waters and Charles L. Adams (Chicago, 1981), xxix–xi.
39. Frans Blom and Oliver La Farge, *Tribes and Temples: A Record of the Expedition to Middle America Conducted by the Tulane University of Louisiana in 1925*, 2 vols. (New Orleans, 1926–27), 44–45.
40. Marcia Merry de Morales, "Chalcatzingo Burials as Indicators of Social Ranking," in *Ancient Chalcatzingo*, ed. David C. Grove (Austin, Tex., 1987), fig. 89.
41. Charlotte Thomson, "Chalcatzingo Jade and Fine Stone Objects," in *Ancient Chalcatzingo*, ed. Grove (as in note 40), 297.
42. Austin (as in note 30), 167.

43. F. Kent Reilly, III, "The Ecological Origins of Olmec Symbols of Rulership," Master's thesis, University of Texas at Austin, 1987, 104.

44. Drucker et al. (as in note 36), 163–73.

45. Elizabeth K. Easby and John F. Scott, *Before Cortés: Sculpture of Middle America* (New York, 1970), fig. 36.

46. Ibid., fig. 40.

47. Philip Drucker, "La Venta, Tabasco: A Study of Olmec Ceramics and Art," *Bureau of American Ethnology*, Bulletin 153 (1952): 72–73; 157–59.

48. Ibid., 156–59.

49. Ibid., fig. 21.

50. Coe and Diehl (as in note 10), 367.

51. Ibid., 327.

52. See Beatriz de la Fuente and Nelly Gutiérrez Solana, *Escultura Monumental Olmeca: Catálogo* (México, D. F., 1973), no. 18.

53. Eliade (as in note 31), 102

54. Willard Z. Park, "Shamanism in Western North America: A Study in Cultural Relationships," *Northwestern University Studies in the Social Sciences*, no. 2 (Chicago, 1938), 77.

55. Martin Pickands, "The Hero Myth in Maya Folklore," in *Symbol and Meaning Beyond the Closed Community: Essays in Mesoamerican Ideas*, ed. Gary H. Gossen (Albany, N.Y., 1986), 101–24.

56. Carolyn E. Tate, *Yaxchilan: The Design of a Maya Ceremonial City* (Austin, Tex., 1992), 131.

57. Drucker (as in note 47), 159.

58. Gordon Bendersky, M. D. assisted in this investigation. Dubious at first about my identification of these figures as fetuses, he presented the images to a group of obstetricians. They said the proportion of the head to the body was the major indicator of a fetus. From a morphological analysis, it would be extremely rare for infantile hydrocephalus to simulate the cranial configuration of a normal fetus. The puffy eyes were characteristic of fourteen- to twenty-one-week-old fetuses. The opinion of the group was that these did indeed represent fetuses to a ninety percent certainty.

59. Reilly (as in note 45), 70.

60. Ibid.

61. Mary Miller and Karl Taube, *The Gods and Symbols of Ancient Mexico and the Maya* (London, 1993), 62, 114. See also A. Romano, cited in Christine Neiderberger, *Paleopaysages et Archeologie Pre-Urbaine du Bassin de Mexico*, vol. 11, bk. 2 (Mexico, 1987), 452.

62. The connection between the pose of these Olmec sculptures with epilepsy was first suggested by Mimi Crossley, based on Hermann Dietering's, an independent scholar in Houston, research into early uses of photography to document psychological abnormalities.

63. Joyce et al. (as in note 35), 146

64. Gordon Bendersky, personal communication, March 1994.

65. Owsei Temkin, *The Falling Sickness: A History of Epilepsy from the Greeks to the Beginnings of Modern Neurology*, 2d ed. (Baltimore, 1970), 151.

66. Quoted in William G. and Margaret A. Lennox, *Epilepsy and Related Disorders*, vol. 1 (Boston, 1960), 278.

67. Quoted in ibid.

68. Ibid., 279.

69. Temkin (as in note 65), 148.

70. *Epilepsy: A Handbook for the Mental Health Professional*, ed. Harry Sands (New York, 1982), 78.

71. Gordon Bendersky, personal communication, March 1994.

72. M-Marsel Mesulam, "Dissociative States with Abnormal Temporal Lobe EEG: Multiple Personality and the Illusion of Possession," *Arch Neurology* 38 (1981): 176–81.

73. Jean Aicardi, *Epilepsy in Children* (New York, 1986), 151.

74. Eliade (as in note 31), 15–31

75. Ibid., 29.

76. Michael A. Persinger, "Religious and Mystical Experiences as Artifacts of Temporal Lobe Function: A General Hypothesis," *Perceptual and Motor Skills* 57 (1983): 1255–62.

77. Swami Vishnudevananda, *The Complete Book of Illustrated Yoga* (New York, 1972), 294.

78. Persinger (as in note 76), 1255–59

79. Aicardi (as in note 73), 146–47.

80. Ibid., 150; Temkin (as in note 65), 142, 144.

Shamanism, Transformation, and Olmec Art

PETER T. FURST

Rereading recently the lecture with which Matthew W. Stirling opened the 1967 Dumbarton Oaks conference on Mesoamerica's first civilization was for me a kind of homecoming after a journey of thirty years.[1] This journey has taken me, by way of West Mexican funerary sculpture and the religions, oral traditions, symbolism, and arts of the Huichols and other Native American peoples, into what many of us who move back and forth between the ethnographic present and the archaeological past believe are shamanistic motifs in the art of the Olmec. Notwithstanding a distance of three millennia, these motifs have analogies in the shamanic religions and symbol systems of living Indian peoples.

Some of the themes that confront us in these societies and in Olmec art—human-animal transformation and qualitative equivalence between humans and animals, ecstatic trance, guardian spirits and animal alter egos, journeys of the soul, animate and sentient physical and metaphysical environments, and the like—seem to come right out of that Archaic circum-northern Pacific shamanistic substratum we understand to be the foundation of all Native American religions.

In a few cases—including the complex religions and symbol systems of the great Classic and Postclassic Mesoamerican civilizations—the remnants of this near-universal substratum stare you in the eye. In others, they are more subdued and attenu-

ated, but still there. They are very much there in those remarkable representations of human-jaguar metamorphosis and animal protectors or alter egos in Olmec lapidary sculpture, which are invariably monumental in visual impact. As Michael D. Coe observed in 1965: "No matter how small the object, it always looks much larger than it really is."[2]

Stirling prefaced his talk on the early history of Olmec scholarship by noting how many colleagues became Olmec enthusiasts as a result of exposure—sight and touch—to a "single fine specimen of Olmec art." For Marshall Saville it was the Kunz Axe; for George Vaillant, the jade jaguar from Necaxa (both objects are now in the American Museum of Natural History, New York). For me it was a little, almost black steatite figurine of a man rising from one knee in the ecstasy of transformation. A work of considerable beauty and technical perfection, it is now in the Los Angeles County Museum of Art (fig. 1; cat. no. 46). Furthermore, the cultural, historical, and ethnographic information it embodies has contributed to our understanding of what some, if not all, of the jaguar symbolism in Olmec art may mean. Its precise origin is uncertain but, like a standing man-jaguar statuette in the Robert Woods Bliss Collection at Dumbarton Oaks Research Library and Collections, Washington, D.C. (fig. 2), also carved from a dark green steatite, it is said to have been found in Tabasco. The two pieces share a number of iconographic details, suggesting that they might have been made in the same workshop; in any event, they clearly express the same underlying concept,

as do two heads missing their bodies, one in a private collection on loan to The Art Museum, Princeton University (fig. 3; cat. no. 47) and the other, found by Stirling near La Venta, now in the National Museum of Anthropology, Mexico City.

Looked at superficially, the Dumbarton Oaks and Los Angeles figures might appear to be wearing jaguar masks, as Samuel K. Lothrop thought was the case with the Dumbarton Oaks statuette, which he identified as female.[3] In fact, looked at more critically, both figures are revealed to be male, notwithstanding the typically Olmec lack of overt sexual characteristics. While this absence of sexual definition has been the subject of much debate, my own theory is that the apparent androgyny in Olmec art, as well as the contrast between feminine facial features and male body characteristics and breechclout demonstrated by the Las Limas Figure, has more to do with the idea of male-female duality or unity. The Quiché Maya, for example, still call their diviners "mother-father," and the holy earth is likewise male and female at the same time, a concept of duality shared by many other traditional Mesoamerican peoples. The perishable clothing many of these now nude statuettes might originally have worn also would have conveyed their gender.

Be that as it may, the Dumbarton Oaks and Los Angeles figurines and the two head fragments make it clear that the jaguar features are not masks but were intended by the artist to be understood as physical phenomena integral to the personages portrayed in stone. True, the jaguar features are set

Figure 1. Crouching Figure of a Man-Jaguar, 800–500 B.C., Tabasco. Dark green serpentine with traces of red pigment, h. 10.5 cm.; w. 7.9 cm. Los Angeles County Museum of Art, gift of Constance McCormick Fearing.

Figure 2. Standing Figure of a Were-Jaguar, 900–600 B.C., Mexico. Serpentine with pyrite inlay, h. 18.8 cm.; w. 10.5 cm.; d. 6.3 cm. Dumbarton Oaks Research and Library Collections, Washington, D.C.

off from the rest of the head by a marked dividing line, but in each case the back of the head is raised, not the jaguar features of the face, which would be elevated were he wearing a mask. This gives the impression that the human features have been peeled away, revealing the feline essence beneath.

Figure 3. Head Fragment from Transformation Figure, 900–700 B.C., Veracruz. Dark serpentine with traces of cinnabar, h. 7.3 cm.; w. 5.2 cm.; d. 5.5 cm. Anonymous loan to The Art Museum, Princeton University.

Despite some stylistic differences the Dumbarton Oaks figure and Mexico City and Princeton heads share the same imagery with the Los Angeles statuette, leaving no doubt that the ancient carvers were representing a physical and metaphysical experience the Olmec believed to be real. I do not think it is coincidental that in every piece the jaguar features are convulsed in a tortured grimace. In my opinion, this is intended to convey, not ferocity and aggressiveness, but emotional stress almost beyond endurance. It is precisely the sort of physically and mentally exhausting crisis—the crossing of the threshold between two worlds, two kinds of reality, if you will, two kinds of being, complementary rather than antithetical—that is integral to the practice of ecstatic shamanism everywhere, and that in the American tropics to this day often expresses itself in complete identification with, and transformation into, the most powerful predator of the rain forest and the savannah.

When I first saw the Los Angeles transformation figure thirty years ago, it struck me as being the single most exciting pre-Columbian stone figure of any size I had ever had the privilege to hold in my hands. That it was Olmec was beyond doubt. That it was the work of a great sculptor, a master lapidary who ranked first in skill, but who also, as I thought then and still do, had personally experienced, not merely observed, the agony and ecstasy of shamanic transformation, was equally obvious. It struck me as either a self-portrait, perhaps of an Olmec artist-shaman undergoing transformation into a jaguar, or a "medicine" figure commissioned by a shaman-priest or priest-chief from the best Olmec sculptor he could find whose skill was informed by personal participation in the techniques and content of shamanic ecstasy.

I went on to speculate how it fit, along with the anthropomorphic jaguars in the Bliss Collection at Dumbarton Oaks, with what we knew of shamanism, including one of its basic tenets, qualitative equivalence between humans and animals, on the one hand, and Stirling's ideas about a possible jaguar ancestry for the Olmec, on the other. I concluded that these figurines could best be understood by analogy to the widespread identification of the shaman with the jaguar, and transformation from the one into the other, in the American tropics.[4] What I did not know at the time was that, in addition to the Bliss Collection pieces, so many other examples of this phenomenon existed in Olmec art that the drama of transformation from human to feline must have had a prominent, not to say dominant, place in the religious ideology and shamanic practice of their makers.

I have long been interested in this aspect of ecstatic shamanism, ever since I enrolled in an anthropology seminar conducted by Johannes Wilbert at the University of California at Los Angeles in 1962, when he shared with us students a whole series of examples from South America of jaguar shamanism and transformation. Wilbert also pointed me in the direction of nineteenth- and early twentieth-century ethnographic writings on South American Indian religion and shamanism. But as a comparative source work for anyone trying to unravel Olmec iconography, nothing seemed to me at the time to have greater potential than the work on mythology and shamanism among the Bolivian Tacana by Karin Hissink,[5] a German ethnologist from the Frankfurt school of cultural morphology founded by the Africanist Leo Frobenius. Her ethnography of Tacana oral poetry and myth, based on two years of fieldwork in the 1950s among these little-known Indians on the eastern side of the Bolivian Andes, is unexpectedly relevant to Meso-america, rich as it is in ethnographic analogies to major motifs in the art of not only Chavín and Moche but, notwithstanding the enormous distance in time and space that divides contemporary Indian South America from ancient Mexico, also the Olmec.[6] There are stories of flying jaguars, jaguar mountain lords, feathered and winged were-jaguars regarded as great *yanaconas* (a word of Quechua origin the Tacana use for shamans), and jaguars as guardians of high gods and the world; of the earth sailing through space on the back of a giant winged jaguar (the world will come to an end when it becomes tired), shamans transforming into jaguars or blowing tobacco powder to repel hostile spirit jaguars threatening their patients or social group, and on and on. In the cosmology of the Tacana there is even a direct analogy, in name and function, to the central Mexican Tlaltecuhtli, "owner of the earth," the deified earth personified as a monstrous toad with fangs and claws who devours the dead. I have no problem with the idea of an essential, underlying unity of Native American religion that is grounded in an "archaic" ecstatic shamanism and crosscuts cultural, temporal, and spatial distances. Frankly, when I read Hissink I was more impressed by the analogies than put off by the great distances involved.

In any event, Tacana mythology and shamanic practice also first suggested to me a possible expla-nation for the so-called acrobats in the art of the Olmec and some other pre-Columbian peoples (figs. 4, 5; cat. no. 40). One of the techniques by which Tacana shamans transform themselves into jaguars is somersaulting, a skill aspiring shamans must acquire in the course of their training. In this they are not always successful. In fact, one of Hissink's informants told her he had been fright-ened out of his plan to become a shaman when he saw his teacher suddenly flip head over heels and stand before him as a jaguar. The technique of

Figure 4. Bottle in the Form of a Contortionist, 1250–900 B.C., Tlatilco. Clay with slip and traces of red pigment, h. 22 cm.; w. 14 cm.; d. 13 cm. Private collection.

Figure 5. Figure with Feet on Head, 900–500 B.C., San Geronimo, Guerrero. Light bluish green steatite, h. 23.5 cm.; w. 13 cm.; d. 26 cm. Private collection.

somersaulting in shamanic metamorphosis is not limited to South America. As I learned years later, certain shamans of the Huichols of the Sierra Madre Occidental, who get their power from wolves, also use somersaulting to transform into their animal alter egos: five jumps forward to assume wolf form, five backward to return to human shape.[7] This sug-gests that techniques of shamanic transformation may account for at least some of the tumbling fig-urines and yogalike poses in the art of both the Olmec and the West Mexican shaft tomb people a millennium later.[8]

An essay on the role of the harpy eagle in eastern South American shamanism by the German ethnologist Otto Zerries, published in 1962, also proved interesting to me,[9] the more so because at the other end of the spatial and cultural continuum in Amazonia, Gerardo Reichel-Dolmatoff was then beginning to unravel the intricacies of harpy eagle symbolism as "the jaguar of the sky" in the shamanic cosmology of the Tukanoan Desana of Colombian Amazonia. So it seemed increasingly likely that although the clues to such apparently incongruous iconographic combinations in Olmec art (and in that of Chavín, their Peruvian contem-poraries) of *Panthera onca* and *Harpia harpyja* (fig. 6) have virtually, or altogether, disappeared from the local environment, they might yet be found in the cosmologies and myths of tropical forest Indians in South America.

THE JAGUAR AS INITIATOR

I remember one session of Wilbert's seminar partic-ularly in relation to our subject here. Wilbert included a graphic description from his own field-work of the ordeal of the young *héwiawan*, literally "Bat Man," a class of Yanomamö shamans who are initiated into their calling in a memorably violent spirit encounter with a huge, supernatural jaguar named Omáokóhe. Having undergone many training sessions in which an experienced older shaman instructs the neophyte in the esoteric knowledge and techniques of Yanomamö shaman-ism, the recruit, whose body is covered with painted jaguar spots and tufts of harpy eagle down, is given a powerful blast of hallucinogenic snuff through a long, blowgun-like tube. Almost at once his scalp

Figure 6. Bottle, 900–400 B.C., Chavín, Peru. Clay, h. 29.2 cm. Private collection.

begins to itch, mucus flows liberally from his nose, and he falls into an ecstatic trance. In this condition he—or his spirit—travels deep into the surrounding rain forest, until he comes face to face with Omáokóhe, master of all the felines. The candidate asks Omáokóhe to strip him of his human flesh. The jaguar does so, without injuring his bones. The neophyte then requests the jaguar to reclothe his skeleton, and the giant feline replaces his flesh with the flesh of a bat. The jaguar also supplants the candidate's vital organs and innards with magical ones made of shiny rock crystal. The initiate's new organs will enable him to sing powerful curing songs and understand the language of animals. He is now a Bat Man (for bat-winged Olmec figurines, see cat. nos. 68, 69).

In his encyclopedic ethnographic and pharmacological study of tobacco and shamanism among South American Indians published in 1987, to which we will return below in relation to the role of tobacco in jaguar shamanism, Wilbert gives another example of the symbolic death and regeneration of a novice Campa shaman at the hands of a super-

natural jaguar. The feline initiator, who is female, becomes the newly initiated jaguar shaman's animal-wife:

> The intimate relationship between the shaman and the jaguar is clearly exemplified by Campa concepts and beliefs. To become one of their jaguar shamans, a novice must ingest an initial dose of tobacco jelly and learn the song of tobacco. When the tobacco "reaches his heat," he receives a vision and meets old woman Tobacco Spirit, whom he asks for one of her daughters. Animals will appear to him in human form pretending to be the jaguar girl he asked for. But if he wants to become a true jaguar shaman and healer, he sees through the sham and lets all disguised animals pass by, until he hears a jaguar roar in the night-darkened jungle. This is the old woman's daughter whom he must go out to meet in the forest. The jaguar attacks the novice and tears him to pieces. If the young man endures the ordeal without retreating, his body will become whole again and his jaguar tormentor will turn into a beautiful young woman.[10]

"JAGUAR CULTS" AND JAGUAR ANCESTORS

From the very first, scholars have generally agreed that Olmec symbolism centers on a "jaguar cult," with the so-called were-jaguar and its corollary, the peculiar combination of infantile and feline features known as the "jaguar-babyface" motif, among the premier distinguishing characteristics of the Olmec style. But there was little consensus on what is actually meant by jaguar cult or even werejaguar. Did the Olmec have a jaguar god? Did they actually consider themselves the "jaguar's children," to borrow the title of Coe's 1965 Museum of Primitive Art book, in the genetic rather than the symbolic sense?[11]

Stirling suggested as much, basing his conjecture on a monumental but badly damaged and fragmentary stone sculpture from Potrero Nuevo he assumed depicted a jaguar copulating with a human female but is now interpreted quite differently by other scholars, including myself.[12] We do in fact find the idea of the jaguar as progenitor among several Amazonian societies who regard themselves as "jaguar people" descended from feline ancestors.

Thus, according to Reichel-Dolmatoff, the Chibchan-speaking Kogi of Colombia are "the People of the Jaguar, their land is the Land of the Jaguar, their ancestors are the Jaguar People." In the Kogi creation myth cycle, a long series of jaguar people were born of the Universal Mother. These first jaguar people were animal and human at the same time and could change at will from one to the other. Jaguars originated and protected all food plants; conversely, they will be instrumental in the end of the present world (just as jaguars caused the destruction of the first creation in the central Mexican myth of four suns that preceded the present creation). Nevertheless, the Kogi respect the jaguar not as a menace but as the essential life force.

The Carib Kaingang of Brazil regard themselves as jaguars in the literal sense, which is why, in preparation for war, they paint themselves with black spots.[13] The identity with the jaguar is taken so literally that occasionally a *minanti*, a man who "dreams" of jaguars, turns into a *mivé*, or "seer" of jaguars. Believing himself to be the intended lover of the daughter of the master of the jaguars, he separates himself from his relatives and friends and prowls the forest alone. He enters a trance state in which he encounters a supernatural jaguar who guides him to the jaguar people or the jaguar woman. The neighboring Apapocúva-Guarani also regard the Kaingang as real jaguars, not because their ancestors were jaguars, but because, even though they have human forms, they have the souls of jaguars.

In his survey of the literature on the jaguar in South American Indian ideology, Heinz Walter found only four groups among whom the feline occurs as a deity in our sense of the term.[14] A closer look at the data showed him that among three of these peoples the putative "jaguar god" was in fact only an institutionalized version of the well-known "master of the species," a being typical of hunting cultures but still found among many tropical forest agriculturalists. The master of the species, or master of the forest, is a powerful being, but not a god. Of the four groups concerned, three are Bolivian— the Arawakan Mojo, the Tacana Araóna, and the Panoan Pacaguára—and the fourth, Brazilian— the Shipáya, a Tupían-speaking people. The Araóna people's religion appears to be strongly influenced by Quechua ideology; indeed, some of their major supernaturals, like their shamans, have Quechua names. The Mojo venerate a jaguar being in a temple attended by a specialized shaman. These jaguar shamans are recruited from among men who survived jaguar attacks in the forest and are thus regarded as favored by the feline deity.

No doubt Walter was right in concluding that this feline god evolved from an original master of the species, who became deified, with his own priest-temple cult, under outside influence, notably the Andean civilizations. For example, the deified jaguar of the Araóna is asked to lead the hunter to his jaguar prey; if the hunter is attacked by the feline and survives, it is taken as a sign of the master of the species's benevolent attitude toward him, and if he succeeds in killing his prey, the god, as master of the jaguar people, must be propitiated. It hardly accords with our idea of a deity that the Araóna jaguar shaman-priest can engage the supernatural jaguar in combat and force his will upon him in behalf of the community. From these spirit battles the shaman often emerges bloodied, exhausted, and with his clothing torn.

In the final analysis, although some deities might be conceived in jaguar form (like the Aztec Tezcatlipoca, as "heart of the mountain" or divine ruler of the interior of the earth), only a single, actual jaguar god appears in the literature on South American Indians: Kumapári, the creator-culture hero and warfare and cannibalism god of the Shipáya.[15] But his is also a special case, since in the origin mythology he starts out in human form and assumes his feline shape only after he becomes disillusioned and angry with humankind.

One thing emerges clearly from the ethnographic literature: the jaguar never derives its supernatural power and mythic qualities purely from the great feline's animal characteristics—from its powerful and cunning predatory nature—but from its inherent supernatural attributes. For many South American Indians the jaguar is not, in fact, an animal, but a human being. And not just any human being, but the technician of the sacred, the master of trance who controls the spirit helpers— that is, the shaman.

Thus it is surely no accident that the jaguar is rarely depicted as solely animal in Olmec art. Even those jaguar effigies that at first sight seem com-

pletely faithful to the natural model turn out to have something human about them. Later—in Maya art, or at Teotihuacan, for example—we do find "naturalistic" jaguars, but their bearing and iconography reveal mystical rather than natural qualities.

Olmec jaguars are virtually exclusively feline anthropomorphs or anthropomorphic felines. The human-jaguar motif ranges conceptually and representationally from effigies where the animal character predominates to those where the anthropomorphic prevails and only the mouth suggests the jaguar. Examples of the first kind include the little upright jaguars that have feline heads, bodies, feet, and tails but human legs, arms, and hands or that stand upright on two legs like people (fig. 7;

Figure 7. Jaguar Standing in Human Position, 900–600 B.C., Tuxtlas region, Veracruz. Light grayish green marble impacted with cinnabar, h. 11.5 cm.; w. 4 cm.; d. 1.5 cm. Private collection.

cat. no. 50). At the other end of the continuum are those in the same class as the Los Angeles statuette in this catalogue (cat. no. 46) and its cousins at Dumbarton Oaks.

Also part of this class is a remarkable jaguar man now at Dumbarton Oaks, reportedly found at Tetlacingo, Puebla (fig. 8). Another example of Olmec human-jaguar transformation, this one takes us one step further into the process. Here the body is completely human, but the bearded face harmoniously blends human and jaguar features, with the ears both of the jaguar and his human equivalent. The whole conveys a sense of completion and contemplative equanimity rather than, as with the Los Angeles transformation figure, a profound crisis of metamorphosis. Given the several known transformation figurines in public and private collections, we now have the entire continuum of human-to-animal "shape-shifting." At one end we have the

Figure 8. Kneeling Figure, 900–600 B.C., Mexico. Serpentine with red pigment, h. 19 cm.; w. 9.7 cm.; d. 10.7 cm. Dumbarton Oaks Research and Library Collections, Washington, D.C.

Figure 9. Shaman in Transformation Pose, 800–600 B.C., Veracruz. Polished gray stone with traces of cinnabar, h. 17.5 cm.; w. 15.5 cm.; d. 9 cm. The Art Museum, Princeton University, gift of Mrs. Gerard B. Lambert, by exchange.

purely human state, with just a hint of the spirit world, represented in the magnificent portrait statuette in The Art Museum, Princeton University (fig. 9; cat. no. 42). The figure, which apparently once wore clothing, is that of an important personage, completely human, but with a toad incised on his bald head (companion animal? clan emblem or "totem"? prototype for Aztec and Mixtec symbol of the divine earth as supernatural toad?) and an expression suggesting, even with the eye inlays now missing, visionary revery.[16] At the other end, in the Los Angeles statuette and its companions, we have the ecstatic agony of transformation and finally the shaman as a two-legged jaguar, striking combative poses similar to that of the boxer challenging his opponent in the ring.

Let us examine the ethnographic evidence for this dramatic process.

SHAMAN-JAGUAR TRANSFORMATION IN SOUTH AMERICA

The ability of shamans to share their identity with the jaguar, to transform at will into the form of their feline companion spirit, or co-essence,[17] and back again, crosses linguistic, geographic, cultural, and temporal boundaries. When jaguars attack people it is believed they do so not because they are by nature aggressive but because they are either shamans in their jaguar form or the soul bearers of deceased shamans.[18] It is noteworthy that among the Bolivian Mojo, the concept of shaman-jaguar transformation persists. Mojo men who have been attacked by a jaguar and escaped unharmed are enrolled in a society of jaguar shamans that comes close to being a specialized, semiprofessional priesthood. Its duties include carrying out rituals connected with jaguars and calling and propitiating their spirits.

In such a society, animals associated with the shaman—mainly the jaguar, but also the harpy eagle—merge with the village chief or headman without, however, losing their role in the shaman's animal transformation. The harpy eagle and the jaguar thus are soul mates not just of the shaman but also of the village rulers, and they validate status and effective leadership.[19] Surely there is a message here for an understanding of the rise of complex societies in Mesoamerica—including that of the Olmec, whose political elites, though on a far different level of authority than South American village headmen, laid claim to the jaguar as the emblem of rulership.

One of the earliest descriptions of jaguar transformation in tribal South America was written by the German priest Martin Dobrizhoffer, who in the early 1800s labored among the Abipon of Paraguay. According to the padre, the Indians were convinced of the power of their "conjurers"—that is, shamans—to transform themselves into their animal familiars and to "inflict disease and death, to cure all disorders, to make known distant and future events; to cause rain, hail, and tempest; to call up the shades of the dead and consult them concerning hidden matters; to put on the form of a tiger, to handle every kind of serpent without danger, etc., which powers, they imagine, are not obtained by art, but imparted to certain persons by their grandfather, the Devil."[20]

It can be said that all the far-flung Carib-speaking tribes of northern Brazil, Venezuela, and the Guianas share the belief in shaman-jaguar equivalence and transformation. The Yucatec Maya use the same word, *balam* (or *bolom*) for shaman-priest and jaguar, and in many places in northern South America the qualitative identification of jaguar and shaman is so complete they are addressed or referred to by a single or closely related term. The Betoi-speaking tribes in the northwestern Amazon basin (eastern and southeastern Colombia and northwestern Brazil) use the same basic term for jaguar and shaman.[21] For example, among the Detuana, the common name for shaman is *dzaika*, for the jaguar, *djaja*. Although separated by the Witoto and a few Carib-speaking groups into western and eastern divisions, with little cultural contact between them, the thirty or so tribes of the Tukanoan-language family share in the concept of shaman-jaguar equivalence and most of them apply the same or a closely related term to both. In the western group, the Siona use the term *yái* and the Corrugaje, *djái* for both.[22] *Djai* is even employed for both by the Witoto, whose language, while classified as independent, includes the Tukanoan term *ikodjai*, meaning "jaguar soul" (*djai* = jaguar, *iko* = soul).[23] In the eastern group, the Cubeo have a concept of supernatural power called *parié*. There are two kinds of shamans, according to the ethnologist Irving Goldman, *pariékokü* (man of power) and *yaví* (jaguar). Every *yaví* is a *pariékokü* but not every *pariékokü* is a *yaví*. Rather, Goldman writes, "the *yaví* is the supreme shaman, the one who can take the form of a jaguar, who consorts with jaguars, who maintains the jaguar as a dog."[24]

Theodor Koch-Grünberg reported that elderly Cubeo shamans can turn themselves into jaguars simply by putting on jaguar skins.[25] This is a magical art the sixteenth-century Franciscan chronicler Fray Bernadino de Sahagún also credited to Aztec "sorcerers" in his encyclopedic work on the Aztecs known as the *Florentine Codex*. The Taurepan of southern Venezuela conceive of different kinds of supernatural jaguars that inhabit the earth or the water. While performing his magical curing chants the shaman merges with the jaguars, who assist him as spirit helpers, and he becomes—indeed, he already is—one of them. In an incantation quoted by Koch-Grünberg, the shaman lists the illnesses sent by various animals of the forest or the savannah to "weaken the flesh." When people are struck by such a disease, the shaman sings: "'they must call upon me, for I am the black jaguar. I drive away the illness. They have to call on me. I am the tapir-jaguar. It is me they have to invoke if they wish to frighten it [the illness] away. I am the puma-jaguar. I too am here. I extract the illness from their backs. It is me they have to call. I am the multi-colored jaguar. I too am here.'"[26]

THE HARPY EAGLE: "JAGUAR OF THE SKY"

It is often said that the jaguar's strong part in Indian cosmology and shamanism results from the fact that it is the most powerful and deadly predator in the savannah and forest. Perhaps an even more compelling reason, according to the ethnologist Peter G. Roe, is that the jaguar "fills so many middleman roles" its nature does not have to be split into separate parts.[27] Indeed, like its human counterpart, the jaguar easily crosses boundaries that restrict most other creatures to specific ecological niches. "The jaguar is an anomalous animal because it participates in a whole set of dimensions that are otherwise contrasted," writes Roe.

The Tukanoan Desana of the Colombian Amazonia, explained Reichel-Dolmatoff, also "emphasize that the jaguar is an animal that lives in a number of different environments; it lives in the deepest part of the jungle, swims in the water, and roams about by day and night. It is then an animal that participates in various dimensions, air, land, and water, and it belongs to light as well as darkness."[28]

Further, in the words of Stephen Hugh-Jones, the Barasana of Colombia "conceive of jaguars essentially as mediators both between the cosmic levels of sky, earth and water and between life and death, the human and spirit worlds, nature and culture."[29]

But the jaguar has a winged counterpart, the strikingly colored harpy eagle, which many Indians in South America consider the "jaguar of the sky," as did, so it seems, the Olmec. In Olmec art we frequently find the feline combined with its celestial

Figure 10. Mask, 900–600 B.C., Tenenexpan, Veracruz. Light green serpentine with traces of cinnabar, h. 17 cm.; w. 17.9 cm.; d. 12 cm. Private collection.

counterpart, the latter often appearing in shorthand form as the misnamed "flame (or plumed) eyebrows" on were-jaguar masks and figurines (figs. 10–12; cat. nos. 194, 117). More than forty years ago Philip Drucker, who helped excavate La Venta, pointed out that the serrated eyebrows "are actually very like the crest of the harpy eagle,"[30] but the former label has proved remarkably resistant to correction. We still find "flame eyebrows" listed as a distinguishing mark of the Olmec style, which is regrettable, since it misses a significant piece of symbolism. Donald Lathrap, a veritable missionary on behalf of tropical forest models for the dominant animal symbolism in the art of Chavín, wrote about the relationship of the jaguar and the harpy in the symbolism of the artists of Chavín, who were contemporaries of the Olmec in the northern Andes. His observations apply equally well to Olmec iconography: "It would appear appropriate, considering what we surmise about Chavín ideology, that the attributes of the most powerful known carnivore, the jaguar, were combined with the attributes of the most powerful raptorial bird, the harpy

Figure 11. Votive Axe in the Form of a Supernatural Were-Jaguar, Veracruz. Stone, h. 18.1 cm. Private collection.

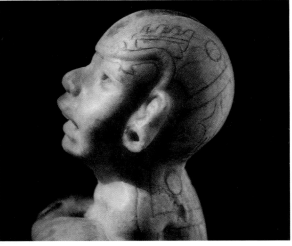

Figure 12. Standing Figure with Incisions (detail), 900–600 B.C., Chiapas. Light grayish green albitite, h. 14 cm.; w. 5.4 cm.; d. 5.8 cm. Private collection.

eagle."[31] Wings, claws, and beaks, and presumably all the rest of the harpy features, also occur in Olmec art, but the characteristic that came to stand more than any other for the bird is the prominent feather crest.

Here again tropical forest peoples can help us with the questions of how the Olmec conceived of the harpy eagle and why they identified it with the jaguar. To the South American shaman, the jaguar is his alter ego on and beneath the earth and in the water (the watery underworld) in the same way the harpy, largest of all American eagles, is his alter ego in the sky (fig. 13). To put it another way, the crested harpy, the most powerful winged predator, which flies in the tall canopy of the tropical forest with incredible agility at speeds up to fifty miles an hour searching for monkeys, its favorite food, is to the upperworld what the jaguar is to the surface of the earth and the world below. The ornithologist Leslie Brown writes this about the great raptor: "The Harpy is unquestionably the world's most formidable bird. A male is impressive enough, weighing 9–10 lb (4.4kg), a female huge, weighing 15–20 lb (6.7–9kg) with a tarsus as thick as a child's wrist; she is about as big as a bird of prey can be while still able to fly easily."[32]

The harpy has yet to be intensively studied by scientists, but its place in the ideological universe in relation to the jaguar and the shaman has been well examined. In *The Shaman and the Jaguar*, Reichel-Dolmatoff offered insightful information on tropical forest shamanism based on his many years of study of the religion and world view of the Tukanoan Desana.[33] One of the first requirements for an aspiring *payé* (the Desana term for shaman) during his initiatory training is to acquire a number of power objects from the celestial sphere to use later in his magical practice. In his first trance, triggered with the aid of *yajé*, a potent psychoactive drink made from the so-called vine of souls, *Banisteriopsis caapi*, or potent snuff made from the inner bark of the Virola tree, the *payé* travels to the House of Thunder.[34] Thunder is a personified being closely related to the spirit jaguar; in fact, he takes on the appearance of a jaguar whenever shamans visit him. His messengers in the sky are harpy eagles and jaguars. On his journey to Thunder's house the initiate sees only the spirit essences of his power objects. These objects include different colored stones; white quartzite and rock crystals; sharp splinters and thorns, which he can use as sickness projectiles to shoot at an enemy or, conversely, as a kind of counter-poison to suck out disease; and psychoactive Virola snuff solidified into resinlike consistency.

Figure 13. Harpy Eagle.

The white hairs from the jaguar's underbelly and the harpy eagle's fluffy white down feathers are essential in shamanic initiation. Stuffed together in his ears, they provide the intiate, who is in an ecstatic trance induced by Virola powder and *yajé*, with magical hearing and the ability to understand the language in which the spirits speak.

The Tukano and other peoples in the South American tropics believe that if jaguars and harpy eagles are especially aggressive, it is not because they are violent by nature, but because they are made so by shamans who enter their bodies. Thus, if a Tukano encounters a jaguar wearing the down feathers of the harpy eagle, he knows he is dealing not with an ordinary feline but with an evil shaman who has entered the jaguar's body and made the animal dangerous. Fortunately, shamans possess

magical incantations and other techniques to ward off these dangers and tame the jaguar. Reichel-Dolmatoff cites a prophylactic spell:

His ears are his ornaments.
They are the white feathers of the harpy eagle.
When he is thus adorned, he is fierce;
Then he is armed with his bow;
Thus he is adorned.[35]

The song goes on to describe how the jaguar is relieved of his feathered ornaments and his weapons by the shaman; without his harpy eagle ornaments and his bow and arrows he is no longer a threat and returns to his home in the forest.

This ambivalence toward the jaguar also applies to his celestial counterpart, the harpy, who may be a transformed sorcerer intent on harming people or the carrier of supernatural illness. While stories abound of shamans becoming jaguars, comparable tales exist of shamanic transformation into the harpy, achieved by means of the bird's feathers. A good example is a Tariana myth cited by Zerries:

In the mythic First Times, when the rocks were still soft and beings, animals and humans, had the same form, three youths wished to become shamans but lacked the necessary harpy eagle feathers. There was a grandmother who hated the harpy eagle people because one of her boys had been devoured by them. She told the three aspiring shamans where the harpy eagle people could be found. To trap and kill them and strip them of their feathers, they should fashion a net of fibers from the *tutru* plant, which grew in the sky in front of the House of Thunder.

They did as they were instructed. Because the material was not of this world, the net they wove was very strong. When they came to the House of the Harpy Eagle People they found only an old woman there, preparing curare (blow gun poison). But they also noticed a trumpet belonging to the harpy eagles. The sound of the trumpet was like that of the harpy eagles. When the harpy eagles heard the trumpet, they came flying to devour the boys. But instead they were trapped in the net and killed. The boys took the dead harpy eagles back to their house, stripped them of their feathers, and used them to make their shaman's costumes.[36]

The Bororo of central Brazil link the harpy and the jaguar because, among other things, they are both carnivores and are considered the only two creatures capable of destroying human beings, according to Jon Christopher Crocker.[37] Killing either a jaguar or a harpy, they believe, is like taking a human life, and involves a whole complex of rituals. To prevent the dead jaguar or harpy eagle from exacting revenge, for example, its tongue is cut out, tobacco smoke is blown over the corpse, and the immediate intervention of two kinds of shamans is sought. These shamans have charge of an antithetical dyad of supernatural forces, one of which is *bope*, the other, *aroe*. Each "is manifested in various 'pure,' undiluted, awful forms, but each is present also in an unstable synthesis within each living creature." For the most part, Bororo symbolic activity, including that of shamans, is devoted to "maintaining and re-creating the balance between each element in this synthesis." Shamans specializing in both these forces are thus required to step in when a harpy eagle or a jaguar has been slain.

The Bororo also regard the harpy eagle as the celestial counterpart to the jaguar and relate them both to shamans. They call the harpy *aroe exeba*, "killer of souls," and say its beak and talons are the same as "the teeth and claws of a jaguar. With them it kills whatever it wishes." Crocker writes that both creatures are deemed as beautiful as they are deadly. Although they are nearly extinct in and around the Bororo territory, they retain their old symbolic and ritual importance and close association "as natural counterparts to man's capacity to slay his own kind."[38]

TOBACCO AND JAGUAR SHAMANISM

Wilbert, the ranking authority on the role of tobacco in South American shamanism, writes: "Like shamans in general, South American tobacco shamans assume a daring posture of combativeness against the powers of disintegration such as evil spirits, sorcerers, sterility, sickness and death. This stance becomes clearly manifested in the widespread shaman-jaguar transformation complex in which tobacco and hallucinogens play an instrumental role."[39]

This raises some interesting questions with respect to chemical "techniques of ecstasy" available in the plant world to Olmec shamans and whether these included, as in South America, tobacco. In 1968 I suggested the possibility that the

Figure 14. Hollow Figure, 100 B.C.–A.D. 200, Colima, Mexico. Clay with slip, h. 27.9 cm. Private collection.

Figure 15. Snuffing pipe in the Form of a Kneeling Figure, 1500–1200 B.C., Xochipala, Guerrero. Clay, h. 14.4 cm.; w. 8.4 cm. The Art Museum, Princeton University, Museum purchase.

Olmec used psychoactive snuff, a practice first observed by Columbus and his men on the island of Hispaniola. I mentioned one likely candidate, *piciétl*, the Nahuatl name for *Nicotiana rustica* tobacco, from whose dried leaves Aztec curers and shamans made a potent powder utilized as a ritual cleanser and ecstatic intoxicant.[40] According to Sahagún, *piciétl* "intoxicates one, makes one dizzy, possesses one."[41] The powder, which could be inhaled directly through the nose, was also mixed with lime and made into wads for chewing and sucking, just as coca leaves and lime are still chewed together in the Andes. I also speculated about a possible Mexican relative of *Anadenanthera peregrina*, a leguminous tree whose seeds, crushed and pulverized, were the probable source of the powerfully psychoactive *cohoba* snuff employed by Taino Indians in the West Indies. The ritual use and extraordinary effects of *cohoba* were described, somewhat fancifully, by the Spanish friar Román Pané, who accompanied Columbus on his second voyage.

My hypothetical Olmec snuffing complex anticipated by several years a good deal of archaeological evidence that in the 1970s confirmed the existence of an early, widespread Mesoamerican snuffing complex.[42] This evidence proved beyond any doubt that ritual intoxication with potent snuff powders was not limited to the Caribbean and Central and South America, but was also practiced in Mexico, at least as long ago as the Early to Middle Formative. A number of figural "nose pipes" dating to about 400–500 B.C. were found at Monte Alban, including an example of a reclining deer with a peyote cactus in its mouth whose erect tail is the nosepiece. A search of West Mexican collections turned up three examples of hollow figurines using snuffing pipes apparently made from small gourds (fig. 14). But the earliest, sculpturally and symbolically most spectacular snuffing pipe—now in the collection of The Art Museum, Princeton University—originated in Xochipala, Guerrero, an Early to Middle Preclassic site rich in artifacts of Olmec manufacture (fig. 15).

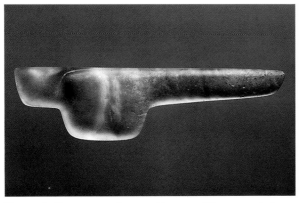

Figure 16. Spoon, 900–600 B.C., Guerrero. Blue-green jade, h. 3.7 cm.; w. 14.4 cm.; d. 15 cm. Anonymous loan to The Art Museum, Princeton University.

Figure 17. Carved Spoon, 1000–500 B.C., Costa Rica. Jade, h. 5 cm.; w. 16 cm.; d. 1 cm. The Denver Art Museum, collection of Jan and Frederick Mayer.

However, all this interesting material only came to light later. In the 1960s all I had to go on to substantiate—or at least suggest—this practice among the Olmec were the characteristic Olmec jade artifacts known as "spoons" (figs. 16, 17; cat. nos. 71, 101). By utilizing the analogy with the large number of wooden, bone, and stone snuff trays from South America (many hundreds of well-preserved wooden ones, dating to the first millennium A.D., about ten percent of which are decorated in a Tihuanaco-related style, the rest plain, have since been excavated in the bone-dry Atacama desert in

northern Chile alone),[43] I suggested that the Olmec "spoons" might have served as trays from which to inhale hallucinogenic snuff and that their shape, which in most instances recalls that of long-tailed birds, was directly related to this use.

Not surprisingly, bird and flight symbolism plays a large part in the practice of snuffing. Birds are widely considered tobacco spirits or patrons of ecstatic intoxication, as well as the shaman's companion spirits and helpers on his celestial journeys. In some cases, such as the harpy eagle effigy "spoon" in fig. 17 and a jade spoon in the American Museum of Natural History, New York, with a bird at one end, the bird symbolism is unmistakable. Coe illustrated a jade spoon with a were-jaguar profile in the bowl and a bird on the handle.[44] I am still convinced that most of the long-tailed "spoons" look like birds in flight because that is what they are. I should add here that it is unlikely that all Olmec—even shamans—would have possessed jade snuff trays. More probably they were owned and used by the religious and political elite. People of lesser status might have used wooden trays or even clam shells. In fact, a small proportion of known jade spoons, including a spoon illustrated here containing a were-jaguar mask (fig. 18; cat. no. 73), resembles the elongated shells of several common species of clams and mussels native to the Gulf Coast. Finally, again by analogy with South American snuffing paraphernalia that include both a tray and a tube, it is possible to surmise that a few of the long, thin jade "beads," some straight and some curved (cat. nos. 208, 211), hitherto classified as jewelry, may in fact have served as snuffing tubes.

Thanks largely to the work of Wilbert, since my article in 1968 first raised the possibility of an Olmec snuffing complex, with tobacco as a prime candidate, we have learned substantially more about the pivotal role of nicotine intoxication in South American shamanism, and, by extension, possibly in Olmec techniques of ecstasy and transformation. Wilbert is particularly interested in whether and how the effects of nicotine—the alkaloid in which *Nicotiana rustica*, the principal species used by Indian shamans, is many times richer than domestic varieties, up to an astonishing 18.6 percent—might explain the combative and

Figure 18. Large Carved Spoon, 900–600 B.C., Chiapas. Light bluish green jadeite, h. 7.1 cm.; w.23 cm.; d. 2.2 cm. Private collection.

aggressive/defensive aspects often noted in South American shamanism and expressed in a few Olmec transformation figurines. In acting on the adrenaline medulla and the centers in the brain that produce chemicals affecting mood, Wilbert writes, nicotine plays an important role precisely in making the jaguar shaman feel and act as aggressively as he often appears in Olmec art and in the ideology and mythology of tropical forest shamanism.[45] Shamans mostly ingest tobacco by smoking, sometimes in truly staggering amounts. I myself watched and photographed a Warao shaman in the Orinoco delta "feeding" the *kanobo* spirits by pointing his burning two-foot-long cigar to the zenith and the cardinal directions (except the west), and smoking it down, swallowing great clouds of smoke with hyperventilation, to a couple of inches and repeating the process with a second one of equal length. Smoking in this manner to trigger the initiatory ecstatic trance is part of shamanic training, and it continues through the shaman's life: "To fulfill the primordial promise of abundant sacrificial tobacco smoke, *wishiratus* smoke incessantly."[46]

Wilbert listed a number of tobacco-related characteristics he believed contributed to shamans becoming identified with jaguars. Among these are acuteness of vision, particularly at night; wakefulness; raspy voice; furred or rough tongue; and a pungent body odor. Thus, he writes:

[T]he shamanic neophyte, who through ingestion of tobacco receives acute near vision during the day, and the mature shaman, who as a result of advanced nicotine intoxication obtains night vision…need little convincing to consider themselves related to such keen-eyed animals as the felines….

Peculiar to jaguar-men is the adoption of either a defensive or an aggressive mode of behavior, although both modes can be fiercely combative. In their protective mode, were-jaguars are powerful chiefs, priests, and gods who defend their territorial boundaries and subjects and have been engaged in doing so in native South America and Mesoamerica since remote prehistoric times.[47]

Wilbert does not suggest that nicotine intoxication accounts by itself for the jaguar transformation complex. Rather, the psychotropic effects of nicotinic action in combination with ideology make it possible, and plausible, for the shaman not merely to enact "but in fact to live his essential jaguarness." Shamans, he observed, are more concerned with "vision" than "seeing" and with "aggression of the mind" than physical combat. In this connection, not only the direct, peripheral, and central action of nicotine on the human body need to be considered, "but also its indirect effects as a liberating agent of epinephrine, norepinephrine, and serotonin, among other compounds…. Taken together, these nicotine-associated psychological, neuropsychological, and cultural factors seem to constitute the essential ingredients of were-jaguar shamanism."[48]

The pharmacology of nicotine is a complex subject beyond the purview of this essay; suffice it to say that regardless of what other psychotropic plants might have been involved in Olmec jaguar-shamanism and transformation, and of whether experienced Olmec shamans even required a chemical trigger to enter ecstatic trance (and we know that many shamans do not), tobacco suffused with the amount of nicotine employed ritually in ancient Mexico would surely have produced the states so graphically depicted in Olmec art. So, if the well-known Olmec jade "spoons" were indeed snuff tablets, as I first suggested in 1968, perhaps the snuff inhaled from them was prepared, as psycho-active snuff still is among some South American Indians, from the crushed and pulverized leaves of *Nicotiana rustica*, alone or with other plants.

THE MAGIC OF WERE-JAGUAR FIGURINES

The one thing missing from the literature on Olmec figurines is any speculation about their purpose and function. What, indeed, might have been their use? Why depict jaguar-men or humans transforming into jaguars? It must have taken the ancient lapidary artist months to produce even one of the many stone figures now in private or public collections. And these are almost certainly only a fraction of the number carved three thousand years ago. Why so many? Why expend so much imagination, effort, and talent on these little masterpieces?

If we were dealing with China rather than Mesoamerica the answer would not be so hard to find or so speculative in nature. Chinese art, too, was functional, but the elite collected carved jades for their own sake—for their beauty, symbolism, and craftsmanship. No doubt the Olmec also admired technical and aesthetic perfection, otherwise the figurines would not be so beautiful and finished. But Native American art is never art for art's sake and never anecdotal, no more than most of the art produced in the "tribal" or "non-Western" world. Olmec artists who through their skills evoked the drama of transformation—in progress or completed—from a piece of jade or steatite or some other mineral of the right color to make it precious or sacred had something other in mind than anecdote, decoration, or status symbol.

For the Olmec, making art was almost certainly no less magical or inspired—no less an act of devotion—than it was for peoples and times for which we have better records. In sixteenth-century Yucatan, for example, it is known that a Maya sculptor who received a commission to make a figurine isolated himself for a lengthy time in a ceremonial house to commune with and receive inspiration from the native gods, thereby ensuring that what he made was correct and embodied the sentiments and power required by his client.[49] There is no reason to think it was different in Olmec times. Olmec figures are as magical as anything produced by pre-Columbian peoples, especially the little jaguar men—the so-called were-jaguars and transformation figures. By analogy with how the diviners of the Quiché Maya in highland Guatemala conceive of and employ in their rituals small archaeo-

logical stone figures called *ralaj alxík* (little *alxíks*), of which some resemble similar stylized anthropomorphic stone sculptures found in Mexico,[50] I propose that the Olmec sculptors simlarly conceived of and employed their figurines. Most, if not all, of the objects made by the Quiché Maya and the Olmec functioned on two interrelated levels: as "household gods" and as familiars or spirit helpers. In the Olmec case, they would have reinforced curing, divination, and religious ritual and intensified the shaman-priest's intimacy with his animal companion spirits, in particular the jaguar, aiding in the reciprocal act of transformation. My interpretation of the Olmec statuettes as spirit helpers, like my explanation of the jaguar motif itself, is thus based on ethnographic analogy. I have used the German ethnographer Leonhard Schultze Jena's discussion of the meaning and ritual use of the little *alxíks* among the highland Guatemalan Indians, whose religion he studied more than sixty years ago, and Reichel-Dolmatoff's informed, if speculative, correlation made between figurines from archaeological Colombian cultures and the large numbers of wooden figures used in the curing practices and beliefs of the Cuna and Chocó Indians. The Cuna live mainly on San Blas and other offshore islands of Panama, the Chocó, along the Colombian Pacific coast between from the Ecuadorean border to Panama. Both were formerly part of a widespread circum-Caribbean and Tropical Forest culture.[51]

We cannot make any direct connection between modern Cuna and Chocó shamanism and the Olmec, so my analogy is based strictly on ideological continuities. Restoration of health is one of the principal responsibilities of Cuna and Chocó shamans, which is why every community, however small, has one or more specialists in the sacred (*haibaná* in Chocó) whose main duty is the prevention and cure of illness. The principal objects used during these curing rites are small, wooden human effigies carved by the shaman, which are placed around the patient. The Chocó shaman may sit on a low animal effigy bench or stool, walk and dance around the patient singing magical incantations, or sit with an assortment of figurines by his side. "While chanting and reciting he then takes one figurine in each hand and, with parallel movements, touches and strokes the patient's body.... After a few minutes the two figures are laid aside and another pair is taken up and used in the same manner, then a third and a fourth pair, until the supply is exhausted."[52] The Cuna shaman does much the same thing. In both cases, the figurines, as the embodiment of the shaman's spirit helpers, are imbued with magical powers "and the shaman calls upon them while singing and reciting."[53]

Two classes of these figurines exist—those discarded after the curing ritual and those, inspected and scrutinized by the shaman after the ceremony, carefully stored in a special box. In both types, some are made from easily worked, soft wood, others from hard, durable wood that must have taken considerable time and skill to carve. These latter figures, which are highly treasured by the shaman, perhaps come closest to the Olmec figures we have considered here.

For their part, the priest-shamans of the Quiché Maya keep their little stone *alxíks* carefully stored with their ritual paraphernalia, taking them out only when they are needed as allies in divination and curing. Imbued with divine power—even treated reverently as "little gods"—the *alxíks* are generally effective allies in the shaman's endeavors. Conversely, if they should feel neglected or treated with insufficient respect, the *alxíks* are capable of inflicting punishment on their guardian.[54] I like to think that their present-day function in the Quiché Maya divinatory system has a long history, thus helping explain the place of such sculptures in former times, perhaps all the way back to the Olmec.

If the ancient figures from Colombia and Panama did, in fact, function in the main as powerful spirit allies in disease-curing and prevention, we can agree with Reichel-Dolmatoff's conclusion that, as ethnographic analogy suggests, "a whole assemblage of prehistoric artifacts would become more intelligible and would, eventually, provide us not only with a better understanding of certain magical attitudes but also of the role these have played in the shaping of an important aboriginal art form."[55]

This insight surely has as good a chance as any to explain what a portion of Olmec portable art, at least, is all about.

NOTES

1. Matthew W. Stirling, "Early History of the Olmec Problem," in *Dumbarton Oaks Conference on the Olmec*, ed. Elizabeth P. Benson (Washington, D.C., 1968), 1.
2. Michael D. Coe, "The Olmec Style and Its Distribution," in *Handbook of Middle American Indians: Archaeology of Southern Mesoamerica, Part Two*, ed. Gordon R. Willey (Austin, Tex., 1965), 749.
3. Samuel K. Lothrop, W. F. Foshag, and Joy Mahler, *Robert Woods Bliss Collection: Pre-Columbian Art* (New York, 1957), 234.
4. Peter T. Furst, "The Olmec Were-Jaguar Motif in the Light of Ethnographic Reality," in *Dumbarton Oaks Conference on the Olmec*, ed. Elizabeth P. Benson (Washington, D.C., 1968), 143–78.
5. Karin Hissink and Albert Hahn, *Die Tacana*, vol. 1 (Stuttgart, 1961).
6. See Tate, this volume.
7. Susana Eger Valadez, personal communication. For details, see also her "Wolf Power and Inter-Species Communication in Huichol Shamanism," in *People of the Peyote: Huichol Indian History, Religion and Survival*, ed. Stacy B. Schaefer and Peter T. Furst (Albuquerque, 1996).
8. See Tate, this volume.
9. Otto Zerries, "Die Vorstellung vom Zweiten Ich und die Rolle der Harpyie in der Kultur Naturvölker SüdAmerikas," trans. Peter T. Furst, *Anthropos* 57 (1962): 889–914.
10. Johannes Wilbert, *Tobacco and Shamanism in South America* (New Haven, 1987), 193.
11. Michael D. Coe, *The Jaguar's Children: Pre-Classic Central Mexico* (New York, 1965), 105.
12. Matthew W. Stirling, "Stone Monuments of the Río Chiquito, Veracruz, Mexico," *Bureau of American Ethnology*, Bulletin 157, no. 43 (1955): 19.
13. Curt Nimuendajú, "Die Sagen von der Erschaffung und Vernichtung der Welt als Grundlage der Religion der Apapocúva-Guarani," *Zeitschrift für Ethnologie* 46 (1914): 371.
14. Heinz Walter, "Der Jaguar in der Vorstellungswelt der südamerikanischen Naturvölkern," Ph.D. diss., University of Hamburg, 1956, 94–96.
15. Curt Nimuendajú, "Tribes of the Lower and Middle Xingu River," in *Handbook of South American Indians*, vol. 3 (Washington, D.C., 1948), 213–43.
16. Lest the apparent patterned balding—usually considered a European, or "Caucasoid," trait—on the Olmec elder portrayed in the Princeton masterpiece set off speculation about an Olmec connection across the Atlantic, it has been noted that this may simply represent the shaving of the head for some customary or specific ritual or magical purpose, or for facilitating the painting or tattooing of the head as the seat of the essential life force. The custom of shaving the head, wholly or partially, and, occasionally, of painting the exposed skin with symbolic designs, is still practiced by Indian tribes in different parts of South America. Cropping the hair short or shaving it off altogether is still practiced as a sign of mourning by both men and women of some groups. Sharp mussel shells are, or were formerly, frequently employed for this purpose. The Princeton figure is clearly a portrait, whose subject may have gone naturally bald. But on the South American evidence, portraying him as bald, and with a toad tattooed or painted where hair would naturally grow, may have a specific meaning to which we are not privy.
17. The general Mesoamerican term for the companion animal a person has from birth, and that shares his or her fate through life, is *nagual*, from the Nahuatl *nahualli*. The term "co-essence" was suggested by John Monaghan, a specialist in the relationship of the Mixtec past to the ethnographic present, as coming closer than *nagual* to the widespread concept of a companion spirit or alter ego, especially for the Maya and other non-Nahuatl-speaking peoples. Stephen Houston and David Stuart adopted "co-essence" as best conveying the meaning of the Maya word *way*, which occurs in closely related forms in various Maya languages with meanings ranging from transformer, familiar, dream, sorcerer, and diviner to "other spirit" in Chol and "animal transformation" or "animal companion" in Tzotzil, in their essay, "The *Way* Glyph: Evidence for 'Co-Essences' among the Classic Maya," in *Research Reports on Ancient Maya Writing*, no. 30 (Washington, D.C., 1989), 5. Houston and Stuart's reading of a glyph with a jaguar component in texts on Maya figure-painted vases as a symbol for *way* has changed in fundamental ways our understanding of the events depicted on many of these vases. They write (ibid., 13): "It indicates that many of the supernatural figures, once described as 'gods,' 'underworld denizens,' or 'deities,' are instead co-essences of supernaturals or humans. More than ever, then, Classic Maya beliefs would seem to coincide with general patterns of Mesoamerican thought."

    In creating their hieroglyphic script, the ancient Maya intellectuals drew on jaguar symbolism to convey the concept of companion spirit, or co-essence, thus bringing the Maya into line with patterns of thought that transcend the boundaries of Mesoamerica.
18. Rafael Karsten, "Studies in the Religion of South American Indians East of the Andes," in *Societas Scientiarium Fennica, Commentationes humanorum litterarum*, ed. Arne Runeberg and Michael Webster, vol. 29 (Helsinki, 1964).
19. Peter T. Furst, "Crowns of Power: Bird and Feather Symbolism in Amazonian Shamanism," in *The Gift of Birds: Featherwork of Native South American Peoples*, ed. Ruben E. Reina and Kenneth M. Kensinger (Philadelphia, 1991), 108.
20. Martin Dobrizhoffer, *An Account of the Abipones, an Equestrian People of Paraguay*, 3 vols. (London, 1822), 67.
21. Theodor Koch-Grünberg, *Zwei Jahre unter den Indianern. Reisen in Nordwest-Brasilien 1903/1905*, vol. 2 (Berlin, 1909–10), 155.
22. Ute Bödiger, *Die Religion der Tukano* (Cologne, 1965), 42–44, 150, 153.
23. Konrad Theodor Preuss, *Die Religion und Mythologie der Witoto. Textaufnahmen und Beobachtungen bei einem Indianerstamm in Kolumbien, Südamerika*, vol. 1 (Göttingen, 1921), 22.
24. Irving Goldman, *The Cubeo: Indians of the Northwest Amazon* (Urbana, 1963), 262–67.

25. Koch-Grünberg (as in note 21).

26. Theodor Koch-Grünberg, *Vom Roroima zum Orinoco*, vol. 3 (Berlin-Stuttgart, 1917–28), 225–26.

27. Peter G. Roe, *The Cosmic Zygote: Cosmology in the Amazon Basin* (New Brunswick, N.J., 1982), 202.

28. Gerardo Reichel-Dolmatoff, *Amazonian Cosmos* (Chicago, 1971), 212.

29. Stephen Hugh-Jones, "Barasana Initiation: Male Initiation and Cosmology among the Barasana Indians of the Vaupés Area of Colombia," Ph.D. diss., Cambridge University, 1974, 103.

30. Philip Drucker, *La Venta, Tabasco: A Study of Olmec Ceramics and Art* (Washington, D.C., 1952). I am indebted to David Joralemon for drawing my attention to this early insight of Drucker.

31. Donald W. Lathrap, "The Tropical Forest and the Cultural Context of Chavín," in *Dumbarton Oaks Conference on Chavín*, ed. Elizabeth P. Benson (Washington, D.C., 1971), 77.

32. Leslie Brown, *Eagles of the World* (New York, 1976), 33.

33. Gerardo Reichel-Dolmatoff, *The Shaman and the Jaguar: A Study of Narcotic Drugs among the Indians of Colombia* (Philadelphia, 1975), 128.

34. Ibid., 78, 100.

35. Ibid., 128.

36. Zerries, trans. Peter T. Furst (as in note 9).

37. Jon Christopher Crocker, *Vital Souls: Bororo Cosmology, Natural Symbolism, and Shamanism* (Tucson, 1985), 121.

38. Ibid., 286–87.

39. Wilbert (as in note 10), 192.

40. Furst (as in note 4), 162.

41. Fray Bernardino de Sahagún, *Florentine Codex, General History of the Things of New Spain*, trans. Arthur J. O. Anderson and Charles E. Dibble, vol. 11 (Santa Fe, 1963), 146.

42. Peter T. Furst. "Archaeological Evidence for Snuffing in Prehispanic Mesoamerica," *Botanical Museum Leaflets, Harvard University* 24 (1974): 1–28.

43. Constantino Manuel Torres, *The Iconography of South American Snuff Trays and Related Paraphernalia* (Göteborg, 1987).

44. Coe (as in note 2), 754, fig. 29.

45. Wilbert (as in note 10), 192.

46. Ibid., 62.

47. Ibid., 195–96.

48. Ibid.

49. For further discussion of the manufacture of idols in sixteenth-century Yucatan, see "Landa's Relacion de las Cosas de Yucatan," *Papers of the Peabody Museum of American Archaeology*, ed. Alfred M. Tozzer, vol. 18 (Cambridge, Mass., 1941).

50. Leonhard Schultze Jena, *Leben, Glaube und Sprache der Quiché von Guatemala*, trans. Peter T. Furst (Jena, Germany, 1933), 54.

51. Gerardo Reichel-Dolmatoff, "Anthropomorphic Figurines from Colombia, Their Magic and Art," in Samuel K. Lothrop et al., *Essays in Pre-Columbian Art and Archaeology* (Cambridge, Mass., 1961), 229–41.

52. Ibid., 231.

53. Ibid., 234.

54. Schultze Jena, trans. Peter T. Furst (as in note 50), 231.

55. Reichel-Dolmatoff, "Anthropomorphic Figurines from Colombia," in Lothrop (as in note 51), 241.

The Rainmakers:
The Olmec and Their Contribution to Mesoamerican Belief and Ritual

As the earliest Mesoamerican civilization based on agriculture, the Olmec developed an elaborate ideology devoted to water and rain and, in addition, religious rituals of sacrifice and supplication designed to ensure agricultural abundance. This precocious and innovative religious complex centered on rain and agricultural fertility profoundly influenced contemporaneous and later Mesoamerican cultures. As the first great "rainmakers," the Olmec created a lasting legacy of deities and rituals devoted to water and agriculture.

THE AVIAN SERPENT

In Olmec iconographic studies, considerable attention has been paid to the chthonic forces of the earth, sea, and underworld. However, relatively little interest has been paid to sky symbolism and its attendant imagery. The strongly terrestrial and underworld focus may partly derive from the clear importance in Olmec ideology of jaguars, which in later Mesoamerican religions are widely identified with the earth and dark, nether regions. In addition, the Massive Offerings and other impressive caches in La Venta Complex A suggest a major Olmec orientation to the earth and underworld. Nonetheless, it should be noted that equally

Frontispiece. Figure Holding a Ceremonial Bar, Fragment, 900–600 B.C., Tuzapan, Veracruz. Dark green serpentine, h. 13.3 cm.; w. 10 cm.; d. 7.5 cm. Collection of Dana B. Martin.

impressive expenditures of effort went into the creation of the great, lofty pyramid that dominates the site of La Venta. Just as the Massive Offerings are oriented to the earth, so the La Venta pyramid offers access to the heavens. In this portion of the study, I will focus on a particular denizen of the Olmec sky, a creature I term the Avian Serpent. Although this composite being is ancestral to the plumed serpent of Classic and Postclassic Mesoamerica, I prefer to use the term Avian Serpent, since it is not simply plumed, but frequently possesses such other bird traits as a beak and wings. While this entity has often been identified as the caiman earth, I will argue that it is primarily a celestial being associated with wind and rain.

THE AVIAN SERPENT AND THE OLMEC DRAGON

In two influential studies Peter David Joralemon isolated a major deity of the Olmec pantheon (figs. 1a–f),[1] describing it as a highly composite creature, or "dragon," an amalgamation of many creatures of the natural world: "The Olmec Dragon is a mythological beast with cayman, eagle, jaguar, human, and serpent attributes. His characteristic features include avian headcrest, flame eyebrows, L-or trough-shaped eyes, bulbous nose, jaws, and dentition of a cayman, bifid tongue, hand-paw-wings, and either a mammalian, saurian, or serpentine

body."[2] Composed of many creatures, the Olmec Dragon also has a wide range of associations, among which Joralemon listed: "earth, maize, agricultural fertility, clouds, rain, water, fire, and kingship."[3] Joralemon suggested that this all-encompassing god may have been ancestral to such high gods as the Maya Itzam Na and the Aztec Ometeotl. Joralemon acknowledged that this Olmec all-encompassing saurian being is quite similar to the Itzam Na or "Iguana House" model of the Maya cosmos proposed by J. Eric S. Thompson.[4] However, it is now clear that Thompson grouped a great number of quite distinct saurian beings under this single category, and his "Itzamnaization" of the Maya universe is now being critically reassessed.[5] Similarly, the question remains whether all forms grouped under the Olmec Dragon category constitute the same being. It is beyond the scope of this study to trace or refute the many suggested permutations of the Olmec Dragon. Instead, I will be concerned with the essential, primary characteristics found in the head region, the most diagnostic area for Mesoamerican deity identification. I will note that the head of this creature is essentially a combination of snake and bird features, in other words, an avian serpent.

Among the Olmec Dragon features that Joralemon listed are a crenelated brow resembling flames or feathers, pawlike wing, and mouth or gum brackets similar to a series of inverted Us.

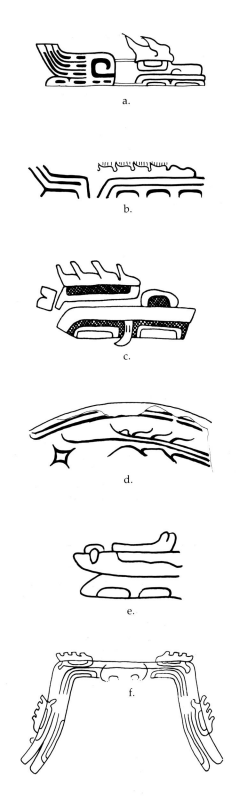

Figure 1. The Olmec Avian Serpent: (a–b) Early Formative examples with paw-wing, Tlatilco. After Joralemon (1971), fig. 101; (c) Early Formative Avian Serpent; (d) Middle Formative example on interior of dish with double-line-break rim. After Niederberger (1987), fig. 514; (e–f) Middle Formative Avian Serpent on incised jadeite objects attributed to Río Pesquero. After Joralemon (1976), fig. 8.

Some of the earliest and most consistent forms appear on the sides of Early Formative incised bowls (figs. 1a–c). For many Early Formative examples, the paw-wing is situated directly behind the head, as if it were an appendage of the cheek or neck (e.g. fig. 1a, b). The faunal make-up of the Olmec Dragon head has been the source of much debate. Although Joralemon initially favored a jaguar-dragon identification, he subsequently noted caiman attributes, and prefers to consider it more reptilian than jaguar.[6] Whereas Joralemon was careful not to link the Olmec Dragon to one specific creature, subsequent researches have identified this entity as a caiman.

In addition to noting caiman attributes, Joralemon also suggested that the Olmec Dragon is associated with the earth, water, and, secondarily, with fire.[7] The caiman is indeed a well-known earth symbol in Mesoamerica, and is also represented in several fire rituals recorded for Postclassic Yucatan.[8] Although the documented association of caimans with the earth and fire seems to support the caiman identification, it is by no means certain that the Olmec Dragon is a terrestrial fire deity. Instead, the head of this creature will be seen to serve as an Olmec sign for the heavens and can be readily related to later Mesoamerican sky imagery.

THE AVIAN SERPENT AND THE PLUMED SERPENT

Both Román Piña Chán and Miguel Covarrubias initially identified the entity now known as the Olmec Dragon as a combination of jaguar and serpent characteristics, an early, ancestral form of the plumed serpent of Classic Mesoamerica.[9] Michael D. Coe was the first to cite several Olmec depictions of serpents with avian characteristics, creatures that he considered as early forms of Quetzalcoatl.[10] In this early analysis, Coe distinguished the plumed serpent from a creature with flamelike crests above the eyes, an entity he regarded as a serpent of fire and drought antithetically opposed to Quetzalcoatl. Among the plumed serpent examples cited by Coe were La Venta Monument 19, Chalcatzinco Petroglyph 5, and a mural from Juxtlahuaca Cave, Guerrero. In a later study, Piña Chán also contrasted

the creature with brow crests, his terrestrial jaguar water serpent, with a sky-dwelling, feathered rain serpent.[11] Although Joralemon initially placed the Olmec plumed serpent under the specific deity category of God VII, he subsequently noted that it was probably but an aspect of the Olmec Dragon.[12] The suggested contrast between the entity with eye crests and the plumed serpent is a false dichotomy; Olmec plumed serpents often have both the crested brow and the paw-wing (see figs. 2a, d, g, 6a). The Olmec plumed serpent and dragon are the same being, a serpent with a range of avian attributes, including a crested eye, beak, and wings as well as body plumage.

A number of researchers have noted that San Lorenzo Monument 47 portrays a person holding an Early Formative plumed serpent.[13] The fanlike feather tufts at the rear of the head are identical in positioning and form to the paw-wing found on contemporaneous depictions of the Olmec Dragon (fig. 2a).[14] During the Middle Formative period, plumed serpents continue to have versions of the paw-wing immediately behind the head (figs. 2b–d). On La Venta Monument 19, the paw-wing has become increasingly attenuated, and clearly relates to the saurian cheek elements appearing on Protoclassic sculpture of the Isthmian and nearby Maya regions (figs. 3a–e). Even in these later instances, the cheek element retains the large curl occurring with the earlier Olmec paw-wing motif.

The paw-wing of the Olmec Dragon (hereafter referred to as the Avian Serpent) is primarily an avian wing, rather than a jaguar paw. The majority of Early Formative examples have paw-wings turning upward to represent feathered wings, not quadruped limbs. Explicit birds with similarly upsweeping paw-wings occur on Laguna de los Cerros Monument 13 and Early Formative aviform effigy vessels.[15] On the Olmec Avian Serpent, the paw-wings are immediately behind the head, like the pectoral fins of fish. But here the feathered wings are not for eel-like transport through standing water, but through the sky, much like contemporary Huichol conceptions of a winged serpent: "the serpent of the Corn Mother has only wings, and 'flies in the rain.'" The modern Mixtec of Nuyoo have a similar concept of a crested or winged rain

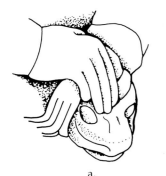

a.

b.

c.

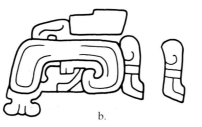

d.

serpent, the *koo savi*: "When a *koo savi* flies, it is surrounded by rain clouds, which it is said to bear on its back."[16]

The Olmec paw-wing evidently serves to transport the Avian Serpent through the heavens, a function that may reveal its underlying meaning in Olmec iconography. In Mesoamerican thought, the wind is recognized as the essential way to carry clouds and rain through the atmosphere. According to the contemporary Huichol, the blue sky serpent is a rain-bringing wind: "When clouds gather from the west, this is one of the serpents, or winds, that bring them along."[17] In Postclassic central Mexican belief, Ehecatl—the duck-billed wind aspect of Quetzalcoatl—is the bringer of the

Figure 2. The appearance of the paw-wing on Olmec Avian Serpents: (a) Early Formative Olmec serpent with feathered paw-wing at back of head, detail of San Lorenzo Monument 47. After Coe and Diehl (1980), fig. 488; (b) Middle Formative Avian Serpent with paw-wing, Chalcatzingo Monument 5. After Joralemon (1971), fig. 244; (c) Middle Formative jade Avian Serpent figure with feather crest and paw-wing. After Joralemon (1971), fig. 246; (d) Late Formative Avian Serpent with paw-wing; detail of San Miguel Amuco Stela (see fig. 7a).

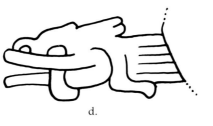

a.

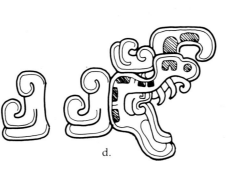

b.

c.

d.

e.

Figure 3. The transformation of the paw-wing motif in southeastern Mesoamerican iconography: (a) Middle Formative attenuated paw-wing, La Venta Monument 19; (b) Protoclassic simplified paw-wing as cheek appendage, Tres Zapotes Stela D; (c) Protoclassic crested serpent with feathered brow and cheek appendage, Izapa Stela 7; (d) Protoclassic Maya stone bowl with crested serpent with feathered brow and simplified paw-wing. After Schele and Miller (1986), pl. 67b; (e) Early Classic Maya serpent with cheek appendage, detail of Leiden Plaque. After Schele and Miller (1986), fig. 12.

fructifying rain: "Quetzalcoatl—he was the wind; he was the guide, the roadsweeper of the rain gods."[18] The Olmec paw-wing motif may be the Olmec sign for wind, the means of transporting the Avian Serpent—and by extension clouds and rain—through the firmament.

Researchers have interpreted the Avian Serpent as a sky serpent, although in this case identified with fire, not rain, due to the so-called flame eyebrows typically displayed by this being.[19] However, no one has provided an argument as to why these brow elements represent flames. In fact, no explicit sign for fire or flames has yet been identified in Olmec art. According to Philip Drucker and Donald W. Lathrap, flame eyebrows are actually plumes, such as occur on the feathered crest of the harpy eagle. Throughout Olmec iconography, sharply beaked raptorial birds display flame eyebrows (fig. 4a–c). Although conceivably such feathers could also refer to flames, it should not be taken as an a priori assumption.[20]

Aside from these bird elements, Olmec serpents also display the crested brow (fig. 4d–g). These reptilian feather-brows probably refer to an intentional blending of bird and serpent, but there is a remarkable snake in the lowland Olmec region with supraorbital crests in the form of several long scales projecting immediately above the eye (fig. 4h). This creature is the much-feared arboreal fer-de-lance (*Bothriechis schlegelii*) known under such epithets as the eyelash, horned, or palm viper.[21] Ranging from southern Mexico to northern South America, this creature is dreaded not only for its terrible venom, but also for its unnerving habit of striking from above at upper portions of the body.[22] Olmec serpents with crested brows are accurate portrayals of the arboreal, "sky-dwelling" palm viper. Although another form of pit viper, the rattlesnake, dominates later Mesoamerican plumed serpent imagery, it is possible that the Early Formative prototype of the feathered serpent is the arboreal palm viper.[23]

THE AVIAN SERPENT AS THE SKY

According to Lathrap, the feather-crested eye is a celestial attribute.[24] Three Early Formative ceramic roller seals from highland Puebla confirm that the

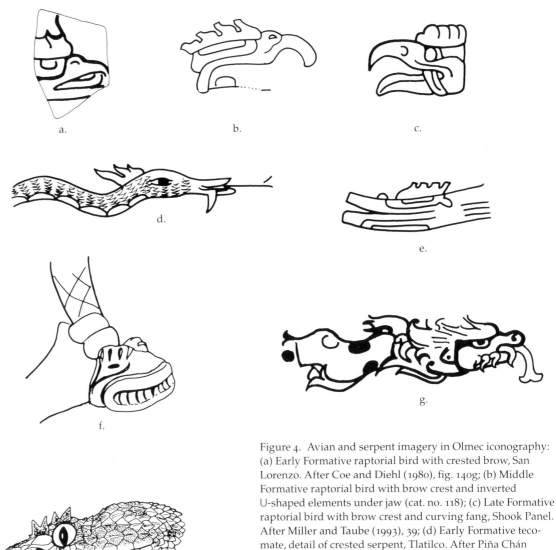

Figure 4. Avian and serpent imagery in Olmec iconography: (a) Early Formative raptorial bird with crested brow, San Lorenzo. After Coe and Diehl (1980), fig. 140g; (b) Middle Formative raptorial bird with brow crest and inverted U-shaped elements under jaw (cat. no. 118); (c) Late Formative raptorial bird with brow crest and curving fang, Shook Panel. After Miller and Taube (1993), 39; (d) Early Formative tecomate, detail of crested serpent, Tlatilco. After Piña Chán (1958); (e) Middle Formative Avian Serpent with brow crest (see fig. 1e); (f) Early Formative serpent with brow crest, detail of jaguar effigy vessel. After Feuchtwanger (1989), pl. 94; (g) Middle Formative Avian Serpent with brow crest, Oxtotitlan. After Grove (1970), fig. 12; (h) palm viper, or arboreal fer-de-lance *Bothriechis schlegelii*. After Campbell and Lamar (1989), fig. 165.

feather-browed eye and the Avian Serpent symbolize the sky, and by extension, rain (fig. 5a–c). Each seal has an undulating, chevronlike form at one end of the scene, which clearly serves as a sign for waves and standing water in the iconography of Teotihuacan and other later Mesoamerican cultures. Along with the wave sign, the first cylinder seal (fig. 5a) also portrays crossed-bands accompanied by paw-wings. Coe suggested that in Olmec and later Maya iconography, the crossed-bands simul-

taneously refer to sky and serpent.[25] Just as the undulating chevron represents the sea and standing water, the crossed-bands and paw-wings depict the sky. Between the crossed-bands sky and the wave motif are teardrop-shaped elements. These devices probably depict falling rain as a mediating force between the overarching heavens and the sustaining sea.

The second roller seal (fig. 5b) also represents the three regions of heaven, falling rain, and

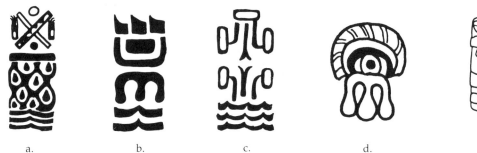

a.   b.   c.   d.   e.

Figure 5. Avian Serpent and sky iconography (a–c) Early Formative roll-out designs of three roller seals attributed to Las Bocas. After Joralemon (1976), fig. 7h,i,n; (d) Classic feathered serpent eye with blue trilobate tear, Teotihuacan. After Berrin, ed. (1988), pls. 1a–f; (e) face from La Venta Monument 6.

standing water. The sky is indicated by the feather-crested eye, below which is the trilobate rain sign of Olmec, Teotihuacan, and later Mesoamerican iconography.[26] Falling from the crested eye, this sign reveals that, like the contact period Aztec, the Olmec compared rain symbolically to tears.[27] The same identification of rain with tears occurs in the recently reported murals at Techinantitla, Teotihuacan. In these murals, which depict a plumed serpent atop a series of glyphically labeled trees, one plant is designated by a blue trilobate tear falling from a feather-crested eye (fig. 5d). Ringed with green feathers, this same crested eye appears with the plumed serpent immediately above the mural scene (see fig. 10e); the eyes are identical in color as well as form—the red eye is topped with a band of yellow and, finally, a green-feathered fringe. In the same way the plumed serpent eye and trilobate sign allude to rain, the great overarching feathered serpent has multicolored rain drops falling from its body and a stream of water pouring from its mouth. Clearly, the Teotihuacan plumed serpent is here portrayed as the celestial rain-bringer.

The crested eye on the Olmec roller seal probably refers to the Avian Serpent ancestral to the plumed serpent of Teotihuacan and subsequent Mesoamerican cultures. However, since only the feathered eye is depicted, it is difficult to determine whether it alludes to a serpent being or simply a bird. On the third roller seal (fig. 5c), the upper sky region obviously possesses serpentine attributes. Directly above the basal waves are two virtually identical, opposed images. In the more intact upper example, the motif can be seen to be of three curv-ing devices bracketed by rectangular forms on three sides. The rectangular bracket enclosure is a specific motif, which Joralemon describes as the rectangular jaw markings of the Olmec Dragon.[28] Once these brackets are identified as a maw, the interior elements are recognizable as the curving fangs and cleft tongue of a serpent. La Venta Monument 6 portrays a flame-browed head with a similar forked tongue and outcurving fangs (fig. 5e). This Avian Serpent face, like the serpent maw on the roller seal, represents the heavens from which the rains come.

One of the finest depictions of the Olmec Avian Serpent appears on La Venta Monument 19 (fig. 6a). A great rattlesnake arches above a seated male wearing a headdress in the image of the same crea-ture. A feather crest projects from the top of the serpent head, which is sharply beaked and displays a simplified form of the crested brow. I have previ-ously noted that the horizontal device immediately below the serpent head is an epigraphic reference to the plumed serpent.[29] The sign is composed of two quetzal birds facing a central sky band represented by crossed-bands (fig. 6b). It is well known that in Mayan languages the words for sky and snake are generally homophonous, tending to be either *chan* or *can*. In the related Mixe-Zoquean languages—the probable language family of the Olmec—the words for serpent (*tsan*) and sky (*tsap*) are similar enough to suggest that both they and the Maya terms may have originally derived from a single Macromayan word denoting both serpent and sky. However, aside from this linguistic possibility, it will be sub-sequently noted that the Olmec Avian Serpent is a symbol of the sky.

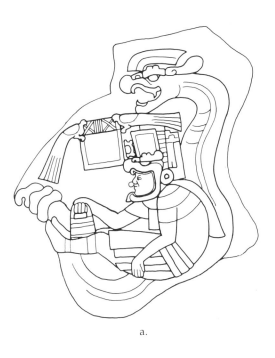

a.

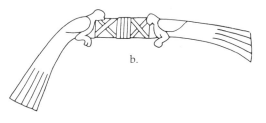

b.

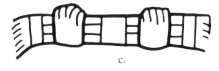

c.

Figure 6. La Venta Monument 19 and the Olmec feather bundle sign: (a) figure with Avian Serpent headdress seated against beaked Avian Serpent, La Venta Monument 19; note quetzal bird and crossed-bands sign at upper left; (b) quetzal birds flanking crossed-bands, a probable reference to the Olmec Avian Serpent, La Venta Monument 19; (c) feather bundle, detail from incised jadeite celt attributed to Río Pesquero. After Joralemon (1976), fig. 8e.

The pair of quetzal birds probably refers not only to the quetzal serpent, but to a particular Olmec artifact, a bound feather bundle, such as the one held in the arms of the standing deity on a Middle Formative celt attributed to Río Pesquero (fig. 6c). The ends of this tied object are not stiff like wood, but hang down, like the quetzal tail feathers on the La Venta Monument 19 sign. A third example occurs on the Olmec-style stela from San Miguel Amuco, Guerrero, on which a striding figure holds the bundle in his left arm (fig. 7a). A glyphic version of the same bundle occurs near the head of the figure, with one end outflaring and tufted, recalling the La Venta and Río Pesquero devices. David C. Grove and Louise C. Paradis described the head at shoulder height as a "feathered serpent head"; the paw-wing, brow crest, and large, curving fang identify it as the Avian Serpent. The same authors also suggested that the figure wears a "bird-serpent mask" with a probable curving fang.[30] This individual then, like the human figure on La Venta Monument 19, is dressed as the Avian Serpent. The feather bundle signs on La Venta Monument 19 and the Amuco stela are probably rare epigraphic references to this Olmec supernatural.

The bound feather bundles are related to the late Olmec crossed-bands sky signs such as appear on the top of Tres Zapotes Stela A and the square incised jadeite tablet in the Dallas Museum of Art (fig. 7b, c; cat. no. 131). Another crossed-bands sky sign—again in the uppermost portion of the scene—occurs on the large incised vessel attributed to Chalcatzingo (fig. 7d; cat. no. 198). Curved and outflaring, the vertical lines resemble flexible long and narrow feathers. A related form, similarly topped with a projecting feather tuft, appears on the Humboldt Celt (fig. 7e). The crossed-bands motif, flanked on either side by triple rain drops, is evidently denoted as a celestial source of rain. On one Protoclassic Maya fuschite vessel (fig. 7f), the crossed-bands appears above an undulating sign for standing water, recalling the Early Formative Puebla roller seals; we will note below that this scene also portrays celestial rain falling upon standing water. This Protoclassic sky band is flanked above and below by feathers, as if the crossed-bands lashes the celestial plumage. The same can be said for the long

a.

b.   c.

d.

e.   f.

Figure 7. Early Mesoamerican feather bundles and sky signs: (a) Late Formative striding male with Avian Serpent head-dress and figure in region of shoulder, San Miguel Amuco Stela; note bundle sign at upper left. After Grove and Paradis (1971), figs. 2, 3; (b) Late Formative figure with brow crests and feather bundle sky sign atop Tres Zapotes Stela A. Detail of drawing courtesy of James Porter; (c) Middle Formative feather bundle sky sign, detail of greenstone tablet, Dallas Museum of Art; (d) Middle Formative sky sign from incised ceramic vessel attributed to Chalcatzingo; (e) Middle Formative feather bundle flanked by triple raindrop motifs, detail of Humboldt Celt. After Joralemon (1971), fig. 32; (f) Protoclassic Maya fuchsite vessel depicting celestial fish-serpent spewing rain upon standing water. After Deletaille (1985), pl. 316.

parallel elements and crossed-bands of the Middle Formative sky sign—all are based on feather bundles secured with cloth and binding.

An incised vessel attributed to Tabasco offers an example of an Olmec feather bundle in which six feathers project from the handle bound with crossed-bands lashing (fig. 8a). A seated albitite

figure in The Cleveland Museum of Art holds a three-dimensional version of this feather object (fig. 8b; cat. no. 200). These two Olmec examples are identical to later bound feather bundles found widely in Classic and Postclassic Mesoamerica, including Tikal, Cacaxtla, and Aztec documents (fig. 8c–i). The cloth, paper, or basketry wrappings

Figure 8. Feather bundles in ancient Mesoamerican trade and tribute: (a) Early Formative Olmec feather bundle with crossed-bands lashing on handle. After Joralemon (1971), fig. 143; (b) Middle Formative jadeite statuette holding feather bundle, The Cleveland Museum of Art. Drawing courtesy of Linda Schele; (c) Early Classic Maya stucco vessel with feather bundle rendered in Teotihuacan style, Tikal. After Culbert (1994); (d) Early Classic Maya incised vessel, detail of figure with quetzal bundle greeting Teotihuacanos, Tikal. After Culbert (1994); (e) Late Classic Maya vase, detail of figure holding quetzal feather bundle and probable manta tribute cloth. After Kerr (1992), 456; (f) Late Classic mural, detail of feather bundle on God L merchant pack, Cacaxtla. After Coe (1993), 109; (g) Postclassic feather bundle, Mendoza Codex, f. 46r; (h) Postclassic quetzal feather bundle, Matricula de Tributos, f. 13r; (i) Postclassic feather bundle placed with Aztec merchant mortuary bundle, Magliabechiano Codex , f. 68r.

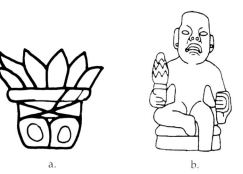

a. b.

c. d. e.

f. g. h. i.

secure the bases of the feathers and provide a means to hold the delicate, precious feathers with a minimum of handling.

Along with serving as an Olmec symbol for the Avian Serpent and the blue diurnal sky, quetzal feather bundles seem to have provided a range of associative meanings, symbolically overlapping with tender green growth, such as grass, shoots, or rushes.[31] The identification of quetzal plumes with green plants is well-documented in Mesoamerica. Thus quetzal feathers are commonly worn in the costume of Mesoamerican maize deities, the Holmul Dancer, a form of the Classic Maya maize god, is an especially developed example. In Yucatec Maya, *k'uk'* signifies sprouts or shoots, and *k'uk'um,* the quetzal.[32] The Aztecs also associated the long quetzal plumes with growing plants: "Those [plumes] which are on its tail are green, herb-green, very green, fresh green, turquoise-colored. They are like wide reeds: the ones which glisten, which bend."[33] Olmec quetzal bundles probably allude to new green growth, a striking, virtually immediate result of rain.

The ambiguity between vegetal growth and quetzal plumes is reflected in the "torch" bundles commonly paired with shell "knuckle-dusters" in Olmec iconography (fig. 9). Whereas I believe that many of these forms represent feather bundles, Linda Schele considers them green vegetal cuttings.[34] The double-merlon or double-step sign, which commonly occurs at the tufted end of these long bundles (figs. 9a–c), also appears repeatedly in the serpentine mosaic masks of the La Venta Massive Offerings (fig. 9d) and in the series of triangular devices often serving as Protoclassic baseline registers, probable representations of the earth (fig. 9e–g). It is difficult to reconcile the appearance of the double merlon with fiery torches, serpentine mask mosaics, and earth signs, but once the reputed "torches" are connected with quetzal plumes and plant growth, the three contexts share a single quality: all are green.

During the Protoclassic period, the double-merlon tabs merge closer together, at times becoming a single unit transected by a vertical line (fig. 9f). With this central division and upside-down T-like form, the Protoclassic double-merlon

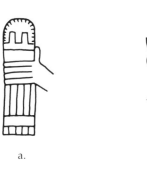

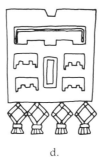
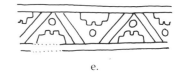

a. b. c. d.

e.

Figure 9. Elongated feather bundles and the double merlon sign: (a–b) Middle Formative bundles with double merlon sign. After Grove (1987), fig. 2c–e; (c) Middle Formative bundle with S-curve cloud form and double merlon sign, Teopantecuanitlan. After drawing courtesy of Linda Schele; (d) Middle Formative double merlons appearing in serpentine mosaic pavement, La Venta. After Coe (1968), 63; (e) Late Formative double merlons in earth band, Alvarado Stela; (f) Protoclassic double merlon in earth band, Chiapa de Corzo Stela 7; (g) Protoclassic double merlons in earth band, Izapa Stela 12; (h) Early Classic Maya *yax* sign, Tikal Stela 31; (i) Late Classic Maya *yax* sign in earth bands, detail of monument. Drawing courtesy of Linda Schele; (j) double merlon cartouches painted in two shades of green, detail of feather cape from Oxtotitlan Mural 1. After Grove (1970), frontispiece, watercolor by Felipé Davalos.

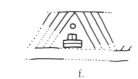

f. g. h.

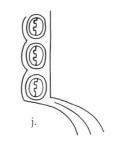

i. j.

Figure 10. Quetzalcoatl and feather bundles: (a–b) Middle Formative stone models of feather bundles with Avian Serpent. After Joralemon (1976), fig. 10; (c) Classic Veracruz style *palma,* detail of Quetzalcoatl figure; note knotted feather bundle at base of scene. After Taube (1986), fig. 6; (d) Late Classic bas-relief scene on carved boulder detail, Maltrata. Drawing by author from object in the Museum of Anthropology, Xalapa; (e) Classic plumed serpent with segmented feather body, Teotihuacan. After Berrin, ed. (1988), fig. VI.2.

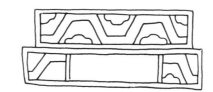

a. b.

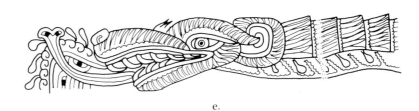

e.

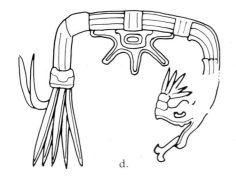

d. c.

resembles the Maya *yax* sign for green (fig. 9h). A Late Classic monument in the Dallas Museum of Art portrays a Maya version of the Protoclassic diagonally banded earth sign with *yax* signs in place of the double-merlon motif (fig. 9i). However, Oxtotitlan Mural 1 provides the best evidence for the meaning of this sign. A series of double-merlon cartouches appears on the feathered costume of the seated figure (fig. 9j). In the color rendition of this mural, all six cartouches are in two shades of *green*: a bluish green and a darker shade of green.[35] Rather than depicting dry, fiery torches, the long bound bundles depict feathers and, by extension, verdant growth.

Two Middle Formative stone examples of the long feather bundles have Avian Serpents placed at the ends, as if this creature is a personification of the bundle (fig. 10a, b). The use of feather bundles to represent plumed serpents is not restricted to the Formative Olmec. One Late Classic Veracruz *palma* depicts a flying anthropomorphic Quetzalcoatl with hands that double as quetzal heads; his body is partly covered by his cut conch wind jewel and a pair of twisted bicephalic serpents (fig. 10c). Projecting below his legs is a probable Late Classic form of the long "torch" bundle—a narrow knotted object containing four long plumes descending to the *palma* base. A roughly contemporaneous Late Classic relief from Maltrata, Veracruz, represents the serpentine form of Quetzalcoatl (fig. 10d). Along with displaying a single large star, the body of the plumed serpent is bound by three bands placed at regular intervals, much like the Olmec feather bundle depicted on the Río Pesquero celt. The Maltrata relief also recalls the plumed serpent of Teotihuacan, which is often portrayed as if it were a segmented series of feather bundles placed in a line (fig. 10e).

AVIAN SERPENT SKY BANDS

Jacinto Quirarte noted a striking similarity between the Olmec Avian Serpent and horizontal band motifs appearing in Protoclassic Izapan-style art, citing as an example the profile depiction of an Avian Serpent from Tlapacoya (fig. 11a).[36] By placing a mirror image of this creature at the tip

of the snout, a frontal image with a pair of outcurving fangs is created, a face notably similar to horizontal bands found in Protoclassic Maya art (fig. 11b, c). Garth Norman rightly identified the Izapan-style motifs as early sky bands, noting that they occur in the upper portions of scenes, at times with clouds and falling rain.[37]

Norman traced the origins of Protoclassic sky bands to as early as the Middle Formative Olmec, observing their presence on Pijijiapan Stone 1 and La Venta Altar 4.[38] The Middle Formative examples, like the Izapan-style sky bands, contain a pair of

Figure 11. The Avian Serpent and early Mesoamerican sky bands: (a) Early Formative Avian Serpent with mirror image. After Quirarte (1981), fig. 2d; (b) Protoclassic Maya sky band, Izapa Stela 12; (c) detail of Protoclassic Maya sky band. After Coe (1973), 27; (d) Middle Formative sky band atop throne, La Venta Altar 4; (e) Early Formative sky band atop throne, Potrero Nuevo Monument 2; (f) Middle Formative sky band at top of La Venta Stela 1; (g) Middle Formative sky band in upper portion of scene incised on Simojovel celt. After Joralemon (1971), fig. 148; (h) Late Formative sky band at top of Alvarado Stela, Veracruz. Drawing by author after object in the National Museum of Anthropology, Mexico City; (i) Middle Formative Zapotec sky band on neck of urn. After Boos (1966), fig. 202a; (j) Classic Zapotec "fauces de cielo," detail of mural from Tomb 105, Monte Alban.

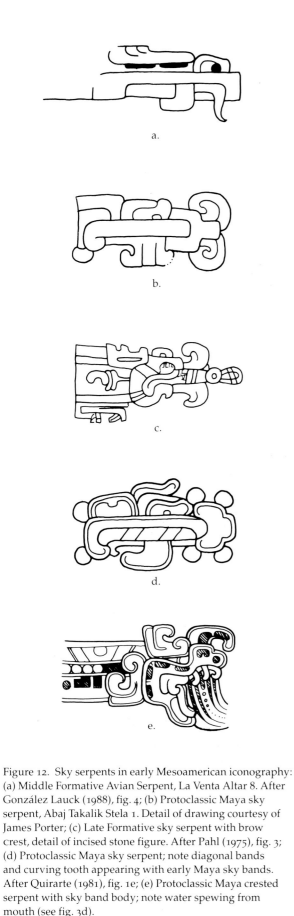

a.

b.

c.

d.

e.

Figure 12. Sky serpents in early Mesoamerican iconography: (a) Middle Formative Avian Serpent, La Venta Altar 8. After González Lauck (1988), fig. 4; (b) Protoclassic Maya sky serpent, Abaj Takalik Stela 1. Detail of drawing courtesy of James Porter; (c) Late Formative sky serpent with brow crest, detail of incised stone figure. After Pahl (1975), fig. 3; (d) Protoclassic Maya sky serpent; note diagonal bands and curving tooth appearing with early Maya sky bands. After Quirarte (1981), fig. 1e; (e) Protoclassic Maya crested serpent with sky band body; note water spewing from mouth (see fig. 3d).

outwardly leaning diagonal bands, creating a form of truncated V. Overlooked by Norman were the inverted U devices on the La Venta monument running along the lower edge of the celestial band (fig. 11d). They are identical to the inverted U-shaped elements commonly accompanying the Olmec Avian Serpent (e.g., fig. 1). Although Joralemon, *après* Lathrap, suggested that the inverted U-shaped element derives from the jaws and teeth of the caiman, the meaning of this device is more complex.[39] This sign can also occur *below* the maw, in the region of the lower chin or belly (e.g., figs. 1e, f, 4b). For the Olmec, this sign clearly had a meaning beyond the dentition of a single species.

Potrero Nuevo Monument 2, an Early Formative San Lorenzo throne, portrays dwarfs supporting a band marked with a series of the inverted U's (fig. 11e). Much like the Palace Throne from Late Classic Palenque, this sculpture portrays atlantean figures supporting the sky. The inverted U elements appear in other Olmec sky bands, again in the uppermost portions of the scenes (figs. 11f, g). Like La Venta Altar 4, the sky band atop La Venta Stela 1 portrays the outwardly leaning diagonal bands above the inverted U-shaped elements. An almost identical program occurs on the uppermost portion of the Alvarado Stela, a Veracruz monument dating to the Late Formative or Protoclassic periods (fig. 11h). For the Zapotec of Oaxaca, the Olmec sky band becomes entirely inverted. Thus, on the upper rim of a Middle Formative effigy vessel representing Cocijo, there are U-shaped elements *above* the diagonal bands (fig. 11i). This may also be seen in the Classic period Zapotec motif labeled as the "fauces de cielo," or "jaws of the sky," by Alfonso Caso. In this clearly celestial motif, a pair of U-shaped elements again appears atop the diagonal bands (fig. 11j).[40]

The series of inverted U-shaped elements are commonly found in Middle Formative Olmec iconography. One of the diagnostic motifs of Middle Formative ceramics, the double-line break, is probably a version of this sky sign. Kent Flannery first suggested that this rim motif is based on the mouth of the "fire-serpent," the figure I identify as the Avian Serpent.[41] The use of sky bands on vessel rims is not restricted to Middle Formative bowls; two

examples of early sky bands appear on the rims of the Middle Formative Zapotec Cocijo urn and a Protoclassic Maya bowl (figs. 11c, i). Of course, it is entirely apt that sky bands occur on bowl rims since they are the uppermost portion of the vessel.

The Olmec Avian Serpent seems to be ancestral to later sky serpents of the Maya and other Mesoamerican cultures. La Venta Altar 8 (formerly termed Stela 4 by Matthew W. Stirling) displays a late example of the Avian Serpent (figs. 12a). Possessing feather-crested brows, these fanged serpents have a long rectangular lip, quite like later Maya examples of sky serpents (e.g., fig. 12b). Another sky serpent appears on an unprovenanced incised stone statuette (fig. 12c). A human figure occurring in the same incised design recalls the Monte Alban II stone reliefs from Mound J, and it is possible that the carving is Late Formative Zapotec. The serpent displays both the feather-crested eye and a flowerlike form at the tip of the snout. Although the meaning of this form is still unknown, sky serpents from Abaj Takalik, Izapa, Cerros, and other Protoclassic Maya sites display similarly tipped snouts (figs. 12b, d, 13c).

An excellent example of the Protoclassic Maya sky serpent appears twice on the sides of a carved stone vessel in the collection of Dumbarton Oaks, Washington, D.C. (fig. 12e). The cylindrical vessel displays two essentially identical serpents with forward-projecting feather crests as well as late versions of the feather-crested eye and paw-wing of the Olmec Avian Serpent. Moreover, the serpent bodies are marked with the diagonal bands and hooked elements typically found with Protoclassic Maya sky bands, thereby labeling these creatures as sky serpents. Gouts of water pour from their mouths, recalling the streams of water spewing from the mouths of Teotihuacan plumed serpents. The head carried on the back of each serpent reinforces the allusion to rain (see fig. 16e). It will be subsequently noted that this is the Protoclassic form of Chac, the Maya god of rain and lightning. Thus much like the Olmec Avian Serpent and Quetzalcoatl of central Mexico, the snake is portrayed as a celestial rain-bringer.

Although sky serpents constitute an essential element of Olmec and Protoclassic Maya sky bands, references to the jaguar also often appear. Stirling first suggested that the upper portions of Tres Zapotes Stela D and Izapa Monument 2 portray frontally facing jaguar heads, with the Izapan sky bands also representing a highly stylized, frontally facing jaguar "mask panel."[42] The upper portion of a number of Izapan sky bands portray a pair of outwardly curving forms flanking a central element (fig. 13a). These probably refer to jaguar whiskers and are virtually identical to those flanking the jaguar snout on Tres Zapotes Stela D (fig. 13b).

Following the initial insights by Stirling, both Quirarte and Norman noted that the Izapan "top-line," or sky-band, motifs contain both serpent and jaguar imagery.[43] The sky-band motifs concern a single major theme: a great cosmic jaguar holding a bicephalic sky serpent in its maw. Izapa Stela 23 portrays a bicephalic serpent hanging from a sky band (fig. 13c). The same basic format appears on Tres Zapotes Stela D, where a pair of profile serpent heads hang down below the frontally facing jaguar face (fig. 13b). Like the Izapa monument, the undersides of the flanking serpents face toward the central scene, just as in Olmec iconography pairs of serpents are portrayed hanging in a similar fashion; for example, the throne appearing in Oxtotitlan Mural 1 displays the fanged frontal face with profile serpents hanging down at the corners of the mouth (fig. 13d). In the Olmec heartland, La Venta Altar 8 also portrays two Avian Serpents facing downward, again with the bellies oriented inward (fig. 13e), as does the recently discovered La Venta Monument 80, although here the Avian Serpents appear as rope-like forms (fig. 13f). According to Rebecca González, the monument represents a seated jaguar holding a bicephalic serpent in its maw.[44] With its crested brow, the snake probably represents the arboreal palm viper.

González compared La Venta Monument 80 to Los Soldados Monument 1 and San Lorenzo Monument 37. Both of these monuments portray seated jaguar figures with ropelike elements hanging down from the sides of their mouths. Although the head of the San Lorenzo monument is missing, the mouth of the Los Soldados sculpture has the same huge pointed tooth or beak element found on the La Venta Monument 80 creature. In the case of

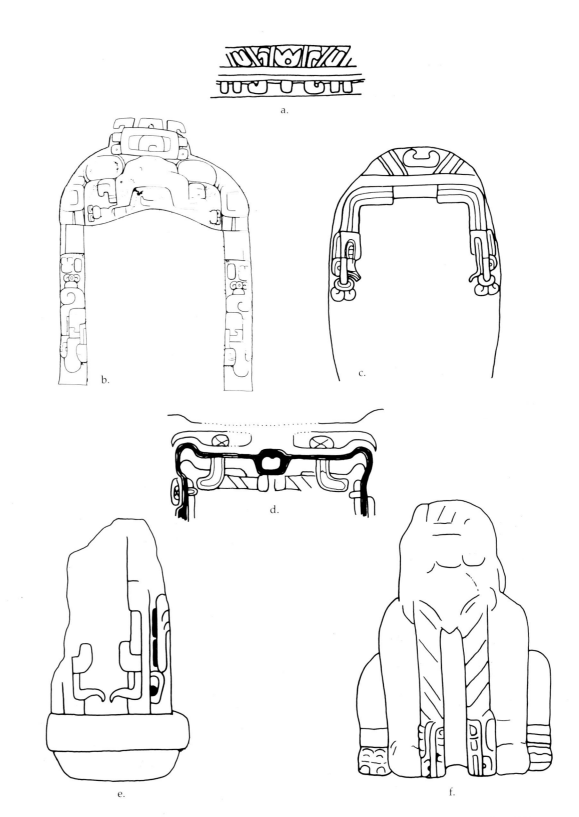

Figure 13. Profile sky serpents and frontal faces in early Mesoamerican iconography: (a) Protoclassic sky band with outcurving teeth and "whiskers" flanking central trefoil device, Izapa Stela 12; (b) Late Formative sky serpents hanging below great jaguar face, Tres Zapotes Stela D; note whiskers flanking central snout. Detail of drawing courtesy of James Porter; (c) Protoclassic bicephalic sky serpent hanging from sky band, Izapa Stela 23; (d) Middle Formative celestial throne with serpent heads hanging from sides of central face, detail of Oxtotitlan Mural 1 (see fig. 9j); (e) Middle Formative pair of hanging Avian Serpents, La Venta Altar 8 (see fig. 12a); (f) Late Formative jaguar holding bicephalic serpent rope, La Venta Monument 80. After González Lauck (1988), cover.

the Los Soldados and San Lorenzo monuments, the pendant elements are of ropelike material with no overt indication of serpent attributes. The aforementioned Early Formative Las Bocas-style effigy vessel portrays a jaguar grasping a crested serpent in its mouth and clasping the snake tail and head below by its talons.[45] The similarity of this sculpture to the three Olmec monuments is immediately obvious, and, as in the case of La Venta Monument 80 and Los Soldados Monument 1, the ceramic jaguar has a central pointed tooth, probably that of a shark (figs. 4f, 20). The theme of the jaguar grasping the sky serpent must have had profound significance for the Formative Olmec. As we shall see below, this cosmic act performed by Olmec gods also may have been performed in actual rites by the Olmec.

Rather than designating the earth, the inherent composite nature of the Avian Serpent suggests that it represents the overarching sky. Although the Classic and Postclassic plumed serpent appears in fairly standardized form as a rattlesnake with a plume-covered body, the form of the Avian Serpent is more varied. Nonetheless, the primary underlying meaning of the Olmec being appears to be the merging of snake and bird, two creatures widely identified with the heavens in Mesoamerica.[46] Transporting the Avian Serpent through the sky, the paw-wing sign may constitute an Olmec wind sign. Like the feathered paw-wing, the crested eye, or "flame eyebrow" serves as a reference to birds and, by extension, the sky. In addition, the arboreal fer-de-lance has similarly crested brows, and may well be the Olmec prototype of the later plumed serpent of Mesoamerica. Frequently displaying the long, curving fangs of vipers along with a serpent body, the Avian Serpent can appear hanging in bicephalic form, much like later Protoclassic sky serpents. Certain Avian Serpent traits, such as the inverted U-shaped elements and curving fangs, occur in Olmec and later Mesoamerican examples of sky signs.

With the recognition of this extensive sky symbolism, Olmec iconography needs to be reappraised in a different light. For example, David C. Grove identified Olmec thrones with the earth and underworld, but I have noted that such thrones as Portrero Nuevo Monument 2 and the one in Oxtotitlan

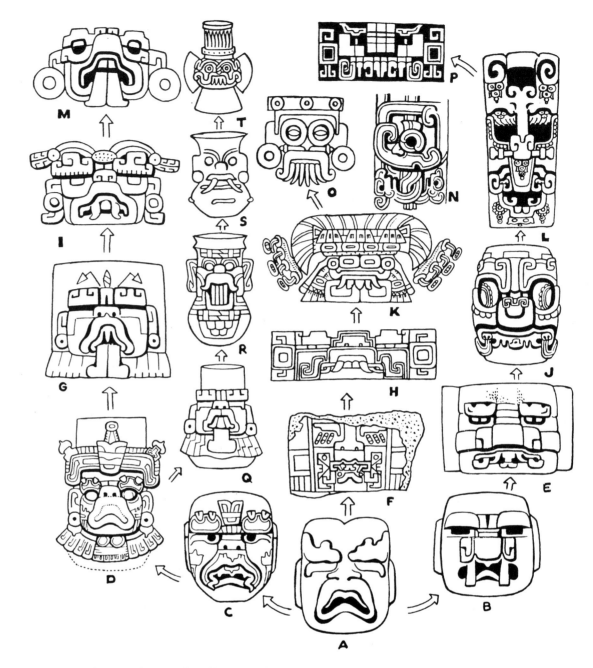

Figure 14. Diagram by Miguel Covarrubias illustrating the origin and evolution of Mesoamerican rain gods. From Covarrubias (1957), fig. 22.

Mural 1 contain explicit references to the sky (figs. 11b, 13d).[47] The figure atop the Oxtotitlan throne, I should like to add, is a feathered birdman in flight. Similarly, La Venta Altar 4 portrays a sky band and, in the niche below it, a man wearing a bird headdress. Ringed with feathers and four quetzal plumed maize ears, this central niche may refer to the later Maya "heart of heaven" concept.[48] However, only to focus upon sky imagery again misses the whole picture. The hybrid animals of the Olmec are a reflection of their and later Mesoamerican peoples' fascination with the interaction and junctures among the sky, earth, and underworld. It is through the passage or exchange among these cosmic realms that rain, the diurnal sun, and other forces of fertility are created.

THE OLMEC RAIN GOD

In an oft-cited and reproduced diagram, Covarrubias traced the evolution of Tlaloc, Chac, Cocijo, and other Mesoamerican rain gods from an Olmec jaguar prototype (fig. 14).[49] While a tacit agreement remains among many researchers that later Mesoamerican rain gods may have evolved from an Olmec jaguar being, the Covarrubias diagram has fallen into some disfavor. Subsequent analysis of the Las Limas Figure and other Olmec objects has revealed that the Olmec had an array of distinct gods, not simply a were-jaguar rain god. The infant or dwarf held in the Las Limas Figure's lap has also been identified as the actual Olmec Rain God— not the mature, squinting entity at the base of the Covarrubias diagram.[50] Nonetheless, the initial insights of Covarrubias do appear to be correct. Chac, Cocijo, and Tlaloc all derive from an Olmec jaguar rain god that is essentially the figure Covarrubias originally placed at the bottom of his evolutionary chart.

Due to epigraphic and iconographic advances provided by David Stuart, Coe, and others, it is now possible to trace the iconography of Chac from the Protoclassic period until the time of the Spanish conquest.[51] The Protoclassic Chac provides a crucial step in tracing the evolution and transformation of the Formative Olmec Rain God. Izapa Stela 1 has been recognized for several decades as a Protoclassic representation of the Maya rain god.[52] The principal theme of this monument concerns rain-making: a gout of water spews from the mouth of Chac, and two other streams fall from his fishing net and the creel slung over his back. It appears that the act of fishing—that is, raising fish into the sky— constituted a form of rain magic.[53]

Norman noted that Izapa Stela 1 contains not simply one but multiple representations of Chac (fig. 15a).[54] A Chac with a ring-tailed fish body occurs as a diadem worn by the principal rain god, evidently an early form of the piscine Jester God jewel (fig. 15b). Other Chac heads occur in the streams falling from the net and creel and flanking the terrestrial water at the base of the scene (fig. 15c–f). This series of Chac heads provides an excellent means to discern some of the basic traits of the Protoclassic Maya Chac. All the heads have

a blunt, at times slightly down-curving, snout with a single, pointed tooth, quite possibly a shark's, and a curling whisker or fish barble at the back of the mouth near the sides of the snout. Especially striking is the tendency of the upper portion of the head to merge into the flanking volutes illustrating clouds and rain. Like our "thunderheads," these Chac heads are probably personfications of great nimbus clouds. Chac's long hair and even his entire upper cranial region blend into the curling cloud volutes; with his eyes shut, his brow area turns into a curling cloud volute.

Protoclassic depictions of Chac are relatively common, and, as in Izapa Stela 1, frequently have the head merging into cloud volutes. This can be seen on El Baul Stela 1 (fig. 16a) and two similar Protoclassic monuments, Kaminaljuyu Stelae 4 and 19, which both portray Chac heads within curling cloud volutes (figs. 16b, 16c). Both Kaminaljuyu heads have the characterstic blunt snout, pointed tooth, and whiskers at the corner of the mouth, with the eyes and upper heads converted into cloud scrolls. In the case of Stela 19, the head is affixed to a serpent tail, a device that appears in other Protoclassic examples. A Protoclassic stucco facade from Uaxactun depicts a Chac head on the tail of a snake belching cloud volutes, quite probably a form of the sky serpent (fig. 16d). A similar scene occurs on the aforementioned stone vessel representing a pair of crested sky serpents spewing water; in both

a.

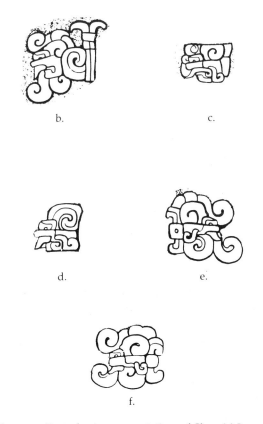

b.

c.

d.

e.

f.

Figure 15. Protoclassic representations of Chac: (a) Izapa Stela 1. Drawing courtesy of James Porter; (b) Chac head worn as Jester God diadem by principal Chac, (c) Chac head in water falling from net; (d) inverted Chac head in water falling from creel; (e–f) Chac heads in standing water at base of scene.

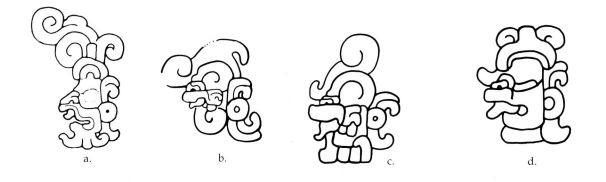

a.   b.   c.   d.

Figure 16. Protoclassic representations of Chac: (a) Chac head in sky, El Baul Stela 1. After drawing courtesy of Linda Schele; (b, c) Chac head in clouds, Kaminaljuyu Stelas 4, 19; (d) Chac head on serpent tail, Structure H-X-Sub-3, Uaxactun; (e) Chac head on sky serpent tail, detail of carved stone vase in the collection of Dumbarton Oaks (see fig. 3f); (f) green-stone carving of Chac, Santa Rita, Campeche. After Ochoa (1983), fig. II.4.2b.

e.   f.

Figure 17. Late Protoclassic stone figurine representing Chac. After sketches courtesy of Linda Schele: (a) profile of kneeling figure; note probable *yax* sign capping top of head; (b) *muyal* cloud curls flanking central *yax* sign; (c) detail of figurine head.

b.

a.   c.

cases, a Chac head rides on the serpent tail (fig. 16e). When the Protoclassic Chac appears frontally or in the round, a bulging and deeply furrowed brow is evident (fig. 16f).

Schele has called my attention to an important late Protoclassic stone carving of Chac (fig. 17a–c). The top of the head contains scrolls much like those appearing on other Protoclassic examples. However, in this instance, the scrolls clearly swirl in opposite directions, and together form the S-curve sign, a device epigraphically identified as *muyal*, or "cloud" in Maya languages.[55] I suspect that the widespread depiction of the upper head with cloud scrolls concerns a metaphoric comparison of nimbus clouds to the gray, convoluted contortions of brains. In this regard, David Freidel has reminded me of an illuminating passage in the Yucatec *Chilam Balam of Chumayel* that refers to copal—the incense from which rain-making clouds of smoke are created—as the "brains of the sky."[56] With the three drops in the region of the chin or beard, the statuette head is notably similar to a series of massive stone censers at Kaminaljuyu, Monuments 16, 17, and 18. Placed in the hollowed top of the head, the burning copal and smoke would literally serve as the "brains" of the censer.

A massive, early boulder sculpture of Chac, Monument 3 at Monte Alto, Guatemala, has the distinctive curling brow and slitted eyes, as well as the thick snout and flanking whiskers (fig. 18a). A possibly Late Formative serpentine artifact attributed to Guerrero depicts a figure with similar slitted eyes and blunt snout flanked by whiskers (fig. 18b). Immediately above the snout is the furrowed brow topped by a bulging cranium. The furrowed brow and swelling cranium also appear on one of the most diagnostic portrayals of the Olmec Rain God, reportedly found near Tuzapan, Veracruz (fig. 18c; cat. no. 199).[57] This Middle Formative figure displays the heavy slitted eyes, large cranial cloud curls, and whisker elements of the Protoclassic Maya Chac. The whisker devices are important, as well, because they are virtually identical to the whisker and cheek markings of early representations of the Zapotec rain god, Cocijo (fig. 18d, e), who also typically has the furrowed brow and, in many early instances, the central pointed tooth.

Figure 18. Rain Gods of Formative and Protoclassic Mesoamerica: (a) Monte Alto Monument 3; (b) serpentine carving of bearded rain god with slitted eyes, furrowed brow, bulging cranium, and whiskers at sides of mouth. After Parsons, Carlson, and Joralemon (1988), no. 19; (c) Rain God holding long bundle, stone figure attributed to Tuzapan, Veracruz, in the American Museum of Natural History. After Joralemon (1971), fig. 255; (d) stone mask of early Zapotec Cocijo, Monte Alban I; note cheek markings and pointed central tooth. After Joralemon (1971), fig. 180; (e) Monte Alban II urn representing Cocijo. After Joralemon (1971), fig. 179.

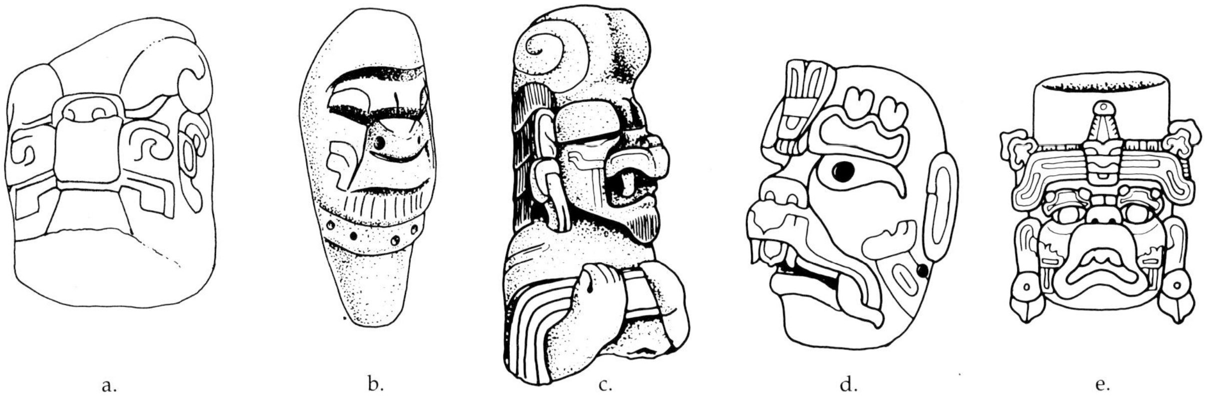

a. b. c. d. e.

Figure 19. The Olmec Rain God: (a) cloud scroll Rain God on Avian Serpent, detail of incision on the Young Lord. After drawing courtesy of Linda Schele; (b) Rain God in rampant jaguar stance; note bulging brow and S-curve cloud scrolls covering body. After Westheim (1957), fig. 1; (c) S-curve cloud scroll with triple rain drop motif, Chalcatzingo (see fig. 24e); (d) Early Formative Las Bocas bottle of Rain God with bulging, furrowed brows and downcurving, slitted eyes. After Feuchtwanger (1989), pl. 68; (e) Early Formative Rain God, San Lorenzo Monument 10.

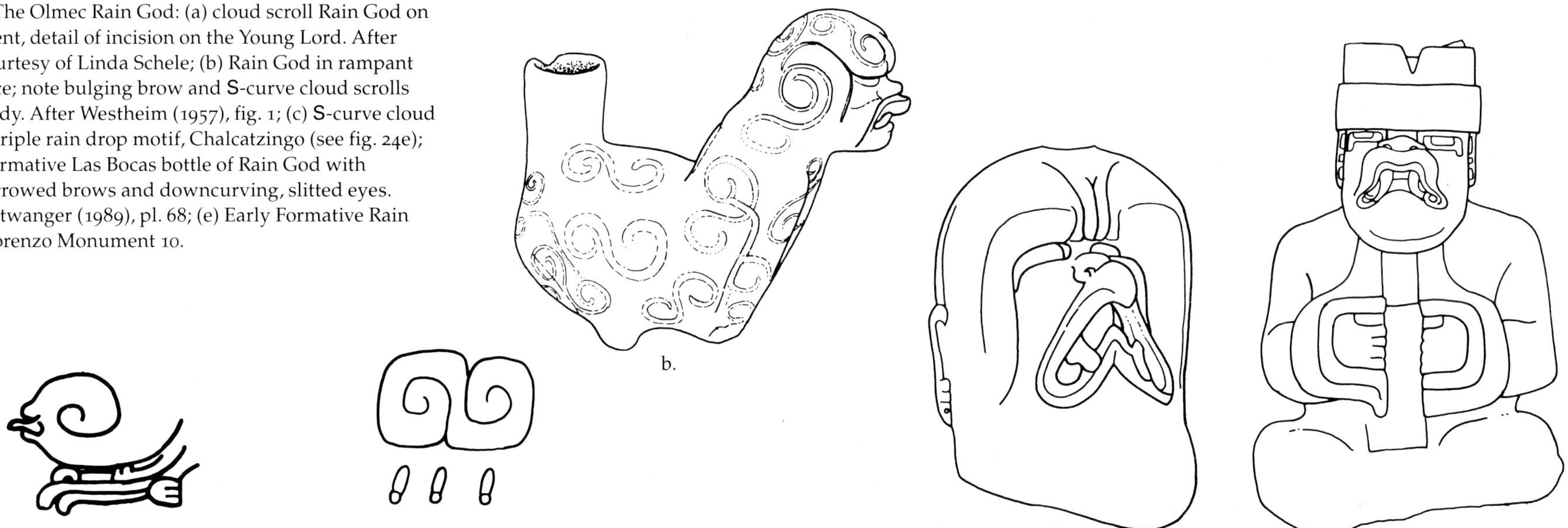

a. b. c. d. e.

An especially elaborate portrayal of Olmec rain gods appears on the late Olmec serpentine statuette of the Young Lord (cat. no. 193). Four cloud-scroll Olmec rain gods are incised on the stauette's upper arms and knees, each god identified with a particular creature, presumably referring to specific sources of rain. Of special interest is the example on the right arm representing the Olmec Rain God atop the Avian Serpent (fig. 19a), which is conceptually identical to the Protoclassic Maya Chacs atop sky serpents (e.g., fig. 16d, e). In all these cases, the serpentine figures are bringers of clouds and rain. Four other Olmec Rain God heads, each different, appear on the inner thighs, with the lower pair repeating in the buttocks region of the statuette.

The two series of four deities probably concern the quadripartite nature of the Olmec Rain God. It is well known that the Maya Chac, Zapotec Cocijo, and central Mexican Tlaloc are strongly quadripartite, a common trait that probably originated in Formative Olmec ideology.

A ceramic effigy vessel, quite possibly dating to the Early Formative Olmec, portrays the Olmec Rain God in a rampant feline stance, with the upper body raised on its forelegs (fig. 19b). Along with having a deeply spiraling and bulging cranium, the vessel figure is covered with S-curve cloud scrolls. A recently discovered relief from Chalcatzingo demonstrates that the S-curve motif signified clouds among the Olmec as well as the Maya.[58] Placed in the upper scene above an avian jaguar, the sign sheds three excalamation-point-shaped rain drops, explicitly denoting it as a rain cloud (figs. 19c, 24c).

In addition to the Avian Serpent, the Rain God is among the more common supernatural beings found in Early Formative Olmec iconography. The Early Formative form also tends to have slitted or downcurving eyes and a deeply bulging, furrowed brow (figs. 19d, e, 20a, b). Since the Early Formative period, the Olmec Rain God displays the typical Olmec "snarl," with the upper lip pulled up to the level of the nostrils, exposing a pair of large curving canines and sometimes a central pointed tooth.

A fragmentary Early Formative figurine from Tlatilco, probably a masked ballplayer, depicts the

Olmec Rain God with the furrowed brow, heavily lidded eyes, and the central pointed tooth flanked by outwardly curving fangs (fig. 20a). The face is very similar to a remarkable Protoclassic Cocijo from San Jose Mogote, Oaxaca (fig. 20b). In this ceramic sculpture, the Zapotec rain god is portrayed in the rearing position of the Las Bocas feline and Olmec Rain God effigy vessels (figs. 19b, 20c). This posture recalls both rearing felines and serpents, and it should be noted that the Las Bocas feline has a serpent belly flanked by the celestial U-brackets.[59] The same combination of jaguar and serpent has been noted in connection with the Zapotec rain god.[60]

Like the major Olmec iconographic theme of a jaguar holding one or a pair of avian serpents in its mouth (see figs. 13f, 20c), Tlaloc also grasps serpents in his jaguar maw. A Classic vessel from Zacuala, Teotihuacan, portrays Tlaloc with a pair of plumed serpents emerging from the corners of the mouth (fig. 21a). A Classic Veracruz palma depicts two intertwined serpents descending from the mouth of a profile Tlaloc (fig. 21b). The raising of celestial rain serpents also occurs in Protoclassic and Classic Maya art. In the upper portion of Izapa Stela 1, a probable Chac holds a serpent rope of twisted fiber (fig. 15) similar to those clasped in the mouths of Olmec jaguar figures (e.g., fig. 13f). Kaminaljuyu Stela 19 portrays a dancing figure holding a writhing snake marked with a Chac head and rain clouds (fig. 22a). The Classic Maya Chac often clasps a serpent in its mouth, reminiscent of the aforementioned scenes of the Olmec Rain God and Tlaloc (figs. 22b–d).

The Classic Maya Cauac Monster, epigraphically identified as *wits* or "mountain," by David Stuart, frequently holds a pair of serpents in the corners of its mouth (fig. 22e). The Cauac Monster and Chac appear to be related; not only do they share similar profiles, but the Cauac Monster can also wear the Spondylus shell earpieces commonly worn by Chac. Chac and the Cauac Monster may both derive from the Olmec Rain God. The Chacs, Tlalocs, and other Mesoamerican rain gods are widely identified with mountains. The Olmec theme of the jaguar biting the Avian Serpent may portray the Olmec Rain God as the pivotal, cosmic mountain integrating the

Figure 21. Classic period representations of Tlaloc holding serpents in its mouth: (a) Teotihuacan Tlaloc with pair of plumed serpents at corners of mouth, detail of incised vessel from Zacuala compound. After Séjourné (1959), fig. 127a; (b) Tlaloc with intertwined snakes in mouth, detail of Classic Veracruz palma, American Museum of Natural History (see fig. 14).

regions of the underworld, earth, and sky.[61]

As Covarrubias suggested, the form and physiognomy of the Olmec Rain God are largely based on the jaguar. Along with its snarling jaguar mouth, the Olmec Rain God has deeply furrowed brows and frequently slitted eyes, perhaps crying tears of rain. Although the feline Olmec Rain God is ancestral to Cocijo and Tlaloc, the latter gods commonly display a lolling, bifurcated serpent tongue. The tendency of the Olmec Rain God cranium to transform into cloud volutes continues with Protoclassic examples of the Maya Chac. However, the faunal makeup of the Protoclassic Chac is somewhat ambiguous. The thick, blunt, often slightly downcurving snout and whiskers at the corner of the mouth suggest the jaguar, but the probable central shark tooth indicates piscine attributes, a trait that continues into the Classic period. The principal Chac on Izapa Stela 1 has fish on its arms and legs (fig. 15), and the Classic Chac frequently has long fish barbels at the corners of its mouth. The Classic Chac's barbels and Spondylus shell earpieces evoke

Figure 20. The ophidian jaguar and Olmec and Zapotec rain gods: (a) Early Formative Olmec Rain God with furrowed brow and pointed central tooth, ceramic figurine, Tlatilco. After Feuchtwanger (1989), fig. 9; (b) Monte Alban II Cocijo with furrowed brow and pointed central tooth, San José Mogote. After Marcus (1992), fig. 9.9; (c) Early Formative effigy vessel of serpentine jaguar with furrowed brow and pointed central tooth grasping crested serpent, Las Bocas (see fig. 4f).

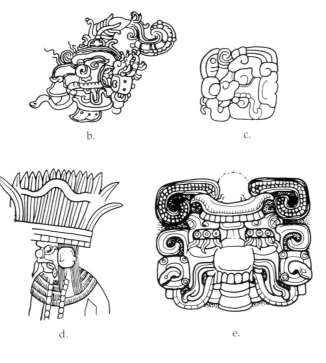

Figure 22. Serpents held by Maya supernatural figures: (a) Protoclassic figure holding celestial serpent; note inverted Chac head to right, Kaminaljuyu Stela 19; (b–c) Early Classic Chacs, each with serpent in mouth. After Taube (1992), figs. 6c,e; (d) Terminal Classic Chac with serpent in mouth, Chichen Itza. After Taube (1992), fig. 5d; (e) Early Classic Cauac Monster with serpents in mouth, stucco facade from Structure 5D-33-2nd, Tikal.

jaguar whiskers and ears. Just as the Maya GI is like an aquatic counterpart of the jaguar sun god, or GIII, so the Classic period Chac appears to be a translation of the jaguar into a fishlike water being.

OLMEC RAIN RITUALS

The layout and orientation of many Formative sites reveal the Olmec concern with the ritual management of rain and water. The elaborate systems of stone drains found at San Lorenzo, La Venta, and Laguna de los Cerros, as well as the highland site of Teopantecuanitlan, Guerrero, probably reflect this ritual orientation. Coe and Richard A. Diehl noted the probable ceremonial use of the drain system at San Lorenzo: "the lagunas, drains, and associated monuments must have been part of a larger system of ritual bathing and rain making involved with Olmec water gods."[62] Citing the importance of caves in Aztec rain lore, Grove suggested that Oxtotitlan Cave was used in Olmec rain and fertility ceremonies.[63] This and the sites of El Manatí and

Chalcatzingo appear to have been loci of rain-making rites oriented to natural bodies or movements of water. Elaborate Olmec offerings were placed in a spring at the base of Cerro Manatí, Veracruz, and at Chalcatzingo, Morelos, where the bas-relief figure known as El Rey, or Monument 1, is situated beside the principal runoff channel of Cerro Chalcatzingo. Portrayed with clouds, cloud scrolls, rain drops, quetzals, and growing plants, the seated figure is presented as a provider of rain.[64]

It is surely no coincidence that the materials most coveted by the Olmec and later Mesoamerican elite—quetzal plumes and jadeite—evoke the verdant, life-giving qualities of water and vegetation. In the Aztec Chimalpopoca Codex, the true "jades" and "quetzal plumes" of the Tlaloque are rain and green husks of tender corn.[65] Bedecked in these precious materials, the elite are the controllers of rain and agricultural fertility as well as of abundance and wealth. Although it is doubtful that the remains of quetzal birds, much less their feathers, will soon be discovered at Olmec sites, explicit

portrayals of these exotic birds occur at La Venta and even Chalcatzingo. In contrast, not only is jade depicted in Olmec art, but is found widely at Middle Formative Olmec sites. As one of its Olmec symbolic referents, jade signified precious rain and water. In fact, the aforementioned Olmec exclamation-point-shaped rain sign is probably based on two strung jade beads, the upper being cylindrical and the lower, spherical.

Grove noted that the beaded raindrop motif, here repeated three times, appears on Olmec masks worn on the brow (fig. 23a), and is ancestral to the Classic Maya Jester God jade diadem, a major symbol of Maya kings. Grove is entirely correct: one form of the Maya Jester God was a symbolic "rain jewel" identified with water and growth.[66] On the recarved back of an Olmec plaque at Dumbarton Oaks, a Protoclassic Maya king wears a Jester God that emanates three beaded elements (fig. 23b). These beads also refer to rain and are virtually identical to the triple tears pouring from the eyes of the frontal face on Tres Zapotes Stela C (fig. 23c). The fishing Chac on Izapa Stela 1 wears an early form of the Jester God, here a combination of Chac with a ring-tailed fish (fig. 15b). The Protoclassic bas-relief at Loltun Cave portrays an explicit ring-tailed, piscine Jester God combined with an anthropomorphic mask, and once again beaded drops emanate from the device (fig. 23d). The piscine Jester God continues into the Classic period, usually with droplets on the face and body (fig. 23e, f). It has been noted that the raising of fish into the sky was a symbolic rain-making act among the Protoclassic Maya, and the piscine Jester God rain-jewel would appear to relate to this magic act. By wearing this item on the brow, the Maya king assumes the duty of rain-maker, the engenderer of water and growth. As Grove and Virginia M. Fields indicated, the ultimate origins of this Maya device derive from Olmec traditions of jade regalia, rulership, and agricultural ritual.

Aside from inorganic artifacts and the ongoing excavations at the wet site of El Manatí, relatively little information is available regarding the types of offerings presented in Olmec rain rituals. It is tempting to associate Olmec bloodletters with imitative rain magic through the sprinkling of blood

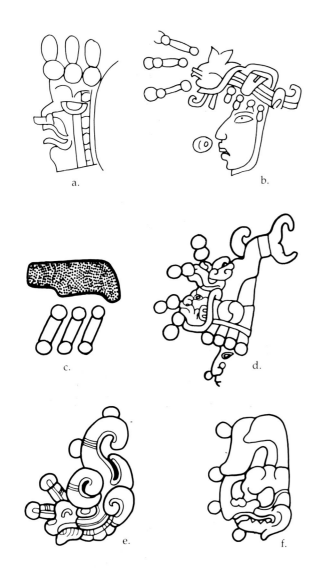

Figure 23. Forms of the Jester God rain jewel in Isthmian and Maya iconography: (a) Middle Formative face with triple rain drop motif worn on brow of Olmec figure. After Grove (1989), fig. 7.7; (b) Protoclassic Maya ruler wearing sky band headband with Jester God. After Schele and Miller (1986), pl. 32a; (c) Late Formative beaded tears from right eye of face, Tres Zapotes Stela C; (d) Protoclassic Jester God as ring-tailed fish, Loltun Cave. After Miller and Taube (1993), 104; (e) Early Classic piscine Jester God, Tikal Stela 31; (f) Late Classic piscine Jester God, Palenque.

or burning it to create fertile clouds of smoke. However, no known Olmec scenes illustrate the ritual significance of bloodletting. Copal or other incense may also have been ritually used to create symbolic rain clouds. Coe notes that the seated figure on La Venta Monument 19 holds an early version of the copal incense bag widely found in Classic and Postclassic Mesoamerica (fig. 6a).

On close inspection, his left hand is seen to present its palm outward, the typical position for scattering blood, incense, and other offerings in Classic Mesoamerica.[67]

Although the ritual significance of blood and incense offerings remains poorly known among the Formative Olmec, human sacrifice was a component of Olmec rain-making rites. Coe and Joralemon suggested that infants were sacrificed to the rain gods, a tradition well known among the later Aztec.[68] Recent excavations at El Manatí spring provide striking corroboration; among its offerings are the disarticulated bodies of infants.[69] Adult captives were also sacrificed in Olmec rain rituals. Reilly noted that the figure incised on the right arm of the Young Lord is an executed bound captive.[70] The figure on the other side is evidently a male holding atlatl darts. Both figures are accompanied by cloud scrolls personified as the Olmec Rain God, indicating that at least by the Middle Formative period, ritual warfare and captive sacrifice served as important means of insuring rain and agricultural abundance.

As with later Mesoamerican peoples, the Olmec performed human sacrifice in conjunction with the ritual ballgame. Although widely cited as a depiction of jaguar and human copulation, Tenochtitlan Monument 1 probably depicts a costumed ballplayer atop a bound victim (fig 24a).[71] Although the head of the ballplayer is missing, contemporaneous ballplayer figurines from both San Lorenzo and Tlatilco frequently wear the mask of the Olmec Rain God (e.g., fig. 20a).[72] For both the Classic Maya and Postclassic central Mexico, ballcourts were regarded as dangerous but also fertile places identified with water and agricultural abundance.

Potrero Nuevo Monument 3 from San Lorenzo concerns the sacrifice of a supine victim by a jaguar complete with talons and a tail (fig. 24b). Similar scenes of humans devoured or attacked by monstrous creatures occur within a specific area on the northern portion of Cerro Chalcatzingo: the bas-relief Monuments 3 and 4 depict felines attacking supine humans, Monument 5 portrays the Avian Serpent devouring a person, and a recently discovered relief from this area depicts an avian jaguar dismembering a human victim with its talons

(fig. 24c). Directly above this bloody scene, rain falls from an S-curve cloud, indicating that the Olmec theme of supernatural beasts devouring human victims had a fertile, rain-making significance.

Human victims were clearly not fed to supernatural rain beasts at Chalcatzingo. Instead, such human sacrifices were surely performed by individuals impersonating these sacred characters. Such an impersonator in jaguar garb menaces a smaller bound person with a clawed instrument in Painting 1 at Juxtlahuaca Cave.[73] However, the term impersonation may not demonstrate the extent to which the participant identified with the supernatural being. It is likely that shamans, who through trance ritually became the supernatural force, performed such sacrificial rain-making rites. In contemporary Mesoamerica, shamans are widely associated with rain and lightning powers.

In his now classic study of 1968, Peter T. Furst demonstrated that a number of Olmec sculptures portray the transformation of shamans into jaguars.[74] But the question remains, just what did these jaguar shamans *do*? They may have performed the important shamanic acts of divination and curing, but they were probably also the pre-eminent Olmec rainmakers. Following the original insights of Covarrubias, I have noted that the Olmec Rain God is essentially a jaguar being. Thus it is not surprising that the more feline of the shamanic transformation figures display the deeply furrowed brow and snarling mouth associated with the rain deity. Certain transformation figures display veinlike, forking brow markings, a trait found on the very example Covarrubias presented as the prototypical Olmec rain deity (fig. 14). In addition, the conventional kneeling position of the transformation figures—arms outstretched to the knees—recalls the rearing stance of the Olmec Rain God (figs. 13f, 19b). The identification of jaguar shamans with the rain deity is best seen in the Tuzapan statuette, which has the same tufted beard and tonsured coiffure typically found on jaguar transformation figures (fig. 18c; cat. no. 199). In other words, the rain deity is portrayed as a shaman.

The cited sculptures from San Lorenzo and Chalcatzingo suggest that human sacrifice was a component of rainmaking rituals performed by Olmec shamans. Another fertility rite seems to have been the lifting of water symbols into the sky. The Tuzapan Olmec Rain God with the shamanic coiffure holds a bundle of quetzal plumes or vegetal growth in his arms (fig. 18c). As I have explained, this long bundle can be transformed into the Avian Serpent, and as such, in referring to the lifting or supporting of the sky, may have cosmic significance. But it may have more immediate meaning as rain magic, with the serpents denoting celestial rain. Two Early Formative monuments from San Lorenzo probably depict this shamanic rainmaking rite: San Lorenzo Monument 47, representing an apparently fully human figure holding the Avian Serpent, and Portrero Nuevo Monument 1, depicting the shaman partly transformed into the jaguar, his clawed hand grasping the undulating serpent.[75] The Las Bocas jaguar effigy vessel seems to represent the same rite, with the viper now grasped in the mouth of the jaguar shaman (figs. 4f, 20c). These scenes immediately recall Protoclassic and Classic rain or lightning serpents held in the hands or mouth of Tlaloc, Chac, and other figures, including actual human individuals (figs. 21, 22).[76] A number of researchers have compared Maya snake dances to similar rainmaking rites of Postclassic central Mexico and the contemporary American Southwest.[77] It would appear that this rite, still performed by the Hopi in the arid regions of the Southwest, has its origins in rainmaking ceremonies of the Formative Olmec.

Conclusions

By the Early Formative period, the Olmec had developed a complex system of ritual and belief pertaining to rain and agricultural fertility. Two major beings of this fertility complex are the Avian Serpent and the Olmec Rain God. Identified with the sky, wind, and rain, the Avian Serpent seems to be ancestral to the plumed serpent of central Mexico. The Avian Serpent compares closely to the Classic Maya Bearded Dragon, an essentially serpentine and frequently plumed being associated with the sky, water, and lightning.[78] The Olmec Rain God readily relates to the Chac, Cocijo, and Tlaloc

rain gods of later Mesoamerica. Aside from the strongly feline origin of these rain gods, it is likely that some of the secondary characteristics of Mesoamerican rain deities, such as their quadripartite nature and identification with mountains, also derive from the Olmec Rain God.

Olmec ceremonies pertaining to agricultural fertility were undoubtedly numerous and complex. Like later Mesoamerican peoples, the Olmec performed rainmaking rites at natural caves, mountains, and springs. Sculpture and monumental architecture at such sites as San Lorenzo and La Venta indicate that rain ceremonies were also enacted in the centers of major communities in the Olmec heartland. Impersonation was an important component of Olmec rainmaking rites, and the many stone masks of the Olmec Rain God probably derive from this phenomenon.[79] It is noteworthy that the later Aztec major masked deities are the fructifying gods of wind and rain—Ehecatl-Quetzalcoatl and Tlaloc. Certain individuals not only impersonated but personified the Olmec Rain God through shamanic trance. Among the rainmaking rites performed by Olmec shamans or priests were human sacrifice and the lifting or carrying of the Avian Serpent, which could be symbolically represented by long bundles of quetzal feathers or vegetation, or by live vipers, such as arboreal fer-de-lances and rattlesnakes.

In terms of Olmec influence on contemporaneous and later Mesoamerican religion, in no area is it more profound than in the propitiation and manipulation of forces of agricultural fertility. Centered in the humid and fertile Gulf Coast lowlands, the Olmec must have been the Formative role models of agricultural success. The power and wealth accrued by their agricultural base is readily seen even today in their monumental art, architecture, and fine objects exquisitely worked in precious and exotic materials. The horticultural knowledge of the Olmec—both real and attributed—was surely coveted by incipient agriculturalists in other areas of Mesoamerica. The situation may be analogous to Mesoamerican influence in the American Southwest during the Postclassic period. By at least Toltec times, Mesoamerican peoples were securing turquoise from the Cerrillos region of northern New

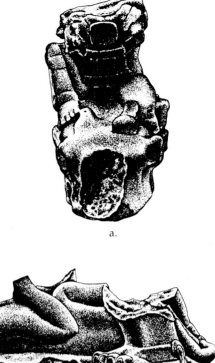

a.

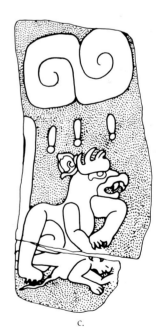

b.

c.

Figure 24. Olmec human sacrifice: (a) Middle Formative ballplayer atop bound victim, Tenochtitlan Monument 1. After Coe and Diehl (1980), fig. 499; (b) Middle Formative jaguar atop supine victim, Potrero Nuevo Monument 3. After Coe and Diehl (1980), fig. 497; (c) Middle Formative Avian jaguar dismembering human victim; note cloud and rain signs above, new monument from Chalcatzingo. Drawing by author from on-site observations.

Mexico.[80] Although inhabiting only a marginally agricultural area, the Puebloan peoples seem to have readily adopted rain ritual and beliefs of their affluent southern neighbors; as examples, the plumed water serpent and the masked mountain rain spirits, or *katsina*, readily come to mind.

For Classic and Postclassic peoples of Mesoamerica, concepts of rulership and wealth were inextricably tied to rain and agricultural fertility. The piscine Jester God, a major emblem of Classic Maya kings, was a symbol of water and growth derived from Olmec regalia. The Aztec Chimalpopoca Codex describes the fall of the Toltec and the rise of the Aztec, the two great empires of Postclassic central Mexico, in terms of the mastery of rain ritual and symbolism. Because the King Huemac refuses the winnings offered by the Tlaloque—green maize husks and rain (their forms of quetzal plumes and jade)—Tollan is destroyed by drought. However, by sacrificing a maiden to the Tlaloque, the Mexica ensure the growth of the Aztec empire.[81] The recognition that power and material wealth ultimately derive from rain and agricultural fertility was not a recent Postclassic innovation, but originated in the interdependent developments of agriculture, ideology, and statecraft among the Formative Olmec.

Notes

During the course of writing this essay, I was greatly assisted by suggestions and comments from many individuals. In particular, I wish to thank Monica Bellas, Elizabeth P. Benson, John Clark, Michael D. Coe, Richard A. Diehl, David A. Freidel, Jill Guthrie, Stephen D. Houston, Peter David Joralemon, Karl Lorenzen, John Pohl, F. Kent Reilly, III, Linda Schele, and Gillian Schultz. I am also indebted to James Porter, who generously contributed some of the illustrations used in this study. A condensed version of this paper was presented in a conference in honor of Michael D. Coe at Yale University on May 7, 1994.

1. Peter David Joralemon, "A Study of Olmec Iconography," in *Studies in Pre-Columbian Art and Archeology*, no. 7 (Washington, D.C., 1971); idem, "The Olmec Dragon: A Study in Pre-Columbian Iconography," in *Origins of Religious Art and Iconography in Preclassic Mesoamerica*, ed. Henry B. Nicholson (Los Angeles, 1976), 27–71.
2. Joralemon, "The Olmec Dragon" (as in note 1), 37.
3. Ibid., 58.
4. Ibid., 61; see J. Eric S. Thompson, *Maya History and Religion* (Norman, Okla., 1970).
5. See David A. Freidel, Linda Schele, and Joy Parker, *Maya Cosmos: Three Thousand Years on the Shaman's Path* (New York, 1993), 46–7, 410–12.
6. Joralemon, "A Study of Olmec Iconography" (as in note 1), 35; idem, "The Olmec Dragon" (as in note 1), 37.
7. Joralemon, "The Olmec Dragon" (as in note 1), 37, 40; idem, "The Olmec," in Lee Parsons, John B. Carlson, and Peter David Joralemon, *The Face of Ancient America: The Wally and Brenda Zollman Collection of Precolumbian Art* (Indianapolis, 1988), 11.
8. See Eduard Seler, *Gesammelte Abhandlungen zur Amerikanischen Sprach- und Alterthumskunde*, vol. 4 (Berlin, 1902–23), 646–53; Karl Taube "*Itzam Cab Ain*: Caimans, Cosmology, and Calendrics in Postclassic Yucatan," *Research Reports on Ancient Maya Writing*, no. 26 (Washington, D.C., 1989).
9. Miguel Covarrubias, *Indian Art of Mexico and Central America* (New York, 1957), 31, 60, 63, 65; Román Piña Chán, *Tlatilco: A través de su cerámica* (Mexico City, 1958).
10. Michael D. Coe, *America's First Civilization* (New York, 1968), 114.
11. Román Piña Chán, *Quetzalcóatl: Serpiente emplumada* (Mexico City, 1977), 19.
12. Joralemon, "A Study of Olmec Iconography" (as in note 1), 82–84; idem, "The Olmec Dragon" (as in note 1), 33.
13. Michael D. Coe and Richard A. Diehl, *In the Land of the Olmec: The Archaeology of San Lorenzo Tenochtitlán*, vol. 1 (Austin, Tex., 1980), 356–57; Joralemon, "The Olmec Dragon" (as in note 1), fig. 9.
14. As the final version of this paper was being prepared for publication, I obtained a copy of Patricia Ann Garbe's Master's thesis entitled "The Olmec Jaguar Paw-Wing Motif: Correspondences in Associated Contexts," University of Arizona, 1971. Garbe independently arrived at many of the same conclusions regarding the paw-wing and an Olmec winged serpent. For examples of serpents with paw-wings, Garbe cited San Lorenzo Monument 47, Chalcatzingo Relief 5, and the San Miguel Amuco Stela. In addition, she also noted that the Olmec Dragon commonly appearing on Early Formative incised vessels is the same winged serpent. However, as far as I am aware, her early insights were not entertained by other researchers.
15. For effigy vessel examples, see Franz Feuchtwanger, *Ceramica Olmeca* (Mexico City, 1989), figs. 98, 101.
16. Carl Lumholtz, *Symbolism of the Huichol Indians* (New York, 1900), 73; John Monaghan, "The Feathered Serpent in Oaxaca," *Expedition* 31 (1989): 12–18.
17. Lumholtz (as in note 16), 41.
18. Fray Bernardino de Sahagún, *Florentine Codex: General History of the Things of New Spain*, trans. Arthur J. O. Anderson and Charles E. Dibble, bk. 1 (Santa Fe, 1950–82), 9.
19. Coe (as in note 10), 114; Joyce Marcus, "Zapotec Chiefdoms and the Nature of Formative Religions," in *Regional Perspectives on the Olmec*, ed. Robert J. Sharer and David C. Grove (Cambridge, 1989), 170, 172; Nanette M. Pyne, "The Fire-Serpent and Were-Jaguar in Formative Oaxaca: A Contingency Table Analysis," in *The Early Mesoamerican Village*, ed. Kent Flannery (New York, 1976), 273.
20. Philip Drucker, "La Venta, Tabasco: A Study of Olmec Ceramics and Art," *Bureau of American Ethnology*, Bulletin 153 (1952): 160, 169, 194–95; Donald W. Lathrap, cited in Joralemon, "The Olmec Dragon" (as in note 1), 40.
21. In Mixe the arboreal palm viper is termed *tsoxc vaj*, meaning "green horn"; Alvin Schoenhals and Louise Schoenhals, *Vocabulario Mixe de Totontepec* (Mexico City, 1965), 120.
22. For descriptions of the arboreal palm viper, see Miguel Alvarez del Toro, *Los reptiles de Chiapas*, 3d ed. (Tuxtla Gutierrez, 1982), 211–12; Jonathan A. Campbell and William W. Lamar, *The Venemous Reptiles of Latin America* (Ithaca, 1989), 162, 168–69.
23. To the Aztec, *quetzalcoatl* could refer not only to the god or the historical king of Tollan, but also to a particular, small venomous snake from the Totonac area, the former region of the Olmec heartland. Although it is unlikely that the creature described can be identified with a specific species, its toxicity and mode of attack are similar to the arboreal palm viper's: "As soon as it appears, it bites one, it strikes one. And he whom it strikes dies suddenly; it is not an hour when he dies—only a very little time. And in order to bite one, first it flies, quite high up; well up it goes; and it just descends upon whom or what it bites. And when it flies or descends, a great wind blows. Wherever it goes, it flies" (Sahagún [as in note 18], bk. 11, 85).
24. Cited in Joralemon, "The Olmec Dragon" (as in note 1), 40.
25. Coe (as in note 10), 114.
26. For a discussion of the trilobate sign in Mesoamerican iconography, see Terrance L. Stocker and Michael W. Spence, "Trilobal Eccentrics at Teotihuacan and Tula," *American Antiquity* 38 (1973): 195–99.
27. According to Aztec belief, the tears of children destined for sacrifice signified the coming rain, Sahagún (as in note 18), bk. 2, 44.
28. Joralemon, "A Study of Olmec Iconography" (as in note 1), 9.
29. Karl Taube, "The Teotihuacan Cave of Origin: The Iconography and Architecture of Emergence Mythology in Mesoamerica and the American Southwest," *Res* 12 (1986): 59.
30. David C. Grove and Louise I. Paradis, "An Olmec Stela from San Miguel Amuco, Guerrero, " *American Antiquity* 36 (1971): 95–102.
31. During the climax of the involuntary kiva initiation of children at Zuni, New Mexico, an image of the plumed serpent Kolowisi is carried from a spring and placed in the kiva entrance. As water actually spews through the mouth of this serpent image, rolls of long green grass are thrown down into the kiva. Led to believe that this grass also comes from the plumed serpent's mouth, the children carry the bundles away as tokens of their initiation (Matilda C. Stevenson, *The Zuni Indians: Their Mythology, Esoteric Fraternities, and Ceremonies* [Washington, D.C., 1904], 101). Although it is beyond the scope of this paper to belabor the similarities between this Zuni being and the Mesoamerican Quetzalcoatl, it should be pointed out that in the Zuni intiation ceremony the conch, which is the voice of Kolowisi, and the morning star, which plays an important ceremonial role, are both significant attributes of Quetzalcoatl (ibid., 95).
32. Alfredo Barrera Vásquez, ed., *Diccionario Maya Cordemex: Maya-Español, Español-Maya* (Mérida, 1980), 420.

33. Sahagún (as in note 18), bk. 11, 19.

34. See Linda Schele, this volume, and "Sprouts and the Early Symbolism of Rulers in Mesoamerica," paper delivered at *Die Welt der Maya*, Hildesheim, Germany, November (1992); manuscript in possession of author (1993).

35. For a color representation of this image, see David C. Grove, "The Olmec Paintings of Oxtotitlan Cave, Guerrero, Mexico," *Studies in Pre-Columbian Art and Archaeology*, no. 6 (Washington, D.C., 1970), frontispiece.

36. Jacinto Quirarte, "Tricephalic Units in Olmec, Izapan-Style, and Maya Art," in *The Olmec and Their Neighbors: Essays in Memory of Matthew W. Stirling*, ed. Elizabeth P. Benson (Washington, D.C., 1981).

37. Garth V. Norman, *Izapa Sculpture: Text* (Provo, 1976), 26.

38. Ibid., 23.

39. Joralemon, "The Olmec Dragon" (as in note 1), 37.

40. Alfonso Caso, *Las estelas Zapotecas* (Mexico City, 1928).

41. Kent Flannery, cited in Stephen Plog, "Measurement of Prehistoric Interaction between Communities," in *The Early Mesoamerican Village*, ed. Kent Flannery (New York, 1976), 272.

42. Matthew W. Stirling, "Stone Monuments of Southern Mexico," *Bureau of American Ethnology,* Bulletin 138 (1943): 14, 62–68.

43. Jacinto Quirarte, "The Relationship of Izapan-Style Art to Olmec and Maya Art: A Review," in *Origins of Religious Art and Iconography in Preclassic Mesoamerica*, ed. Henry B. Nicholson (Los Angeles, 1976), 77–78; and Norman (as in note 37), 28.

44. Rebecca González Lauck, "Proyecto arqueológico La Venta," *Arqueología* 4 (1988): 155.

45. See Feuchtwanger (as in note 15), figs. 94–97.

46. The quadruped aspect of the Avian Serpent described by Joralemon could be a cosmic being encompassing both earth and sky. In this case, the quadruped form may refer to the caiman earth, the head serving as the Avian Serpent. The actual faunal identity of the quadruped is still uncertain, but it is entirely possible that it represents a caiman, or else a jaguar or toad. In addition, Linda Schele (personal communication, 1994) called my attention to one of the animal burdens carried by the Classic Maya Holmul Dancer. Bearing the celestial name *wak ka'an*, or "raised up sky," this entity is essentially a quadruped serpent.

47. David C. Grove, "Olmec Altars and Myths," *Archaeology* 26 (1973): 128–35; idem, "Olmec Monuments: Mutilation as a Clue to Meaning," in *The Olmec and Their Neighbors*, ed. Benson (as in note 36), 64; idem, "The Olmec Legacy: Updating Olmec Prehistory," *National Geographic Research and Exploration* 8 (1992): 156–57.

48. The Olmec niche figure holds a rope, recalling the sky rope cords of Maya iconography. For a discussion of the Maya celestial conduit, or "heart of heaven," see Freidel, Schele, and Parker (as in note 5), 59, 99, 103, 105, 425.

49. Although this diagram is best known from Covarrubias's 1957 *Indian Art of Mexico and Central America* (as in note 9), it was previously published in his article entitled "El arte 'Olmeca' o de La Venta," *Cuadernos Americanos* 28 (1946): fig. 4.

50. See Coe (as in note 10), 111, 114, Joralemon, "A Study of Olmec Iconography" (as in note 1), 71–76, 90; idem,

"The Olmec Dragon" (as in note 1), 29, 33.

51. See Michael D. Coe, *Lords of the Underworld: Masterpieces of Classic Maya Ceramics* (Princeton, N.J., 1978), 76–78; David Stuart, "Ten Phonetic Syllables, *"Research Reports on Ancient Maya Writing*, no. 14 (Washington, D.C., 1987), 17–23; Karl Taube, "The Major Gods of Ancient Yucatan," *Studies in Pre-Columbian Art and Archaeology*, no. 32 (Washington, D.C., 1992), 17–27.

52. Michael D. Coe, *Mexico* (New York, 1962), 99; Rafael Girard, *Los Mayas: Su civilización, su historia, sus vinculaciones continentales* (Mexico City, 1966), 40.

53. On Izapa Stela 5, a seated figure holds a ring-tailed fish with an S-curve cloud hovering immediately above, see Norman (as in note 37), fig. 4.21, Individual 7. Citing unpublished epigraphic research by Nikolai Grube, Freidel, Schele, and Parker note that the Classic Maya "fish-in-hand" glyph denotes the term *tsak*, a Mayan word that signifies 'to conjure clouds' (as in note 5), 436, n. 65.

54. Norman (as in note 37), 91.

55. Stephen D. Houston and David Stuart, "T632 as *muyal*, 'Cloud,'" *Central Tennessean Notes in Maya Epigraphy*, no. 1 (1990).

56. Ralph L. Roys, *The Book of Chilam Balam of Chumayel*, Publication 438, Carnegie Institution of Washington (Washington, D.C., 1933), 96.

57. This remarkable statuette seems to have had, even in recent times, a rather convoluted history. Reportedly taken in 1918 from a Veracruz household where it was being used for a handy punch block, it subsequently served as a Packard automobile hood ornament. After the car had a major accident in British Columbia, the piece was removed and eventually became part of the Guennol Collection. Alastair Martin, "Pardon a Hunter," in *The Guennol Collection*, ed. Ida Elly Rubin, vol. 1 (New York, 1975), xxiii–xxv.

58. In 1992, Kent Reilly first mentioned to me the cloud and rain significance of this Middle Formative relief.

59. See Feuchtwanger (as in note 15), fig. 94.

60. Alfonso Caso and Ignacio Bernal, *Urnas de Oaxaca* (Mexico City, 1952), 25.

61. Karl Lorenzen pointed out to me that the common Postclassic convention of feathered serpent balustrades might involve the concept of the cosmic mountain. Since pyramids were widely considered symbolic mountains in Mesoamerica, the pair of descending feathered serpents flanking the central stairway could depict celestial serpents raised by the pivotal sacred mountain.

62. Coe and Diehl (as in note 13), 393.

63. Grove (as in note 35), 31.

64. In the Chalcatzingo scene, the figure sits in a cave represented as the profile face of the Avian Serpent. Cloud volutes emanating from the cave mouth may portray the breath, or wind, of the Avian Serpent. In Late Postclassic Central Mexico, the wind temple of Ehecatl-Quetzalcoatl was marked with a serpent mouth doorway, see Taube (as in note 29), 68.

65. John Bierhorst, *History and Mythology of the Aztecs: The Codex Chimalpopoca* (Tuscon, 1992), 156–57.

66. Grove, "Chalcatzingo and its Olmec Connection," in *Regional Perspectives*, ed. Sharer and Grove (as in note 19), 134; see also, Virginia M. Fields, "The Iconographic

Heritage of the Maya Jester God," in *Sixth Palenque Round Table, 1986*, ed. Virginia M. Fields (Norman, Okla. 1991).

67. Coe (as in note 10), 114.

68. Michael D. Coe, *The Jaguar's Children: Pre-Classic Central Mexico* (New York, 1965), 14; Joralemon, "A Study of Olmec Iconography" (as in note 1), 91. For Aztec child sacrifice, see Sahagún (as in note 18) bk. 1, 68; bk 2, 1–2.

69. Ponciano Ortiz and María del Carmen Rodríguez, "Olmec Ceremonial Behavior Seen in the Offerings at El Manatí," paper delivered at the Pre-Columbian Symposium at Dumbarton Oaks, Washington, D.C., 1993.

70. F. Kent Reilly, III, this volume, and "Olmec Iconographic Influences on the Symbols of Maya Rulership: An Examination of Possible Symbols," in *Sixth Palenque Round Table, 1986*, ed. Fields (as in note 66), 156.

71. The ballplayer identification has been recently proposed by Mary Miller and Karl Taube, *The Gods and Symbols of Ancient Mexico and the Maya: An Illustrated Dictionary of Mesoamerican Religion* (London and New York, 1993), 158, and independently by Douglas E. Bradley and Peter David Joralemon, *The Lords of Life: The Iconography of Power and Fertility in Preclassic Mesoamerica* (Notre Dame, 1993), 21.

72. For examples of ballplayers wearing Olmec Rain God masks, see Christine Niederberger Betton, *Paleopaysages et Archeologie Pre-urbaine du Bassin de Mexico*, 2 vols. (Mexico City, 1987), fig. 282; Bradley and Joralemon (as in note 71), illus. 1b; Coe and Diehl (as in note 13), fig. 334.

73. See F. Kent Reilly, III, "The Shaman in Transformation Pose: A Study of the Theme of Rulership in Olmec Art," *Record of The Art Museum, Princeton University* 48, no. 2 (1989): 16–17.

74. Peter T. Furst, "The Olmec Were-Jaguar Motif in the Light of Ethnographic Reality," in *Dumbarton Oaks Conference on the Olmec*, ed. Elizabeth P. Benson (Washington, D.C., 1968), 143–74.

75. For views of Portrero Nuevo Monument 1, see Coe and Diehl (as in note 13), figs. 487, 495.

76. Nikolai Grube notes that in one Late Classic Maya snake dance scene from the Usumacinta area, the serpent is epigraphically labeled a "sky snake," Nikolai Grube, "Classic Maya Dance: Evidence from Hieroglyphics and Iconography," *Ancient Mesoamerica* 3 (1992): 212.

77. Claude-François Baudez, "The Maya Snake Dance: Ritual and Cosmology," *Res* 21 (1992): 37–52; Samuel K. Lothrop, "Further Notes on Indian Ceremonies in Guatemala," *Indian Notes* 6 (1929): 1–25; Karl Taube, "Ritual Humor in Classic Maya Religion," in *Word and Image in Mayan Culture*, ed. William Hanks and Donald Rice (Salt Lake City, 1989), 351–82; .

78. On Uaxactun Stela 7, a Late Classic Bearded Dragon appears atop a plumed sky band, recalling the celestial feather bundles of the Formative Olmec.

79. For examples of Olmec Rain God masks, see Lin and Emile Deletaille, *Trésors du Nouveau Monde* (Brussels, 1992), figs. 84, 85; Joralemon; "A Study of Olmec Iconography" (as in note 1), figs. 152–58.

80. Garman Harbottle and Phil C. Weigand, "Turquoise in Pre-Columbian America," *Scientific American* 266, no. 2 (1992): 78–85.

81. Bierhorst (as in note 65), 156–57.

The Olmec Mountain and Tree of Creation in Mesoamerican Cosmology

LINDA SCHELE

Since the work of Miguel Covarrubias and Matthew W. Stirling, the Olmec of the Gulf Coast have been viewed by most scholars as the mother culture of ancient Mesoamerica. Proponents of these views, led by Michael D. Coe, point to the wide distribution of cultural artifacts created in a recognizable style and carrying a common array of symbols as evidence of an Olmec horizon in Mesoamerica during the Early and Middle Preclassic periods. Since the earliest manifestations of this symbol system and its accompanying style have been excavated in Gulf Coast sites, they point to that region as the source of the cultural tradition. Other scholars, led principally by David C. Grove, challenge this view by showing that the widely distributed artifactual arrays in Olmec style were created by artists speaking different languages and living within different cultural traditions.[1] Moreover, they refer to the absence of evidence supporting the existence of a central political authority linking these diverse regions into a larger political structure as proof that there were separate and independent regional cultures that borrowed selectively from the "Olmec" symbol system.

To me, both views are productive ways of thinking about the problem: the "Olmec" were the mother culture of Mesoamerica, but they were not a centrally organized society dominated by a single governing structure. Instead, I prefer the suggestion of F. Kent Reilly, III's, that a Middle Formative

Period Ceremonial Complex unified Mesoamerica from 900 to 500 B.C.[2] This complex included shared cosmology, symbolic arrays, artistic style, and ritual performances that were combined with regional and local versions. In this view, groups from different cultural traditions, speaking different languages, and living in different areas of Mesoamerica adopted both the symbols and the style of art objects first developed by the Olmec on the Gulf Coast and the highlands of Guerrero, and by other groups in different parts of Mesoamerica, such as the Pacific coast of Guatemala and Chiapas. The primary means of ideological transfer among these cultural regions seems to have been small portable objects, mainly made of jade, shell, clay, and, we can deduce, wood. Drawings on boulders and rock faces throughout the Soconusco area of Chiapas and Guatemala also suggest that exotics were carried on trade routes from highlands to lowlands and along pilgrimage routes to and from highland and lowland areas as far south as western El Salvador and central Honduras. Certainly, Olmec-style objects—especially jade—were valued heirlooms and power objects during the Formative period and throughout the remainder of Mesoamerican history.

After spreading through Mesoamerica during the Middle Formative period, these symbols, deities, and cosmology functioned in subsequent Mesoamerican history like a fugal variation on a set of original themes. Covarrubias first showed that early Olmec symbols could be traced from their earliest forms through transformations in the var-

ious cultural traditions that followed.[3] Coe accepted the same premises and connected Olmec and Aztec royal symbolism.[4] Karl A. Taube, in this volume, revisits Covarrubias's original genealogy of rain deities in Mesoamerica. The present paper falls within this same tradition, but I will follow three great cosmological themes—the mountain of creation, the world tree, and the king as the tree—from their earliest forms through the conquest.

THE OLMEC

In his analyses of the Olmec symbol system, Peter David Joralemon first systematized the nomenclature used to refer to Olmec supernaturals.[5] Especially important to the system he proposed was the Las Limas Figure and a series of celts showing a supernatural he designated God I. He identified this supernatural as the central being held by the Las Limas ruler and on the series of celts (fig. 1a–d). He also demonstrated a principle in Olmec art in which the complex detail of a full program could be reduced to a single symbol standing for the whole.

Reilly built upon Joralemon's original classification and identified this god as the personification of the center axis, especially in its form as a tree.[6] In a particularly important insight, he realized that the four seeds regularly occurring in the corners of the composition create the Olmec quincunx symbol, with the tree as its center and the seeds at the four corners of the world (fig. 2a, b). Following Joralemon and Virginia M. Fields, he also demonstrated how the entire composition of the personified crocodile

Frontispiece. Celt with Incisions, 900 – 600 B.C., Río Pesquero, Veracruz. Jade with traces of red pigment, h. 24.8 cm.; w. 10.2 cm. Private collection.

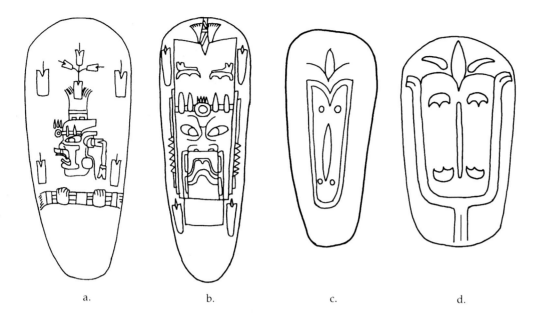

Figure 1. (a) Celt from Río Pesquero; (b) celt from Río Pesquero; (c–d) celts from La Venta Offering 1942-C.

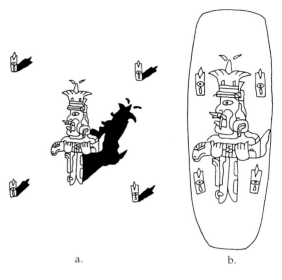

Figure 2. (a) Reilly's cast shadows; (b) celt from Río Pesquero.

tree with its four corner sprouts could be reduced to a simple sprouting seed with the Olmec quincunx inside.[7] Finally, all three researchers deduced that the Olmec ruler was the personification of the world tree.

Fields identified the headdress worn by this deity as the prototype of the Jester God headdress of the Maya.[8] She showed that the four seeds of the composition discussed by Reilly become the four cleft seeds on the headband of this god, while the tree or sprout becomes the central vegetal element (fig. 3a). Using the celt from El Sitio, Guatemala (fig. 3b), she went on to identify the plant as an ear of corn, its kernels clearly delineated and the leaves sitting on either side of it.[9] Many other versions of this deity reveal the maize emerging from the cleft as a sprout before the anatomy of the ear has developed, with both single-unit sprouts and the more mature plant shown.

Matthew Looper and I added to this original identification by demonstrating that the plants coming from these cleft seeds represent monocot (single leaf [figs. 1c; 3c, d]) and dicot (triple leaf [figs. 1d; 3a, b]) plants.[10] Thus, the two types of plants appearing in the Olmec "crown" incorporate the three major cultigens of Mesoamerican agriculture—the monocot maize and the dicot beans and

squash. By the time of the Classic period, the Maya and other Mesoamerican groups reworked the original symbol from a sprouting plant to a flower, but the genetic line of the symbol evolution is clear.

Moreover, I suggested that the bundled sticks carried by Olmec gods and rulers represent cuttings used to reproduce trees both in grafting and planting.[11] In her study of these symbols, Fields indicated that the bound objects are not torches, but banded maize.[12] I think her identification is the most likely one, although others offered include torches, and Grove further associated them with bloodletting because of the pointed shapes in the upper zone of an incised vessel example (fig. 4a; cat. no. 198).[13] However, I think these shapes are just as likely to be emerging sprout formations as perforators. The crowns of some bundles resemble fruits or other plant forms (fig. 4b; cat. no. 200) like the set of greenstone shapes found in the tomb at the center of the Temple of Quetzalcoatl at Teotihuacan. Others, such as the deities of the Teopantecuanitlan monoliths (fig. 4c), have leaflike forms on their crowns.

The extraordinary statue of a Young Lord (cat. no. 193) is depicted holding two scepters in his arms. His arms and legs carry incised designs documenting the supernatural foundation of his political

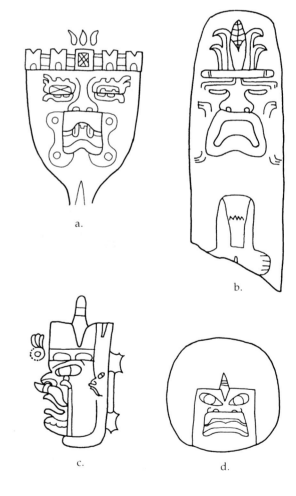

Figure 3. (a) Jade from Las Tuxtlas; (b) celt from El Sitio, Guatemala; (c) celt from La Venta Offering 2; (d) incised plaque from Guerrero.

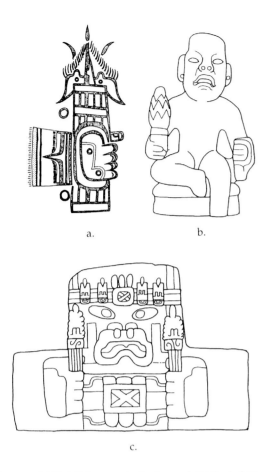

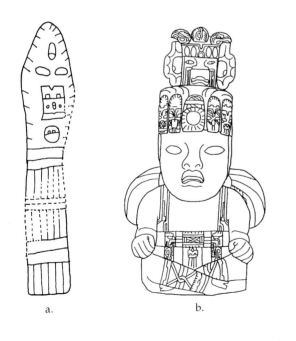

Figure 4. (a) Detail from an incised vessel; (b) Seated Figure; (c) Travertine Monolith, Teopanicaunitlan.

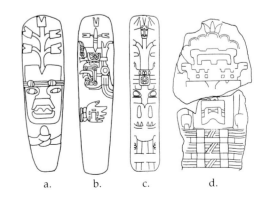

Figure 5. (a) Staff held by the Young Lord; (b) Seated Figure of a Man in the collection of Dumbarton Oaks.

power.[14] The head of the bundle scepter held in his right arm has a ticked contour (fig. 5a), but it also displays in its center one of the cleft-seed symbols and the bound cuttings. I take the presence of this seed icon to support Field's plant identification of the stick-bundle icon. More importantly, the seeds mounted on the headband of a figure in the collection of Dumbarton Oaks, Washington, D.C., have the same ticked contour emerging from the cleft (fig. 5b; see cat. no. 193, figure 3). Since monocot and dicot sprouts rise from these same cleft seeds in other examples, I understand the ticked contour to be another symbol for sprouts.

This bundle of cuttings often occurs alongside an object called a knuckleduster. Such an arrangement is found on an incised vessel, where disembodied hands hold a cuttings bundle in the right and a knuckleduster in the left (fig. 6a). Grove and Rosemary Joyce et al. identified the knuckleduster as a bloodletter.[15] Following this identification, E. Wyllys Andrews suggested that the knuckledusters were large conch shells, probably the Milk Conch, *Strombus costatus*.[16] Olmec figurines regularly depict both humans and supernaturals holding these objects as emblems of authority. If correctly identified, they are evidence that the Olmec rulers and lords carried staffs of cuttings and conch shells as implements of political and religious power (fig. 6b).

A Río Pesquero celt reveals another aspect of Olmec political authority central to an understanding of the evolution of Mesoamerican cosmology. Reilly recognized that the figure on this and other similar celts represents the tree at the center of the cosmos (fig. 7a). He has shown that lines on the legs of the Young Lord represent the crocodile head appearing at the base of many tree images, such as Izapa Stela 25 (fig. 7b). His identification indicates that the Olmec defined their ruler as the embodiment of the world tree.

Fields and Reilly identified other representations of this center tree.[17] Among these, one celt shows a three-branched tree and another a five-branched tree emerging from the cleft-headed god (fig. 8a, b). Fields recognized the image of the tree on Celt 1 from Offering 4 at La Venta. Reilly doubled the image and showed that it represented the three-branched tree rising from the cleft-headed

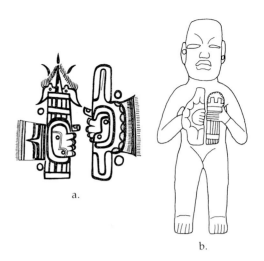

Figure 6. (a) Details from an incised vessel; (b) Standing Figure from San Cristobal Tepotlaxco, in the collection of Dumbarton Oaks.

Figure 7. (a) Celt from Río Pesquero; (b) detail from Izapa Stela 25.

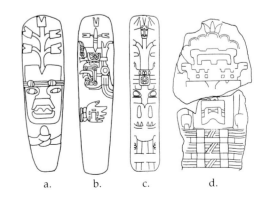

Figure 8. (a) Celt from Río Pesquero; (b) celt, The Metropolitan Museum of Art; (c) doubling of celt fragment from La Venta Offering 4; (d) La Venta Stela 25–26.

god resting on a bundle (fig. 8c). He identified the same bundle and tree on La Venta Stelae 25–26 (fig. 8d) and an opened version of the bundle on an incised vessel.

The raising of this tree played a crucial role in Olmec symbolism. The life-size figure, which once sat in a cleft leading into the crater atop San Martín Pajapán, has human features, anthropomorphic earflares, and a cleft anthropomorphic headdress with its rear surface cut into quadrants by deep notches (fig. 9a). He squats with one leg up and the other under him as he leans forward to grip a pole. Reilly pointed out that one of his hands is below the post and the other above it in exactly the position needed to raise it into vertical position. This being sat on top of the most sacred mountain in the Olmec sacred landscape—a volcano that was probably the source of creation—raising the pole at the center of the cosmos.

The people of La Venta built a replica of a volcano, probably San Martín itself, with their main pyramid (fig. 10), as Robert F. Heizer first argued.[18] Lake Catemaco, the great crater lake at the base of San Martín, must have been seen by the Olmec as a fragment of the primordial sea, and it, too, has its analogue at La Venta in the sunken court with its great serpentine mosaic offerings.[19] A fragment of another probable tree-raising sculpture was also found at La Venta (fig. 9b).[20]

An extraordinary tablet in the Dallas Museum of Art combines all these symbols into one cosmological image (fig. 11a; cat. no.131). Reilly first interpreted this image accurately as a mountain with a tree on its summit surrounded by the four seeds at the corners of the world. The sign above the tree corresponds to the designs on top of an incised vessel (fig. 11b) and on the Humboldt Celt (fig. 11c), which Reilly has identified as a directional sign, most likely "north." If he is correct, the tree represented for the Olmec, as it did for the Maya, a north-south axis. The plaque is framed with a design that may refer either to a plaza space or the four sides of the earth. Below the mountain sits three round objects Reilly and I have independently associated with the three stones mentioned in the accounts of creation at the Classic Maya sites of Quirigua and Palenque. If this correspondence is right, this plaque records the Olmec version of the order of the

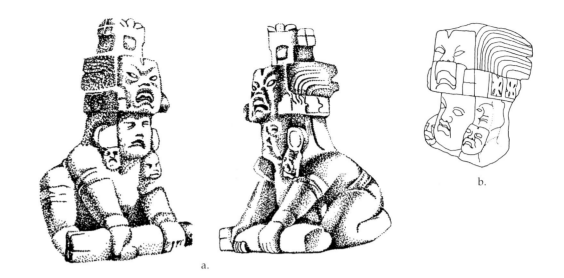

Figure 9. (a) San Martín Pajapán Monument 1; (b) fragment from La Venta Monument 44.

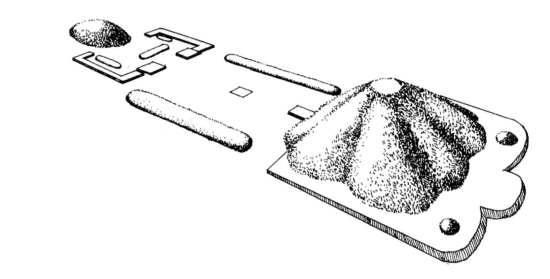

Figure 10. La Venta Complex A. The pyramid (C-1) is an effigy of San Martín Pajapán; the bounded court to the far right is the primordial sea.

cosmos established when the tree of the center was raised over the mountain of creation.

Reilly has also identified another image of the raising of the tree closely associated with a sacred mountain—this time, the cleft mountain at Chalcatzingo. Stela 21 shows a female personage standing with her hands against an upright post bound with horizontal bands mounted with cleft seeds (fig. 12a). This post and the groundline below are marked by diagonal lines and ovals, the diagonals closely resembling the pattern designating "stone" in the Mixtec codices. Reilly has pointed out to me that the Chalcatzingo region was probably

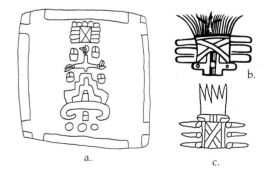

Figure 11. (a) Incised Tablet from the Dallas Museum of Art; (b) detail from an incised vessel; (c) detail from the Humboldt Celt.

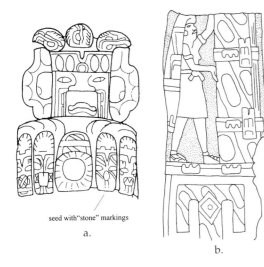

seed with "stone" markings

a.

b.

Figure 12. (a) detail from Seated Figure of a Man in the collection of Dumbarton Oaks; (b) Chalcatzingo Stela 21.

Figure 13. Stucco façade from Group H at Waxaktun, Guatemala. The lower band represents fish swimming in the primordial sea; the lower mask is the mountain of Creation; the upper mask is the human-made Snake Mountain.

a.

b.

c.

Figure 14. (a) Tree from the Sarcophagus lid, Temple of Inscriptions, Palenque; (b) shell from Yaxchilan; (c) detail of the world tree from a Maya pot.

Otomangean-speaking. Although a great time span divides the Chalcatzingo monument and the Mixtec codices, we may have here a very ancient sign for "stone" that survived as a shared feature within the same language family. Moreover, this diagonal pattern also occurs on the inner seed on the right side of the headband of the Dumbarton Oaks figure (fig. 12b). If these identifications are true, the Chalcatzingo monument depicts a stone tree being raised by a Creatrix.

The contrast in the genders of these tree-raisers may represent a pattern that persisted to the time of the conquest. The principal actor in the raising of the world tree and the creation of the cosmos was male in the imagery of Maya and Mixe-Zoque regions and female in the Otomangean and Nahuatl regions. The myths in all these regions have both male and female participants, but they differ according to which gender plays the principal roles.

THE MAYA

The images of this world tree, the creation mountain, and the primordial sea persisted in subsequent cultural traditions in Mesoamerica. In Maya art, one of the earliest manifestations of the mountain of creation was built in Group H at Waxaktun (fig. 13),

an eight-meter-high stucco facade flanking in pairs the stairway of the principal building of a Late Preclassic acropolis.[21] On the lower level, the creation mountain called Yax-Hal-Witz, the "First True Mountain," floats in the primordial sea, with fish swimming in the swirls of the roiling water. On the second level sits the human-made replica of the creation mountain, a pyramid snake mountain marked by a *tzuk*-partition head in its mouth and a vision serpent penetrating from side to side. This is the earliest known example of the snake mountain, Coatepec, which symbolized the sustenance mountain that permeates Mesoamerican architectural symbolism.

In Maya symbolism, some artists emphasized the features of the Yax-Hal-Witz by marking the pyramid mountain with maize god or maize foliation, as at Copan Temple 22. Others focused on the snake mountain aspect of the human-made side, of which the most spectacular examples are the High Priest's Grave and the Castillo at Chichén Itza, but I suspect that many of the pyramids with four directional stairways may be snake mountains.

The Maya also manifested their own version of the world tree, which they called the Wakah-Chan, or "Raised-up Sky" (fig. 14a–c). This tree was, in addition, the Milky Way, stretching from north to

south, with the constellations Sagittarius and Scorpio at its base.[22] The double-headed serpent draped around its arms represents the ecliptic as well as the path of travel between the human world and the sacred world of the gods and the ancestors (fig. 14a, b). The form of the tree can vary from emulating the great ceiba tree to multiple branches growing from a trunk stub. I have associated this latter representation with the tree forms that result from the harvesting of branches for charcoal, house-building, fence-making, and other such uses.[23]

In tracking the cosmic tree through Mesoamerican imagery, Alfredo López Austin assembled references to the tree and its erection at the beginning of the last creation in the *Chilam Balam of Mani* and the *Chilam Balam of Chumayel*.[24] He also called attention to Francisco Nuñez de la Vega's description of the ceibas in central plazas throughout Chiapas: "las raíces de aquella ceiba son por donde viene su linaje."[25] Today, many of the names of the militias among the Cruzob Maya (their equivalent of lineages) are named for trees, and tree metaphors and names play equally important roles among the K'iche' ("Many Trees") and the Kaqchikel in the highlands of Guatemala.

The Classic-period glyph for lineage and its founding member was *ch'ok te na*, "sprout tree house." Moreover, the Maya king was the embodiment of the world tree, and he dressed to show it: the serpent-fretted-sungod apron is, in fact, the trunk of the tree with the branches folded down by its sides; the double-headed serpent held in the ruler's arms shows that he commands the sky and the path of the moving stars; and the divine bird called Itzam Yeh perches on his headdress (fig. 15).[26] This world tree is still central to the origin stories of the Maya of Santiago Atitlan, Guatemala. Robert Carlsen and Martin Prechtel described how the people of the town talk about this ancestral tree:

> [B]efore there was a world (what we would call the "universe"), a solitary deified tree was at the center of all there was. As the world's creation approached, this deity became pregnant with potential life; its branches grew one of all things in the form of fruit. Not only were there gross physical objects like rocks, maize, and deer hanging from the branches, there were also such elements as types of lightning, and even individual segments of time. Eventually this abundance became too much for the tree to support, and the fruit fell. Smashing open, the fruit scattered their seeds; and soon there were numerous seedlings at the foot of the old tree. The great tree provided shelter for the young "plants," nurturing them, until finally it was crowded out by the new. Since then, this tree has existed as a stump at the center of the world. This stump is what remains of the original "Father/Mother" (*Ti Tie Ti Tixel*), the source and endpoint of life.[27]

The people of Santiago Atitlan gave this great central concept of life a physical representation in the main altar of their church:

Figure 15. Quirigua Stela F shows the king Butz'-Tilwi dressed as the world tree.

This altar, constructed when the church was without a resident priest and under full *cofradia* control, is dominated by a mountain carved in wood. To either side of the mountain are carvings of *cofradia* members, complete with their staffs of office and shown ascending the mountain. Atop the mountain is a world tree in the form of a sprouting maize plant. Atitekos believe that as long as the primal ancestral element, as "Flowering Mountain Earth," is "fed," it will continue to provide sustenance. In Atiteko religion, this "feeding" can be literal. For example, some Atitekos will have an actual hole on their land through which offerings are given to the ancestor. In the Tzutujil dialect, this hole is called *r'muxux* ("umbilicus"). More commonly, "feeding" is accomplished through ritual, *costumbres*. For instance, dancing, sacred bundles, burning copal incense, or praying can feed ancestral form.[28]

The cord that spirals around world trees (figs. 14c, 16a) is the pre-Columbian prototype of the Atiteko umbilical cord. I think an Olmec prototype also exists in the snake-headed ropes that hang in the mouths of jaguars in sculptures from La Venta (fig. 16b), Tres Zapotes, and San Lorenzo.

TEOTIHUACAN

This description of the central tree as the source of creation and life was shared by many other peoples in Mesoamerica. The Tepantitla murals in Teotihuacan show a tree emerging from the top of a female goddess (fig. 17). Taube associated this image with the spider woman, a Creatrix found throughout the mythology of Uto-Aztecan-speaking people in North America.[29] Now called the Great Goddess by most Teotihuacan scholars, this being symbolizes the generative source of creation in the Teotihuacan mode. A group of my students in 1982 suggested that the Tepantitla image is in fact a scene of creation.[30] They also proposed that the lower talud scene replicates the scene above with the city of Teotihuacan as the materialization on earth of this creation (fig. 18). I have tested their ideas for a decade and found them to be extraordinarily productive.

The Great Goddess wears a distinct headdress; it is marked here by an owl and in other examples by knives of sacrifice and the hearts and intestines

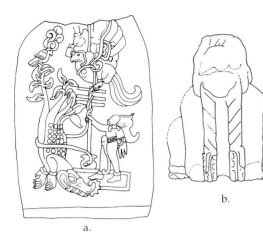

Figure 16. (a) Izapa Stela 25; (b) La Venta Altar 8.

Figure 17. Mural, Tepantitla, Teotihuacan, showing the Great Goddess and the world tree.

are not included in the illustration here), Teotihuacanos cavort in the spaces around the mountain, conducting their daily lives and the sacred rituals that make the world run.[31]

Moreover, as with the Olmec and the Maya, I think the ruler of Teotihuacan was very likely seen as the embodiment of this tree. This idea came to me while another of my graduate students, Nancy Deffenbach, presented an analysis of Atetelco in a 1993 seminar in which she pointed to the special iconography of the mural in the center building of the three in the courtyard. She noted that the net pattern on this wall occurs without mirrors and with blood signs in it. As I watched her presentation, I realized that the person inside the net carries a staff and is dressed like a male human rather than the Great Goddess (fig. 19). He wears her special nose ornament and owl-mounted headdress, but he carries a staff and conch shell, which appear to be instruments of his office. Moreover, these objects replicate, as Reilly pointed out to me in conversa-

Figure 18. The mountain, streams, and lakes from the Talud Panel in the Tepantitla mural. The left half is reconstructed.

Figure 19. Detail of mural, Atetelco, Teotihuacan.

of sacrificial victims. In the Tepantitla mural, she has geometric face markings, round earflares, and a distinctive nose ornament consisting of a bar with multiple toothlike projections hanging from it. Scrolls of blue and red liquid emerge from her body orifices and water drips from her hands; complementary liquids of blood and water flow from her womb to create the sacred liquids of the cosmos.

The tree emerging from her head is composed of two intertwined trunks that branch out into water-seeping flowers. Birds and butterflies flitter among the branches. The tree halves are distinguished by spiders on one side and butterflies on the other. Spiders are generally taken to represent weaving and thus female aspects of creation, while butterflies are associated with the souls of dead

warriors in the later symbolism in central Mexico. If these associations hold also for Teotihuacan, the tree intertwines male and female aspects of creation to create the axis at the center of the world.

The image in the talud below replicates the upper image, but in human space. As a depiction of the natural environment, the mountain represents Cerro Gordo and the other mountains of the valley with springs emerging from their bases. This water flowed from the mountains into the Río San Juan, which ran through cultivated fields to the lakes of the Valley of Mexico. In the human-made world, the mountain is Teotihuacan's Pyramid of the Sun with the four-lobed cave below it, and the water is the channeled part of the San Juan and the lakes are still the lakes. In the full talud (these details

Figure 20. The Teotihuacan ruler/Great Goddess, West Group, Avenue of the Dead, Teotihuacan.

tion, the staffs and conch shells carried by Olmec rulers (fig. 6). Another version of the Teotihuacan image I believe is a ruler rather than the Goddess holds handfuls of sprouting cuttings directly analogous to those held by Olmec kings (figs. 20, 4c). Thus, like the Olmec before them and the Maya contemporary to them, the Teotihuacanos portrayed their ruler as the world tree. This meant a male ruler took on the guise of the Great Goddess, who stood at the center of Teotihuacan's cosmos. Thus, the ruler of Teotihuacan became the embodiment of the tree and the creative principal of the universe, wielding the same symbols of authority as his Olmec predecessors.

The emblems associated with the Goddess/ruler are found in other contexts that support this identification. The Goddess/ruler's nose ornament was discovered in the tomb under the center of the Temple of Quetzalcoatl, exactly where a ruler would have been buried if Teotihuacan followed known Mesoamerican patterns for royal burial. In addition, this nose ornament can be juxtaposed with the eye rings of warriors at Teotihuacan. Perhaps the most important of these juxtapositions occurs on the façade of the Temple of Quetzalcoatl with Taube's recognition of the feathered snake as the serpent of sacred war. Mark Parsons and Taube identified the image attached to the tail of this war serpent as a mosaic headdress.[32] Taube further connected this mosaic headdress to warfare and warriors throughout Mesoamerica, especially in the Maya region. The prototypical image of this headdress at Teoti-

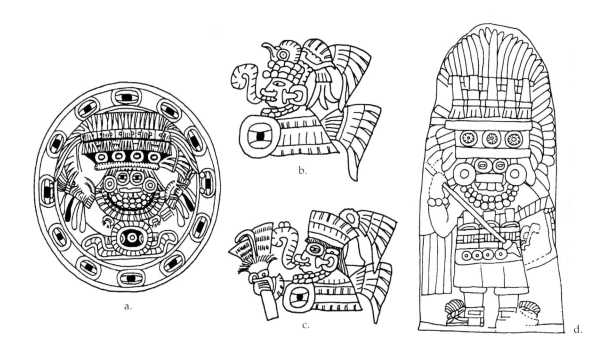

Figure 22. (a) back of mirror, Kaminaljuyu, Guatemala; (b–c) details from a pot in Burial 10, Tikal, Guatemala; (d) Yaxha Stela 11.

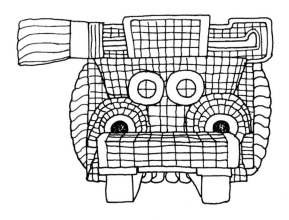

Figure 21. The mosaic headdress, Temple of Quetzalcoatl, Teotihuacan.

huacan has the eye rings of the warrior mounted on its forehead and, as Taube noted, the nose ornament of the Great Goddess hanging under its muzzle (fig. 21). Thus, the symbolism of war combines with the nose piece of the Goddess/ruler on a building that may have contained the burial of a man who wore the nose ornament in his costume. I suspect he was a king, perhaps a ruler who was critically important to the early history of the city—a founder.

These images of the "Teotihuacan ruler" as the Great Goddess-tree are also prominent among Maya images with Teotihuacan affinity. A mirror-back from Kaminaljuyu shows the frontal-view image of a person wearing rings around his eyes and the Great Goddess nose ornament, and holding what appears to be bundles of cuttings (fig. 22a). Several pots from Burial 10 of Tikal, believed to be the tomb of Curl-Snout, also have images of males wearing the eye-rings and nose ornament, one of which wears a mosaic headdress with an owl attached and another, the prototype of the drum-major headdress (fig. 22b, c). And finally, Stela 11 of Yaxha, which is roughly contemporary to the Tikal tomb, shows an armed person wearing the

nose ornament, eye-rings, and tasseled headdress (fig. 22d).

The presence of these Teotihuacan images in the Maya heartland has been assumed by many scholars to signal the dominance of Teotihuacan among Maya kingdoms from A.D. 375 to A.D. 450. I have always resisted this interpretation and sought different explanations for what is clearly an interaction of profound importance to both sides of the exchange. I suggest that the proposed identification of this cluster of symbols—the eye-rings, nose ornament, and warfare—with the Teotihuacan ruler offers an explanation of why the Maya adopted them with such enthusiasm: as images of royalty they reinforced the Maya kings' own power and associated them with a widely distributed complex of war and royalty.

THE MIXTEC

Like the world tree at Teotihuacan, the tree in the Mixtec codices of the Postclassic period is bifurcated. The Mixtec version of creation detailed in the Vindobonensis Codex features the birth tree of

Apoala, which appears twice in the codex, on pages 50 and 37.[33] On page 50, the tree is tended by children of the Mixtec creator couple, 1 Deer and 1 Deer (fig. 23a). Among these children are tree men, a pair of stone men (not shown), and two anthropomorphs, 7 Rain and 7 Eagle, who carry bags toward the tree. A second pair of stone men descends toward it carrying smoking braziers. The tree grows from a plain most researchers have associated with the ethnohistorical myth of the Apoala. The dotted disk with emerging scrolls marks the codical place of creation. The tree, which is white with colored flowers on the ends of its multiple branches, has scrolls of blood emerging from a cut at its base and a curving stream of red flowing from its swollen trunk like blood or an umbilical cord.

As Jill Furst noted, the tree reappears on page 37 with some of the same attendants, including both pairs of stone men and the tree men.[34] The anthropomorphs 7 Eagle and 7 Rain appear twice: first proceeding to the tree in the company of another pair of beings carrying plant cuttings in their hands (not shown), then on either side of the tree as it rises from the feather plain (fig. 23b). The tree now splits open to give birth to a nude man and woman. A severed headed Furst identified as female replaces the bloody tendrils at its base on page 50.[35] Most importantly, the tree's flowers now have pistils and stamen and it is covered with red line patterns. The left side has disks, perhaps spindle whorls, and the right, atlatl javelins. Furst also recognized one side as female and the other as male, similar to the Mixtec analogue of the spider-butterfly sides on the Teotihuacan tree.

The two attendants seem to be striking the tree with odd implements. On the right, 7 Rain holds a tool Alfonso Caso identified as a copper chisel.[36] On the left, 7 Eagle holds one that David Stuart associated with a sculptural tool in a panel from the Palenque region.[37] Furst connected these implements with the scene of the cutting open of the tree in the Mixtec myth Man of Fourteen Strengths.[38] This may be correct, since the tree is clearly split open in order to give birth to the nude man emerging from it. However, I would like to follow Stuart's suggestion that 7 Eagle and 7 Rain are carving the trunk with the red line patterns. In the Maya *Popol Vuh*, objects and people are acti-

a.

b.

Figure 23. The Tree of Life: (a) Vindobonensis Codex 50; (b) Vindobonensis Codex 37.

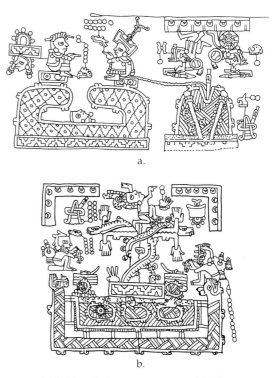

a.

b.

Figure 24. (a) Selden Codex page 1, scene of the lineage founder 11 Water Smoking-Ballcourt being born from a split mountain; (b) Selden Codex page 2, the lineage founder 2 Grass being born from the world tree.

vated by painting and decorating them. I think the sculpting of the tree—the dressing of it with its proper imagery—may activate it so that it can give birth to the first man and woman.

Maarten Jansen suggested that the Vindobonensis nude figures are not so much the Mixtec Adam and Eve as metaphors for the descent of kingship from the founding ancestors.[39] His idea is supported by the reappearance of a birth tree and the split mountain of creation in the depiction of the founding of the first dynasty of Jaltepec in the first two pages of the Selden Codex.[40] Page 1 has a male named 11 Water-Smoking Ballcourt being born from a cleft in a mountain split open by an atlatl dart (fig. 24a); above the mountain hangs 1 Motion, the Mixtec Venus, and 1 Death, the Mixtec sun god, who are ready to fire more javelins. After 11 Water-Smoking Ballcourt's marriage to a woman named 7 Eagle, the couple gives birth to a daughter, who marries 4 Eagle-Ballcourt from Coixtlahuaca. They in turn give birth to a daughter, 8 Rabbit-Sundisk.

A second lineage-founding occurs on page 2, where the flowering Mixtec world tree is split down the middle, but this time it has an eye on its trunk (fig. 24b). The tree sits on a place band floating on the primordial sea, which is contained inside a double-headed stone creature with a snake head on one end and a jaguar on the other. Two priest attendants, 10 Lizard and 10 Flint, make offerings to the tree; a star snake and a cloud snake intertwine with the branches. Three stones float in the water under the tree, in what may be an analogue of the three stones of creation in the Dallas tablet (fig. 11a) and in Maya creation myths. The scene is enframed by star bands. The figure who emerges from the split in the tree remains attached to it by his umbilical cord. The image is clearly one of birth, but the newborn is neither naked nor an unnamed primordial human being: he is 2 Grass, the founder of this lineage. In the next scene (not shown), he sits on a marriage mat with Lady 8 Rabbit-Sundisk, whose grandfather was born from the split mountain. Mixtec sources do not to my knowledge manifest the king as the tree as do the Olmec, Teotihuacano, and Maya, but the relationship among birth from trees, mountains, the Venus and sun twins, and the founding of lineages is explicit.

THE BORGIA CODEX

The Borgia Codex has many trees in it, but the most important one for us is on page 53, at the end of

a.

the pages on which the world directions are set, which shows the tree at the center of the world (fig. 25). The tree rises from the opened belly of a death god who lies on the crocodile mouth of the world. The swirl of the primordial sea creates a disk behind it. The tree is a maize plant with pairs of red and yellow ears emerging from its base, central shaft, and two branches. A quetzal bird sits on its summit.[41] The tree is fertilized and perhaps animated by streams of blood arching from the perforated penises of a Venus god nicknamed Strip-Eye by researchers (on the left) and 5 Flower (on the right). Their self-sacrifice generates the tree. Here, as in the Mixtec version, at least one of the actors is a Venus god.

THE MEXICA

Mexica symbolism is also full of references to the snake mountain, Coatepec, and the world tree. For example, the Templo Mayor in Tenochtitlan was a model Coatepec, a place that was critical to the founding myth of the city and the Aztec right to rule. Miguel León-Portilla examined all the ethnohistorical records about the temple and its meaning, concluding that "the Coatepec complex of symbols became so intrinsically associated with the temple that in several texts the Huey Teocalli is only referred to as the Coatepec."[42] The Azcatitlan Codex shows this relationship in a form that echoes the Late Preclassic stucco at Waxaktun discussed above (figs. 13, 26a). The natural mountain, with snakes emerging from several sides, sits below the temple mountain on which the god Huitzilopochtli stands wielding a spear and shield. To the right is another pyramid with a Xiuhcoatl, or fire snake, which parallels the stairs in an image similar to the Castillo, the "snake mountain" of Chich'en Itza. A war banner and shield stand behind the descending snake.

The world tree also appears in Aztec imagery. The symbol of Tenochtitlan itself is a cactus rising from the clefted belly of the Earth Goddess, who is on her back in water that is at once the lakes of Mexico and the primordial sea (fig. 26b). An eagle sits atop the tree with a serpent in its mouth. While this image derives from the Aztec foundation

Figure 25. The world tree from the Borgia Codex.

b.

Figure 26. (a) Codex Azcatitlan (pl. vi) showing the Aztec capital of Tenochtitlan as Coatepec; (b) Temple Stone, Tenochtitlan, showing the world tree manifested as the cactus and eagle myth of the founding of the city.

myth, it is also a replay of an ancient Mesoamerican symbol for the center axis of the world.

Richard Townsend used a ceremonial mosaic shield from the British Museum, London, to illustrate another version of this central axis in the Aztec cosmos (fig. 27).[43] He identified the world tree on the upper level, the sun symbol with the four directions and the center laid out in the quincunx pattern on the middle level, and the Earth Mother's toothy maw at the base of the image. A serpent rears up from the base of the central axis, spiraling upward as it moves through the levels of the cosmos. Four sky-bearers stand in the corners of the world.

Figure 27. Mosaic Shield from the British Museum. After Townsend (1979).

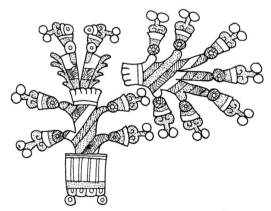

Figure 28. Borbonicus Codex 15 showing Tamochan.

Figure 29. The Tota tree ceremony. After Duran, trans. Heyden and Horcasitas (1971).

López Austin identified another image of the world tree from the Borbonicus Codex (fig. 28).[44] According to him, the broken tree of four colors on page 15 is the place the Aztec called Tamoanchan. Scholars have long recognized that this place name was borrowed from the Maya, but the meaning was not well understood. In the Maya language of Classic Chol, Ta Moan Chan means "At Cloudy Sky." Wak Muyal Chan (or Wak Muwan Chan), "Six-Cloudy-Sky," is one of the names of the tree at the center of the world and the Milky Way in its north-south orientation. In studying the astronomical configurations associated with this Maya creation cosmology and the creation days of August 13 and February 5, I discovered that the most perfect alignments for the astronomical symbolism occurs at 1000 B.C. at 18 degrees north latitude. This is the position of La Venta, San Lorenzo, Tres Zapotes, and Chalcatzingo. I believe that the Milky Way associations with creation mythology and the world tree were set during Olmec times. If I am right, the Aztec Tamoanchan and the Maya Wak Muyal Chan have their roots in Olmec symbolism.

Finally, the Tota tree was erected by the Aztec in ceremonies honoring Tlaloc (fig. 29).[45] A tree on the mountain of Colhuacan was chosen, bound up so that its branches would not be damaged, and cut and carried to the temple of Tlaloc where it was set upright in a deep hole. Four smaller trees were then erected around the Tota, or Father, tree and bound to it by a straw rope. Tassels made of the same straw as the ropes hung from them as symbols of the penance and harshness of the lives of those who served the gods. The ceremony ended with the sacrifice of a child and the depositing of the Tota in Pantitlan, the whirlpool at the center of the lakes. Today, this setting up of the Tota tree is reflected in the erection of the ceiba tree by the Cruzob Maya of Quintana Roo and the Volador ceremonies throughout Mexico and Guatemala. The erection of world trees was probably a pan-Mesoamerican ritual of ancient origin.

CONCLUSION

In this study, I have taken two themes—the world tree and the mountain of creation—central to the cosmology of the Olmec and other Early and Middle Formative peoples and shown how they remained at the heart of Mesoamerican ideology until the conquest—and still do, even today. Rex Koontz has detailed their function at other sites, including El Tajin and Xochicalco,[46] while Maria Elena Bernal Garcia has traced other parts of the cosmology through Mesoamerican cultural history.[47] Taube and Freidel have shown similar development histories with other symbol complexes. In a very real way, the Olmec and their contemporaries were the mother culture of Mesoamerica. As they created an array of symbols to define the sacred nature of the cosmos and the relationship of political authority and the human community to it, they established the basic themes that continued at the heart of Mesoamerican cosmological and political thought in all their successor cultures. I surmise that much of the mythology associated with this cosmology descended from far more ancient ideologies evolved in the context of both hunter-gatherer and early agricultural societies. Nevertheless, the Early and Middle Formative cosmology established the themes for the great cultural fugue that is Mesoamerican cultural history. These voices still sound today among the many indigenous communities in Mexico, Guatemala, Belize, Honduras, and El Salvador.

1. Many of these questions are debated in *Regional Perspectives on the Olmec*, ed. Robert J. Sharer and David C. Grove (Cambridge, 1989).

2. F. Kent Reilly, III, "Visions to Another World: Art, Shamanism, and Political Power in Middle Formative Mesoamerica," Ph.D. diss., University of Texas at Austin, 1994.

3. Covarrubias argued this in many publications, but the principal one in English is *Indian Art of Mexico and Central America* (New York, 1957).

4. Michael D. Coe, "Olmec Jaguars and Olmec Kings," in *The Cult of the Feline* (Washington, D.C., 1972), 1–18.

5. David Joralemon's work is published in "A Study of Olmec Iconography," *Studies in Pre-Columbian Art and Archaeology*, no. 7 (Washington, D.C., 1971) and "The Olmec Dragon: A Study in Pre-Columbian Iconography," in *Origins of Religious Art and Iconography in Preclassic Mesoamerica*, ed. Henry B. Nicholson (Los Angeles, 1976), 27–71.

6. Reilly's work appears in "The Ecological Origins of Olmec Symbols of Rulership," Master's thesis, University of Texas at Austin, 1987; "Olmec Iconographic Influences on the Symbols of Maya Rulership: An Examination of Possible Sources," in *Sixth Palenque Round Table, 1986*, ed. Virginia M. Fields (Norman, Okla., 1991), 151–66; "Cosmos and Rulership: The Function of Olmec-Style Symbols in Formative Period Mesoamerica," informal paper prepared for the *First Sibley Family Symposium on World Traditions of Culture and Art, The Symbolism of Kingship: Comparative Strategies around the World*, University of Texas at Austin, April 18–21, 1991.

7. Virginia M. Fields first analyzed the iconography of God GI in "Political Symbolism among the Olmecs," paper prepared for a seminar, Department of Art History, University of Texas at Austin, 1982.

8. Fields worked on the origin of the Jester God and other important political iconography in "Political Symbolism among the Olmecs" (as in note 7) and "The Origins of Divine Kingship among the Lowland Classic Maya," Ph.D. diss., University of Texas at Austin, 1989.

9. One of the Río Pesquero celts points toward two other aspects of Olmec sprout symbolism. This celt has its four seeds marked with the images of eyes. I spoke with Brian Stross about homophonies in the Mixe-Zoquean languages that might relate to this appearance of eyes. He informs me that the proto-Mixe-Zoquean term for "eye" is *wi tam*, "face seed." This usage is consistent with Mayan languages and, we suspect, with most Mesoamerican languages.

10. Matthew Looper published his observations in "Observations on the Morphology of Sprouts in Olmec Art," *Texas Notes on Precolumbian Art, Writing, and Culture*, no. 58 (Austin, Tex., 1994). I presented these arguments in "Sprouts and the Early Symbolism of Rulers in Meso-america," a paper delivered at the symposium held in connection with the exhibition *Die Welt der Maya*, in Hildesheim, Germany, November 1992. Looper informed me the terms monocot (monocotyledons) and dicot (dicotyledons) refer to the subclasses of angiosperms or flowering plants. These subclasses have very different forms that effect the way they are represented in imagery.

For example, the embryo of a monocot seed has only one seed leaf, or cotyledon, while that of a dicot has two. Other differences are that monocot leaves have parallel veins and smooth sides, while dicot leaves have branching and rebranching veins and lobed or indented edges. The parts of monocot flowers—including petals, leaves, stamen, pistils—exist in threes or multiples of three, while those of dicots occur in fours and fives or their multiples.

Looper also explained to me that a monocot sends a single shoot up through the ground, and, since the leaves grow and unfold in a spiral pattern, no two leaves can emerge parallel to each other on the stem. Grasses, including maize, are monocot. The single-shoot icons are maize, just as Fields originally proposed. On the other hand, dicot seeds send up two cotyledons. The first leaf emerges between them to make a trileaf form in the earliest sprout stage. This yields both the trifurcated and bifurcated forms of the central icon. The bifurcated form represents the sprout before the first leaf emerges between the cotyledons and the trifurcate represents the sprout after it emerges. Most interesting, both beans and squash, the other two members of the Mesoamerican agricultural triad, are dicots. In fact, squash, with the indented leaves typical of dicots, is clearly represented at Chalcatzingo in the sculpture sequence associated with Relief 1.

11. Schele (as in note 10).

12. Fields (as in note 7).

13. Michael Coe ventured this identification in *The Jaguar's Children: Pre-Classic Central Mexico*, (New York, 1965). David Grove also argued this identification in "'Torches,' 'Knuckle-Dusters' and the Legitimization of Formative Period Rulership," *Mexicon* 9 (1987): 60–65. Rosemary Joyce, et al. presented this interpretation in "Olmec Bloodletting: An Iconographic Study," in *Sixth Palenque Round Table, 1986*, ed. Fields (as in note 6), 143–50. Both the Grove article and Joyce et al. associate the object with bloodletting rituals.

14. Reilly presented detailed arguments on the political meaning of the images in "The Ecological Origins of Olmec Symbols of Rulership" (as in note 6) and "Cosmos and Rulership" (as in note 6).

15. This identification was made in Grove (as in note 13) and Joyce et al. (as in note 13).

16. E. Wyllys Andrews made this identification in "Spoons and Knuckle-Dusters in Formative Mesoamerica," a paper delivered at the "III Texas Symposium, Olmec, Izapa, and the Development of Maya Civilization," Texas Meeting on Maya Hieroglyphic Writing, Austin, Tex., 1987.

17. Fields (as in note 7) and Reilly in "The Ecological Origins of Olmec Symbols of Rulership" (as in note 6), "Cosmos and Rulership" (as in note 6), and "Olmec Iconographic Influences on the Symbols of Maya Rulership" (as in note 6).

18. Robert F. Heizer's excavations are published in "New Observations on La Venta," in *Dumbarton Oaks Conference on the Olmec October 28th and 29th, 1967*, ed. Elizabeth Benson (Washington, D.C., 1968), 9–40.

19. Reilly made this identification in "Enclosed Ritual Space and the Watery Underworld in Formative Period Architecture: New Observations on the Function of La Venta Complex A," in *Seventh Palenque Round Table, 1989* (in press).

20. C. William Clewlow, Jr., published this fragment in "A Comparison of Two Unusual Olmec Monuments," *Contributions of the University of California Archaeological Research Facility*, no. 8 (Berkeley, 1970), 35–40.

21. The most complete publication on this building to date is Juan Antonio Valdés, "El Grupo H de Uaxactún: evidencias de un centro de poder durante el Preclásico Temprano," *Memorias el Segunda Coloquio International de Mayistas, Vol. 1* (Mexico City, 1989), 603–24. The interpretation is discussed in Linda Schele, David Freidel, and Joy Parker, *Maya Cosmos: Three Thousand Years on the Shaman's Path* (New York, 1993), 139–43.

22. This identification was first made by the present author in the *Workbook for the XVIth Maya Hieroglyphic Workshop at Texas, with Commentaries on the Group of the Cross at Palenque* (Austin, Tex., 1992). Full details and the context in which the Milky Way operated were expanded in Schele et al. (as in note 21), 59–122.

23. Schele (as in note 10).

24. Alfredo López-Austin presented his ideas in "El Arbol cosmico en las tradición Mesoamericana," *iichiko intercultural*, no. 5 (1993).

25. A new edition of Fray Francisco Nuñez de la Vega's *Constituciones diocesanas de obispado de Chiapa* has been published in *Fuentes para el estudio de la cultura Maya*, no. 6 (Mexico City, 1988).

26. The present author and Mary Miller made this observation in *The Blood of Kings: Dynasty and Ritual in Maya Art* (New York, 1986), 77.

27. Robert Carlsen and Martin Prechtel, "The Flowering of the Dead: An Interpretation of Highland Maya Culture," *Man*, n.s. (1991), 26–27.

28. Carlsen and Prechtel describe this altar and how the cofradistas came to carve it in ibid. Cofradia are organizations that care for the statues of saints, oversee associated rituals, pageants, and maintain the traditional customs of the highland Maya.

29. Karl A. Taube, "The Teotihuacán Spider Woman," *Journal of Latin American Lore* 9 (1984): 107–89.

30. This interpretation was first presented by a team of students working in a seminar on "The Transition from Preclassic to Classic Times," held in 1982 at the University of Texas at Austin. Elements of the full interpretation were subsequently presented in several of the seminar papers, including Amy Oakland, "Teotihuacan: The Blood Complex at Atetelco"; Dorie Reents-Budet, "Pre-classic Development in the Valley of Teotihuacan and Teotihuacan and Maya Contacts as Evidenced in the Maya Iconographic Programs"; and Mark Parsons, "Three Thematic Complexes in the Art of Teotihuacan." These three papers remain some of my primary sources for the interpretation of Teotihuacan art.

31. For a detailed study of these activities, see Esther Pasztory, *The Murals of Tepantitla, Teotihuacan* (New York, 1976).

32. Mark Parsons made the argument in "Three Thematic Complexes in the Art of Teotihuacan," a seminar paper at

the University of Texas at Austin, 1985. Karl A. Taube discussed the same idea and identified the feathered serpent as a war serpent in "The Temple of Quetzalcoatl and the Cult of Sacred War at Teotihuacan," *Res* 22 (1992): 53–87.

33. The tree of Apoala is discussed extensively by Jill Leslie Furst, *Codex Vindobonensis Mexicanus I: A Commentary* (Albany, 1978) and Maarten E. R. G. N. Jansen, *Huisi Tacu, estudio interpretativo de un libro mixteca antiguo: Codex Vindobonensis Mexicanus I* (Amsterdam, 1983).

34. Furst (as in note 33), 132–34.

35. Ibid., 135.

36. Alfonso Caso, *Reyes y reinos de la Mixteca*, 2 vols. (Mexico City, 1979).

37. David Stuart made this identification in "A New Carved Panel from the Palenque Area," *Research Reports on Ancient Maya Writing*, no. 32 (Washington, D.C., 1990).

38. Furst (as in note 33), 135.

39. Jansen (as in note 33), 110.

40. My interpretation of these pages derives from a seminar given by Robert Williams at the University of Texas at Austin in 1993 and from the study groups on the Mixtec codices held under the direction of Robert Williams and John Pohl at the Texas Meetings in 1992–94.

41. Birds in the Borgia Codex are sometimes difficult to identify, but the type of crest, detail of feathers, color, and other features of this bird are similar to those long identified by Borgia scholars. Eagles have different kinds of crests and color patterns on their feathers.

42. Miguel León-Portilla, "The Ethnohistorical Record for the Huey Teocalli of Tenochtitlan," in *The Aztec Templo Mayor*, ed. Elizabeth Boone (Washington, D.C., 1987).

43. Richard Townsend, "State and Cosmos in the Art of Tenochtitlan," *Studies in Pre-Columbian Art and Archaeology*, no. 20 (Washington, D.C., 1979).

44. López-Austin (as in note 24).

45. This ceremony is described in Fray Diego Duran, *Book of the Gods and Rites and the Ancient Calendar*, trans. Fernando Horcasitas and Doris Heyden (Norman, Okla., 1971), 162–63.

46. Rex Koontz, "Aspects of Founding Central Places in Postclassic Mesoamerica," in *Cosmology and Natural Modeling Among Aboriginal American Peoples* (Austin, Tex., 1993).

47. Maria Elena Bernal-Garcia, "Carving Mountains in a Blue/Green Bowl: Mythological Urban Planning in Mesoamerica," Ph.D diss., University of Texas at Austin, 1993.

The Olmec World

RITUAL AND RULERSHIP

Glossary of Olmec Motifs

The Olmec Dragon

The Olmec Dragon is the principal zoomorphic supernatural in Olmec art. The features of the dragon are a composite of the crocodilian and harpy eagle, which endow it with the power to navigate the land, water, and air, the three levels of the cosmos. The eyes, often surmounted by flame eyebrows derived from the plumage of the harpy eagle, are trough-shaped from the front and L-shaped in profile. The nose is broad and flattened and the gum line of the upper jaw is shown with downturned brackets. The dragon is usually depicted without a lower jaw and teeth. When viewed from the front, the maw of the dragon is represented by a rectangular bracket, and is associated with caves and entrances to the underworld. The creature's limbs are sometimes represented by the hand-paw-wing motif, a composite of human and animal forms. The Olmec Dragon is often represented *pars pro toto*, in abbreviated form by an abstracted motif based on a single feature.

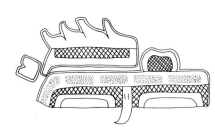

Olmec Dragon — front view

Olmec Dragon — profile view

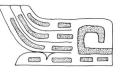

hand-paw-wing motif

flame eyebrows

L-shaped eyes

downturned gum brackets

trough-shaped eyes

The Olmec Supernatural

The Olmec Supernatural, the principal anthropomorphic denizen of the supernatural world, controls the rain and the growth of maize. It may be represented as an infant were-jaguar, diminutive and with a toothless upper gum, and is identified with agricultural regeneration. The forehead is cleft, eyes almond-shaped, and nose broad and flattened. The wide, trapezoidal mouth with flaring upper lip is turned down at the corners. The creature is often depicted with a headdress, which may be cleft, comprising a headband with two dots or nodules and two crenellated elements that hang to either side of the face. The Olmec Supernatural may be represented *pars pro toto* and is often shown in profile.

were-jaguar

forehead with cleft and almond-shaped eyes

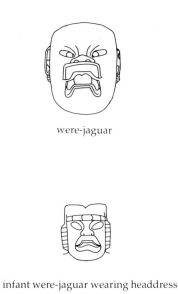

infant were-jaguar wearing headdress

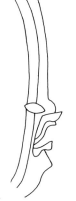

profile motif

headdress with cleft and two nodules and two crenellated earflaps

The Terrestrial Realm

The surface of the earth is represented by the back of the Olmec Dragon, the dragon's gum brackets, an inturning gum bracket, or a single or double groundline. The cleft, a symbol for which many interpretations have been offered, is most likely an abstraction drawn from nature representing organic growth such as corn leaves, the opening of the parted earth, or a husk from which a sprout or cob emerges, symbolizing passage from one state to another, from the natural to the supernatural. The motif of the double merlon may be drawn from the crenellated enclosures of sacred precincts and, like the cleft, may represent the passage between the natural and supernatural realms.

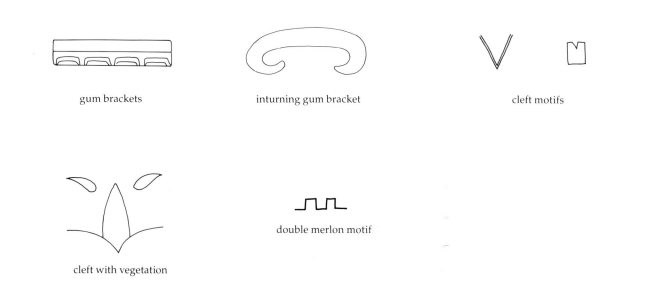

gum brackets

inturning gum bracket

cleft motifs

cleft with vegetation

double merlon motif

The Sky Realm

Representations of avians or avian motifs such as wings or talons symbolize the sky realm and flight to the supernatural world. Crossed-bands motifs are also symbols of the sky and identify the wearer or object with the center of the sky or cosmos. Diamond motifs with straight or concave sides may represent stars and the celestial sphere. The lazy-S or scroll represents clouds or water; exclamation-point motifs are symbols of rain.

avian talon

diamond motifs

crossed-bands motif

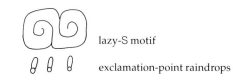

lazy-S motif

exclamation-point raindrops

The Underworld

The underworld is the watery realm represented by the crocodilian or the Olmec Dragon, aquatic creatures, shells, or circles. Ceramic and stone objects in the form of water creatures placed in Middle Formative burials identified the grave within the watery underworld.

shark

shell with circles

The *Axis Mundi*, the World Tree, and Maize

The *axis mundi* is at the center of the three cosmic realms. Represented as either a symbolic maize plant or other vegetative motif, it is sometimes surrounded by four sprouting maize seeds, symbols of the four corners of the earth. This five-point cosmic configuration may be represented by the four-dots-and-bar motif. The ruler may be represented in symbolic costume as the world tree, crowned by a headdress with sprouting maize motifs, thus proclaiming and validating his power to unify the cosmos and, as the *axis mundi*, the conduit between the natural and supernatural realms. Vegetative symbolism may be abbreviated to a trefoil motif, probably derived from the parting leaves and corn silk at the top of the husk of maize.

Vegetation and maize are also represented by bundles, sometimes bound, shown singly or with the "knuckleduster" motif, identified as a cut conch shell. The bundles have been referred to as "torches," are associated with bloodletting, and are often carried by "fliers" or shamanic rulers as they travel through the supernatural portal.

ruler costumed as the world tree
surrounded by four maize seeds

vegetative bundle or "torch"

"knuckleduster"

four-dots-and-bar motif

sprouting vegetation

Rocks and Minerals Employed by the Olmec as Carvings

George E. Harlow

Ascribing meaningful and correct labels to natural carving materials is important in the study of lithic artifacts. In addition to determining the constitution of a material, labeling typically requires sifting through a complex web of overlapping jargon and nomenclatures from various fields, including petrology, mineralogy, archaeology, art history, conservation, and the building trades. The one or two words finally selected are rarely satisfactory to all parties, so a definition of terms is necessary. One term, *jade*, with which I am especially acquainted, is particularly problematic. Another, greenstone, is commonly used for a variety of green rocks. Both of these terms are discussed below.

Without a microscopic analysis of a sliced sample, a ticklish endeavor with a priceless artifact, determining carving material is subject to error. Even then, the precise rock name, thus yielded, may be meaningless except to specialists. A level of understanding somewhere between the specialist and the layman is preferred. My goal here is to provide a working list of material types using the fewest number of names possible. Since most of the samples were examined without the aid of a petrographic microscope (used for examining sections of rocks), chemical analysis, or other definitive techniques, this simplification is also inevitable. Some microsamples were studied by X-ray diffraction, a definitive, mineral identification technique, hence the artifacts from which these come are partially or well constrained. The trained eye, while powerful, can be deceived, and mistakes may have been made in my analysis, particularly in the cases of materials with microscopic or smaller constituent grains and/or deceptively similar appearance and properties belonging to more common rocks. Though representative of Olmec carvings as a whole, the following list of materials, which covers the broad categories encountered in this volume, is not comprehensive.

Albitite: A medium-hard rock composed predominantly of albite, a common sodium feldspar. The white feldspar matrix of visibly discernible to microscopic grains can be pigmented green by minor disseminations of actinolite, diopside, or chlorite, or various ochre shades by oxides (rusts) of iron and manganese. Albitite is a common, lesser-quality cultural jade in Middle America without the durability of true jades.

Basalt: A common, hard, black igneous rock found as solidified outpourings from volcanoes and rifts. Variations can be slightly green, gray, or brown. Empty vesicles or distinctive vitreous crystals can be found in the otherwise microcrystalline rock.

Breccia: A rock composed of angular fragments naturally cemented together. The term is usually used in combination with a descriptor of the rock type or origin, e.g., greenstone breccia.

Chloromelanite: A black pyroxene mineral similar to jadeite in its properties and potential for forming a dense, durable rock used as jade. The rock form is blue black to green black and typically shows veining. There is a continuum of materials between chloromelanite and metabasite in Middle American jades.

Compacted Clay or Claystone: A soft carving stone composed of clay minerals. Colors are typically gray to green or tan but, because of the absorbent nature of clays, can darken with handling or application of pigments or oils. Claystones can be evenly colored, banded, or speckled.

Granite: An overall light-colored (gray to tan to pink), hard igneous rock with grains identifiable to the naked eye. Quartz and one or two feldspars (typically orthoclase and a sodic plagioclase) are the distinctive constituents; black minerals such as hornblende or biotite are typical—while low in abundance they provide a "salt and pepper" texture to some granites.

Greenstone: A medium-to-dark (leek) green, usually moderately soft rock of such fine grain size that little else can be said; a catchall term for green rocks when a better term is not known. Geologically, greenstone denotes a low-grade (low temperature, low pressure) metamorphic rock derived from an iron-rich precursor, typically a basaltic rock; the color is usually derived from an abundance of a chlorite mineral.

Hard rock: A rock with an aggregate Mohs's hardness of approximately six or above. The distinction is based on the difficulty of abrasion and polishing relative to quartz, the most common abrasive and tool material, which has a hardness of 7; and jadeite jade, the abundant hardstone carving and tool with a hardness of 6–6.5. Hard stones require considerable effort and man hours to fashion without the use of harder abrasives (e.g., emery or diamond), which were unknown in pre-Columbian America.

Jade: A lapidary term that describes two distinctly different kinds of supremely durable carving materials used for over three thousand years: nephrite and jadeite. In Middle America the overarching term "cultural jade" has been applied to materials employed in a similar fashion to or in place of the finer jadeite jade, including albitite, green mica rock, and possibly chrysoprase. Other materials used like jade (or as substitutes) worldwide include serpentine, green chalcedonies besides chrysoprase, green jasper, vesuvianite, thulite, green grossular rock, and, occasionally, metamorphic greenstones.

Jadeite: The true jade of Middle America; the original material to which the term *jade* is applied in Western culture. Jadeite, *sensu stricto*, is a mineral species in the pyroxene family with nominal composition $NaAlSl_2O_6$, and the rock form where jadeite is predominant is correctly termed jadeitite (the technical rock name) or jadeite jade. In a pure state jadeite is white but chemical substitution of iron yields green to blue-green coloring. Emerald green color requires substitution of some chromium for aluminum. Jadeite jade is a hard, dense stone, among the most durable of rocks, and an excellent, often beautiful carving material. A very rare rock, it is formed at high pressure in abundance in only a handful of localities worldwide; the Motagua Valley of Guatemala is the only source identified so far in Middle America. It occurs in a variety of green to blue-green to gray hues ranging to almost white in Middle America. Among the most splendid varieties is the "Olmec" or "Olmec blue-green," which is pale to deep blue green, slightly to moderately translucent, usually with light-colored turbid or cloudy spots in the translucent matrix. As the name suggests, this jade, which is almost absent, for example, among Maya jades, is typical of fine Olmec jades. The source of Olmec jadeite jade, probably Guatemala, is still in dispute. Alleged sources in Guerrero have not been described in any detail or verified geologically. See Frederick W. Lange, ed., *Precolumbian Jade: New Geological and Cultural Interpretations* (Salt Lake City, 1993), 378, for a more complete discussion.

Lapilli tuff: A volcanoclastic rock composed of small fragments, typically rounded, thrown out in a volcanic eruption. Usually dark gray to tan, it is easy to shape in to pieces, breaking or separating along the lapilli boundaries.

Marble: A moderately soft coarse- to fine-textured metamorphic rock composed primarily of calcite. White in its pure form, marbles are naturally pigmented to any color and may show planar or undulating "marble" banding and patterns or cross-cutting veins with different colors and texture. Sometimes limestone, a sedimentary rock constituted primarily of calcite, is called marble, and in the building stone trades marble covers all non-igneous rocks and granite covers the rest.

Metabasalt or metabasite: A basalt or basaltic rock that has been metamorphosed (modified geologically by deep burial). The Middle American materials usually are a very dark green to blue black rock related to and found with true jade. These metabasalts are hard and have even greater toughness and durability than basalt. They contain a blue-black amphibole and dark green omphacite or chloromelanite (pyroxenes similar to jadeite, also geologically formed at high pressure). Contemporary lapidaries refer to the Middle American metabasite as "black jade."

Mica Rock: A rock composed of one or more mica minerals. Among cultural jades it is a soft fine-grained rock with apple to emerald green color composed entirely of ferroan and/or chromian muscovite mica. Sometimes this material has been called fuchsite, which is a particular variety of green chromian muscovite; the variety attribution may or may not be correct.

Nephrite: A hard massive rock consisting of felted, intergrown, fiberlike crystals of the minerals tremolite and/or actinolite, $Ca_2(Mg,Fe)_5Si_8O_{22}(OH)_2$, members of the amphibole family of minerals. It is the toughest known rock, the classic jade of China, and unknown in Mesoamerica.

Omphacite: A pyroxene mineral intermediate in composition between jadeite and diopside $CaMgSi_2O_6$ (or hedenburgite $CaFeSi_2O_6$), usually conspicuous by its medium to dark green color (also an indicator of high-pressure formational conditions). It is a common component of metabasites and a minor component of some jadeitites.

Onyx marble: A fine-grained banded form of calcite or limestone (the term is a strange misnomer because it is neither onyx—flat banded agate—nor marble—it may be calcite but is not a metamorphic rock). This soft lapidary material is usually translucent white to tan but can be stained various colors.

Quartzite: A very hard rock constituted primarily of quartz, and, like albitite, can be pigmented by minor amounts of other minerals gray, green, brown, ochre, and other colors. Because it is composed of quartz (Mohs' hardness of 7), this stone requires laborious slow grinding to fashion without an abrasive harder than quartz, such as emery, which was unknown in pre-Columbian Middle America.

Serpentine or serpentinite: A popularly used, moderately soft, fine-grained black to green to bluish rock composed primarily of one or more of the three common serpentine minerals: chrysotile, lizardite, and antigorite—nominally $(Mg,Fe)_3Si_2O_6(OH)_4$. Serpentinite, the proper lithologic term, is a metamorphic rock formed from numerous possible igneous precursor rocks rich in magnesium and iron. Textures may mimic the precursor with apparently large included crystals, veining is very common, and alteration (both geologic and post manufacture) can yield blotchiness with ochre staining and even near-white bleaching. Antigorite rocks can be semi-translucent with dark green to black color. Varieties of serpentinite are nearly as commonly used as jadeite jade for Olmec carvings observed here.

Soft Rock: Rocks with an aggregate Mohs' hardness below 6, which are easily and quickly worked compared to hard rocks (see hard rock for comparison).

Steatite or Soapstone: A very soft, usually fine-textured rock formed of talc. Colors range from white to gray to apple green to black with possible ochre to black staining patinas; the luster is usually waxy. Inclusions of other minerals like pyrite or its rusty oxidation products are common. A curious feature of some steatite artifacts is tooth marks suggesting being bitten or eaten. This feature may relate to a behavior of animals (and humans) in tropical environments known as lithophagy, where clays are eaten for the nutritional potassium and sodium they can provide.

Volcanic or Volcano-clastic Rock: A non-specific term for rocks formed by volcanic processes either as a hardened lava, like basalt, but of a paler color so that a specific rock name is not readily assigned, or as an air-fallen or water-deposited ash or pumaceous rock. These rocks can be full of vesicles and soft pieces that make them much softer or more easily fashioned than solid basalts.

Catalogue of the Exhibition

Introduction

Olmec art was the symbolic means by which the peoples of Formative period Mesoamerica visualized their ritual and spiritual relationship with the supernatural. The mediator in this relationship was the shaman or ruler who claimed shamanic power. Whether ministering to the quotidian needs of a village, effecting cures and divinations, or as the ritual performer resplendent in symbolic costume in the sacred precincts of the great ceremonial centers, the shaman ensured the well-being and continuity of the community through his power of access to the supernatural. That well-being and continuity rested on a fundamental issue, sustenance. All Olmec ritual leads to and ultimately converges on the maize and the rain on which the harvest depends.

The shamanic ruler journeyed to the supernatural world to propitiate and manipulate the cosmic forces that determined the harvest. Through transformation into a nagual, the animal alter ego or spirit companion, or into the world tree or *axis mundi,* which linked the three levels of the shamanic cosmos, the shaman became the conduit between the earthly and supernatural realms.

In Olmec art we witness the creation of an archetypal style. In comparison to that of the Maya, the Olmec style may be characterized as more sculptural and iconic than pictorial and narrative. The later, more discursive and anecdotal tradition may be a correlation of the writing system developed by the Classic period Maya. The Olmec developed a more encoded symbol system charged with the appositions of perceived and unseen reality. Transformation is the central mystery of Olmec ideology and ritual, and informs

the art style at its most fundamental level. *Pars pro toto* images reduced to increasingly abstract motifs; the declension of symbols; the absence or vacancy of attributes; and the symbolic significance of a void embody and are completed in the reality of the supernatural. Images and symbols magically transform and empower the ritual object as the medium, and the shamanic ruler as the locus of access to the supernatural world.

Transformation is the narrative subject of Olmec art and can only be made visible in intervals or stages, as it is in representations of figures changing into jaguars. Less explicit depictions of transformation are encoded in figures in ritual postures and by their gestures. The sequence of a ritual action may be represented by figures in the same pose but with different attributes; an infant or a bundle of vegetation similarly cradled in the arms of ritual performers may be understood as stages in the transformation of the sacrificial victim into the harvest. The central motif of the maize plant is transformed in stages of growth from germinating seeds and sprouts emerging from the kernel or earth and the cob from the husk, into the symbolic world tree. The representation of infants, fetuslike figures, young birds, and infant were-jaguars, signs of nascent life and the cycle of regeneration, are the symbolic equivalents of seeds and sprouts, signs of agricultural renewal.

All art styles that extend over time and geographical areas evolve and are subject to regional interpretations, as are the systems of beliefs and ritual practices for which art styles are created. Centuries may separate the colossal heads and monuments of the Gulf

Coast ceremonial centers and the portable objects in greenstone and jade. We have no visual record or system of language from which we can reconstruct causes or events to which we can attribute such a dramatic change in the scale and physiognomic types of the Olmec ideal of rulership. The monuments of the ceremonial centers and the portable objects found throughout Formative period Mesoamerica, however, reflect such a consistent mode of representation and system of symbols that despite regional expressions one can speak of an Olmec style. The great discovery of the peoples of the Formative period was the power of images to embody, codify, and communicate a shamanic ideology, ritual system, and political charter. Through portable objects the style was diffused, absorbed, and adapted by other peoples according to their own traditions and social and political development, thereby participating in what was, in effect, a far-flung but cohesive ceremonial complex. The interpretation of the ritual of the Formative period, its ideological foundation and political implications, provides insight into how the Olmec saw themselves within their world and the forces that shaped their lives.

The thematic organization of the catalogue was determined in collaboration with Carolyn E. Tate and F. Kent Reilly, III, consulting curators, and their research, writings, and interpretations are the bases for the introductory sections and individual entries. Contributions also have been made by Gillett G. Griffin, Matthew H. Robb, and Karl A. Taube.

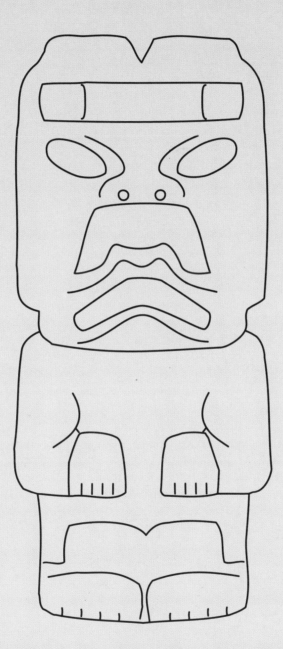

I

Regeneration and Shamanism

Among the most enigmatic objects executed in the Olmec style in the Early Formative period are hollow ceramic figures. Often of indeterminate age, many of the figures are infants, while others are clearly adolescents and adults. Because of similarities in anatomy and pose, due most likely to the physical and technical requirements of modeling and firing hollow clay figures, the generic term "hollow baby" has been somewhat indiscriminately applied to these effigies. While few of these figures have been archaeologically excavated, Suzannah and George Vaillant excavated two hollow clay figures at the site of Gualupita, Morelos, in 1932: one was found between the legs of a skeleton, and the other, a fragmentary figure, in a more indeterminate context.[1] These infants have been variously interpreted as the result of the union of a jaguar and a human—"the jaguar's children"[2]—or as figures with deformities that marked them as imbued with supernatural powers, rain spirits or sacrifices to a rain god, or simply as well-fed infants.[3] Informed with a gravity that precludes the possibility of simple genre subjects, the figures of infants, either depicted with supernatural features, wearing headdresses, or simply naturalistically observed, signal the significance of infants and their effigies in Olmec ideology and ritual. As funerary objects, they may symbolize the spirits of the deceased. But based on the little archaeological evidence available, it cannot be assumed that these effigies had only a funerary function.

Small ceramic representations of infants shown in the care and protection of old women led Peter David Joralemon to suggest that the old women, as shamans, are performing a curing or birth ceremony[4] or perhaps preparing the infants in shamanic mysteries and ritual. In more hieratic contexts, as on the Las Limas Figure, La Venta Altar 5, and a small sculpture of a figure seated on a throne included here, the infants are held by figures with ceremonial bearing

dressed in symbolic costume, incised with cosmic symbols or enthroned.

The infants held by these seated figures are conspicuously inanimate, heads and legs falling limply over the arms of the Las Limas Figure and the figure on the front of La Venta Altar 5, or wooden and stiff on the enthroned figure. Cosmic symbols are incised on the body of the Las Limas Figure. The figure on the front of La Venta Altar 5 is seated within a cave mouth, the entrance to the supernatural realm, and wears a cone-shaped headdress decorated with a were-jaguar plaque and three exclamation-points symbolizing rain. In the small sculpture the throne identifies the figure as the ruler and the interface between the earthly and supernatural; the sides of the throne are decorated with scrolled extensions, symbols of clouds. The child bearers, identified by costume, setting, or attribute, sit in stilled anticipation at the intersection of the natural and supernatural worlds.

It has been suggested that the bearers of infants and of ceremonial bars or bundles may be related.[5] On Chalcatzingo Monument 1, a figure wearing an elaborate headdress marked with exclamation-point raindrops, similar to those on the headdress of the figure on La Venta Altar 5, sits on a low throne in a cave mouth surrounded by symbols of clouds, rain, and vegetation. The lazy-S motif, identified as a cloud symbol,[6] marks the bar cradled in the arms of the figure and the throne. A fragmentary stone figure in this catalogue wearing a scrolled cloud headdress cradles a vegetative bundle that hangs limply over its arms, like the feet and heads of the infants on the Las Limas Figure and La Venta Altar 5. The transmutation of the symbols within the motif of the ceremonial bearer—infant, rain clouds, and vegetation—signifies the mystical interval in which the infants are transformed into rain and vegetation. Symbols of procreation and the cycle of regeneration, the infants are

ritually sacrificed, either actually or in effigy, for rain and agricultural fertility.

Infant bones found at El Manatí, Veracruz, may indicate that the Olmec considered infants propitious offerings and practiced child sacrifice.[7] The swampy site at El Manatí reinforces the association of the sacrifice with water or rain, and Chalcatzingo Monument 1 is situated near the runoff channel of Cerro Chalcatzingo.[8]

Scenes depicting animated infants on the sides of La Venta Altar 5 are most likely sequential to the ceremony recorded on the front of the altar. In a discussion of large, standing hollow ceramic infants from Xochipala, Joralemon suggested that they may have been carried in ceremonies or placed in the laps of larger statues,[9] and the ritual performed through the animation of the effigies. The hollow clay infants may have been surrogates for living infants, sacrificed in effigy.

The hollow clay figures of adolescents and adults appear to be images of the elite. If they are funerary objects, the distinction in ages may be those at which they died. Their attributes, the signs and symbols with which they are marked, and their bearing and gestures may indicate their position or power in life, which would be restored in death. They are considered here with the stone statuettes of male figures. The order in which they are presented, ceramic to stone, is not intended to impose a chronological sequence of materials, although it does agree with the generally accepted view that stone superseded clay as the medium of elite expression.[10]

The predominantly small figures in stone are rarely of a size to be displayed with any public impact, and the standing figures do not support themselves independently. These must have been placed in sand, as is the group of sixteen small stone figures with celts that make up La Venta Offering 4. Effigies, carved in precious materials, are empowered objects and may have been animated in ritual or deposited in burials or caches with other magical objects in sacred precincts. Elizabeth P. Benson speculated that figures like those in La Venta Offering 4 may have been "buried as gifts to the earth," and that "to know the motivation for their manufacture and use would mean the possession of real insight into the Olmec mind."[11]

While there may be actual portraits, and idealized images of particular persons, among the group of figures assembled here, they are less records of the appearances of individuals than portraits of the shamanic power they possessed and on which their temporal authority rested. Several of the figures are incised with signs and symbols that mark them with special powers; others are characterized by their bearing and physicality as men of rank and authority.

The majority, however, are posed standing, sitting, or kneeling with no ostensible signs or attributes of power. As positions, they are hardly remarkable in themselves, but a defined and canonical pattern of details and emphases emerges within the group. Though writing on Aztec ideology, Alfredo Lopez-Austin has observed, "there is nothing in Meso-american thought to authorize our believing that there existed a body-soul dichotomy. To the contrary, according to indigenous thought, the embodiment of psychic entities is quite apparent." [12] It is clear from Lopez-Austin's study that the Aztecs cultivated a knowledge of systems for describing the functions of the bodily organs and the movement of breath and "animistic entities" through and within the body.

Through formal analysis of the human figure in Olmec art, Carolyn E. Tate has proposed that the Olmec also conceived of the body as a conduit for animistic energies. There is visual evidence that the human body in Olmec art was divided into the levels of the shamanic cosmos. The lower part of the body was identified with the watery underworld, the torso with the terrestrial realm, occupied by humans, and the head and shoulders with the sky or celestial sphere.

The colossal heads of the great ceremonial centers of the Gulf Coast are the grandest testament to the centrality of the head in Olmec ideology and iconography. Heads broken from full-length figures sufficed as prized heirlooms, and a fragmentary torso shown here was incised with a face to restore its power. The heads in images of the elite are elongated, shaped by binding, and are also often large in proportion to the body. The degree of detail concentrated in the head is in

striking contrast to the more stylized modeling of the body, with only the slightest indications of skeletal or muscular definition. The areas of raw, unpolished stone on the heads of otherwise highly finished and polished figures may be interpreted as a gesture to the magical properties of the stone itself and the head as the conduit for animistic forces.

The meaning of the pervasive absence of genitalia in Olmec art has long been a subject of debate. In many instances, statues may have actually been clothed, thus eliminating the need to depict genitalia. But some scholars have interpreted the absence as a sign of the negation of normal human bodily activity and devotion to the spiritual.

The standing, sitting, or kneeling postures of, the body may have specific shamanic associations and convey ideological content. Tate has described these poses as ritual postures, disciplined meditative exercises conducive to concentration and a steady flow of energy through the body. Inducing a state of trance through which the body becomes transformed, the shaman gains access to the supernatural realm. Figures seated cross-legged, with the spine straight or in variations in which the feet touch closing the circuit of the body, are interpreted as in poses of shamanic meditation. F. Kent Reilly, III, noted the parallels and continuity between kneeling human and jaguar transformation figures.[13] The kneeling position may be specific to transformation of the shaman into the nagual, the animal spirit companion that transports him to the otherworld. Stages of trance may even be indicated by the position of the hands, open and resting on the knees or clenched, resting on the thighs. Standing figures consistently are shown with legs flexed, pelvis thrust forward, the back rigidly straight, and arms slightly extended to the sides, a position associated with the transformation of the ruler into the *axis mundi*, the conduit through which the natural and supernatural worlds intersect.

The outcome of the shamanic journey is vividly conveyed in a jade statuette of a standing figure in the meditative posture holding a small creature. Almond-shaped eyes, short, wide nose, and gaping mouth with flared upper lip turned down at the sides, revealing a toothless gum line, identify the diminutive creature as an infant were-jaguar. The head is cleft and the creature wears a headband decorated with two nodules and crenellated earflaps. The infant in the lap of the Las Limas Figure has the same physiognomy and attire; and the infant on the front of La Venta Altar 5 and the infants on the sides of the altar may

share this physiognomy. These infants are costumed as the supernatural to whom the sacrifice is addressed. Through the sacrifice, the ruler transformed gains access to the otherworld to procure the rain. He holds the supernatural, identified with the rain and the maize, that must be propitiated and manipulated to effect the favorable outcome of the harvest. In the jade statuette, the ruler stands transfixed, holding this empowered and empowering image, which demonstrates his shamanic powers, access to the supernatural through ritual performance that validates his rulership.

NOTES

1. Susannah B. Vaillant and George C. Vaillant, "Excavations at Gualalupita," *American Museum of Natural History Anthropological Papers* 35, pt. 1 (1934).

2. Michael D. Coe, *The Jaguar's Children: Pre-Classic Central Mexico* (New York, 1965), 105.

3. Peter David Joralemon, "The Old Woman and the Child: Themes in the Iconography of Preclassic Mesoamerica," in *The Olmec and Their Neighbors: Essays in Memory of Matthew W. Stirling*, ed. Elizabeth P. Benson (Washington, D.C., 1981), 176; Francis Robiscek, "Of Olmec Babies and Were-Jaguars," *Mexicon* 5 (1983), 7–19.

4. Joralemon (as in note 3).

5. Peter David Joralemon (as in note 3), 175.

6. F. Kent Reilly, III, "Visions to Another World: Art, Shamanism, and Political Power in Middle Formative Mesoamerica," Ph.D. diss., University of Texas at Austin, 1994, 77–87.

7. Ponciano Ortiz, María del Cármen Rodríguez, and Paul Schmidt, "El Proyecto Manatí, Temporada 1988: Informe Preliminar," *Arqueología* 3 (1988): 141–54; Ponciano Ortiz and María del Cármen Rodríguez, "Proyecto Manatí 1989," *Arqueología* 1 (segunda época 1989): 23–52.

8. David C. Grove and Jorge Angulo, v, "Catalog and Description of the Monuments," in *Ancient Chalcatzingo*, ed. David C. Grove (Austin, Tex., 1987), 115.

9. Joralemon (as in note 3), 175.

10. James F. Garber, David C. Grove, Kenneth G. Hirth, John W. Hoopes, "Jade Use in Portions of Mexico and Central America," in *Precolumbian Jade: New Geological and Cultural Interpretations*, ed. Frederick W. Lange (Salt Lake City, 1993), 213.

11. Elizabeth P. Benson, "Some Olmec Objects in the Robert Woods Bliss Collection at Dumbarton Oaks," in *The Olmec and Their Neighbors: Essays in Memory of Matthew W. Stirling*, ed. Elizabeth P. Benson (Washington, D.C., 1981), 98.

12. Alfredo López-Austin, *The Human Body and Ideology: Concepts of the Ancient Nahuas* (Salt Lake City, 1988), 163.

13. F. Kent Reilly, III, "The Shaman in Transformation Pose: A Study of the Theme of Rulership in Olmec Art," *Record of The Art Museum, Princeton University* 48, no. 2 (1989): 4–21.

1. Crawling Hollow Figure

1200–900 B.C.
Provenance: Las Bocas, Puebla
Material: clay with white to ivory slip
Dimensions: h. 30.1 cm.; w. 40.2 cm.; d. 23.8 cm.
Private collection

The depiction of pronounced physical activity in three-dimensional figures is rare in Olmec art. This figure crawling forward, pausing to raise the right arm as if in recognition or response, is not simply a playful infant, nor is its expression childlike (fig. 1). The face, ears, and shape of the head are stylized to conform to the Olmec ideal. The secure sense of balance, firm body, and taut chest and abdomen suggest physical strength and coordination. There is no indication of genitalia, and only the small depression of the navel interrupts the fluid lines and forms of the sculpture. The gesture of the right arm is calm and reassuring; the lips are parted as though about to speak.

The overall appearance of this figure is similar to one illustrated in Miguel Covarrubias's *Indian Art of Mexico and Central America.*[1] The body and limbs in both objects are smooth and the face shows the same distant expression. While the crawling pose is unusual, it is not unique: a ceramic figure now in The Saint Louis Art Museum (fig. 2) also depicts a crawling infant with an elongated skull, but its execution, particularly the slanting eyes and punctuated pupils, is more representative of Tlatilco figurines.

The figure is constructed of a rough, grayish brown clay, masterfully worked in thin sheets for the body, painted with a white to ivory slip, once highly burnished but now deteriorated and stained with iron oxide, impacted with mineral deposits, and etched by soil acids. Maintaining the balance of the figure in wet clay in preparation for the kiln must have been a challenge. Two holes in line through the chest indicate that a wooden stick, which burned out in firing, was passed through the clay body to support it in the kiln. The figure, which was broken into eight large pieces and a dozen smaller ones, has been repaired to its original form. A ceramic sculpture, not a vessel, the only openings to the interior, aside from those mentioned, are the mouth, eyes, and two firing holes in each ear.

BIBLIOGRAPHY
Unpublished.

NOTE
1. Miguel Covarrubias, *Indian Art of Mexico and Central America* (New York, 1957), pl. 1, mislabeled.

Figure 1. Detail.

Figure 2. Hollow Crawling Baby Figure, Central Highlands, Mexico, buff earthenware, h. 16 cm.; w. 21 cm. The Saint Louis Art Museum, gift of Morton D. May.

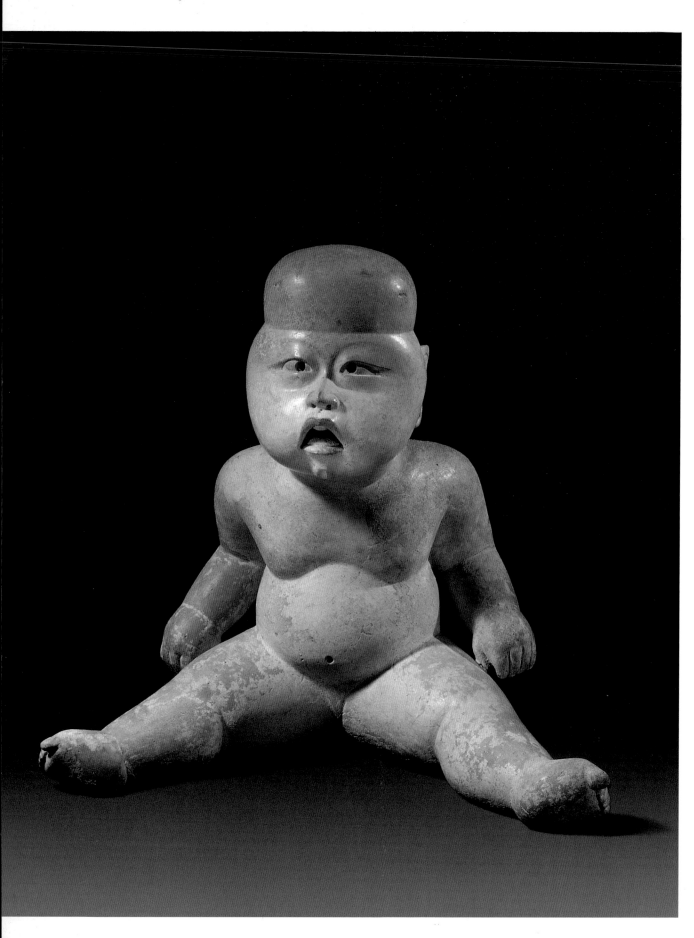

2. Seated Hollow Figure

1200–900 B.C.
Provenance: Area of Xochipala and Zumpango del Río,
Guerrero
Material: clay with ivory slip
Dimensions: h. 28.9 cm.; w. 33.1 cm.; d. 18.8 cm.
Private collection

The drawn-back shoulders, tense arms, curled fingers,
and widespread legs with arched feet and clenched
toes of this infant all indicate the muscle tension
required to keep it upright, although in precarious
balance.[1] The staring, crossed eyes and open mouth
seem to suggest surprise and apprehension at its
achievement. The head shows the result of having
been bound from birth. The skull is shaped into a form
that is either an early stage or a stylization of the elongated head the Olmec must have regarded as elegant
or a sign of power. The earlobes of the flange ears were
pierced for jewelry or ornaments now lost.

   The only openings to the interior are the mouth, the
eyes, and two tiny holes: one in the navel and one at
the bottom of the figure. The figure is modeled of a
rough, reddish brown clay with an ivory slip, which
retains some of the original burnishing in the upper
portion of the face. Lower down on the figure the slip
has deteriorated, exposing the base ceramic in spots
on the arms and legs. The body of the figure had few
breaks and has been repaired; a small area on the left
foot has been restored.

BIBLIOGRAPHY
Unpublished.

NOTE
1. For a similar figure, see *Trésors du nouveau monde*, Royal
   Museum of Art and History (Brussels, 1992), fig. 77.

3. Seated Hollow Figure

1200–900 B.C.
Provenance: Las Bocas, Puebla
Material: clay with white slip and traces of red pigment
Dimensions: h. 35.1 cm.; w. 32.8 cm.; d. 25.1 cm.
Private collection

The latent energy in this seated figure is more sensed than seen. Glancing inquiringly upward and to the left, the youth's sudden movement in an otherwise relaxed position is observed in the barest hint of torsion in the shoulders. The inclination of the body and tilt of the head subtly animate the entire figure.

The torso is far longer than the legs, proportions appropriate to an infant but not a child of a clearly more advanced age. These proportions are perhaps a convention of hollow figures also found in representations of adults. The slender arms taper to small hands with delicately modeled fingers; the feet are hardly more than gracefully curved and closed terminations of the legs. The highly individualized head has a somewhat disquieting expression, the eyes set beneath arching brows and the sweeping lines of the eyelids, the pupils focused and attentive (fig. 1). The cheeks below the gently modeled cheekbones have a sensual fleshiness, the lips are parted, and teeth are indicated

Figure 1. Detail of head.

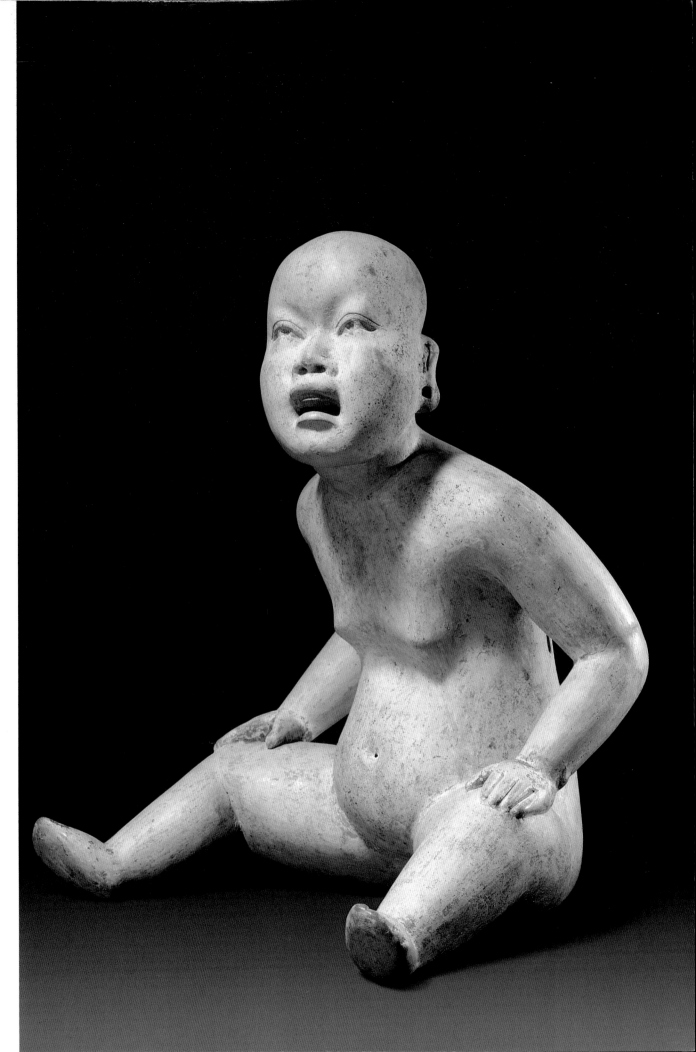

in the open mouth. Unusual care was taken with the modeling of the ears. the helices are realistically rendered and the firing holes are ingeniously incorporated in the concha openings.

This would seem to be a portrait of a specific youth, who sits with confidence. The elegant shape of the skull is the result of earlier binding; the elongated torso, apart from the soft fall of the breasts, is free of baby fat; the arms are lean and attenuated. The earlobes appear to have been pierced to accept large earplugs and stretched over time. Here again, as in cat. nos. 1 and 2, the genitals are not depicted.

The slip, over a fine tan-to-pinkish clay body, has been uniformly eroded from a more highly polished grayish white. Traces of red pigment appear on the feet, hands, and ears. Soil stains, mineral deposits, and bits of hard, brownish calcification have married with the powdery surface, which is also etched in places by roots. The sculpture survived in the kiln with a minimum of firing holes: one in the mouth, one in each ear, one rectangular slit on either side of the chest, and a hole one-half inch in diameter in the base.

BIBLIOGRAPHY
Unpublished.

4. Old Woman Holding Infant in Lap

1200–900 B.C.
Provenance: Las Bocas, Puebla
Material: clay with traces of red and black pigment
Dimensions: h. 7.6 cm.; w. 4.2 cm.; d. 7.2 cm.
Private collection

An aged woman gazes adoringly at the infant she tenderly cradles in her arms. The binding to deform the skull is still in place around the head of the infant, who also appears to be wearing a practical diaper. The lips of the trapezoidal mouth are parted, the upper lip flared, and the eyes treated in the "eyeless style" of a small group of figurines from Las Bocas in this catalogue (fig. 1; cat. no. 239).

Too old perhaps to be the infant's mother, the woman's back, with pronounced vertebrae, is bowed with years, her abdomen slack, breasts flaccid, and face deeply creased. She may be a grandmother or a formal guardian or a protector of children designated for elevation to a position of importance in Olmec society. In discussing the occurrence of old women in later Mesoamerican iconography, Peter David Joralemon hypothesized that they "may indeed be images of female shamans, and the hags with infants may represent some sort of child-curing ceremonies or rituals of childbirth."[1]

This sculpture is solid, made of a fine-grain, unslipped, but highly polished, light reddish brown clay. The figures were modeled separately, but fired together in the kiln. The red and black pigment are original.

BIBLIOGRAPHY
Peter David Joralemon, "The Old Woman and the Child: Themes in the Iconography of Preclassic Mesoamerica," in *The Olmec and Their Neighbors: Essays in Memory of Matthew W. Stirling*, ed. Elizabeth P. Benson (Washington, D.C., 1981), figs. 19, 20.

NOTE
1. Peter David Joralemon, "The Old Woman and the Child: Themes in the Iconography of Preclassic Mesoamerica," in *The Olmec and Their Neighbors: Essays in Memory of Matthew W. Stirling*, ed. Elizabeth P. Benson (Washington, D.C., 1981), 178.

Figure 1. Back view.

5. Old Woman Holding Infant in Lap

1200–500 B.C.
Provenance: Las Bocas, Puebla
Material: clay with white slip and traces of red pigment
Dimensions: h. 12.5 cm.; w. 11 cm.
Private collection

The theme of the elderly woman with an infant is represented again (see cat. no. 4) in this slightly larger, vigorously modeled, clay sculpture from Las Bocas. The woman's age is difficult to determine, but the elongated, flattened breasts would indicate she is beyond childbearing age. The strong features, articulated in broad, sharp planes, are sheltered by the overhanging, helmetlike hair. The lower lip protrudes and the high cheekbones are dressed with what seem to be plaquettes with furrowed decoration. The cylindrical, barely tapered limbs terminate in toes and fingers that are no more than mechanical impressions of the modeling tool in the soft clay. The woman cups the head of the child in her right hand, rests her left hand on the child's breast, and gazes down at the infant lying across her lap.

Despite the brute, geometric style of the piece and the massiveness of the woman looming over the child, there is a sense of tender solicitousness in her regard for the child no less moving than the overt attentions of the woman in the more naturalistically rendered group previously discussed. The child's rigid, straight right arm falls over the woman's outer crossed leg, meeting her foot in a pronounced pattern of indented fingers and toes. The child's face with what seem to be closed eyes and the inert pose with the dropped arm suggest sleep or a state of suspended consciousness. The head is elongated and appears to be shaped by binding; the hair is shaved into a crest. The child's features are similar to those of another figure in the catalogue exemplifying the Olmec style (cat. no. 8). The commingling of the genrelike and hieratic, maternal and ceremonial makes this ceramic figure at once appealing and auspicious and may reflect a regional interpretation of Olmec iconographic and stylistic elements.

The sculpture is modeled from a dense, brownish clay with a highly burnished white slip and retains a considerable amount of the original red pigment used to accent the hair, facial decoration of the woman, and extremities: ears, fingers, and toes.

BIBLIOGRAPHY
Peter David Joralemon, "The Old Woman and the Child: Themes in the Iconography of Preclassic Mesoamerica," in *The Olmec and Their Neighbors: Essays in Memory of Matthew W. Stirling*, ed. Elizabeth P. Benson (Washington, D.C., 1981), figs. 21, 22.
Gillett G. Griffin, "Olmec Forms and Materials Found in Central Guerrero," in *The Olmec and Their Neighbors: Essays in Memory of Matthew W. Stirling*, ed. Elizabeth P. Benson (Washington, D.C., 1981), fig. 9.
Emile Deletaille, *Rediscovered Masterpieces* (Boulogne, 1985), no. 115.
Franz Feuchtwanger, *Ceramica Olmeca* (Mexico City, 1989), no. 54.

BIBLIOGRAPHY
Record of The Art Museum, Princeton University 42, no. 1 (1983): 68 (illus.).
Peter David Joralemon, "The Old Woman and the Child: Themes in the Iconography of Preclassic Mesoamerica," in *The Olmec and Their Neighbors: Essays in Memory of Matthew W. Stirling*, ed. Elizabeth P. Benson (Washington, D.C., 1981), figs. 17, 18.
Gillett G. Griffin, "Olmec Forms and Materials Found in Central Guerrero," in *The Olmec and Their Neighbors: Essays in Memory of Matthew W. Stirling*, ed. Elizabeth P. Benson (Washington, D.C., 1981), fig. 8.

7. Seated Hollow Figure with ▶ Raised Right Arm

1200 – 900 B.C.
Provenance: Morelos
Material: clay with traces of red pigment
Dimensions: h. 26.7 cm.; w. 20.3 cm.; d. 13.3 cm.
Private collection

This hollow figure is illustrative of the marked difference in style and craftsmanship between the delicately modeled clay sculptures from Las Bocas and those associated with local workshops in Tlapacoya and Tlatilco or more distant Guerrero, Morelos, and Veracruz. The thickness of the coarse clay and the broad modeling and rough surface texture, especially of the face, contribute to an effect of raw vitality. The swollen volumes are not limited to the fat belly; the arms and legs are meaty and even the stubby hands are plump. The right arm is forcefully extended, the fist clenched. The age is indeterminate, but given the helmet or headdress and aggressive posture, it seems safe to assume that this figure, though in the form of an infant, is intended to represent an adult.

The piece bears comparison with the highly refined Baby Figure in The Metropolitan Museum of Art (fig. 1) in the convincingly organic rolls of flesh and the pronounced navel. Crescent-shaped openings on the back of the head (fig. 2) may have had symbolic meaning and almost certainly functioned as firing holes, as did the holes under each shoulder.

BIBLIOGRAPHY
Unpublished.

6. Old Woman Holding Infant in Lap

1200 – 900 B.C.
Provenance: Xochipala, Guerrero
Material: clay
Dimensions: h. 10.2 cm.; w. 7.4 cm.; d. 7.1 cm.
The Art Museum, Princeton University, gift of Mr. and Mrs. Peter G. Wray

This sculpture is not Olmec. It is from the village of Xochipala, situated to the south of Las Bocas. Xochipala produced solid clay figurines distinctive to its workshops and probably contemporary with the apogee of the Olmec ceramic production in the central highlands. Though not of Olmec workmanship, this sculpture is akin in subject and composition to the two figures of old women with infants from Las Bocas (cat. nos. 4 and 5).

While the old woman cradles the head of the child lying across her lap, she lacks the tenderness the old women show toward the infants in the two previous examples. There are no affectionate gazes or tender caresses. Sitting bolt upright, looking straight ahead, the woman seems fiercely protective of her charge. She glowers forbiddingly from deep-set eyes and her mouth is open, as if issuing a warning. Her cheeks are marked with crosshatching, intended to represent scarification. The child wears a necklace, perhaps an emblem of high status. His genitalia are indicated, and the area around the knees is curiously detailed. The child does not have any of the features associated with Olmec infants.

The finely detailed faces of the child and the woman and her delicately incised hair are characteristic of this regional style. The old woman is a particularly stark and harsh example of the realism and singular style developed at Xochipala. The sculpture is roughly modeled in unslipped clay.

Figure 1. Baby Figure, Mexico, ceramic, h. 34 cm. The Metropolitan Museum of Art, the Michael C. Rockefeller Memorial Collection, bequest of Nelson A. Rockefeller, 1979.

Figure 2. Back view of head.

137

◄ 8. Seated Hollow Figure with Raised Left Hand

1100–900 B.C.
Provenance: Zumpango del Río, Guerrero
Material: clay with ivory slip and traces of red and
black pigment
Dimensions: h. 36 cm.; w. 31 cm.; d. 19 cm.
The Denver Art Museum, gift of various donors

The flexed left leg, left arm with elbow resting on knee
and hand raised, and the tilt of the head introduce
movement to this otherwise rigidly composed sculpture. The right arm thrust out, the formal, upright
bearing, and the confident expression of the face speak
of a self-possessed young man of some authority.
In contrast to the stylized body, the face has been modeled with sensitivity; great care has been taken to
define the features, suggesting that the figure represents an ideal of masculine beauty. The eyebrows and
hairline were painted black and the crown of the head
colored red, perhaps to indicate a helmet or other
headdress. The surface of the ceramic is especially well
preserved, with the burnished, deep ivory slip
retaining its original luster.

BIBLIOGRAPHY
Denver Art Museum, *Major Works in the Collection* (Denver, 1981),
    122–23.
Emile Deletaille, *Rediscovered Masterpieces* (Boulogne, 1985), no. 53.
Franz Feuchtwanger, *Ceramica Olmeca* (Mexico City, 1989), no. 8.

9. Seated Figure ►

1150–900 B.C.
Provenance: Tlapacoya, Mexico
Material: gray clay with white slip
Dimensions: h. 16.5 cm.; w. 13 cm.; d. 11 cm.
Private collection

This stocky seated figure is one of the finest examples
of ceramic sculpture from the site of Tlapacoya. The
weight of the figure rests on its massive thighs and
extended right arm; the left arm across the lap, the
tilt of the head, and the slightly open mouth imply
a shifting of weight that lends a sense of movement
to the piece. The shoulders are broad, the torso thick,
with a noticeable puncture for the navel. The head
shows little evidence of skull deformation. The eyes
are pitted to indicate pupils. Michael D. Coe originally
placed this object with other hollow figures; Elizabeth
K. Easby, however, later noted that it was "heavy
for its size" and "probably solid."[1]

The face gives few clues to the age or sex of the figure, and while the breasts would seem to suggest a woman, they could also represent the comfortable plumpness of a male member of the elite. A ceramic figure in the Antigua Colleción Sáenz and a group of six figures from Las Bocas, which share many of the same physical traits with this Tlapacoya figure, are almost certainly male.[2] While there are no specific indications of social rank in the Tlapacoya figure, the naturalism and relaxed pose imply a personage of some importance.

BIBLIOGRAPHY
Michael D. Coe, *The Jaguar's Children: Pre-Classic Central Mexico* (New York, 1965), no. 190.
Elizabeth K. Easby, *Ancient Art of Latin America from the Collection of Jay C. Leff* (New York, 1966), no. 130.
Pre-Columbian Art of Mesoamerica from the Collection of Jay C. Leff (Allentown, Pa., 1972), no. 10.
Kathryn M. Linduff, *Ancient Art of Middle America* (Huntington, West Virginia, 1974), pl. 47.

NOTES
1. Michael D. Coe, *The Jaguar's Children: Pre-Classic Central Mexico* (New York, 1965), 105; Elizabeth K. Easby, *Ancient Art of Latin America from the Collection of Jay C. Leff* (New York, 1966), 30.
2. Franz Feuchtwanger, *Ceramica Olmeca* (Mexico, 1989), figs. 44, 58.

10. Seated Hollow Figure with Incisions

1000–500 B.C.
Provenance: Las Bocas, Puebla
Material: clay with buff slip and traces of red pigment
Dimensions: h. 34 cm.; d. 18 cm.; w. 33 cm.
Private collection

This confident young man raises his hand to the back of his neck, drawing attention to the scalloped cartouche of incised symbols running from the upper back to the buttocks (fig. 1). The modeling of the body is similar to that of the figure in the Denver Art Museum (cat. no. 8), with its tapering, cylindrical limbs and fingers and toes defined by short impressions in the clay. The broad shoulders and well-defined pectoral muscles are those of a strong adult, but the hands, legs, and small feet are stylized as in images of infants and males of indeterminate age. The fleshy, smiling mouth and cheeks contrast with the sharp angle at which the brows meet, lending an intense, almost calculating effect to the face. The head is supported by a neck thicker at the top than at the bottom, adding to the forcefulness of the expression. Traces of red pigment are evident on the face, chest, and what remains of the forehead. The surface is not

Figure 1. Back view.

divided by a diagonal bar with opposed, curved extensions flanked by triangles with concave sides and crosshatched semicircles. The motif of the bar and extensions appears to the left of the doorway on an effigy vessel in the form of a temple (cat. no. 245). The closest comparison to the crosshatched semicircles, perhaps also seen on the helmet of the Metropolitan figure, is a similar motif on some blackware ceramics.[1] The two bands separating the zones contain pairs of flaring lines, suggestive of the flame eyebrows of the Olmec Dragon.[2]

BIBLIOGRAPHY
Emile Deletaille, *Rediscovered Masterpieces* (Boulogne, 1985), no. 41.
Franz Feuchtwanger, *Ceramica Olmeca* (Mexico City, 1989), no. 7.

NOTES
1. See Michael D. Coe, *The Jaguar's Children: Pre-Classic Mexico* (New York, 1965), fig. 24; Michael D. Coe and Richard A. Diehl, *In the Land of the Olmec: The Archaeology of San Lorenzo Tenochtitlán* vol. 1 (Austin, Tex., 1981), figs. 140b, e, f; Franz Feuchtwanger, *Ceramica Olmeca* (Mexico, 1989), fig. 116; this volume, cat. no. 208. In "Olmec Bloodletting: An Iconographic Study" (*Sixth Palenque Round Table, 1986,* ed. Virginia M. Fields, Norman, Okla., 1991), Rosemary Joyce et al. identify this motif as part of a bloodletting symbol set.

2. See cat. nos. 99–106.

smooth, the limbs marked by faceted modeling. Firing holes can be seen underneath the right arm, at the navel, and at the calves.

The design at the back of the head may indicate that when intact the figure wore a helmet, similar to that on the Baby Figure in The Metropolitan Museum of Art (cat. no. 7, fig. 1). The insignia painted on the back of the Metropolitan figure appears to be a variation of the hand-paw-wing motif. The cartouche on the back of this figure is composed of three fields, each

11. Seated Bearded Hollow Figure

900 – 600 B.C.
Provenance: Tenenexpan, Veracruz
Material: clay with deep ivory slip and traces of red pigment
Dimensions: h. 40.6 cm.; w. 33.2 cm ; d. 22.2 cm
Private collection

This imposing personage is among the most distinctive of the large, hollow clay figures. The beard and especially the mustache are seldom seen in Olmec clay sculptures, and the large ear spools, the particular shape or deformation of the head, and the design of the hair are unusual. The smallness of the head in proportion to the torso emphasizes the powerful modeling of the chest, the thick arms and broad shoulders. A small patch of red coloring, perhaps a loincloth, covers the groin.

The long, narrow, intensely focused eyes, short nose, and open mouth with bared teeth give the figure an almost declamatory quality. The somewhat pugnacious bearing is expressed in the pose—hands on thighs, arms akimbo, and shoulders slightly hunched. The short, sturdy legs follow the convention of most seated hollow figures, probably more a result of the potter's need to produce a stable ceramic form than any attempt to model realistic infant legs.

This highly particularized figure may be a portrait of an individual, a ruler, or important functionary. Such

Figure 1. Back view of head.

141

an identification would be clarified if the incisions on the back of the head could be deciphered (fig. 1): two horizontal bands, which actually pierce the clay, below which are three vertical lines to the right and three circles to the left.

The slip has taken on a deep ivory patina, somewhat eroded and etched in places with root marks. This figure was broken into several pieces, which have been repaired and the cracks filled.

BIBLIOGRAPHY
Unpublished.

12. Kneeling Bearded Figure

900–400 B.C.
Provenance: Puebla
Material: dark greenish gray serpentine
Dimensions: h. 29.3 cm.; w. 18 cm.; d. 16 cm.
Private collection

Unusually large for a figure carved from serpentine, this impressive figure of a kneeling man exudes stability, dignity, and authority. Much of the strength and monumentality of the piece comes from the compact, geometric clarity of the pyramidal form. The body is carved in simple units, unarticulated except for the slight modeling of the chest, and there is almost no neck. All of the detail resides in the head and face. The high, tapered skull is emphasized by the wide projecting jaw line. The pointed beard, which begins with short incised lines along the jawbone, consists of straight descending lines. The hint of a mustache and a small drilled hole can be seen above the partly opened mouth. The empty eye sockets might have originally held inlays.[1] Generally speaking, in Olmec stone sculpture the eye is made by drilling holes at either side and removing the stone between them, sometimes leaving a hole to mark the pupil or, more rarely, a fully realized, carved eyeball incised with an iris.

The kneeling posture is a practical position from a sculptural point of view, as the foreshortened flexed position of the legs is for hollow ceramic figures. But this position with hands resting on the knees is also associated with shamanic transformation (see cat. nos. 42 and 43) and may be implied here in a more secular representation of a ruler's power.[2]

The hands and feet have been broken off; a large section of the figure's left arm is missing. There is damage to the top of the head and the surface of the stone is heavily marked and abraded.

BIBLIOGRAPHY

Carnegie Institute of Fine Arts, *Exotic Art from Ancient and Primitive Civilizations: Collection of Jay C. Leff* (Pittsburgh, 1959), no. 341.

American Federation of Arts, *Exotic Art from Ancient and Primitive Civilizations: A Selection from the Collection of Jay C. Leff* (New York, 1960), no. 43.

Elizabeth K. Easby, *Ancient Art of Latin America from the Collection of Jay C. Leff* (New York, 1966), no. 3.

Hasso von Winning, *Pre-Columbian Art of Mexico and Central America* (New York, 1968), fig. 49.

Pre-Columbian Art of Mesoamerica from the Collection of Jay C. Leff (Allentown, Pa., 1972), no. 2.

Katheryn M. Linduff, *Ancient Art of Middle America* (Huntington, West Virginia, 1974), pl. 9.

F. Kent Reilly, III, "The Shaman in Transformation Pose," *Record of The Art Museum* 48, no. 2 (1989): fig. 15a.

NOTES

1. This is probably true for many Olmec stone sculptures in which the eyes are left as roughly excavated cavities.
2. See F. Kent Reilly, III, "The Shaman in Transformation Pose," *Record of The Art Museum* 48, no. 2 (1989): 4–21.

13. Kneeling Bearded Figure

900–600 B.C.
Provenance: Tuxtlas region, Veracruz
Material: close-grained blue-green basalt with dark green speckling and rusty patina
Dimensions: h. 20 cm.; w. 15 cm.; d. 10 cm.
Private collection

The sculptor of this powerful figure modeled the muscles of the chest, the outline of the ribcage, and even the shoulder blades with extraordinary subtlety and gave great detail to the arrangement of the hair: the crosshatched design to the front, with slender, loose, ribbonlike strands falling over the hair to the shoulders at the back.

The figure most closely relates to the kneeling bearded figure of cat. no. 12. The beards on these two sculptures indicate a Late Formative date.[1]

BIBLIOGRAPHY
Unpublished.

NOTE

1. Elizabeth P. Benson, "Some Olmec Objects in the Robert Woods Bliss Collection at Dumbarton Oaks," in *The Olmec and Their Neighbors: Essays in Memory of Matthew W. Stirling*, ed. Elizabeth P. Benson (Washington, D.C., 1981), 97–98.

14. Kneeling Figure, Fragment

1200 – 600 B.C.
Provenance: Mexico
Material: stone
Dimensions: h. 26 cm.; w. 19.6 cm.; d. 20 cm.
The Cleveland Museum of Art, the Norweb Collection

The size of this figure, even in its fragmentary state, and the quality of its carving suggest that the person depicted was of considerable importance. The modeling of the body and distinctive details—the deeply carved line defining the calves pressing against the backs of the thighs, the curve of the feet adhering to the buttocks, and the arcs of the shins on which the sculpture rests, the knees and feet suspended— resemble features of the Shaman in Transformation Pose (cat. no. 42).

The sculpture is refined down to the finger and toenails and, most remarkably, the short carved line on the underside that indicates the heel turned back against the ankle (fig 1.). The hands rest open on the knees, as in cat. no. 13 and, in all likelihood, cat. no. 12, differentiating these kneeling figures from those with clenched fists, who appear already to be in the early stages of transformation (cat. nos. 42 and 43). Genitalia are indicated on this kneeling figure, a rare feature in Olmec sculpture, and a drill hole exists on the underside, possibly remaining from the pointing of the stone.

BIBLIOGRAPHY
William M. Milliken, *Art of the Americas Picture Book Number Two* (Cleveland, 1946), 27.
Handbook of The Cleveland Museum of Art (Cleveland, 1978), 392.

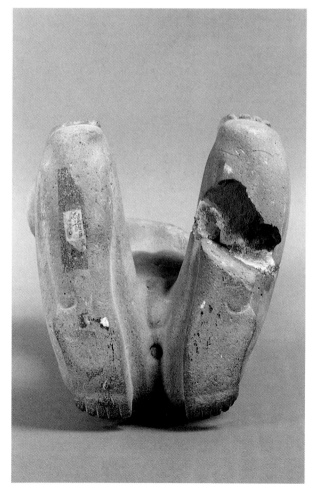

Figure 1. View of underside.

15. Seated Ruler in a Ritual Pose

900–500 B.C.
Provenance: San Martin Texmelucan, Puebla
Material: dark green serpentine with traces of cinnabar
Dimensions: h. 18 cm.; w. 13.6 cm.; d. 7.8 cm.
Dallas Museum of Art, gift of Mrs. Eugene McDermott, the
Roberta Coke Camp Fund, and the Art Museum League Fund

The haughty bearing and magnificent workmanship
of this statue would suggest a person of some con-
sequence, perhaps a young lord. The left hand rests
on the horizontal left thigh and the right arm hangs
casually over the raised right knee. An interesting
detail is the joining of the feet, which closes the circuit
of the limbs. The hands and feet are small and, despite
the great refinement of the carving of this jade, the
toes and fingers are schematically indicated. The thick
waist belies the thin, tapered arms; no musculature on
the chest interrupts the smooth surface of the stone.
The figure wears a band around his elongated head
and a narrow loincloth, held in place by a belt. While
no regalia is shown, faint traces of incisions above the
right eye and on the cheek below it may identify the
source of the figure's power. The features of the face—
the fine nose, large, downturned eyes, and grimacing
mouth exposing well-defined teeth—reflect the Olmec
ideal. The brilliant polish of the stone enhances the
fluidity of the carving. Probably covered with cinnabar
when it was buried, the eerie effect of the color on the
face may be due to the residue of cinnabar in the
crevices.[1]

BIBLIOGRAPHY
Andre Emmerich, *Art Before Columbus* (New York, 1963), 51.
Román Piña Chán and Luis Covarrubias, *El Pueblo del Jaguar*
    (Mexico City, 1964), fig. 29.
Ann R. Bromberg, *Selected Works from the Dallas Museum of Art*
    (Dallas, 1983), no. 4.
Emile Deletaille, *Rediscovered Masterpieces* (Boulogne, 1985), no. 7.
Román Piña Chán, *The Olmec: Mother Culture of Mesoamerica*
    (New York, 1989), no. 53.

NOTE
1. A line drawing of this piece appears in one of Miguel Covarrubias's sketchbooks with the phrase "Huezotzingo, Pue," a
   town near San Martin, thus providing a possible provenance.

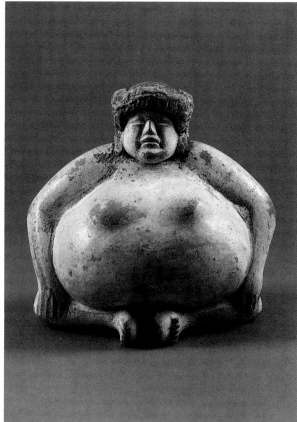

Figure 1. Seated Obese Figure, 1200–950 B.C., Las Bocas, clay with white slip, black pigment, and cinnabar, h. 10.5 cm. The Art Museum, Princeton University, Museum purchase, Fowler McCormick, Class of 1921, Fund.

16. Seated Figure

1200–900 B.C.
Provenance: Las Bocas, Puebla
Material: clay with white slip and traces of cinnabar
Dimensions: h. 11 cm.; w. 10.8 cm.; d. 8.9 cm.
Raymond and Laura Wielgus Collection, on extended loan to Indiana University Art Museum

The head of this figure sits atop a mass of flesh that slopes down the back and front and pools around the legs. The flabby arms and outsized hands rest on the sides of the body. The stomach, punctuated by a navel, folds over the feet, which lie one on top of the other. The face generally conforms to the Olmec type with a greatly extended chin. The tip of the peaked cap has been restored to curve to the front.

Two other potbellied figurines from Las Bocas are cited here.[1] The example in the Zollman collection has a shaved head with elaborate, curved extensions, hair or ornaments, at the sides. The head of the figure in the collection of The Art Museum, Princeton University, is framed by an ornate cap, and the grotesquely attenuated arms hang limply over the great swollen body (fig. 1). The feet in both these objects are again joined, but at the heels. Michael D. Coe and Peter David Joralemon identified these fat figures, which may represent excess and abundance, as distant antecedents of the potbellied sculptures from the Pacific Coast of Guatemala of some five hundred years later.[2]

BIBLIOGRAPHY
Michael D. Coe, *The Jaguar's Children: Pre-Classic Central Mexico* (New York, 1965), fig. 193a, b.

NOTES
1. Lee A. Parsons, John B. Carlson, and Peter David Joralemon, *The Face of Ancient America: The Wally and Brenda Zollman Collection of Precolumbian Art* (Indianapolis, 1988), no. 7; *Record of The Art Museum, Princeton University* 47, no. 1 (1988): 51 (illus.).
2. Ibid., 28; Michael D. Coe, *The Jaguar's Children: Pre-Classic Central Mexico* (New York, 1965), 105.

17. Seated Figure

1000 – 500 B.C.
Provenance: Honduras
Material: dark green serpentine
Dimensions: h. 10.5 cm.; w. 10 cm.; d. 10 cm.
Private collection

This portly figure, wearing a tight-fitting cap incised with straight lines on the left side, reclines with a sense of luxury and ease. While the facial type is characteristic of Olmec sculpture, the representation of corpulent figures in stone is unusual. Though Olmec male figures are more characteristically slim, conversely, girth also appears to have been prized for its own sake and as a sign of position. Perhaps this sculpture was intended to represent both personal well-being and a ruler's ability to procure material wealth. The arms and legs are separated from the body only by straight carved lines, reinforcing the overall mass of the figure and the bulge of the chest and stomach. The large recessed navel is similar to that on the Seated Hollow Figure with Raised Right Arm (cat. no. 7) and may be a convention used for fat figures.

The sculpture was found in Honduras, but it reflects the influence of the great ceremonial centers of the Middle Formative period to the north.[1] Most likely, objects carved in the north found their way south through various trade routes. We will probably never know, however, if these motifs had the same meaning for residents in Honduras as they did for the people of San Lorenzo and La Venta.

BIBLIOGRAPHY

Julie Jones, *Pre-Columbian Art in New York: Selections from Private Collections* (New York, 1969), no. 2.

Emile Deletaille, *Rediscovered Masterpieces* (Boulogne, 1985), no. 11.

NOTE

1. A concave plaque with unmistakably Olmec motifs was found at the site of Salitrón Viejo, Honduras. For a discussion of heirloom jades from Salitrón Viejo, see Kenneth G. Hirth and Susan Grant Hirth, "Ancient Currency: The Style and Use of Jade and Marble Carvings in Central Honduras," in *Precolumbian Jade: New Geological and Cultural Interpretations*, ed. Frederick W. Lange (Salt Lake City, 1993), 186–87, fig. 13.13c.

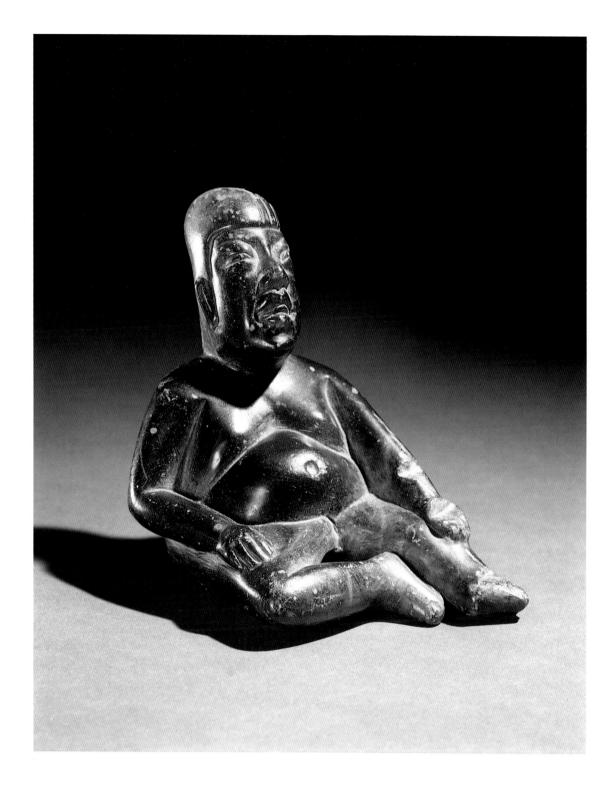

18. Standing Figure

900 – 600 B.C.
Provenance: unknown
Material: blue-green jade
Dimensions: h. 14 cm.; w. 3.8 cm.; d. 2.5 cm.
Lent by Landon T. Clay to the Worcester Art Museum

This standing figure is distinguished by a great deli-cacy in the overall form, the extreme slimness of the limbs, and elongation of the arms. The contour and surface of the body is subtly modulated and undulates slightly from the high, narrow shoulders and chest to the gentle swell of the abdomen, where the highly polished surface is interrupted only by the incised penis sheath. The carving of the jade is extremely refined. Only the inside surfaces of the arms are left unpolished, which demonstrate the use of slab sawing to create the form. The ears seem prominent against the smooth, contained oval shape of the head and the eyes give the subject a slightly pinched expression. A figure in the collection of the American Museum of Natural History is similar in the exaggerated thinness.[1]

BIBLIOGRAPHY
Unpublished.

NOTE
1. N. C. Christopher Couch, *Pre-Columbian Art from The Ernest Erickson Collection at the American Museum of Natural History* (New York, 1988), frontispiece.

19. Standing Figure ▶

900 – 600 B.C.
Provenance: Southern Veracruz
Material: fine-grained, blue-green jadeite with white-to-green inclusions and traces of cinnabar
Dimensions: h. 15.9 cm.; w. 6 cm.; d. 2.5 cm.
Private collection

The sensuous curve of this jadeite figure, with its knees flexed forward, spine very straight, and arms extended slightly at the sides, expresses the state of relaxed yet precise equilibrium achieved in standing meditation. Through this position, as Carolyn E. Tate proposes in this volume, union with the axis of the Olmec cosmos is accomplished. The synthesis of realistic and abstract elements in this figure produces a human image grounded in reality yet suggestive of the archetypal.

Exquisitely poised on the attenuated body, the prominent head counterbalances the curve of the back and thrust of the pelvic area. The hooked nose, flaring upper lip, and pronounced cleft chin jut aggressively forward and the high forehead rises to a bulge at the back of the skull. The concentrated expression of the face is enlivened with subtle details, for example, the incised lines that make the eyes seem deeper than they actually are and cheeks that join the jaw in a smooth curve toward the chin. Teeth can be seen in the slightly open mouth, which is formed by the trapezoidal upper lip characteristic of the Olmec style.

In contrast to the detailed face, the body is reduced to simple forms; only incised curving lines define the creases at the elbows, wrists, knees, and pectoral mus-cles. The tapered arms terminate in large blocks with lightly incised lines indicating curled fingers. The long, gracefully curved legs end in abbreviated feet, the toes rendered schematically. Perhaps in order not to break the long, flowing line from the back to the legs, the supporting belt of the narrow loincloth is not continued around the waist.

From the quality of the workmanship, it would seem that this jadeite was entrusted to the most skilled carvers. Certainly this sculpture is an example of daring virtuosity; working with stone tools and fiber saws, the stone has been chiseled, ground, and pol-ished to create a torso and limbs so slender and fragile that there must have been a constant risk of breakage. Even the nasal septum and earlobes have been metic-ulously perforated, perhaps for attaching jewelry. For reasons unclear, the back of the head is roughly polished with a patch of jade left in its natural state, possibly in deference to the prized, magical material in which it was worked.

BIBLIOGRAPHY
Unpublished.

bent legs from the body has left clear evidence of saw marks from the sculpting process. All detail is concentrated in the compact head and blunt face: the line of the nostrils descends to outline the trapezoidal mouth. The ears are simply incised, scarcely raised rectangles, and there is evidence of a drilled pupil in the left eye. The broad shoulders and upper arms of the figure appear to flex backward, imparting a hint of motion.

The faceting, the penultimate stage of carving, and an unworked patch of stone are visible on the crown of the head, as in cat. no. 26.

BIBLIOGRAPHY
Unpublished.

▲
20. Miniature Standing Figure

900 – 600 B.C.
Provenance: Guerrero
Material: deep green steatite
Dimensions: h. 5 cm.; w. 1.5 cm.; d. 1 cm.
Private collection

Olmec small sculptures of human beings are invested with a monumentality and presence all out of proportion to their size. The geometric organization of the figure and the features of the face, the ears, and the head itself are rendered in the stone tradition of Guerrero, particularly Mezcala, where sculptors carved the compact yet fluid forms of stone celts into rudimentary human images. The rough edges of the broken arms were sawed even and roughly polished to make the damage less distracting. This cosmetic work seems to be of some antiquity, an indication that the figure was prized even in its damaged state.

BIBLIOGRAPHY
Unpublished.

▲
21. Standing Figure

900 – 600 B.C.
Provenance: Michoacan
Material: serpentine
Dimensions: h. 12.7 cm.; w. 5 cm.; d. 2.5 cm.
Private collection

This statue contains all the stylistic elements associated with Olmec standing figures, but in abbreviated form. The separation of the tapered arms and slightly

22. Standing Figure, Fragment ▶

900 – 600 B.C.
Provenance: Mexico
Material: mottled green jade
Dimensions: h. 13.33 cm.; w. 10.16 cm.; d. 4.3 cm.
Private collection

This fragmentary, but refined sculpture with a high, regal head and incised loincloth probably once stood in a position similar to that of the jade figure in the collection of Dumbarton Oaks, which Robert Woods Bliss purchased in 1912 (fig. 1). The arms thrust out from the body suggest the commanding gesture of a ruler and an image of political power. Elizabeth P. Benson speculated that the Dumbarton Oaks figure may have held ritual objects, thereby identifying the projecting arms as a ceremonial posture.[1] The design incised above the figure's right eye and on the cheek below it (fig. 2) perhaps represents the supernatural forces justifying this ruler's power.[2]

BIBLIOGRAPHY
Unpublished.

NOTES
1. Elizabeth P. Benson, "Some Olmec Objects in the Robert Woods Bliss Collection at Dumbarton Oaks," in *The Olmec and Their Neighbors: Essays in Memory of Matthew W. Stirling*, ed. Elizabeth P. Benson (Washington, D.C., 1981), 97.
2. For the same design, see a maskette in this catalogue (cat. no. 153) and a mask in Miguel Covarrubias, *Indian Art of Mexico and Central America* (New York, 1957), 80, pl. 10.

Figure 1. Standing Figure, jadeite, h. 23.9 cm. Dumbarton Oaks Research Library and Collections, Washington, D.C.

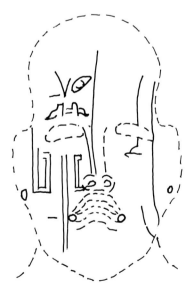

Figure 2. Drawing of incisions.

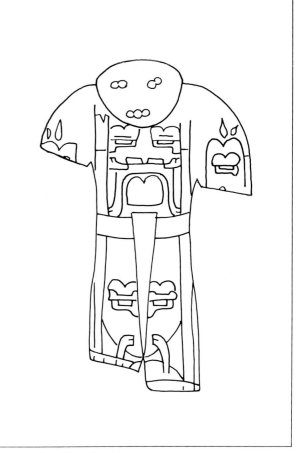

Figure 1. Back view.

Figure 2. Drawing of incisions.

23. Standing Figure with Incisions, Fragment

900–600 B.C.
Provenance: Guerrero
Material: mottled blue-green-to-white jadeite with traces
of red pigment
Dimensions: h. 8.9 cm.; w. 5.5 cm.; d. 2 cm.
Private collection

This fragmentary figure, carved in a rare and precious stone, must have been one of the masterpieces — and the most realistic — of Olmec small sculpture. The chest and leg muscles are defined, the shoulder blades are outlined, and even the loincloth band is shown tied at the back in a knot (fig. 1). The figure, broken in antiquity, was later found and revivified by drilling shallow markings in the repolished broken neck to recreate eyes and mouth. The rough edges of the broken legs were polished smooth and banded and the left arm, now missing, was reattached with a dowel fitted into a hole bored in the upper arm.[1] The two sprouting maize seeds on the shoulders and the stylized supernatural mask emblazoned on the chest are delicately incised. A hollow drill, a tool more com-monly associated with later stone technology, was used to mark the new eyes and mouth, suggesting this torso was cherished as an heirloom.

Though incomplete, the incisions can be identified as motifs associated with the earth and vegetative fertility (fig. 2). The face incised on the chest is similar to the version of the Olmec Dragon on a vase from Tlapacoya (see F. Kent Reilly, III, this volume, fig. 17). The gaping mouth with a cleft motif in the center is the same as that seen on the scepter held in the right arm of the Young Lord (cat. no. 193). The motifs flanking the loincloth, opposed L-shaped eyes and cleft elements, are a more abbreviated version of the dragon, and incorporate variations on the motifs on the shoulders and chest.

BIBLIOGRAPHY
Peter David Joralemon, "The Olmec Dragon: A Study in
Pre-Columbian Iconography," in *Origins of Religious Art and
Iconography in Preclassic Mesoamerica*, ed. Henry B. Nicholson
(Los Angeles, 1976), fig. 10a₁.

NOTE
1. For an example of this technique, see Lee A. Parsons,
*Pre-Columbian Art: The Morton D. May and The Saint Louis
Art Museum Collections* (Saint Louis, 1980), no. 48.

24. Head from a Figure

900–600 B.C.
Provenance: Palenque, Chiapas
Material: jade
Dimensions: h. 7 cm.; w. 4 cm.; d. 4 cm.
National Museum of the American Indian,
Smithsonian Institution

The elongated head, almond-shaped eyes, fine aquiline nose, and downturned mouth of this fragment
from a figure is among the most refined representations of an idealized physical type of a ruler or
member of the elite. The head, found at Palenque at
the end of the nineteenth century, may have sufficed
more readily as an empowered heirloom than that
of a headless fragment (see cat. no. 23), where the
head has been reinstated by the crudely incised face
on the neck.

BIBLIOGRAPHY
Pál Kelemen, *Medieval American Art: Masterpieces of the New World
Before Columbus*, 3d ed. (New York, 1969), 306, pl. 245e.
Masterworks from the Museum of the American Indian Foundation,
The Metropolitan Museum of Art (New York, 1973), no. 28.

25. Incised Maskette

900–600 B.C.
Provenance: Tabasco
Material: dark olive green serpentine with milky green patina
Dimensions: h. 13.5 cm.; w. 10 cm.; d. 5 cm.
Private collection

Despite this mask's small size and the fact that neither
the eyes nor the mouth are cut through, the back has
been deeply hollowed out as if it was intended to be
worn. The area just behind the nose has been bored
through the drilled nostrils, and expanded by grinding
to enable breathing.

The elegant face, with sensuous parted lips, puffy
eyes, and aquiline nose, is recognizable in other small
sculptures, but the resemblance to the standing figure
from the coast of Guerrero (cat. no. 26) is particularly striking. While the mask is reliably reported to
have been found in Tabasco, near La Venta, both it and
the Guerrero sculpture were carved with identical
lithic techniques to extract the living image from the
stone. Whether or not their similar appearance means

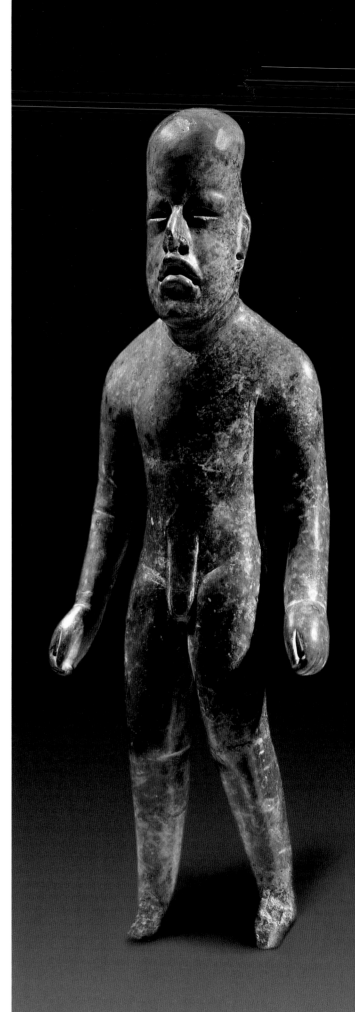

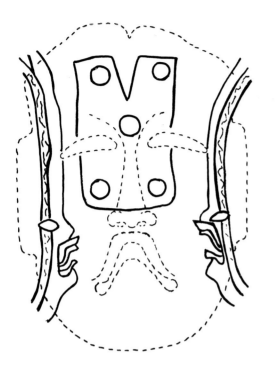

Figure 1. Drawing of incisions.

ished and polished, has a hole drilled in it later to open the skull.

The profiles incised on the cheeks imbue the image with supernatural power (fig. 1). They appear on other stone masks in similar style, heads of human figures carved in the round (cat. no. 32), were-jaguar sculptures, and stone plaques such as the pectoral of multiple profiles in the National Museum in Mexico City.[4] The profile heads are usually extended by narrow bands, terminating in cleft elements similar to a sprouting corn plant's split leaves. The bands may vary in detail as does the treatment of the eyes and mouth of the profiles.

The design on the upper face, five circles set in a cleft rectangle, has been identified by Peter David Joralemon as a distinct motif,[5] but it may be a variation on the "four-dots-and-bar" icon. This motif varies widely; for example, the central element may be in the form of a diamond and the cleft top stepped up twice (see cat. no. 124), or turned sideways and curved to end in a double clefted tip (see cat. no. 93), or, in its most complex form, transformed into a standing figure with the four dots representing sprouting seeds. This last design has been interpreted by F. Kent Reilly, III, as a diagram of Olmec cosmology: the ruler a personification of the world tree and the four seeds the four corners of the universe (see Reilly, this volume, fig. 26).

The refined features on this maskette are the antithesis of the broad-faced, flat-nosed, thick-lipped faces of the Gulf Coast colossal heads, perhaps representing the ascendency of two distinct physical types as the aesthetic ideal of the elite.[6]

they were carved in the same place or is due to technical considerations or an attempt to depict an ideal physical type or possibly even the same person, we do not know.

The extension at the top of the head is broken, but the beginning of a V-shaped cleft can be seen. The meaning of this motif, a defining attribute of the Olmec style, is much debated. Various interpretations have been offered, i.e., that it is the result of a blow to the head from an axe, the fontanel of a newborn baby, the furrow of jaguar's head, or the split in the skin of a toad beginning the molting process.[1] It also is read as a "generalized deity head" or symbol of fertility, perhaps the corn plant itself,[2] or the parted earth from which the plant emerges, a symbol of passage from the terrestial to the supernatural realms.

The V-shaped cleft appears in so many different contexts that it cannot represent an attribute of a specific deity,[3] but it is an all-powerful one for a shamanic ruler to appropriate and incorporate into his own image. Perhaps there is a parallel here with the lithic tradition in figural sculptures where a raw patch of the original stone is left unfinished, or when a head, fin-

BIBLIOGRAPHY
Unpublished.

NOTES
1. Peter Furst, "Jaguar Baby or Toad Mother: A New Look at an Old Problem in Olmec Iconography," in *The Olmec and Their Neighbors: Essays in Memory of Matthew W. Stirling*, ed. Elizabeth P. Benson (Washington, D.C., 1981), 150.
2. Lee A. Parsons, John B. Carlson, and Peter David Joralemon, *The Face of Ancient America: The Wally and Brenda Zollman Collection of Precolumbian Art* (Indianapolis, 1988), 40.
3. Peter David Joralemon, "A Study of Olmec Iconography," *Studies in Pre-Columbian Art and Archaeology*, no. 7 (Washington, D.C., 1971), 7.
4. Michael D. Coe, "The Olmec Style and Its Distribution," in *Handbook of Middle American Indians: Archaeology of Southern Mesoamerica*, vol. 3, ed. Gordon R. Willey (Austin, Tex., 1965), fig. 20.
5. Peter David Joralemon, "A Study of Olmec Iconography," *Studies in Pre-Columbian Art and Archaeology*, no. 7 (Washington, D.C., 1971), motif 187.
6. For a maskette of similar size and incisions, see *Trésors du nouveau monde*, Royal Museum of Art and History (Brussels, 1992), no. 71.

◄ 26. Standing Figure

900 – 600 B.C.
Provenance: Guerrero
Material: blue-green serpentine with milky inclusions and
cloudy patina
Dimensions: h. 25 cm.; w. 9 cm.; d. 4 cm.
Private collection

This male figure exemplifies the Olmec sculptor's skill
in carving serpentine with both precision and fluidity.
The pronounced slope of the shoulders emphasizes the
elongation of the head. The huge, deformed skull, long
line of the torso, and poise of the arms lend the figure
an air of lofty self assurance. Subtleties of detail set the
figure apart from more conventionalized renderings of
the human form. Rather than being simply terminals
with incised fingers, the hands are fully carved, and
the slight upward bend at the wrists gives the figure a
sense of controlled alertness. The carved groin area is
an unusual detail and, although minimally rendered,
seems to be a rare effort on the part of a sculptor to
render genitalia. The indentations at the knees appear
to be an attempt to model moveable, functioning
joints; the legs are not symmetrically fixed but slightly
opposed to suggest movement: the right leg is held
straight and the left is drawn back as if the man were
about to take a step. The feet are damaged, but there is
sufficient indication that they were originally extended
and articulated.

The head is finished in a fashion similar to that of
the standing figure from Michoacan (cat. no. 21). There
is a small spot of unworked stone at the top of the
head, and the faceting in the final shaping of the head,
from just above the eyebrows all the way round to the
back, is unpolished and still visible. The right hand
from midpalm to fingertips was broken off and reattached in antiquity by inserting a dowel into a hole
drilled into the broken surface of the wrist. The feet
were also broken; sawed grooves in the bottom of the
feet indicate they were reattached by a similar method.

This figure, whose remarkable naturalism places
it in a different category from other standing figures,
seems closer in rendering to the standing figure in the
collection of Dumbarton Oaks (see cat. no. 22, fig. 1),
particularly in the hands, knees, and genitalia.

BIBLIOGRAPHY
Unpublished.

27. Seated Figure ►

900 – 600 B.C.
Provenance: Oaxaca
Material: olive-to-pale green serpentine with black oxide
inclusions and cinnabar encrustation
Dimensions: h. 14.2 cm.; w. 8.1 cm.; d. 6.3 cm.
Private collection

Broadly defined and minimally articulated by carving,
drilling, and incising, the human form in this sculpture has been reduced to rudimentary elements. The
carving here consists in simply blocking out the head,
the upright slab of the body onto which the arms and
hands have been scratched, and the crossed legs.
The features are defined by two drilled holes for the
eyes and a rough gash for the mouth, which is circumscribed by an incised line that economically
serves to define the bottom of the nose. This line is
probably best understood as a mouth mask (see
cat. nos. 179, 180).

Contrary to appearances, the rough area at the top
of the figure's head is not damaged. Close inspection
reveals that the area is polished and finished and
that the surface sloping in from the edges and on the
high spots of the rough area are identical to the overall
polish of the rest of the figure. The appearance of such
rough areas on the heads of other, finer and highly
polished small jade sculptures indicates that these
"unfinished" patches are deliberate and significant.

BIBLIOGRAPHY
Unpublished.

28. Seated Figure ►

900 – 600 B.C.
Provenance: Veracruz
Material: light green serpentine
Dimensions: h. 4.45 cm.; w. 2.2 cm.; d. 2.5 cm.
Private collection

A slice of stone was sawed from the bottom of this
figure, but enough of the legs remain to indicate that
this venerable old man is in a cross-legged posture
conducive to meditation. The back, hunched with age,
is not held erect, but is balanced by the slightly lifted,
oversized head. It is unclear whether the eyes are
closed or open, but the figure seems lost in thought
and might well be an aged shaman in a trance.

BIBLIOGRAPHY
Unpublished.

31. Mask ▶

1150–550 B.C.
Provenance: Río Pesquero, Veracruz
Material: gray jadeite with black inclusions
Dimensions: h. 21.6 cm.; w. 19.4 cm.; d. 5.5 cm.
Museum of Fine Arts, Boston, gift of Landon T. Clay

The stone's thickness and weight raise the question whether this mask could have been practical to wear. The back, however, is hollowed out, the eyes and mouth have been carved through, and there are holes drilled below the ears, probably for attachment.

The heavy, fleshy features strongly suggest a portrait and a temporal presence of authority. The face also bears a general physiognomic resemblance to the rulers memorialized in the colossal heads found at San Lorenzo. Whether or not this is a portrait of a historical individual, in its naturalism it is distinct from the other anthropomorphic masks in this catalogue, with no suggestion of an otherworldly, trancelike expression.

The cache of masks and celts from Río Pesquero apparently was not found in a funerary context.[1] This mask may have been intended to preserve the image of a deceased ruler in a material that would not perish and appropriated and worn or displayed by descendants as a claim to the legitimacy of lineage.

BIBLIOGRAPHY
Charlotte Thomson, *Ancient Art of the Americas from New England Collections* (Boston, 1971), no. 7.
Beatriz de la Fuente, "Order and Nature in Olmec Art," in *The Ancient Americas: Art from Sacred Landscapes*, ed. Richard F. Townsend (Chicago, 1992), no. 212.

NOTE
1. See Lee A. Parsons, John B. Carlson, and Peter David Joralemon, *The Face of Ancient America: The Wally and Brenda Zollman Collection of Precolumbian Art* (Indianapolis, 1988), 40.

29. Seated Obese Figure

900–600 B.C.
Provenance: Veracruz
Material: deep bluish green meta-basalt speckled with black
Dimensions: h. 8.3 cm.; w. 5.1 cm.; d. 4.2 cm.
Private collection

The head of this rotund figure is almost the same length as the mound of the torso. The modeling of the body is soft and unarticulated; the crossed legs are reduced to a coil on which the figure sits. The head is held high and the facial features are more sharply defined than the anatomy. The ears were drilled for attachments and the hole of the left ear is broken.

Small stone figures like this may have been carried about with other shamanic or talismanic objects. This one in particular may have been held in the hand and experienced from all angles, especially since the legs are fully carved on the underside.

The figure bears comparison with ceramic seated figures in the treatment of the arms and hands (see cat. no. 16).

BIBLIOGRAPHY
Unpublished.

30. Seated Figure

1000–600 B.C.
Provenance: Puebla
Material: solid buff clay
Dimensions: h. 4.5 cm.; w. 3.5 cm.; d. 2.5 cm.
Private collection

The pose of this diminutive figure of an old man, although a more modest work in clay and very different in subject, recalls that of the Seated Ruler in the Dallas Museum of Art (cat. no. 15). The variations on the pose can perhaps be explained by the more naturalistic observance of the old man, who is hunchbacked with several vertebrae showing. The legs are spindly and the skin on the chest and stomach falls in loose folds.

It is difficult to determine the state of the man. The treatment of each eye differs: the left is tortoiselike, with only a slit between the heavy lids; the right is only slightly more open. These variances, which might simply be the result of the vagaries of the modeler's tool, give the effect of a trancelike state.

BIBLIOGRAPHY
Unpublished.

▲
32. Head with Incisions

900–600 B.C.
Provenance: Puebla
Material: light greenish gray marble with black veins, hornblende and phlogopite encrustations
Dimensions: h. 12.7 cm.; w. 8.1 cm.; d. 6.9 cm.
Private collection

This head was apparently broken from a relatively large figure. The jowly, broad-nosed, thick-lipped face is reminiscent of the colossal heads, although the skull is elongated and shaved, leaving one long lock of hair falling over the headband. Ear spools are incised and drilled in the ears, which are set back and flare from the head. Animating profiles of supernaturals are incised well back on the sides of either cheek, the one on the left now almost completely obliterated. A shallow depression in the crown of the head has been ground out exposing the raw stone.

BIBLIOGRAPHY
Unpublished.

157

33. Figure Holding Infant

900–600 B.C.
Provenance: Tabasco
Material: light green compacted clay
Dimensions: h. 5 cm.; w. 3 cm.; d. 3 cm.
Private collection

The seated adult male figure supporting the infant is hunchbacked; the back is severely deformed on one side, where the shoulder blade and ribs protrude. The head, under which the infant is sheltered, is massive, the skull, elongated. The figure may wear a tight-fitting cap or have close-cropped hair. The features are heavy, particularly the fleshy, pronounced lips. With the support of the adult figure, the infant stands with both feet on the ground. Its head has already been deformed by binding, and the navel is pronounced in the plump belly.

It is easy to see this as a simple vignette of familial affection, but this miniature group must be understood in the context of images of child-bearers and in anticipation of shamanic rituals where infants, effigies of infants, or infants in the guise of a supernatural are presented (cat. nos. 4–6, 34, 35).

BIBLIOGRAPHY
Unpublished.

34. Seated Figure Holding Infant

900–500 B.C.
Provenance: Mexico
Material: serpentine
Dimensions: h. 11.4 cm.; w. 5.7 cm.; d. 5.4 cm.
Lent by The Metropolitan Museum of Art, the Michael C. Rockefeller Memorial Collection, bequest of Nelson A. Rockefeller, 1979

In contrast to the group of ceramic figures of old women holding infants (cat. nos. 4–6), this stone object shows a man seated on a throne with an infant across his lap. Scholars have noted the similarities among the infant-bearing sculptures in both ceramic and stone, but the nature of their relationship is a source of debate. Peter David Joralemon stated that "despite

Figure 1. La Venta Altar 5.

Figure 3. La Venta Altar 5, side view.

Figure 2. Las Limas Figure.

the formal similarities shared by all the infant-bearers, I see no reason to believe that the sculptures necessarily have the same meaning."[1] Gillett G. Griffin speculated that the stone monuments were "later evolutions of the theme" first seen in the ceramic figures, and felt that the iconography of the motif had "changed radically."[2]

The statue evokes a sense of monumentality disproportionate to its size. The face, which is not idealized, has an expression of intense anticipation. Teeth can be seen in the deeply carved mouth. Centrally parted with incised locks, the hair resembles a tight-fitting cap. Other than at the chest, which is softly rounded, the body shows few signs of definition. Short, incised lines indicate the fingers and toes. Random, shallow drill holes separate the arms from the chest. Flangelike ears are pierced, presumably for ornaments. The figure has sustained some damage at the crown of the head and the upper lip; a gash to the left of the lower lip extends to the cheek; and the right leg is missing below the knee.

The left side of the infant, who appears lifeless and rigid, merges into the torso of the seated figure. The infant's right arm and hand are barely defined; its large, square head, framed by rectangular ears, is joined directly to the body. The face displays shallow indentations for eyes, a flat nose, curled upper lip, and downturned mouth. Simple saw lines define the legs. Two incised parallel lines cross the chest and right arm.

The image of a seated male holding a prone infant is seen on two monuments from the Gulf Coast: La Venta Altar 5 and the Las Limas Figure (figs. 1 and 2).[3] In all the three images, the infants have similar faces, the seated figures hold the infants in the same position, and the adult figures are identified as ritual performers: the La Venta Altar 5 figure by the costume; the Metropolitan figure by the throne; the Las Limas Figure by the incised symbols of the supernatural on the face, shoulders, and knees. While the body of the Metropolitan infant is stiff, and the infants on the Las Limas Figure and on the front of La Venta Altar 5 are draped limply across the arms of the supporting figures, all are depicted as lifeless. On the Las Limas Figure, the infant wears two crossed-bands pectorals, a headband, and crenellated earflaps, attributes of the Olmec Supernatural that controls the rain and harvest.

On the left and right sides of La Venta Altar 5 are scenes of seated figures holding animated infants in contrast to the lifeless infant on the front (fig. 3). These scenes appear to represent stages in a sacrificial ritual, either actual or ceremonial, in which infants are presented in the image of the supernatural, offered as symbols of agricultural renewal.

BIBLIOGRAPHY
Bradley Smith, *Mexico: A History in Art* (New York, 1968), 33.
Robert Goldwater et al., *Art of Oceania, Africa, and the Americas from the Museum of Primitive Art* (New York, 1969), no. 551.
Muriel P. Weaver, *The Aztecs, Maya, and Their Predecessors* (New York, 1972), pl. 1a.
Gillett G. Griffin, "Olmec Forms and Materials Found in Central Guerrero," in *The Olmec and Their Neighbors: Essays in Memory of Matthew W. Stirling*, ed. Elizabeth P. Benson (Washington, D.C., 1981), fig. 11.
Beatriz de la Fuente et al., *Mexico en el mundo de las colecionnes de arte 1: Mesoamerica* (Mexico City, 1992), 42.

NOTES
1. Peter David Joralemon, "The Old Woman and the Child: Themes in the Iconography of Preclassic Mesoamerica," in *The Olmec and Their Neighbors: Essays in Memory of Matthew W. Stirling*, ed. Elizabeth P. Benson (Washington, D.C., 1981), 176.
2. Gillett G. Griffin, "Olmec Forms and Materials Found in Central Guerrero," in *The Olmec and Their Neighbors: Essays in Memory of Matthew W. Stirling*, ed. Elizabeth P. Benson (Washington, D.C., 1981), 214.
3. The motif is also seen on La Venta Altar 2 and San Lorenzo Monument 20, although these monuments are too mutilated to interpret further. The badly eroded San Lorenzo Monument 12 depicts a seated, cross-legged figure holding an infant who seems to be alive.

35. Standing Figure Holding Supernatural Effigy

800–500 B.C.
Provenance: Mexico
Material: jade
Dimensions: h. 21.9 cm.; w. 8.1 cm.; d. 4.1 cm.
The collection of Robin B. Martin, currently on loan to
The Brooklyn Museum

For sheer power of presence, symbolic significance, and technical brilliance, this statue is one of the most charged icons of Olmec art. Although the original provenance of the piece cannot be determined, it is said to have been in France at least as early as the mid-nineteenth century before it came to the United States.[1] While its iconographic affinities to other major touch-stones of Olmec art, including the Las Limas Figure and La Venta Altar 5, have long been recognized, the exact nature of its meaning and relationship to those objects remain unclear.

The emphatic symmetry of the composition inten-sifies the mystical drama embodied in the sculpture. With legs parted and solidly planted, the standing figure has a ceremonial bearing. Looming large in relation to the body, the finely and richly carved face is in striking contrast to the smooth volumes of the arms and legs. The head narrows and flattens at the top, the brow is high, and the cranium is extended and shaped at the back. Set under arching brows, the eyes are deeply excavated with drilled pupils. The back is straight and the knees slightly flexed in the position associated with standing meditation.[2] An immaterial presence is lent to the figure by the mirrorlike polish of the surface and the translucency of the material.

The standing figure holds the body of a diminu-tive creature with a V-shaped cleft in its head, almond-shaped eyes, foreshortened broad nose, and wide, open mouth with heavy, downturned fleshy lips. The fiercely animated expression is sharply contrasted with the transfixed gaze of the adult figure. The drilled navel of the small being is conspicuous and would correspond to the height of the navel of the adult figure, marking the exact center of the composition.[3]

A headband with two nodules and wavy crenel-lations at the sides identifies the creature with the Olmec Supernatural,[4] among the most prominent and recognizable images in Olmec art. Whether its appearance in this sculpture is to be understood as a masked human baby about to be sacrificed, a carved ritual object, or the supernatural itself, it is intended to represent the power of this creature.

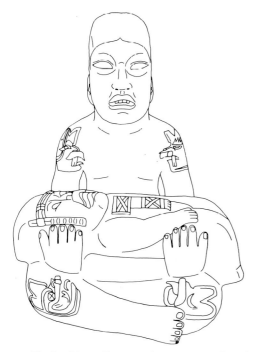

Figure 1. The Las Limas Figure, indicating incised profiles on the shoulders and knees.

In discussing the incisions of the Las Limas Figure, Peter David Joralemon noted that the profile heads incised on each of the seated figure's shoulders are raptorial birds, hence sky symbols (fig. 1).[5] Following Joralemon's association of the incised raptors with the sky realm, F. Kent Reilly, III, noted that the incised profiles on the Las Limas Figure's knees derive from a shark and a serpent, representatives of the watery underworld.[6] The upper and lower parts of the body of the seated figure are thereby identified with the upper and lower levels of the shamanic cosmos. The incised profiles on the seated figure's shoulders face inward, those on the knees, upward. Were the Las Limas Figure to stand and hold the supernatural against the chest, its posture would correspond to the statue under discussion here, whose shamanic meditative stance provides access to supernatural power that transforms the body into the axis linking the levels of the cosmos. No incisions serve to identify this figure explicitly with different cosmic levels, but the creature held in his arms is a visible manifestation of his possession and manipulation of supernatural powers.

BIBLIOGRAPHY

Maxwell Sommerville, *Engraved Gems: Their History and Place in Art* (Philadelphia, 1889), 89.
J. Pijoan, *Arte Precolombiano, Mexicano, y Maya* (Madrid, 1946), fig. 450.
Herbert J. Spinden, "An Olmec Jewel," *Brooklyn Museum Bulletin* 9, no. 1 (1947): 1–12.
H. Comstock, "The Connoisseur in America," *The Connoisseur* 127 (April, 1951): 41.
D. F. Rubín de la Borbolla, *Mexico: Monumentos Históricos y Arqueológicos* (Mexico, 1953), fig. 229.
S. Linné, *Treasures of Ancient Mexico*, trans. A. Read (Stockholm, 1956), 50–51.
Herbert J. Spinden, *Maya Art and Civilization* (Colorado, 1957), pl. 56c.
Jane Powell, *Ancient Art of the Americas* (New York, 1960), 32.
William Spratling, *Escultura Precolumbina de Guerrero* (Mexico City, 1964), fig. 54.
Alfonso M. Zenil, "La Escultura de las Limas," *Boletin Instituto Nacional de Antropología y Historia* 21 (1965), 8.
Michael D. Coe, "The Olmec Style and Its Distribution," in *Handbook of Middle American Indians: Archaeology of Southern Mesoamerica*, vol. 3, ed. Gordon R. Willey (Austin, Tex., 1965), fig. 7.
Michael D. Coe, *The Jaguar's Children: Pre-Classic Central Mexico* (New York, 1965), fig. 4.
E. Dávalos Hurtado, *Tema de Antropologia Fisica* (Mexico City, 1965), pl. 6.
Ferdinand Anton, *Alt-Mexiko und seine Kunst* (Leipzig, 1965), no. 30.
Hasso von Winning, *Pre-Columbian Art of Mexico and Central America* (New York, 1968), fig. 53.
Louis Zara, *Jade* (New York, 1969), fig. 29.
Elizabeth K. Easby and John F. Scott, *Before Cortés: Sculpture of Middle America* (New York, 1970), no. 41.
Peter David Joralemon, "A Study of Olmec Iconography," *Studies in Pre-Columbian Art and Archaeology*, no. 7 (Washington, D.C., 1971), fig. 208.
Samuel K. Lothrop and Gordon F. Ekholm, "Pre-Columbian Objects," in *The Guennol Collection* vol. 1, ed. Ida Ely Rubin (New York, 1975), 307.
Mary Miller, "Pre-Hispanic Jade," *Latin American Art* (Spring 1991): fig. 1.
Ronald L. Bishop, Frederick W. Lange, and Elizabeth K. Easby, "Jade in Mesoamerica," in *Jade*, ed. Roger Keverne (London, 1991), fig. 25.
Beatriz de la Fuente et al., *Mexico en el mundo de las colecionnes de Aarte 1: Mesoamerica* (Mexico City, 1992), 41.
Richard F. Townsend, ed., *The Ancient Americas: Art from Sacred Landscapes* (Chicago, 1992), 126; no. 206.

NOTES

1. Samuel K. Lothrop and Gordon F. Ekholm, "Pre-Columbian Objects," in *The Guennol Collection* vol. 1, ed. Ida Ely Rubin (New York, 1975), 315.
2. See Carolyn E. Tate, this volume.
3. This correspondence of human and supernatural navels is significant in Aztec thought. The navel was considered the central nexus, the conjunction of all parts of the body, and a conduit through which the individual was connected to the magic-cosmic world. See Alfredo López Austin, *The Human Body and Ideology: Concepts of the Ancient Nahuas* (Salt Lake City, 1988), 167. The umbilical cord is described as a symbol of connection in Maya iconography in Linda Schele, David A. Freidel, and Joy Parker, *Maya Cosmos: Three Thousand Years Down the Shaman's Path* (New York, 1993), 99–107.
4. See cat. nos. 83–88 for further interpretation of this supernatural.
5. Peter David Joralemon, "The Olmec Dragon: A Study in Pre-Columbian Iconography," in *Origins of Religious Art and Iconography in Preclassic Mesoamerica*, ed. Henry B. Nicholson (Los Angeles, 1976), 33, 37.
6. F. Kent Reilly, III, "Visions to Another World: Art, Shamanism, and Political Power in Middle Formative Mesoamerica," Ph.D. diss., University of Texas at Austin, 1994, 128.

36. Supernatural Effigy Plaque

900–400 B.C.
Provenance: Cuautla, Morelos
Material: greenstone
Dimensions: h. 14.9 cm.; w. 6.7 cm.; d. 2 cm.
William P. Palmer III Collection, Hudson Museum, University of Maine

Allowing for differences in format and pose, this plaque is identical in the features of the face, V-shaped cleft, headband, and projections on the sides of the head to the supernatural discussed in the preceding entry (cat. no. 35). The almost square head and body are in approximately the same proportion. More attention was paid to the rendering of the face than the body; only cursory lines indicate fingers and toes. The legs are framed by a relief carving in the form of a crenellation with a pendant tri-lobed motif in the center. The plaque lacks any holes for attachment, and, if not worn, may have been held or displayed in a shamanic ritual as a symbol of supernatural power.

BIBLIOGRAPHY

Marjorie Smith Zengel et al., *The Art of Ancient and Modern Latin America* (New Orleans, 1968), fig. 10.
Hasso von Winning, *Pre-Columbian Art of Mexico and Central America* (New York, 1968), fig. 41.

II
The Shamanic Landscape and Journey

In the shamanic world of ancient Mesoamerica, no dichotomy exists between the natural and the supernatural. The body of the shamanic ruler through ritual meditation and transformation becomes the conduit depicted as the *axis mundi*, the conduit between the natural and supernatural, and the features of the natural landscape — mountains, caves, rivers, and springs — are manifestations of portals to the otherworld. The Olmec cosmos is structured in three levels: the terrestrial, inhabited by humans, and the watery underworld and celestial realm, inhabited by supernaturals, who control the cosmic forces that determine the outcome of human events, most importantly rain and agricultural fertility. Those worlds could only be bridged and access gained to the supernatural through shamanic ritual claimed by Olmec rulers.

The supernatural world, the sacred landscape, was made manifest in the great ceremonial centers and through the ritual manipulation of magically empowered objects. Ceremonial centers may have been established where the terrain suggested the topography of the supernatural realm, natural equivalents of the watery underworld and celestial sphere. In Morelos, Cerro Delgado and Cerro Chalcatzingo rise above the floor of the Río Amatzinac Valley, and on the slopes of Cerro Chalcatzingo a relief depicts a ruler in the mouth of a cave, the portal to the underworld, in the form of the great maw of a zoomorphic supernatural. At the ceremonial center of La Venta, a sacred mountain was erected rising one hundred feet into the sky over the flat landscape of the Gulf Coast. The underworld was defined by great caches and pavements of precious greenstone, symbolizing water, buried to the north of the mountain.

Transformation of the shaman or ruler into his nagual, the animal spirit companion, was a means of entrance to the otherworld. As the standing meditative posture may be associated with the transformation of the ruler into the *axis mundi*, so the kneeling meditative posture may be specifically identified with and preparatory to transformation into the nagual. Neither fully human nor animal, figures in transformation are represented in varying degrees of fusion with the nagual. The prevalence of jaguar transformation figures and the likelihood that such effigies represented or were made for powerful figures suggest that shaman-jaguar transformation was a validation of Olmec rulership. The rulers of the Formative period, transformed into the powerful predator, overcame the dangers of the otherworld in search of ancestral communication and the power to manipulate the cosmic forces.

Hallucinogens were probably ingested in transformation ritual to induce the trance state. Ceramic vessels in the forms of animals may have been containers for hallucinogenic substances and effigies of the animal spirit companion; objects in stone, identified as spoons by their bowllike chambers, may have been receptacles used to ingest the hallucinogens. The existence of perforators, sharp objects in jade and greenstone, would indicate that blood was a causative agent that opened the portal between the natural and supernatural worlds. Spoons and perforators were carved in greenstone, a magical material symbolizing water for ancient Mesoamericans. Red pigment, such as cinnabar, was often used to heighten the incised images on these objects and functioned symbolically as blood. The spoons and perforators carried images and symbols of supernatural flight, the shamanic journey across the portal, sometimes depicted in the form of "fliers," figures in horizontal positons wearing headdresses and short skirts, winged or wearing short capes, with arms outstretched holding a shaft of bound vegetation, identified variously as a torch, bound vegetation or feathers, and bloodletters. The shamanic journey is also depicted in small sculptures showing humans and supernaturals riding on the backs of their animal spirit companions or a supernatural zoomorph that had the power to travel between the levels of the cosmos.

The construction of ceremonial centers and the creation of magically empowered objects of precious and exotic materials animated in ritual performance gave visible form to the shamanic powers of Olmec rulers as a validation to their claim to rulership.

37. Chalcatzingo Monument 9

700–500 B.C.?
Provenance: Chalcatzingo, Morelos
Material: granodiorite
Dimensions: h. 183 cm.; w. 142 cm.; d. 15.2 cm.
Munson-Williams-Proctor Institute, Museum of Art, Utica,
New York

Monument 9, a carved slab of stone from the site of
Chalcatzingo, was removed from its original location
above a tomb on Plaza Central Structure 4 sometime in
the 1960s. David C. Grove and Ann Cyphers-Guillén
dated Structure 4 to the Cantera Phase of occupation at
Chalcatzingo, approximately 700–500 B.C., providing
a possible date for Monument 9.[1]

Monument 9 depicts a frontal-faced, open-mouthed,
zoomorphic monster (fig. 1). The quatrefoil mouth,
large enough for an individual to crawl through, is
surrounded by three separate framing elements. The
somewhat worn bottom part of the mouth led Grove
to suggest that the monument "may have served
as a ritual passageway."[2] Above the mouth, the ovoid
eyes are surmounted with eye ridges ending in cleft
projections.[3] Although drawings show the eyes reconstructed with the crossed-bands motif in the pupils,
close examination reveals no such elements.[4] An
oval cartouche between the eyes and above the nose
surrounds a damaged motif, possibly a face. Two

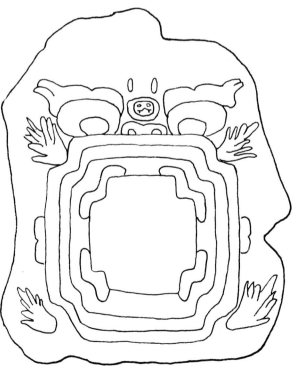

Figure 1. Revised drawing of Monument 9.

Figure 2. Chalcatzingo Monument 1.

Figure 3. Bowl with incisions, 900–600 B.C., Xochipala, stone, h. 6.4 cm.; diam. 15.5 cm. Private collection.

Peter David Joralemon, "A Study of Olmec Iconography," *Studies in Pre-Columbian Art and Archaeology*, no. 7 (Washington, D.C., 1971), figs. 141, 266.

Peter David Joralemon, "The Olmec Dragon: A Study in Pre-Columbian Iconography," in *Origins of Religious Art and Iconography in Preclassic Mesoamerica*, ed. Henry B. Nicholson (Los Angeles, 1976), figs. 6b, 10q, 17b.

David C. Grove, *Chalcatzingo: Excavations on the Olmec Frontier* (New York, 1984), 50; figs. 8, 9.

David C. Grove, ed., *Ancient Chalcatzingo* (Austin, 1987), 124–25, 141.

Beatriz de la Fuente et al., *Mexico en el mundo de las colecionnes de arte 1: Mesoamerica* (Mexico City, 1992), 36.

Beatriz de la Fuente, "Order and Nature in Olmec Art," in *The Ancient Americas: Art from Sacred Landscapes,* ed. Richard F. Townsend (Chicago, 1992), no. 211.

NOTES

1. David C. Grove and Ann Cyphers-Guillén, "The Excavations," in *Ancient Chalcatzingo*, ed. David C. Grove (Austin, Tex., 1987), 30–32. In the catalogue of the monuments of Chalcatzingo, Grove and Jorge Angulo, V, stated that "our excavations atop P[laza] C[entral] Structure 4's northern edge uncovered an area of disturbed soil near the mound's northern edge. Several workers informed us that the monument [9], in fragments, had been found there," David C. Grove and Jorge Angulo, V, "Catalog and Description of the Monuments," in *Ancient Chalcatzingo*, ed. Grove, 124. See also David C. Grove, *Chalcatzingo: Excavations on the Olmec Frontier* (New York, 1984), fig. 9, for a map of the Plaza Central and the location of Monument 9. The area of disturbed soil is labeled "looted" by Grove and Guillén ("The Excavations," fig. 4.9) and "looted crypt" by Marcia Merry de Morales ("Chalcatzingo Burials as Indicators of Social Ranking," in *Ancient Chalcatzingo,* ed. Grove, 100, 462–63).

2. Grove and Angulo (as in note 1), 125.

3. The source of these strangely configured eye ridges may be the bony plates over the protruding eyes of crocodilians. Crocodilians have been repeatedly shown to be the source of much of the Olmec Dragon imagery. For further discussion of the Olmec Dragon, see Reilly, this volume, and Peter David Joralemon, "The Olmec Dragon: A Study in Pre-Columbian Iconography," in *Origins of Religious Art and Iconography in Preclassic Mesoamerica*, ed. Henry B. Nicholson (Los Angeles, 1976), 27–71.

4. This finding was confirmed by Virginia M. Fields and F. Kent Reilly, III, upon examination of Monument 9 in June 1993.

5. See Karl A. Taube, this volume.

6. Joralemon (as in note 3), 36–37.

7. Grove and Angulo (as in note 1), see fig. 9.13.

8. Philip Drucker, "La Venta, Tabasco: A Study of Olmec Ceramics and Art," *Bureau of American Ethnology* Bulletin 153 (1952), fig. 22, pl. 18.

9. David C. Grove, "Chalcatzingo and Its Olmec Connection," in *Regional Perspectives on the Olmec*, ed. Robert J. Sharer and David C. Grove (Cambridge, 1989), 132.

10. Joralemon first discussed the function of the gaping maw in "The Olmec Dragon" (as in note 3), 37–40.

11. For the identification of Mesoamerican rulers as supernatural portals and pathways of communication, see Linda Schele and David Freidel, *A Forest of Kings: The Untold Story of the Ancient Maya* (New York, 1990); David Freidel, Linda Schele, and Joy Parker, *Maya Cosmos: Three Thousand Years on the Shaman's Path* (New York, 1993); and Reilly, this volume.

elements above this cartouche may represent exclamation-point rain motifs.[5] Vegetative elements resembling bromeliads emerge from the four corners of the mouth.

The same cave mouth is seen in profile, with crossed-bands in the eyes, on Chalcatzingo Monument 1 (fig. 2). Peter David Joralemon demonstrated that the use of frontal and profile variants was a fundamental principle of Olmec art.[6] The monster on Chalcatzingo Monuments 1 and 9 appears on a variety of objects. For example, the surviving segment of Chalcatzingo Monument 13 shows a figure with a cleft head in profile seated inside the monster in the same position as on Monument 1.[7] A stone bowl, allegedly from Xochipala, has the monster incised on its underside (fig. 3) and a fragment of a bowl from La Venta displays the monster mouth in relief.[8] Iconographic connections between the monuments at La Venta and Chalcatzingo, and the lack of a tradition of monumental sculpture in central Mexico, imply that the carvings of Chalcatzingo were "executed in an imported technique and display imported messages and narratives."[9] In this manner, Monument 9 relates to another Olmec tomb monument, La Venta Monument 6, a sandstone sarcophagus depicting the Olmec Dragon. Here the buried person rode on the back of the dragon to the otherworld. In a similar fashion, in Monument 9 the buried person in the tomb below "traveled" through it, marking the transition from life to death.

The gaping maw on Monument 9 functioned symbolically as a portal between the natural and supernatural aspects of the cosmic order.[10] It was both a path of communication and a point of access to supernatural power. The Olmec conceived of these portals as thin, membranelike doors separating the living, natural order from the supernatural realm of the ancestors. The portals could exist not only as sculptures, such as Monument 9, but also as geographic features in the Mesoamerican landscape, such as caves and mountains. Smaller objects, manipulated by the shamanic ruler, also could function in rituals to open portals to the supernatural world.[11] Monument 9's worn bottom ledge strongly suggests that it was employed as a passageway for objects or people journeying into or emerging from the supernatural realm during this ritual activity.

BIBLIOGRAPHY

David C. Grove, "Chalcatzingo, Morelos, Mexico: A Reappraisal of the Olmec Rock Carvings," *American Antiquity* 33, no. 4 (1968): 486–91.

Elizabeth K. Easby and John F. Scott, *Before Cortés: Sculpture of Middle America* (New York, 1970), no. 32.

CONTORTION AND TRANSFORMATION

At least five monumental sculptures from Mesoamerica depict figures with bodies arched backward and feet placed on the head (see Tate, this volume). It is not known if these contorted positions represent actual postures taken by shamans or are metaphors for the rigors and discipline, the inversion of the mind and body, necessary to achieve a state of ecstatic trance and transformation into a spirit form through which to gain access to the supernatural world. Peter T. Furst observes in this volume that Huichol shamans somersault to transform themselves into animal alter egos. In the series of human figures changing into jaguars, some express by their movements the physical and psychic exertion of transformation; and the well-known sculpture, referred to as a "wrestler," with arms raised in a seemingly combative position, has recently been interpreted as a shaman.[1]

Human figures, in a kneeling position of stilled equilibrium, may represent the preparatory stage of transformation, possibly specific to conjuring the nagual, the spirit form through which the shaman is transported to the supernatural world.

NOTE
1. Roy C. Craven, Jr., "An Iconographic Note: 'Wrestler' or 'Shaman'?" *Mexicon* 17 (April 1995): 30–32.

38. Vessel in the Form of a Contortionist ▶

1250–900 B.C.
Provenance: Tlatilco, Mexico
Material: redware
Dimensions: h. 38.1 cm.
Private collection

The legs of this contortionist, one straight up and the other with the foot resting on the head, form the spout and handle of a vessel. It is one of a number of examples from Tlatilco employing this conceit.[1] A variation on the theme shows a figure, who wears a grotesque mask, lying feet up on the drum-shaped body of the vessel, the hands supporting the legs, which are joined to form the spout (fig. 1).

Whether symbolic or functional, these vessels embody the principle of transformation through their

contorted poses and may have contained a substance that helped induce the shamanic trance. The use of a human form may signify that the body is a vessel for animistic energies.

BIBLIOGRAPHY
Trésors d'art précolombien (Paris, 1959), no. 6.
Michael D. Coe, *The Jaguar's Children: Pre-Classic Central Mexico*
    (New York, 1965), no. 75.

NOTE
1. Román Piña Chán, *The Olmec: Mother Culture of Mesoamerica*
    (New York, 1989), figs. 6, 8; Emile Deletaille, *Rediscovered*
    Masterpieces (Boulogne, 1985), no. 117.

▲ 39. Figures in Contorted Postures

1250–900 B.C.
Provenance: Las Bocas, Puebla
Material: buff clay with white slip and traces of red pigment
Dimensions: left: h. 3 cm.; w. 2 cm.; d. 4 cm.; middle and right:
h. 5.1 cm.; w. 2.5 cm.; d. 2.5 cm.
Private collection

These three small solid clay sculptures, said to have been found together at Las Bocas, kneel with their arms across their chests, bodies thrown back in progressive degrees of contortion until the head of one figure touches the ground. It is tempting to see them as a sequence in the stages of an ecstatic trance. Varying only slightly in detail, as, for example, in the treatment of the hair, all three are rendered without eyes, perhaps to emphasize the trance state. Needlelike holes are drilled through the torsos to permit the insertion of a slender stick with which to manipulate them.

BIBLIOGRAPHY
Unpublished.

Figure 1. Bottle in the form of a contortionist, 1250–900 B.C., Tlatilco, ceramic with slip and traces of red pigment, h. 22 cm.; w. 14 cm.; d. 13 cm. Private collection.

◀ 40. Figure with Feet on Head

900 – 500 B.C.
Provenance: San Geronimo, Guerrero
Material: light bluish green steatite with the surface mineral
stained brown
Dimensions: h. 23.5 cm.; w. 13 cm.; d. 26 cm.
Private collection

With the greatest of ease, this figure, lying on its
stomach and leaning on its elbows, turns its legs back
so that the feet rest on the back of the head, creating an
enclosed form. With no signs of the physical exertion
demanded of such a posture, the figure's expression is
calm and reflective, the arms comfortably crossed
over the chest. The hands gripping the arms provide
the only indication of leverage. The finely polished
surface of the stone appears to have been gnawed by
an animal.

Elegant, almost feminine in the refinement of its
features, the face has a long, thin nose, arched brow,
narrow eyes, and soft lips. On the top of the head, like
a cap made of an open, inverted shell, are two symmetrical, rounded forms incised with a fish-scale pattern. Cut low and straight across the forehead with
long sideburns, the hair is indicated by finely incised
vertical lines. The torso, chest, ribcage, and ribs are
clearly defined on the underside, a measure of the
quality and refinement of this stone sculpture. This
contortionist wears a loincloth, which is extended
in the back to form a short skirt often associated with
the "fliers," symbols of the shaman's magic flight
to the otherworld.[1]

Clearly a member of the elite, not merely a contortionist or acrobat, the figure's position is not idle
exercise.[2] Seen from the side, the figure forms an
enclosed void, which may symbolize an opening to
the otherworld. A stone bas-relief from San Antonio
Suchitepequez, Guatemala, depicts two figures in
similar postures (see Tate, this volume, fig. 28). One
of the figures, extremely attenuated, grasps its ankles
with its hands, forming a circle. A regal personage
is seen from the front in the void enclosed by the
figure's body. The soles of the feet appear to either
side of the headdress, indicating that the figure is in
the same posture as the statue illustrated here. The
ruler or shaman seated in a cave mouth or niche, symbolic portals to the otherworld, is a motif most often
associated with the altars of La Venta and the reliefs of
Chalcatzingo. The San Antonio Suchitepequez relief
and this sculpture may record this concept in the
metaphorical form of these contortionists.

BIBLIOGRAPHY
Unpublished.

NOTES
1. F. Kent Reilly, III, "The Shaman in Transformation Pose: A Study of the Theme of Rulership in Olmec Art," *Record of The Art Museum, Princeton University* 48, no. 2 (1989): 16.
2. A similar posture is recorded in a ceramic vessel from Tlatilco, Román Piña Chán, *The Olmec: Mother Culture of Mesoamerica* (New York, 1989), fig. 6.

41. Figure with Incised Feet on Head and Crossed Arms

900 – 500 B.C.
Provenance: Mexico
Material: stone
Dimensions: h. 5.7 cm.; w. 9.5 cm.; d. 3.8 cm.
Private collection

Unlike the languid ease of the contortionist in cat. no. 40, the pose of this figure is more abstract and vigorous. There is a deft handling of the stone, as if it were a pliable material, and a quick sureness to the incisions consistent with the immediacy, power, and vitality of the sculpture. The crossed arms, which project well in front of the figure, appear to provide greater balance, but the large, padlike feet are impossibly turned back on themselves. The position of

the heels forms the same scalloped design as the hairline in cat. no. 40. The unarticulated body and legs sweep around between the incised lines that define the arms and the feet. The columnar head rises abruptly from the plane of the back; the aggressive jut of the hooked nose and the thick, protruding lips provide the only carved relief in the otherwise contained form of the contortionist.

The symbols on the soles of the feet, a crossed-bands on the right and a dotted bracket on the left, most often appear in place of eyes on larger Olmec sculptures. Their meaning is debated.[1] The juxtaposition and union of head and feet are unusual (see cat. no. 67). Disembodied feet, which appear repeatedly in Olmec art (cat. nos. 126, 198, and La Venta Monument 13), may refer to the shamanic journey.

BIBLIOGRAPHY
"Arte / Rama," *Editorial Codex, S.A.* 60 (1961): 33.
Ferdinand Anton and Frederick Dockstader, *Pre-Columbian Art* (New York, 1968), 25.
Peter David Joralemon, "A Study of Olmec Iconography," *Studies in Pre-Columbian Art and Archaeology,* no. 7 (Washington, D.C., 1971), fig. 23, motif 114.
Peter David Joralemon, "The Olmec Dragon: A Study in Pre-Columbian Iconography," in *Origins of Religious Art and Iconography in Preclassic Mesoamerica,* ed. Henry B. Nicholson (Los Angeles, 1976), fig. 18f.
Ferdinand Anton, *Primitive Art* (New York, 1979), 25.
Everett McNear, *High Culture in the Americas Before 1500* (Chicago, 1982), 3.

NOTE
1. Rosemary Joyce et al., "Olmec Bloodletting: An Iconographic Study," in *Sixth Palenque Round Table, 1986,* ed. Virginia M. Fields (Norman, Okla., 1991); Peter David Joralemon, "The Olmec Dragon: A Study in Pre-Columbian Iconography," in *Origins of Religious Art and Iconography in Preclassic Mesoamerica,* ed. Henry B. Nicholson (Los Angeles, 1976), fig. 18f; idem, "A Study of Olmec Iconography," *Studies in Pre-Columbian Art and Archaeology,* no. 7 (Washington, D.C., 1971), fig. 23, motif 114.

42. Shaman in Transformation Pose

800 – 600 B.C.
Provenance: Veracruz
Material: polished gray stone with traces of cinnabar
Dimensions: h. 17.5 cm.; w. 15.5 cm.; d. 9 cm.
The Art Museum, Princeton University,
gift of Mrs. Gerard B. Lambert by exchange

This kneeling figure provides a crucial link between kneeling bearded figures (cat. nos. 12, 13) and the group of figures depicting stages in the transformation from human to jaguar. Where the kneeling bearded figures almost certainly depict rulers or important members of society, their shamanic content is implied only when one connects the pose of this figure with a kneeling figure with a head of a jaguar in the collection of Dumbarton Oaks (fig. 1).

This individual, surely a specific person, kneels with his arms resting on top of his knees, hands clenched, in quiet, intense concentration. Except for two tiers of finely incised hair curving back from the ears and temples, the high sloping head is shaved. The upper tier meets in a scallop design at the center of the back of the head. The face is startling in its commingling of the individual and the ideal. Heavily lidded without the inlays that originally filled them, the eyes are set in deep cavities under the strongly defined eyebrows. The fine line of the nose widens to a fleshy point; the nostrils and parted lips are gracefully shaped. Enhancing the naturalistic effect are the convincing bone structure and organic overlay of the skin, the fleshy planes and creases, the high cheekbones, and the hollowed cheeks. Although the characteristic flangelike forms are softened and set close to the head, the ears are the only stylized element. The chin is damaged where there might have been a small beard or goatee.

The body, more simply rendered, is still subtly carved in the softly modeled torso, indication of the collarbone, and barely perceptible hunch of the shoulder blades. If the sculpture appears monumental

Figure 1. Kneeling Figure, serpentine with red pigment, h. 19.0 cm.; w. 9.7 cm.; d. 10.7 cm. Dumbarton Oaks Research Library and Collections, Washington, D.C.

seen from the front, subtle details of the design can be most appreciated in profile (fig. 2). The noble bearing lies in the poise of the head, the cantilevered projection of the profile, and the angle of the head where it meets the long curve of the back. The profile view also reveals the arabesque of the back of the leg, the foot curving upward, pressed against the thigh and buttocks. The curved line of the shins allows a gentle rocking motion.

The smooth, shaved forehead provides a surface for incisions indicating this figure is in a shamanic trance. The incisions depict a toad identified as *Bufo marinus* (fig. 3).[1] Whether or not *Bufo marinus* is specifically represented, the toad surely relates to the ritual of transformation either as the animal spirit companion of the shaman or as a symbolic identification of the natural transformation of the toad itself. The lozenge-shaped form surrounded by an open band of hatched lines at the center of both the toad's and the shaman's

Figure 2. Side view.

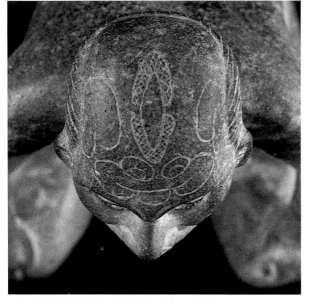

Figure 3. Detail of head with incisions.

heads has been interpreted as the splitting of the skin of the toad when it molts, sheds its skin, and is transformed.[2]

Traces of cinnabar are everywhere except at the waist, where a loincloth or short kilt would have been worn, perhaps explaining the shallow drill holes in this area and the lack of genitalia. In the first article on transformation figures, however, Peter T. Furst pointed out that there were "strong sexual taboos which seem to be almost universally associated with shamanic initiation, ecstatic transport, and other shamanic ritual."[3]

BIBLIOGRAPHY
Record of the Art Museum, Princeton University 36, no. 1 (1977): 32 (illus.).
Jan Van der Marck, *In Quest of Excellence: Civic Pride, Patronage, Connoisseurship* (Miami, Fl., 1984), 186–87.
Selections from The Art Museum, Princeton University (Princeton, N.J., 1986), 249.
Emile Deletaille, *Rediscovered Masterpieces* (Boulogne, 1985), fig. 19.
F. Kent Reilly, III, "The Shaman in Transformation Pose: A Study of the Theme of Rulership in Olmec Art," *Record of The Art Museum, Princeton University* 48, no. 2 (1989): 4–21.
Trésors du nouveau monde (exhib. cat., Royal Museum of Art and History, Brussels, 1992), no. 74.
Beatriz de la Fuente et al., *Mexico en el mundo de las colecionnes de arte 1: Mesoamerica* (Mexico City, 1992), 48.

NOTES
1. F. Kent Reilly, III, identified the toad as *B. marinus* and hypothesized that bufotenine, a chemical component of the secretions of the toad, could induce hallucinogenic reactions, thus relating the toad to shamanic ritual practice. Wade Davis and Andrew T. Weil, however, related that most of the hallucinogenic reports associated with bufotenine probably indicate normal physiological reactions to toxicity. See F. Kent Reilly, III, "The Shaman in Transformation Pose," *Record of The Art Museum, Princeton University* 48, no. 2 (1989): 4–21; and Wade Davis and Andrew T. Weil, "Identity of a New World Psychoactive Toad," *Ancient Mesoamerica* 3 (1992): 51–59.
2. Reilly (as in note 1), 11; Peter T. Furst, "Jaguar Baby or Toad Mother: A New Look at an Old Problem in Olmec Iconography," in *The Olmec and Their Neighbors: Essays in Memory of Matthew W. Stirling*, ed. Elizabeth P. Benson (Washington, D.C., 1981), 158–60.
3. Peter T. Furst, "The Olmec Were-Jaguar Motif in the Light of Ethnographic Reality," in *Dumbarton Oaks Conference on the Olmec*, ed. Elizabeth P. Benson (Washington, D.C., 1968), 166.

43. Kneeling Bearded Figure

600–400 B.C.
Provenance: La Lima Farm, Ulua Valley, Honduras
Material: jadeite
Dimensions: h. 9.3 cm.; w. 8.1 cm.
Courtesy of the Middle American Research Institute, Tulane University, New Orleans

The energy with which the sculptor carved this forceful figure is reflected in the broad proportions of the body and the way the huge head is thrust forward and socketed in the hunched shoulders. Large drill holes are left in the flaring nostrils, corners of the mouth, and hands, creating the impression that the stone is as much quarried as carved. The mouth is formed with great care, a sensitive line defining the fleshy lips and indications of a mustache and beard. The feet, however, are simply incised lines. Though still wholly human, the kneeling posture and the clenched fists associate this figure with the early stages of transformation.

Figures such as this, which display stylistic elements more commonly associated with the ceremonial centers of the Gulf Coast, have often been called Olmecoid." Elizabeth K. Easby and John F. Scott noted this statue had an affinity with heads from Tres Zapotes, usually assigned a later date than heads from San Lorenzo and La Venta.[1] While the figure probably dates to the end of the Late Formative, its apparent formal and iconographic similarities to the other kneeling bearded figures identify it as Olmec.

BIBLIOGRAPHY
Doris Stone, "The Archaeology of Central Southern Honduras," *Papers of the Peabody Museum* 49, no. 3 (1957): fig. 84b.
Ferdinand Anton, *Mexiko: Indianerkunst aus Präkolumbisherzeit* (Munich, 1961), pl. 9.

Ferdinand Anton, *Alt-Mexiko und seine Kunst* (Leipzig, 1965), no. 26.

Marjorie Smith Zengel et al., *The Art of Ancient and Modern Latin America* (New Orleans, 1968), fig. 9.

Ignacio Bernal, *The Olmec World*, trans. Doris Heyden and Fernando Horcasitas (Berkeley, 1969), 185, fig. 102.

Pál Kelemen, *Medieval American Art: Masterpieces of the New World Before Columbus*, 3d ed. (New York, 1969), 306, pl. 253c.

Elizabeth K. Easby and John F. Scott, *Before Cortés: Sculpture of Middle America* (New York, 1970), no. 65.

NOTE

1. Elizabeth K. Easby and John F. Scott, *Before Cortés: Sculpture of Middle America* (New York, 1970), 105.

44. Kneeling Figure Wearing Jaguar Helmet

900 – 500 B.C.
Provenance: Chiapas
Material: mottled olive-to-light-green serpentine with white inclusions and a milky-to-chalky patina
Dimensions: h. 12.5 cm.; w. 5 cm.; d. 6 cm.
Private collection

It is uncertain if this figure is actually in the process of transformation into a jaguar. No effort was made to merge human and animal characteristics: the figure seems to be wearing a large, helmetlike mask, distinct from the body. The body is that of an elegantly slim youth. Strikingly narrow when seen from the front, an effect exaggerated by the smallness of the waist and the length of the arms, the figure is drawn up, aristocratic in bearing, even in this kneeling position. The emphatic distinction between head and body, deliberate in a work of such skill, might indicate that the statue depicts a figure who has donned a mask for a transformation ceremony rather than an actual transformation. The mask is jaguarian, with ears, chin whiskers, and fangs. The stylization of the upper part of the face is similar to the clearly defined mask seen in cat. no. 220.

Drilling and abrasion undercut the area between the torso and the arms. Pits can be seen where the drills entered farther than the intended surface. The large hole directly in the center of the groin (fig. 1) may be one of these, but its size and placement might have special meaning. With the exception of the areas of

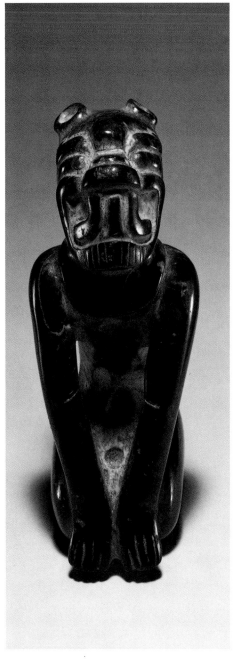

Figure 1. Front view.

the lap and groin, backs of the forearms, and recessed areas of the face, which are encrusted with soil scale and etched with root marks, the surface of the stone retains its original polish. Actual husks of calcified roots are evident as well.

BIBLIOGRAPHY
Unpublished.

45. Crouching Transformation Figure

900–600 B.C.
Provenance: Veracruz
Material: mottled bluish green jadeite with heavy cinnabar encrustation
Dimensions: h. 10 cm.; w. 10.5 cm.; d. 7 cm.
Private collection

This unfinished sculpture, blocked in and faceted, might simply be taken for a straightforward model of a crouching jaguar, complete with tail (fig. 1). Closer inspection, however, reveals that the forepaws rest on the knees, the position taken by shamans in transformation posture. In addition, the back, with broad, hunched shoulders tapering to a narrow waist, could be a man's.

The piece reveals a great deal about Olmec lithic technology. Work stopped on this sculpture, except for the back, after the roughing-in stage. The approximate form of the piece was quarried from the block in a triangular mass, the longest sloping side chiseled down to shape the back of the head, the front shaped by cutting back to the vertical line of the arms. Solid stone drills were used to define the arms from the torso, separate the legs, and excavate the front of the block inward to the chest. Reaming out the drill holes had only just begun: the raw, spiral cuts of the drills are still visible, along with notches from stone saws and grooves from string cutting with an abrasive and water. The sculptor had started working the stone to rough in the facial features; pitting from that procedure survives, as well. A similar form can be seen in a crouching figure whose face and body appear more finished (fig. 2).

The emergence of the image from the raw stone may be seen as a metaphor for transformation, the change in form from human to jaguar.

BIBLIOGRAPHY
Unpublished.

Figure 1. Back view.

Figure 2. Crouching figure, 900–600 B.C., Mexico, serpentine, h. 9 cm.; w. 5 cm.; d. 4.5 cm. Private collection.

46. Crouching Figure of a Man-Jaguar

1000 – 600 B.C.
Provenance: Tabasco
Material: dark green serpentine with traces of red pigment
Dimensions: h. 10.8 cm.; w. 7.9 cm.
Los Angeles County Museum of Art, gift of
Constance McCormick Fearing

In no other transformation figure are the human and feline so brilliantly fused as in this were-jaguar. About to rise from a kneeling position, the powerful, still human body is already informed with the suppleness and stealthy grace of the great cat. The head and ears remain human,[1] the crown of the head is smooth, as if shaved. The features of the face flow into one another, and the polished surface takes the light in a sensuous and complex pattern. The eye sockets are deeply bored; traces of the material with which they were inlaid has stained the stone. Extended by incised lines above the eyes, the carved brows are reminiscent of the flame eyebrows, or perhaps they signify the shedding of the human skin.

BIBLIOGRAPHY
Peter T. Furst, *Selections from the Pre-Columbian Collection of Constance McCormick Fearing* (Santa Barbara, California, 1967), 13.
Peter T. Furst, "The Olmec Were-Jaguar Motif in the Light of Ethnographic Reality," in *Dumbarton Oaks Conference on the Olmec,* ed. Elizabeth P. Benson (Washington, D.C., 1968), fig. 3.
Lorna Price, *Masterpieces from the Los Angeles County Museum of Art* (Los Angeles, 1988), 37.
Beatriz de la Fuente, "Order and Nature in Olmec Art," in *The Ancient Americas: Art from Sacred Landscapes,* ed. Richard F. Townsend (Chicago, 1992), no. 209.

NOTE
1. In many of the transformation figures, human ears are rendered more naturalistically than the stylized, flangelike ears seen on other Olmec sculpture.

BIBLIOGRAPHY
Julie Jones, *Pre-Columbian Art in New York: Selections from Private Collections* (New York, 1969), no. 1.

NOTE
1. Peter T. Furst, "The Olmec Were-Jaguar Motif in the Light of Ethnographic Reality," in *Dumbarton Oaks Conference on the Olmec*, ed. Elizabeth P. Benson (Washington, D.C., 1968).

is thematically identical. Each figure stands with one leg forward to counterbalance the slight torsion of the body; the arms are extended, the left slightly at the side and the right crooked and raised. The thick body, balled fists, heavy, blunted features, and the menacing expression of the Dumbarton Oaks figure, are found in this figure. The outsized, clenched feet and hands anticipate the heavy padded paws of the jaguar, the spread nose and large mouth, the snout and muzzle. In both figures the right hand is drilled for the insertion of an object.

Of the two, this figure is perhaps more human in aspect. The face is powerfully expressive and carved in clearly defined broad planes, notably those of the high cheekbones that set off the deeply drilled eyes. The incised wavy lines above the eyebrows are similar to the ridges seen in cat. no. 46. The three short lines incised directly above the nose mark the furrowed brow.

BIBLIOGRAPHY
Unpublished.

47. Transformation Figure, Fragment

900 – 700 B.C.
Provenance: Veracruz
Material: dark serpentine with traces of cinnabar
Dimensions: h. 7.3 cm.; w. 5.2 cm.; d. 5.5 cm.
Anonymous loan to The Art Museum, Princeton University

This impressive head of a were-jaguar is in the same stage of transformation as those of the standing were-jaguars in the collection of Dumbarton Oaks and cat. nos. 46 and 48. Given the size of this head, the intact figure could have been as large as the Dumbarton Oaks statue. The features of the face are poised mid-point in the transformation from human to jaguar. Round and drawn to points at the outside corners, the deeply excavated eyes probably held inlays of a dark, reflective material such as pyrite. The human nose has broadened and the nostrils are slightly flared; the wide, open mouth, with indications of sharp fangs, takes on the aspect of a growl. The ears are completely human. The brow is knitted and creased with ridges above the eyes and another ridge, beginning above the ear and running over the smooth crown of the head, that may indicate the emergence of the jaguar from the human shell. The remarkable consistency of features among these figures lends support to Peter T. Furst's insight that "we are dealing not with a stylistic aberration but with a well-defined mode of representing a phenomenon."[1]

48. Standing Transformation Figure

900 – 600 B.C.
Provenance: Tuxtlas region, Veracruz
Material: dark green steatite with hematite and red pigment
Dimensions: h. 10.2 cm.; w. 5 cm.; d. 3.5 cm.
Private collection

Though smaller, carved in a different stone, and more schematically rendered than the standing were-jaguar in the collection of Dumbarton Oaks (fig. 1), this figure

Figure 1. Standing Figure of a Were-Jaguar, Mexico, serpentine with pyrite inlay, h. 18.8 cm.; w. 10.5 cm.; d. 6.3 cm. Dumbarton Oaks Research Library and Collections, Washington, D.C.

Figure 1. Rear view.

49. Standing Figure with Tail

800–500 B.C.
Provenance: Southern Veracruz, Mexico
Material: felsite
Dimensions: h. 6 cm.; w. 3.8 cm.; d. 1.9 cm.
From the collection of Christopher B. Martin, currently on loan to The Brooklyn Museum

This assertive little figure, with the features of an animal, is perhaps in the costume of its animal spirit companion. The line across the brow indicates a cap with feline ears, shaped behind with two lobes that form a cleft. Enclosed in circles, the small, drilled eyes give the face a somewhat quizzical expression. The nose is pug and at the corners of the downturned mouth are two drill holes. A long bushy tail extending from the point of the coccyx, possibly of an animal other than the jaguar, might also be part of a costume (fig. 1).

BIBLIOGRAPHY
Hasso von Winning, *Pre-Columbian Art of Mexico and Central America* (New York, 1968), fig. 46.
Elizabeth K. Easby and John F. Scott, *Before Cortés: Sculpture of Middle America* (New York, 1970), no. 44.
Mary Ann Durgin, "Felsite Jaguar," in *The Guennol Collection* vol. 2 (New York, 1982), 119–20.

50. Standing Jaguar ▶

900–600 B.C.
Provenance: Tuxtlas region, Veracruz
Material: light grayish green marble with pronounced white veins; oxidized surface impacted with cinnabar
Dimensions: h. 11.5 cm.; w. 4 cm.; d. 1.5 cm.
Private collection

Rather than a human being with the attributes of a jaguar, this transformation figure is more jaguar than human. It stands on its hind legs like a man and has hands, not claws, cupped and raised to the mouth. The drill hole through the hands was meant for the insertion of an object. Since no comparable image is known in Olmec art, we can only speculate what the object might have been. Given the distance from the end of the hands to the mouth, it must have had an extension, like the neck of a vessel, a gourd, or a conch shell.

Another anthropomorphic jaguar, very similar in feeling, is in the collection of Dumbarton Oaks (fig. 1). Tiny but monumental, it retains some of the posture of the standing were-jaguars, with both fists raised (see cat. no. 48). Its lines are fluid and sleek, the mouth parted in a growl. The jaguar here is comfortably

Figure 1. Standing jaguar, serpentine, h. 8. cm. Dumbarton Oaks Research Library and Collections, Washington, D.C.

padded and amiably absorbed with whatever object was held to its mouth. In both cases, the tails hang down and curve around the hind paws to stabilize the figures. A more unusual, shared detail are the recesses in the hind paws, in all likelihood for inlays. The eyes of this jaguar, which are deeply drilled, may also have been inlaid.

BIBLIOGRAPHY
Unpublished.

CERAMIC ANIMAL EFFIGY VESSELS

Masterpieces of pottery, in which design and function are often ingeniously incorporated into the natural form of the animal—the mouth of a vessel, the perforations of a brazier—ceramic animal vessels are among the most sculptural and expressive forms created in the Olmec world.

While some animal vessels are given fantastic or stylized form, for the most part they are carefully observed, naturalistic renderings. Movement is often brilliantly captured, whether of a fish rising to the surface or a jaguar guardedly at rest. Some are anthropomorphized by their gestures, such as a toad, arms outstretched, offering up a shallow vessel, or by human details, such as the tonsured coiffure of a *tlacuache* or the ears of a young bird.

Creatures of the water, earth, or air—the three levels of the cosmos—are represented. The vessels may have been containers for substances inducive to shamanic trance and transformation, in the form of the animal spirit companion, the nagual, who accompanied the shaman on his journey to the supernatural world.

51. Jaguar Effigy Vessel

1200–900 B.C.
Provenance: Las Bocas, Puebla
Material: reddish brown clay with brownish black slip
Dimensions: h. 29.3 cm.; w. 21 cm.; d. 34.1 cm.
Private collection

Although naturalistic representations of the jaguar are surprisingly uncommon in Olmec art, the physical and magical powers with which the Olmec endowed the jaguar are magnificently captured in this effigy vessel from Las Bocas. With hind legs crouched and forelegs upright, one placed slightly in advance of the other, implying movement, the animal rests its paws on pads, practical supports for the extended claws. Rising upward from the coccyx, the spout, an accommodation to the function of the vessel, is conceived here as an abbreviated tail. The sleek thickness of the powerfully muscled body is most vividly expressed in the massing of the shoulders and the short, strong forelegs.

Naturalism and elegant stylization are fused in the head and fearsome face. The mouth is wide open,

revealing a flat line of teeth with two sharp fangs and a long pointed tongue curling out from the center. The snout and muzzle are two rounded forms defined by sweeping incised lines. Curving incisions mark the deeply carved eyes set under arching brow lines, which extend over the high cheekbones to meet the lines of the muzzle in a long arabesque. The irises are modeled and the whites lightly hatched. Despite the definitive feline features, the expression of the face appears strangely human.

The highly burnished slip is somewhat eroded and etched with roots, and the pads of the feet are worn down to the base clay. The only significant damage is in the vulnerably extended ears, which probably functioned as whistles: a liquid poured into the tail spout would have forced air out of the vessel through the ears causing them to whistle. While vessels such as this almost certainly were included in elite burials, they were surely used in rituals before internment. The authority of the modeling and the expressive power of this jaguar vessel have few equals in Olmec ceramic sculpture.

BIBLIOGRAPHY
Unpublished.

52. Fish Effigy Vessel

1200–900 B.C.
Provenance: Mexico
Material: blackware with red pigment
Dimensions: h. 18.2 cm.; w. 17.1 cm.; d. 9.8 cm.
Private collection

BIBLIOGRAPHY
Unpublished.

53. Fish Effigy Vessel

1200–900 B.C.
Provenance: Las Bocas, Puebla
Material: clay with highly burnished black slip
Dimensions: h. 6.6 cm.; w. 11.2 cm.; d. 11 cm.
Private collection

BIBLIOGRAPHY
Unpublished.

54. Fish Effigy Vessel

1200–900 B.C.
Provenance: Las Bocas, Puebla
Material: blackware with traces of red pigment
Dimensions: h. 20.5 cm.; w. 17 cm.; d. 14.5 cm.
Private collection

52

53

BIBLIOGRAPHY
Michael D. Coe, *The Jaguar's Children: Pre-Classic Central Mexico* (New York, 1965), no. 59.
Elizabeth K. Easby, *Ancient Art of Latin America from the Collection of Jay C. Leff* (New York, 1966), no. 66.
Katheryn M. Linduff, *Ancient Art of Middle America* (Huntington, W. Va., 1974), fig. 19.
André Emmerich Gallery and Perls Galleries, *Masterpieces of Pre-Columbian Art from the Collection of Mr. and Mrs. Peter G. Wray* (New York, 1984), no. 8.

The mouths of these ceramic vessels are conceived as open mouths of fish breaking to the surface of the water. The fish in cat. nos. 52 and 53 lie on their sides, heads turned up from the flat bodies. The bodies of the fish are made from thin sheets joined to form the opening for the mouth. This process is more evident in cat. no. 53, the simpler of the two vessels, at the angled joints of the upper and lower parts of the mouth. Covered in a fine black slip, the fin and tails are incised. The eye is rendered by gouging a circular shape into the hard clay, leaving a circle of the original black surface for the iris. Cat. no. 52 is more sculptural, especially in the modeling and convincing torsion of the fish's head and the definition of the lips and eyes. A diagonal section in the lower part of the body, heightened with red pigment, is scored with scrolls to represent water. In cat. no. 54, the fish rises from a hollow, circular base, also decorated with scrolls to represent water. Scored lines and incising define the scales, fins, gills, and tail of the ample body; a deeply scored line delineates the circular eye. This object is similar in style to two other blackware fish vessels: one from Las Bocas and the other from Tlatilco.[1]

55

54

NOTE

1. For the Las Bocas fish, see Michael D. Coe, *The Jaguar's Children: Pre-Classic Central Mexico* (New York, 1965), no. 60; for the Tlatilco fish, see Román Piña Chán, *The Olmec* (New York, 1989), fig. 10.

55. Fish Effigy Vessel

1200–500 B.C.
Provenance: Central Highlands
Material: polished black-brown earthenware with red paint
Dimensions: h. 9.5 cm.; w. 19 cm.; d. 5.1 cm.
The Saint Louis Art Museum, gift of Morton D. May

Unlike the naturalistically depicted fish in cat. nos. 52–54, this is a fish of a more fantastic order. Horizontally oriented, on its own bottom, the mouth of the vessel is cut into its back. The protruding, heavy-lidded eyes are set within circles and incised with irises. Shallow holes indicate the nares; the gills, which are in slight relief, and the finlike scales covering the body are edged with feathery, radial lines. A coiled design on the sides depicts the pectoral fins. Encircled with an incised line and red lips, the open mouth reveals a row of surprisingly human teeth. The lidded eyes and the teeth point to an identification of this curiously hybridized creature as a denizen of the watery supernatural underworld.

BIBLIOGRAPHY

Lee A. Parsons, *Pre-Columbian Art: The Morton D. May and The Saint Louis Art Museum Collections* (Saint Louis, 1980), no. 13.

56. Toad Effigy Vessel

1200 900 B.C.
Provenance: Zumpango del Río, Guerrero
Material: reddish brown-to-black clay
Dimensions: h. 20.3 cm.; w. 14.8 cm.; d. 22.1 cm.
Private collection

This vessel takes the form of a toad, probably a member of the *Bufo* genus, judging from its prominent parotid glands. The rounded mass of the toad tapers toward the mouth. The bulging eyes, pockmarked glands, and crouching hind legs are modeled in relief. Marked by a long depression, the mouth ends with incised curlicues. The incised band from the nostrils along the length of the back, grooved to either side and marked with short incised strokes, indicates the split skin of the toad and the beginning of the molting process. Once the skin is cast off, the toad consumes it, vividly symbolizing transformation.[1] Reduced to curved, hollow tubes, the forelegs function as conduits from the hollow body to the bowl. The shallow bowl is carved and incised with a band of stylized, frontally faced cleft heads with trident-shaped mouths that flank a pair of lazy-S motifs (fig. 1).

F. Kent Reilly, III, has speculated that this vessel could have held a potent hallucinogenic brew, derived from the venom of the *Bufo marinus*.[2] Wade Davis and Andrew T. Weil, however, have concluded that "it is highly unlikely that *Bufo marinus* could, under any circumstances now or in the past, be employed as a psychoactive agent."[3] Peter T. Furst has argued that the toad's long life span, the molting and eating of its skin, prominent V-shaped cleft, and presence in the faunal remains of San Lorenzo indicate that it lies at the core of the images long associated with the Olmec "'were-jaguar baby face.'"[4]

BIBLIOGRAPHY
F. Kent Reilly, III, "The Shaman in Transformation Pose: A Study of the Theme of Rulership in Olmec Art," *Record of The Art Museum, Princeton University* 48, no. 2 (1989).

NOTES
1. Peter T. Furst, "Jaguar Baby or Toad Mother: A New Look at an Old Problem in Olmec Iconography," in *The Olmec and Their Neighbors: Essays in Memory of Matthew W. Stirling*, ed. Elizabeth P. Benson (Washington, D.C., 1981), 158–60.
2. F. Kent Reilly, III, "The Shaman in Transformation Pose: A Study of the Theme of Rulership in Olmec Art," *Record of The Art Museum, Princeton University* 48, no. 2 (1989): 10–11.
3. Wade Davis and Andrew T. Weil, "Identity of a New World Psychoactive Toad," *Ancient Mesoamerica* 3 (1992): 56.
4. Furst (as in note 1), 150.

Figure 1. Drawing of incised pattern on bowl.

57. Toucan Effigy Vessel

1000–500 B.C.
Provenance: Las Bocas, Puebla
Material: dark gray clay with black slip and traces of
red pigment
Dimensions: h. 12.8 cm.; w. 16 cm.; d. 13.8 cm.
Private collection

The bird on this blackware vessel has been identified
by its beak as a toucan, and, because of the exaggerated size of the head, a nestling. Much of the charm of
the piece lies in the somewhat baleful expression of
the large eyes, set under heavy, protective brows. Not
integrated with the natural form of the bird, the mouth
of the vessel is simply a wide opening at the top of the
head. On the sides of the head, two vertical flanges
may indicate human ears. The wings and tail flow
smoothly out of the body. Three textured knobs above
the brows may be schematic renderings of the beginnings of the more characteristic head plumage of the
adult bird, and appear on cat. nos. 58 and 242.

BIBLIOGRAPHY
Samuel K. Lothrop, *Treasures of Ancient America* (Cleveland, 1964), 15.
Franz Feuchtwanger, *Ceramica Olmeca* (Mexico City, 1989), no. 83.

58. Bird Effigy Vessel

1200–900 B.C.
Provenance: Tlatilco, Mexico
Material: kaolin
Dimensions: h. 14 cm.; w. 11 cm.; d. 15.9 cm.
Private collection

This vessel is similar in conception and execution
to cat. no. 57, although modeled in kaolin, a rare white
clay. Both use the *tecomate* (a bowl in the form of a
round gourd) as the basic vessel form, which, in this
example, is set on an unadorned, drum-shaped base.
Modeled on one side with the broad beak and face of a
bird, the vessel has vertical flanges at the sides that
appear to be human ears, perhaps symbols of transformation. Set under heavy, overhanging brows, the
flat, medallionlike eyes are less expressive than those
of the toucan. Textured knobs are similar to those on
cat. no. 57.

BIBLIOGRAPHY
Muriel Noé Porter, "Tlatilco and the Pre-Classic Cultures of the
    New World," *Viking Fund Publications in Anthropology*, no. 19
    (New York, 1953), pl. 8a.

59. Duck Effigy Vessel

1250–900 B.C.
Provenance: Las Bocas, Puebla
Material: dark gray clay with black slip and traces of
red pigment
Dimensions: h. 23 cm.; w. 19 cm.; d. 13 cm.
Private collection

A creature of the air, land, and water, the strata of
the natural and supernatural worlds, the duck is cele-
brated in many vessels.

The duck's natural form has been ingeniously reinvented in the design of this blackware brazier, which
may have been used for incense and other ceremonial
purposes. The bird's parted bill, closed with a finely
crosshatched gusset, forms the mouth of the vessel;
the thrown-back head is enlarged to contain a burning
substance. Fumes would have traveled through the
arched neck, which also serves as a handle, and
escaped through the pierced breast. The duck stands
triumphantly, breast thrown forward, on a four-sided
pedestal base, a conflation of the webbed feet.

The design of the bill is carefully observed from the
nostrils down to the bean at the tip. Sharply accented
against the black sheen of the head, the raised and
incised eye is extended into the contour of the auric-
ular region. The interlaced breast is separated from
the wings by a black band that curves and widens
from the neck to the base. Short tail feathers enliven
and balance the silhouette. The contrast of surface and
texture, including the gray, matte areas of the breast
and feathers and other accented details, is achieved by
abrading the fired surface.

BIBLIOGRAPHY
Emile Deletaille, *Rediscovered Masterpieces* (Boulogne, 1985), no. 38.
Franz Feuchtwanger, *Ceramica Olmeca* (Mexico City, 1989), no. 82.
Trésors du nouveau monde, Royal Museum of Art and History
(Brussels, 1992), fig. 83.
Beatriz de la Fuente et al., *Mexico en el mundo de las colecionnes de
arte 1: Mesoamerica* (Mexico City, 1992), 69.

61. Bird Effigy Vessel

1150–975 B.C.
Provenance: Las Bocas, Puebla
Material: clay with incised black decoration and traces
of cinnabar
Dimensions: h. 14.6 cm.; w. 13 cm.; d. 15.2 cm.
Museum of Fine Arts, Boston, William Francis Warden Fund

The characteristics of a young raptor are well observed
in this blackware vessel. Around the eyes, the concave
areas, similar to cat. nos. 57 and 58, convey the sense
of the actual, feathery hollows. The narrow, sharply
slanted eye with carved iris and the small hooked beak
are those of the keen-sighted infant raptor.[1] The wings
are folded back, and the bottom of the vessel, which
coincides with the underside of the bird, is stabilized
by the tail feathers. The opening of the vessel is at the
crown of the head. Puffed out, the breast is incised
with a scroll design similar to the one seen on the base
of the fish effigy vessel in cat. nos. 52, 54.

BIBLIOGRAPHY
Unpublished.

NOTE
1. See Franz Feuchtwanger, *Ceramica Olmeca* (Mexico City, 1989),
   no. 100, for a similar example.

60. Bird Effigy Vessel

1200–900 B.C.
Provenance: Tlatilco, Mexico
Material: mottled gray-to-ivory kaolin
Dimensions: h. 19.5 cm.; w. 10.9 cm.; d. 15.8 cm.
Private collection

Seeming to have alighted on the circular base, this
bird's long, elegant talons grasp the sides. The head is
turned up, as if in song, to balance the spout, which is
flanked by the tail feathers. Simply modeled, the bird
is incised with a minimum of detail: the eye, inside
corner of the beak, and a single line, branched at the
top, to indicate the spine of the tail plumage. No more
is needed to evoke the spirit of what must be a song-
bird. A blackware vessel of similar form carries more
explicit symbolism associated with shamanic flight.[1]

BIBLIOGRAPHY
Muriel Noé Porter, "Tlatilco and the Pre-Classic Cultures of the
   New World," *Viking Fund Publications in Anthropology*, no. 19
   (New York, 1953), pl. 8b.

NOTE
1. See Michael D. Coe, *The Jaguar's Children: Pre-Classic Mexico*
   (New York, 1965), fig. 61.

62. *Tlacuache* Effigy Vessel

1200–900 B.C.
Provenance: Las Bocas, Puebla
Material: clay
Dimensions: h. 17.8 cm.; w. 10.4 cm.; d. 10.2 cm.
The Art Museum, Princeton University, gift of the estate of
Minnie V. Robinson

Sitting on its haunches, the *tlacuache*, or opossum, is about to bite into the gourd held in its fore-paws. The open snout reveals a row of long, sharp teeth and the tongue that hangs over the side. Hollowed, narrowed slits with punctuated irises, the eyes are intently focused, the incised furrowed brow adding to the impression of concentration. A small rectangular hole occurs below the right shoulder on the back. The fringe of roughly modeled hair runs from ear to ear around the back of the head. This human tonsure, and perhaps the lack of a tail, may mark the *tlacuache*

as an animal spirit companion. The vessel is open at the leveled, bald pate and might have contained a substance used in transformation ritual.

Representations of the gourd, one of the oldest cultivated plants, appear on many vessels (see cat. nos. 248, 249),[1] indicating its importance to early Mesoamerican peoples.

BIBLIOGRAPHY
Record of The Art Museum, Princeton University 52, no. 1 (1993): 77 (illus).

NOTE
1. Elizabeth K. Easby and John F. Scott, *Before Cortés: Sculpture of Middle America* (New York, 1970), no. 22.

FLIERS AND THE PARAPHERNALIA OF FLIGHT

Access through the portal to the otherworld is represented by images of flight: the shaman transported on the back of a supernatural or a "flier" dressed in cape and short kilt holding an object variously described as a torch or bound vegetative bundle.

Objects in greenstone and other precious lithic materials found at Olmec sites, identified as spoons and perforators, may indicate that transformation and supernatural flight were induced not only through meditation, but also by hallucinogenic substances and ritual bloodletting. Unadorned or carved and incised with images of transformation and flight, the spoons may also symbolize wings. Spoons are frequently pierced to be worn as pendants and, in addition, as both functional instruments and emblems of shamanic power. Later examples, in which function becomes increasingly vestigial to the form of the spoon as a symbol of empowerment, evolve into large pendants or pectorals worn as articles of regalia.

The sharp, pointed objects, plain or carved and incised with images of the supernatural, some symbolizing flight, may be evidence that ritual bloodletting, practiced by the Classic Maya and Postclassic Mesoamerican civilizations, was also practiced by the Olmec in the Formative period.

63. Supernatural Riding a Jaguar

900–600 B.C.
Provenance: Río Pesquero, Veracruz
Material: gray-green jadeite with a milky patina and vein of a softer mineral
Dimensions: h. 8.9 cm.; w. 3.1 cm.; d. 5 cm.
Private collection

A rare and vivid example of narrative action in Olmec art, this small object is dense in meaning central to the larger themes of Olmec ideology and ritual. With its head thrown back, its soft, toothless mouth agape as if

the seasons, wind and rain; as guardian or emissary of the deities. . .; as earth bearer or supporter of the earth bearers; as regulator of darkness and light. . .; and as the initiatory being of shamans."[1]

The figure atop the jaguar, with slanted almond-shaped eyes, widespread nose, and gaping, down-turned mouth, is the Olmec Supernatural. The small creature with the headband with two raised nodules, the vertical, horizontally divided panels sometimes referred to as crenellated earflaps at the sides of the head, and the cleft, whether in the head or headdress, is the figure held by the shamanic ruler in cat. no. 35 and also seen in cat. nos. 85–88, on the Las Limas Figure (see cat. no. 35, fig. 1) and San Lorenzo Monument 52, and in other variations and manifestations.

The supernatural grips the tail of the jaguar, right hand over left, in the same manner rulers hold ceremonial bars or scepters (see cat. nos. 144–147). This grip on the tail is equated with control of the spirit of the jaguar, the powerful animal spirit companion of shamanic rulers. While the gesture of the hands has many parallels, the riding position is unusual. Other objects depict the shamanic journey with figures lying on their stomachs on the backs of supernatural animals (see cat. no. 64, and Reilly, this volume, fig. 35). The Olmec Supernatural lying in the curve of the back of the jaguar, with its head at the tail end, corresponds to the position of the ruler who was interred in La Venta Monument 6, the sandstone sarcophagus depict-

63

wailing, the infantlike creature rides on the back of a jaguar, firmly holding its tail. The shadowed hollow of the mouth of the infant is balanced by the deeply carved eyes and mouth of the jaguar. Though this is an unusually naturalistic representation of a jaguar, flight is suggested in the curve of the compact body and upturned head; the forelegs project to the sides and the hind quarters are tucked within the body. The magic jaguar has the ability to swim and fly; he may journey through the watery underworld to the celestial realm, an explanation, perhaps, for the conflation of avian and jaguarian elements in many Olmec objects. Peter T. Furst pointed out that for the Tacana of the Bolivian Andes the flying jaguar is an ambivalent power; it can be either benevolent or antagonistic to humans, functioning "as a danger to man and the universe as a whole, and as master or guardian of the air, earth, water, and all animal and plant species; as bringer of

64

ing the Olmec Dragon. The front of the dragon faced north, its back hollowed out to hold a human body, long since dissolved in the acidic soil of the Gulf Coast; only the jade jewelry remained. F. Kent Reilly, III, has observed that "the elite occupant of the Olmec Dragon coffin was laid out with his head to the south—jade earspools were found at that end—or tail end, and his feet to the north, or mouth end."[2]

In death, the ruler buried in La Venta Monument 6 is transported to the watery underworld on the back of the dragon. The rider here is the Olmec Supernatural, identified with rain and corn, in whose image infants are offered by the shaman-ruler as a sacrifice in kind (see cat. nos. 34 and 35). The rider journeys to the otherworld to return with the maize, which it is shown carrying in a sack on its back in cat. no. 119.

BIBLIOGRAPHY
Unpublished.

NOTES
1. Peter T. Furst, "The Olmec Were-Jaguar Motif in Light of Ethnographic Reality," in *Dumbarton Oaks Conference on the Olmec*, ed. Elizabeth P. Benson (Washington, D.C., 1968), 159.
2. F. Kent Reilly, III, "Visions to Another World: Art, Shamanism, and Political Power in Middle Formative Mesoamerica," Ph.D. diss., University of Texas at Austin, 1994, 157.

This creature carrying a human figure not only depicts a shaman engaged in the journey to the supernatural otherworld, but also indicates that crocodilians were guides to the watery underworld. This association is reinforced by La Venta Monument 6.

BIBLIOGRAPHY
Unpublished.

▲
65. Hunchbacked Figure Emerging from Mouth of Beast

1000–500 B.C.
Provenance: Mexico
Material: green jadeite
Dimensions: h. 7.5 cm.; w. 3.5 cm.; d. 6 cm.
Private collection

A hunchback with a goatee and distended chest (see cat. no. 213), his arms drawn tightly against his sides, sits in what seems to be the gaping mouth of a bird, whose long beak curves into a bead at the tip to form a canopy over the figure. In profile, the folded legs of the hunchback merge with the lower jaw of the bird. The head of the bird is faintly incised with a fat-bellied figure, upside down in relation to the hunchback. The head of the incised figure is not discernible. On the bottom of the piece is a drilled depression, around which runs an incised line that terminates in a diamond, or star, design. On the back is a large, drilled concavity, somewhat rougher in finish than the rest of the piece.

As in Chalcatzingo Monument 1, the gaping maw of this beast is identified as an entrance to the otherworld. The hunchback, marked by its unnatural form as a creature with special gifts, occupies or emerges from the gaping mouth as a sign of its power of access to the supernatural.

BIBLIOGRAPHY
Emile Deletaille, *Rediscovered Masterpieces* (Boulogne, 1985), no. 32.

▼ ### 66. Standing Figure with Serpent Costume

900–600 B.C.
Provenance: Guatemala
Material: mottled light-to-dark green jadeite with mica and albite inclusions
Dimensions: h. 11.1 cm.; w. 5.1 cm.; d. 4.9 cm.
Private collection

A shaman stands constricted in the coils of a great serpent, his head emerging from its jaws. Though the face is worn, it seems to be anthropomorphic, not supernatural. His belted, feathered skirt is incised at the center with the crossed-bands motif on a flap with scalloped edges and a U-shaped bracket below. The serpent's stylized bifurcated fangs, at some remove from the mouth of the serpent, hangs from its lowest

◄ ### 64. Figure Riding a Crocodilian

900–600 B.C.
Provenance: Mexico
Material: serpentine
Dimensions: h. 7.5 cm.; w. 4.5 cm.; d. 11.5 cm.
Private collection

This crocodilian is mostly head and snout, with curled nostrils and bared teeth; its abbreviated body and legs are carved in low relief. Compressed flame eyebrows can be seen above the creature's eyes. A shaman straddles the beast's back, his legs to either side, echoing the position of the crocodile, and holds fast to the snout, rider and carrier merged. Carved in compact, simple volumes, the stone is incised with geometric clarity. The shaman's mouth and nose are a continuous plane; the heavy lids are created by incised curved lines around the eyes, which are hollowed for inlays. Comprised of bands across the brow and over the top of the head, the headdress is enclosed at the back. A band is also incised across the back. The lack of drill holes distinguishes this piece as a self-contained amulet.

coil on either side over the skirt. The feet are broken off and only the upper part of blocky legs extends from under the skirt. The serpent's body is marked with circles and cross-hatching representing the scaly skin.

The crossed-bands belt is seen on a number of monuments associated with the Olmec Supernatural. La Venta Monument 19 depicts an elaborately costumed and helmeted personage surrounded by the curved body of a plumed rattlesnake. The statuette illustrated here may represent a shaman wearing an elaborate costume or merged and transported with his avian serpent animal spirit companion.

BIBLIOGRAPHY
Unpublished.

67. Crouching Figure with Incisions

1500–800 B.C.
Provenance: Tabasco
Material: greenstone
Dimensions: h. 15 cm.; w. 10.4 cm.; d. 11.8 cm.
Private collection

This wide-snouted creature crouches with arms wrapped around its body. The right hand grips the left shoulder, the arm covering the lower part of the face, which is encircled by a slight ridge. A human footprint with five toes and toenails, incised around the hollowed-out eyes, marks the creature as a magical being, perhaps a shaman's animal spirit companion.

Disembodied feet, which appear on a small number of Olmec objects (see cat. nos. 127, 198, and La Venta Monument 13), may relate to the shamanic journey. The placement of the foot over the eye on this object metaphorically equates vision and journey. Though not as exaggerated as in cat. nos. 39–41, the contorted position of the creature may be a manifestation of shamanic transformation.

BIBLIOGRAPHY
Unpublished.

68. Winged Figure ▶

800–500 B.C.
Provenance: Guanacaste-Nicoya region, Costa Rica
Material: jade
Dimensions: h. 6.3 cm.; w. 4.8 cm.; d. 1.2 cm.
Anonymous loan to The Brooklyn Museum

BIBLIOGRAPHY
Jorge Lines, "Dos nuevas Gemas en la arqueologia de Costa Rica," *Proceedings of the Eighth American Scientific Congress: Anthropological Sciences*, no. 2 (1942): 117–222.
Miguel Covarrubias, "El arte 'Olmeca' o de La Venta," *Cuadernos Americanos* 28 (1946): fig. 18.
Jane Powell, *Ancient Art of the Americas* (New York, 1960), frontispiece.
Carlos Balser, "La Influencia olmeca en algunos motivos de la arqueologia de Costa Rica," *Informe Semestral: Instituto Geografico de Costa Rica* (Costa Rica, 1961), fig. 2.
André Emmerich, *Art Before Columbus: The Art of Ancient Mexico from the Archaic Village of the Second Millennium B.C. to the Splendor of the Aztecs* (New York, 1963), 64.
Jorge Lines, *Costa Rica: Land of Exciting Archaeology* (Costa Rica, 1964), 22.
Michael D. Coe, "The Olmec Style and Its Distribution," in *Handbook of Middle American Indians: Archaeology of Southern Mesoamerica*, vol. 3, ed. Gordon R. Willey (Austin, Tex., 1965), fig. 16.
W. J. Moreno, "Mesoamerica before the Toltecs," in *Ancient Oaxaca: Discoveries in Mexican Archaeology and History*, ed. John Paddock (Stanford, Cal., 1966), fig. 16.
Hasso von Winning, *Pre-Columbian Art of Mexico and Central America* (New York, 1968), fig. 54.
Ignacio Bernal, *The Olmec World*, trans. Doris Heyden and Fernando Horcasitas (Berkeley, 1969), fig. 103.
Peter David Joralemon, "A Study of Olmec Iconography," in *Studies in Pre-Columbian Art and Archaeology*, no. 7 (Washington, D.C., 1971), fig. 196.

Samuel K. Lothrop and Gordon F. Ekholm, "Pre-Columbian Objects," in *The Guennol Collection*, vol. 1, ed. Ida Ely Rubin (New York, 1975), 320–24.
Anatole Pohorilenko, "The Olmec Style and Costa Rican Archaeology," in *The Olmec and Their Neighbors: Essays in Memory of Matthew W. Stirling*, ed. Elizabeth P. Benson (Washington, D.C., 1981), fig. 7.
Ronald L. Bishop, Frederick W. Lange, and Elizabeth K. Easby, "Jade in Mesoamerica," in *Jade*, ed. Roger Keverne (London, 1991), fig. 9.

69

◄ 69. Small Winged Figure

800–500 B.C.
Provenance: Union de Guapiles, Linea Vieja, Costa Rica
Material: jade
Dimensions: h. 4.8 cm.; w. 3.8 cm.; d. 1.2 cm.
From the collection of Robin B. Martin, currently on loan to
The Brooklyn Museum

BIBLIOGRAPHY
Carlos Balser, "Los 'Baby Faces' olmecas de Costa Rica," *Acta del
XXXIII Congreso Internacional de Americanistas*, no. 2 (San Jose,
Costa Rica, 1959), fig. b.
Carlos Balser, "Some Costa Rican Jade Motifs," in Samuel K.
Lothrop et al., *Essays in Pre-Columbian Art and Archaeology*
(Cambridge, Mass., 1961), fig. 2e.
Carlos Balser, "La Influencia olmeca en algunos motivos de la
arqueologia de Costa Rica," *Informe Semestral: Instituto Geografico
de Costa Rica* (San Jose, Costa Rica, 1961), fig. 1.
Samuel K. Lothrop and Gordon F. Ekholm, "Pre-Columbian
Objects," in *The Guennol Collection*, vol. 1, ed. Ida Ely Rubin
(New York, 1975), 320–24.
Anatole Pohorilenko, "The Olmec Style and Costa Rican
Archaeology," in *The Olmec and Their Neighbors: Essays in Memory
of Matthew W. Stirling*, ed. Elizabeth P. Benson (Washington, D.C.,
1981), fig. 5.

Although from Costa Rica, these two jade figures bear
the hallmarks of the Olmec style, including the immediately recognizable elongated heads and facial features. Both show relief carving only on the head, with
all other significant detail rendered in incised lines,
and have drill holes for suspension as well as smaller
perforations for sewing to clothing and headdresses.

The wings have been identified by many scholars
as those of a bat, a night flier that may be equated with
the darkness of the otherworld.[1] While the wings in
cat. no. 68 are notched in a geometric fashion, suggesting those of a bat, those in cat. no. 69 have scalloped edges, heightened by the fine incised line that
follows their contours, recalling the wings of a butterfly, a potent symbol of transformation (see cat. no.
175). The standing figure in cat. no. 68 wears a short,
fringed skirt belted with a wide, flat, double merlon
motif and a central cleft element, almost certainly
symbolizing a corn plant (see cat. no. 172). The skirt's
fringe may represent feathers or corn silk. The headdress has been variously identified as the face of a leaf-
nosed bat or a tripartite corn motif; the latter seems
more likely.

NOTE
1. Samuel K. Lothrop and Gordon F. Ekholm, "Pre-Columbian
Objects," in *The Guennol Collection*, vol. 1, ed. Ida Ely Rubin
(New York, 1975), 320–23.

▲ 70. Oblong Spoon with Incisions

900–600 B.C.
Provenance: Veracruz
Material: translucent blue-green jadeite
Dimensions: h. 2.7 cm.; w. 6.7 cm.; d. 0.5 cm.
Private collection

With its concave surface and two drill holes at the top
edge, this jade spoon may have functioned as both a
pendant and a practical implement for dispensing or
ingesting a hallucinogenic powder. Shown horizontally, the incised figure wears a short, fringed skirt and
a wing projecting from the back, identifying the figure
as a "flier." The figure's left arm is crooked at a sharp
angle and the extended right arm holds an object consisting of two vertical elements surmounted by two
concentric triangles, perhaps representing a torch or a
bound bundle of vegetation. The figure has an Olmec-
style mouth and wears earspools.

Depictions of fliers holding bound bundles are seen
on a variety of Olmec objects: Chalcatzingo Monument
12 (fig. 1) and La Venta Monument 19 (see Taube, this
volume, fig. 6a) are the largest examples; two celts
from La Venta Offering 4 and a celt-shaped spoon are
the best-known, small-scale versions.[1] These figures
represent shamanic flight to the otherworld, the object
of their journey symbolized by the bound, vegetative
bundle.

BIBLIOGRAPHY
Unpublished.

NOTE
1. See Peter David Joralemon, "A Study of Olmec Iconography," in
Studies in Pre-Columbian Art and Archaeology, no. 7 (Washington,
D.C., 1971), fig. 36.

Figure 1. Chalcatzingo Monument 12.

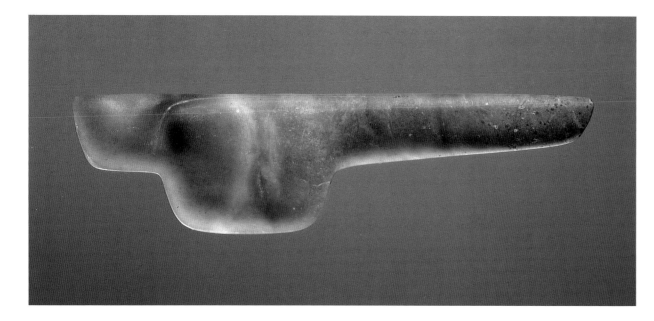

an abbreviated supernatural face with cleft and eyes and a squared spiral similar to that seen on the fragmentary figure in cat. no. 22. The entire profile is shown wearing a mask cut away to reveal the human face beneath. This method of depicting humans in supernatural costume, commonly referred to as X-ray style, may have parallels with Oxtotitlan Mural 1 and hollow figures wearing the pelts of supernaturals (see cat. no. 204).[1] The mask here consists of an eyeless profile in front, flame eyebrows above the head, and a hand-paw-wing motif behind the head, representing an abbreviated version of the Olmec Dragon. Three lobed designs incised in concentric lines on either side of the bowl and an inverted version at the end of the handle have been interpreted as "jaguar pelage,"[2] and may relate to the costume over the profile head.

BIBLIOGRAPHY
Peter David Joralemon, "The Olmec Dragon: A Study in Pre-Columbian Iconography," in *Origins of Religious Art and Iconography in Preclassic Mesoamerica*, ed. Henry B. Nicholson (Los Angeles, 1976), fig. 14h.
Mary Ann Durgin, "Two Jade Spoons," in *The Guennol Collection*, vol. 2 (New York, 1982), 117–19.

NOTES
1. Mary Ann Durgin, "Two Jade Spoons," in *The Guennol Collection*, vol. 2 (New York, 1982), 117. For examples of the X-ray style on Classic Maya objects, see Justin Kerr, "A Maya Vase from the Ik Site," *Record of The Art Museum, Princeton University* 48, no. 2 (1989): 32–34.
2. Mary Ann Durgin (as in note 1).

71. Spoon

900–600 B.C.
Provenance: Guerrero
Material: blue-green jade
Dimensions: h. 3.7 cm.; w. 14.4 cm.; d. 0.5 cm.
Anonymous loan to The Art Museum, Princeton University

Few objects in Olmec art can be admired more for pure unadorned form than the jade spoon seen here. The subtly angled long handle, the dip of the bowl, and the shorter projection suggest a symbolism beyond functional considerations. The concavity is finely graded from the handle to the half curve, which marks the deepest point. Two holes along the top edge indicate that the spoon could also have been worn as a pendant.

The form of these asymmetrical spoons has been interpreted as the body of a tadpole or a long-tailed bird, and many are incised with avian symbols.[1] These receptacles may have been used for hallucinogens to induce the shaman's meditative trance and flight.

BIBLIOGRAPHY
Unpublished.

NOTE
1. Anatole Pohorilenko, "The Olmec Style and Costa Rican Archaeology," in *The Olmec and Their Neighbors: Essays in Memory of Matthew W. Stirling*, ed. Elizabeth P. Benson (Washington, D.C., 1981), 311; Peter T. Furst, this volume, and "The Olmec Were-Jaguar Motif in the Light of Ethnographic Reality," in *Dumbarton Oaks Conference on the Olmec*, ed. Elizabeth P. Benson (Washington, D.C., 1968), 162.

72. Spoon with Incisions

800–500 B.C.
Provenance: Veracruz
Material: jade with traces of red pigment
Dimensions: h. 3 cm.; w. 12.1 cm.; d. 1.1 cm.
Anonymous loan to The Brooklyn Museum

The slim handle of this jade spoon widens into a bowl, then narrows into a smaller concave extension. The bowl is incised with a face in profile with a second, eyeless profile on the cheek, and what may be

74. Oval Carved Spoon

900–600 B.C.
Provenance: Guatemala
Material: green serpentine with rusty white inclusions
Dimensions: h. 2.1 cm.; w. 5 cm.; d. 1.2 cm.
Private collection

Almost filling the concavities to either side of the face carved in the center of this spoon, the foreshortened curled hands create the effect of a crouching or prone figure, perhaps in flight. The suggestion of an arm or sleeve is visible above the hands. The sure carving of the head and well-defined features are all the more remarkable on such a small scale. The hair is parted in the middle, combed behind the ears, and worn long. Small holes perforated along the top edge for suspension are not visible from the front.

BIBLIOGRAPHY
Unpublished.

▲
73. Large Carved Spoon

74

900–600 B.C.
Provenance: Chiapas
Material: light bluish green jadeite speckled with white
Dimensions: h. 7.1 cm.; w. 23 cm.; d. 2.2 cm.
Private collection

This double-chambered spoon with a face in relief in the center was probably carved from a celt. At the nose and lips, the thickest portion is approximately the depth of the original celt. The chambers to the sides have been hollowed out to form practical spoon depressions. The face is carved in a blunt, blocky style. The eye cavities, formed by three drill holes for inlays, have been incised to regularize the full almond shape. The squared mouth with protruding tongue is the most geometric feature. The headdress, with what appear to be ear flaps and an incised, fringed headband with a central circular motif surmounted by a cleft, frames the face. Along the upper edge, two suspension holes are carefully bored so they will not be seen from the front. Though the modified form of the spoon bears a resemblance to flanged pectorals with faces carved in relief, smaller spoons of similar design exist (see cat. no. 75).

BIBLIOGRAPHY
Unpublished.

75. Oval Spoon with Incisions

900–600 B.C.
Provenance: Veracruz
Material: dark green jade with white specks of chloromelanite
Dimensions: h. 2.6 cm.; w. 7 cm.; d. 0.6 cm.
Private collection

This spoon, a simple oblong shape, is incised in the center of the concavity with an Olmec face. The head is distinctive in the narrowed, close-set, concentrated eyes, earflares, and arrangement of the hair, parted in the middle and worn long, the strands incised. Placed abruptly below the chin, a bar contains what appears to be the upper half of a crossed-bands pectoral. Drill holes mark the centers of the incised earspools and nostrils, and the corners of the down-turned mouth.

BIBLIOGRAPHY
Unpublished.

75

76. Carved Ornament

900–600 B.C.
Provenance: Río Pesquero, Veracruz
Material: light green jade
Dimensions: h. 12.3 cm.; w. 5.4 cm.; d. 3.2 cm.
Dr. and Mrs. Wally Zollman

With the exception of the angular cuts that define the juncture of the chest and folded arms, this figure is softly rendered. The hands, closed over the chest, and the facial features, particularly around the closed eyes, are fleshy and slightly puffy. The full cheeks weigh on the slack, unformed mouth, perhaps of an infant. The lower half of the sculpture is carved and incised in the form of a maize kernel, from which the figure emerges (see cat. no. 172). The motif of the kernel is echoed in the shape of the cleft head and reinforced by the triangular form incised above the crossed-bands headband, interpreted by Peter David Joralemon as a corn symbol.[1]

Though many other objects of this type are clearly perforator handles,[2] comparison with an incised celt (cat. no. 128) makes it probable that this object is not a perforator handle, finial, or attachment of any kind,[3] but complete in itself. Allowing for the obvious differences between the two objects, the shape of the celt—a cleft at the top and small projection at the bottom—agrees with the form seen here. On the celt, the incised figure is confined within the stone—arms and legs drawn in and eyes closed, as if sleeping. The figure here has emerged from the cleft. Taken together, the objects may represent different stages in a germinating seed. The equation of the infant with the young maize plant may support the interpretation of the ceremonial or sacrificial presentation of infants discussed in cat. nos. 33–36.

BIBLIOGRAPHY
Brian A. Dursum and Robert Sonin, *Jade East and West* (Miami, 1980), no. 215.
Lee A. Parsons, John B. Carlson, and Peter David Joralemon, *The Face of Ancient America: The Wally and Brenda Zollman Collection of Precolumbian Art* (Indianapolis, 1988), no. 18.

NOTES
1. Lee A. Parsons, John B. Carlson, and Peter David Joralemon, *The Face of Ancient America: The Wally and Brenda Zollman Collection of Precolumbian Art* (Indianapolis, 1988), 40.
2. Emile Deletaille, *Rediscovered Masterpieces* (Boulogne, 1985), nos. 5, 8.
3. Parsons et al. (as in note 1).

77. Perforator ▼

900–600 B.C.
Provenance: Guerrero
Material: olive green clay
Dimensions: h. 11.45 cm; w. 2 cm.; d. 2.1 cm.
Private collection

In this compacted clay piece, a stingray spine is represented emerging from the head or headdress of this standing figure. Natural stingray spines, the remains of which are found in quantity in Olmec burials,[1] may have been the actual instruments used for drawing blood.

BIBLIOGRAPHY
Unpublished.

NOTE
1. Philip Drucker, "La Venta, Tabasco: A Study of Olmec Ceramics and Art," *Bureau of American Ethnology*, Bulletin 153 (1952), 26.

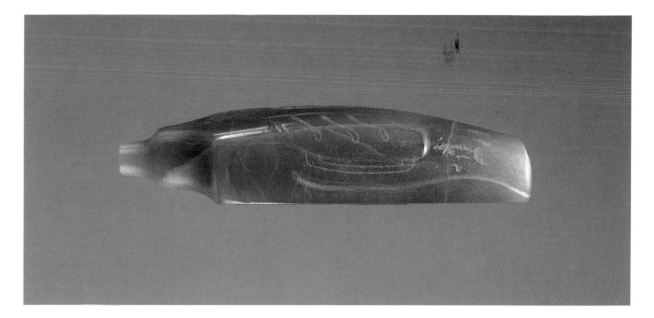

▲
78. Perforator Handle

900–600 B.C.
Provenance: Guerrero
Material: blue-green jade
Dimensions: h. 1.2 cm.; w. 7.2 cm.; d. 2.5 cm.
Anonymous loan to The Art Museum, Princeton University

The top side of the handle of this exquisite blood-letter, whose blade was broken off sometime in antiquity, is incised with the form of a harpy eagle's head, a creature associated with the celestial realm. Above the whiplash line indicating a beak, which reinforces the eagle connotation, is a trough-shaped eye surmounted by flame eyebrows.

The incisions on the underside of the handle—the cleft, scalloped element, and four-dots-and-bar motif—represent the Olmec cosmic diagram (fig. 1). The four-dots-and-bar motif has been shown to be an abstract representation of the Olmec Dragon.[1] One side of the perforator handle represents the sky, the other, the earth. The blood shed by the now missing blade would have been the magical substance that allowed access to the power inherent within these supernatural realms. With its incised motifs, the perforator handle is dramatic proof that even small objects could carry complex symbolic information.

A hole runs from the tip to the underside of the handle, indicating that after it was broken the blood-letter was treasured, possibly as a pendant.

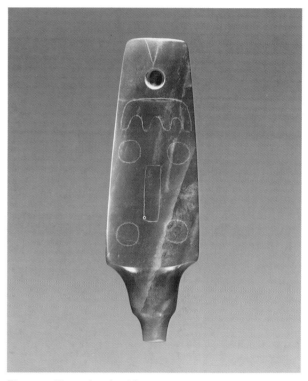

Figure 1. View of underside.

BIBLIOGRAPHY
Carlo T. E. Gay, *Chalcacingo* (Graz, Austria, 1971), fig. 45.
Peter David Joralemon, "The Olmec Dragon: A Study in Pre-Columbian Iconography," in *Origins of Religious Art and Iconography in Preclassic Mesoamerica*, ed. Henry B. Nicholson (Los Angeles, 1976), figs. 10i$_1$, 19e.

NOTE
1. Peter David Joralemon, "The Olmec Dragon: A Study in Pre-Columbian Iconography," in *Origins of Religious Art and Iconography in Preclassic Mesoamerica*, ed. Henry B. Nicholson (Los Angeles, 1976), 47.

79. Perforator ▼

900–600 B.C.
Provenance: Puebla
Material: mottled dark-to-light green serpentine
Dimensions: h. 2.5 cm.; w. 18 cm.; d. 2.4 cm.
Private collection

This long pick with a handlelike head seems more a practical tool than a ritual object. Because the point is duller than one would expect in a bloodletter, Peter T. Furst has suggested that it may be a weaving pick.[1] Like yokes and other paraphernalia of the ritual ball-game carved in stone (cat. nos. 134, 136–38), this object may be an effigy, with no reason for the needle-sharp point of an actual bloodletting instrument.[2]

BIBLIOGRAPHY
Unpublished.

NOTES
1. Peter T. Furst, personal communication, April 1994.
2. For jade perforators recovered from Tomb A at La Venta, see Diehl, this volume, fig. 14.

80. Perforator Handle ▶

900–600 B.C.
Provenance: Tabasco
Material: mottled dark-to-light green serpentine
Dimensions: h. 4.5 cm.; w. 2.4 cm.; d. 1.9 cm.
Private collection

The heavy, flat features combined with the close-fitting helmet in this carved bust recall the colossal heads from the Gulf Coast, the region of origin of this piece. A deeply bored hole in the bottom creates a socket into which the shank of a perforator could have been inserted. A double band crosses the brow and continues down the sides of the face, perhaps the upper jaw of a serpent with nostrils and eyes above. The cross-hatched skin falls along the back to the waist.

BIBLIOGRAPHY
Unpublished.

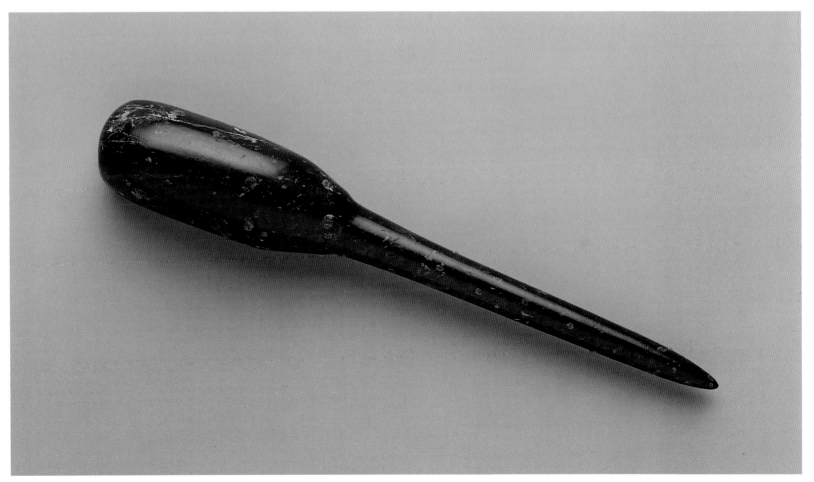

81. Canoe Effigy

1150–550 B.C.
Provenance: Mexico
Material: Jade
Dimensions: h. 13.9 cm.; w. 4.4 cm.; d. 1.27 cm.
Anonymous loan, Museum of Fine Arts, Boston

BIBLIOGRAPHY
Unpublished.

82. Hand Vessel

800–500 B.C.
Provenance: Mexico
Material: jade with traces of red pigment
Dimensions: h. 20.6 cm.; w. 6.7 cm.; d. 2.9 cm.
Anonymous loan to The Brooklyn Museum

BIBLIOGRAPHY
André Emmerich, *Art Before Columbus: The Art of Ancient Mexico from the Archaic Village of the Second Millennium B.C. to the Splendor of the Aztecs* (New York, 1963), 67.
Michael D. Coe, *America's First Civilization* (New York, 1968), 150.
Samuel K. Lothrop and Gordon F. Ekholm, "Pre-Columbian Objects," in *The Guennol Collection*, vol. 1, ed. Ida Ely Rubin (New York, 1975), 316–19.
Trésors du nouveau monde, Royal Museum of Art and History (Brussels, 1992), no. 92.
Beatriz de la Fuente et al., *Mexico en el mundo de las colecionnes de arte 1: Mesoamerica* (Mexico City, 1992), 46.

In 1941 Matthew W. Stirling discovered a cache of several hundred jade objects at the site of Cerro de las Mesas, Veracruz. Though this cache was buried sometime in the Early Classic, it contained at least two objects unmistakably Olmec in style—a figurine of a dwarf and a piece resembling a dugout canoe with incised faces on the bow and stern. Philip Drucker, writing on the Cerro de las Mesas jades, described the stone of the canoe as "very similar to that from which the Olmec figurine was made," and felt that "it may be entirely fortuitous, but the Olmec figurine . . . fit[s] snugly into the 'canoe' and it stands up very solidly in the little vessel."[1]

Cat. nos. 81 and 82 are of the same form as the Cerro de las Mesas canoe, though no. 81 shows no signs of incisions and no. 82 is in the form of a hand. These troughlike forms with sloping sides at the ends may have been ceremonial vessels. Cat. no. 81, which is pierced with drill holes on the long sides in the same fashion as the Cerro de las Mesas canoe, could have been worn as a pendant. Cat. no. 82 has drill holes in approximately the same location, as well as others

between the thumb and forefinger and at the knuckle of the little finger, which could have been threaded with an attachment. A platform at one end of the vessel is recarved to form the tips of the fingers; perhaps the other platform was cut off to form the wrist (fig. 1). A detail that reflects the great refinement of the hand is the incised fingernails. The jade is highly polished and retains traces of red pigment in the drill holes and grooves between the fingers. The hand may have been recarved from a canoe form at a later time. If the hand and vessel were originally carved as one, they may represent an offering. Disembodied hands are often represented in Olmec art (see cat. no. 96, fig. 1; cat. no. 172, fig. 1; cat. no. 198; and San Lorenzo Monument 41). Though relatively uncommon in Olmec art, canoes can be related to certain aspects of Olmec iconography, particularly the notion of crossing to the watery underworld.

NOTE
1. Philip Drucker, "The Cerro de las Mesas Offering of Jade and Other Materials," in *Bureau of American Ethnology*, Bulletin 157 (1955): 48.

81

82

Figure 1. Underside of hand vessel.

195

III

Images of Supernaturals

The anthropomorphic and zoomorphic supernaturals that inhabit the otherworld of the Olmec are the agents of intersection between the natural and supernatural realms and the means of access between man and the cosmic forces. Fantastic hybrid zoomorphs such as the Olmec Dragon are composites of the most powerful predators of the natural world: the jaguar, the harpy eagle, and the crocodilian, able to negotiate the terrestrial level, the watery underworld, and celestial realm of the shamanic cosmos.

The other principal inhabitant of the supernatural world is an anthropomorphic creature, an infant were-jaguar, characterized by slanted almond-shaped eyes, cleft head, and a trapezoidal, downturned, toothless mouth with flared upper lip and short, broad nose, which create the effect of the jaguarian muzzle. It is the image of the face that is most often represented on portable Olmec objects. Its most canonical attributes are a headband decorated with two nodules, crenellated earflaps, and a crossed-bands pectoral. Others include maize symbols and zoomorphic features including flame eyebrows, bifurcated fangs, and trough-shaped eyes.

In explanation of the fusion of jaguar and human traits, Matthew W. Stirling proposed that two monumental but damaged sculptures from the vicinity of San Lorenzo depicted the sexual union of jaguars and human females, resulting in what Michael D. Coe called "the jaguar's children."[1] While the integration of jaguar and human features is integral to Olmec ideology, Stirling's hypothesis has been shown to be highly unlikely; the "copulation" scenes are in all probability scenes of jaguars vanquishing humans, mythic or symbolic representations relating to blood sacrifice. As the most powerful predator of the tropical jungle, the jaguar was no doubt perceived by the Olmec as the animal spirit companion par excellence, a natural creature able to negotiate all levels of the cosmos. The suggestion of the jaguarian muzzle in the conformation of the downturned mouth with flaring upper lip in wholly human representations is an expression of the Olmec ideal.

The infant were-jaguar was grouped by Miguel Covarrubias with other infantile and dwarflike creatures, linking them with contemporary myths of *chaneques*, dwarfs who lived in caves and controlled powerful natural phenomena such as rain, lightning or thunderbolts, and the growth of corn.[2] In his first major study of Olmec iconography, Peter David Joralemon distinguished among the various representations of the infant were-jaguar, and created a pantheon of ten distinct deities. The creature in fullest regalia, with the headband, earflaps, and pectoral, was God IV in his system, "the rain god thought to be the chief divinity of the Olmec culture."[3] The association with rain, endorsed by Coe, was based primarily on an ethnographic analogy with the Aztec sacrifices of children. By sympathetic magic, as the children cried, so too would the clouds rain. San Lorenzo Monument 52, a particularly diagnostic example of Joralemon's God IV, was discovered near a drainage trough, reinforcing the connection with water.[1]

These interpretations have been and continue to be re-evaluated. Coe has questioned the association of the infant supernatural with rain and Joralemon has revised his system and reduced the pantheon from ten deities to six.[5] Karl A. Taube has reinterpreted many of Joralemon's categories, proposing that Gods II, IV, and VI represent the Olmec Maize God at different stages of growth of the maize plant.[6]

Rather than distinct deities or supernatural entities, the variations and permutations on the underlying image of the infant were-jaguar may represent different manifestations of the elemental force associated with rain and maize. Referred to here as the Olmec Supernatural, it is incised on the faces of humans and masks, animating and empowering the stone and images. It is depicted on ritual regalia worn and held by rulers as signs of access to supernatural power.

The fiercest manifestation of the supernatural is carved on the hefts of effigy axes, with bifurcated fangs projecting from the usual toothless mouth of the infant were-jaguar. These imposing objects are ceremonial representations of axes and celts used to clear the land for cultivation and symbolize the power of agriculture over untamed nature. The Olmec Supernatural may also be shown riding through the cosmos on the back of a jaguar or carrying a sack of maize on its back. Infants wearing the distinctive headband and earflaps may have been offered in sacrifice in the image of the supernatural. As the primary bearer of rain and corn, the Olmec Supernatural was the most powerful ally and patron sought by Olmec rulers, the elemental force they must propitiate and manipulate to ensure a favorable harvest.

NOTES

1. Matthew W. Stirling, "Stone Monuments of the Río Chiquito, Veracruz, Mexico," *Bureau of American Ethnology* Bulletin 157 (1955): 19–20; Michael D. Coe, *The Jaguar's Children: Pre-Classic Central Mexico* (New York, 1965), 105.
2. Miguel Covarrubias, *Indian Art of Mexico and Central America* (New York, 1957), 56–58.
3. Peter David Joralemon, "A Study of Olmec Iconography," *Studies in Pre-Columbian Art and Archaeology*, no. 7 (Washington, D.C., 1971), 91.
4. Michael D. Coe and Richard A. Diehl, *In the Land of the Olmec: The Archaeology of San Lorenzo Tenochtitlán*, vol. 1 (Austin, Tex., 1980), 363.
5. Michael D. Coe, "The Olmec Heartland: Evolution of Ideology," in *Regional Perspectives on the Olmec*, ed. Robert J. Sharer and David C. Grove (Cambridge, 1989), 75; Peter David Joralemon, "The Olmec Dragon: A Study in Pre-Columbian Iconography," in *Origins of Religious Art and Iconography in Preclassic Mesoamerica*, ed. Henry B. Nicholson (Los Angeles, 1976), 33.
6. Karl A. Taube, "The Olmec Maize God: The Face of Corn in Formative and Late Preclassic Mesoamerica," paper delivered at the Thirteenth Annual Maya Weekend, Philadelphia, April 9, 1995.

83. Plaque ▶

800–500 B.C.
Provenance: Isla Piedras, Campeche
Material: light green jade
Dimensions: h. 8.4 cm.; w. 12.1 cm.; d. 2.9 cm.
Anonymous loan to The Brooklyn Museum

This large jade plaque with a face carved in the center was most likely originally an ornament or a two-chambered spoon. As in cat. no. 73, the beveled edge at the top may have extended around the plaque. The notch in the lower left corner and the holes in the upper corners signify that the plaque was worn, probably as a pectoral.

While the face has the features associated with the ideal Olmec Supernatural, it lacks the characteristic headband and earflaps. The eyes have been drilled at the corners and somewhat roughly finished. A tooth is suggested where the arches of the gum line converge. The incised pattern for the ears is also seen on the Kunz Axe (see Diehl, this volume, fig. 17) and the were-jaguar mask in cat. no. 194.

The back of the plaque is incised with Maya hieroglyphs, identified by Linda Schele and Mary Ellen Miller as the name of a Late Preclassic Maya lord,[1] indicating that it was prized as an heirloom hundreds of years after it was made. Two other Olmec pectorals — one in the British Museum and the second in the collection of Dumbarton Oaks — are also incised with Maya hieroglyphs.[2]

BIBLIOGRAPHY
Miguel Covarrubias, *Indian Art of Mexico and Central America* (New York, 1957), fig. 94.
Jane Powell, *Ancient Art of the Americas* (New York, 1960), 6.
Michael D. Coe, "The Olmec Style and Its Distribution," in *Handbook of Middle American Indians: Archaeology of Southern Mesoamerica*, vol. 3, ed. Gordon R. Willey (Austin, Tex., 1965), fig. 21.
Samuel K. Lothrop and Gordon F. Ekholm, "Pre-Columbian Objects," in *The Guennol Collection*, vol. 1, ed. Ida Ely Rubin (New York, 1975), 311.
Linda Schele and Mary Ellen Miller, *The Blood of Kings: Dynasty and Ritual in Maya Art* (Fort Worth, 1986), pl. 45.

NOTES
1. Linda Schele and Mary Ellen Miller, *The Blood of Kings: Dynasty and Ritual in Maya Art* (Fort Worth, 1986), 151.
2. Ibid., pls. 31, 32.

84. Standing Figure ▶

900–600 B.C.
Provenance: Veracruz
Material: blue-green jadeite with white inclusions
Dimensions: h. 6.1 cm.; w. 2.2 cm.; d. 1.5 cm.
Private collection

With the face of an infant feline, and fleshy, undeveloped features, this figure stands on two legs, arms and hands held over the front of the body. The head, which shows signs of binding, is deeply indented by two grooves that intersect on the top at right angles. A scalloped line over the shoulders appears to be a four-paneled shawl or cape, the front of which, incised with a circle, hangs over the chest. Similarly incised panels cover the shoulders, but the back panel is undecorated. Small ovals are incised on the bottoms of the feet.

The face is consistent with numerous representations in Olmec art of creatures in nascent, transitional form. The indented skull may be an abbreviated cleft, or the unclosed fontanel of an infant (see cat. no. 25). The pose recalls that in cat. nos. 76 and 128, depictions of sprouting maize, associating the infant supernatural with symbols of transformation and growth.

BIBLIOGRAPHY
Unpublished.

85. Maskette with Incisions

900–600 B.C.
Provenance: Area of La Venta, Tabasco
Material: pale green stone
Dimensions: h. 6.5 cm.; w. 6.2 cm.; d. 3.4 cm.
Private collection

Almost archetypal in its depiction of the infant were-jaguar—cleft head, almond shaped eyes, short, flat nose, and trapezoidal mouth with flared upper lip drooping at the corners—this creature also wears the headband and crenellated earflaps associated with the Olmec Supernatural. The eyes are deeply hollowed with drilled pupils. The open mouth, upper and lower lips carved as separate elements, bares a toothless gum line. Two holes at the top of the maskette are drilled for attachment.

BIBLIOGRAPHY
Unpublished.

85   86

86. Plaque

900–600 B.C.
Provenance: Veracruz
Material: mottled bluish green-to-black jadeite
Dimensions: h. 4.5 cm.; w. 3.7 cm.; d. 1.5 cm.
Private collection

Severe in form and countenance, this image projects some of the fierceness of the faces on ceremonial axes (cat. nos. 91 and 92). The head is cleft and the head-band separated from the face by a deep ridge over-shadowing the U-shaped eyes, which are placed low in relation to the precisely delineated nose. The deeply drilled mouth balances the heavy carving above. Crenellated earflaps cover the ears and extend from the middle of the brow to the corners of the mouth. Since it has no attachment or suspension holes and the back is unfinished, this tiny plaque might once have been fastened to a more perishable material.

BIBLIOGRAPHY
Unpublished.

87

87. Plaque

900–600 B.C.
Provenance: Mexico
Material: serpentine
Dimensions: h. 6 cm.; w. 8 cm.; d. 3.5 cm.
Private collection

This creature, with the requisite cleft, almond-shaped eyes, trapezoidal mouth, flat nose, headband, and earflaps, appears to crouch, shoulders hunched, arms and hands drawn to the sides of the face. A repetition of the band and cleft can be seen above the head. The projections above the arms, comprised of stepped and curved planes, may represent the compressed hind quarters.

The architectural quality of this object recalls the monoliths decorated with supernatural faces found at Teopantecuanitlan, Guerrero (see Tate, this volume, fig. 6) and the headdress worn by the seated figure from Río Pesquero (see cat. no. 193, fig. 3). This plaque is unperforated and may have functioned as an amulet.

BIBLIOGRAPHY
Unpublished.

▲

88. Standing Figure

900–600 B.C.
Provenance: Tajumulco, Guatemala
Material: blue-green jade
Dimensions: h. 9.5 cm.; w. 5.1 cm.; d. 2.8 cm.
Private collection

While the headband, with raised squared nodules, and the crossed-bands pectoral identify this figure as the Olmec Supernatural, the full, softly rectangular head and broad, flattened features are characteristics of what appears to be a regional style. There is nothing fierce in the bulging eyes or the gaping mouth with its deep gum line. A carved line below the pectoral may indicate a modeled chest; a heavy band around the waist is perhaps the belt of a loincloth. Saw lines separate the arms from the body and the insides of the short wide legs curve in at the thighs and out at the feet. The left foot is chipped.

Such isolated, static depictions of the Olmec Supernatural are rare in small sculptures.

BIBLIOGRAPHY
Unpublished.

◄ 89. Head from a Figure

900–600 B.C.
Provenance: unknown
Material: gray and pinkish granite
Dimensions: h. 31.5 cm.; w. 22.5 cm.; d. 17 cm.
The Art Museum, Princeton University, Museum purchase

Probably broken from a life-size statue, this eroded
stone head is one of many variations on the representation of a supernatural. The relatively small nose
and upper lip, carved in relief, are the best-preserved
features. The ears are no more than rounded mounds
with the suggestion of incisions on the left one. The
badly eroded eyes are narrowed by the rise of the full
cheeks. The stepped headdress may be akin to the high
headdress worn by the Young Lord in cat. no. 193.

BIBLIOGRAPHY
Elizabeth K. Easby, *Ancient Art of Latin America from the Collection
of Jay C. Leff* (New York, 1966), no. 1.

90. Effigy Axe ►

1000–500 B.C.
Provenance: Veracruz
Material: granite
Dimensions: h. 30 cm.; w. 16 cm.; d. 11 cm.
National Museum of the American Indian,
Smithsonian Institution

This ceremonial axe depicts a supernatural wearing
the earflaps and headband associated with the Olmec
Supernatural. The eyes are lightly scored in shallow
recesses set off by the projections of the headband and
bridge of the nose. The prominent flat band of the
upper lip appears detached from the lower lip by the
large drill holes at the softly defined corners; two fangs
bridge the gap, merging with the upswept curve of the
lower gum line. The hands are incised, in the right-
hand-over-left position (see cat. nos. 145, 146). Faint
incised lines define the legs. The addition of the fangs
adds a fierce aspect to the image of the supernatural
appropriate to the symbolic meaning of the axe.[1]

BIBLIOGRAPHY
Muriel P. Weaver, *The Aztecs, Maya, and Their Predecessors*
(New York, 1972), pl. 1f.
Masterworks from the Museum of the American Indian Foundation,
exhib. cat., The Metropolitan Museum of Art (New York, 1973),
no. 29.

NOTE
1. Peter David Joralemon initially defined the two fangs as an
attribute of God V, but later identified God V as a false category.

Peter David Joralemon, "A Study of Olmec Iconography," in *Studies in Pre-Columbian Art and Archaeology*, no. 7 (Washington, D.C., 1971), 77; idem, "The Olmec Dragon: A Study in Pre-Columbian Iconography," in *Origins of Religious Art and Iconography in Preclassic Mesoamerica*, ed. Henry B. Nicholson (Los Angeles, 1976), 33.

91. Votive Axe

900–500 B.C.
Provenance: Tabasco
Material: dark gray stone with white veins
Dimensions: h. 26.4 cm.; w. 14.6 cm.; d. 11.9 cm.
Dallas Museum of Art, gift of Mr. and Mrs. Eugene McDermott, the Eugene McDermott Foundation, and Mr. and Mrs. Algur H. Meadows and the Meadows Foundation, Incorporated

BIBLIOGRAPHY
Ann R. Bromberg, *Selected Works from the Dallas Museum of Art* (Dallas, 1983), no. 2.

92. Effigy Axe

1000–500 B.C.
Provenance: Tabasco
Material: dark gray stone with white veins
Dimensions: h. 26 cm.; w. 15 cm.; d. 12.
Private collection

BIBLIOGRAPHY
Emile Deletaille, *Rediscovered Masterpieces* (Boulogne, 1985), no. 4.

Close in handling and style, and approximately the same size, these two axes are carved from dark gray, white-veined stone.[1] The join of the head, the haft, to the body or blade is deeply undercut on both. The heads are cleft and the high brows are divided into two fields, with carved faces in low relief on cat. no. 91 and barely visible incised faces on cat. no. 92. On cat. no. 91, the faces are damaged at the top, but trapezoidal mouths can be seen; on cat. no. 92, faint outlines of clefts and almond-shaped eyes remain. The brows on both axes are joined by a motif, which may be a furrowed brow over the bridge of the nose. The eyebrows on cat. no. 91 are in the form of rectangular bars in relief, those on cat. no. 92 are unarticulated, although the brow projects over the eye. The eyes on both are U-shaped: rectangular on cat. no. 91, rounded on cat. no. 92. The compressed noses are damaged, but drill holes for the nostrils are evident.

The mouths are the dominant and most sculptural elements. The mouth on cat. no. 91 is more rectangular

91

than that on cat. no. 92, but both show three large drill holes at the corners and center of the mouth. Two sets of bifurcated fangs can be seen in each mouth; the interlocking fangs flare up and down on the lips and flank the deeply drilled center. Peter T. Furst interpreted these projections as the foreleg skin of the molting *Bufo marinus* as it eats its molting skin (see cat. no. 56), and as a symbol of "the drama of cyclical death and rebirth in the earth."[2] If these axes are effigies of tools used to clear wide swaths of land for agriculture, the cyclical molting of the toad may have served as a symbol for agricultural regeneration.

The right-hand-over-left position evident on both axes is more obvious on cat. no. 92. Slight incisions below the hands on both axes may indicate they originally held objects, as on the Kunz Axe (see Diehl, this volume, fig. 17) and cat. no. 90. The position is sometimes conveyed without an object or instrument (see cat. nos. 146, 147) and may be related to the figures holding batons (see cat. nos. 145, 148). The configuration of the hands on these axes may define their ritual and symbolic function.

NOTES

1. A strikingly similar axe can be seen in *Trésors du nouveau monde*, exhib. cat., Royal Museum of Art and History (Brussels, 1992), fig. 87. Peter David Joralemon stated there that "this axe was part of a group of three discovered in Olmec territory nearly twenty-five years ago." Given the stylistic similarities, it may well be that the two axes illustrated here are of that group.
2. Peter T. Furst, "Jaguar Baby or Toad Mother: A New Look at an Old Problem in Olmec Iconography," in *The Olmec and Their Neighbors: Essays in Memory of Matthew W. Stirling*, ed. Elizabeth P. Benson (Washington, D.C., 1981), 160.

93. Effigy Axe ▶

900–600 B.C.
Provenance: Oaxaca
Material: dark green serpentine with lighter green veins
Dimensions: h. 28 cm.; w. 13 cm.; d. 10 cm.
Private collection

While similar in form and mass to other effigy axes, the imagery here is more incised than carved. The head, which is not cleft, is encircled by a headband whose central element may be a corn symbol. Flanking this motif are two brows that flare upward and end in a small cleft. The downturned, L-shaped saurian eyes, and short nose sit atop the large, trapezoidal mouth. Faint incisions form rectangles for the ears. Barely discernible squared spirals are incised around the mouth; these markings and the two distinct fangs may

BIBLIOGRAPHY

Peter David Joralemon, "The Olmec Dragon: A Study in Pre-Columbian Iconography," in *Origins of Religious Art and Iconography in Preclassic Mesoamerica*, ed. Henry B. Nicholson (Los Angeles, 1976), fig. 190.

NOTE

1. Peter David Joralemon has argued that the four-dots-and-bar motif is itself a symbol for the Olmec Dragon. See Peter David Joralemon, "The Olmec Dragon: A Study in Pre-Columbian Iconography," in *Origins of Religious Art and Iconography in Preclassic Mesoamerica*, ed. Henry B. Nicholson (Los Angeles, 1976), 52.

94. Carved Tusk ▶

900–600 B.C.
Provenance: Veracruz
Material: tusk
Dimensions: h. 12.7 cm.; w. 2 cm.; d. 2 cm.
Private collection

Carved from what appears to be a boar's tusk, this object depicts a supernatural, with flame eyebrows and upraised arms. The fierce expression is due in part to the deeply carved eyes, nostrils, and mouth, accentuated by some loss to the surface.

The object is almost a miniature replica of La Venta Monument 12, which has often been interpreted as a monkey.[1] The unusual physiognomy and raised arms on both objects are suggestive of such an animal. La Venta Monument 12, however, has extensive incisions, including a necklace with bifurcated fangs and what may be the face of a supernatural around its waist. While the object here lacks such elaborate incisions, it does have a wide, broad necklace. The curved band that seems to form the base of Monument 12 is extended in this object to two serpentlike coils, suggesting that Monument 12 may have been similarly constructed. La Venta Monument 12 was found on the northern side of a red clay cap covering the South Central Platform. This cap dates to La Venta Phase IV, indicating a later date for the monument, and perhaps for this carving as well.

BIBLIOGRAPHY
Unpublished.

NOTE

1. Philip Drucker, "La Venta, Tabasco: A Study of Olmec Ceramics and Art," *Bureau of American Ethnology,* Bulletin 153 (1952), pl. 62; Philip Drucker, Robert F. Heizer, and Robert J. Squier, "Excavations at La Venta, Tabasco, 1955," *Bureau of American Ethnology,* Bulletin 170 (1959), 34.

relate this image to the incised faces seen on cat. nos. 22 and 153.

The arms are at the side, freeing the torso for a series of incisions: two vertical parallel lines down the center of the axe and a variation on the four-dots-and-bar motif. The bar, a flared element similar to that on the brow of the figure, is decorated with a small incised oval. This isolated flared element appears on a number of other objects (see cat. nos. 171, 199, 216) and may be an abbreviated version of the Olmec Dragon.[1]

95. Carved Celt ▶

900–600 B.C.
Provenance: Chiapas
Material: mottled bluish green-to-white jadeite (or omphacite)
with black amphibole crystals
Dimensions: h. 26.8 cm.; w. 11.5 cm.; d. 5.5 cm.
Private collection

This object, carved in the form of a celt, conveys a
monumentality disproportionate to its actual size.
The softly carved face, with downcast eyes, flattened
nose, round cheeks, and full lips, relate the celt to the
colossal heads of the Gulf Coast, but the two incised
fangs, similar to those in cat. nos. 90 and 93, indicate
a supernatural association.

Above the head is a helmet or headdress divided into three tiers: the central and dominant element is a carved cleft corn symbol surrounding a more pronounced, incised cleft. This motif is crowned by an ornate vegetative form, the incised horizontal lines on the shaft and tassellike effect at the top suggesting a schematic rendering of an ear of maize. Virginia M. Fields interpreted similar examples of tripartite elements in headbands as maize emerging from clefts.[1] The area of low relief just above the face has incised lines slanted toward the face. Incised lines slant away from the face in a band above this area. F. Kent Reilly, III, in this volume, discusses the sky bands formed by diagonal lines in Olmec and Izapan art. The incised lines seen here may serve a similar function; the maize motif grows above the sky band and the ruler resides below as the protector and provider of the harvest.

BIBLIOGRAPHY
Unpublished.

NOTE
1. Virginia M. Fields, "The Iconographic Heritage of the Maya Jester God," in *Sixth Palenque Round Table*, *1986*, ed. Virginia M. Fields (Norman, Okla., 1991), 168–69.

96

96. Incised Bowl

1200–900 B.C.
Provenance: Tlapacoya, Mexico
Material: clay with black firing blushes
Dimensions: h. 11 cm.; diam. 15 cm.
Private collection

BIBLIOGRAPHY
Unpublished.

97. Incised Bowl

1200–900 B.C.
Provenance: Tlapacoya, Mexico
Material: clay with ivory-tan slip
Dimensions: h. 9 cm.; diam. 16 cm.
Private collection

BIBLIOGRAPHY
Unpublished.

97

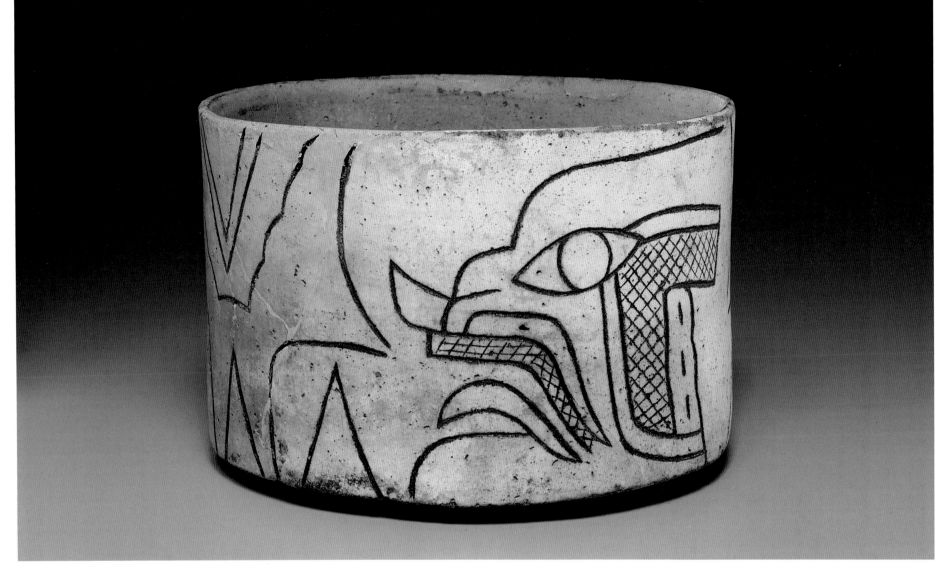

98. Incised Bowl

1200–900 B.C.
Provenance: Morelos
Material: clay with cream slip and black pigment
Dimensions: h. 11.2 cm.; diam. 18.4 cm.
Raymond and Laura Wielgus Collection, Indiana University
Art Museum

These three bowls are incised on both sides with images of a cleft-headed supernatural. The profile in cat. no. 96 is turned back and facing up, the gaping mouth identified, as in the fish effigy vessels (cat. nos. 52–54), with the mouth of the bowl. The eye is almond-shaped and incised with an iris; the cleft head is formed by two elongated projections, one rectangular and the other slightly curved. The gum line at the roof of the mouth is incised with a cross-hatched pattern, perhaps to suggest texture. The profiles on both sides are enclosed in rectangular fields in the lower register of the bowl that alternate with rectilinear and scalloped designs, perhaps symbols of the creature's habitat.

The images in cat. nos. 97 and 98 are carved in the same vigorous style, but the profiles have different orientations: the head in cat. no. 97 faces up, as in cat. no. 96, while the head in cat. no. 98 is in a vertical position. The creatures on both bowls have projecting, sharp-tipped snouts, which in cat. no. 97 presses against the rim of the bowl. A curved line defines the chins of both faces; cross-hatching at the gum lines is similar to that seen in cat. no. 96 and is repeated behind the eyes. The profiles are separated in cat. no. 97 by simple curved lines, in cat. no. 98, by areas of cleft and scalloped incisions.

Many other vessels, all of which have been reported to come from the state of Morelos or the nearby site of Tlapacoya, Mexico, display similar profiles. While most depict the profile vertically, some depict it at an angle, or horizontally, as in cat. nos. 96 and 97.[1] The profiles are similar to those on the vertical bands on some masks (see cat. no. 25), and probably represent the same cleft-headed supernatural (see cat. no. 233).

The formal problem of representing the cleft in profile is solved by rotating the cleft ninety degrees. The function of these vessels and their iconographic significance elude specific interpretation, but they demonstrate the use of Olmec motifs at an early date in the highlands of Mexico.

BIBLIOGRAPHY
Michael D. Coe, *The Jaguar's Children: Pre-Classic Central Mexico* (New York, 1965), no. 21.
Michael D. Coe, Douglas Newton, and Roy Sieber, *African, Pacific, and Pre-Columbian Art in the Indiana University Art Museum* (Indianapolis, 1986), no. 1.

NOTE
1. See Michael D. Coe, *The Jaguar's Children* (New York, 1965), nos. 19, 20; Franz Feuchtwanger, *Ceramica Olmeca* (Mexico City, 1989), nos. 152–55.

THE OLMEC DRAGON

The Olmec Dragon is a composite zoomorph with avian, saurian, and jaguarian attributes, which define the dragon's ability to move through and link the different levels of the cosmos. First defined by Peter David Joralemon as a "mythological hybrid par excellence,"[1] the Olmec Dragon is examined further by F. Kent Reilly, III, and Karl A. Taube in this volume. Reilly separates the dragon into celestial and terrestrial aspects; Taube suggests that many representations previously identified as dragons belong to a distinct category he terms the Avian Serpent.

The crocodilian body of the dragon is the "chassis" onto which all other attributes are attached.[2] The snout is usually blunt; nostrils are often depicted with half-circles. The eye is depicted in a varity of forms, including a U-shaped trough and backward-L surmounted by flame eyebrows, stylizations of the plumes of the harpy eagle, indicating the dragon's ability to fly. The dragon's teeth, if present at all, are often reduced to a curved fang flanked by brackets indicating the gums; the lower jaw is usually absent or ill-defined. The gum brackets have been identified with earth symbols and the open mouth of the dragon with the mouths of caves, symbols of entrance to the otherworld. Mobility is provided by the hand-paw-wing motif, a conflation of a human hand, crocodilian limb, and bird wing. While scutes are sometimes depicted

Figure 1. Supernatural Effigy, 900–600 B.C., Guerrero, Mexico, green jade, h. 11 cm.; w. 5 cm.; d. 2.7 cm. Anonymous loan to The Art Museum, Princeton University.

(fig. 1), tails are conspicuously lacking on most Olmec Dragons, perhaps due to the observation of crocodilians floating with their tails hidden just below the surface.

Representations of the dragon range from small amulets of greenstone to incised images on ceramics to the sandstone sarcophagus of La Venta Monument 6. Many depictions are *pars pro toto*, highly abstract abbreviations of parts of the dragon's body. The dragon may be identifed with the four-dots-and-bar motif, the five-point cosmogram of the Olmec.[3]

On La Venta Monument 6, vegetation sprouts from the dragon's back, and in a series of reliefs related to Chalcatzingo Monument 1 small dragons atop cloud scrolls with clouds and raindrops above them identify the Olmec Dragon with agricultural fertility.

NOTES
1. Peter David Joralemon, "The Olmec Dragon: A Study in Pre-Columbian Iconography," in *Origins of Religious Art and Iconography in Preclassic Mesoamerica*, ed. Henry B. Nicholson (Los Angeles, 1976), 37.
2. Ibid.
3. Ibid.

99. Supernatural Effigy

800–500 B.C.
Provenance: Mexico
Material: jade
Dimensions: h. 3.9 cm.; w. 12.1 cm.; d. 3.9 cm.
From the collection of Robin B. Martin, currently on loan to The Brooklyn Museum

In this small jade statue, the natural form of an iguana has been enhanced with the L-shaped eyes and flame eyebrows of the Olmec Dragon. The eyes are incised and the eyebrows carved in relief with three small circular depressions. The iguana crouches, legs drawn close to the body and head raised; drilled nostrils mark the blunt snout. The overhanging upper jaw suggests the powerful hinged jaw of a crocodilian. While the form of the object indicates the handle of a bloodletter, as in cat. no. 78, the abrupt truncation of the short, cleft tail may represent a lizard whose tail has been broken off.

BIBLIOGRAPHY
Peter David Joralemon, "The Olmec Dragon: A Study in Pre-Columbian Iconography," in *Origins of Religious Art and Iconography in Preclassic Mesoamerica*, ed. Henry B. Nicholson (Los Angeles, 1976), figs. 9d, 24m.
Mary Ann Durgin, "Jade Iguana," in *The Guennol Collection*, vol. 2 (New York, 1982), 114–15.

100. Carved Lid ▼

1500–900 B.C.
Provenance: Las Bocas, Puebla
Material: gray clay with cream-colored slip and traces of yellow pigment
Dimensions: h. 3.5 cm.; w. 5.3 cm.; d. 4.8 cm.
Dr. and Mrs. Wally Zollman

This lid in the form of the Olmec Dragon may once have covered a container used in shamanic rituals (see cat. no. 209). Like many dragon images it lacks a lower jaw; the upper jaw is rendered in the shape of a down-turned L. Descending from the jaw is a single pair of cleft fangs and a large central tooth. The nose and head are angular in comparison to the smooth curve of the forelimbs. Underneath barlike eyebrows, which flare at the back, are two small projections defining the eyes. A line of scutes runs along the spine, suggesting the comb of an iguana.[1] Small holes in the shoulder of the piece indicate that it was attached to a vessel.

BIBLIOGRAPHY
Lee A. Parsons, John B. Carlson, and Peter David Joralemon, *The Face of Ancient America: The Wally and Brenda Zollman Collection of Precolumbian Art* (Indianapolis, 1988), no. 9.

NOTE
1. Lee A. Parsons, John B. Carlson, and Peter David Joralemon, *The Face of Ancient America: The Wally and Brenda Zollman Collection of Precolumbian Art* (Indianapolis, 1988), 29–30.

▲

101. Carved Spoon

1000–500 B.C.
Provenance: Costa Rica
Material: jade
Dimensions: h. 5 cm.; w. 16 cm.; d. 1 cm.
The Denver Art Museum, collection of Jan and Frederick Mayer

This spoon is carved in the shape of an Olmec Dragon in profile. The downturned beak and flame eyebrow derive from the harpy eagle, the curved front tooth and descending serpent's fang underlining the hybrid character of this zoomorph. The bowl of the spoon is perforated with three small holes, probably for suspension.[1]

Several Olmec-style, small-scale objects show humans and supernaturals being carried on the backs of dragons (see cat. nos. 63, 64 and Reilly, this volume, fig. 35). Like cat. nos. 70–75, this spoon may have been used for holding hallucinogens. By taking such a substance, the shaman would generate or summon the zoomorphic supernatural who would carry him on his celestial journey.

BIBLIOGRAPHY
Emile Deletaille, *Rediscovered Masterpieces* (Boulogne,1985), no. 21.

NOTE
1. For a similar spoon, see Anatole Pohorilenko, "The Olmec Style and Costa Rican Archaeology," in *The Olmec and Their Neighbors: Essays in Memory of Matthew W. Stirling*, ed. Elizabeth P. Benson (Washington, D.C., 1981), fig. 4.

102. Carved Bowl

1500–900 B.C.
Provenance: Las Bocas, Puebla
Material: blackware with traces of red pigment
Dimensions: h. 8.9 cm.; diam. 19 cm.
Dr. and Mrs. Wally Zollman

BIBLIOGRAPHY
Franz Feuchtwanger, *Ceramica Olmeca* (Mexico City, 1989), no. 123.
Lee A. Parsons, John B. Carlson, and Peter David Joralemon,
*The Face of Ancient America: The Wally and Brenda Zollman
Collection of Precolumbian Art* (Indianapolis, 1988), no. 12.

103. Carved Bowl

1200–900 B.C.
Provenance: Mexico
Material: blackware with traces of red pigment
Dimensions: h. 6.6 cm.; diam. 10 cm.
Anonymous loan to The Art Museum, Princeton University

BIBLIOGRAPHY
Unpublished.

104. Carved Bowl

1200–900 B.C.
Provenance: Tenenexpan, Veracruz
Material: coarse black clay
Dimensions: h. 7 cm.; diam. 12 cm.
Private collection

BIBLIOGRAPHY
Peter David Joralemon, "The Olmec Dragon: A Study in Pre-
Columbian Iconography," in *Origins of Religious Art and
Iconography in Preclassic Mesoamerica*, ed. Henry B. Nicholson
(Los Angeles, 1976), figs. 6e, 7g, 10d, 15w.

105. Carved Bowl

1200–900 B.C.
Provenance: Morelos
Material: dark gray clay with red and buff slip
Dimensions: h. 6 cm.; diam. 13 cm.
Private collection

BIBLIOGRAPHY
Unpublished.

Each of these bowls is carved with *pars pro toto* representations of the Olmec Dragon.

The linear design of the dragon on the large, highly burnished bowl (cat. no. 102) is dominated by the file of curved forms, angled at the top, that constitutes the flame eyebrows. Immediately below, separated from the body and the nose by vertical lines to either side, is

102

103

104

105

the U-shaped eye. To the left of the eye, the creature's body is depicted by horizontal bands. In front of the eye, the square snout encloses an unusual pinwheel design, variously described as a nostril and possible antecedent of a Zapotec earthquake symbol.[1] L-shaped fangs are incised in front of the nose. The carved design retains considerable traces of red pigment.

The long, diagonal lines representing the dragon on cat. no. 103 suggest a rising movement. Flame eyebrows are indicated by curved lines to the left, the gum line by two downturned brackets separated by an L-shaped fang. The crisp, graphic design, carved with an obsidian blade or similar tool, was made when the clay was leather hard.[2]

The dragon on the bowl of cat. no. 104 is represented frontally, flanked by extensions incorporating the hand-paw-wing motif (fig. 1). Flame eyebrows

Figure 1. Side view of cat no. 104.

surmount the L-shaped eyes; the nostrils are indicated by two simple curves. The U-shaped mouth encloses two smaller brackets similar to those seen on the gum line of cat. no. 103 and probably carry the same meaning. The hand-paw-wing motif usually points away from the front of the dragon; its placement on cat. no. 104 is suggestive of the crouching posture of cat. no. 99 or even the plaque of cat. no. 87. The hand-paw-wing motif ends with a rectangle enclosing a diamond shape, most likely a celestial symbol (see Reilly, this volume). The design is sketchily incised and the surface roughened between the outlines of the L-shaped eyes, mouth and gum line, and hand-paw-wing motifs.

The use of *pars pro toto* is carried to a schematic minimum in the low, elegant bowl of cat. no. 105.[1] Carved through a red slip, the design consists of long, thin bands over a series of rectangles. The bands correspond to the horizontal lines in cat. nos. 102 and 103 representing the body of the dragon; the rectangles contain the downturned brackets of the gum line in cat. nos. 103 and 104. The brackets are enclosed in a larger decorative motif of brackets linked by vertical rectangles. This symbolic abbreviation of the gum bracket is interpreted as a groundline defining the earth (see Reilly, this volume).

NOTES
1. Lee A. Parsons, John B. Carlson, and Peter David Joralemon, *The Face of Ancient America: The Wally and Brenda Zollman Collection of Precolumbian Art* (Indianapolis, 1988), 32; F. Kent Reilly, III, "Visions to Another World: Art, Shamanism, and Political Power in Middle Formative Mesoamerica," Ph.D. diss., University of Texas at Austin, 1994, 195–96.
2. Michael D. Coe and Richard A. Diehl, *In the Land of the Olmec: The Archaeology of San Lorenzo Tenochtitlán*, vol. 1 (Austin, Tex., 1980), 162.
3. Similar vessels can be seen in Franz Feuchtwanger, *Ceramica Olmeca* (Mexico City, 1989), no. 125; Román Piña Chán, *The Olmec: Mother Culture of Mesoamerica* (New York, 1989), fig. 17.

106. Supernatural Effigy

300–100 B.C.
Provenance: Mexico
Material: greenstone
Dimensions: h. 2.25 cm.; w. 13. 5 cm.; d. 4.5 cm.
Private collection

The ornately carved saurian here is identified as a supernatural principally by the flame eyebrows. The incised round eye is recessed under the brow, and the undulating line of the upper jaw turns into tightly curled nostrils in the high, blunt snout. The deeply incised line of the lower jaw is accentuated by descending fangs. The hunched forelegs extend in relief with incisions that suggest the hand-paw-wing motif; the scrolled hind legs are incised. A series of chevrons down the creature's spine probably represents its scutes. With no apparent functional form or holes for attachment or suspension, this small object may have been an amulet.

The configuration of the mouth is similar to the profile of the dragon in cat. no. 101, and its snout resembles that of the dragon carrying a human figure in cat. no. 64. In contrast to the dragons on ceramic objects, these dragons seem to have well-defined lower jaws. The curved snout recalls the fluid scrolls of Preclassic Izapan art. The image of the Olmec Dragon in this late piece from Mexico indicates the longevity of Olmec-style motifs and concepts despite regional variations.

BIBLIOGRAPHY
Unpublished.

107. Carved Bottle ▶

1150–550 B.C.
Provenance: Las Bocas, Puebla
Material: blackware
Dimensions: h. 23.5 cm.; diam. 14.5 cm.
Private collection

A two-headed, serpentlike creature curves around the walls of this blackware bottle, one head facing up, the other down (fig. 1). A line decorated at regular inter-

Figure 1. Roll-out of cat. no. 107.

vals with diamond-shaped star symbols bisects the body. The heads are incised with nostrils and eyes that are curved at the bottom in what seems to be a scalloped design. Two long fangs and a V-shaped tooth or beak project from the heads. Four pairs of limbs, carved along the sides of the body, correspond to each head.

While the creature lacks the flame eyebrows and other diagnostic traits of the Olmec Dragon, the diamond shapes on the back are associated with depictions of the dragon (see cat. no. 104). These symbols may represent the skin pattern of a lizard or snake, but they also appear in a variety of contexts as star or celestial symbols (see Reilly, this volume).

Rare in the Formative period, bicephalic images are common in Classic Maya art, frequently symbolizing the ecliptic in the form of double-headed serpents.[1] Jacinto Quirarte discussed the relationship between the imagery of Izapan and Olmec art and interpreted many Olmec objects as "'ancestral' bicephalic creature[s],"[2] and the standing figure of a Young Lord (cat. no. 193) holds two scepters decorated with supernatural faces in a posture seeming to foreshadow that seen on later Classic Maya stelae. With one head turned to the lower regions, the other to the celestial, this creature may be an ancient depiction of the Mesoamerican belief in the serpent as a symbol of the sky.

BIBLIOGRAPHY
André Emmerich Gallery and Perls Galleries, *Masterpieces of Pre-Columbian Art from the Collection of Mr. and Mrs. Peter G. Wray* (New York, 1984), no. 7.

NOTES
1. Linda Schele, David Freidel, and Joy Parker, *Maya Cosmos: Three Thousand Years on the Shaman's Path* (New York, 1993), 78–79.
2. Jacinto Quirarte, "Tricephalic Units in Olmec, Izapan-Style, and Maya Art," in *The Olmec and Their Neighbors: Essays in Memory of Matthew W. Stirling*, ed. Elizabeth P. Benson (Washington, D.C., 1981), 294.

108a. Carved Bottle

1200–900 B.C.
Provenance: Las Bocas, Puebla
Material: blackware
Dimensions: h. 19.7 cm.; diam. 14.4 cm.
Anonymous loan to The Art Museum, Princeton University

BIBLIOGRAPHY
Unpublished.

108b. Carved *Tecomate*

1200–900 B.C.
Provenance: Las Bocas, Puebla
Material: blackware heightened with cinnabar
Dimensions: h. 7.3 cm.; diam. 11.7 cm.
Anonymous loan to The Art Museum, Princeton University

BIBLIOGRAPHY
Peter David Joralemon, "The Olmec Dragon: A Study in Pre-
Columbian Iconography," in *Origins of Religious Art and
Iconography in Preclassic Mesoamerica*, ed. Henry B. Nicholson
(Los Angeles, 1976), fig. 21c.

The symbols on these two vessels are boldly incised
raptorial claws. The foot on the bottle in cat. no. 108a
has three front claws and a single talon at the back.
A diamond-shaped symbol identifies the claw as that
of a creature of the air. The central section of the claw
in the spherical bowl (cat. no. 108b) is in the form of
an uneven bracket enclosing a scored, raised circle;
the longer arm of the bracket is perhaps the front of
the claw. The three front claws and single back one
are rendered as circles and curves. The carving on the
bottle is contrasted between the highly burnished
black slip and the buff clay underneath. The design
on the bowl is contrasted with the black by the application of cinnabar.

Talons appear most frequently on ceramics from the
highlands, but they are also seen as footwear on the
relief carving at Xoc, Chiapas (now destroyed),[1] and
as headdress ornaments on La Venta Colossal Head 4
and a figure on the side of San Lorenzo Monument 14.
David C. Grove has argued that the talon identifies
the latter two figures as the same person;[2] the talon
may also identify the source of that person's power—
an avian supernatural.

NOTES
1. Susanna Ekholm-Miller, "The Olmec Rock Carving at Xoc,
   Chiapas, Mexico," *Papers of the New World Archaeological
   Foundation*, no. 32 (Provo, Utah, 1973).
2. David C. Grove, "Olmec Monuments: Mutilation as a Clue to
   Meaning," in *The Olmec and Their Neighbors: Essays in Memory
   of Matthew W. Stirling*, ed. Elizabeth P. Benson (Washington,
   D.C., 1981), 66.

109. Carved Bottle

1200–900 B.C.
Provenance: Las Bocas, Puebla
Material: blackware with traces of red pigment
Dimensions: h. 21 cm.; diam. 14 cm.
Private collection

The composition of the avian supernatural encompasses the body of this bottle, leaving the wide, flaring neck undecorated. The bottom of the bird corresponds to that of the bottle and the tip of the beak touches its shoulder. The bird has flame eyebrows, but the beak is long, not that of a raptor. An angled line defining the back of the neck curves and extends along the top of the hand-paw-wing motif and is more heavily carved than the lighter incisions of the feathers. The complicated pattern is perhaps a stylization of the understood structure of the wing. The lower extension is more abstract and includes a crossed-bands motif. Red pigment applied to the carved and incised design contrasts with the black surface.

BIBLIOGRAPHY
Unpublished.

110. Carved *Tecomate*

1000–500 B.C.
Provenance: Las Bocas, Puebla
Material: burnished black clay
Dimensions: h. 10 cm.; diam. 13.8 cm.
Anonymous loan to The Art Museum, Princeton University

This blackware *tecomate* bears the carved image of a supernatural serpent, defined by alternating areas of burnished and unburnished clay. A small, semicircular band surrounding a raised circle defines the eyebrow and eye of this serpent, whose head is cropped at the vessel's opening. An incised, somewhat perfunctory fang descends from the large, curved jaw. Behind the head, the body tapers to several narrow bands with small, scalloped incisions, probably symbolizing scales, but also corresponding in position to the hand-paw-wing motifs seen behind the heads of Formative period avian serpents (see Taube, this volume). Though it lacks the plumes associated with avian serpents, this creature may belong to the same category.

BIBLIOGRAPHY
Emile Deletaille, *Rediscovered Masterpieces* (Boulogne, 1985), no. 49.
Franz Feuchtwanger, *Ceramica Olmeca* (Mexico City, 1989), no. 117.
Trésors du nouveau monde, Royal Museum of Art and History
  (Brussels, 1992), fig. 99.

Dwarfs

Because of their deformity, dwarfs may have been perceived as possessing special powers and able to travel between the earthly and supernatural realms. Dwarfs are represented on a monumental throne, Portero Nuevo Monument 2, supporting the ledge on which the ruler sat. The ledge is banded with earth symbols and the dwarfs are depicted within this cosmic schema and the context of rulership as a mediator. Miguel Covarrubias, who first noted the prevalence of dwarf and fetuslike figures in Olmec art, speculated that they played a similar role to that of the *chaneques* of Veracruz and Guerrero folklore, the bringers of rain and thereby fertility.[1]

Within the broad category established by Covarrubias, distinctions can perhaps be made between achondroplastic figures, true dwarfs, and those with more pronounced fetoid features, even, in one example, the convincing effect of a covering membrane. If indeed fetuses, creatures between worlds, their agitated gestures may be equated with the trauma of transformation and passage.

Note
1. Miguel Covarrubias, *Indian Art of Mexico and Central America* (New York, 1957), 57.

111. Seated Figure

900–600 B.C.
Provenance: Mexico
Material: hematite
Dimensions: h. 11 cm.; w. 8 cm.; d. 6 cm.
Wadsworth Atheneum, Hartford. The Henry D. Miller Fund

This figure of a dwarf is carved in hematite, an iron ore used for making concave mirrors. Powerfully massed, it stands with arms extended and hands clenched and turned down, a position commonly taken by Olmec stone figures (see cat. nos. 177, 178). Except for folds of skin pressed under the jaw, the massive, unadorned head sits directly on the body. The Olmec idealized face is evident in the long narrow eyes, compact nose, and drooping mouth. The flat ears are set close to the head. The short, thick torso is settled on the bent, compressed legs, which, separated by a wide cut from the stone, end in flattened, incised feet. The outside of the right foot is chipped.

An auspicious aura is lent to the figure by the highly reflective surface and dark sheen of the hematite, which the Olmec may have related to the surface of standing water, a place of interface between the earthly and otherworldly realms. The material, therefore, reinforces the role of the dwarf as an intercessor between the natural and supernatural.

Bibliography
Peabody Museum and the William Hayes Fogg Art Museum, Harvard University, *An Exhibition of Pre-Columbian Art* (Cambridge, Mass., 1940), no. 156.
Wadsworth Atheneum Handbook (Hartford, 1958), 173.
Trésors d'art précolombien, Galerie Charpentier (Paris, 1959), no. 17.
Ferdinand Anton, *Alt-Mexiko und seine Kunst* (Leipzig, 1965), no. 31.

112. Figure Holding Head ▶

900–600 B.C.
Provenance: Mexico
Material: stone
Dimensions: h. 26.4 cm.; w. 13.3 cm.; d. 15.6 cm.
Lent by The Metropolitan Museum of Art, the Michael C. Rockefeller Memorial Collection, bequest of Nelson A. Rockefeller, 1979

This figure holds its abnormally enlarged head as if in pain. The helmet it wears is carved with reliefs too abraded to be read. Soft and without any particular character, the features are as unformed as those of an infant or perhaps a fetus. The legs are separated by a large drill hole, and the wide, joined feet serve as a pedestal base.

Bibliography
Unpublished.

113. Figure Holding Head ▲

900–600 B.C.
Provenance: Orizaba, Veracruz
Material: light greenish blue steatite with dark patina
Dimensions: h. 13 cm.; w. 9.1 cm.; d. 9.9 cm.
Private collection

This crouching figure strains to support its massive head, which is extended horizontally and slightly squared off. The eyes are squinted and the mouth is open in a wail. A single incised line across the brow may be intended to reinforce the pained expression, but the head is so badly gnawed and clawed, perhaps by animals, it is difficult to be precise about such a detail. The size and shape of the head in this piece suggest an abnormal affliction.

BIBLIOGRAPHY
Unpublished.

Wrapped up and around the head, the gesture of the arms defines the character of this small figure. The swollen belly, bulging out from an articulated ribcage, rests on drawn-up knees. The legs are cut straight on the inside; the short, turned-up feet are indicated by a carved line.

BIBLIOGRAPHY
Emile Deletaille, *Rediscovered Masterpieces* (Boulogne, 1985), no. 12.

114. Figure Holding Head

1000–500 B.C.
Provenance: unknown
Material: blue-green jade
Dimensions: h. 6 cm.; w. 2.2 cm.; d. 2 cm.
Private collection

The effect of a membrane covering the arms and the face of this curving figure indicates the deliberate intention of representing a fetuslike creature. The face displays a pronounced Olmec physiognomy in the small, almond-shaped eyes; high, drilled nostrils; deeply undercut, downturned mouth; and full muzzle. Two small, shallow, hemispherical recesses occur above each eye, and a central incised ridge divides the head, as in cat. no. 181.

115. Figure with Raised Arms

1100–500 B.C.
Provenance: Mexico
Material: basalt
Dimensions: h. 24 cm.; w. 14.5 cm.; d. 9 cm.
Private collection

BIBLIOGRAPHY
Unpublished.

116. Figure with Crossed Arms

900–600 B.C.
Provenance: Mexico
Material: basalt
Dimensions: h. 20.6 cm.; w. 8 cm.; d. 10 cm.
Private collection

BIBLIOGRAPHY
Unpublished.

These two basalt figures belong to a distinct category of dwarflike and fetoid figurines. The erect posture of the figure in cat. no. 116 with deeply flexed legs is typical of this category of childlike creatures with receding chins carved in stone.[1] The head is large, the bald crown balanced against the deep curve of the back; the features are completely human, down to the ears. The arms are crossed over the chest; the legs are separately carved with wide, flattened feet. Cat. no. 115 is more animated, with arms raised as if presenting an offering of some sort. The body is human, but the long-snouted head resembles an animal. The back is rigidly straight and the head sharply angled. Akin to these figurines is a later, large basalt sculpture of a seated figure with hair, teeth, and crossed arms from Cate-maco, Veracruz, now in the collection of the Smith-sonian Institution (fig. 1).

NOTE
1. See Román Piña Chán and Luis Covarrubias, *El Pueblo del jaguar* (Mexico City, 1964), 75; Philip Drucker, "La Venta, Tabasco: A Study of Olmec Ceramics and Art," *Bureau of American Ethnology*, Bulletin 153 (1952), pl. 51; *Handbook of the Robert Woods Bliss Collection of Pre-Columbian Art* (Washington, D.C., 1963), no. 22.

Figure 1. Sitting Figure, Catemaco, Veracruz, basalt. Department of Anthropology, Smithsonian Institution.

117. Standing Figure with Incisions

900–600 B.C.
Provenance: Chiapas
Material: light grayish green albitite, one side charred by fire
Dimensions: h. 14 cm.; w. 5.4 cm.; d. 5.8 cm.
Private collection

Unusual care is given to anatomical detail in this standing, dwarflike figure, particularly in the delicate modeling of the face, the rendering of the neck and clavicle, and the flexed shoulder muscles. The naturalistic ears are drilled for earspools. The large, erect head is balanced by the extended belly and low-slung, small buttocks. The big hands, short, muscular legs, and pawlike feet seem not so much exaggerations or deformities of human anatomy as the appendages of a young animal. The figure's extended arms and downturned hands recall those of the figures in cat. nos. 177 and 178; the paunch and large feet those of the standing jaguar in the collection of Dumbarton Oaks (see cat. no. 50, fig. 1). It is said that the figure was turned up in a milpa that had been burned over prior to planting, a possible explanation for the charred right side.

Incisions on the head and down the back depict the Olmec Dragon, the dragon's open jaws framing the figure's face, and flame eyebrows, nose, and pronounced serpent fangs appearing on the sides of the figure's head. Rectangular compartments containing either a circle or a diamond-shaped sign resembling the Formative period star symbol divide the back (fig. 1; see cat. nos. 107, 201, 210). A deep groove from the forehead to the base of the neck, excavated by drilling and then grinding out the stone between the holes, might have supported feathers in a harpy eagle headdress (see Furst, this volume, fig. 13).

The incisions on the back of this figure resemble the saurian pelt worn by the hollow figure from Atlihuayan, Morelos,[1] and a hollow figure in this catalogue (cat. no. 204). In all three instances, the pelt represents the wearer's ability to journey to the supernatural realm.

BIBLIOGRAPHY
Unpublished.

NOTE
1. Ignacio Bernal, *The Olmec World*, trans. Doris Heyden and Fernando Horcasitas (Berkeley, 1969), pl. 59.

Figure 1. Drawing of incisions on the back of cat. no. 117.

118. Kneeling Figure with Incisions

1000–500 B.C.
Provenance: Tabasco
Material: brown stone
Dimensions: h. 9 cm.; w. 6.5 cm.; d. 5.1 cm.
Private collection

Within the category of dwarfs, hunchbacks, and fetus-like beings, this figure is among the most physically exaggerated and the most densely inscribed with iconography. The richly carved and incised ovoid head, rubbery mouth, bulging eyes and nostrils, and round, pendulous cheeks that hang well below the mouth are all outsized and fleshy. The lower part of the legs and arms are broken; it is not clear whether the figure is crouching or kneeling, but since the chest and abdomen are highly finished and polished, the fragmentary arms appear to have been extended and not held close to the body.

So closely are the carving and incisions on the top of the head merged with the figure that it is difficult to determine if they are to be read as a headdress in the form of a supernatural creature, a conflation of a rapto-rial bird and the feathered dragon, or the externalized spirit companion of the dwarflike creature. The con-verging profiles of sharply curling beaks form the furrowed brow of the figure, and behind the pitted nostrils on the beaks are the elongated saurian eyes and flame eyebrows associated with the harpy eagle and the Avian Serpent (see Taube, this volume, fig. 4b). The lobes of the strangely contorted ears are drilled into the head, possibly for the attachment of earspools.

Incisions on the body of the figure may correspond to the symbols on the back of cat. no. 117. On the right knee, shoulder, and buttock is an oval with three pro-jections at the top. On the left knee, shoulder, and but-tock is a somewhat architectural motif consisting of an inverted U surmounted by a rectangle divided in the center. The motif on the right knee is seen again on the lower left leg; and, though only a fragment, the inci-sion on the lower right leg is clearly the motif from the left knee.

The figure wears a sack on its back, textured, it would seem, to indicate the material from which it was made. Attached to the headdress, the sack is secured by a tumpline visible at the sides of the head and deco-rated with incised ascending chevrons and diamond-shaped motifs. The contents of the sack are identified by the rounded form cleft at the top, most likely a maize kernel, as in cat. nos. 119 and 172, the gift borne by the creature in its commerce between the earthly and supernatural realms.

BIBLIOGRAPHY
Peter David Joralemon, "The Olmec Dragon: A Study in Pre-Columbian Iconography," in *Origins of Religious Art and Iconography in Preclassic Mesoamerica*, ed. Henry B. Nicholson (Los Angeles, 1976), fig. 2of.
Emile Deletaille, *Rediscovered Masterpieces* (Boulogne, 1985), no. 13.

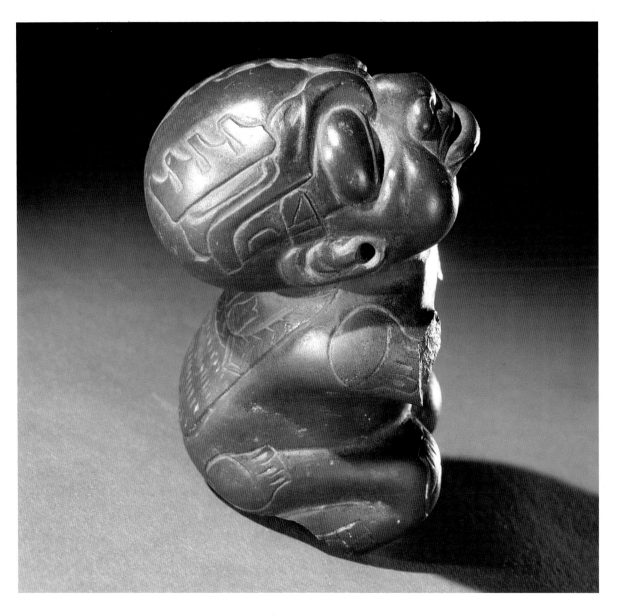

119. Standing Figure with Sack ▶

900–600 B.C.
Provenance: Guerrero
Material: jade
Dimensions: h. 8.3 cm.; w. 3.8 cm.; d. 3.5 cm.
The Metropolitan Museum of Art, anonymous loan

Arms raised to hold a tumpline, this small figure carries a sack similar to the one seen on cat. no. 118 (fig. 1). Incised chevrons and diamond elements, as well as U-shaped brackets, decorate the line and the top of the sack. Two rows of small ovals probably represent the textured surface. A carved, cleft element emerging from the sack, a corn symbol, is drilled through horizontally, indicating that the object could have been worn as a pendant; the ears are drilled for attachments. A ridged band hangs around the waist with a long, wide flap at the back covering the buttocks.

The features of this infantlike creature are those of the Olmec Supernatural. It wears the headdress with two nodules and two crossed-bands pectorals, and the head is cleft. The supernatural is explicitly shown as the *cargador* bearing the precious maize.

BIBLIOGRAPHY
Mary Ann Durgin, "Jade Burden Bearer," in *The Guennol Collection*, vol. 2 (New York, 1982), 115–17.

Figure 1. Back view.

120. Crouching Figure with Bundle ▶

900–600 B.C.
Provenance: Catemaco, Veracruz
Material: dark gray-to-black volcanic rock with inclusions of hornblende
Dimensions: h. 12.7 cm.; w. 7.1 cm.; d. 10.9 cm.
Private collection

The volcanic rock from which this squatting figure is carved, and its possible erosion, give this sculpture an unfinished appearance. Rough hewn coarse features, with a large head, pot belly, and large hands and feet, the dwarf sits with his left arm wrapped around what seems to be a large bundle resting on his shoulder. Given the symbolism associated with the packs in cat. nos. 118 and 119, it may be a sack of maize or, as has been suggested, a bundle containing the paraphernalia of a shaman (see cat. nos. 198–215). Perhaps due to the quality of the stone, the figure here is similar in handling to the basalt figures in cat. nos. 116 and 117; however, this object is unusual in its informal pose.

BIBLIOGRAPHY
Unpublished.

of objects at La Venta were deposited in layers of cinnabar and red sand: Tomb D was defined by a rectangle of cinnabar approximately 30 by 50 centimeters, not large enough for an adult but large enough for a child or a dwarf.[1] There is evidence, too, that carved objects were covered in cinnabar, as in cat. no. 15. Traces of cinnabar on objects are probably residue caught in incisions.

The placement of the hunchbacked dwarf in the vessel may be an effigy burial.

BIBLIOGRAPHY
Unpublished.

NOTE
1. See Tate, this volume; Philip Drucker, "La Venta, Tabasco: A Study of Olmec Ceramics and Art," *Bureau of American Ethnology*, Bulletin 153 (1952): 72–73; 157–59.

121. Hunchbacked Figure and Vessel ▶

900–600 B.C.
Provenance: Las Bocas
Material: eroded onyx and cinnabar
Dimensions: h. 9 cm.; w. 8.9 cm.; d. 9.1 cm.
Private collection

This figure and vessel, said to have been found together, recall the Cerro de las Mesas dwarf and canoe (see cat. nos. 81, 82). While the surfaces of the figure and bowl are severely eroded, it is safe to assume they were once as highly polished as the hematite dwarf of cat. no. 111. The shape of the head and the facial features also would have been nearly the same, though this figure is a hunchback.

The vessel is filled with a red powder, probably cinnabar. Cinnabar, a mercuric sulfide ore, was frequently used in Formative period burials, liberally covering the body and funerary objects. Buried caches

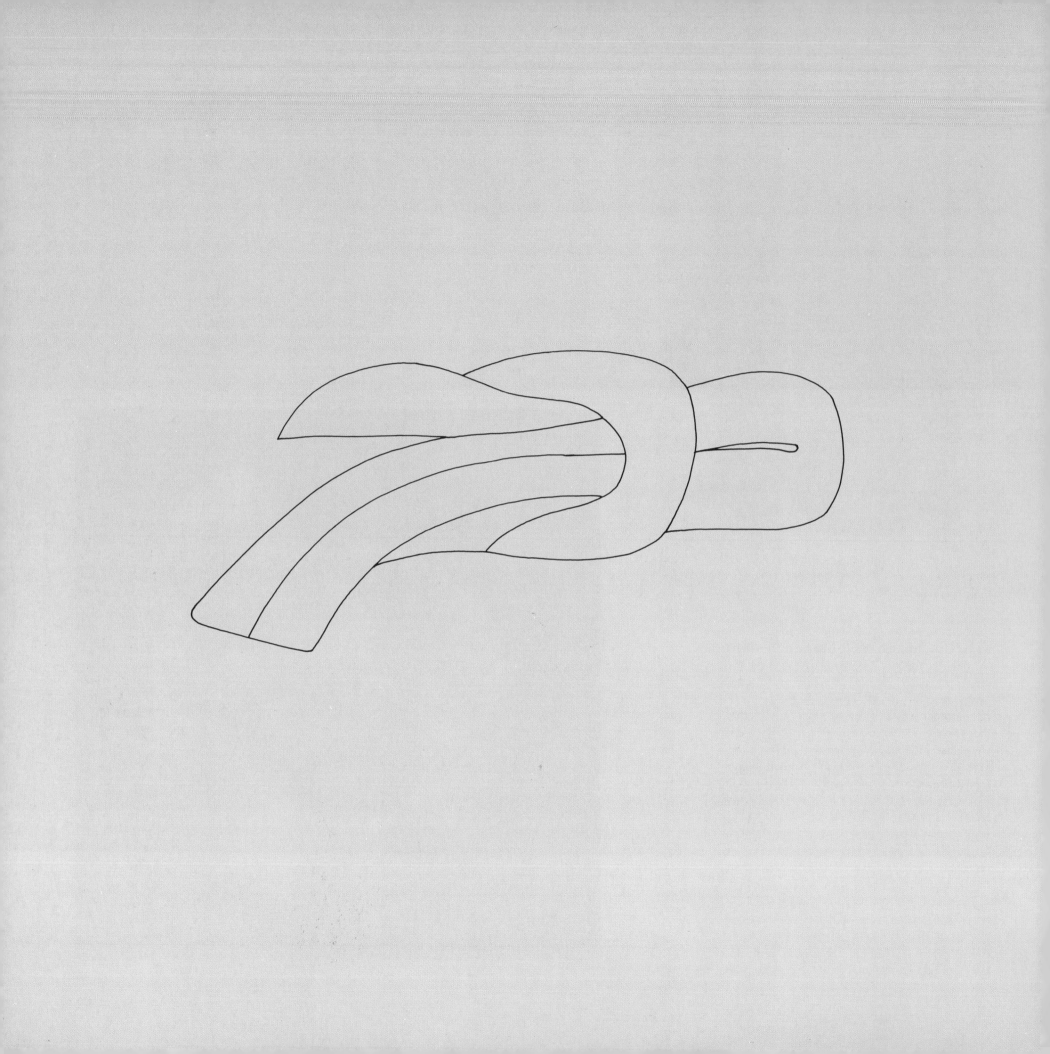

IV

The *Axis Mundi*

The point of alignment and intersection of the three levels of the cosmos — the earth, sky, and underworld — was the *axis mundi*, the place of entrance and conduit between the natural and supernatural worlds. In Mesoamerica, the *axis mundi* was conceived as a world tree, often rendered as cruciform vegetation, sprouting from the headdresses of rulers on the surfaces of celts or appearing in cruciform-shaped arrangements of celts. The wearers are identified as occupants of the cosmic center and the interface of the natural and supernatural oppositions in nature.

In Olmec ceremonial centers, celts were buried as caches to designate plazas, platform mounds, and ballcourts as ritual spaces, and defined them as portals to the otherworld. These deposits marked the cosmic stage on which the ruler performed the rituals of both the *axis mundi* and the journey into the otherworld.

Celts

Celts, or ground stone axe heads, played a major role in both Olmec economy and religion. They were an essential means of clearing wood and brush for the preparation of fields for farming. However, the Olmec were far more interested in the symbolism of the naked blade than the hafted axe. For the Olmec, celts were closely identified with agriculture and food production. In addition, vertically planted celts served to define the central *axis mundi* and the corners of the four-sided world, commonly regarded as a cosmic maize field. When rendered in jade and serpentine, celts symbolized precious ears of harvested corn, and thus maize iconography is often carved or incised on celts.[1]

Celts and much of their attendant iconography were already present among the Early Formative Olmec. At San Lorenzo, there are both the actual stone tools and representations of celts in monumental art. Whereas Monument 8 bears a series of celt outlines carefully carved into its surface, Monument 18 portrays two dwarfs holding vertical celts against the centerlines of their bodies.[2] Celts are even more common in the Middle Formative art of La Venta. James Porter has observed that a number of stelae at La Venta and later sites are in the form of vertically placed celts, with the narrower poll end planted in the ground. Such monuments seem to serve as symbolic *axis mundis*, thematically overlapping with world trees. At La Venta, caches of jade and serpentine celts are planted vertically like miniature stelae, or horizontally in the form of a cross, probably alluding to the four directions. In Olmec costume, celts in groups of four are also placed against the body or donned as a headband, delineating the wearer as a personification of the *axis mundi*.

Among the Middle Formative Olmec, celts were also widely identified with ears of corn. Frequently, the blade is portrayed with a V-shaped cleft from which a cob emerges. In these representations, the celts are maize ears partly projecting out of their enclosing green husk. Although the many Olmec celts carved from serpentine and jadeite clearly allude to maize, these objects had other meanings as well. Clearly a great deal of Olmec jade and serpentine was widely traded in the form of compact and easily transported celts to be recarved into statuettes and other items. The greenstone celts, however, may have

also constituted forms of wealth and even primitive money, much like the copper axe heads of Postclassic highland Mexico. These precious stone celts were perhaps considered concentrated embodiments of agricultural surplus and wealth, items worth many times their weight in actual corn.

The Ballgame

The ballgame was a defining feature of Mesoamerican culture from the Formative period to the Conquest. While the Olmec did not record ballgames on their monuments, numerous figurines depict the attire and equipment associated with the game, and rubber balls have been found at El Manatí. Ballcourts may have been present at La Venta and an early I-shaped court has been reported at Teopantecuanitlan. A large mosaic pavement of greenstone was unearthed between the two range mounds at La Venta, probably a ballcourt, suggesting the pavement marked the center of the court as the portal to the otherworld, and the *axis mundi.*

Many of the objects here, effigies of ballgame equipment made of lighter, perishable materials, may have been trophies for victorious players or buried with rulers to play the ballgame against the gods of the otherworld.

NOTES

1. Lee A. Parsons, John B. Carlson, and Peter David Joralemon, *The Face of Ancient America: The Wally and Brenda Zollman Collection of Precolumbian Art* (Indianapolis, 1988), 16.
2. Michael D. Coe and Richard A. Diehl, *In the Land of the Olmec: The Archaeology of San Lorenzo Tenochtitlán*, vol. 1 (Austin, Tex., 1980), 313, 327.

122. Three Celts

900–600 B.C.
Provenance: Mexico
Material: jade
Dimensions: left: h. 14 cm.; w. 5.3 cm.; d. 2 cm.; middle: h. 17.5
cm.; w. 3.5 cm.; d. 2 cm.; right: h. 14 cm.; w. 4.8 cm.; d. 3 cm.
Private collection

BIBLIOGRAPHY
Unpublished.

123. Two Celts

900–600 B.C.
Provenance: left: Río Pesquero, Veracruz; right: Guerrero
Material: left: dark green jade; right: greenstone
Dimensions: left: h. 20.5 cm.; w. 11 cm.; d. 5.9 cm.;
right: h. 22 cm.; w. 7.1 cm.; d. 5.7 cm.
left: The Art Museum, Princeton University, gift of Bernard
Sperling; right: Anonymous loan to The Art Museum,
Princeton University

BIBLIOGRAPHY
Unpublished.

124. Incised Celt

900–600 B.C.
Provenance: Veracruz
Material: blue-green jadeite with white inclusions and traces
of red pigment
Dimensions: h. 12.7 cm.; w. 6.5 cm.; d. 2 cm.
Private collection

The upper motif incised on this celt consists of a deep
cleft formed by two projecting arms with horizontal
lines, two brackets, and a small diamond surrounded
by four circles on the top and bottom of a hexagonal
shape (fig. 1). Similar to the motif on the mosaic pavements of La Venta, where it was laid out with hundreds of serpentine blocks, it has been interpreted as
an abstract representation of the Olmec Dragon.[1]
Below, a clover design with a central diamond and
smaller ovoid shapes in each petal may correspond
to the diamond shapes on the La Venta pavements,
which F. Kent Reilly, III, has suggested may represent
blossoming water lilies, part of the watery habitat of
the Olmec Dragon.[2]

BIBLIOGRAPHY
Peter David Joralemon, "The Olmec Dragon: A Study in Pre-
    Columbian Iconography," in *Origins of Religious Art and
    Iconography in Preclassic Mesoamerica*, ed. Henry B. Nicholson
    (Los Angeles, 1976), fig. 19l.

123

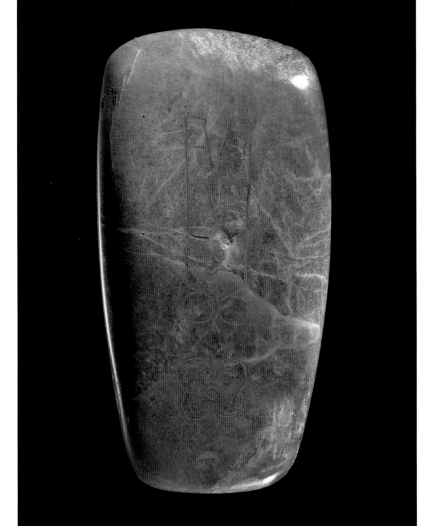

124

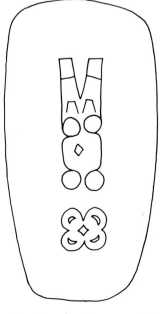

Figure 1. Drawing of incisions on cat. no. 124.

NOTES
1. Peter David Joralemon, "The Olmec Dragon: A Study in Pre-Columbian Iconography," in *Origins of Religious Art and Iconography in Preclassic Mesoamerica,* ed. Henry B. Nicholson (Los Angeles, 1976), 52.
2. F. Kent Reilly, III, "Visions to Another World: Art, Shamanism, and Political Power in Middle Formative Mesoamerica," Ph.D. diss., University of Texas at Austin, 1994, 169.

125. Incised Celt

900–600 B.C.
Provenance: Area of Chalcatzingo, Morelos
Material: bluish green serpentine with milky patina
Dimensions: h. 17.5 cm.; w. 7 cm.; d. 3 cm.
Private collection

The front side of this celt is convex and curves around to a flat back, suggesting that it was cut down from a larger celt. The image incised on the front is anthropomorphic (fig. 1); human hands hold ritual implements usually referred to as "knuckledusters," probably cut conch shells (see Schele, this volume). Extending from the upper part of each knuckleduster is a curved bracket enclosing two circles, which may be a variation on the four-dots-and-bar motif. An avian creature's flame eyebrows overlap these brackets; horizontal curves below the eyebrows appear to be the eyes and, further below, a prominent beak hangs over a wide, gaping mouth (see cat. no. 170).[1] Two small ovals to either side of the beak may depict knots, indicating

Figure 2. Back of cat. no. 125.

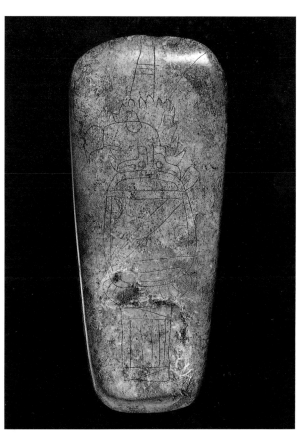

Figure 3. Drawing of incisions on back of cat. no. 125.

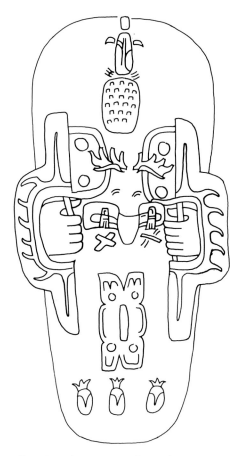

Figure 1. Drawing of incisions on front of cat. no. 125.

that the mouth is to be understood as a mask. Under each side of the mouth are two crossed-bands symbols. The six fingers on the hand at the right are a significant detail. The deformity possibly marks the shaman as one touched by supernatural forces.

At the top of the celt is a maize plant; the larger oval from which it emerges, incised with small marks, may represent seeds. The maize plant is echoed in three ovals, incised with clefts and trefoil elements, at the bottom of the celt. Above the three ovals is a cartouche with the four-dots-and-bar motif, an abstract representation of the Olmec Dragon. The cartouche is cleft at the bottom and top and closed on the sides by brackets. U-shaped brackets are incised in the lower projections of the celt and cleft elements in the upper arms. The incisions may represent the levels of the

cosmos the Olmec Dragon traverses: the cartouche is thus to be understood as a cosmic diagram. Alternating between the descriptive elements of the hands and the abstract elements of the cartouche, the overall composition represents a ruler or shaman wearing and manipulating the symbols that identify him as the conduit connecting the levels of the cosmos. Headdresses with vegetative motifs are often interpreted as the world tree (see cat. no. 95), the flame eyebrows and beak as symbols of the sky, and the knuckledusters as water symbols, completing the depiction of a person capable of moving through the three levels of the cosmos.

The imagery on the back of the celt is also avian (figs. 2, 3). A flamboyantly crested bird with raptorial beak, from whose head a tall, tapering spike rises to

229

the edge of the celt, is seen at the top. Banded, as the symbol of the maize plant often is (see cat. no. 233), the spike's extreme elongation to a sharply pointed tip suggests it may be a bloodletter. Below the bird's head are two smaller profiles surmounting a large oval cartouche, which appears to be the central knot of a bundled scepter, the loops of which are in the upper left and lower right corners and just behind the crest of the bird. Feathers of the bird fan out below the knot and are bound in a shaft. As a bloodletter, the incised image symbolizes access to the supernatural realm; as a bound bundle it may relate to the vegetative bundle or torch motif carried by shamanic flyers.

BIBLIOGRAPHY
Peter David Joralemon, "The Olmec Dragon: A Study in Pre-Columbian Iconography," in *Origins of Religious Art and Iconography in Preclassic Mesoamerica*, ed. Henry B. Nicholson (Los Angeles, 1976), fig. 191.

NOTE
1. A celt from La Venta Offering 2 depicts a seated figure wearing a similarly incised bird mask. See Philip Drucker, Robert F. Heizer, and Robert J. Squier, "Excavations at La Venta, Tabasco, 1955," *Bureau of American Ethnology*, Bulletin 170 (1959): fig. 35.

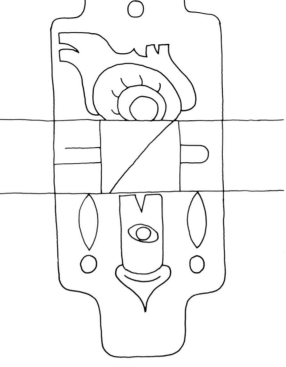

Figure 1. Drawing of incisions on cat. no. 126.

126. Incised Celt

900–600 B.C.
Provenance: Area of Chalcatzingo, Morelos
Material: greenish white albite rock with dark green pyroxene or amphibole crystals
Dimensions: h. 17.8 cm.; w. 7 cm.; d. 2.9 cm.
Private collection

Cut from a customary form to an unusual configuration, this celt represents a shaman's bundle fastened with a wide band secured by a large knot (see cat. no. 125, fig. 2, and cat. no. 198). Such bundles contained implements and substances imbued with magic powers pertaining to the shaman's access to the supernatural, forces alluded to in the eye above and cleft element below the knot (fig. 1). That this celt represents a bundle or scepter is confirmed by the image of the Young Lord (cat. no. 193) who holds a scepter in the crook of his right arm marked with the same eye motif.

In the upper register, the huge eye, with its flame eyebrow and lines radiating from the iris, appears on Monuments 1 and 9 at Chalcatzingo (see cat. no. 37), suggesting that the celt was carved in the vicinity of that highland site. The exclamation-point forms, one above and two below, also seen at Chalcatzingo, represent rain (see Taube, this volume).

A further association with vegetative fertility is made by the central element below the knot: a cleft cartouche marked with an eye. A similar conflation of the eye and cleft element occurs on a celt from Río Pesquero (see Reilly, this volume, fig. 25). The eye identifies the cartouche as a seed.[1] The pointed element descending from the cartouche may represent an emerging root.

BIBLIOGRAPHY
Unpublished.

NOTE
1. The word for eye in proto-Mixe Zoquean is *wi tam*, or "face seed" (see Schele, this volume). This homophony is perhaps an explanation for the unusual depressions on the maize symbols in cat. nos. 172 and 173, which may be intended to represent eyes.

127. Incised Celt ▶

900–600 B.C.
Provenance: Guerrero
Material: green jadeite with traces of red pigment
Dimensions: h. 16.5 cm.; w. 4.5 cm.; d. 2 cm.
Private collection

The most prominent incisions on this celt, a headdress and a human foot, are a *pars pro toto* representation of a ritual performer. The headdress is similar
to that seen on a celt in The Metropolitan Museum
of Art (see cat. no. 172, fig. 1) and one from Simojovel, Chiapas.[1] Curved lines, surmounted by an oval,
possibly a cloud symbol, mark the top of the headdress; a double-merlon motif is incised in the band
below; a crossed-bands may represent a knot at
the rear, where a high, vase-shaped element can be
seen. Small pointed ovals are incised above, which
on the Simojovel celt appear to be parts of vegetative
motifs. Descending from the back of the headdress
is a curved band.

The disembodied foot on the lower half of the celt
stands on an inturning gum bracket, interpreted by
Reilly (this volume) as a groundline. The foot is
marked by a crossed-bands flanked by three small
nubbins. Similar crossed-bands and nubbins are seen
on cat. nos. 131 and 198 and in the Humboldt Celt.

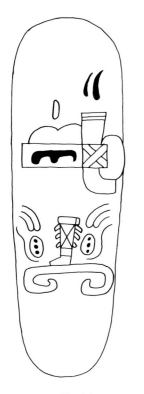

Figure 1. Drawing of incisions on cat. no. 127.

(Schele, this volume, fig. 11 b, c). A foot atop an intur-
ing gum bracket can be seen on the Incised Vessel (cat.
no. 198). The incised motifs on either side of the foot
have not been identified.

BIBLIOGRAPHY
Unpublished.

NOTE
1. Michael D. Coe, "The Olmec Style and Its Distribution," in
*Handbook of Middle American Indians: Archaeology of Southern
Mesoamerica*, vol. 3, ed. Gordon R. Willey (Austin, Tex., 1965),
fig. 17.

128. Incised Celt ▼

900–600 B.C.
Provenance: Río Pesquero, Veracruz
Material: jade
Dimensions: h. 15 cm.; w. 6.3 cm.; d. 2.5 cm.
Private collection

The form of this deeply cleft celt, with its flange projecting from the bottom, is similar to cat. no. 76, where
a three-dimensional figure emerges from the stone,
like a sprout from a seed. Here, a human figure is
depicted within the body of the celt, the face, with
closed eyes and trapezoidal mouth, incised in an oval.
The incised arms are tight to the body, the hands in
front. The curled feet, three toes separated by a curved

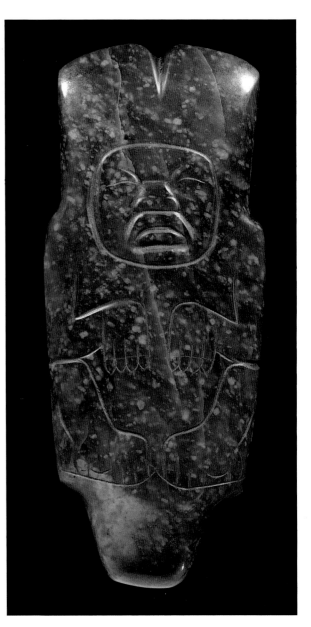

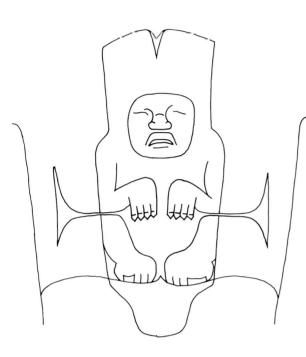

Figure 1. Drawing of incisions on cat. no. 128.

line with another toe at the rear, resemble the bird claws described in cat. no. 108 a, b (fig. 1). It is not clear whether celtlike objects such as this, with flanges at the bottom, are complete as we see them now. In some cases the flanges appear to be polished and patinated, but in others they are rougher, perhaps indicating breakage. If these objects are intact they may have served as scepters or hand-held ritual objects; or they may have been handles of ritual bloodletters.

If, as Peter David Joralemon and Karl A. Taube have suggested, jade and greenstone celts may represent ears of maize,[1] and the images on these celts may symbolize different phases in the annual cycle of corn,[2] then this celt may represent a germinating seed and the actual husk containing the ear of corn.

BIBLIOGRAPHY
Unpublished.

NOTES
1. Lee A. Parsons, John B. Carlson, and Peter David Joralemon, *The Face of Ancient America: The Wally and Brenda Zollman Collection of Precolumbian Art* (Indianapolis, 1988), 38.
2. Karl A. Taube, "The Olmec Maize God: The Face of Corn in Formative and Late Preclassic Mesoamerica," paper delivered at the Thirteenth Annual Maya Weekend, Philadelphia, April 9, 1995.

129. Two Celts

900–600 B.C.
Provenance: left: Guerrero; right: Río Pesquero, Veracruz
Material: jade
Dimensions: left: h. 10 cm.; w. 2.2 cm.; d. 1.4 cm.;
right: h. 9.3 cm.; w. 4.2 cm.; d. 0.6 cm.
Anonymous loans to The Art Museum, Princeton University

The holes perforating these celts indicate they were worn as part of a ceremonial costume, as for example, on the flying figures on La Venta Stela 2.[1] The celt on the left, which is perforated along the side, probably hung as a pectoral. The flat back and hole at the bit end of the celt on the right suggest that it was a belt dangle. Middle Formative belt celts may be antecedents of the Early Classic versions seen on incised pendants.[2]

BIBLIOGRAPHY
Unpublished.

NOTES
1. Karl A. Taube, in "The Olmec Maize God: The Face of Corn in Formative and Late Preclassic Mesoamerica," a paper delivered at the Thirteenth Annual Maya Weekend, Philadelphia, April 9, 1995, pointed out that the flying figures on La Venta Stela 2 wear pendant belt celts.
2. See Emile Deletaille, *Rediscovered Masterpieces* (Boulogne, 1985), nos. 330–33; Linda Schele and Mary Ellen Miller, *The Blood of Kings: Dynasty and Ritual in Maya Art* (Fort Worth, 1986), pls. 22, 33.

130. Mirror

900–600 B.C.
Provenance: Río Pesquero, Veracruz
Material: ilmenite
Dimensions: h. 10.9 cm.; w. 15.5 cm.; d. 1 cm.
Anonymous loan to The Art Museum, Princeton University

One of the largest known concave iron-ore mirrors, this example has an almost spherical figure. It is thought that many Gulf Coast monuments show figures wearing mirrors — a statue from La Venta Tomb A depicts a seated woman with a small mirror at her chest,[1] —and most known mirrors are perforated for suspension.[2] The concave iron-ore mirrors both reflect and invert images, lending them a mysterious power. Mirrors are known as tools for shamanic divination in later Mesoamerican cultures, which may have been true for the Olmec as well. Large concave iron-ore mirrors like this one may also have been used to start fires.[3]

Similar mirrors were found buried with celts at La Venta. In one instance, the mirror was placed near the end of the northernmost arm of a cruciform layout of celts.[4] Michael D. Coe, making an analogy with the Aztec myth of Tezcatlipoca, suggested that this deposit represented the world tree and the mirror a "symbol of the quadripartite god who raised the world tree."[5] The association between mirrors and lineage, which may have its roots in the Formative period (see cat. nos. 155, 156),[6] is also found in the Classic Maya God K, who is often identified by a mirror placed in his forehead.[7]

BIBLIOGRAPHY
John B. Carlson, "Olmec Concave Iron-Ore Mirrors: The Aesthetics of a Lithic Technology and the Lord of the Mirror (with an Illustrated Catalogue of Mirrors)," in *The Olmec and Their Neighbors: Essays in Memory of Matthew W. Stirling,* ed. Elizabeth P. Benson (Washington, D.C., 1981), fig. 15.

NOTES
1. Philip Drucker, "La Venta, Tabasco: A Study of Olmec Ceramics and Art," *Bureau of American Ethnology,* Bulletin 153 (1952): pl. 46.
2. John B. Carlson, "Olmec Concave Iron-Ore Mirrors: The Aesthetics of a Lithic Technology and the Lord of the Mirror (with an Illustrated Catalogue of Mirrors)," in *The Olmec and Their Neighbors: Essays in Memory of Matthew W. Stirling,* ed. Elizabeth P. Benson (Washington, D.C., 1981), 119.
3. Ibid.
4. Offerings 9 and 11 were found near the centerline of Complex A, above Massive Offering 2; the cruciform deposit of Offering 1943-E was found above Mosaic Pavement 1. See Philip Drucker, Robert F. Heizer, and Robert J. Squier, "Excavations at La Venta, Tabasco, 1955," *Bureau of American Ethnology,* Bulletin 170 (1959): 176–84; pls. 42–46.
5. Michael D. Coe, "Olmec Jaguars and Olmec Kings," in *The Cult of the Feline,* ed. Elizabeth P. Benson (Washington, D.C., 1972), 9–10.
6. Carlson (as in note 2), 130.
7. Linda Schele and Mary Ellen Miller, *The Blood of Kings: Dynasty and Ritual in Maya Art* (Fort Worth, 1986), 49.

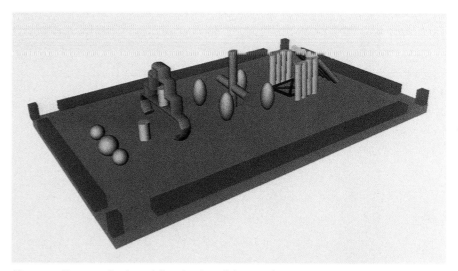

Figure 1. Computerized spatial projection of the motifs on cat. no. 131.

131. Tablet with Incised Glyphic Inscription

900–500 B.C.
Provenance: Ahuelican, Guerrero
Material: mottled greenstone
Dimensions: h. 8.9 cm.; w. 8.9 cm.; d 1.9 cm.
Dallas Museum of Art, Dallas Art Association purchase

The elements of the cosmic diagram on this small stone tablet are sufficiently consistent with those of the creation myth of the Classic Maya that the myth can be taken as a valid point of departure for interpretation of the imagery.[1]

The Y-shaped corners and incised brackets define the center as a sacred precinct. The surface of the greenstone symbolizes the primal waters of creation, the watery underworld of the Olmec; greenstone in all its manifestations was and is used as a ritual symbol of water by pre-Columbian cultures and their modern descendants. The three circles at the bottom of the tablet, centrally positioned within the waters, correspond to the three stones of creation, which the gods set in place as the first act of creation: the separation of water from sky. Above the stones is the earth, represented by the inturning groundline, from which rises a stepped mountain, analogous to the Yax-Hal-Witz, or

"First True Mountain," of Maya myth. From the mountain springs a cruciform-shaped foliated maize plant, the Olmec world tree, the center of the universe, surrounded by four ovals, each divided into three parts, perhaps seeds marking the four corners of the universe.

Above the tree is an enigmatic motif, a rectangular cartouche with a crossed-bands surrounded by thirteen projecting nubbins, which has been compared with similar motifs on cat. no. 198 and the Humboldt Celt (see Schele, this volume, fig. 11) and may represent a sign for north. The nubbins have been identified as a bundle of feathers or leaves, but Karl A. Taube, in this volume, points out that there is considerable overlap between the symbols of green quetzal feathers and green vegetative bundles. Another possible interpretation of the motif, given the cosmological content of the incisions, has been proposed by David Friedel, who identifies it as the "sky-house of the Olmec," a parallel to the Maya "house of the north."[2]

The incisions also recall the organization of tombs and monuments at the site of La Venta (fig. 1).[3] F. Kent Reilly, III, has interpreted the triadic formation of mounds in Complex A as analogous to the three stones of creation; the sandstone sarcophagus of Tomb B carved with the Olmec Dragon, a symbol of the world tree; the basalt column Tomb A, the "house of the

north"; and the Massive Offering of greenstone below Tomb A, the primordial sea from which the world tree is raised.[4] In her analysis of the astronomical associations of the Maya creation myth, Linda Schele discovered that the best alignments for the astronomical symbolism occurs at 1000 B.C. at 18 degrees north latitude, the position of La Venta, and suggests that the symbolism of "the Milky Way associations with creation mythology and the world tree were set during Olmec times."

Despite the spatial distance between Guerrero and La Venta and the chronological distance between the Olmec and the Classic Maya, the continuity from the incisions on this tablet to the alignment of La Venta Complex A to the creation myth of the Classic Maya indicates that all three derive from a common source. Perhaps even more striking than this proposed continuity is the ability of the artists and sages of the Formative period to reduce their most fundamental myth, the myth of creation, onto this small tablet.

BIBLIOGRAPHY
Carlo T. E. Gay, "Olmec Hieroglyphic Writing," *Archaeology* 26, no. 4 (1973): 286.
Brian Stross, "Maize and Blood," *Res* 22 (1992): fig. 15.

NOTES
1. For a summary of the Maya creation myth, see Linda Schele, David Freidel, and Joy Parker, *Maya Cosmos: Three Thousand Years on the Shaman's Path* (New York, 1993), 59–172.
2. Ibid, 73.
3. F. Kent Reilly, III, personal communication, January 1995.
4. F. Kent Reilly, III, "Visions to Another World: Art, Shamanism, and Political Power in Middle Formative Mesoamerica," Ph.D. diss., University of Texas at Austin, 1994, 92–93; 161–62; 169.

132. Hollow Seated Figure Holding Ball

1200–900 B.C.
Provenance: Las Bocas, Puebla
Material: buff clay with orange-brown slip and traces of red pigment
Dimensions: h. 28 cm.; w. 22 cm.; d. 16.9 cm.
Private collection

The balance and torsion of the body of this figure about to hurl a ball are convincingly observed, and the expression on the face is consistent with the action. The teeth are filed and the head shaped according to the Olmec ideal. Three roughly modeled tufts of hair resemble the knobs on the heads of the young birds in cat. nos. 57 and 58. Traces of red paint over the genital area, at the neck, and on the legs may indicate a costume or are perhaps purely decorative. Small firing holes were punched in the navel, in the sides of the head, and where the arms join the torso.

The eight equal vertical segments of the ball are divided horizontally at the center into upper and lower zones, the sections alternately hatched and plain. Four equally spaced firing holes in the shape of diamond celestial symbols pierce the circumference. The hatching possibly reflects the construction or texture of the ball. Most likely made for funerary purposes, the effigy figure would have ensured the participation of the deceased in the ritual ballgame in the otherworld.

BIBLIOGRAPHY
Unpublished.

133. Tenon, Fragment

1000–600 B.C.
Provenance: Area of Tres Zapotes, Veracruz
Material: volcanic stone
Dimensions: h. 28.8 cm.; w. 19.5 cm.; d. 19 cm.
The Art Museum, Princeton University, gift of Samuel Merrin

Broadly modeled from pitted lava stone, this compact head is a cluster of swelling forms that cohere into a fierce, demonic presence. The figure is bust length; the small hands at the base grip the body, presupposing

133

134. Standing Figure, Fragment ▼

900–600 B.C.
Provenance: Guerrero coast
Material: mottled light-to-dark green serpentine with chalky
patina and calcifications
Dimensions: h. 9.7 cm.; w. 5.4 cm.; d. 3.5 cm.
Private collection

Wearing a yoke incised with Olmec symbols, this
small fragment of a standing figure is strong evidence
that the ballgame was played in the Formative period,
and of the possible perils of the ritual contest. The face
is grotesquely deformed. The bony brow is deeply
furrowed and the face lined and creased. The nose is
twisted to the side and appears to have been broken.
The mouth is drawn up in what seems to be a crooked
grin or pained grimace, the lip literally split. The
crown of the elongated head is rough hewn and damaged and the ears are simple flanges incised with parallel lines and pierced for attachments.

The right arm and hand are incised with parallel
lines, apparently to suggest some sort of protective
wrapping (fig. 1). In this instance, the crossed-bands
on the back of the right hand is thus probably not a
celestial symbol, but a direct observation of this wrapping. Folded over the body and resting on the yoke,
the left arm and hand are not incised. Part of the yoke

crossed arms and a resolute bearing consistent with
the dour set of the face. The sculpture is broken at the
back; when intact it was probably a tenon, smaller but
similar to Tres Zapotes Monuments F and G.[1] These
tenons may have served as markers in ballcourts.

BIBLIOGRAPHY
Record of The Art Museum, Princeton University 53, no. 1 (1994):
    85, illus.

NOTE
1. Matthew W. Stirling, "Monumental Sculpture of Southern
    Veracruz and Tabasco," in *Handbook of Middle American Indians:
    Archaeology of Southern Mesoamerica*, vol. 3, ed. Gordon R. Willey
    (Austin, Tex., 1965), fig. 22.

Figure 1. Back view.

is incised with a basket weave, indicating that it was made of a perishable material or wrapped with a fabric where it was worn close to the body.

Though the figure's legs are broken, enough remains of the body to show that the yoke was worn around the waist, with the closed end resting on the right hip. The kilt on which the yoke rests, similar to that on cat. no. 147, is decorated with short incised lines at the edges indicating fringed cloth and floral designs (see cat no. 124).[1] Just under the tip of the yoke is a tiny profile image of a supernatural with flame eyebrows. The central element of the kilt may have been the means by which the yoke was attached to the figure's waist.

BIBLIOGRAPHY
Unpublished.

NOTE
1. See also David C. Grove, "The Olmec Paintings of Oxtotitlan Cave, Guerrero, Mexico," in *Studies in Pre-Columbian Art and Archaeology*, no. 6 (Washington, D.C., 1970), fig. 7.

135. Yoke

900–600 B.C.
Provenance: Río Pesquero, Veracruz
Material: greenstone
Dimensions: h. 11.5 cm.; w. 33 cm.; d. 39.5 cm.
The Art Museum, Princeton University, gift of Gillett G. Griffin

Bare of any decoration, this deep green, highly polished stone yoke is a beautiful example of pre-Columbian lithic work. The only intrusions on the purity of the form are triangular notches on the upper outside edges, where the curve begins, and the shallow indentations on the insides of the arms. Its weight renders moot any discussion of its being worn ceremonially, much less used in an actual ballgame. It may have been a trophy or funerary object.

BIBLIOGRAPHY
Mary Ellen Miller, "The Ballgame," *Record of The Art Museum, Princeton University* 48, no. 2 (1989): fig. 9.
Record of The Art Museum, Princeton University 51, no. 1 (1992): 73, illus.

136. *Yugito*

900–600 B.C.
Provenance: Veracruz
Material: granite
Dimensions: h. 13 cm.; w. 12 cm.; d. 14 cm.
The Art Museum, Princeton University, Museum purchase, gift of the Wallace S. Whittaker Foundation in memory of Wallace S. Whittaker, Yale Class of 1914

The *yugito*, a cuff-shaped effigy used for protection in the ballgame, was formed to fit over the hand or knee, and often carved in the form of parts of the body or face. The design on this *yugito* closely follows the plane of the stone, the nose lying flat to the face. Most striking is the large hollow right eye, which may have been inlaid with another material, a sign of the punishing and fateful results of the ballgame. The forked tongue of a serpent extending from the wide, U-shaped mouth may indicate that the battered face is that of a supernatural defeated by a human ball-player. The back is carved with a horizontal band and vertical scrolls similar to motifs on blackware vessels (see cat. no. 54). The *yugito* is broken at the back, rendering a modern inscription unreadable.

BIBLIOGRAPHY
Emile Deletaille, *Rediscovered Masterpieces* (Boulogne, 1985), 31.
Mary E. Miller, "The Ballgame," *Record of The Art Museum, Princeton University* 48, no. 2 (1989): fig. 12.

137. *Yugito* with Incisions

900–600 B.C.
Provenance: North Central Guerrero
Material: hard green-black granular stone, mostly feldspar
Dimensions: h. 10.4 cm.; w. 11 cm.; d. 11.9 cm.
Private collection

This small effigy of a *yugito* is carved in the form of a cupped hand. The fingers extend over half the surface; the raised, rounded form that corresponds to the back of the hand and the squared spiral at the wrist form the hand-paw-wing motif as seen on blackware vessels.[1]

BIBLIOGRAPHY
Unpublished.

NOTE
1. See Miguel Covarrubias, *Indian Art of Mexico and Central America* (New York, 1957), fig. 10.

138. *Yugito* with Carved Face and Incisions

900–600 B.C.
Provenance: Mexico
Material: stone
Dimensions: h. 19 cm.; w. 14.9 cm.; d. 15.2 cm.
Lent by The Metropolitan Museum of Art, the Michael
C. Rockefeller Memorial Collection, gift of Nelson A.
Rockefeller, 1963

Except for the eyes, which suggest a different lineage, the full lips, splayed nose, and human ears on this *yugito* appear to be directly descended from the colossal heads of the Gulf Coast. The curving recesses that frame the face and extend into the domed head also recall the helmets and headdresses of the great heads.

The shape is distinctive. Unlike the low arc in which other examples are formed, such as cat. nos. 136 and 137, this *yugito* is taller and more compressed, the underside taking the shape of a high, narrow arch. The holes at the ear lobes were probably fitted with large ornaments in a different material.

An extensive system of incisions covers the face. Over the eyes appear supernatural faces, with almond-shaped eyes. The mouths can be seen just above the eyebrows; the finely incised bands flanking the carved face may represent fangs. A network of lines and brackets, two lines of which coincide with the sides of the nose, forms a grid over the face. On either side of the mouth the designs become more complicated, but small diamonds, circles, and scrolls are evident. The incisions imbue the *yugito* with supernatural power for the mythic ballgame played in the otherworld.

BIBLIOGRAPHY

Miguel Covarrubias, *Indian Art of Mexico and Central America* (New York, 1957), fig. 35; pl. 9.
Román Piña Chán and Luis Covarrubias, *El Pueblo del jaguar* (Mexico City, 1964), fig. 55.
Robert Goldwater et al., *Art of Oceania, Africa, and the Americas from the Museum of Primitive Art* (New York, 1969), no. 561.
Beatriz de la Fuente et al., *Mexico en el mundo de las colecionnes de arte 1: Mesoamerica* (Mexico City, 1992), 66.

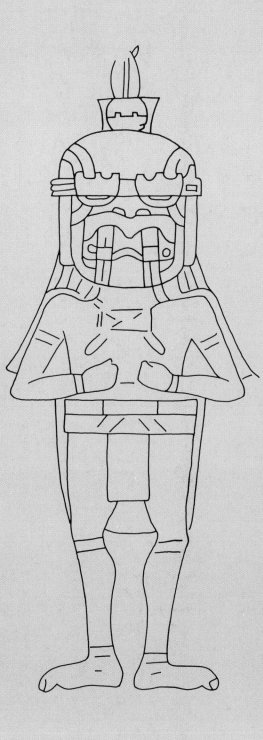

V

Rulers and Regalia

Shamanic power and authority of the standing figures discussed earlier was embodied principally through the representation of a ritual meditative posture. While ceremonial and ritual positions and gestures convey religious and political meaning, monuments and portable objects of Middle Formative Mesoamerica provide evidence that elaborate costume and ritual paraphernalia functioned as a visualization of shamanic ideology and identified the ritual performer as the focus and intersection of cosmological power.

The iconography of the monumental thrones, or so-called altars, of the Gulf Coast—sky and earth bands and niches symbolizing caves—identifies the throne as the juncture of the earthly and supernatural realms and the portal to the otherworld. The ruler enthroned is positioned at this intersection and identified as the *axis mundi*: an attribute and symbol of that power. When depicted enthroned and ritually engaged, holding ceremonial objects, offering an infant or vegetative bundle, the ruler is activating that power to gain access to the supernatural objects.

The scepters, ceremonial bars, and celts, and the position in which they are held also convey the image of the ruler as the *axis mundi*. The damage to many of the monumental works of figures holding staffs precludes certain identification, but some of the staffs are carved with vegetative motifs,[1] and the celt is a potent symbol of agricultural fertility, maize, and power over nature. Standing figures, human and supernatural, holding such ceremonial or ritual objects vertically and close to the chest, right hand over the left, are identified as the world tree. On some axes and a small sculpture shown here, the hands are in this position but without a visible object. The gesture of the hands alone conveys the power of the ritual object. Figures also may be shown, seated and kneeling, holding staffs or ceremonial bars horizontally or, as on La Venta Stela 2, standing, holding the bar diagonally across the chest.[2] The right-hand-over-left position, the right cupped under the upper part of the shaft and the left gripping the base as if to stabilize it, has been interpreted as the raising of the world tree to a vertical position.[3]

Monuments and portable objects attest to the elaborate costumes and articles of regalia of the ritual performer through which the identity of the rulers as the world tree, the *axis mundi,* was also symbolized and conveyed. Maskettes, plaques incised with cosmic symbols, mirrors made of magnetic ores, necklaces in the form of human body parts, and ritual objects such as spoons worn as pendants, earspools, and buckles were elements of the symbolically charged ritual costume. Usually found in burials, the ceremonial and ritual objects, most likely worn in life, were arrayed with the deceased. Perishable materials of the costumes, textiles, wood, feathers, and vegetation, into which many of these jade and greenstone objects were incorporated, have not survived. Headdresses, as represented on monuments and portable objects, particularly celts, varied from simple headbands with attachments of sprouting or trilobed vegetative elements to towering structures, may have incorporated feathers and vegetation. Other headdresses, probably made of cloth, were shaped in symbolic forms, as on La Venta Altar 5, and various types of caps, cylindrical, brimmed, or helmetlike, perhaps representing a clan or status, also are represented. Earspools and flares were worn through the ear and were often so large and heavy that they required counterbalances or may have been suspended from headdresses. Masks of human faces and supernaturals, carved in jade, were drilled for the attachment of ear ornaments, and possibly headdresses. One surviving mask in wood has remnants of jade inlay.

Ritual costume and paraphernalia were visual statements of the supernatural power of the performer on which the legitimacy of rulership rested. Made of rare and precious materials, jade, shell, quetzal feathers, and possibly specially woven and dyed textiles and pelts of animals, ceremonial and ritual costume was also a conspicuous statement of the material power of the ruler.

Notes

1. The staff held by the figure on San Martín Pajapan Monument 1 is carved in a four-way cleft, a vegetative symbol. See Diehl, this volume, fig. 15.
2. See Ignacio Bernal, *The Olmec World*, trans. Doris Heyden and Fernando Horcasitas (Berkeley, 1969), pl 17.
3. F. Kent Reilly, III, "Visions to Another World: Art, Shamanism, and Political Power in Middle Formative Mesoamerica," Ph.D. diss., University of Texas at Austin, 1994, 171.

139. Enthroned Figure

300–100 B.C.
Provenance: Tres Zapotes, Veracruz
Material: dark green mica rock marbled with white and light
greenstone rich in chromium and/or iron
Dimensions: h. 22.3 cm.; w. 14.1 cm.; d. 6.5 cm.
Private collection

The most obvious attribute of authority is the throne
on which this ruler or dignitary sits. The massive proportions and powerful modeling of the head, shoulders, torso, and arms diminish dramatically in the legs,
which are no more than relief elements of the throne,
with the pointed projections of the feet suspended well
above the groundline. The arms extend straight down,
cut away from the body, and the hands, reduced to
pads, rest squarely on the seat of the throne. The body
is articulated only by the rounded projections of the
shoulders and the short incised line on the inside of
the elbow. The assertive head sits low on the shoulders
and the expression of the face is gravely fixed. The
closely spaced, hollowed out oval eyes form dark
pools; the nose, hooked at the bridge, widens and
flattens, and the firmly set mouth is circumscribed by
an incised line. The ears are rounded and incised.

While rich with symbolic meaning, the throne is a
simple construction — a horizontal support with
stepped side projections that curve down to slightly
tapered legs the same depth as the seat. The composition is remarkably close in conception, execution, and
detail to four figures seated on benches from the highlands of Guatemala.[1] Similarly rendered thrones are
illustrated in cat. nos. 34 and 223. La Venta Monument
40 and Laguna de los Cerros Monument 8 are two Gulf
Coast monuments that depict this motif in large scale,
and it is thought that the famed "altars" of La Venta
and San Lorenzo functioned as thrones.[2]

BIBLIOGRAPHY
Unpublished.

NOTES
1. See Elizabeth K. Easby and John F. Scott, *Before Cortés*
   (New York, 1970), no. 66; Susan Milbrath, "A Study of Olmec
   Sculptural Chronology," *Studies in Pre-Columbian Art and
   Archaeology*, no. 23 (Washington D.C., 1979), fig. 60; Lee Parsons,
   "The Origins of Maya Art," *Studies in Pre-Columbian Art and
   Archaeology*, no. 28 (Washington D.C., 1986), fig. 36. The
   fourth bench figure is in the Museum of Mankind, London
   (1938.10.21.214).
2. David C. Grove, "Olmec Altars and Myths," *Archaeology* 26
   (1973): 128–35.

A semicircular line incised under the chin may be the abbreviated description of a necklace, pendant, or collar line. A band or sash, possibly of a tunic, wraps over the legs, crosses the body behind the joined arms, and extends to the armpits. The grid incised on the upper body and face may represent a painted or tattooed design, or scarification. Horizontal lines extend from either side of the mouth onto the headcloth and from the corners of the eyes. The pedestal or throne and the headband with face plaque point to a figure of some importance, but the other distinctive details of costume and grid elude interpretation and a more specific identification.

BIBLIOGRAPHY
Unpublished.

140. Figure Standing on Throne

900–600 B.C.
Provenance: Veracruz
Material: light green serpentine with brown patina and black mineral inclusions
Dimensions: h. 6.6 cm.; w. 2.9 cm.; d. 2.4 cm.
Private collection

The pedestal or abbreviated throne on which the figure stands has been drilled from the bottom, leaving a hole for mounting on a staff or other support. Standing squarely, the figure's legs are separated by a large drill hole: the hands either are joined in front or hold an object. Uniformly eroded, some details have been lost: a delicately incised iris is preserved only on the left eye, and the features of the face plaque set in the center of the wide headband, recalling that on the niche figure of La Venta Altar 5, are faint. A groove around the head separates the headband from the caplike arrangement, with its knob or top knot from which incised radial lines extend in the front and a headcloth falls to the shoulders at the back. If the headband is not taken as a separate unit, the figure appears to be wearing an elaborate helmet.

141. Figure Standing on Throne

900–600 B.C.
Provenance: Honduras
Material: greenstone
Dimensions: h. 31 cm.; w. 7.6 cm.; d. 5.1 cm.
The Jay I. Kislak Foundation

Strangely proportioned, this figure standing on a throne closely adheres to the form of a celt, from which it appears to be carved. This accounts for the contained, economical articulation of the features, no more than beveled or notched from the stone. The head sinks deeply into the shoulders, the arms fall straight to the sides, angling abruptly to clasp the body, and the short, blocky legs are one with the four-legged throne, the toes gripping the front edge.

Although from Honduras and in what appears to be a distinctive, regional style, the figure reflects the Guerrero lithic tradition of recarving celts into compact human figures that retain the integrity of the original form. The pose evokes the identification of the ruler as the *axis mundi* and the persistent memory of the celt imbues the figure with the power of that symbol of authority (see cat. nos. 76, 122–129).

BIBLIOGRAPHY
Unpublished.

142. Standing Figure

900–600 B.C.
Provenance: Puebla
Material: mottled light-to-dark green serpentine with
rust-to-red veins and inclusions
Dimensions: h. 28.1 cm.; w. 9.8 cm.; 5 cm.
Private collection

The many kinds of headdresses and hair arrangements
on Olmec statues are very likely specific attributes of
temporal or religious authority or identified with a
particular clan or person. The cylindrical hat worn by
this declamatory figure must reflect his position. It
cannot be determined if the cufflike effect at the wrists
is meant to indicate a costume, ornaments, or articulation of the joints; the area around the waist is similarly
ambivalent, but the more clearly defined rings around
the ankles appear to be ornaments. Genitalia are prominently represented under a loincloth or sheath. The
stance is assertive. The head, whose face is broadly
carved and aggressive, is as large as the torso. The ears,
which project sharply, are set very high and could
almost be read as attachments to the hat. A notch in
the hat may relate to the areas of unfinished stone on
the heads of other Olmec statuettes.

   The blocky, muscular treatment of the body recalls
another Late Formative statue from Puebla;[1] both are in
marked contrast to the fluid lines of the standing figures usually associated with La Venta (see cat. nos. 18,
19). A similar sculpture from Teotihuacan suggests a
regional tradition of stone carving in the highlands.[2]

BIBLIOGRAPHY
Unpublished.

NOTES
1. Román Piña Chán and Luis Covarrubias, *El Pueblo del jaguar*
    (Mexico City, 1964), fig. 32.
2. See Samuel K. Lothrop, *Treasures of Ancient America*
    (Cleveland, 1964), 43.

143. Figure Holding Crossed-Bands

900–600 B.C.
Provenance: Guerrero
Material: light green serpentine with surface oxidized white
with raised pyrites
Dimensions: h. 7.8 cm.; w. 4 cm.; d. 3.5 cm.
Private collection

Associated with meditation and shamanism, the
seated crossed-legged position of this figure forms a

143

scribed ritual manner, as in other images (see Diehl, this volume, fig. 15; and cat no. 147), the visual focus of the gesture is accentuated by the absence of distracting details of clothing or other regalia, although the head might have been adorned. The ears are pierced, and the raised concavity above the center of the upper lip might have held an inset such as a nose bead suspended from the septum. While rare in Olmec art, nose beads are present on major Olmec monuments, including the Oxtotitlan mural in Guerrero and La Venta Monument 13.

BIBLIOGRAPHY
Unpublished.

coiled base, as in cat. no. 29. The head is unusually flat, and the ambivalent expression, similar to that of the maskette in cat. no. 154, is associated with rain, an interpretation reinforced by the band held across the stomach with the crossed-bands sky symbol.

BIBLIOGRAPHY
Unpublished.

144. Standing Figure Holding Staff

900–600 B.C.
Provenance: Upper Balsas River Basin, Guerrero
Material: bluish green serpentine with milky patina
Dimensions: h. 12.1 cm.; w. 5.5 cm.; d. 4 cm.
Private collection

Hefting a heavy ceremonial bar with a convincing sense of movement, this muscular figure from Guerrero shifts his shoulders, bringing his right arm under it to bear the weight. The middle section of the bar is cross-hatched, probably to denote the texture of its material, whose nature is unclear. Held in the pre-

145. Standing Figure, Right Hand Over Left

900–600 B.C.
Provenance: Chiapas
Material: fine-grained, light green serpentine with bluish inclusions and rust-to-red mineral stains
Dimensions: h. 9.6 cm.; w. 4.5 cm.; d. 2.4 cm.
Private collection

This solemn figure, wearing a loincloth with a broad, apronlike front flap, stands with his hands against his body, right hand over left, as if holding a staff, baton, or celt. The features of the face are sharply defined; the hair, parted in the middle, falls to the shoulders, the strands incised in a similar fashion to those on a bust now in the collection of Dumbarton Oaks.[1] Incised lines define the spine, the backs of the knees, and the cloth covering the buttocks. Drill holes separating the arms from the shoulders do not penetrate the object.

The same position of the hands is found on standing, seated, and enthroned figures, as well as on ceremonial axes (see Diehl, this volume, fig. 17, and cat. nos. 90 93).[2] The motif of the hands alone carries the symbolic significance of the ritual instrument and its power.

BIBLIOGRAPHY
Unpublished.

NOTES
1. Michael D. Coe, "The Olmec Style and Its Distribution," in *Handbook of Middle American Indians: Archaeology of Southern Mesoamerica*, vol. 3, ed. Gordon R. Willey (Austin, Tex., 1965), fig. 15.
2. See also La Venta Figurine No. 1, now in the National Museum of Anthropology, Mexico City.

146. Standing Figure, Right Hand Over Left

900–600 B.C.
Provenance: Guerrero
Material: light green serpentine with mineral-stained chalky patina
Dimensions: h. 9 cm.; w. 4.5 cm.; d. 2.6 cm.
Private collection

The geometrically interpreted, downturned Olmec mouth and small peak of a nose form a trapezoid. The brows and eyes are summarily formed, the ears unarticulated. Incised lines divide the arms from the chest and define the squared hands.

This rudimentary carving is from the Lower Balsas, and is as removed stylistically from the figure in cat. no. 145 as it is geographically, yet the symbolic ritual position of the hands is the same.

BIBLIOGRAPHY
Unpublished.

147. Standing Figure Holding Ceremonial Staff

900–600 B.C.
Provenance: Veracruz
Material: light green jadeite oxidized or stained brown
Dimensions: h. 11.5 cm.; w. 4.4 cm.; d. 3 cm.
Private collection

Slightly hunched and intensely focused, this figure clasps the ceremonial bar with a sense of purpose. The coiffure is one of the most elaborate in Olmec art. Bound by a band decorated at the back with a disk,

Figure 1. Back view.

Figure 2. Standing figure, 900–400 B.C., Veracruz, gray-green jade, h. 10.5 cm. Private collection.

perhaps representing a mirror (fig. 1), the hair is swept in a dome high above the band and gathered to the left side of the face. Bangs cover the brow to the eyelids. A long, flat lock falls to the right side of the face, decorated with a hatched or scored oval disk that balances the large earspool on the left side of the face. The triangular loincloth is overlapped at the back by the tip of a flat, triangular backrack that is supported by a frame across the shoulders and decorated with a disk divided into thirteen irregular sections with a diamond-shaped central element. The figure also wears a wide, fringed or radial collar, extending from shoulder to shoulder, that overlaps an

irregular-shaped ornament with a depressed center, probably a pendant.

Neither the formal detail nor the symbolic weight of this paraphernalia overwhelms the power and dignity of the figure. The body is tightly muscled, the pectorals, shoulders, and biceps clearly defined; the hands and toes are articulated, albeit schematically. The lean jaw line tapers sharply from the high cheekbones to the squared, firmly set chin. While the shape of the face is more angular and taut than the rounded format of the boulders from which the colossal heads of the Gulf Coast were carved, the eyes with incised irises, the short, wide nose, and the protu-

berant, voluptuous lips, and the treatment of the chin suggest some lineage, if only formal, from the colossal portraits.

Another figure in jade, differing in detail but replete with similar paraphernalia, including the staff held in the same position, is a small sculpture from Veracruz in a private collection (fig. 2). The staffs held by the rulers on La Venta Stela 2 and San Martin Pajapan Monument 1 appear identical to the staffs in these small portable sculptures. F. Kent Reilly, III, has suggested that the kneeling figure on San Martin Pajapan Monument 1 is in the process of raising the world tree to help create the current universe. The standing figures holding staffs in the same position may be related to a ritual of "centering the world itself."[1]

BIBLIOGRAPHY
Unpublished.

NOTE
1. F. Kent Reilly, III, "Visions to Another World: Art, Shamanism, and Political Power in Middle Formative Mesoamerica," Ph.D. diss., University of Texas at Austin, 1994, 171.

148. Mask with Incisions

900–600 B.C.
Provenance: Mexico
Material: white jade
Dimensions: h. 12.7 cm.; w. 9.5 cm.; d. 5 cm.
Courtesy of The Cleveland Museum of Art

The eyes of this highly refined mask are drilled in the inner and outer corners and excavated with no indication of irises. The softening of the raised edges throughout must have resulted from an intentional final polishing rather than from handling and wear over time. The earlobes are pierced and there are holes for attachment, indicating that the mask may have been mounted on a costume or headdress. Shading to a light green, the white jade creates a creamy effect. Contact with minerals, probably iron oxide, in the soil in which the mask was buried has caused the rust-colored stain on the left cheek, mouth, and chin.

A section on the right side of the face from the ear to the back of the jaw was lost and restored in modern times. The broken edge was polished down, apparently in antiquity, a measure of the value placed on the mask for its importance as a magic, ritual object, as an heirloom, or as a beautiful piece in itself.

A resemblance has been noted between this mask and the face of the Seated Ruler in Ritual Pose (cat. no. 15). The downturned eyes, long nose, and upper row of scalloped teeth are similar. Faint incisions are evident above the right eye of each object. Whether or not there is a connection between the two, this mask is also certainly the image of a young ruler or member of the elite.

BIBLIOGRAPHY
Carnegie Institute of Fine Arts, *Exotic Art from Ancient and Primitive Civilizations: Collection of Jay C. Leff* (Pittsburgh, 1959), no. 421.
André Emmerich, *Art Before Columbus: The Art of Ancient Mexico from the Archaic Village of the Second Millennium B.C. to the Splendor of the Aztecs* (New York, 1963), 61.
André Emmerich Gallery and Perls Galleries, *Masterpieces of Pre-Columbian Art from the Collection of Mr. and Mrs. Peter G. Wray* (New York, 1984), no. 3.

149. Mask

900–600 B.C.
Provenance: Coast of Guerrero
Material: dark green-to-black antigorite serpentine rock
with traces of cinnabar
Dimensions: h. 17 cm.; w. 15.2 cm.; d. 8.1 cm.
Private collection

The face of this mask is as striking as the highly
polished dark stone from which it was carved. The
underside of the nose and the upward flaring nostrils
so closely echo the dip in the upper lip that they must
have been determined by the same cut in the stone.
The sensuous, parted lips are accentuated by dimples
bracketing the cleft in the chin. Fine sweeping lines
define the browlines. The treatment of the eyes—
narrowed arched grooves with bored holes to indicate
the iris and not intended for insets—is associated with
the Guerrero-Puebla lithic tradition and the widely
used technique for modeling the eye in clay. The ears
are nearly plain flanges with only a line to define the
helix and a shallow drill mark for the concha.

Four holes, two on either side of the top of the mask
and two along the bottom, coupled with the lack of
piercings for eyes and nostrils, indicate that this object
was not worn as a mask but was part of a ceremonial
costume or headdress. Root marks cover the surface
and there are traces of cinnabar in the eyes, mouth,
and drill holes.

BIBLIOGRAPHY
Unpublished.

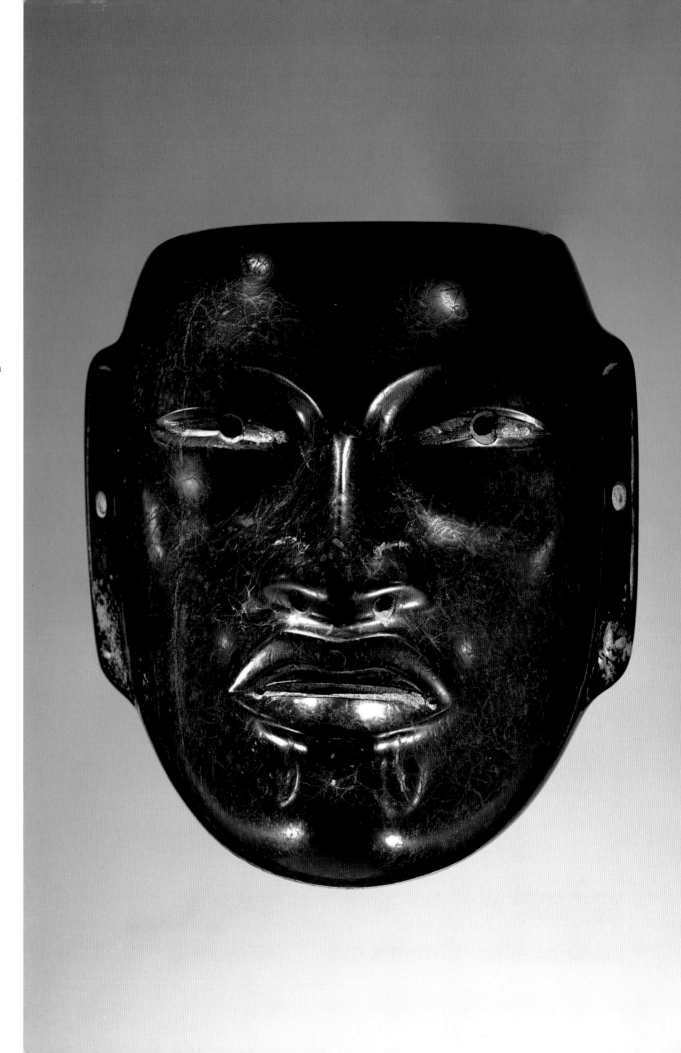

151. Maskette

900–600 B.C.
Provenance: Veracruz
Material: dark green jadeite with white inclusions, pronounced veins of albite, and traces of cinnabar
Dimensions: h. 4.4 cm.; w. 4.5 cm.; d. 2.1 cm.
Private collection

The geometric organization of the features within the sharply tapered oval of this maskette produces a tightly designed, intense image. The lines of the eyebrows are carved in relief but continue as incised lines that sweep beneath the hollowed out eyes and extend to the ears. The nose and mouth are unified in a trapezoidal shape, the nostrils directly echoing the highly arched upper lip. The wide planes of the cheeks are slightly drawn to converge on the corners of the mouth. The ears are small and pierced. A white vein crosses the forehead from left to right and traces of cinnabar are evident in the incised and carved lines and in the drilled interstices in the stone.

BIBLIOGRAPHY
Unpublished.

150. Maskette

900–600 B.C.
Provenance: Campeche
Material: mottled light-to-dark green jadeite with white inclusions and hematite staining
Dimensions: h. 9.6 cm.; w. 8 cm.; d. 4.1 cm.
Private collection

While the naturalism of the face suggests that a particular individual is depicted, it is more likely an ideal visage of an Olmec ruler. The prominent drill holes at the corners of the mouth and the sharply delineated expression lines contrast with the overall fleshiness of the face and the softly carved thick nose, lips, and full cheeks. The earlobes are pierced and two holes at the top indicate it may have been worn as a pendant. It is hollowed out at the back, probably to reduce the weight of the stone.

BIBLIOGRAPHY
Unpublished.

152. Incised Mask

600–400 B.C.
Provenance: Veracruz (?)
Material: greenstone
Dimensions: h. 12 cm.; w. 9 cm.
Peabody Museum of Archaeology and Ethnology,
Harvard University

The human aspect of this mask provides a foil for the
florid designs incised all over the face. A chevron
marks the center of the brow. The cheeks are decorated
with vertical, opposed scrolls that extend from a horizontal variation of the motif, permutations of which
are used on the brow, bridge, and tip of the nose and
chin. Unlike incisions found on other masks and maskettes, the impression here is of actual scarification.

Jacinto Quirarte identified these incisions as a
tricephalic unit, with the U-element on the nose representing a "feline serpent (?)" and dragon-heads
"incised on the cheeks of the mask and presented
upside down."[1] Peter David Joralemon grouped the
incisions with other representations of God II.[2] The
convergence of curved and diagonal lines at the base
of the chevron, if halved, resembles the configuration
atop the jade representation of an element from a headdress, identified as a corn symbol (cat. no. 173). The
ears are pierced at the lobe and two holes are drilled
at the temple just above the ears.

BIBLIOGRAPHY

Peabody Museum and the William Hayes Fogg Art Museum,
    Harvard University, *An Exhibition of Pre-Columbian Art*
    (Cambridge, Mass., 1940), no. 152.
William M. Milliken, *Art of the Americas Picture Book Number Two*
    (Cleveland, 1946), 23.
Miguel Covarrubias, *Indian Art of Mexico and Central America*
    (New York, 1957), fig. 35, pl. 10.
Roman Piña Chan and Luis Covarrubias, *El Pueblo del jaguar*
    (Mexico City, 1964), 85.
Pál Kelemen, *Medieval American Art: Masterpieces of the New World
    Before Columbus*, 3d ed. (New York, 1969), 306, pl. 248b.
Peter David Joralemon, "A Study of Olmec Iconography," in
    Studies in Pre-Columbian Art and Archaeology, no. 7 (Washington,
    D.C., 1971): fig. 187.

NOTES

1. Jacinto Quirarte, "Tricephalic Units in Olmec, Izapan-Style, and
   Maya Art," in *The Olmec and Their Neighbors: Essays in Memory of
   Matthew W. Stirling*, ed. Elizabeth P. Benson (Washington, D.C.,
   1981), 293.
2. Peter David Joralemon, "A Study of Olmec Iconography," in
   Studies in Pre-Columbian Art and Archaeology, no. 7 (Washington,
   D.C., 1971), 66.

153. Bearded Maskette with Incisions

900–600 B.C.
Provenance: Tabasco
Material: green serpentine
Dimensions: h. 7.6 cm.; w. 5.4 cm.; d. 3 cm.
Private collection

Despite the damages to this small, bearded maskette, it retains a distinctive, fleshy character, with full pendant cheeks and deeply set downturned eyes. The nose is destroyed down to the drill holes for the nostrils and the mouth and beard also have suffered. The puffy mouth is segmented; and a pronounced goatee extends from below the projecting lower lip. All that remains of the right ear is the stone surrounding the drill hole in the lobe. The maskette is concave in the back and perforated for suspension.

   The authority of this image is confirmed by the incisions (fig. 1). A vertical band encloses two ovals along the left cheek. Above the right eye is an image of a cleft head with almond-shaped eyes and two fangs projecting from the mouth; below the right eye is a squared spiral. The incisions depict a supernatural similar to the one seen on the face of cat. no. 22. It cannot be determined if the long incised line on the right cheek bears any relation to the other incisions.

BIBLIOGRAPHY
Unpublished.

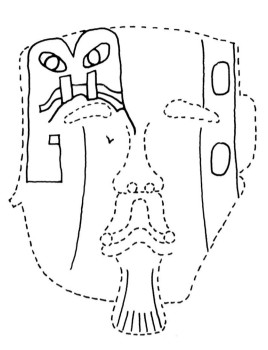

Figure 1. Drawing of incisions.

154. Maskette

900–600 B.C.
Provenance: Tabasco
Material: greenstone
Dimensions: h. 8.5 cm.; w. 10.5 cm.; d. 4.4 cm.
Private collection

The features on this maskette stand out with etched clarity against the softly graded planes of the face. Incised lines follow the upper lids of the narrowed, hollowed-out eyes, and the rounded nose with high drilled nostrils appears to be drawn up into the face. The downturned mouth is locked in a grimace emphasized by the large drill holes. The broad, moon-like face narrows at the temples; the ears are simply rendered in an incised, stylized pattern on the sides at the widest part of the mask. The expression is ambivalent, smiling or weeping. Similar smiling or weeping maskettes have been associated with the niche figure from La Venta Altar 5, who wears a headdress adorned with a maskette with such an expression. Peter David Joralemon has suggested that these images may be associated with rain making rituals.[1]

BIBLIOGRAPHY
Unpublished.

NOTE
1. See cat. no. 228; Elizabeth K. Easby, *Ancient Art of Latin America from the Collection of Jay C. Leff* (New York, 1966), no. 4; Lee A. Parsons, John B. Carlson, and Peter David Joralemon, *The Face of Ancient America: The Wally and Brenda Zollman Collection of Precolumbian Art* (Indianapolis, 1988), no. 16.

155. Mask

500 B.C.
Provenance: Mexico
Material: jade
Dimensions: h. 13.6 cm.; w. 4.7 cm.; d. 2.8 cm.
The Cleveland Museum of Art, gift of Mr. and Mrs. James
B. Wadhams in memory of Miss Helen Humphreys

It is difficult to determine whether the eyes in this curious mask are open or closed, although the curved perforation along the bottom of them creates the impression of heavy, closed lids. The nose and mouth are de-emphasized. The high, smooth dome of the head is encircled by a headband decorated with a round medallion containing a shallow depression, resembling small mirrors made of ilmenite and hematite. Somewhat puzzling is a bowlike arrangement at the neck, with a crescent-shaped clasp and a bib with incised concentric lines. The incised lines, which seem to pass behind the crescent in combination with those on the bib, may be diagrammatic or costume details. Holes exist in the corners of the knot and along the sides of the head. Despite the exaggerated size of the eyes, it cannot be assumed that this image depicts a supernatural. It may be a late work reflecting increasingly complicated ceremonial regalia and attempts to convey some spiritual state through the bizarre treatment of the eyes.

BIBLIOGRAPHY
Trésors du nouveau monde, Royal Museum of Art and History (Brussels, 1992), no. 70.

157a. Miniature Mask

900   600 B.C.
Provenance: Guerrero
Material: greenstone
Dimensions: h. 1.1 cm.; w. 1.2 cm.; d. 0.2 cm.
Private collection

BIBLIOGRAPHY
Unpublished.

157b. Miniature Mask

900 – 600 B.C.
Provenance: Veracruz
Material: serpentine
Dimensions: h. 1.5 cm.; w. 1 cm.; d. 0.7 cm.
Private collection

BIBLIOGRAPHY
Unpublished.

157c. Miniature Mask

900 – 600 B.C.
Provenance: Guerrero
Material: greenstone
Dimensions: h. 1.9 cm.
Private collection

BIBLIOGRAPHY
Unpublished.

These miniature carvings must have been incorporated into larger costume elements, perhaps as insets in the center of earflares.

It is difficult to interpret expressive intention on such a small scale, but the features of cat. no. 157a—the slack, slit eyes, soft, flat nose, and barely open mouth, sagging on the chin—are finely carved and not the least rudimentary. The enormous hollows of the eyes on cat. no. 157b, bored down to the sockets, dominate this wizened face and suggest a figure turned to spirit, perhaps that of an ancestor. The nose, prominent against the sunken cheeks, and the tapered chin and beard extend beyond the mouth, with its rubbery lower lip, a naturalistic detail in an aged face. In marked contrast to this face, cat. no. 157c is no more than an asymmetric funnel punctured by three drill holes. The largest hole locates the mouth in the drawn-out snout and the two smaller ones, the eyes of this little creature. The mask's depth may indicate it was actually fashioned to fit over a tiny face, perhaps to animate a small effigy.

156. Mirrors

900 – 600 B.C.
Provenance: Guerrero
Material: magnetite
Dimensions: large: h. 8.6 cm.; w. 13 cm.; d. 1.1 cm.;
small: h. 5 cm.; w. 6 cm.; d. 0.5 cm.
Anonymous loan to The Art Museum, Princeton University

The term "mirror" should not be taken to mean a looking glass in the modern sense of the word, but a descriptive term for these highly polished, concave objects (see cat. no. 130). A small mirror, very similar in appearance to the smaller of the two illustrated here, was found at Chalcatzingo near the head of a skeleton.[1] The sizes of these two mirrors suggest they could have been worn on a headdress, perhaps in a similar configuration to cat. no. 155, or used as pendants.

BIBLIOGRAPHY
John B. Carlson, "Olmec Concave Iron-Ore Mirrors: The Aesthetics of a Lithic Technology and the Lord of the Mirror (with an Illustrated Catalog of Mirrors)," in *The Olmec and Their Neighbors: Essays in Memory of Matthew W. Stirling*, ed. Elizabeth P. Benson (Washington, D.C., 1981), figs. 17, 18.
Gillett G. Griffin, "Olmec Forms and Materials Found in Central Guerrero," in *The Olmec and Their Neighbors: Essays in Memory of Matthew W. Stirling*, ed. Elizabeth P. Benson (Washington, D.C., 1981), fig. 15.

NOTE
1. Marcia Merry de Morales, "Chalcatzingo Burials as Indicators of Social Ranking," in *Ancient Chalcatzingo*, ed. David C. Grove (Austin, Tex. 1987), 100.

a.

b.

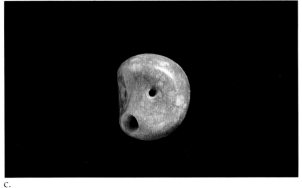

c.

159. Mask, Fragment ▶

1000–500 B.C.
Provenance: Costa Rica
Material: blue-green jade
Dimensions: h. 12.5 cm.; w. 3.7 cm.; d. 3.1 cm.
Private collection

Cut down at the sides and tapering to include only the broad, strong nose and mouth of the original mask, this fragment has a monumentality perhaps greater than that of the work from which it was fashioned. The small holes at the sides of the nose may be the drilled inner corners of the eyes of the full mask. A particularly beautiful effect is the change in the color of the stone, which is darkest at the top and gradually becomes lighter from the tip of the nose down. The stone is pierced at the top. The working of the stone may have been the best means of salvaging an heirloom from a broken but prized work.

BIBLIOGRAPHY
Emile Deletaille, *Rediscovered Masterpieces* (Boulogne, 1985), no. 20.

158. Halved Maskette ▶

900–600 B.C.
Provenance: Costa Rica
Material: jade
Dimensions: h. 5.1 cm.; w. 2.8 cm.; d. 1.2 cm.
The Denver Art Museum, collection of Jan and
Frederick Mayer

The carving of this face is extremely soft and the expression almost somnolent. It is not known whether this maskette was broken accidentally or for a ritual purpose. The broken edge has been smoothed and a small hole has been drilled in the forehead, indications that the maskette was valued after it was damaged.

BIBLIOGRAPHY
Unpublished.

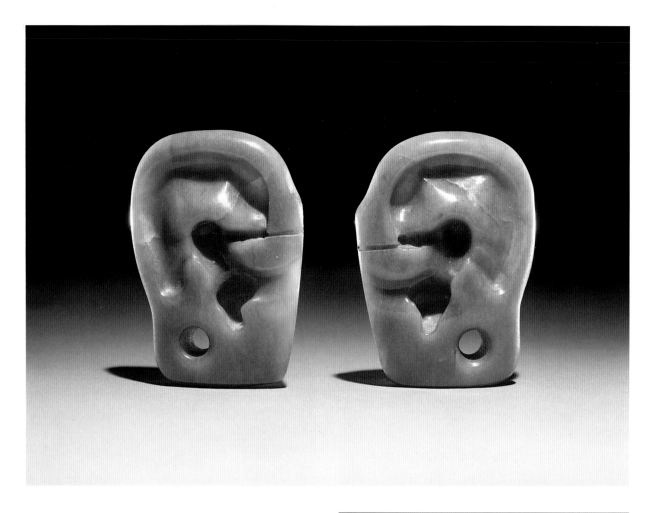

texture, is in marked contrast to that of the flangelike ears typical on even the most realistic Olmec images. The only intrusions on this verisimilitude are the incisions at the tragus. No holes exist for mounting or suspension except those in the lobes, which may have held attachments. If worn as pendants they would have hung upside down. The ears are flat at the bottom, most likely a formal expediency. Four shallow holes are drilled along the front edge of each ear; the third hole from the top is drilled through horizontally. Practically identical in carving and detail to the pair, the single ear is slightly different in size and color, which is a mottled green rather than blue-gray. It is not known if the single ear was originally one of a pair or carved alone. The significance of such isolated body parts is unknown, although they perhaps functioned as trophies or, as has been suggested, funerary regalia.[1]

NOTE
1. Mary Ann Durgin, "Jade Ears," in *The Guennol Collection*, vol. 2 (New York, 1982), 121.

160. Ear Effigies

800–500 B.C.
Provenance: Mexico
Material: jade
Dimensions: h. 5.8 cm.; w. 4.5 cm.; d. 0.8 cm.
From the collection of Robin B. Martin, currently on loan to The Brooklyn Museum

BIBLIOGRAPHY
Mary Ann Durgin, "Jade Ears," in *The Guennol Collection*, vol. 2 (New York, 1982), 121.

161. Ear Effigy

900–600 B.C.
Provenance: Guerrero
Material: mottled greenstone
Dimensions: h. 6 cm.; w. 4.2 cm.; d. 1 cm.
Anonymous loan to The Art Museum, Princeton University

BIBLIOGRAPHY
Unpublished.

The remarkable, naturalistic carving of these human ears, which conveys the cartilaginous structure and

162. Leg-Shaped Beads

950–600 B.C.
Provenance: Guerrero
Material: jadeite
Dimensions: h. 3.8–4.6 cm.; l. 35 cm. (reconstructed)
The Art Museum, Princeton University, Museum purchase, gift of Mrs. Walter L. Weil, by exchange

As in the case of the ears in cat. nos. 160 and 161, the meaning of these detached body parts is unknown, but they are clearly elements of a necklace. The seventeen carved blue-green jade legs and four irregular-shaped stones are drilled across the top so that the legs face to the front when strung.[1] Slightly bent at the knobby knees, the legs are shaped at the back of the thighs and calves and terminate in flat rectangular feet. The tips of the feet are drilled for attachments, perhaps feathers.

BIBLIOGRAPHY
Record of The Art Museum, Princeton University 47, no. 1 (1988): 52, illus.

NOTE
1. When purchased by The Art Museum, the beads were strung with discs of spondylus shell.

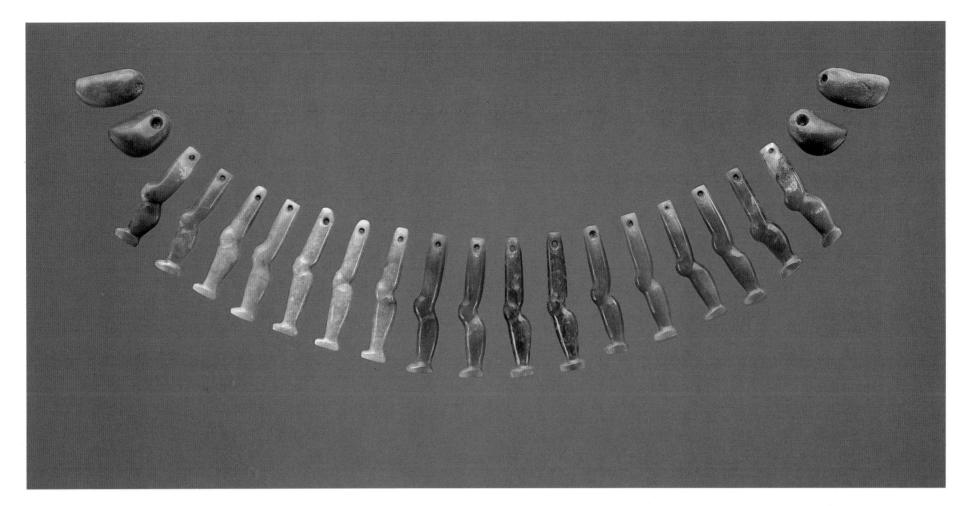

163. Earflare

600–200 B.C.
Provenance: Michoacan
Material: calcified jadeite with cinnabar
Dimensions: d. 5 cm.; diam. 8.8 cm.
Anonymous loan to The Art Museum, Princeton University

Earflares and earspools are sometimes represented on altar figures, colossal heads, and standing figures as part of the regalia worn by Olmec rulers and important personages (see cat. no. 147). Though calcified, this large earflare conveys the dramatic effect these ornaments must have had. The flare is pitted for inlays at eight equidistant points around the edge. The inside of the tubular flange is covered with cinnabar, arguing in this instance against the addition of a central element. A hole in the flange possibly indicates that these large flares were suspended or counterbalanced if drawn through the ear.

BIBLIOGRAPHY
Unpublished.

164. Carved Ornament

1150–550 B.C.
Provenance: Guerrero
Material: mottled sea green jade
Dimensions: h. 3.8 cm.; w. 4.4 cm.; d. 0.2 cm.
Anonymous loan, Museum of Fine Arts, Boston

This plaque features two supernatural profiles carved in relief, their cleft heads bent around the top corners, almost meeting. The overall shape suggests an earspool, but the two holes at the top, asymmetrically placed, must be attachment holes. The void at the center, like that created by the position of the contortionist in cat. no. 40, may represent the cosmic portal, flanked here by supernaturals. The star shape formed by the juncture of the cleft heads recalls the Classic Maya glyph for Venus, which has its roots as a celestial symbol in the Formative period (see Reilly, this volume, and cat. nos. 107, 251).

BIBLIOGRAPHY
Charlotte Thomson, *Ancient Art of the Americas from New England Collections* (Boston, 1971), no. 2.

165. Reworked Maskette

900–600 B.C.
Provenance: Línea Vieja, Costa Rica
Material: grayish blue translucent jadeite
Dimensions: h. 7.2 cm.; w. 7.2 cm.; d. 1.6 cm.
The Denver Art Museum, collection of Jan and Frederick Mayer

Since this piece seems to have been extensively reworked, it is not possible to determine if its demonic appearance was originally intended. The relief is low

in the upper part of the face, and in the flat pug nose, which merges with the upper lip. Shallow drill holes mark the pupils and nostrils. An incised line, broken at the bridge of the nose, runs from the forehead to the bottom of the upper lip. The mouth is deeply excavated and masterfully carved with receding ridges that create an illusion of depth beyond the thickness of the stone. The left ear, smaller than the right, may have been broken and repolished. At the top of the maskette, the small, uneven projections, a feature commonly associated with Costa Rican bird celts, are perforated horizontally.[1] Holes at the upper corners, below the ears, under the chin, and on top of the forehead "suggest that this carved piece could have been worn either as a pendant or been sewn or attached to some unspecifiable surface."[2] Highly unusual are the frondlike forms incised on the cheeks.

BIBLIOGRAPHY
Anatole Pohorilenko, "The Olmec Style and Costa Rican Archaeology," in *The Olmec and Their Neighbors: Essays in Memory of Matthew W. Stirling*, ed. Elizabeth P. Benson (Washington, D.C., 1981), fig. 9.

NOTES
1. Anatole Pohorilenko, "The Olmec Style and Costa Rican Archaeology," in *The Olmec and Their Neighbors: Essays in Memory of Matthew W. Stirling,* ed. Elizabeth P. Benson (Washington, D.C., 1981), 319–20.
2. Ibid.

166. Maskette ▶

900–600 B.C.
Provenance: Veracruz
Material: mottled blue-green jadeite with milky patina
Dimensions: h. 6.4 cm.; w. 9.5 cm.; d. 1.5 cm.
Private collection

The features of this feline face are generously proportioned, wide set, and softly rendered. Formed by deep cavities, the large, open eyes are flat across the top and deeply curved at the bottom; they flare and dissolve at the outside corners. The wide, short nose with sharply splayed nostrils abuts the high, puffy upper lip, which shows a toothless gum ridge. Mouth and nose are carved as a unit in shallow relief, separated only by a narrow line. The tongue hangs over the lower lip onto the chin. The nostrils are drilled and holes on the flangelike ears probably served for suspension.

BIBLIOGRAPHY
Unpublished.

168. Bird Pendant

1150 – 550 B.C.
Provenance: unknown
Material: blue-green jadeite
Dimensions: h. 9.5 cm.; w. 4.7 cm.; d. 0.6 cm.
Museum of Fine Arts, Boston, gift of Lavinia D. Clay

This pendant is carved as a naturalistic representation of a bird. The brow is furrowed; the eye is indicated by a long, deeply carved slit. The beak has the unmistakable curve of a raptor's, perhaps a vulture, hawk, or eagle. The wing, tail, and claws have been fused in a design no doubt dictated by the size of the jade from which it was carved. Claws are drawn up to the body and rest on top of the tail; the wing is tightly folded along the back as if in a position of death or sleep. Two holes drilled through the wing indicate that the bird hung face down when worn. This object may have represented the wearer's avian spirit companion.

BIBLIOGRAPHY
Elizabeth K. Easby and John J. Scott, *Before Cortés: Sculpture of Middle America* (New York, 1970), no. 46.

167. Pendant with Incisions ▼

900 – 600 B.C.
Provenance: Guerrero
Material: serpentine
Dimensions: h. 4.1 cm.; w. 7 cm.; d. 0.5 cm.
Private collection

This object falls somewhere between two Olmec forms: the spoon (cat. nos. 70 –75, 221a, b) and the flanged

pectoral (cat. no. 231a, b).[1] The two holes at the top of this piece indicate that it could have been worn as a pendant, and a plain spoon is seen as a chest ornament on the San Antonio Suchitepequez relief (see Tate, this volume, fig. 28).

Human and supernatural faces are often incised in the bowls of spoons (cat. no. 72). Here, the supernatural face has been reduced in design and execution to a fine line drawing. Its position at the center of the spoon, flanked by two, smaller symmetrical projections, presages the prominence of the face in compositionally similar, though larger objects (cat. nos. 73, 231a, b), as the spoon evolves from a ritual utilitarian object to a more symbolic emblem of power. This shaped pendant and the incised image incorporate the means and end of the shamanic ritual: access to the supernatural realm through the use of ritual objects.

BIBLIOGRAPHY
Unpublished.

NOTE
1. See also Emile Deletaille, *Rediscovered Masterpieces* (Boulogne, 1985), no. 25, for a similar object, and Linda Schele and Mary Ellen Miller, *The Blood of Kings: Dynasty and Ritual in Maya Art* (Fort Worth, 1986), pl. 32, for a flanged pectoral in the collection of Dumbarton Oaks.

169. Incised Celt

800–500 B.C.
Provenance: Costa Rica
Material: jade
Dimensions: h. 20 cm.; w. 4.2 cm.; d. 1.3 cm.
Anonymous loan to The Brooklyn Museum

Although this jade was found in Costa Rica, the carving and incisions on its front and back are rendered in the Olmec style. On the back, the truncated design (fig. 1), which is upside down in relation to the front, suggests that the present celt was cut down from an object with an incised profile of an Olmec face. Incisions, too abraded to be deciphered, can be seen on the eyes and forehead of this face. The front is carved and incised in the form of an avian creature, whose round eyes and browline, cleft and rising to peaks at the sides, appear to represent a horned owl. Rounded, not sharp and curved like the raptorial bird's in cat. no. 168, the beak's shape may be the result of a frontal rather than profile view or the use of another bird's beak in this already hybridized creature. The celtlike form inserted in the cleft of the head may be the central plume seen in many avian masks used in transformation ceremonies (see cat. nos. 178–180). The hole drilled above the head suggests that the celt was a pendant or costume attachment.

It is possible that this represents a human figure wearing a bird costume in a ritual performance of shamanic flight. Incised lines emerge from beneath the long, folded wings. The overall composition of the piece recalls the Tuxtla statuette, itself an Epi-Olmec statue.[1]

BIBLIOGRAPHY
Mary Ann Durgin, "Olmec Jade Celt," in *The Guennol Collection,* vol. 2 (New York, 1982), 124.

NOTE
1. See Robert L. Rands, "Jades of the Maya Lowlands," in *Handbook of Middle American Indians: Archaeology of Southern Mesoamerica,* vol. 3, ed. Gordon R. Willey (Austin, Tex., 1965), fig. 47, for the Tuxtla statuette.

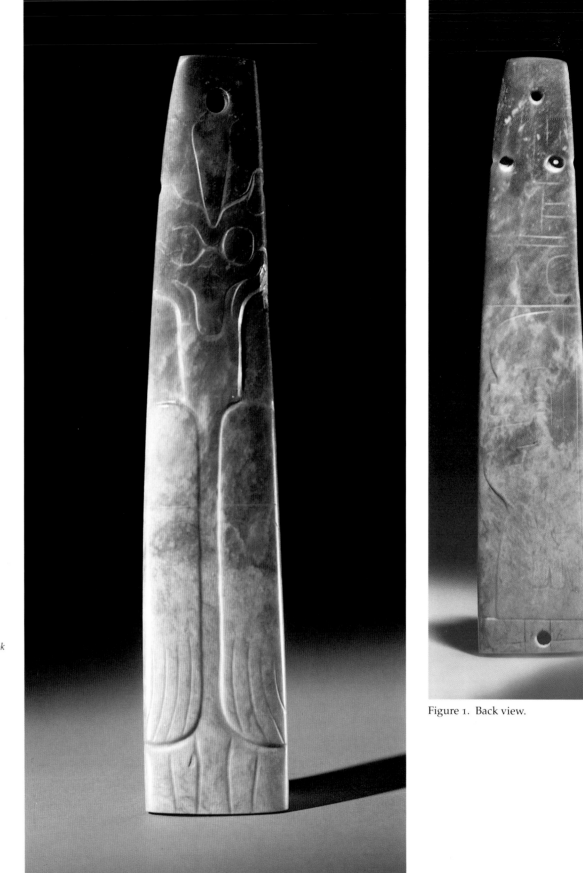

Figure 1. Back view.

170. Mirror with Incisions

900–600 B.C.
Provenance: Guerrero
Material: translucent blue-green jadeite
Dimensions: h. 9 cm.; w. 9.6 cm.; d. 1.5 cm.
Private collection

The concave surface of this jade is highly polished, indicating that it was used as a mirror in the same way as cat. nos. 130 and 156. The obverse is incised with a continuous line in the image of an avian. The horizontal eyes are surmounted by flame eyebrows; the pointed, raptorial beak hangs over the open mouth. Forty-two holes drilled in the surface may have been inlaid, but their pattern is too calculated to be purely decorative.

BIBLIOGRAPHY
Peter David Joralemon, "The Olmec Dragon: A Study in Pre-Columbian Iconography," in *Origins of Religious Art and Iconography in Preclassic Mesoamerica*, ed. Henry B. Nicholson (Los Angeles, 1976), fig. 20 o.

171. Incised Plaque

1150–550 B.C.
Provenance: Guerrero
Material: jade
Dimensions: h. 12 cm.; w. 11.4 cm.; d. 1.4 cm.
Private collection

The incisions and carvings on this object are similar to those on the Olmec Dragon on an incised vase from Tlapacoya (see Reilly, this volume, fig. 17). Flame eyebrows meet in a cleft over the recessed, L-shaped eyes. Below the eyes are two deeply carved nostrils and a trapezoidal mouth with two bifurcated fangs hanging over the lower lip. Lightly incised lines form a bracket around the mouth and three cleft rectangles line the chin.[1] Two small holes below the nostrils were probably for attachments.

While the overall appearance is similar to the Tlapacoya vase, the image as it is applied here belongs to a distinct category of objects incised with supernatural faces (see cat. no. 233).[2] The lower two-thirds of the plaque could be seen as another supernatural face, with almond-shaped eyes and a small, V-shaped cleft between them. Abbreviated flame eyebrows just below the eyes indicate the presence of the Olmec Dragon. Three incised horizontal lines on either side of the mouth form a pattern similar to that on cat. no. 193, there interpreted as straps for attaching a mask.

BIBLIOGRAPHY
Peter David Joralemon, "The Olmec Dragon: A Study in Pre-Columbian Iconography," in *Origins of Religious Art and Iconography in Preclassic Mesoamerica*, ed. Henry B. Nicholson (Los Angeles, 1976), fig. 10 o.

NOTES
1. F. Kent Reilly, III, has pointed out that similar brackets may indicate an entrance to the Olmec underworld. The three cleft rectangles may correspond to three cleft four-dots-and-bar motifs that line the chin of a mask from Río Pesquero. See Peter David Joralemon, "The Olmec Dragon: A Study in Pre-Columbian Iconography," in *Origins of Religious Art and Iconography in Preclassic Mesoamerica*, ed. Henry B. Nicholson (Los Angeles, 1976), fig. 8b.

2. See also Emile Deletaille, *Rediscovered Masterpieces* (Boulogne, 1985), no. 30; Peter David Joralemon, "A Study of Olmec Iconography," in *Studies in Pre-Columbian Art and Archaeology*, no. 7 (Washington, D.C., 1971), fig. 186.

172. Ornament ▾

900–600 B.C.
Provenance: Guerrero
Material: jade
Dimensions: h. 3.1 cm.; w. 2 cm.; d. 1 cm.
Anonymous loan to The Art Museum, Princeton University

BIBLIOGRAPHY
Gillett G. Griffin, "Olmec Forms and Materials Found in Central Guerrero," in *The Olmec and Their Neighbors: Essays in Memory of Matthew W. Stirling*, ed. Elizabeth P. Benson (Washington, D.C., 1981), fig. 22.

173. Ornament ▸

800–500 B.C.
Provenance: Mexico
Material: jade
Dimensions: h. 8 cm.; w. 3.8 cm.; d. 0.5 cm.
From the collection of Christopher B. Martin, currently on loan to The Brooklyn Museum

BIBLIOGRAPHY
Mary Ann Durgin, "Jade Corn Symbol," in *The Guennol Collection*, vol. 2 (New York, 1982), 122–23.

These two jades have been identified with headdress ornaments because of their close resemblance to motifs on a jade celt incised with the profile of a figure wear-

ing an elaborate ritual costume in The Metropolitan Museum of Art (fig. 1). Cat. no. 172 has a cleft at the top, a small circular depression in the center, and two drill holes on the right side. The trapezoidal form in cat. no. 173 is crowned at the top with a triangle on the right and curved scroll on the left; parallel lines below are carved in relief. There is a small round indentation near the top, but no drill holes. Both forms illustrated here have been interpreted as corn symbols. Cat. no. 172 matches the cleft motif attached to the tripartite element emerging from the profile figure's headdress in figure 1, identified as a maize plant, and the cleft element carried by the dwarfs in cat. nos. 118 and 119.[1] Cat. no. 173 appears to be the mirror image of the trapezoidal outline that forms the back of the headdress.

NOTE
1. Peter David Joralemon, "A Study of Olmec Iconography," in *Studies in Pre-Columbian Art and Archaeology*, no. 7 (Washington, D.C., 1971), motif 89.

Figure 1. Celt incised with profile face, Mexico, jade, 900–600 B.C., h. 31.4 cm.; w. 7.9 cm.; d. 1.9 cm. The Metropolitan Museum of Art, the Michael C. Rockefeller Memorial collection, gift of Nelson A. Rockefeller, 1963.

174. Pendant: Crocodilian

900–500 B.C.
Provenance: Guerrero
Material: jadeite
Dimensions: h. 13.9 cm.; w. 5.7 cm.; d. 0.9 cm.
Dallas Museum of Art, gift of Mr. and Mrs. Eugene McDermott, the McDermott Foundation, and Mr. and Mrs. Algur H. Meadows and the Meadows Foundation, Incorporated

This pendant is carved in the form of a crocodilian seen from above. The head is at the bottom, with two drill holes for the nostrils; the four small projections on either side of the long snout are teeth; and the legs consist of four irregular projections, the slightly larger rear legs consistent with the graduated width of the jade. The top of the pendant ends in a slightly curved horizontal line where the tail of the crocodilian is rendered as an incised, squared spiral on the right side. Two drill holes show that it hung vertically, recalling the imagery of the upended saurian as the world tree (see Reilly, this volume, and cat. no. 193).

BIBLIOGRAPHY
Unpublished.

175. Carved Celt

900–600 B.C.
Provenance: Puebla
Material: translucent blue-green jadeite with traces of cinnabar
Dimensions: h. 35 cm.; w. 7.9 cm.; d. 1.9 cm.
Private collection

This large celt is carved, drilled, and incised in the form of a caterpillar. The segmented plates and three-pronged sense organs, as well as the head, mouth, and eyes, are detailed. The tail segment is incised with long striations dimpled with fine holes. The back of the stone is carved to suggest the undulating movement of the caterpillar. At the top, the three projections have prompted an identification of the celt as a hornworm, a hawkmoth caterpillar, but if so, there should be a single projection at the tail. Liberties may have been taken, however, and rather than a biological detail, the three projections may represent the vegetation on which the caterpillar feeds. The transformation of the caterpillar into a moth or butterfly probably had special meaning for the Olmec. If combined in a ritual object or a ruler's ceremonial regalia with an image of the crop it destroys, the caterpillar takes on apotropaic significance, symbolizing the ruler's shamanic power to protect the harvests.

BIBLIOGRAPHY
Elizabeth K. Easby, *Ancient Art of Latin America from the Collection of Jay C. Leff* (New York, 1966), no. 17.

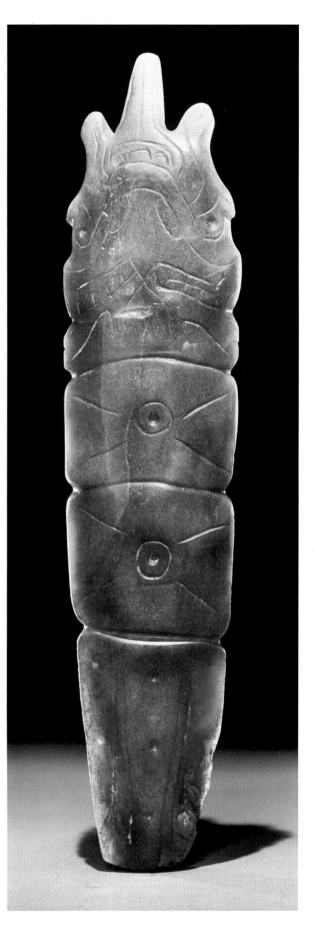

176. Knot

900–600 B.C.
Provenance: Guerrero
Material: light green serpentine
Dimensions: h. 4.1 cm.; w. 10.4 cm.; d. 3.9 cm.
Anonymous loan to The Art Museum, Princeton University

A virtuoso example of Olmec stonework, these two separate loops, which appear to have been carved from a single piece of stone, interlock to form a knot. The drilled holes at the ends of the piece could have been used to attach strings or cords for tying. From the appearance of the knot at the small of the back on cat. no. 193, these loops also could have functioned as a buckle or clasp by pulling a cloth or sash through the center of the knot.

A glyph representing knotted cloth on the Epi-Olmec monument La Mojarra Stela 1 has been asso-ciated by John Justeson and Peter Mathews with "accession to royal power."[1] Similar knots appear on the backs of San Lorenzo Monuments 1 and 2. The function of the knot as a symbol of royal power appears to have had its origin in the Formative period. The intertwined loops are suggestive of the interconnection of the supernatural and natural worlds manifest in the charismatic person of the shamanic ruler.

BIBLIOGRAPHY
Emile Deletaille, *Rediscovered Masterpieces* (Boulogne, 1985), no. 22.

NOTE
1. John S. Justeson and Peter Mathews, "Evolutionary Trends in Mesoamerican Hieroglyphic Writing," *Visible Language* 24, no. 1 (1990): 112–13; John S. Justeson and Terence Kaufman, personal communication, April 1995.

MASKS

The quantity, variety, and quality of the surviving Olmec masks, which range from lifesize to miniature and include full, half, and mouth masks representing humans, animals, and supernaturals, attest to the centrality of this quintessential icon of transformation in Olmec ritual. Masks are shown on objects, clearly delineated from the wearer by such details as attachment straps or hinged jaws. The distinction between mask and wearer renders visible the power of the mask and of the charismatic and shamanic ritual performer, the ruler, who possesses and animates the talismanic object.

The masks depict animals, the wearer's nagual or spirit companion, and supernaturals and zoomorphs, fantastic fusions of saurian, jagaurian, and avian features, attributes of creatures of the Olmec natural world with dominion over the water, earth, and air, summoned to negotiate the shamanic journey through the levels of the cosmos.

The lifesize, wearable masks in human form present what appears to be another aspect of transformation. Carved from large cobbles of precious stone with daunting refinement, given the simple tools—wood and stone drills and abrasives—these masks can only be the images of rulers. While the masks are distinct, some share similar features, which may reflect technical and local traditions. With rare exceptions, however, no specific personality emerges. The expressions of otherworldly focus suggest a transcendent, ecstatic state, the idealized and eternal face of the ruler, and may have had both ceremonial and funerary associations. A great number of known masks are said to have come from a cache with other precious objects at Río Pesquero, perhaps as an offering similar to those at La Venta.

As empowered objects of the greatest luxury, masks embodied the shamanic, political, and economic power of the ruler and legitimized his status in life and death or, by appropriation, the claims of his successors.

Figure 1. Back view of cat. no. 178.

The mask worn by cat. no. 178 is not identical to the wearable mask in cat. no. 194, nor to the mask worn by the Young Lord (cat. no. 193), but it carries essentially the same meaning. In this case, a single plume is used instead of feathered eyebrows to express the avian aspect of the fanged feline.[1] Care has been taken to show that the mask is held in place on the face by a string, which cuts into the hair across the back of the head (fig. 1).

NOTE
1. See Peter David Joralemon, "The Olmec Dragon: A Study in Pre-Columbian Iconography," in *Origins of Religious Art and Iconography in Preclassic Mesoamerica*, ed. Henry B. Nicholson (Los Angeles, 1976), figs. 20d, g, for similar examples of the avian plume.

177. Standing Figure ▲

900–600 B.C.
Provenance: Chiapas
Material: mottled dark green-to-black serpentine
Dimensions: h. 8.9 cm.; w. 3.9 cm.; d. 2.4 cm.
Private collection

BIBLIOGRAPHY
Unpublished.

178. Standing Figure Wearing Mask ▲

900–600 B.C.
Provenance: Valley of Mexico
Material: fine-grained, olive green serpentine with red-brown inclusions
Dimensions: h. 10.2 cm.; w. 4.4 cm.; d. 3.5 cm.
Private collection

BIBLIOGRAPHY
Unpublished.

179. Standing Figure ▶

1200–700 B.C.
Provenance: Mexico
Material: serpentine with black inclusions
Dimensions: h. 8 cm.; w. 3.5 cm.; d. 3 cm.
Private collection

BIBLIOGRAPHY
Unpublished.

Made in different stones and found at considerable distances from one another, these three figures are thematically related. The shaman in cat. no. 177, with his oversized head and sensuously carved, down-turned Olmec mouth, the full upper lip flared, stands in a formal ritual position with bent arms thrust out and hands clenched. Cat. nos. 178 and 179 are in the same ritual pose. Cat. no. 178 wears a mask with avian and jaguar attributes; cat. no. 179 has passed beyond the masked phase into a state of complete transformation: the human form, save for the pose, has given way to that of the supernatural avian jaguar.

180. Standing Figure

900 600 B.C.
Provenance: Las Bocas, Puebla
Material: ceramic with traces of cinnabar
Dimensions: h. 3.5 cm.; w. 1.9 cm.; d. 1.7 cm.
Private collection

The deft balancing of the head, belly, and legs of this miniature figure provides it with a sense of movement. The great paunch hangs over the cone-shaped bit of clay defining the legs. The arms are bent up close to the body, the head thrown back. The lower jaw is set well back beneath the heavy beak on which the short, upturned nose sits; the eyes are indicated by the ridge of the brow and the line of the upper beak. The figure wears large, spherical ear ornaments. A possibly significant detail is the ridge of clay applied to the brow. Broken at the tip, but perhaps a plume, as in cat. nos. 178 and 179, it may identify this miniature figure as either wearing a mask of a harpy eagle or being in a state of transformation into that animal spirit.

BIBLIOGRAPHY
Unpublished.

181. Duck Bill Pendant

900–600 B.C.
Provenance: Veracruz
Material: blackstone
Dimensions: h. 7.8 cm.; w. 3.7 cm.; d. 2.9 cm.
The Art Museum, Princeton University, gift of Gillett G. Griffin

This carving of a human head wearing a duck bill mask is pierced through the sides of the head to be worn as a pendant. The turbanlike headdress, arranged in receding, diagonal rows flanking a band of concentric inverted chevrons, is separated from the face by a soft groove, which, since it is unpolished, may have been wound with additional decoration. Almost certainly originally inlaid, the large oval eyes slope to the finely shaped nose, providing a fluid transition to the duck bill. The head and bill are beautifully counterbalanced. The curved, raised edge that

conforms to the shape of the face is echoed by incised lines that converge on the raised spine of the bill.

As a creature of the land, water, and sky of the natural world, the duck is often represented in ritual objects (see cat. no. 59).[1] The pendant perhaps depicts a shaman wearing the mask of his animal spirit companion.

BIBLIOGRAPHY
Unpublished.

NOTE
1. See also Michael D. Coe, "The Olmec Style and Its Distribution," in *Handbook of Middle American Indians: Archaeology of Southern Mesoamerica,* vol. 3, ed. Gordon R. Willey (Austin, Tex., 1965), fig. 25 for a similar pendant in the collection of Dumbarton Oaks; Robert L. Rands, "Jades of the Maya Lowlands," in *Handbook of Middle American Indians,* ed. Willey, fig. 47, for the Tuxtla statuette; Elizabeth K. Easby and John F. Scott, *Before Cortés: Sculpture of Middle America* (New York, 1970), figs. 49, 50.

182. Mask ▶

900–600 B.C.
Provenance: Veracruz
Material: jade
Dimensions: h. 15.5 cm.; w. 14 cm.; d. 6.9 cm.
Private collection

This startling image is one of the most direct expressions of the magic, animating power of the mask in Olmec art. The round, fleshy face is richly carved and sparingly incised along the contours of the upper eyelid and the mouth. The mask bears the physiognomy of the infant were-jaguar, the Olmec Supernatural: the sharply slanted almond-shaped eyes, short, somewhat pug nose, and jaguarian muzzle. The sensuously carved lips are parted to reveal a conspicuously toothless gum line. The eyes are the most hypnotic feature; the large pierced irises are close set within lids that converge in sharp points and flare at the outer corners.

While the irises are pierced and the nostrils drilled through the stone, the mouth, while deeply carved, is not open to the back. The attachment holes at the top and at the sides below the ears, however, would indicate that this was a wearable mask, and the size and weight suggest that it might have been worn by a child. The ears, set back and close to the face, are drilled for attachments.

BIBLIOGRAPHY
Thomas Dickey, Vance Muse, and Henry Weincek, *The God-Kings of Mexico* (Chicago, 1982), 28.

183. Miniature Mask

900–600 B.C.
Provenance: Mexico
Material: greenstone
Dimensions: h. 2.5 cm.; w. 3.2 cm.; d. 1 cm.
Private collection

BIBLIOGRAPHY
Unpublished.

184. Miniature Mask

900–600 B.C.
Provenance: Mexico
Material: greenstone
Dimensions: h. 1.5 cm.; w. 2 cm.; d. 0.25 cm.
Private collection

BIBLIOGRAPHY
Unpublished.

185. Miniature Mask

900–600 B.C.
Provenance: Mexico
Material: greenstone
Dimensions: h. 4.5 cm.; w. 6.1 cm.; d. 0.5 cm.
Private collection

BIBLIOGRAPHY
Unpublished.

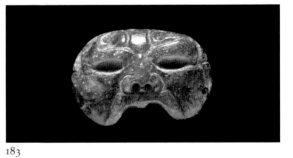

183

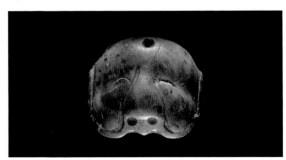

184

These miniature half masks are variations on the face of the jaguar, and may have been appliqués, pendants, or ear ornaments incorporated in larger ensembles, or, if independent objects, used to dress and animate small figures in ritual reenactments.[1]

In cat. no. 183 the upper half of the trapezoidal mouth is visible. A lower half might have been hinged at the two holes on the sides, completing and animating the mask. In cat. no. 184, the drooped, slit eyes and overall fleshiness of the features have been said to represent a flayed jaguar. Except for the slit eyes, all of the detail of the softly modeled face is concentrated in the nose and the mouth, which terminates in the elegant flourish of the upper lip. The nostrils are drilled and a pierced hole occurs at the center of the brow. Cat. no. 185 is slightly larger and more abstractly

185

rendered than cat. nos. 183 and 184. The eyes are circles carved in low relief with drill holes at the centers; the incised snout, a triangle rounded at the bottom, abuts the complicated geometric interpretation of the cleft mouth. Reduced to oval, padlike shapes, the ears wrap around the face, with separate sections corresponding to lobes, just large enough to accommodate drill holes. Two holes are drilled at the top of the maskette for suspension.

NOTE
1. See Beatriz de la Fuente, "Order and Nature in Olmec Art," in *The Ancient Americas: Art from Sacred Landscapes*, ed. Richard F. Townsend (Chicago, 1992), no. 207; and *Trésors du nouveau monde,* Royal Museum of Art and History (Brussels, 1992), no. 96.

186. Mask with Incisions

900–600 B.C.
Provenance: Río Pesquero, Veracruz
Material: white and gray jadeite with red pigment
Dimensions: h. 17 cm.; w. 16 cm.; d. 9 cm.
Private collection

The strong, precisely carved features of this visage are set within subtly modulated curves and planes. The flared eyes and nostrils and the open mouth are concentrated in an expression of suspended wonder.

The mask is hollowed out at the back and the mouth, nostrils, and irises of the eyes are pierced. Several drill holes are not visible from the front. Two are drilled below and behind the ears. Four are found on the top edge of the mask: two lining up approximately with the nostrils, the other two further to the side above the eyes. The long, flangelike ears, cut on the diagonal at the bottom, are not pierced for ornaments, but, consistent with the great refinement of the carving, are hollowed out to give them stylized definition. A hairline crack runs from the lower right ear through the right eye and to the left eye. There is some exfoliation below the right eye.

Superimposed on the face are incisions that animate it with shamanic power (fig. 1). Made legible by the red pigment rubbed into the fine lines, the incisions are divided into four major elements: an irregular, rectangular cartouche surrounding the right eye, a T-shaped element below the right eye, and vertical bands on either side of the face. The rectangular cartouche around the right eye begins just below the upper edge of the mask, crosses the lower lid of the eye, and has a narrow band running down the side of the nose. The top of the cartouche takes the form of a U-shaped bracket, the projecting arms incised with supernatural profiles; the left profile is cleft. In the center of the bracket is a small, raised point. Resting on the eyelid is a triple-pronged motif, the obverse of the element above.[1] On either side of this motif are circles containing double merlons. Directly below the eye is another U-shaped bracket, whose underside contains three rectangular projections with small incised circles. Inside the thin band descending from the center of the U is a supernatural profile as seen on cat. no. 25. Along the sides of the mask are similar bands with matching half-faces of supernaturals, this time with cleft-heads and concentric incisions indicating the hand-paw-wing motif. When the bands are viewed horizontally, one can more readily see gum brackets, *pars pro toto* representations of the Olmec Dragon.

While the element below the right eye is to our knowledge the only known instance of a T-shaped motif, the hand descending from it also has gum brackets and may be an abbreviated version of the upended saurian as the world tree (see Reilly, this volume, fig. 24). The profile heads of the cartouche recall the T-shaped monoliths of Teopantecuanitlan (see Tate, this volume, fig. 6). The encircled double merlons suggest the portal and passage to the supernatural realm. The triple-pronged element between them may be a cloud motif and symbol of the celestial realm. The cartouche may then be understood to represent an enclosed court, a sacred precinct, in which the wearer of this mask was a ritual performer. These incisions speak to the shamanic empowerment of both the mask itself and its wearer.

BIBLIOGRAPHY
The Merrin Gallery, *Works of Art from Pre-Columbian Mexico and Guatemala* (New York, 1971), no. 6.
Peter David Joralemon, "The Olmec Dragon: A Study in Pre-Columbian Iconography," in *Origins of Religious Art and Iconography in Preclassic Mesoamerica*, ed. Henry B. Nicholson (Los Angeles, 1976), 8c.
Emile Deletaille, *Rediscovered Masterpieces* (Boulogne, 1985), no. 1.

NOTE
1. See Peter David Joralemon, "A Study of Olmec Iconography," *Studies in Pre-Columbian Art and Archaeology*, no. 7 (Washington, D.C., 1971), motif 137.

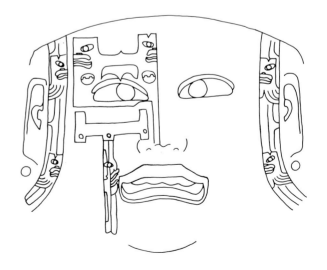

Figure 1. Drawing of incisions.

187. Mask

900–500 B.C.
Provenance: Río Pesquero, Veracruz
Material: white and gray jadeite
Dimensions: h. 18 cm.; w. 16.7 cm.; d. 10 cm.
Dallas Museum of Art, gift of Mr. and Mrs. Eugene McDermott,
the McDermott Foundation, and Mr. and Mrs. Algur H.
Meadows and the Meadows Foundation, Incorporated

The shaping of the inner brows, the most intense
aspect of this serene face, accentuates the fixed, trancelike expression of the eyes. The features are concentrated in the wide, long face. The upper lids weighing
drowsily on the closely set almond-shaped eyes with
perforated irises. The aquiline nose is finely made with
drilled nostrils; the lips are parted. The stone's light,
luminous color lends an ethereal aura to this powerful,
grandly composed visage. Drill holes exist behind the
ears and one hole is drilled through the top of the
mask. The ears are pierced, most likely for the attachment of ornaments.

BIBLIOGRAPHY
Ann R. Bromberg, *Selected Works from the Dallas Museum of Art*
    (Dallas, 1983), no. 3.
Emile Deletaille, *Rediscovered Masterpieces* (Boulogne, 1985), no. 23.

188. Mask

900 – 600 B.C.
Provenance: Río Pesquero, Veracruz
Material: serpentine
Dimensions: h. 17.8 cm.; w. 13.9 cm.; d. 10.2 cm.
Private collection

This mask closely resembles the mask in the collection of the Dallas Museum of Art (cat. no. 187), both of which are of a distinctive type associated with Río Pesquero. The features of this example, which is proportionally narrower than the Dallas mask, appear more sharply accentuated and the planes more emphatically assertive, an effect perhaps due in part to the darker color of the stone. Longer and flatter, the eyes appear to be set more closely together, on the verge of crossing. The heavy upper lids slant down as they converge on the nose. The line of the upper lip is straighter and broader than in cat. no. 187 and the perforation that joins the drill holes at the corners of the mouth is slightly awry with the line of the lower lip. The ears are perforated at the lobes, probably for attachments.

BIBLIOGRAPHY
Unpublished.

189. Mask

900–600 B.C.
Provenance: Puebla
Material: greenstone
Dimensions: h. 18.3 cm.
Private collection

From Puebla, this striking mask is a broader, more vigorous interpretation of the idealized types found in Río Pesquero. The eyes, fully shaped and open at the outer edges, have large perforations; the nose is broad; and the wide, open mouth reveals two teeth. The trancelike state conveyed in the closely set eyes is offset by the assertive, even fierce demeanor. Short, straight cuts indicate the eyebrows, but the mask is more fully modeled below the eyes, around the nose, and on the mouth, cheeks, and chin, which has sustained the only conspicuous damage. Holes below the ears and behind the forehead indicate the mask could have been worn. Hollowed out, semicircular areas at the middle of the pierced ears might have been inlaid with another material, which would have heightened the coloristic effect of the greenstone.

BIBLIOGRAPHY
Elizabeth K. Easby, *Ancient Art of Latin America from the Collection of Jay C. Leff* (New York, 1966), no. 6.

190. Mask with Furrowed Brow

1150–550 B.C.
Provenance: Playa de los Muertos, Honduras
Material: jade
Dimensions: h. 17.6 cm.; w. 15.3 cm.; d. 9 cm.
Private collection

While the stone carving technique is consistent with that of the heartland, this mask from Honduras seems to represent the stylized image of a local cacique or shaman. A bluntness and immediacy characterize the carving and subject. The face, broken into a pattern of broadly carved planes, with large and emphatic features, is contorted into an expression of concentration, indicated by the deep furrows and ridges of the brow, which converge and press down on the bridge of the nose. This impression is reinforced by the deep pouches under the eyes and the turn of the malleable lips. The perforated irises are set deep into the recesses of the eyes. Unarticulated, the ears are pierced at the bottom.

BIBLIOGRAPHY
André Emmerich Gallery and Perls Galleries, *Masterpieces of Pre-Columbian Art from the Collection of Mr. and Mrs. Peter G. Wray* (New York, 1984), no. 1.

191. Mask

900–600 B.C.
Provenance: Veracruz
Material: light green-to-gray-blue quartzite with inclusions of pyrite and chlorite
Dimensions: h. 15.9 cm.; w. 15.5 cm.; d. 9 cm.
Private collection

Short, quizzical brows extending from the bridge of the nose lend an almost bemused cast to this face. The perforated eyes echo the curve of the faint smile that crosses the lips. This compositional and expressive element is further emphasized by the precise, shadowed curve of the perforated space between the teeth and the lower lip. The effect of a smile might be simply an attempt to infuse life into the effigy.

The lithic techniques used in the manufacture of this mask are at once typical and unusual: typical in that the back is deeply excavated and the upper ridge curved to fit the forehead, unusual in that the interior of the cavity is polished to the same degree as the face itself. The interior of a mask is customarily left with the cuts from quarrying the stone and only roughly dressed. The holes bored for the nostrils and earlobes, and the attachment holes at the top and on either side below the ears, were made with the usual solid stone drills, but those for the teeth and hollows of the ears seem to have been made with small hollow drills. The marks of these drills, which appear to represent a late phase of Olmec lithic technology, may have been considered attractive in themselves, since no effort was made to polish them out. A narrow vein of softer stone in a line from the left cheek through the lower nose eroded out completely, forming an open crack in the stone, which has been repaired.

BIBLIOGRAPHY
Unpublished.

192. Mask with Filed Teeth and Opening in Forehead

900–600 B.C.
Provenance: Río Pesquero, Veracruz
Material: light green jadeite
Dimensions: h. 20 cm.; w. 18 cm.; d. 12 cm.
Private collection

There is a palpable fleshiness and an aura of barely contained feral intensity about this mask. The directness of the gaze is due to unmodeled, fully pierced openings of the eyes, set flat to the face with only an incised line to indicate the upper lid. The lines of the brow narrow smoothly into the ridge of the nose, which broadens into wide, flaring nostrils. Sinuous lines rise from the corners of the mouth to form the curled upper lip; the gum follows the inner curve of the lip, arches and converges on the filed bicurcated fang. The projecting lower lip dissolves at the corners; the stone immediately behind is roughly finished. The ears are incised with a stylized pattern and pierced biconically at the bottom.

The mask was cut from the cobble of luminous white stone, shaded to pale blue-green, so that the dark veins fall either peripherally in the right ear or at the exact center over the bridge of the nose. The square hole in the center of the forehead, ending in a small circle at the back (fig. 1), while unusual, is found on another mask from Río Pesquero,[1] and the only known Olmec wooden mask has a recess in the forehead, and in all

Figure 1. Back view of cat. no. 192.

Figure 2. Wooden Mask, Canon de la Mano, Guerrero, h. 18 cm. Courtesy American Museum of Natural History.

three instances were most likely for inlay (fig. 2).

Holes are drilled for the attachment of the mask below the ears and in the deep flange extending behind the top of the mask, where additional holes may have held headdress elements.

BIBLIOGRAPHY
Emile Deletaille, *Rediscovered Masterpieces* (Boulogne, 1985), no. 4.

NOTE
1. See *Trésors du nouveau monde*, Royal Museum of Art and History (Brussels, 1992), no. 88.

VI
The Young Lord

193. Young Lord

900–600 B.C.
Provenance: Border of El Salvador/Guatemala
Material: mottled dark-to-light green serpentine, light milky patina with traces of cinnabar
Dimensions: h. 65.5 cm.; w. 11 cm.; d. 5.4 cm.
Private collection

No other portable work of Olmec art makes as powerful a statement or carries as complete a program of the mythic and political ideology serving as the foundation for Olmec rulership as this large serpentine figure. Standing over half a meter tall and carved with a refinement usually reserved for smaller objects, this imposing icon is extensively incised with complex images. The precise modeling of the clavicle, ribcage,

Figure 1. Detail of face.

knees, and shoulder blades contrasts with the extreme attenuation of the figure, unnaturally elongated and narrow, thus the figure's familiar sobriquet of "Slim," under which it has been published.[1]

The pose is rigidly frontal and symmetrical, the arms holding two scepters against the chest. Carved in the form of a scepter, a symbol of the power he wields, the Young Lord is incised with images of the ceremonial and ritual practices through which he exercises his shamanic powers and demonstrates his right to rule. The incisions on the head, arms, hands, scepters, and legs form a unified ideological program, and the head, torso and lower body correspond to the three levels of the cosmos. The ruler is the *axis mundi,* the conduit between the earthly and supernatural realms, a charismatic being who integrates the levels of the cosmos. The extensive incisions may identify him as a specific person, perhaps a young ruler at the time of his investiture, but that is coincidental to the primary meaning encoded in the statue.

The figure wears a bell-shaped headdress with a narrow brim, rectangular plaque in the center, and stepped projection at the top. This headdress, the only part of the figure not incised, has an architectural quality recalling the headdress worn by the supernatural in cat. no. 89 and may have been a support for ephemeral decoration, perhaps vegetation or feathers. The flange-shaped ears end in large earflares. The face is completely covered by a mask (fig. 1), a combination of carved and incised elements, attached by side straps indicated by three lines on each cheek. The hollowed-out eyes, perhaps originally inlaid, contrast with the conjoined nose and gaping mouth that project from the plane of the face. Flame eyebrows are incised to either side of the furrowed brow. Two bars are incised under the left eye and one long and three short bars beneath its right. The snarling, fanged mouth of a jaguar and the subtly carved raptorial beak and flame eyebrows of

the harpy eagle incorporate aspects of the principal avatars of shamanic power. On a recently discovered relief at Chalcatzingo (see Taube, this volume, fig. 24c), a feline adorned with flame eyebrows and a projecting beak is shown clawing a human beneath its feet. This relief, the mask shown in cat. no. 194, and the Young Lord's own mask indicate that the Young Lord is capable of transforming into an avian jaguar and performing sacrificial rituals, an interpretation confirmed by the incisions on the body.

The incisions represent the central ritual of the shamanic ruler in the terrestrial realm: bloodletting through human sacrifice, allowing access to the supernatural world, and the making of rain (fig. 2). The lower half of the scepter held in the crook of the right arm is composed of a shaft made of bound vertical sticks, perhaps vegetative stalks, and a blade. The shaft is bound at the top and near the bottom.[2] Tic marks on the edge of the blade have been interpreted as both sprout symbols and the edge of a flint knife.[3] A face consisting of an exclamation-point raindrop, two half-oval eyes, and a mouth in the form of a cleft rectangle containing a double merlon over three ovals imbues the head of this scepter with supernatural power; a smaller circle below the rectangle also contains a double merlon. Similar tic marks and double merlons on the headband of the seated figure in the collection of Dumbarton Oaks (fig. 3; see Schele, this volume, fig. 5b) have been identified by Karl A. Taube as greenstone celts symbolizing corn.[4] This scepter may symbolize a bloodletting instrument as well as the crop propitiated by blood sacrifice.

The victim on which such an implement was used is incised on the bent right arm. The human face is framed with a headdress surmounted by a radial design; scalloped lappets meet under the chin. The arms, bound above the elbow, are twisted behind the figure's arched back. Bands at the waist support a

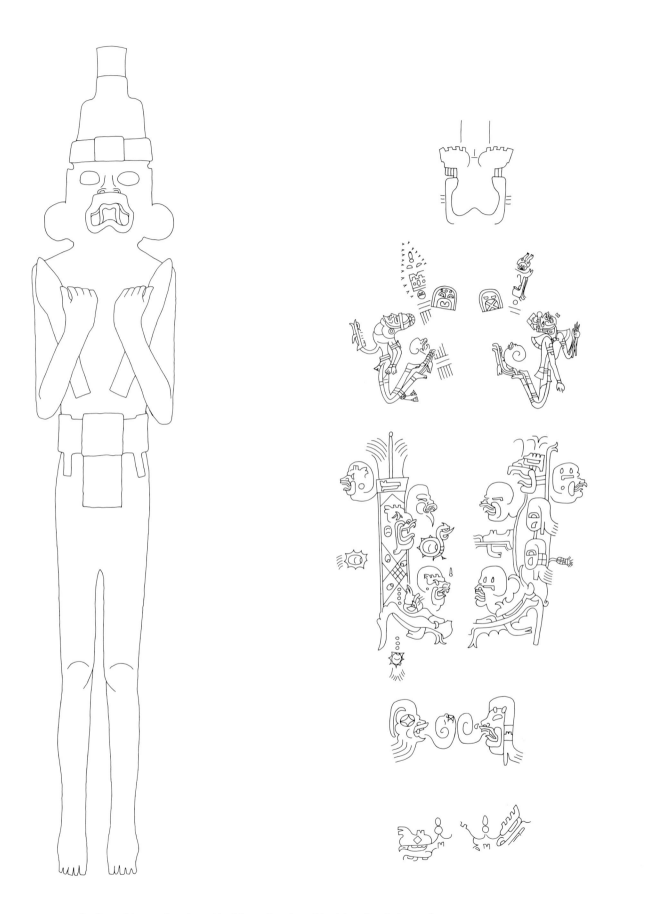

Figure 2. Outline of figure; drawing of incisions; drawing of incisions in relation to figure.

cleft loincloth; the legs are banded and small tassels hang from the shins. The most conspicuous attribute is the long-necked zoomorph with downturned saurian eyes and feathered brows emerging from the figure's chest; the head of a similar creature extends from the right foot, above which is an eyeless profile with a long snout and gaping mouth. As interpreted on Monument 6 at La Venta (see cat. no. 63), these supernatural zoomorphs transport the victim to the otherworld.

The scepter held in the left arm is incised with the eye and flame eyebrows seen in cat. no. 126 and Chalcatzingo Monuments 1 and 9 (cat. no. 37) over an open mouth shown in profile, with a small band and circle underneath. Chalcatzingo Monument 1 depicts a ruler seated inside a cave mouth, from which volutes emerge while raindrops fall from clouds above. The Young Lord, rather than being placed inside a cave mouth to demonstrate his shamanic rainmaking powers, is shown holding a scepter marked with the symbolic abbreviation of the cave.

The figure curving around the left arm holds three long, sharp sticks and wears an elaborate costume and mask identifying him as a ritual performer, who perhaps sacrificed the victim incised on the right arm. He wears a cape and short kilt similar to those worn by the winged figure on a carved celt now in the Xalapa Museum (see cat. no. 216, fig. 1),[5] and the Dumbarton Oaks seated figure. The cape, the figure's pose, and the darts he holds indicate that this is a "flier" (see cat. no. 70). The headdress also recalls those on the Dumbarton Oaks seated figure and the sculptures of El Azuzul (see Diehl, this volume, fig. 8). The squared top of the headdress has been compared to a similar headdress on a mural from Monte Alban Tomb 104, associated with the Zapotec Maize God by Taube. A cleft form floats near the figure's chin. The legs are banded, and celts, symbols of power and possibly maize, are bound to the upper arms.[6] A supernatural zoomorph again emerges from the figure's foot; above this is another profile defined by a whiplash line. The blood of the sacrificial victim opens the portal; the zoomorph transports the figure through the portal to the otherworld (see cat. no. 64).

The incisions on the backs of the hands of the Young Lord depict bracketed faces. On the right hand, three dots are incised over two semicircular eyes and a U-bracket mouth, recalling a face incised on the loincloth of a greenstone figure from Puebla and the overhanging beaks of cat. nos. 125 and 170.[7] On the left hand, the crossed-bands motif in the mouth of the face

recalls a carved vessel from Tlapacoya (see Reilly, this volume, fig. 17) and may represent a sky symbol and the unity of the cosmos.

The Young Lord holds implements used in sacrifice, and the arms and hands are incised with images of the ritual performer and victim, and symbols of transport to the otherworld. While the back of the Young Lord is not incised, it is carved at the waist with a knot (fig. 4) like those seen in cat. nos. 22, 176, and 198. A symbol of rulership, the knot is a sign of legitimacy in the natural world only obtained by performing the rituals recorded on the front of the figure.[8]

Supernatural zoomorphs are incised down the lengths of the thighs. The heads of the monsters face each other with gaping jaws, bared fangs, and forked tongues. The snouts are different, long and low on the left and blunt on the right. The brows are variations on flame eyebrows. F. Kent Reilly, III, has described the zoomorphs as "symbols of the underworld power—water and vegetative fertility—that the earthly ruler ritually insures to sustain the life of his people."[9] He has identified the creature on the right leg as a fish zoomorph, possibly derived from a gar, with its bulbous nose and diamond-shaped scales, an inhabitant of the watery underworld. It lacks legs for locomotion and the symbols issuing from its mouth and behind its back are probably shells; the small circles in front of the open mouth and behind the head also may be water symbols. The shell motif to the right of the midsection has a serpentlike creature wrapped around it, probably "an abbreviation for the full-figured zoomorph below it."[10] The crosshatched pattern behind the creature's head may represent fish scales, as proposed above, or snake scales (see cat. no. 66), but these are not mutually exclusive; such hybridization is a common aspect of Olmec zoomorphs.[11] The crosshatching is located in a larger crossed-bands motif, the continuation of which is implied by the angled line under the tail. On Chalcatzingo Monument 5, a serpent's body is marked with crossed-bands and floats above a cloud symbol indicating that it is a sky serpent; the crossed-bands may have the same meaning here. The fringed eye of this zoomorph recalls the eye of the avian serpent, indicating that, though the shell motifs locate the creature in the watery underworld, it is capable of moving through the levels of the cosmos.[12]

On the zoomorph's upper back is a profile with two fangs and an eye formed by two intersecting crescents resembling the crescent eye of the raptor incised on the right shoulder of the Las Limas Figure (see cat. no.

Figure 3. Seated Figure of a Man, 900–600 B.C., Río Pesquero, Veracruz, diopside, h. 16.3 cm.; w. 9.3 cm.; d. 5.7 cm. Dumbarton Oaks Research Library and Collections, Washington, D.C.

35, fig. 1). An oval with curved lines behind the profile repeats the shell forms . The motif at the base of the tail combines two Olmec eye symbols: a downturned L-shaped eye, a saurian and water symbol, and a single cleft flame eyebrow, an avian attribute and symbol of flight, and probably serves as an abbreviation of the Olmec Dragon who traversed all levels of the cosmos. The fanlike tail, which reinforces the association of a fish and the watery underworld, also suggests vegetative fronds or feathers (see cat. no. 198 and Taube, this volume) and may relate to the plumes associated with the avian serpent (see cat. nos. 107–10). Three profile heads are attached to this zoomorph—the first above the creature's head; the second above the profile on the back; and the third on the other side, connected to the tail by an incised line. The first and third heads appear to be related to the profile on the back of the fish, with the same eyebrow, mouth, and crescent eye, but the second head has a simpler eye and a beard, a feature seen on many Olmec figures (see cat. no. 213). Whether the profiles represent ancestors or sacrificed victims,

Figure 4. Detail of back.

they appear to be denizens of the otherworld accompanying the creature on its journey.[13]

The creature on the Young Lord's left leg is a crocodilian, an elaborate version of the Olmec Dragon, which has the ability to move between the watery and terrestrial worlds, and is affiliated with earth, rain, and vegetation. A blossoming plant extends from the underside of the dragon, confirming its association with fertility. An abbreviated dragon head emerging from the back of the body corresponds compositionally to the serpent-shell motif on the right leg. A large profile with flame eyebrows and attachment straps near the tail of the dragon reprises the mask worn by the Young Lord; simple lines above this mask recall the cleft forms seen on many Olmec headdresses and are probably plant symbols, as is the cleft form at the back of the mask. Again, three scrolled heads extend from the body of the dragon—the first above the creature's head; the second and third below and behind the mask, respectively. The heads have the same mouth and downturned L-shaped eye in common, but differ in the addition of tear-shaped markings; none in the head at the top, two above the eye in the lower head, and two, with the addition of a circle on the cheek, in the head at the back of the mask. These markings most likely represent water or rain. Incised on the dragon's legs are semicircular eyes like

those on the back of the Young Lord's right hand; beneath them, the teardrops may depict seeds (see Reilly, this volume, fig. 25) or rain. The feet are in the form of the hand paw-wing motif A habit of male crocodilians, so-called water dancing, specifically relates these creatures to rain and fertility. Angling their heads and tails out of the water, they inhale with mouths closed. As their bodies vibrate, water splashes into the air like rain, and the bellow of the crocodile resembles thunder.[14]

The incisions on the shins of the Young Lord continue the theme of the journey to the otherworld, but more enigmatically. The head on the right shin has a long extension curving from the top, perhaps a cleft, as seen in the heads on incised bowls (see cat. nos. 96–99). The hand-paw-wing motif at the lower jaw resembles a beard. The eye is formed by a concave diamond enclosed in a circle. A scroll profile with a crossed-bands motif issues from the mouth; the star and crossed-bands are sky symbols. On the left shin, a hand-paw-wing motif with a double merlon behind the head echoes the form of the dragon's legs. Two ovals joined by a line may be an abbreviation of the headdress worn by the figure on the left arm; the mouth is consistent with those on the profiles around the dragon. A simple spiral projects from the mouth and a small teardrop is incised in front of the nose; combined, these symbols may represent a rain cloud. The incisions on the feet, which are difficult to read, are to be understood to continue symmetrically around the sides. The same variants of the flame eyebrow are evident on both feet. Small exclamation-point raindrops repeat the motif on the right-hand scepter. The diamond motif in the eye of the head on the right shin and on the back of the creature above is repeated in the right flame eyebrow.

As we have seen, the Young Lord is divided horizontally into the three levels of the cosmos. The elements incised on either side of the figure are at once juxtaposed and continuous. If read from the right arm down the right leg and up the left side, the incisions may be seen as a sequence beginning with ritual sacrifice and journey to the watery underworld and ending with the ritual performer emerging from the cave mouth with the power to bring rain and abundant harvest for which the sacrifice was performed.

The bicephalic composition of the Young Lord, with a masked face on the top and incised supernatural profiles on the feet, is repeated on the Young Lord's arms incised with figures with zoomorphs emerging from their feet, and on the Young Lord's legs incised

with zoomorphs with masks attached to their tails. This formal and symbolic structure corresponds to the bicephalic compositions in cat. no. 63, where the Olmec Supernatural rides the back of a jaguar, and in La Venta Monument 6, where the body of the deceased lies in the dragon sarcophagus. The opposing, hybridized beasts incised on the legs of the Young Lord, both able to traverse all levels of the cosmos, represent different stages of the journey; the two scepters signify access and return through the portal.

In addition to his detailed analysis of the iconographic program of the Young Lord, Reilly has drawn a significant parallel between the organization and symbolism of the statue and the series of carved monuments at Chalcatzingo. The carvings at Chalcatzingo manifest on a monumental, public scale the same charter of shamanic rulership incised on the Young Lord: the alignment and unity of the cosmos in the person of the ruler and the blessings of rain and harvest through the performance of ritual sacrifice and journey through the cosmos.[15] This fundamental ideology underlies and unifies the monuments and portable objects of the Olmec world.

BIBLIOGRAPHY
Emile Deletaille, *Rediscovered Masterpieces* (Boulogne, 1985), nos. 35, 36.
F. Kent Reilly, III, "Olmec Iconographic Influences on the Symbols of Maya Rulership: An Examination of Possible Sources," in *Sixth Palenque Round Table, 1986*, ed. Virginia M. Fields (Norman, Okla., 1991).

NOTES
1. For further discussion of the Young Lord and his incised symbols, see F. Kent Reilly, III, "The Ecological Origins of Olmec Symbols of Rulership," Master's thesis, University of Texas at Austin, 1987; idem, "Olmec Iconographic Influences on the Symbols of Maya Rulership: An Examination of Possible Sources," in *Sixth Palenque Round Table, 1986*, ed. Virginia M. Fields (Norman, Okla.), 1991), 151–66.
2. F. Kent Reilly, III, has proposed a third binding, concealed by the arm, because of the evident association with bloodletters of three knots or bindings. Reilly, "Olmec Iconographic Influences" (as in note 1, 1991), 156.
3. See Schele, this volume, and Elizabeth K. Easby and John F. Scott, *Before Cortés: Sculpture of Middle America* (New York, 1970), no. 256.
4. Karl A. Taube, "The Olmec Maize God: The Face of Corn in Formative and Late Preclassic Mesoamerica," paper delivered at the Thirteenth Annual Maya Weekend, Philadelphia, April 9, 1995.
5. *The Bogousslavsky Collection of Pre-Columbian Art*, Sotheby Parke Bernet Inc. (New York, Dec. 4, 1981), no. 53.
6. Taube (as in note 4).
7. Román Piña Chán and Luis Covarrubias, *El Pueblo del jaguar* (Mexico City, 1964), fig. 32.
8. For further discussion on knots in the Formative period, see cat. no. 176.

9. Reilly "Olmec Iconographic Influences" (as in note 1), 159.
10. Ibid.
11. Peter David Joralemon, "The Olmec Dragon: A Study in Pre-Columbian Iconography," in *Origins of Religious Art and Iconography in Preclassic Mesoamerica*, ed. Henry B. Nicholson (Los Angeles, 1976), 33.
12. See Taube, this volume, and cat. nos. 107–110.
13. Reilly "Olmec Iconographic Influences" (as in note 1), 160.
14. Ibid., 162.
15. Ibid., 162–66.

194. Mask

900–600 B.C.
Provenance: Tenenexpan, Veracruz
Material: light green serpentine with black striations and speckling and traces of cinnabar
Dimensions: h. 17 cm.; w. 17.9 cm.; d. 12 cm.
Private collection

This avian jaguar mask is essentially the same as that worn by the Young Lord (cat. no. 193), differing principally in the addition of bifurcated fangs, which descend from the upper gum line over and into the curve of the lower lip, framing the large drill holes at the corners of the mouth, as in cat. nos. 91 and 92. Profiles of supernaturals, represented by gaping mouths and cleft heads, are joined with the upper pair of fangs. Though facing each other, they recall an incised plaque with back-to-back profiles that surround a defined void (cat. no. 164), perhaps a symbolic opening to the otherworld. The downturned, U-shaped bracket incised in the recessed gum line may identify the mouth as a cave opening to the underworld, similar to the gaping maw of Chalcatzingo Monument 9 (cat. no. 37).

The flat nose, with large drilled nostrils, projects onto the upper lip, which is drawn to a point like the beak of a raptorial bird. The trough-shaped eyes and brow line are similar to cat. nos. 91 and 92, though here flame eyebrows flank the furrowed brow. The incisions on each ear flange may represent, rather than parts of the ear, half a diagram that, if joined with the other ear, repeats the bracket incised on the upper gum line. The double bars beneath the bracket and the triangles at the bottom of the ears may then signify different cosmic levels. The same pattern is incised on the ears of the Kunz Axe (see Diehl, this volume, fig. 17) and an axe in the British Museum.[1]

The mask was carved leaving a heavy ridge of stone for support all around the back, and hollowed out to a depth of less than one quarter of an inch in some areas

of the stone. Holes for attachment can be seen at the top of the mask and below the ears. Surprisingly light, it could have been worn comfortably; the eyes, nose, and mouth are pierced so that the wearer could see, breathe, and speak. The mask was broken into three pieces and fitted together with negligible losses along the cracks. The traces of cinnabar are original to the piece.

BIBLIOGRAPHY
Peter David Joralemon, "The Olmec Dragon: A Study in Pre-Columbian Iconography," in *Origins of Religious Art and Iconography in Preclassic Mesoamerica*, ed. Henry B. Nicholson (Los Angeles, 1976), fig. 20b.

NOTE
1. Michael D. Coe, *The Jaguar's Children: Pre-Classic Central Mexico* (New York, 1965), fig. 5.

195. Incised Celt

900–600 B.C.
Provenance: Río Pesquero, Veracruz
Material: jade with traces of red pigment
Dimensions: h. 28.5 cm.; w. 11.5 cm.; d. 3 cm.
Private collection

Two-dimensional frontal representations of standing figures are rare in Olmec art, perhaps because of the difficulties presented by foreshortening. The feet of the standing figure on this celt are shown in profile to avoid this problem. The figure stands with arms and hands held in front of the chest in a pose similar to the Young Lord (cat. no. 193), but without scepters. However, scepters may be implied by the position of the hands, as in the figures of cat. nos. 145 and 146, whose hands appear as though holding celts or other ceremonial objects.

The figure is elaborately costumed and wears a mask similar to that worn by the Young Lord. The upper lip of the gaping mouth, from which two bifurcated fangs descend, is drawn to a point resembling the beak of a raptorial bird. Two small circles are incised in the corners of the mouth, indicating the presence of large drill holes like those on cat. no. 194. Nostrils are incised above the mouth; the shallow curve of the eyes continues into the flame eyebrows. The bifurcated curves at the outer corners of the face may be part of the decoration of the figure's domed helmet, which appears to extend down the back of the head. Parallel lines above the shoulders may indicate long hair, and the lines around the upper arms, a cape, fastened over the chest by an eroded crossed-bands pectoral. Atop the helmet is a rectangular projection enclosing a circle incised with a double merlon. The oval form that extends to the top of the celt is a vegetative symbol, most likely a maize plant. The arms at the wrists and upper arms, legs, ankles, and above the knees, are banded. The belt attaching the loincloth is divided into two bands, the first consisting of three rectangular fields and the second of incised diagonal lines. Lines around the upper legs and between the knees signify a long apron covering the buttocks. A small line indicates the ankles; the toes are bent and incised with toenails.

Standing in the same position as the Young Lord, this figure also acts as the *axis mundi,* the vertical conduit connecting the levels of the cosmos. Incised celts often contain cosmic diagrams (cat. nos. 124–127); here the ruler embodies that concept.

BIBLIOGRAPHY
Unpublished.

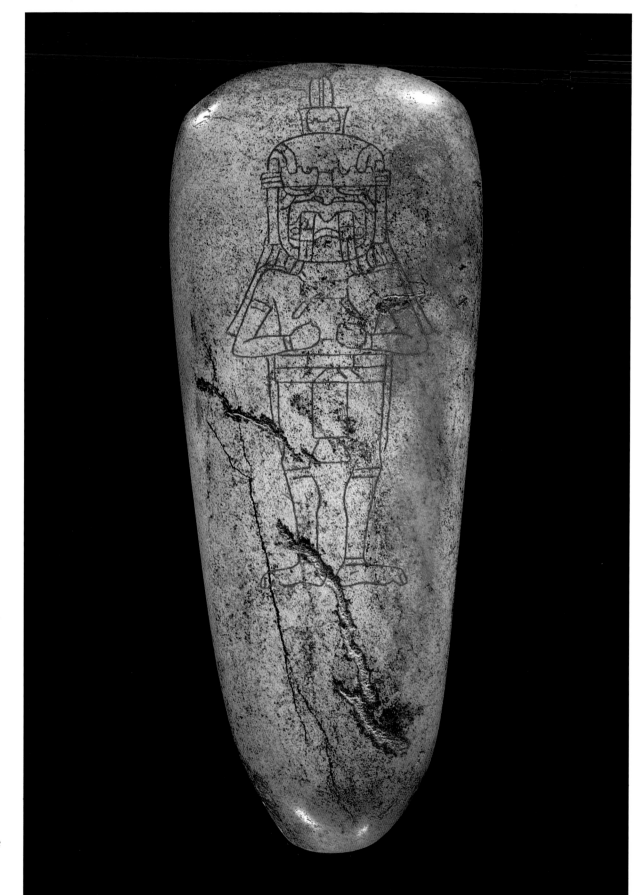

Olmec: water and the harvest. Though there is no known image of an Olmec ruler wielding a conch-shell scepter, both bound stalks and conch shells appear separately as ritual objects. For example, the figure in cat. no. 199 holds a vegetative bundle across its arms and "knuckledusters," identified as cut conch shells, are common elements in Olmec iconography (see Schele, this volume; and cat. nos. 198, 200, 202, 216). The "torch" motif, often seen with the knuckleduster, is probably bound vegetation (see Taube, this volume).

BIBLIOGRAPHY
Unpublished.

197. Standing Figure

900–600 B.C.
Provenance: Guerrero
Material: dark green serpentine with whitish green inclusions
Dimensions: h. 46 cm.; w. 12.1 cm.; d. 4.9 cm.
Private collection

Unadorned and carved in the simple lithic traditions of Guerrero and Mezcala, this elongated figure of a man is carved in the form of a scepter. The elongated head is flattened at the top; the deeply drilled eyes may have been inlaid; the nose is small; and the downturned mouth is carved in the Olmec style. The ears are set close to the head, the lobes pierced for attachment. Broken above the elbow, the arms may have been held closely to the sides, observing the limits of the original thick block of stone. The body is schematically rendered with horizontal lines and subtle indentations to model the chest, waist, and knees. The waist band of the long, triangular loincloth is shown only on the front. The legs terminate with projecting feet incised with toes.

Though the face and loincloth are similar to those on other Olmec standing figures (cat. nos. 18, 19, 26), the rigid posture contrasts with the fluid, relaxed stances of those figures. Rather than a ruler or shaman assuming a meditative posture, this figure incorporates the image of the ruler into a scepter, a symbol of the power he wields.

BIBLIOGRAPHY
Unpublished.

196. Scepter

900–600 B.C.
Provenance: Upper Balsas River Basin, Guerrero
Material: mottled serpentine
Dimensions: h. 34 cm.; w. 10 cm.; d. 7 cm.
Private collection

The shaft of the scepter, carved in the form of spiraling, vegetative stalks bound by rings and crowned by a conch shell, embodies the principal themes of the

VII
The Shamanic Bundle

The term "bundle" in Olmec ideology may refer to grouped objects in burials and sacred locations; shafts of bound vertical elements described as torches, vegetative or feather bundles, and bloodletters; similar banded bundles held horizontally across the arms; and bundles as containers for the implements of shamanic ritual. There is archaeological and visual evidence that magically empowered objects like masks, human figures, and shamanic apparatus were kept in so-called bundles. Objects found in two burials at the southern end of the basalt column tomb of La Venta Monument 7 appear to have been placed or arranged in bundles. The objects included a seated and standing figure in each bundle, one of the seated figures wearing a hematite mirror; actual and effigy stingray spines, and the handle of a perforator, objects relating to bloodletting; and a jade shell effigy. Human bones were also found, stained brown and reduced to splinters by soil acids, which would have destroyed any cloth wrapping or wooden container. On the basis of their size and weight, and the small teeth found with the second group or bundle of objects, Philip Drucker speculated that they were the bones of children.[1]

Such bundles may have functioned as shamanic "kits" containing equipment for the performance of rituals, divinations, and cures with which the deceased were furnished to empower them in death as they had been in life. Graves at Tlatilco contained *pulidores*, shells, greenstone necklaces, carved clay roller seals, and whistles. Similar objects are illustrated here as well as *candeleros*, small clay boxes used to hold sacred substances, a symbolic metate, and other objects that may have formed part of the shaman's paraphernalia. Also included are figures holding ritual objects that

may have been included in bundles and images of hunchbacks and wizened old men who perhaps carried and used such bundles.

Representations of bundles have been identified on a number of monuments and objects. A relief from Xoc, Chiapas, now destroyed, depicted a striding figure holding a large rectangular tablet bound with three knots and surmounted by a trilobed vegetative motif. Relief carvings from El Salvador show striding figures holding long objects with double merlons enclosed within a circle at the top. The figure carved on the San Miguel Amuco stela carries a tablet with a fringed top in its left arm.

The incised image on a large ceramic vessel from the vicinity of Chalcatzingo, included here, is perhaps the most extensive and explicit representation of a shamanic bundle. It is identifiable with the object held in the relief from Xoc by the three knots that bind a boxlike structure and the fringed vegetative motif at the top. The bundle is depicted as if unwrapped, the middle knot untied, and the contents displayed: a profile head resting on a foot, a *pars pro toto* representation of a ritual performer. To either side of the bundle, a disembodied hand holds a ritual object. The left hand holds a "knuckleduster," made from a cut conch shell. The object held by the right hand is a shaft of vertical elements bound at the top, bottom, and middle like the larger bundle. David C. Grove has identified such bundled shafts as "torches" and bloodletting symbols.[2] Blood is the causative agent of access to the supernatural, and "fliers," figures in shamanic flight through the portal to the otherworld are sometimes shown carrying bundled shafts. Linda Schele interprets the motif as bound vegetation. Karl A. Taube suggests they are actually feather bundles, but indi-

cates that feathers and vegetation may overlap symbolically, and Brian Stross has pointed out that blood and maize are metaphorical equivalents.[3] These interpretations, vegetation and feathers, blood and maize, and flight, all intersect in an image of another bundled, scepterlike object incised on a celt in the section on the *axis mundi*: a bird in profile, with tail feathers projecting from the bound body and a large spike, a perforator, banded as a maize symbol extending from the head. Smaller avian profiles are seen above the knotted binding of the body. The bundled shaft on the Incised Vessel reiterates this conflated symbolism. The shaft is crowned by what may be understood as a perforator in the form of a bird's head, a spike flanked by a winged motif with a double merlon over the "eyes," surmounted in turn by a vegetative motif.

The bound shafts symbolize the transformation of the blood offering into the maize. The larger bundle is a symbolic representation of the ritual; the shamanic ruler is flanked by the bloodletter and the conch shell, a symbol of water and rain. The three knots on the shaft and on the large bundle symbolize the levels of the cosmos, opened through the sacrifice and unified in the person of the ruler as the *axis mundi*; the world tree, the elaborate vegetative motif at the top, rises above this cosmic image.

Notes

1. Philip Drucker, "La Venta, Tabasco: A Study of Olmec Ceramics and Art," *Bureau of American Ethnology*, Bulletin 153 (1952): 23; see Diehl, this volume, fig. 14.
2. David C. Grove, "'Torches,' 'Knuckledusters,' and the Legitimization of Formative Period Rulership," *Mexicon* 9 (June, 1987), 60–65.
3. See Schele, this volume; Taube, this volume; Brian Stross, "Maize and Blood," *Res* 22 (1992): 101.

198. Incised Vessel

1150–800 B.C.
Provenance: Area of Chalcatzingo, Morelos
Material: clay
Dimensions: h. 45 cm.; diam. 25.4 cm. at base; 14 cm. at neck
Private collection

Reportedly from the vicinity of Chalcatzingo, this large, gray, tear-shaped ceramic vessel is incised with a complex scene understood to be an open bundle, a boxlike structure bound by three knots. A tablet with three horizontal bands held by the figure in the relief from Xoc, Chiapas (now destroyed) has been identified as a bundle, and the trefoil motif surmounting the tablet in the relief may agree with the elaborate projection at the top of the bundle on this incised vessel.[1]

The open bundle is defined by vertical bands to either side of a cleft profile head. Knots at the top and bottom are represented with curved bands at the center and long horizontal bands enclosing loops to either side. A third, open knot is partly obscured by the head. The profile head is flanked by a hand on the right holding a vertical bound bundle, identified as a "torch," vegetation, or feathers, and on the left by a hand holding a "knuckleduster," an object identified as a cut conch shell.

The profile in the center sits atop a rectangle intersected by crossed-bands with three loops extending to either side. Attached to the rectangle is a profile foot standing on the knot binding the lower part of the bundle, which rests on an inturned gum bracket. The central image within the bundle is a *pars pro toto* representation of a ritual performer as on the celt in cat. no. 127.

Circles at three points on the jaw may indicate that the figure is wearing a hinged, articulated buccal mask; and an S-curve loop and fringed ties at the back of the head may be the knot by which the mask is fastened. The mask incorporates elements of two profiles incised on the Las Limas Figure (see cat. no. 35, fig. 1),[2] the profile on the left knee with a crescent eye and prominent fang and the one on the right shoulder with a series of vertical lines and circles through the eye. The profiles represent creatures with access to the sky and watery realms.

Flanking the *pars pro toto* image of the masked figure are disembodied hands holding implements as on the celt of cat. no. 125. The knuckleduster is often shown as part of a ritual costume and identified as a symbol of rulership and water. Curved at the back with vertical extensions at the top and bottom, it is incised to suggest the interior structure of a conch shell.

288

Figure 1. Roll-out of cat. no. 198.

knots may symbolize the three levels of the cosmos. The seeds and roots develop into the sprouting plant that emerges from the cleft head and into the fuller vegetation atop the bundled shaft.

The crowning element, extending from the center of the top knot of the bundle, on axis with the profile head, and supported by a tripartite flange decorated with three circles along the horizontal with a vertically divided central band, is a crossed-bands motif surmounted by fanned lines and a central triangular motif with branching arms, a corn symbol. Three long loops extend to either side of the rectangle, similar to the configuration joining the head and foot below. This element has been interpreted as a bundle of vegetation or feathers (see Schele, this volume; Taube, this volume) and is similar to the motif above the world tree on the plaque in cat. no. 131.

The image of the open bundle on the Incised Vessel reprises the ideology and ritual embodied in the Young Lord (cat. no. 193). The ritual performer on the vessel, standing masked as a supernatural and holding ritual objects, is identified as the world tree and the axis linking the three levels of the cosmos. The knuckleduster symbolizes water or rain as does the scepter held in the left hand of the Young Lord; and in the right hands both hold the instruments of the blood sacrifice that will be transformed into rain and maize.

BIBLIOGRAPHY

Carlo T. E. Gay, *Chalcacingo* (Graz, Austria, 1971), fig. 43, pl. 23.
Jacques Soustelle, *The Olmec* (New York, 1979) pl. 30.
Emile Deletaille, *Rediscovered Masterpieces* (Boulogne, 1985), no. 46.
David C. Grove, "'Torches,' 'Knuckledusters,' and the Legitimization of Formative Period Rulership," *Mexicon* 9 (3): fig. 6.
Franz Feuchtwanger, *Ceramica Olmeca* (Mexico City, 1989), no. 161.
Brian Stross, "Olmec Vessel with a Crayfish Icon," in *Word and Image in Maya Culture*, ed. William F. Hanks and Don S. Rice (Salt Lake City, 1989).
Rosemary Joyce et al., "Olmec Bloodletting: An Iconographic Study," in *Sixth Palenque Round Table, 1986*, ed. Virginia M. Fields (Norman, Okla., 1991).
Brian Stross, "Maize and Blood," *Res* 22 (1992).

NOTES

1. Susanna Ekholm-Miller, "The Olmec Rock Carving at Xoc, Chiapas, Mexico," in *Papers of the New World Archaeological Foundation*, no. 32 (Provo, Utah, 1973); F. Kent Reilly, III, "Visions to Another World: Art, Shamanism, and Political Power in Middle Formative Mesoamerica," Ph.D. diss., University of Texas at Austin, 1994, 127–30.
2. David C. Grove, "'Torches,' 'Knuckledusters,' and the Legitimization of Formative Period Rulership," *Mexicon* 9 (3): 60–65; Rosemary Joyce et al., "Olmec Bloodletting: An Iconographic Study," in *Sixth Palenque Round Table, 1986*, ed. Virginia M. Fields (Norman, Okla., 1991), 145.
3. Brian Stross, "Maize and Blood," *Res* 22 (1992): 93.
4. Stross (as in note 3), 101.

The "cuff" that extends beyond the curve of the shell is decorated with short, finely incised lines that suggest the fringe of a costume; the cuff of the right hand is similar to that on the upraised left arm of Oxtotitlan Mural 1. The circles above and below these cuffs may be water or blood symbols.[3]

The right hand is wrapped around a shaft of vertical bands bound at the top and bottom. An elaborate configuration at the top of the shaft, with winglike extensions marked with circles on either side of a central, pointed element, is bordered by a fringe of fine lines from which extends a maize symbol. Two small projections atop the wing forms may be a double merlon motif symbolizing passage to the supernatural world, commonly seen on the top of bundled shafts identified as bound vegetation or feathers, and interpreted as both bloodletters (see cat. no. 126) and torches. A fringed shaft is carried in the left arm of the figure depicted on the San Amuco Stela (see Taube, this volume, fig. 7a), and bound shafts are held by "fliers,"

shamans in flight through the portal to the supernatural world (see cat. no. 70). Brian Stross has pointed out that "maize and blood symbolism. . . are metaphorical equivalents, the one alluding to and sometimes even substituting for the other."[4] Bloodletting is concomitant to flight through the portal, as is blood sacrifice for rain and maize in the program incised on the figure of the Young Lord (cat. no. 193).

The winged, pointed configuration at the top of the shaft of the Incised Vessel, crowned by a maize symbol, may graphically and symbolically identify the bundle with bloodletting or sacrifice and the transformation of blood into rain and maize. Vegetative or maize motifs progress from the bottom to the top of the composition: small tripartite forms in the openings of the inturned gum bracket, a symbol of the earth, may be seeds; the four root motifs surrounding the central profile may be read as the four points of the cosmos surrounding the ritual performer as the world tree (see Reilly, this volume, fig. 25); and the three

199. Figure Holding a Bundle, Fragment

900–600 B.C.
Provenance: Tuzapan, Veracruz
Material: dark green serpentine
Dimensions: h. 13.3 cm.; w. 10 cm.; d. 7.5 cm.
Collection of Dana B. Martin

The slight sloping projection at the chest suggests this figure, when intact, was sitting or kneeling. The figure cradles a bundle of vegetation that hangs limply over its arms. Flexible tassels with cleft ends hang through the spools in the elaborately carved ears; drill holes separate the tassels from the body. A cape incised across the back extends from shoulder to shoulder, decorated with a band with ovals at the top, a row of scallops below, and fringed lines just above the break. Two shallow drill holes in the top of the head might have held extensions of perishable material.

The jaguarian face, with projecting muzzle, gaping mouth, fangs, and deep furrow at the bridge of the nose, is, with the exception of the eyes, similar to the fierce supernatural faces carved on ceremonial axes. The large eyes seem to be heavy, lowered lids as on the plaque in cat. no. 155. The incised, tiered arrangement of the hair, an elaborate variation of the tonsured coiffure on the Shaman in Transformation Pose (cat. no. 42), the contrast between the face and the soft, naturalistically modeled shoulders, clavicle, and hands, and the cape worn by "fliers" indicate the transformation of a shaman into his jaguar spirit companion. The head rises and swells at the sides, curving in a bulbous projection over the front of the face, with an incised scroll on the sides. The shape recalls the headdress decorated with rain symbols worn by the figure on the front of La Venta Altar 5, and the roof of an incense burner decorated with cloud and water symbols (see cat. no. 245). The incisions to either side of the figure's mouth are symbols of the gaping maw of the Olmec Dragon, associated with caves, entrance to the underworld and the source of rain as in Chalcatzingo Monument 1, where the figure in the cave mouth wears a headdress marked with rain symbols and holds a ceremonial bar with cloud symbols.

On two celts from Río Pesquero, ritual performers hold bundles; in one a serpentlike creature and in the other, vegetation bound with three knots that falls limply at the ends like the bundle held with ceremonial solemnity in this figure here. The figures in both celts wear elaborate headdresses surmounted by maize motifs and are flanked by four cleft elements, the four corners of the cosmos. Both figures are identified as the world tree and *axis mundi*, the interface

Figure 1. Side view.

between the natural and supernatural worlds, as are the infant bearers of the Las Limas Figure, the figure on the front of La Venta Altar 5, and the enthroned figure in cat. no. 34. The sacrifice of the infants begets the rain and the vegetation cradled in the arms of the figure in this statuette.

BIBLIOGRAPHY

Miguel Covarrubias, *Indian Art of Mexico and Central America* (New York, 1957), pl. 11.
Gordon F. Ekholm, "Art in Archaeology," in *Aspects of Primitive Art*, ed. Robert Redfield (New York, 1959), pl. 10.
Román Piña Chán and Luis Covarrubias, *El Pueblo del jaguar* (Mexico City, 1964), 94.
Michael D. Coe, "The Olmec Style and Its Distribution," in *Handbook of Middle American Indians: Archaeology of Southern Mesoamerica*, vol. 3, ed. Gordon R. Willey (Austin, Tex., 1965), fig. 14.
A. Warman and C. S. de Bonfil, *Olmecas, Zapotecas, Mixtecos* (Mexico City, 1967), 12.
Samuel K. Lothrop and Gordon F. Ekholm, "Pre-Columbian Objects," in *The Guennol Collection*, vol. 1, ed. Ida Ely Rubin (New York, 1975), 326.

200. Seated Figure

900–500 B.C.
Provenance: Mexico
Material: albitite
Dimensions: h. 11 cm.; w. 6.2 cm.; d. 3.9 cm.
The Cleveland Museum of Art, purchase from the J. H. Wade Fund

With one leg hanging over a throne and the other folded in front of the body, the pose of this figure may be identified with the Classic Maya "posture of royal ease."[1] The figure holds a knuckleduster and an incised conical bundle similar to the two instruments on either side of the profile head on cat. no. 198, identifying him as a shamanic ruler.

201. Metate and Mano

900–600 B.C.
Provenance: Area of La Venta, Tabasco
Material: stone
Dimensions: metate: h. 5.6 cm.; w. 30.8 cm.; d. 18.5 cm.;
mano: diam. 5.8 cm.; d. 23.5 cm.
Anonymous loan to The Art Museum, Princeton University

Maize could have been ground on the curved surface of this metate with the mano, a long stone roller. Since the top is polished, with one end carved in a trilobe motif, and a star design is incised on the underside (fig. 1), this four-legged metate may have had a ceremonial function.

The star, read in conjunction with the four circles formed by the legs of the metate, is a variant of the four-dots-and-bar motif, a symbol of the *axis mundi* and the Olmec Dragon. The symbolism on this metate may cast light on the similarities between low thrones and metates (see cat. nos. 223, 224); and ceremonial bars and manos (see cat. no. 148). The star symbol ascribes a cosmic dimension to the metate on which the maize is ground and transformed.

Figure 1. Underside of metate.

BIBLIOGRAPHY
Unpublished.

BIBLIOGRAPHY
William M. Milliken, *Art of the Americas Picture Book Number Two* (Cleveland, 1946), 29.
Michael D. Coe, "The Olmec Style and Its Distribution," in *Handbook of Middle American Indians: Archaeology of Southern Mesoamerica*, vol. 3, ed. Gordon R. Willey (Austin, Tex., 1965), fig. 12.
Pál Kelemen, *Medieval American Art: Masterpieces of the New World Before Columbus*, 3d ed. (New York, 1969), pl. 253d.
Handbook of The Cleveland Museum of Art (Cleveland, 1978), 392.
Masterpieces from East to West (Cleveland, 1992), 180.
Beatriz de la Fuente et al., *Mexico en el mundo de las colecionnes de arte 1: Mesoamerica* (Mexico City, 1992), 39.

NOTE
1. Anne-Louise Schaffer, "The Maya 'Posture of Royal Ease,'" in *Sixth Palenque Round Table, 1986*, ed. Virginia M. Fields (Norman, Okla., 1991), 215–16.

203. Bottle with Incisions

1200–900 B.C.
Provenance: Las Bocas, Puebla
Material: clay with traces of red pigment
Dimensions: h. 21 cm.; diam. 14 cm.
Private collection

In form and essence the image incised on this black-ware vessel resembles the vegetative headdress crowning the composition on cat. no. 198. The central cleft motif rising from the base of this vessel is incised with a crossed-bands and fine lines rising from the top. The areas to either side of the stem are stippled, possibly to indicate the earth. This vegetative motif is flanked by truncated knuckledusters with areas of crosshatching at the base similar to the band on the back of cat. no. 10 and the ovals on the blackware box in cat. no. 209.

A variant of this composition on a vessel of similar form is in the Saint Louis Art Museum (fig. 1). A hollow cylinder across the inside of the neck acts as a handle on this unusual and possibly unique vessel.

BIBLIOGRAPHY
Unpublished.

Figure 1. Decorated Jar with Interior Hollow Handle, 1000–500 B.C., Las Bocas, Puebla, burnished black earthenware, h. 15.5 cm. The Saint Louis Art Museum, gift of Morton D. May.

204. Seated Figure

1200–900 B.C.
Provenance: Upper Balsas Region, Guerrero
Material: hollow brownish red clay with some yellow color
Dimensions: h. 21 cm.; w. 23 cm.; d. 13 cm.
Private collection

This hollow ceramic figure is visually and thematically related to the Atlihuayan figure in the National Museum of Anthropology in Mexico City (fig. 1). Both figures lean forward with elbows resting on their knees, small hands held in front of the chest. Here the figure is seated with legs apart, whereas the Atlihuayan figure's legs, while broken at the thighs, indicate a more cross-legged position. The figures differ primarily in the treatment of the headdress and eyes. The Atlihuayan figure wears a cape and head-dress in the form of the pelt of the Olmec Dragon. This figure wears only a headdress, with a brim that lacks the clearly defined gum brackets evident on the Atlihuayan figure. Small circular depressions on the forehead flanked by finely incised chevrons, ear flaps

Figure 1. Atlihuayan figure, h. 23 cm. National Museum of Anthropology, Mexico City.

with circles, and earflares complete the headdress. Tufts (see cat. nos. 58, 59, and 242) indicate that a supernatural with more avian attributes may be represented. The two figures appear to be in a trance state; the eyes of the Atlihuayan figure are incised scalloped lines resembling those on cat. no. 237; here, the blank space of each eye is surmounted by three small circles of clay.

BIBLIOGRAPHY
Unpublished.

205. Four Pairs of *Pulidores*

1200–900 B.C.
Provenance: Mexico
Material: top left: agate; top right: redstone; bottom left: chalcedony; bottom right: stone
Dimensions: top left: w. 3.3 cm.; top right: w. 4.4 cm.; bottom left: w. 4.3 cm.; bottom right: w. 4.7 cm.
Anonymous loan to The Art Museum, Princeton University

Pairs of polished stones such as these, known as *pulidores*, or "polishing stones," are found almost exclusively in the highlands.[1] It was once thought that these objects were used as polishers, but Tlatilco Burial 154, the grave containing the ceramic "acrobat" vessel (see Tate, this volume, fig. 24), also contained *pulidores*, indicating that they were the property of a shaman.

Two distinct shapes are represented here: oblong and faceted and a more irregular horizontal shape, straight or concave at the top, curved at the sides with the lower edge in the form of a shallow chevron. Beautifully worked, they have been carefully paired in the same material, including veined stones, as in the two carved from a milky blue stone with a white vein, and contrasting colors. The faceted and rounded sides allow the stones to spin on an axis; they may have been cast for shamanic divination.

BIBLIOGRAPHY
Gillett G. Griffin, "Olmec Forms and Materials Found in Central Guerrero," in *The Olmec and Their Neighbors: Essays in Memory of Matthew W. Stirling*, ed. Elizabeth P. Benson (Washington, D.C., 1981), fig. 17.

NOTE
1. Charlotte W. Thomson, "Chalcatzingo Jade and Fine Stone Objects," in *Ancient Chalcatzingo*, ed. David C. Grove (Austin, Tex., 1987), 303; Michael D. Coe and Richard A. Diehl, *In the Land of the Olmec: The Archaeology of San Lorenzo Tenochtitlán*, vol. 1 (Austin, Tex., 1980), 238.

206. *Pulidor* with Wooden Handle

1200–900 B.C.
Provenance: Mexico
Material: stone and wood
Dimensions: h. 15.5. cm.; w. 4.5 cm.; d. 3.2 cm.
Anonymous loan to The Art Museum, Princeton University

This object, with a finely shaped and highly polished stone mounted on a long tapering handle, is extremely rare because the wooden handle has survived. The large, translucent stone, shading to amber in the center, is attached to the hollowed-out top of the handle with sinew and pitch. Perhaps a *pulidor* in the literal sense of the word, the object may have been used to burnish clay or other stones. It may also have been used by a shaman to effect cures.

BIBLIOGRAPHY
Gillett G. Griffin, "Olmec Forms and Materials Found in Central Guerrero," in *The Olmec and Their Neighbors: Essays in Memory of Matthew W. Stirling*, ed. Elizabeth P. Benson (Washington, D.C., 1981), fig. 16.

207. Three Standing Figures ▶

900–600 B.C.
Provenance: left: Zumpango del Río, Guerrero; middle:
Río Pesquero, Veracruz; right: Guerrero
Material: left: dark bluish green steatite with iron oxide stains
overall; middle: light green jadeite with dark green-to-blue
inclusions, milky patina; right: dark green serpentine
Dimensions: left: h. 6 cm.; w. 3 cm.; d. 2 cm.; middle: h. 8 cm.;
w. 3.5 cm.; d. 2.5 cm.; right: h. 8 cm.; w. 2.5 cm.; d. 2 cm.
Private collection

These three geometricized figures are derived from the
tradition of incised celts. All three clasp their hands
across their midsections and have faces defined by
trapezoidal noses and mouths. The figure in the center
is the most Olmec in style. The cleft head and physiognomy recall the incised figure in cat. no. 128, interpreted as a germinating plant. The minimalism of the
two other figures, which may reflect a more regional
influence, makes interpretation more difficult. As
amulets, they may have been used in shamanic rituals.

BIBLIOGRAPHY
Unpublished.

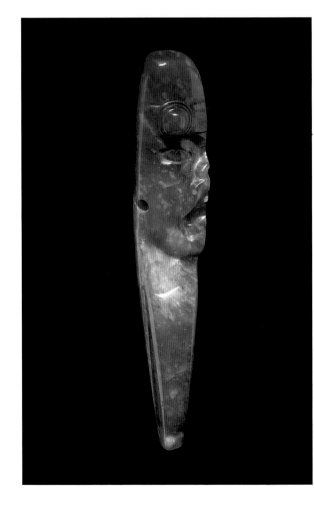

◀ 208. Split Axe

900–600 B.C.
Provenance: Veracruz
Material: blue-green jadeite with white inclusions, some of
which are stained by iron oxide
Dimensions: h. 8.9 cm.; w. 1.2 cm.; d. 1.5 cm.
Private collection

Carved in the form of a miniature axe, with the head of
the Olmec Supernatural on the upper half, this object
was sawed down the middle at a later date. When
intact, the object probably resembled the standing
figure of the Olmec Supernatural in cat. no. 84. A drill
hole at the back of the head at the position of the earlobe probably held ornaments.

　　The object is drilled through from top to bottom,
perhaps for suspension as a pendant, or possibly for
sniffing a hallucinogenic substance.

BIBLIOGRAPHY
Unpublished.

209. Two Boxes

1400–1200 B.C.
Provenance: Las Bocas
Material: left: clay with traces of cinnabar;
right: burnished clay
Dimensions: left: h. 2.9 cm.; w. 6.9 cm.; d. 3.8 cm.;
right: h. 2.7 cm.; w. 8.1 cm.; d. 2.6 cm.
Anonymous loans to The Art Museum, Princeton University

Sometimes referred to as *candeleros*, these two com-
partmented clay boxes probably contained substances
used in rituals. Both have small holes between the two
chambers, indicating that a lid was once attached to
the box. The buff-colored box is in the form of a two-
legged throne with scrolled extensions at the sides and
U-brackets incised above the legs. The latter arrangement recalls Portero Nuevo Altar 2, which depicts two
dwarfs holding a line of U-brackets above their heads.
The small box here may be a miniature throne, with
the brackets defining the earth and the scrolls indicating clouds. Similar thrones can be seen in cat. nos.
34 and 223.

　　The gray box is incised with an abstract image of the
ascendant Olmec Dragon, with saurian profile and

flame eyebrows similar to those on the blackware vessel in cat. no. 103. The ends are incised with areas of crosshatching surrounded by scalloped lines, a motif commonly seen on blackware ceramics from the Gulf Coast and the highlands (see cat. no. 10). While its meaning remains unclear, similar motifs appear on the right leg of the Young Lord (cat. no. 193), interpreted there as shell symbols. Their presence here may indicate that the dragon is emerging from the watery underworld.

BIBLIOGRAPHY
Unpublished.

210. Two Roller Seals; One Stamp

1200–900 B.C.
Provenance: Las Bocas, Puebla
Material: left: clay with burnished kaolin slip; center: clay; right: clay with traces of specular hematite
Dimensions: left: h. 8.7 cm.; diam. 5 cm.; center: h. 8.4 cm.; diam. 5.8 cm.; right: h. 3.5 cm.; diam. 4.6 cm.
Left and right: Anonymous loans to The Art Museum, Princeton University; center: The Art Museum, Princeton University, gift of Gillett G. Griffin

Roller seals may have been used to print sacred symbols on the body. The rollout of the wider of the two seals, in reddish clay, is carved with a pointed polygonal form with concave sides, similar to those on the sides of the chambered blackware box in cat. no. 209, but here enclosed in a curve with open work between. A curved band within the pointed polygon is filled with pelletlike forms. The same oval motif on the right leg of the Young Lord (cat. no. 193) has been interpreted as a shell. This shell motif is held by an open hand; a T-shaped symbol appears underneath the hand.

The full width of the roller seal in light grayish clay is carved with two diamonds with concave sides; four-petal flowers mark the center of each diamond. The spaces in between the points at which the diamonds touch are filled with half-flowers, which, if complete, would have eight petals.

The stamp seal is carved with a four-pointed star with concave sides enclosed within a diamond shape and encircled by two concentric bands. This is a common motif on Olmec objects and appears to be a celestial symbol.

BIBLIOGRAPHY
Unpublished.

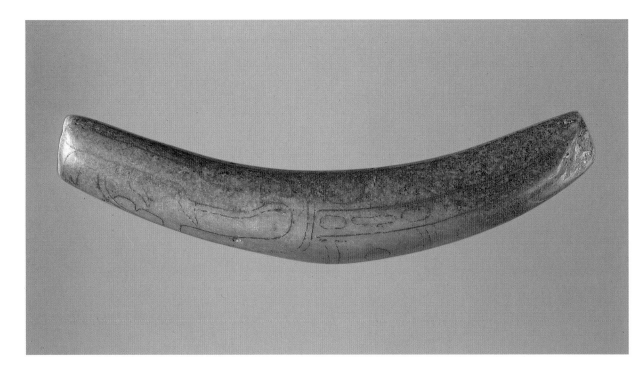

ing the object may have been suspended and worn by a shaman. The unusual treatment of the mouth recalls the jade pendant head in the collection of Dumbarton Oaks.[1] Both objects may record a specific stage in a shamanic ritual.

BIBLIOGRAPHY
Unpublished.

NOTE
1. Elizabeth P. Benson, "Some Objects in the Robert Woods Bliss Collection at Dumbarton Oaks," in *The Olmec and Their Neighbors: Essays in Memory of Matthew W. Stirling*, ed. Elizabeth P. Benson (Washington, D.C., 1981), fig. 8.

211. Incised Bead ▲

1250–400 B.C.
Provenance: Mexico
Material: jade with traces of cinnabar
Dimensions: w. 18 cm.; diam. 3 cm.
The Art Museum, Princeton University, Museum purchase

The Olmec Dragon incised on this bead is shown in profile with a long snout and open jaw revealing a forked tongue, fang, and cleft form; a flame eyebrow or plumage is indicated by the ornate cleft motif at the back of the head. The body is divided by a band incised with irregular ovals. Above the band is an inward-angled sky band; below it are three compartments containing circles. A similar pattern is incised on the back of the dwarf in cat. no. 117.

The bead is biconically drilled through from each end and may have been worn as a pendant or pectoral. But, as in the case of spoons (see cat. nos. 70–72), pierced to be worn as shamanic emblems, the bead may also have had a ritual function as a nose snifter for a powdered hallucinogen. The hole at the left end of the bead agrees with the snout of the dragon; any substance inhaled would travel through the dragon's "body," reinforcing the interpretation of the dragon as a conduit between the natural and supernatural realms.

BIBLIOGRAPHY
Lois Dubin, *History of Beads from 30,000 B.C. to the Present* (New York, 1987), no. 253.

212. Vessel ▼

900–600 B.C.
Provenance: Upper Balsas River Basin, Guerrero
Material: greenstone
Dimensions: h. 3 cm.; w. 5.5 cm.; d. 4.5 cm.
Private collection

This miniature vessel in the form of a human head is remarkable in the detail of the extended lower jaw and tongue. An incised line that curves from the ears around the back of the head recalls the tonsures in cat. no. 42. Short lines define the eyes and ears. The bowl is drilled through on the sides behind the ears, suggest-

213. Standing Bearded Figure ▶

900–600 B.C.
Provenance: Veracruz
Material: light green serpentine with dark green specks and striations
Dimensions: h. 8.5 cm.; w. 3.5 cm.; d. 3.5 cm.
Private collection

This stooped bearded figure, with knees flexed, compressed torso leaning forward, appears to be a hunchback (see Tate, this volume, fig. 19), although if viewed from a particular angle the hunch resembles a bundle or pack.[1] Hunchbacks, beings with access to the supernatural realm and associated with rain (see cat. nos. 65, 235), usually lack beards, a trait more often associated with rulers and transformation figures (cat. nos. 11–13; 42–43). The incorporation of the beard with the hunched back may indicate that this statue depicts a shaman impersonating a hunchback. The pack recalls the supernatural bearers of maize in cat. nos. 118 and 119. This figure may carry a similarly precious cargo or a bundle containing objects for shamanic rituals.

BIBLIOGRAPHY
Unpublished.

NOTE
1. A figurine from the Cerro de las Mesas cache (see cat. no. 82) stands in a similarly ambiguous posture; see Philip Drucker, "The Cerro de las Mesas Offering of Jade and Other Materials," in *Bureau of American Ethnology*, Bulletin 157 (1955): 32.

214. Head from a Figure

900–600 B.C.
Provenance: Veracruz
Material: mottled dark-to-light green jadeite
Dimensions: h. 4 cm.; w. 2 cm.; d. 2.5 cm.
Private collection

Broken from a full figure, this wizened head of an old, bearded man is drilled through the base of the head, and may have been worn as a pendant. The dimmed eyes, sunken cheeks, and toothless mouth form a moving portrait of dignified, venerable old age. This finely carved piece may be a portrait of a shaman, worn as an amulet.

BIBLIOGRAPHY
Unpublished.

215. Crouching Male Figure ▶

900–500 B.C.
Provenance: Puebla
Material: steatite
Dimensions: h. 7.6 cm.; w. 4.6 cm.; d. 5.1 cm.
Dallas Museum of Art, gift of Mr. and Mrs. Eugene McDermott, the McDermott Foundation, and Mr. and Mrs. Algur H. Meadows and the Meadows Foundation, Incorporated

Hunched over, this crouching figure draws his legs apart and close to the body, revealing genitals and a defined cavelike space at the midsection. Two large drill holes at the sides separate the arms and legs from the body. The head and features are powerfully carved with large, hollowed-out eyes, a broad, hooked nose, and wide, slightly open mouth. He is bearded and wears a tight-fitting cap that covers the ears, similar to the one in cat. no. 17. A fine fillet is incised on the brow just below the edge of the cap and at the sides, where holes have been drilled for the attachment of ornaments. Two lines are incised to either side of the outer corners of the eyes, and the brow is furrowed in what appears to be a grimace consistent with exertion. A circle is incised on each buttock.

The pose, associated with birthing, also approximates the pose taken by some performers of blood-letting rituals in Classic Maya art. Given the explicit depiction of genitalia, rare in Olmec art, a similar emphasis may be indicated here. David A. Friedel, in this volume, discusses the birthing pose of this figure as an exploration of the paradox of the mother-father in Mesoamerican mythology, and proposes that the circles on the buttocks, with the figure's scrotum, may be symbols of the three stones of creation (see cat. no. 131).

BIBLIOGRAPHY
Unpublished.

NOTE
1. Linda Schele and Mary Ellen Miller, *The Blood of Kings: Dynasty and Ritual in Maya Art* (Fort Worth, 1986), pl. 72.

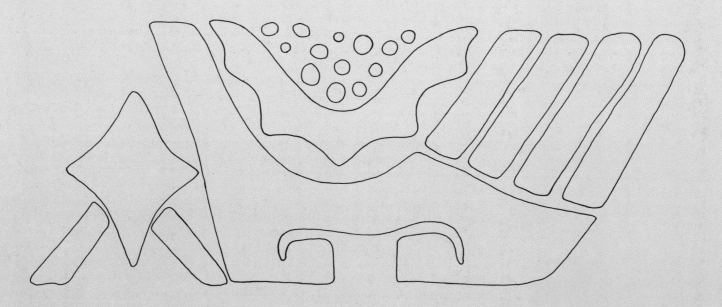

VIII
Regional Manifestations of the Olmec Style

One of the most debated issues in Mesoamerican studies is the relationship between the culture of the people of the Gulf Coast, identified as the Olmec, and other societies of Formative period Mesoamerica. The archaeological cultures of southern Veracruz and Tabasco from 1500 to 600 B.C. are generally regarded as Olmec and for many years have been accepted as the source of an art style and iconography that emerged in the Formative period. While some scholars insist that the Gulf Coast is the heartland of the Olmec style,[1] other views have emerged in recent years.

One school of thought holds that the term Olmec has been applied indiscriminately to objects and symbols found outside the Gulf Coast. Its proponents believe that culture traits commonly called Olmec either originated outside the southern Gulf Coast or were so widely distributed that they cannot be considered Olmec.[2]

Another view maintains that the peoples of Middle Formative Mesoamerica participated in a far-flung ceremonial complex. Based on shared beliefs, rituals, and symbols having their roots in the culture of the Gulf Coast, this complex was adapted by diverse ethnic groups and cultures to suit the conditions and needs of their own traditions.[3]

The attempt has been made, and a bias expressed, in this catalogue to reconstruct a view of the ritual landscape of ancient Mesoamerica on the basis of the formal and iconographic consistencies of objects from the various regions, which, it would seem, record the influence of the Olmec style and the regional traditions with which it intersected. Objects from the Gulf Coast, Guerrero, and the central highlands have been juxtaposed throughout the catalogue, and in the following section, additional examples from Guerrero and the central highlands further demonstrate the strongly shared artistic traditions, ideology, and ritual of Formative period Mesoamerica.

Guerrero

Due to lack of scientific excavation, the degree to which the populations of Guerrero participated in the Middle Formative Ceremonial Complex is not well understood, but the parallels, in both form and content, in monumental works and an abundance of portable objects, strongly suggest direct familiarity with the Olmec style. Cave and wall paintings in the Olmec style have been found at Juxtlahuaca, Oxtotitlan, and Cacahuaziziqui, and a stela from San Miguel Amuco displays Olmec motifs. Excavations at Teopantecuanitlan have yielded evidence of monumental works and structural elements associated with Gulf Coast sites—massive sculptures carved with the image of the Olmec Supernatural, a drainage system similar to those found at La Venta and San Lorenzo, and a large, although not colossal, stone head.[4] Figures of contortionists, dwarfs and fetus-like creatures, masks, maskettes and plaques, perforators, spoons, pendants, beads, earspools, and other objects mirroring the style and themes of Olmec art have also been found to such an extent, in fact, that some scholars have argued that the Olmec style originated in Guerrero.

Although the only geologically confirmed source of jade in Mesoamerica lies in the Motagua River Valley of Guatemala, an important unresolved question is whether Guerrero was a source of jade, serpentine, and greenstone in the Formative period. Reports of jade and serpentine cobbles in the riverbeds of Guerrero and the strong lithic tradition in the region suggests that it was.[5]

Ceramics from the Central Highlands

If stone is the more characteristic material of Guerrero, clay is the medium of artistic expression in the highlands. In an analysis of ceramic figurines from Tlatilco, Douglas Bradley and Peter David Joralemon have posited that "Tlatilco culture used the Olmec format for the presentation of fertility symbolism to carry a new religious message throughout the Central Mexican Highlands."[6] The highly sophisticated ceramics from Las Bocas, hollow clay figures, animal effigy vessels, and incised bottles, clearly reflect stylistic elements and motifs associated with the Gulf Coast. Vessels from Tlapacoya incised with profiles of Olmec supernaturals demonstrate an understanding of the Olmec system of *pars pro toto* motifs. The objects considered here are evidence of a wide range of local traditions that absorbed and reinterpreted the Olmec style.

NOTES
1. See Diehl, this volume.
2. See *Regional Perspectives on the Olmec*, ed. Robert J. Sharer and David C. Grove (Cambridge, 1989).
3. See Reilly, this volume; Schele, this volume.
4. For a summary of these and other discoveries in Guerrero, see Guadalupe Martinez Donjuán, "Los olmecas en el estado de Guerrero," in *Los olmecas en Mesoamérica*, ed. John E. Clark (Mexico City, 1994).
5. See Gillett G. Griffin, "Formative Guerrero and Its Jade," in *Precolumbian Jade: New Geological and Cultural Interpretations*, ed. Frederick W. Lange (Salt Lake City, 1993), 203–10.
6. Douglas Bradley and Peter David Joralemon, *The Lords of Life* (Notre Dame, Ind., 1992), 28.

216. Incised Celt: Masked Figure

1200–600 B.C.
Provenance: Guerrero
Material: jadeite
Dimensions: h. 28 cm.; w. 7.8 cm.; d. 3.8 cm.
Dallas Museum of Art, Dallas Art Association Purchase

The incised image of an elaborately costumed figure striding to the viewer's left extends slightly around the sides of this gray-green jade celt. The head and legs are in profile, while the torso is shown frontally. The right arm is extended in front of the figure, the left arm, crooked toward the body, holds a staff.

Small, fringed wings extend from behind the shoulders and may be attached to the figure's collar. The upper section of the long, rectangular loincloth is quartered and surmounted by a cleft symbol. A longer, wider apron, which falls down the back, is visible between the legs. The arms and legs are banded.

The figure appears to be wearing a mask, indicated by the line that runs parallel to the back of the neck and curves around to form the jaw and mouth. A notched circle, probably an earspool, is suspended from the back of the headdress. A large fang descends from the upper jaw. If completed in a frontal view, the formation of the jaw would take the form of a U-bracket, often incised around the mouths of supernatural zoomorphs. The cross symbol quartering the eye is unusual, as most crossed-bands in eyes are oriented diagonally.[1]

The headband, with a short, angled appendage at the front, is decorated with two of what would be four cleft forms if seen from the front. Above and in front of the headband is an oval drawn in a fine line, which may be a profile view of a stone mirror.

Dominating the towering headdress is a zoomorphic face with a gaping mouth. The lower jaw, cleft at the back, is a motif often associated with the Olmec Dragon (see cat. no. 93). The nose sits directly on the upper lip and brackets intersect the oval eye. On the forehead is a profile cleft form with a circle and a curved extension. At the back, almost the full height of the headdress, is a banded vaselike form similar to that on cat. no. 127. Overlapping this motif is a hand gripping a knuckleduster as on cat. no. 198. If seen frontally, the headdress would resemble that of a

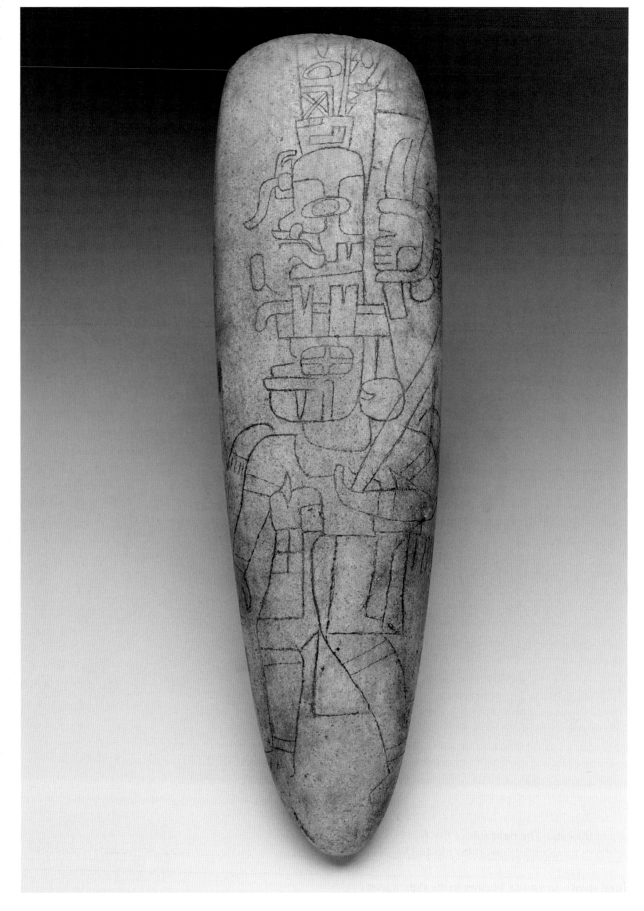

Figure 1. Drawing of carved celt, 900–600 B.C., Mexico, bluish greenstone, h. 22.7 cm. Museum of Anthropology, Xalapa, Veracruz.

seated figure from Río Pesquero with a supernatural face flanked by knuckledusters (see Schele, this volume, fig. 5b).

The supernatural face here is surmounted by a headdress of another more abstract face in profile. A rectangle enclosing a free-floating eye symbol, similar to the motif forming the lower jaw of the mask below, provides the base for this face. The mouth is marked by a crossed-bands motif; and above the eye a pointed oval, a sprouting seed, emerges from the cleft at the top of the head. The right side of this face is banded with sawtooth projections at the top and bottom, probably the crenellated earflaps of the Olmec Supernatural shown in profile. Further to the right a motif

appears to be an inverted version of the corn symbol of cat. no. 173, flanked by two circles. The overall sense of headdress upon headdress recalls a towering plant; the brackets on the lower profile intersecting the eye may represent the parted earth from which the plant emerges as in cat. no. 203.

Walking or striding figures holding a bundle or staff are seen on many monumental and portable objects throughout Formative period Mesoamerica, including a carved celt of unknown provenance (fig. 1),[2] the San Miguel Amuco stela from northwestern Guerrero (see Taube, this volume, fig. 7a), and the carving on the relief at Xoc, Chiapas (now destroyed). The main figure on the carved celt lacks the mask seen here, but his towering headdress shows a similar supernatural face in profile. The bundles held by the figures in the latter two examples are considerably thicker than the staff here, but a standing figure from Viejón Stela 1, Veracruz, holds a thin staff like this one.[3]

BIBLIOGRAPHY
Peter David Joralemon, "A Study of Olmec Iconography," *Studies in Pre-Columbian Art and Archaeology*, no. 7 (Washington, D.C., 1971), fig. 33.
Virginia M. Fields, "The Iconographic Heritage of the Maya Jester God," in *Sixth Palenque Round Table, 1986*, ed. Virginia M. Fields (Norman, Okla., 1991), fig. 6c.

NOTES
1. See Peter David Joralemon, "The Olmec Dragon: A Study in Pre-Columbian Iconography," in *Origins of Religious Art and Iconography in Preclassic Mesoamerica*, ed. Henry B. Nicholson (Los Angeles, 1976), figs. 18b, c, e.
2. *The Bogousslavsky Collection of Pre-Columbian Art*, Sotheby Parke Bernet Inc. (New York, Dec. 4, 1981), no. 53.
3. For the Xoc carving, see Susanna Ekholm-Miller, "The Olmec Rock Carving at Xoc, Chiapas, Mexico," in *Papers of the New World Archaeological Foundation*, no. 32 (Provo, Utah, 1973); for Viejón Stela 1, see Ignacio Bernal, *The Olmec World*, trans. Doris Heyden and Fernando Horcasitas (Berkeley, 1969), pl. 70.

217. Standing Figure

900–600 B.C.
Provenance: Upper Balsas River Basin
Material: light bluish green serpentine stained brown by hematite
Dimensions: h. 14 cm.; w. 5 cm.; d. 2.5 cm.
Private collection

This figure, viewed in profile, with knees flexed, pelvis thrust forward and back held rigidly straight, is in the posture of standing meditation, a position that induces a trancelike state. The elongated head and features conform to the Olmec ideal and the flange ears are drilled for ornaments. The body is minimally articulated, the nostrils and loin cloth are incised. The wrists are connected to the body at the hips and the feet joined at the ankles, possibly to strengthen the legs. Somewhat bottom heavy, the figure's legs are disproportionately thick and the feet seem suspended from the lower legs. The central line of the spine divides at the base of the skull to form a sheathlike shape with a circle on either side. The figure cannot stand independently and was most likely intended to be supported by sand in burials or offerings.

BIBLIOGRAPHY
Unpublished.

218. Standing Figure ▼

900–600 B.C.
Provenance: Upper Balsas River Basin
Material: mottled dark-to-light green albite mica rock with white veins and milky inclusions; green caused by chlorite or edidote
Dimensions: h. 7 cm.; w. 3.5 cm.; d. 2 cm.
Private collection

BIBLIOGRAPHY
Unpublished.

219. Standing Figure ▼

900–600 B.C.
Provenance: Guerrero
Material: mottled brown-to-olive green serpentine with black striations
Dimensions: h. 18 cm.; w. 8 cm.; d. 6 cm.
Private collection

BIBLIOGRAPHY
Unpublished.

220. Standing Figure ▲

900–600 B.C.
Provenance: Western Veracruz
Material: mottled dark green serpentine with broad bands of lighter green and calcified roots and cinnabar
Dimensions: h. 22 cm.; w. 9 cm.; d. 6 cm.
Private collection

From the refined treatment of cat. no. 26 to the more minimal treatment of cat. no. 218, Olmec standing figures from Guerrero display the same range of styles found in other areas of Mesoamerica during the Formative period.

Many objects from Guerrero are also influenced by the geometric style of Mezcala, as seen in the carved figure of cat. no. 219. The head, cut horizontally at the top and jutting forward, almost detached from the body, gives the impression of a mask. With its narrowed eyes extending to the outer edges, large, deeply ridged nose, and widely flaring mouth, the rough-hewn face appears contorted in a grimace. The arms are surprisingly diminutive in relation to the broad shoulders and chest, but the legs create a greater sense of stability.

The geometric treatment of cat. no. 220 more emphatically reflects the influence of Mezcala, despite its reported provenance. The small, tapering legs seem cursory in comparison to those of cat. no. 219. Bluntly carved, this figure stands with legs separated, and arms attached and angled back and down the sides of the body. The head is sunk into the shoulders, and the brow, eyes, and nose are organized on a deeply carved grid projecting abruptly from the domed top of the head. The squared mouth is turned up in the center of the upper lip in a rectangle that abuts the nose. The projections at the lower jaw and at the brow indicate that the figure is to be read as wearing a mask, similar in the gridlike treatment to the upper part of the mask in cat. no. 44.

BIBLIOGRAPHY
Unpublished.

221a. Spoons and Perforator

900–600 B.C.
Provenance: Upper Balsas River Basin
Material: blue-green jadeite
Dimensions: upper: h. 1.5 cm.; w. 6 cm.; d. 0.5 cm.;
middle: h. 0.7 cm.; w. 9 cm.; d. 0.4 cm; lower: h. 3 cm.;
w. 11.5 cm.; d. 1 cm.
Private collection

BIBLIOGRAPHY
Unpublished.

221b. Spoons

900–600 B.C.
Provenance: Upper Balsas River Basin
Material: upper: mottled light-to-dark green serpentine with oxidized softer stone inclusions; surface stained and etched by roots; lower: very fine compact, bluish green serpentine stained and etched by root action
Dimensions: upper: h. 4 cm.; w. 16 cm.; d. 1 cm.; lower: h. 2 cm.; w. 11 cm.; d. .25 cm.
Private collection

a.

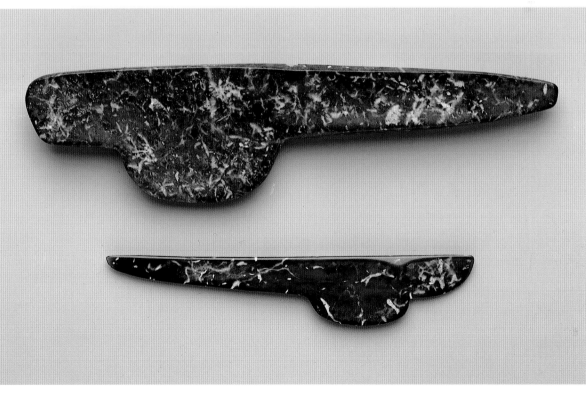

b.

The largest of the three objects in cat. no. 221a is a spoon in the unadorned but elegant form produced in Guerrero (see cat. no. 71). The extensions to either side of the bowl are concave, the longer of the two slightly turned up at the end, suggestive of a stylized wing form. The two indentations at the blunted end of the slim, sharp, pointed shaft of jade in the center are too shallow to hold a substance and probably were notched for a firmer grip, indicating that this object was a bloodletter. The smallest of the objects is rudimentary in form, and takes the general shape of the spoon discussed above, with a long and short projection to either side of the bowl, although it is hollowed out the full length in the same plane. Pierced at the top, in the center, and to either side at the bottom, the jade was probably worn as a pendant.

The two spoons of cat. no. 221b are in the same form as cat. nos. 71 and 72. Scholars have suggested that this form represents tadpoles or razor clams. Peter T. Furst has speculated that they were used to hold a powerful tobacco such as *Nicotiana rustica* L.[1]

BIBLIOGRAPHY
Unpublished.

NOTE

1. Peter T. Furst, this volume, and "The Olmec Were-Jaguar Motif in the Light of Ethnographic Reality," in *Dumbarton Oaks Conference on the Olmec*, ed. Elizabeth P. Benson (Washington, D.C., 1968), 162; Gillett G. Griffin, "Olmec Forms and Materials Found in Central Guerrero," in *The Olmec and Their Neighbors: Essays in Memory of Matthew W. Stirling*, ed. Elizabeth P. Benson (Washington, D.C., 1981), 219; Anatole Pohorilenko, "The Olmec Style and Costa Rican Archaeology," in *The Olmec and Their Neighbors: Essays in Memory of Matthew W. Stirling*, ed. Elizabeth P. Benson (Washington, D.C., 1981), 311.

222. Perforator

900–600 B.C.
Provenance: Upper Balsas River Basin
Material: translucent blue-green jadeite
Dimensions: h. 10 cm.; w. 1.7 cm.; d. 1.5 cm.
Private collection

Separated from the shaft by a small flange, the handle of this perforator is carved in the form of a figure with short legs and arms held close to the body. With its small flat nose and deep muzzle, the blunted face is strongly simian; the open mouth suggests a scream. The undercut plane around the mouth, which con-

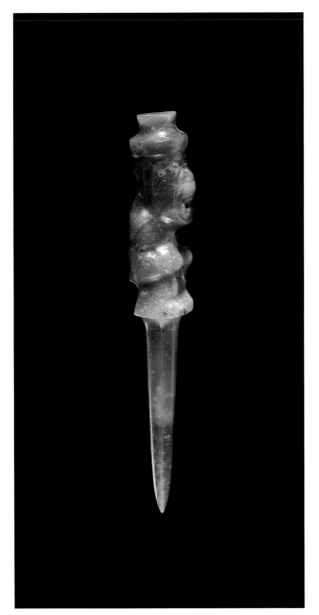

tinues under the eye, may indicate a buccal mask. The finial is a hat or headdress secured by bands on either side of the head.

BIBLIOGRAPHY
Unpublished.

223. Enthroned Figure ▶

900–600 B.C.
Provenance: Guerrero
Material: light greenish gray steatite patinated a deep brown by iron oxides
Dimensions: h. 18 cm.; w. 9 cm.; d. 7.5 cm.
Private collection

Although transformation and rulership are merged in this enthroned figure, no trace of the characteristic Olmec features is evident. The face and body, including the ear on the right side, are human; however, the projecting animal ears and the sloping forehead give the figure a feline aspect. The arms, held close to the sides and drawn across the chest, meet over a slight paunch. Carved in low relief, the schematically rendered legs are truncated and do not touch the ground. The legs of the throne form the four dots-and-bar motif, placing the ruler at the center of the cosmos as the *axis mundi*.

BIBLIOGRAPHY
Unpublished.

224. Throne with Incisions

900–600 B.C.
Provenance: Guerrero
Material: light greenish gray steatite with reddish brown patina
Dimensions: h. 7 cm.; w. 21 cm.; d. 9 cm.
Private collection

This metate is identified by its symbolic incsions as a throne, as in cat. no. 201. The slightly concave surface is incised with a profile of a supernatural, with a protruding forehead, overhanging upper lip, and deeply carved eye, emerging from a knuckleduster (fig. 1).

The four legs are each incised with a variation of the four root symbols seen on cat. no. 198. The motif here is comprised of a half circle enclosing a dot over a vertical line. The sides of the throne are lightly incised with identical designs; at the right end is a four-dots-and-bar motif and at the left end a cleft, possibly with eyes, as in cat. no. 91. Below the cleft are trident elements similar to the brackets in cat. no. 126. The four-dots-and-bar motif may indicate that the legs of this throne are the four dots and the throne itself is the bar.

Throne and metate are equated in this object, conflating imagery of rulership with an object fundamental to the daily lives of ancient Mesoamericans.[1]

BIBLIOGRAPHY
Unpublished.

NOTE
1. For metates from Olmec sites, see Michael D. Coe and Richard A. Diehl, *In the Land of the Olmec: The Archaeology of San Lorenzo Tenochtitlán,* vol. 1 (Austin, Tex., 1980), 227–32; David C. Grove, "Ground Stone Artifacts," in *Ancient Chalcatzingo,* ed. David C. Grove (Austin, Tex., 1987), 331–32.

Figure 1. View of incisions.

225. Standing Figure

900–600 B.C.
Provenance: Upper Balsas River Basin
Material: dark green serpentine with coarse and flaky grains and pyrite inclusions; surface oxidized to a whitish patina
Dimensions: h. 31 cm.; w. 9 cm.; d. 6 cm.
Private collection

The otherworldly quality of this figure, drawn within itself, is due in part to the smallness of the body in relation to the large head, a common characteristic of Olmec figures. Drawn up over a swelling paunch as on cat. no. 223, the arms hold an oval object, perhaps a celt or bundle. The high cheekbones and slightly drawn cheeks give the broad face a gaunt aspect. The overhanging brows cast deep shadows on the shallow eyes; the narrow nose and mouth are minimally defined. The tall headdress is in the form of the upturned head and open mouth of a zoomorphic supernatural.

BIBLIOGRAPHY
Unpublished.

226

226. Maskette

900–600 B.C.
Provenance: Upper Balsas River Basin
Material: light green serpentine with darker green veins; surface oxidized white and impacted with cinnabar
Dimensions: h. 7.6 cm.; w. 7.5 cm.; d. 4 cm.
Private collection

Faint ovals under the broad span of the deeply undercut brows define the eyes on this maskette; small pits are drilled immediately to either side of the bridge of the nose. While the geometric treatment of the nose and mouth is strong evidence of a Mezcala influence, the flaring upper lip reduced to a trapezoidal band indicates an Olmec influence. Shallow holes are drilled in the corners of the upper lip, which is carved in relief and divided from the hollowed-out lower part of the mouth. The ears are flat to the head. Traces of red pigment in the crevices of the face may show that the maskette was completely covered with this material, most likely in a burial. The top of the maskette is broken and unevenly worn.

BIBLIOGRAPHY
Unpublished.

227

227. Maskette

900–600 B.C.
Provenance: Upper Balsas River Basin
Material: dark green serpentine with chalky patina stained
with hematite
Dimensions: h. 11.4 cm.; w. 8 cm.; d. 3 cm.
Private collection

While still exhibiting the influence of Mezcala, this
maskette is not rigidly geometric in the delineation
of the features. The face has a decidedly soft, fleshy
appearance, particularly under the eyes, cheeks, chin,
and brow. The nose is carved as a flat triangle, but
the mouth, although still highly schematic, retains
some aspect of the puffy, flared upper lip of purer
Olmec representations. With an incised line above, the
slit eyes are sharply angled down toward the outside
corners. The ears are flat to the head. The maskette has
been broken, abraded, and has numerous small chips
and losses. The back has been partially hollowed out,
leaving a narrow ridge at the top, drilled with two
holes for suspension.

BIBLIOGRAPHY
Unpublished.

228

228. Maskette

900–600 B.C.
Provenance: Upper Balsas River Basin
Material: mottled light-to-dark green serpentine, eroded
oxidized-to-white surface stained brown by minerals
Dimensions: h. 11 cm.; w. 10 cm.; d. 5 cm.
Private collection

While more vertical than the maskette in cat. no. 154,
the expression here is similarly ambiguous, as if weeping and smiling. The soft planes of the brow sweep
into the bridge of the nose and out into the cheeks.
The puffy eyes appear half shut, and the short, broad
nose is separated from the grimacing, fleshy lips by
a carved line; both gum lines and tongue are articulated. The flange ears are pierced at the lobe. Despite
the size, a cavity at the back of the mask would have
allowed the wearer to breathe through the drilled
nostrils.

BIBLIOGRAPHY
Unpublished.

229. Head from a Figure

900–600 B.C.
Provenance: Guerrero
Material: mottled light-to-dark green serpentine
Dimensions: h. 7.5 cm.; w. 4.5 cm.; d. 3 cm.
Private collection

This head, broken from a full figure, can be included
among works of the purest Olmec style and compared
favorably with such finely carved examples as cat. nos.
19 and 24. The interlocking treatment of the nose and
upper lip and the articulation of the tongue and lower
lip are especially subtle. The crease lines defining the
block of the mouth are an unusual detail. The eyes are
deeply hollowed, probably for inlays. While the
optical orbit is not modeled, the undercut, roughly
finished areas beneath the eyes may have been fitted
with insets. The ears are pierced at the bottom for
ornaments.

BIBLIOGRAPHY
Unpublished.

229

231b. Flanged Pectoral

900–600 B.C.
Provenance: Upper Balsas River Basin
Material: eroded dark green serpentine with chalky patina
Dimensions: h. 3 cm.; w. 4 cm.; d. 2 cm.
Private collection

BIBLIOGRAPHY
Unpublished.

These two pendants are carved and incised with supernatural images. In cat. no. 231a, the head has a small cleft, deeply carved eyes, and trapezoidal mouth; faintly visible flame eyebrows indicate that it may be an avian jaguar (see cat. no. 194). The flanges, marked by cross-shaped incisions, are reduced to short projections only half the height of the face. The roughly incised face, with cleft head, almond-shaped eyes, and trapezoidal mouth of cat. no. 231b, may represent the Olmec Supernatural.[1] The central image of a head with lateral extensions is derived from the form of ritual spoons (see cat. nos. 221a and b), the hollowed chambers in this pendant reduced to two-dimensional, curved forms.

NOTE
1. A fragment of a similar pectoral was found in San Lorenzo. Michael D. Coe and Richard A. Diehl, *In the Land of the Olmec: The Archaeology of San Lorenzo Tenochtitlán*, vol. 1 (Austin, Tex., 1980), fig. 247.

230. Pendant ▲

900–600 B.C.
Provenance: Upper Balsas River Basin
Material: bluish-green jadeite with white inclusions
Dimensions: h. 4 cm.; w. 14.8 cm.; d. 1 cm.
Private collection

This exquisite piece of jade is carved with a horizontal tube at the top, drilled to be strung for suspension as a pendant. A similar object is reportedly from La Venta.[1]

BIBLIOGRAPHY
Unpublished.

NOTE
1. Ignacio Bernal, *The Olmec World*, trans. Doris Heyden and Fernando Horcasitas (Berkeley, 1969), pl. 42.

a.

231a. Flanged Pectoral

900–600 B.C.
Provenance: Upper Balsas River Basin
Material: mottled dark-to-light green serpentine with hematite stains
Dimensions: h. 4.7 cm.; w. 12.8 cm.; d. 1 cm.
Private collection

BIBLIOGRAPHY
Unpublished.

b.

232. Pendant with Inlays

900–600 B.C.
Provenance: Upper Balsas River Basin
Material: mother-of-pearl with obsidian inlays
Dimensions: h. 13.9 cm.; w. 9 cm.; d. 0.5 cm.
Private collection

Fashioned of mother-of-pearl with obsidian insets, this unusual object depicts a bearded figure in profile wearing a low headdress with a curved, hornlike extension. The area of the eye is marked by four rectangular and four circular cavities, all but one inlaid with obsidian, surrounding a tiny perforation. The bottommost of these inlays is curved, possibly to repeat the shape of the extension from the head. The nostril is also inlaid with obsidian. Five small drill holes at the top of the head and along the jaw may have held attachments of some perishable material. Two larger holes drilled high at the back of the head and another near the earlobe may have been used to incorporate this object into a costume. Other lines define the thick lips, cheek, and chin, as well as the large ear and earspool at the back of the head and elements of the headdress. Fine incisions on and to the side of the lips may indicate a mustache.

BIBLIOGRAPHY
Unpublished.

233. Plaque with Incisions

900–600 B.C.
Provenance: Upper Balsas River Basin
Material: mottled light-to-dark green serpentine with surface calcifications
Dimensions: diam. 15.2 cm.; d. 2 cm.
Private collection

Incised on the convex side, this object may have been an effigy of a mirror, similar to cat. no. 130, or a mirror back, perhaps a support for a mosaic of obsidian or jade. The concave side is heavily calcified. The incisions, which occupy the lower half of the surface, recall the composition on the lower half of cat. no. 171; a number of other, similarly incised plaques are reportedly from Guerrero.[1] The face is contained in a cleft rectangle; the almond-shaped eyes are incised with irises and the nostrils sit atop the trapezoidal mouth. A sharp, banded triangle emerging from the cleft, similar to the pointed elements inside fringed motifs on cat. no. 198, is most likely a symbol of vegetation (see Schele, this volume, fig. 3d).

BIBLIOGRAPHY
Peter David Joralemon, "A Study of Olmec Iconography," *Studies in Pre-Columbian Art and Archaeology*, no. 7 (Washington, D.C., 1971), fig. 185.
Virginia M. Fields, "The Iconographic Heritage of the Maya Jester God," in *Sixth Palenque Round Table, 1986*, ed. Virginia M. Fields (Norman, Okla., 1991), fig. 5c.

NOTE
1. See Emile Deletaille, *Rediscovered Masterpieces* (Boulogne, 1985), no. 30; Peter David Joralemon, "A Study of Olmec Iconography," in *Studies in Pre-Columbian Art and Archaeology*, no. 7 (Washington, D.C., 1971), fig. 186.

234. Plaque with Incisions

900–600 B.C.
Provenance: Upper Balsas River Basin
Material: greenstone breccia with distinctly separate zones
of light and dark green
Dimensions: h. 20 cm.; w. 10 cm.; d. 2 cm.
Private collection

This slightly concave, oval slab of greenstone has a
subtly raised, tapering ridge along one side, forming
an effigy of a clam shell. The center is incised with
the profile of a supernatural with a deeply cleft head,
downturned L-shaped eye, projecting upper lip,
and bifurcated fang descending from the upper jaw.
A similar, unincised effigy was discovered in Offering
1942-A at La Venta.[1] The eye and flame eyebrow repeat
motifs on the wooden mask from Canon de la Mano,
Guerrero (see cat. no. 92, fig. 2). A hole is drilled off
center toward the back of the profile.

BIBLIOGRAPHY
Peter David Joralemon, "The Olmec Dragon: A Study in
Pre-Columbian Iconography," in *Origins of Religious Art and
Iconography in Preclassic Mesoamerica*, ed. Henry B. Nicholson
(Los Angeles, 1976), fig. 14b.

NOTE
1. Philip Drucker, Robert F. Heizer, and Robert J. Squier, "Excavations at La Venta, Tabasco, 1955," *Bureau of American Ethnology,*
Bulletin 170 (1959): 272.

235. Hunchback

900–600 B.C.
Provenance: Guerrero
Material: mottled very dark-to-light green serpentine
Dimensions: h. 7.5 cm.; w. 2.5 cm.; d. 3 cm.
Private collection

Combining the rounded head of a dwarf and the
pigeon-chested posture of a hunchback, this figure
is conceived in geometric terms that may reflect the
influence of Mezcala. The head, upper torso, stomach,
legs, and feet are distinct units. The large sphere of
the head and the bulbous upper torso seem inade-
quately supported by the lower body and diminutive
feet. Though undifferentiated, the mass of the hands,
extended from spindly arms, suggests something held
or offered, as in cat. no. 213. The softly rounded triangular belly articulates the otherwise solid block of the
legs. The face exhibits the same geometric organization as the body, with the nose and mouth formed by
horizontal divisions inside a trapezoid. The eyes are
treated in a curious manner. The eyeballs are grotesquely exaggerated and project as if too large to be
contained within the sockets.

BIBLIOGRAPHY
Unpublished.

236. Seted Figure

1200–900 B.C.
Provenance: Las Bocas, Puebla
Material: solid buff clay with traces of red pigment
Dimensions: h. 6 cm.; w. 5 cm.; d. 4 cm.
Private collection

With the right hand touching the left shoulder, this figure leans forward over crossed legs. The head is tilted and the expression on the face is animated, the mouth open as if in conversation. While there is no clear indication of gender, the delicate features, long ponytail down the back, and small breasts point to a female.

Topped with a large button, the domed headdress (fig. 1) is decorated on the front with a floral motif framed by red pigment. Downturned, L-shaped eyes surmounted by incised flame eyebrows incised on the headdress, attributes of the Olmec Dragon, are strong evidence of the incorporation of the Olmec symbol system into a regional tradition of ceramic figures.

Flame eyebrows, gum brackets, and crossed-bands—*pars pro toto* representations of the Olmec

Figure 1. Detail of head.

Dragon—appear on blackware ceramic vessels from the centers of San Lorenzo, Veracruz, Chalcatzingo, Morelos, and San Jose Mogote, Oaxaca.[1] While the mode of depicting the dragon was constant throughout Formative period Mesoamerica, the peoples of these centers appropriated the symbols in various ways. In an analysis of ceramic sherds from the Valley of Oaxaca, Nanette M. Pyne concluded that these symbolic motifs were associated with a particular family or group of families.[2] Kent V. Flannery and Joyce Marcus have noted that, "In Oaxaca, excised fire-serpents are associated with men's burials. . . . In the Basin of Mexico, they are associated with women's burials."[3]

These motifs were the visualization of a shared ideology and symbols taken by families, perhaps to establish mythic ancestry under the aegis of the supernatural. The incorporation of these motifs into the headdress of this figure indicate her supernatural associations and may identify her as a member of a specific clan.

BIBLIOGRAPHY
Unpublished.

NOTES
1. Michael D. Coe and Richard A. Diehl, *In the Land of the Olmec: The Archaeology of San Lorenzo Tenochtitlán*, vol. 1 (Austin, Tex., 1980), 162–71; Ann Cyphers Guillén, "Ceramics," in *Ancient Chalcatzingo*, ed. David C. Grove (Austin, Tex., 1987), 210–11; Kent V. Flannery and Joyce Marcus, *Early Formative Pottery of the Valley of Oaxaca, Mexico* (Ann Arbor, 1994), 157–80; 259–68.
2. Nanette M. Pyne "The Fire-Serpent and Were-Jaguar in Formative Oaxaca: A Contingency Table Analysis," in *The Early Mesoamerican Village*, ed. Kent V. Flannery (New York, 1976), 272–80.
3. Flannery and Marcus (as in note 1), 390; see also Paul Tolstoy, "Western Mesoamerica and the Olmec" in *Regional Perspectives on the Olmec*, ed. Robert J. Sharer and David C. Grove (Cambridge, 1989), 275–302.

237. Reclining Hollow Figure ▶

1200–900 B.C.
Provenance: Las Bocas, Puebla
Material: hollow buff clay with red pigment
Dimensions: h. 6.5 cm; w. 13 cm.; d. 5 cm.
Private collection

This slender figure with compact breasts reclines languidly, head supported by the left hand, right leg drawn up and right hand draped over the hip. The carved cosmic motifs on her body belie her casual pose. Feathery flame eyebrows are pierced above the breast, two holes on the torso indicate nostrils, and a mouth with a long central tooth flanked by L-shaped brackets is cut into her abdomen. Similar brackets pierce her head. A small band cuts through the right leg; diagonal slashes with a diamond on the left thigh are probably a partial crossed-bands motif. The motif on the abdomen may indicate her status or bloodline. A similar motif on a roller seal from Puebla has been associated with rain (see Taube, this volume, fig. 5c). The small piece of stone under the left arm is not original to the piece.

A standing male figure (fig. 1) is pierced with a similar, but more elaborate pattern of cosmic symbols. On the right side of the chest is an inverted form of the bracket that appears on the head and abdomen of this figure; on the left side, a long triangular form with incised radiating lines at the bottom recalls elements incised on the sides of cat. nos. 118 and 224. A four-sided star shape is placed directly at the center of the chest. On the right side of the stomach, pierced and incised, is a three-pronged bar seen on the backs of the heads of cat. nos. 238 and 239c. A crossed-bands motif, with a central star symbol and radiating incised lines, cut into the right thigh completes the motif on the left thigh of the figure here. A cosmic configuration of a cleft above and below a four-sided star symbol is incised on the right shin.

In both objects, the incised designs may reflect the actual decoration of the body with pigment-covered roller seals (see cat. no. 210).

BIBLIOGRAPHY
Unpublished.

Figure 1. Standing figure with incisions, 1000–500, Mexico, beige slipped earthenware, h. 27 cm. Private collection.

238. Two Standing Figures ▶

1200–900 B.C.
Provenance: Las Bocas, Puebla
Material: solid buff clay with traces of red pigment
Dimensions: left: h. 12.5 cm.; w. 5 cm.; d. 3 cm.;
right: h. 12.5 cm.; w. 6.5 cm.; d. 3 cm.
Private collection

Judging by their silhouettes, two matrons are represented here. The short-waisted figures have ample hips, full abdomens, and fleshy thighs accentuated by incised lines that separate them from the stomachs and define the groin area. The lower legs taper to small feet in both figures. The thin arms of the figure on the left, which fall to either side and slightly forward of the body, are attached at the hips probably for support; the raised arms of the figure on the right are attached below the breasts by small struts of clay.

Each face is distinctive: broad and open on the left; more refined and haughty, with pursed lips, on the right. The former figure, wearing earrings, has her hair swept forward and tied in a knot at the front with a long tress trailing down the back. The latter, with two shells on her high forehead, perhaps prized ornaments imported from a distant coast, is modeled without hair. These figures are carved with what seem to be sky symbols: the back of each head is hollowed out in a horizontal bar with three vertical spikes that may be a stylization of a cloud (fig. 1). A similar motif is carved into the back of a large hollow figure in The Metropolitan Museum of Art (see cat. no. 7, fig. 1). The placement and appearance of this motif on these figures may be symbolic and identify them as members of the same family or clan.

BIBLIOGRAPHY
Unpublished.

Figure 1. Back view.

239a. Reclining Figure

1200–900 B.C.
Provenance: Las Bocas, Puebla
Material: solid buff clay with red color
Dimensions: h. 6 cm.; w. 12.2 cm.; d. 3 cm.
Private collection

BIBLIOGRAPHY
Unpublished.

239b. Reclining Figure

1200–900 B.C.
Provenance: Las Bocas, Puebla
Material: solid buff clay
Dimensions: h. 6.5 cm.; w. 14.5 cm.; d. 3 cm.
Private collection

BIBLIOGRAPHY
Unpublished.

239c. Seated Figure

1200–900 B.C.
Provenance: Las Bocas, Puebla
Material: solid buff clay
Dimensions: h. 8.5 cm.; w. 7 cm.; d. 7 cm.
Private collection

BIBLIOGRAPHY
Unpublished.

239d. Seated Figure

1200–900 B.C.
Provenance: Las Bocas, Puebla
Material: solid clay, ivory slip with red color
Dimensions: h. 9 cm.; w. 7 cm.; d. 6.5 cm.
Private collection

BIBLIOGRAPHY
Unpublished.

239e. Seated Figure

1200–900 B.C.
Provenance: Las Bocas, Puebla
Material: solid buff clay with red color
Dimensions: h. 7 cm.; w. 6.5 cm.; d. 5 cm.
Private collection

BIBLIOGRAPHY
Unpublished.

a.

b.

c.

d.

e.

f.

g.

h.

i.

239f. Standing Figure

1200–900 B.C.
Provenance: Las Bocas, Puebla
Material: solid buff clay with red color
Dimensions: h. 12 cm.; w. 5.5 cm.; d. 2.5 cm.
Private collection

BIBLIOGRAPHY
Unpublished.

239g. Standing Figure

1200–900 B.C.
Provenance: Las Bocas, Puebla
Material: solid ceramic, traces of slip and red pigment
Dimensions: h. 7 cm.; w. 2.5 cm.; d. 3 cm.
Private collection

BIBLIOGRAPHY
Unpublished.

239h. Standing Figure

1200–900 B.C.
Provenance: Las Bocas, Puebla
Material: solid buff clay with red color
Dimensions: h. 13.4 cm.; w. 5.5 cm.; d. 3.5 cm.
Private collection

BIBLIOGRAPHY
Unpublished.

239i. Two Standing Figures

1200–900 B.C.
Provenance: Las Bocas, Puebla
Material: solid buff clay, ivory slip, traces of red pigment
Dimensions: left: h. 9.6 cm.; w. 5.5 cm.; d. 2.5 cm.;
right: h. 10 cm.; w. 5 cm.; d. 2.5 cm.
Private collection

BIBLIOGRAPHY
Unpublished.

The movement and gestures, the vivacity and expressive range, of the figures in this group set them apart from previously published ceramic figures from the highlands. With few exceptions, the proportions of the figures are naturalistically observed, if somewhat exaggerated, and the finely modeled faces are individually and delightfully characterized. In almost all cases, and most emphatically in the male figures, the mouth with filed teeth is characteristically Olmec and remarkable in its detail, as are the hair, headdresses, and ornaments in figures of such small scale. The abstract treatment of the eyes—blank, slightly raised areas under arching brows, neither incised nor painted, and, in the figure on the right, cat. no. 239i , completely flat—is curiously at odds with the otherwise highly expressive faces. Although no trace remains, the eyes may have been painted on with a fugitive pigment that has disintegrated, although the red coloring on the figures has remained remarkably intact. It is more likely that the "eyelessness" of these figurines is symbolic in a way that does not contradict their informal, genrelike appearance. Unified stylistically, cat. nos. 235 through 239i form an ensemble, a cast of characters of types and possibly individuals in an extended family, clan, or highland village community. The eyelessness may indicate they are deceased, ancestral archetypes or spirit counterparts and companions of a familial or social group. While it is more likely they form a generalized community, they may represent members of a particular family or clan: some possibly mythic, identified by the pierced symbols, historic, or recently deceased and individualized by their physical appearance, a telling gesture, or some other familiar or identifying detail.

Not always easy to characterize, the figures have vivid and distinctive personalities: cat. no. 239a reclines with voluptuous languor while cat. 239b is stretched out rather stiffly and scowls. The thickset figure in cat. no. 239c is intent on something originally held in his broken right hand; while cat. no. 239d appears to be engaged in nothing more eventful than scratching his back. The women provide the most varied and charming repertory. While the general pose of cat. no. 239h may recall the "pretty ladies" of Tlatilco (see Tate, this volume, fig. 3), the softly feminine movement of her right hand as she adjusts her headdress and the way she holds the long lock of hair with her left is more naturalistic and individualized than in comparable types from Tlatilco. The unusual gesture of cat. no. 239e, seated cross-legged, leaning forward with her head raised and holding her right breast, takes on a certain significance because of the pierced diagonal bars on her chest. The most disarming of the female figures is the coquettish young woman in cat. no. 239g, with her tall, soft body, peculiarly elongated head, pouty lips, and long, drawn-out eyes. Holding an object behind her back, possibly a gourd or toadstool, she seems to mince forward, her head slightly projected in the direction of the object of her attentions, the recipient of her "surprise." This coy figure is in sharp contrast to the pugnacious stances of the figures in cat. no 239i and the matronlike sturdiness of cat. no. 239f.

The figures sport a wonderful range of hair styles from pompadours to sidelocks and long ponytails. There is great diversity in the patterns of hair on otherwise shaved heads, but the most interesting are the variations on the spondyllus motif on cat. nos. 239c, e, g, and i. Because of the incised texture, it is not clear if they are actual shells, as in cat. no. 238, or hair cut in the form of a shell. The hair styles may be ceremonial, signs of status or other form of identification, or simply reflect actual fashion. These animated and expressive figurines put a human, familiar face on the people of the highlands in the Formative period and, apart from their possible symbolic or mythic content, provide a rare and tantalizing picture of a community of social beings, individualized by physical type and subject to a range of emotions, foibles, and vanities.

240. Two Figures Embracing ▶

1200–900 B.C.
Provenance: Las Bocas, Puebla
Material: solid buff clay with dark ivory slip and traces of red pigment
Dimensions: h. 9 cm.; w. 4.9 cm.; d. 6 cm.
Private collection

An old man, his mouth contorted into a leer, embraces a young woman. Straddling her open thighs, he thrusts his left hand under her belt to grab her buttocks as if to draw her closer. Heads pressed side to side, they look over each other's shoulders. She has Olmec features and long hair; he, a bald pate, bulbous nose, sunken cheeks, slanted eyes, and ridged brows drawn out to prominent ears. Except for the face of the old man, which is modeled in detail, the figures are broadly handled with heavy, unarticulated limbs. A residue of red pigment covers the body of the woman and the left arm of the man.

Rather than simply a bawdy genre scene, this couple from Las Bocas may have a mythic dimension.[1] A universal theme, it is often humorously and more discreetly represented in Classic Maya figurines from Jaina, where beautiful women appear with underworld deities in the form of old men.[2]

BIBLIOGRAPHY
Unpublished.

NOTES
1. A similar composition is reported in another Las Bocas
   figurine in the National Museum of Anthropology in Mexico
   City. See Franz Feuchtwanger, *Ceramica Olmeca* (Mexico City,
   1989), 39–40.
2. Linda Schele and Mary Ellen Miller, *The Blood of Kings: Dynasty
   and Ritual in Maya Art* (Fort Worth, 1986), 153, pl. 53.

241. Two Standing Figures ▶

1200–900 B.C.
Provenance: Las Bocas, Puebla
Material: solid buff clay with cream slip and traces of red
and black pigment
Dimensions: left: h. 5.1 cm.; w. 2.5 cm.; d. 1.8 cm.;
right: h. 5.1 cm.; w. 3.3 cm.; d. 1.9 cm.
Private collection

These miniature figures, whose costumes are rendered
in sharp detail, are most likely ballplayers. One figure
is painted principally black with accents of red and the
other, red with accents of black, perhaps to identify
their teams or positions on the court. Since most Olmec
three-dimensional figures are depicted without clothing save the occasional loincloth or headwear, these
offer a remarkable glimpse into Olmec costuming.[1]
Each figure wears a thick belt at the waist, probably a
yoke, attached in a fashion similar to cat. no. 135. The
broad band looped around the front appears to be
connected to a loincloth draped between the legs and
over the buttocks. Each figure holds in the right hand
an object that may be a counterweight. The black
figure wears a short cape with a high, striated collar;
the red figure seems to have hip-length hair cascading
down the back from a headdress or cloth attachment.

The two figures wear masks covering their faces to
the narrow slits of their eyes. Ear dangles worn by the

red figure are broken on the black figure. Small furrows on the browlines are similar to those on stone
masks and axes. Both headbands have curved, arched
bands, but they differ at the top: a tripartite plaque
occurs on the black figure and a thick band surmounted by a curved horizontal object, convex in the
center and pinched at the ends, on the red figure.

The tilt of the hip and shoulder and the position
of the legs in the black figure display a keen understanding of bodily motion; the red figure, despite the
loss of the left leg, shows a similar sense of movement.
While the elaborate costumes are similar in appearance to those worn by ballplayer figurines from
Tlapacoya, the active postures of these two figures
contrast with the stiff stances seen in other examples,
who seem weighed down by their towering headdresses and bulky attire.[2]

BIBLIOGRAPHY
Unpublished.

NOTES
1. See Franz Feuchtwanger, *Ceramica Olmeca* (Mexico City, 1989),
   no. 72 and cat. no. 180 for objects of similar size and treatment.
2. See Michael D. Coe, *The Jaguar's Children: Pre-Classic Mexico*
   (New York, 1965), nos. 151, 152, 158; Christine Niederberger
   Betton, *Paleopaysages et archeologie pre-urbaine du Bassin de
   Mexico*, vol. 1 (Mexico City, 1987), figs. 281–90.; Douglas Bradley
   and Peter David Joralemon, *The Lords of Life* (Notre Dame, Ind.,
   1992), no. 1.

242. Seated Hollow Figure

1200–900 B.C.
Provenance: Tlatilco, Mexico
Material: clay with traces of red pigment
Dimensions: h. 22.8 cm; w. 23.5 cm.; d. 13 cm.
Private collection

This hollow ceramic figure depicts a rotund infant with avian attributes. The eyes themselves, long incisions articulated with irises, are human, but the concave areas surrounding them, raised at the edges, recall the circular plumage around the eyes of an owl or owlet. The nose tapers to a small hooked beak. The open mouth is human, with a sharp tooth visible at the top, possibly an egg tooth. On the forehead are two roughly textured shell-shaped mounds similar to the downy tufts on the heads of the young birds in

cat. nos. 57 and 58. The dimpled chin, all but lost in the fleshy jowls, overhangs the fat body. Striped on the sides with a grid pattern at the groin, the unusual diaperlike costume is pulled taut under the distended belly with protruding navel. The stubby, fleshy arms and legs are extended, the toes curled and nails incised. The earlobes are pierced.

The seated, upright pose with arms extended is similar to that of the infant in cat. no. 2. Shamanic flight is represented in this infantlike creature as it transforms into the shaman's avian spirit companion.

BIBLIOGRAPHY
Unpublished.

243a. Seated Figure

1200–900 B.C.
Provenance: Tlapacoya, Mexico
Material: clay with white slip
Dimensions: h. 14 cm.; w. 9 cm.; d. 8 cm.
Private collection

BIBLIOGRAPHY
Unpublished.

243b. Seated Figure

1200–900 B.C.
Provenance: Las Bocas, Puebla
Material: clay with white-ivory slip and traces of red pigment
Dimensions: h. 13.5 cm.; w. 8 cm.; d. 10 cm.
Private collection

BIBLIOGRAPHY
Emile Deletaille, *Rediscovered Masterpieces* (Boulogne, 1985),
   no. 132.

243c. Seated Figure

1200–900 B.C.
Provenance: Tlatilco, Mexico
Material: clay with white-ivory slip and traces of red pigment
Dimensions: h. 10 cm.; w. 6.5 cm.; d. 6.5 cm.
Private collection

BIBLIOGRAPHY
Unpublished.

243d. Standing Figure

1200–900 B.C.
Provenance: Las Bocas, Puebla
Material: clay with slip and traces of red pigment
Dimensions: h. 13.2 cm.; w. 5 cm.; d. 2 cm.
Anonymous loan to The Art Museum, Princeton University

These comfortably, almost nonchalantly, posed figures from Las Bocas, Tlapacoya, and Tlatilco exhibit a remarkable uniformity of style. The broad shoulders and the soft breasts and torso of the male figure in cat. no. 243a are in sharp contrast to his stiff, unarticulated limbs. Sitting in a cross-legged position, the right arm clasps the right leg, the left arm is drawn across the thighs. The right foot is broken. The elongated head and features of the face are strongly Olmec.

The fuller breasts of cat. nos. 243b and c would indicate they are women. Broad shouldered, the bodies and limbs are also thicker than those of the male figure from Tlapacoya. Wearing a short fringed skirt and a tall, close-fitting cap, the figure in cat. 243b sits with the left leg drawn under the extended right leg; the right arm, whose elbow appears to bend forward, rests on the ground. The figure from Tlatilco, cat. no. 243c, wears a turbanlike coiffure, parted down the middle and hanging to the right side. She sits cross-legged, the left arm touching the left knee, the right arm against the right thigh. Both the faces are similar except for the angle of the eyes. The surfaces of the figures are abraded and pitted, though the red pigment on the headdresses is well-preserved.

Standing male figures in clay from Las Bocas (see cat. no. 237, fig. 1) may be comparable in refinement to their counterparts in jade and greenstone. The figure (cat. no. 243d) wears a plain short kilt and stands with legs apart, firmly planted and the feet angled; the arms hang straight at the sides with hands slightly curled. The head and face are purely Olmec in style and expression. The narrow and elongated head, with long flange ears is in sharp contrast to the stocky body. The upper lip is full, the lower lip punctuated by four sharp triangular teeth, which were probably filed as a sign of elite status similar to deformation of the head (see cat. no. 239a–i).[1]

BIBLIOGRAPHY
Unpublished.

NOTE
1. Romàn Piña Chán, *The Olmec* (New York, 1989), 47.

a.

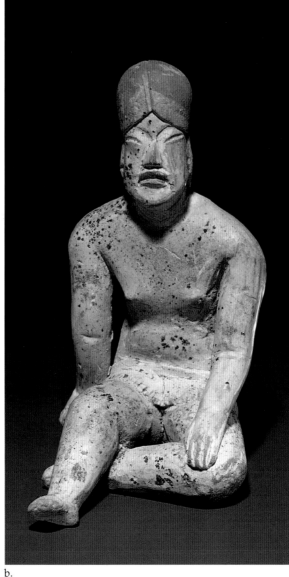

b.

c.

244. Peccary Effigy Vessel

d.

1000–700 B.C.
Provenance: Tlatilco, Mexico
Material: clay with traces of red-brown pigment
Dimensions: h. 19 cm.; w. 24.5 cm.; d. 15 cm.
National Museum of the American Indian, Smithsonian
Institution

Very different in sprit from animal effigy vessels
from Las Bocas, the peccary is vividly captured in the
simple volumes and exaggerated proportions of this
effigy vessel from Tlatilco. The compressed, hunched
body tapers to a cone to form the opening of the vessel.
The nostrils on the blunt snout and the slit eyes with
small indentations for irises are incised. Small, peaked
ears are perched atop the large head, and four stumpy
legs support the great hulking mass. The vessel is
painted with a red-brown pigment and impressed
with rocker-stamp decorations.

BIBLIOGRAPHY

Muriel Noé Porter, "Tlatilco and the Pre-Classic Cultures of the
New World," *Viking Fund Publications in Archaeology*, no. 19
(New York, 1953), pl. 9h.
Muriel P. Weaver, *The Aztecs, Maya, and Their Predecessors* (New
York, 1972), pl. 4k.
Masterworks from the Museum of the American Indian Foundation
(New York, 1973), no. 32.

245. Bottle in the Form of a Temple

1200–900 B.C.
Provenance: Tlatilco, Mexico
Material: mottled white-to-buff clay with kaolin slip and traces of cinnabar
Dimensions: h. 22 cm.; w. 11.7 cm.; d. 10.6 cm.
Collection of Herbert L. Lucas, Class of 1950, on loan to The Art Museum, Princeton University

A rare Formative period representation of an architectural structure, perhaps a temple or house, this vessel was most likely used as an incense burner. It is divided into three tiers: a high, plain base or foundation marked at the edges by incised lines; a chamber with the front and side walls executed in an openwork of incised bands, with a rectangular opening at the front and closed at the back. The roof with a curved overhang contains the mouth of the vessel. The interior is chambered to form a flue from the top to the bottom; the small rectangle on the right side of the base would create the draft and send the fumes up through the mouth of the vessel.

The rectangular opening on the middle tier is flanked by opposed Z-shaped motifs with curved bands on the right and scrolled bands on the left. The latter motif, found on the bases of fish vessels (see cat. no. 54), is probably a symbol of water and clouds. The meaning of the former symbol is not clear but may lie in its opposition to the cloud and water symbol.

The open work on the sides is in the form of two crossed bars forming a diamond in the center, pierced by a four-pointed star with concave sides, symbolic of the celestial level of the cosmos. At the front of the vessel, the sloped roof rises to form a curved overhang. The shape of the roof is the same as the headdress of the supernatural in cat. no. 199 and the headdress of the niche figure on La Venta Altar 5, which have been interpreted as symbols of clouds and rain.[1] If this is indeed an incense burner, the smoke would have risen through the opening in the roof like clouds. Empowered with symbols of the cosmos, clouds, and water, this vessel may have been used in rain rituals.

BIBLIOGRAPHY

Michael D. Coe, *The Jaguar's Children: Pre-Classic Central Mexico* (New York, 1965), no. 80.

Elizabeth K. Easby, *Ancient Art of Latin America from the Collection of Jay C. Leff* (New York, 1966), no. 68.

Franz Feuchtwanger, *Ceramica Olmeca* (Mexico City, 1989), no. 109.

NOTE

1. See David C. Grove, "Chalcatzingo and Its Olmec Connection," in *Regional Perspectives on the Olmec*, ed. Robert J. Sharer and David C. Grove (Cambridge, 1989), 134, and Taube, this volume.

a.

246a. Dish

1200–900 B.C.
Provenance: Las Bocas, Puebla
Material: clay with traces of cinnabar
Dimensions: h. 3.2 cm.; diam. 14.5
Anonymous loan to The Art Museum, Princeton University

This small, simple plate is remarkable in the subtle range of colors and random pattern created by fire-clouding. The linear elements may have been created by the application of vegetative fibers.

BIBLIOGRAPHY
Emile Deletaille, *Rediscovered Masterpieces* (Boulogne, 1985), no. 50.
Trésors du nouveau monde, Royal Museum of Art and History (Brussels, 1992), fig. 81.

246b. *Tecomate*

1200–900 B.C.
Provenance: Tlatilco, Mexico
Material: clay with kaolin slip
Dimensions: h. 10 cm.; diam. 12.5 cm.
Anonymous loan to The Art Museum, Princeton University

BIBLIOGRAPHY
Unpublished.

246c. *Tecomate*

1200–900 B.C.
Provenance: Las Bocas, Puebla
Material: clay with kaolin slip
Dimensions: h. 10.3 cm.; diam. 13.8 cm.
Anonymous loan to The Art Museum, Princeton University

BIBLIOGRAPHY
Emile Deletaille, *Rediscovered Masterpieces* (Boulogne, 1985), no. 50.
Trésors du nouveau monde, Royal Museum of Art and History (Brussels, 1992), fig. 82.

Among the most elegant and striking ceramics produced at Tlatilco and Las Bocas are *tecomates*, subspherical bowls with eggshell-thin, pale, cream-slipped walls. *Tecomates* take their form from gourds used as water containers. The thin trail of orange fire-clouding on cat. no. 246b may have been produced by the application of a wet blade of grass to the bowl in the firing; cat. no. 246c is unusual in the extent and prominence of the fire-clouding in orange and black.

b.

c.

248. Spouted Tray

1200–900 B.C.
Provenance: Tlatilco, Mexico
Material: clay with kaolin slip and traces of cinnabar
Dimensions: h. 30 cm.; w. 24.2 cm.; d. 4 cm.
Anonymous loan to The Art Museum, Princeton University

Several of these low-sided, spouted trays were found in burials at Tlatilco; smaller, circular ones without spouts are also known. While the function of these objects is uncertain, this example still has a considerable amount of cinnabar visible on its surface, and may have been a pallet for mixing this pigment.

BIBLIOGRAPHY
Unpublished.

247. Bottle with Lattice Base

1200–900 B.C.
Provenance: Las Bocas, Puebla
Material: clay with traces of red pigment
Dimensions: h. 22.3 cm.; diam. 12.5 cm.
Private collection

The highly burnished, long-necked blackware vessel sits on a latticework base. Whether the design is functional or decorative cannot be determined. The elegant proportions of the bottle are heightened by the contrasting color of the stand, which still has extensive traces of the red pigment with which it was covered.

BIBLIOGRAPHY
Michael D. Coe, *The Jaguar's Children: Pre-Classic Central Mexico* (New York, 1965), no. 35.
Franz Feuchtwanger, *Ceramica Olmeca* (Mexico City, 1989), no. 145.

249. Pumpkin Effigy Vessel

1000–500 B.C.
Provenance: Las Bocas, Puebla
Material: polished black earthenware
Dimensions: h. 9.5 cm.; w. 16.5 cm.
The Saint Louis Art Museum, gift of Morton D. May

BIBLIOGRAPHY
Lee A. Parsons, *Pre-Columbian Art: The Morton D. May and The Saint Louis Art Museum Collections* (Saint Louis, 1980), no. 15.

250. Squash Effigy Vessel

1200–900 B.C.
Provenance: Las Bocas, Puebla
Material: greenish-white onyx/marble with veins oxidized to rusty brown
Dimensions: h. 22 cm.; diam. 20 cm.
Private collection

These vessels, like the *tecomates* (see cat. nos. 246b, c), are derived from natural forms. Effigy vessels in the form of pumpkins and squash were common productions in the local traditions of Tlatilco and Las Bocas. They appear also in ritual objects and images like the *tlacuache* of cat. no. 62 and Chalcatzingo Monuments 6, 14, and 15, where they are associated with fertility and rain.[1]

The blackware vessel of cat. no. 249 in the shape of a pumpkin stands on its side, with a wide wedge cut into it to form the mouth of the bowl. The stem at the top of the pumpkin can be seen just below the center of the mouth. The onyx vessel of cat. no. 250 is in the form of a complete gourd; the stem is the lid handle.[2]

Pumpkins and squash, among the earliest cultivated crops in the Americas, must have been important sources of food for the Olmec, as they were for later Mesoamerican cultures, who also made effigies of these crops.

BIBLIOGRAPHY
Unpublished.

NOTES
1. Jorge Angulo, v, "The Chalcatzingo Reliefs: An Iconographic Analysis," in *Ancient Chalcatzingo*, ed. David C. Grove (Austin, Tex., 1987), 139.
2. Ronald L. Bishop (personal communication, May 1995) has suggested that many of the vessels previously classified as onyx may in fact be made from stalactitic stone.

251. Heart-Shaped Effigy Vessel

1200–900 B.C.
Provenance: Las Bocas, Puebla
Material: clay with slip and traces of red pigment
Dimensions: h. 11.4 cm.; w. 7.6 cm.; d. 5.1 cm.
Private collection

It is not clear if this vessel represents a personified heart or a victim offering its heart. The figure is seated, the right leg folded back and the left bent flat to the ground, the foot touching the right thigh. The head is modeled in the Olmec style and the hair or cap, composed of three wide bands, resembles the shell head ornaments seen in cat. nos. 238 and 239c. The arms are folded over the chest, or lid, of the container.

The anatomical details of the heart are correctly observed. Divided vertically into the right and left ventricles, the curved projections emerging from the rounded part of the lid correspond to the pulmonary veins and arteries. Curved raised areas enclosing circles are carved above and below the lid.

There are no known representations in Olmec art of the act of human sacrifice, suggested by the image of this vessel, other than the possible interpretation of the zoomorph projected from the breast of the sacrificial victim incised on the right arm of the Young Lord (cat. no. 193). It was perhaps anathema to the Olmec to show such an act or, more characteristically, to show such explicit narrative action. Human sacrifice may be encoded in representations symbolizing the transformation of the blood sacrifice into rain and vegetation.

BIBLIOGRAPHY
Franz Feuchtwanger, *Ceramica Olmeca* (Mexico City, 1989), nos. 61, 62.

252. Vessel in the Form of a Kneeling Skeletonized Woman

1200–900 B.C.
Provenance: Santa Cruz, Morelos
Material: clay with white slip
Dimensions: h: 21.6 cm.; w. 12.5 cm.
Raymond and Laura Wielgus Collection

In the form of a kneeling, skeletonized figure, this vessel is one of the most powerful and haunting images to have survived not just from the Early Formative period but from all pre-Columbian Mexico. While this vessel from the highlands shows little Olmec stylistic influence, it embodies themes at the heart of Olmec ritual and central to the lives of the peoples of Formative period Mesoamerica.

Although depicted as an ancient crone with dry, sagging breasts, the swollen belly has been taken to indicate pregnancy, and the yawning mouth, the spout of the vessel, with the greatly distended lower jaw and lip as a howl of pain. Peter David Joralemon has pointed out that the figure is in the traditional Mexican Indian birthing position and has proposed that this is an image of "the mother of all gods and humans, a deity appearing throughout ancient Mesoamerican cultures, who, along with her consort, determines exactly when each person will be born."[1]

The bald head is thrown back and the face contorted; the eyes, indented irises under modeled lids or brows, are reduced to long slits and the cheeks drawn into myriad creases. The nose is blunt with two prominent nostrils, and the flange ears, the only detail that reflects the Olmec style, are modeled with earspools in the lobes. Pulled up by the thrust of the head, the loose skin of the neck forms deep cavities between the central ridge of skin and the taut tendons to either side; scalloped folds of skin below the clavicle follow the lines of the upper rib cage and recede into the deep hollows formed by the fall of the flat breasts.

The sharply delineated rib cage continues at either side of the breasts and into the deformed back. Thin arms hug the sides of the body, the hands grabbing the sides of the folded-back legs. The form of the feet may be an attempt to articulate the turned-out heels. The thighs are parted and the triangular pubic area delineated from the overhanging stomach with distended navel.

If the figure is giving birth, an act of regeneration, this brings us full circle to the infants with which the catalogue began and those in the care of women, in one instance, cat. no. 5, with flat sagging breasts and possibly characterized as beyond child-bearing age, and in another, cat. no. 6, an old hag with her mouth open as if uttering a sound or cry. Human procreation and vegetative regeneration may be as inextricably linked in this figure as they seem to be in images on La Venta Altar 5 and in infants costumed as the Olmec Supernatural. Vegetative fertility, the central preoccupation of the Olmec, informs their sacred objects and images and is the principal issue of their rituals.

But why such a devastating image? Even where clearly of advanced age, none of the examples of women tending infants are as pointedly ravaged as this creature, who seems to transcend human gender and sexuality. The swollen belly may be a sign of pregnancy, but the desiccated, skeletal body, may also show the effect of hunger, of starvation; the kneeling position, with the head thrown back, may be that of supplication. There is convincing visual evidence in Olmec art of the ritual focus on rain, and drought

must have been a seasonal and constant concern. Perhaps this creature "in extremis" addresses such a desperate time and implores the heavens for the rain on which the harvest and the survival of its issue depends. The exaggeration of the mouth, due in part certainly to its function as the mouth of the vessel, may also reflect such an interpretation; the head is thrown back and the mouth held open, waiting to be filled. If the archetypal "mother of all gods and humans" is represented, the meaning of the image is enlarged from temporal to mythic time and the creature may await the primordial rains that will give life to the earth and her loins, vegetative and human fertility. The old woman embraces the cycle of life, as it is through the blood sacrifice of the progeny she bears that the blessings of rain and vegetation will issue and nourish life. If the image of the vessel is an earth figure, it is the primeval, parched earth, a still empty vessel, and, like the Olmec rulers, it must procure the life-giving waters.

BIBLIOGRAPHY
Michael D. Coe, *The Jaguar's Children: Pre-Classic Central Mexico* (New York, 1965), no. 77.
Peter David Joralemon, "The Old Woman and the Child: Themes in the Iconography of Preclassic Mesoamerica," in *The Olmec and Their Neighbors: Essays in Memory of Matthew W. Stirling*, ed. Elizabeth P. Benson (Washington, D.C., 1981), fig. 12.

NOTE
1. Peter David Joralemon, "The Old Woman and the Child: Themes in the Iconography of Preclassic Mesoamerica," in *The Olmec and Their Neighbors: Essays in Memory of Matthew W. Stirling*, ed. Elizabeth P. Benson (Washington, D.C., 1981), 179.

Photography Credits

The principal photographers for this catalogue are John Bigelow Taylor, Justin Kerr, and Bruce M. White. Other photographs were provided by the owners or curators of these works of art, and also by the photographers listed below.

John Bigelow Taylor: catalogue frontispiece; p. 5 fig. 2; p. 28 fig. 1b; p. 29 fig. 2, fig. 3, fig. 4; p. 34 fig. 9; p. 36 fig. 18; p. 42 fig. 34; p. 50 fig. 2; p. 51 fig. 3, fig. 4; p. 53 fig. 7, fig. 8, fig. 10; p. 55 fig. 12; p. 56 fig. 14; p. 59 fig. 18; p. 60 fig. 19; p. 71 fig. 4, fig. 5; p. 73 fig. 7; p. 75 fig. 10; p. 78 fig. 18; cat. nos.: 1, 1 fig. 1, 2, 3, 3 fig. 1, 4, 4 fig. 1, 7, 7 fig. 2, 11, 11 fig. 1, 13, 19, 20, 21, 22, 23, 23 fig. 1, 25, 26, 27, 28, 29, 30, 32, 33, 38 fig. 1, 39, 40, 41, 44, 44 fig. 1, 45, 45 fig. 1, 45 fig. 2, 48, 50, 51, 53, 54, 56, 58, 60, 63, 64, 66, 70, 73, 74, 75, 77, 79, 80, 84, 86, 93, 94, 95, 96, 97, 104, 104 fig. 1, 105, 106, 109, 113, 115, 117, 120, 121, 122, 124, 125, 125 fig. 2, 126, 127, 128, 132, 134, 134 fig. 1, 137, 139, 140, 142, 143, 144, 145, 146, 147, 147 fig. 1, 149, 150, 151, 153, 156, 157a, 157b, 157c, 166, 167, 170, 171, 172, 176, 177, 178, 178 fig. 1, 179, 180, 183, 184, 190, 191, 193, 193 fig. 1, 193 fig. 4, 194, 195, 196, 197, 203, 204, 206, 207, 208, 212, 213, 214, 217, 218, 219, 220, 221a, 221b, 222, 223, 224, 224 fig. 1, 225, 226, 227, 228, 229, 230, 231a, 231b, 232, 233, 234, 235, 236, 236 fig. 1, 237, 238, 238 fig. 1, 239a, 239b, 239c, 239d, 239e, 239f, 239g, 239h, 239i, 240, 241, 242, 243a, 243b, 243c, 247, 250.

Justin Kerr: frontispiece; p. 6 fig. 3; p. 8 fig. 9b; p. 35 fig. 16; p. 38 fig. 23; p. 42 fig. 35; p. 46 fig. 1; p. 54 fig. 11; p. 57 fig. 15; p. 59 fig. 17; p. 78 fig. 17; p. 104; cat. nos: 9, 10, 10 fig. 1, 12, 17, 34, 35, 37, 49, 49 fig. 1, 52, 57, 59, 65, 67, 68, 69, 72, 76, 82, 82 fig. 1, 83, 85, 87, 88, 92, 99, 100, 101, 102, 107 fig. 1, 112, 114, 116, 118, 119, 138, 141, 147 fig. 2, 154, 159, 160, 165, 169, 169 fig. 1, 173, 175, 182, 185, 186, 188, 189, 192, 192 fig. 1, 198, 198 fig. 1, 202, 237 fig. 1, 251.

Bruce M. White: cover; p. 28 fig. 1a; p. 34 fig. 10, fig. 11; p. 53 fig. 9; p. 70 fig. 3; p. 74 fig. 9; p. 77 fig. 15; p. 78 fig. 16; p. 208 fig. 1; cat. nos.: 6, 42, 42 fig. 2, 47, 62, 71, 78, 78 fig. 1, 89, 103, 108a, 108b, 110, 123, 129, 130, 133, 135, 136, 161, 162, 163, 181, 201, 201 fig. 1, 205, 209, 210, 211, 243d, 245, 246a, 246b, 246c, 248.

American Custom Maps: p. 2 fig. 1; p. 10 fig. 1; **American Museum of Natural History, Courtesy Department of Library Services:** p. 21 fig. 17 (neg. 326909, photo by Alex Rota); p. 82 fig. 1 (neg. 124109, photo by Alex Rota); cat. no. 192, fig. 2 (neg. 320582, photo by Alex Rota), cat. no. 199 (trans. 5333[3], photo by Craig Chesek), cat. no. 199 fig. 1 (neg. 124108, photo by Alex Rota); **E. Wyllys Andrews, v:** cat. no. 43; **John Blazejewski:** p. 40 fig. 29; cat. no. 37 fig. 3; **Peter Brenner:** cat. no. 107; **Stephen Briggs:** cat. no. 18; **Hillel Burger:** cat. no. 152; **James A. Campbell:** p. 33 fig. 7a, fig. 7b; cat. nos. 22 fig. 2, 23 fig. 2, 25 fig. 1, 124 fig. 1, 125 fig. 1, 125 fig. 3, 126 fig. 1, 127 fig. 1, 128 fig. 1, 153 fig. 1, 216 fig. 1; **Michael Cavanagh and Kevin Montague:** cat. nos. 16, 98, 252; **The Cleveland Museum of Art:** cat. nos. 14, 14 fig. 1, 148, 155, 200; **Courtesy of Michael D. Coe :** p. 14 fig. 5, fig. 6; p. 15 fig. 7; **Miguel Covarrubias:** p. 94 fig. 14; **The Dallas Museum of Art:** p. 7 fig. 5, fig. 6, fig. 7; p. 8 fig. 8, fig. 9a; cat. nos. 15, 91, 131, 174, 187, 215, 216; **Richard A. Diehl:** p. 14 fig. 4; p. 17 fig. 10; p. 18 fig. 13; p. 19 fig. 15; **Dumbarton Oaks Research Library and Collections, Washington, D.C.:** p. 20 fig. 16; p. 70 fig. 2; p. 73 fig. 8; cat. nos. 22 fig. 1, 42 fig. 1, 48 fig. 1, 50 fig. 1, 193 fig. 3; **Susan Einstein:** cat. no. 5; **Clem Fiori:** cat. no. 16 fig. 1, 42 fig. 3; **Peter T. Furst:** p. 72 fig. 6; p. 75 fig. 11, fig. 12; p. 77 fig. 14; **Kenneth Garrett:** p. 16 fig. 8, fig. 9; p. 17 fig. 11; **Carlo T. E. Gay:** p. 55 fig. 13; **Irmgard Groth-Kimball:** p. 52 fig. 5; cat. no. 34 fig. 2; **Courtesy of Gillett G. Griffin:** p. 58 fig. 13; cat. no. 204 fig. 1; **Robert Heizer/National Geographic Image Collection:** p. 18 fig. 12; **Carmelo Guadagno:** cat. no. 244; **Peter David Joralemon:** cat. no. 119 fig. 1; **Bob Kolbrener:** cat. nos. 1 fig. 2, 55, 203 fig. 1, 249; **Los Angeles County Museum of Art:** p. 68 fig. 1; cat. no. 46; **The Metro-politan Museum of Art:** cat. no. 7 fig. 1, 173 fig. 1; **Museum of Fine Arts, Boston:** cat. nos. 31, 61, 81, 164, 168; **Tina Najbjerg:** p. 13 fig. 3; p. 128, p. 162, p. 196, p. 224, p. 240, p. 277, p. 286, p. 300; Glossary; cat. no. 35 fig. 1, 56 fig. 1, 117 fig. 1; 186 fig. 1; cat. no. 193 fig. 2; **National Museum of the American Indian, Smithsonian Institution:** p. 60 fig. 20; cat. nos. 24, 90; **Keary Nichols:** p. 32 fig. 5; cat. no. 36; **Maggie Nimkin:** cat. no. 38; **Bill O'Connor:** cat. no. 8; **Kevin Perry, Interactive Computer Graphics Laboratory, Princeton University:** cat. no. 131 fig. 1; **James Porter:** p. 88 fig. 7b; p. 92 fig. 12b; p. 93 fig. 13b; p. 95 fig. 15a; **Frances Pratt:** p. 34 fig. 8; **F. Kent Reilly, III:** p. 26; p. 32 fig. 6; p. 35 fig. 12, fig. 13, fig. 14, fig. 15; p. 36 fig. 17, fig. 19; p. 37 fig. 20a, fig. 20b, fig. 21a, fig. 21b, fig. 22a, fig. 22b, fig. 22c; p. 38 fig. 24, fig. 25; p. 39 fig. 26, fig. 27; p. 40 fig. 28; p. 40 fig. 30; p. 41 fig. 31, fig. 32; p. 42 fig. 33; p. 52 fig. 6; cat. nos. 34 fig. 1, 37 fig. 1, 37 fig. 2, 70 fig. 1; **Neil Rettig:** p. 76 fig. 13; **Lloyd Rule:** cat. no. 158; **Linda Schele:** p. 89 fig. 8b; p. 90 fig. 9i; p. 106 fig. 1, fig. 2, fig. 3; p. 107 fig. 4, fig. 5, fig. 6, fig. 7, fig. 8; p. 108 fig. 9, fig. 10, fig. 11; p. 109 fig. 12, fig. 13, fig. 14; p. 110 fig. 15, p. 111 fig. 16, fig. 17, fig. 18, fig. 19, fig. 20; p. 112 fig. 21, fig. 22; p. 113 fig. 23, fig. 24; p. 114 fig. 25, fig. 26; p. 115 fig. 27, fig. 28, fig. 29; **David Stansbury:** p. 60 fig. 21; cat. no. 111; **Richard Stewart/National Geographic Image Collection:** p. 65 fig. 29; cat. no. 34 fig. 3; **Matthew W. Stirling/National Geographic Image Collection:** p. 18 fig. 14; **Carolyn E. Tate:** p. 61 fig. 22, fig. 23; p. 62 fig. 24, fig. 25; p. 63 fig. 26, fig. 27, fig. 28; **Karl A. Taube:** p. 84 fig. 1; p. 85 fig. 2, fig. 3; p. 86 fig. 4; p. 87 fig. 5, fig. 6; p. 88 fig. 7a, fig. 7c–f; p. 89 fig. 8a, fig. 8c–i; p. 90 fig. 9a–h, fig. 9j, fig. 10; p. 91 fig. 11; p. 92 fig. 12a, fig. 12c–e; p. 93 fig. 13a, fig. 13c–f; p. 95 fig. 15b–f; p. 96 fig. 16, fig. 17; p. 97 fig. 18, fig. 19; p. 98 fig. 20, fig. 21; p. 99 fig. 22; p. 100 fig. 23; p. 101 fig. 24.

Alison Speckman, Princeton, New Jersey, printed many of the black and white illustrations.

Selected Bibliography

Aicardi, Jean
1986   *Epilepsy in Children* (New York).
The Allentown Museum
1972   *Pre-Columbian Art of Mesoamerica from the Collection of Jay C. Leff* (Allentown, Pa.).
American Federation of Arts
1960   *Exotic Art from Ancient and Primitive Civilizations: A Selection from the Collection of Jay C. Leff* (New York).
Anderson, Benedict R. O'G.
1972   "The Idea of Power in Javanese Culture," in *Culture and Politics in Indonesia*, ed. Claire Holt (Ithaca, N.Y.), 1–69.
Anderson, James E.
1967   "The Human Skeletons," in *The Prehistory of the Tehuacan Valley: Environment and Subsistence*, vol. 1, ed. Douglas S. Byers (Austin, Tex.).
Andrews, E. Wyllys
1987   "Spoons and Knuckle-Dusters in Formative Mesoamerica," paper delivered at "III Texas Symposium: Olmec, Izapa, and the Development of Maya Civilization," Texas Meeting on Maya Heiroglyphic Writing.
Angulo V., Jorge
1987   "The Chalcatzingo Reliefs: An Iconographic Analysis," in *Ancient Chalcatzingo*, ed. David C. Grove (Austin, Tex.).
Anton, Ferdinand
1961   *Mexiko: Indianerkunst aus Präkolumbisherzeit* (Munich).
1965   *Alt-Mexico und seine Kunst* (Leipzig).
1979   *Primitive Art* (New York).
Anton, Ferdinand, and Frederick Dockstader
1968   *Pre-Columbian Art* (New York).
Balser, Carlos
1959   "Los 'Baby Faces' Olmecas de Costa Rica," in *Actas del XXXIII Congreso Internacional de Americanistas*, no. 2 (San José, Costa Rica).
1961a   "Some Costa Rican Motifs," in Samuel K. Lothrop et al., *Essays in Pre-Columbian Art and Archaeology* (Cambridge, Mass.).
1961b   "La influencia olmeca en algunos motivos de la arqueologia de Costa Rica," in *Informe Semestral* (Costa Rica).
Baudez, Claude-François
1992   "The Maya Snake Dance: Ritual and Cosmology," *Res* 21: 37–52.
Benitez, Susana Villasana
1988   "La Organización social de los Zoques de Tapalap, Chiapas," in *Estudios Recientes en el Area Zoque* (Chiapas).
Benson, Elizabeth P.
1968   (ed.) *Dumbarton Oaks Conference on the Olmec, October 28th and 29th, 1967* (Washington, D.C.).
1971a   (ed.) *Dumbarton Oaks Conference on Chavín* (Washington, D.C.).

1971b   "An Olmec Figure at Dumbarton Oaks," in *Studies in Pre-Columbian Art and Archaeology*, no. 8 (Washington, D.C.).
1972   (ed.) *The Cult of the Feline* (Washington, D.C.).
1981a   (ed.) *The Olmec and Their Neighbors: Essays in Memory of Matthew W. Stirling* (Washington, D.C.).
1981b   "Some Olmec Objects in the Robert Woods Bliss Collection at Dumbarton Oaks," in *The Olmec and Their Neighbors: Essays in Memory of Matthew W. Stirling*, ed. Elizabeth P. Benson (Washington D.C.), 95–108.
Benson, Elizabeth P., and Gillett G. Griffin
1984   (eds.) *Maya Iconography* (Princeton, N.J.).
Bernal, Ignacio
1969   *The Olmec World*, trans. Doris Heyden and Fernando Horcasitas (Berkeley).
Bernal-Garcia, Maria Elena
1993   "Carving Mountains in a Blue/Green Bowl: Mythological Urban Planning in Mesoamerica," Ph. D. diss., University of Texas at Austin.
Beyer, Hermann
1927   "Nota bibliográfica sobre 'Tribes and Temples' de F. Blom y O. La Farge," *El México Antiguo* 2: 305–13.
Bierhorst, John
1992   *History and Mythology of the Aztecs: The Codex Chimalpopoca* (Tucson).
Bishop, Ronald L., Frederick W. Lange, and
Elizabeth K. Easby
1991   "Jade in Mesoamerica," in *Jade*, ed. Roger Keverne (London).
Blom, Frans, and Oliver LaFarge
1926   *Tribes and Temples: A Record of the Expedition to Middle America Conducted by the Tulane University of Louisiana in 1925*, 2 vols. (New Orleans).
Bödiger, Ute
1965   *Die Religion der Tukano* (Cologne).
Borbolla, D. F. Rubín de la
1953   *Mexico: Monumentos historícos y arqueológicos* (Mexico City).
Bradley, Douglas E., and Peter David Joralemon
1992   *The Lords of Life: The Iconography of Power and Fertility in Preclassic Mesoamerica* (Notre Dame, Ind.).
Brodzky, Ann T., Rose Daneswich, and Nick Johnson
1974   "Stones, Bones, and Skin: Ritual and Shamanic Art," *Artscanada*, nos. 184–87.
Bromberg, Ann R.
1983   *Selected Works from the Dallas Museum of Art* (Dallas).
Brown, Leslie
1976   *Eagles of the World* (New York).
Bundage, B. C.
1979   *The Fifth Sun: Aztec Gods, Aztec World* (Austin, Tex.), 31–32.

Campbell, Jonathan A., and William W. Lamar
1989   *The Venomous Reptiles of Latin America* (Ithaca, N.Y.), 162–69.
Campbell, Lyle R., and Terrence S. Kaufman
1976   "A Linguistic Look at the Olmec," *American Antiquity* 41 (1): 80–89.
Capitaine, Fernando Winfield
1988   "La Estela 1 de La Mojarra, Veracruz, México," *Research Reports on Ancient Maya Writing*, no. 16 (Washington, D.C.).
1990   *La Estela 1 de La Mojarra* (Mexico City).
Carlsen, Robert, and Martin Prechtel
1991   "The Flowering of the Dead: An Interpretation of Highland Maya Culture," *Man* 26: 23–42.
Carlson, John B.
1981   "Olmec Concave Iron-Ore Mirrors: The Aesthetics of a Lithic Technology and the Lord of the Mirror (with an Illustrated Catalogue of Mirrors)," in *The Olmec and Their Neighbors: Essays in Memory of Matthew W. Stirling*, ed. Elizabeth P. Benson (Washington, D.C.), 117–38.
Carnegie Institute of Fine Arts
1959   *Exotic Art from Ancient and Primitive Civilizations: Collection of Jay C. Leff* (Pittsburgh).
Caso, Alfonso
1928   *Las estelas Zapotecas* (Mexico City).
1942   "Definición y extensión del complejo 'Olmeca,'" in *Mayas y Olmecas: Segunda Reunión de Mesa Redonda Sobre Problemas Antropológicos de México y Centro América* (Tuxtla Gutiérrez), 43–46.
1979   *Reyes y reinos de la Mixteca*, 2 vols. (Mexico City).
Caso, Alfonso, and Ignacio Bernal
1952   "Urnas de Oaxaca," in *Memorias del Instituto Nacional de Antropología e Historia*, vol. 2 (Mexico City).
Chang, K. C.
1983   *Art, Myth, and Ritual: The Path to Political Authority in Ancient China* (Cambridge, Mass.).
1988   "An Introduction to Korean Shamanism," in *Shamanism: The Spirit World of Korea*, ed. Richard W. I. Guisso and Chai-shin Yu (Berkeley), 30–51.
Clark, John E.
1990   "Olmecas, olmoquismo, y olmequización en mesoamérica," *Arqueología* 3: 49–54.
Clark, John E., and Michael Blake
1989   "El Origen de la civilización en Mesoamerica: Las Olmecas y Mokaya de la Soconusco de Chiapas, México," in *El Preclasico o formativo: avances y perspectivas*, ed. Martha Carmona Macías (Mexico City), 385–403.
Clewlow, C. William, Jr.
1970   "A Comparison of Two Unusual Olmec Monuments," in *Contributions of the University of California Archaeological Research Facility*, no. 8 (Berkeley), 35–40.

331

1974 "A Stylistic and Chronological Study of Olmec Monumental Sculpture," in *Contributions of the University of California Archaeological Research Facility*, no. 19 (Berkeley).

Cleveland Museum of Art
1978 *Handbook of the Cleveland Museum of Art* (Cleveland).
1992 *Masterpieces from East to West* (Cleveland).

Cobean, Robert H., et al.
1971 "Obsidian Trade at San Lorenzo Tenochtitlan," *Science* 174: 666–71.

Coe, Michael D.
1962 *Mexico* (New York and London).
1965a *The Jaguar's Children: Pre-Classic Central Mexico* (New York).
1965b "The Olmec Style and Its Distributions," in *Handbook of Middle American Indians: Archaeology of Southern Mesoamerica*, vol. 3, ed. Gordon R. Willey (Austin, Tex.), 739–75.
1965c "Archaeological Synthesis of Southern Veracruz and Tabasco," in *Handbook of Middle American Indians: Archaeology of Southern Mesoamerica*, vol. 3, ed. Gordon R. Willey (Austin, Tex.), 679–715.
1968 *America's First Civilization* (New York).
1972 "Olmec Jaguars and Olmec Kings," in *The Cult of the Feline*, ed. Elizabeth P. Benson (Washington, D.C.), 1–18.
1976 "The Iconology of Olmec Art," in *The Iconography of Middle American Sculpture* (New York), 1–12.
1977 "Olmec and Maya: A Study in Relationships," in *The Origins of Maya Civilization*, ed. Richard E. W. Adams (Albuquerque), 183–96.
1978 *Lords of the Underworld: Masterpieces of Classic Maya Ceramics* (Princeton, N.J.).
1989 "The Olmec Heartland: Evolution of Ideology," in *Regional Perspectives on the Olmec*, ed. Robert J. Sharer and David C. Grove (Cambridge), 68–82.

Coe, Michael D., and Richard A. Diehl
1980a *In the Land of the Olmec: The Archaeology of San Lorenzo Tenochtitlán*, vol. 1 (Austin, Tex.).
1980b *In the Land of the Olmec: The People of the River*, vol. 2 (Austin, Tex.).

Coe, Michael D., Richard A. Diehl, and Minze Stuiver
1967 "Olmec Civilization, Veracruz, Mexico: Dating of the San Lorenzo Phase," *Science* 155: 1399–1401.

Coe, Michael D., Douglas Newton, and Roy Sieber
1986 *Asian, Pacific, and Pre-Columbian Art in the Indiana University Art Museum* (Indianapolis).

Coe, William R., and Robert Struckenroth, Jr.
1964 "A Review of La Venta, Tabasco and Its Relevance to the Olmec Problem," in *Kroeber Anthropological Society Papers*, vol. 31 (Berkeley), 1–43.

Comstock, Helen
1951 "The Connoisseur in America," *Connoisseur* 127: 41.

Cortez, Constance
1986 "The Principal Bird Deity in Preclassic and Early Classic Maya Art," Master's thesis, University of Texas at Austin.

Couch, Christopher
1988 *Pre-Columbian Art from The Ernest Erikson Collection of the American Museum of Natural History* (New York).

Covarrubias, Miguel
1942 "Origen y Desarrollo del estilo artístico 'Olmeca'," in *Mayas y Olmecas: Segunda Reunión de Mesa Redonda Sobre Problemas Antropológicos de México y Centro América* (Tuxtla Gutiérrez), 46–9.
1943 "Tlatilco, Archaic Mexican Art and Culture," *DYN* 4–5: 40–46.
1946a "El arte 'Olmeca' o de La Venta," *Cuadernos Americanos* 28: 153–79.
1946b "Olmec Art or the Art of La Venta," trans. Robert Thomas Pirazzini, in *Pre-Columbian Art History: Selected Readings*, ed. Alana Cordy-Collins and Jean Stern (Palo Alto, Cal.), 1.
1957 *Indian Art of Mexico and Central America* (New York).

Crocker, Jon Christopher
1985 *Vital Souls: Bororo Cosmology, Natural Symbolism, and Shamanism* (Tucson).

Croix, Horst de la, with Richard G. Tansey and Diane Kirkpatrick
1991 *Gardener's Art through the Ages*, 9th ed. (New York).

Davis, Wade, and Andrew T. Weil
1992 "Identity of a New World Psychoactive Toad," *Ancient Mesoamerica* 3: 51–59.

Deletaille, Emile, Gerald Berjonneau, and Jean-Louis Sonnery
1985 *Rediscovered Masterpieces of Mesoamerica: Mexico-Guatemala-Honduras* (Boulogne).

Deletaille, Lin, and Emile Deletaille
1992 *Trésors du Nouveau Monde* (Brussels).

Demarest, Arthur
1989 "The Olmec and the Rise of Civilization in Eastern Mesoamerica," in *Regional Perspectives on the Olmec*, ed. Robert J. Sharer and David C. Grove (Cambridge), 303–44.

Denver Art Museum
1981 *Major Works in the Collection* (Denver).

Dickey, Thomas, Vana Muse, and Henry Weincek
1982 *The God-Kings of Mexico* (Chicago).

Diehl, Richard A.
1981 "Olmec Architecture: A Comparison of San Lorenzo and La Venta," in *The Olmec and Their Neighbors: Essays in Memory of Matthew W. Stirling*, ed. Elizabeth P. Benson (Washington, D.C.), 69–82.
1989 "Olmec Archaeology: What We Know and What We Wish We Knew," in *Regional Perspectives on the Olmec*, ed. Robert J. Sharer and David C. Grove (Cambridge), 23–26.

Dillehay, Thomas D.
1989 *Monte Verde: A Late Pleistocene Settlement in Chile* (Washington, D.C.).

Dobrizhoffer, Martin
1822 *An Account of the Abipones, an Equestrian People of Paraguay*, trans. Sara Coleridge from the Latin edition of 1784, 3 vols. (London).

Drucker, Philip
1943 "Ceramic Sequences at Tres Zapotes, Veracruz, Mexico," in *Bureau of American Ethnology*, Bulletin 140.
1952 "La Venta, Tabasco: A Study of Olmec Ceramics and Art," in *Bureau of American Ethnology*, Bulletin 153, 72–73, 157–59.
1955 "The Cerro de las Mesas Offering of Jade and Other Materials," in *Bureau of American Ethnology*, Bulletin 157.
1981 "On the Nature of Olmec Polity," in *The Olmec and Their Neighbors: Essays in Memory of Matthew W. Stirling*, ed. Elizabeth P. Benson (Washington, D.C.), 29–48.

Drucker, Philip, Robert F. Heizer, and Robert J. Squier
1959 "Excavations at La Venta, Tabasco, 1955," in *Bureau of American Ethnology*, Bulletin 170.

Drury, Nevill
1989 *The Elements of Shamanism* (Longmead, Eng.).

Dubin, Lois
1987 *History of Beads from 30,000 B.C. to the Present* (New York).

Dumbarton Oaks and the Trustees for Harvard University
1963 *Handbook of the Robert Woods Bliss Collection of Pre-Columbian Art* (Washington, D.C.).

Duran, Fray Diego
1971 *Book of Gods and Rites and the Ancient Calendar*, trans. Doris Heyden and Fernando Horcasitas (Norman, Okla.), 162–63.

Durgin, Mary Ann
1982 "Olmec Jade Celt," "Jade Corn Symbol," "Jade Ears," "Jade Burden Bearer," "Jade Iguana," "Two Jade Spoons," and "Felsite Jaguar," in *The Guennel Collection*, vol. 2 (New York).

Dursum, Brian A., and Robert Sonin
1980 *Jade East and West* (Miami).

Easby, Elizabeth Kennedy
1966 *Ancient Art of Latin America from the Collection of Jay C. Leff* (New York).

Easby, Elizabeth Kennedy, and John F. Scott
1970 *Before Cortés: Sculpture of Middle America* (New York).

Ekholm, Gordon F.
1959 "Art in Archaeology," in *Aspects of Primitive Art*, ed. Robert Redfield (New York).

Ekholm-Miller, Susanna
1973 "The Olmec Rock Carving at Xoc, Chiapas, Mexico," in *Papers of the New World Archaeological Foundation*, no. 32 (Provo, Ut.).

Eliade, Mircea
1959 *Cosmos and History: The Myth of the Eternal Return* (New York).
1970 *Shamanism: Archaic Techniques of Ecstasy*, trans. Willard R. Trask (Princeton, N.J.).

Emmerich, André
1963 *Art Before Columbus: The Art of Ancient Mexico from the Archaic Village of the Second Millenium B.C. to the Splendor of the Aztecs* (New York).

The André Emmerich Gallery and Perls Galleries
1984 *Masterpieces of Pre-Columbian Art from the Collection of Mr. and Mrs. Peter G. Wray* (New York).

Evans-Wentz, W. Y.
1981 *Cuchama and Sacred Mountains*, ed. Frank Waters and Charles L. Adams (Chicago).

Fabbri, Dino, and Nicolas J. Gibelli
1965 "El Arte en America precolombina, en Africa y Oceania," in *Arte/Rama* 9.

Fash, William
1987 "The Altar and Associated Features," in *Ancient Chalcatzingo*, ed. David C. Grove (Austin, Tex.), 82–94.

Feuchtwanger, Franz
1989 *Ceramica Olmeca* (Mexico).

Fields, Virginia M.
1982 "Political Symbolism among the Olmecs," paper prepared for a seminar, Dept. of Art History, University of Texas at Austin.
1989 "The Origins of Kingship among the Lowland Classic Maya," Ph.D. diss., University of Texas at Austin.

1991a "The Iconographic Heritage of the Maya Jester God," in *Sixth Palenque Round Table, 1986*, ed. Virginia M. Fields (Norman, Okla.), 167–74.

1991b (ed.) *Sixth Palenque Round Table 1986* (Norman, Okla.).

Flannery, Kent V.

1968 "The Olmec and the Valley of Oaxaca: A Model for Inter-regional Interaction in Formative Times," in *Dumbarton Oaks Conference on the Olmec, October 28th and 29th, 1967*, ed. Elizabeth P. Benson (Washington, D.C.), 79–110.

1976 (ed.) *The Early Mesoamerican Village* (New York).

Freidel, David A.

1986 "Terminal Classic Lowland Maya: Successes, Failures, and Aftermaths," in *Late Lowland Maya Civilization, Classic to Postclassic*, ed. Jeremy A. Sabloff and E. Wyllys Andrews, v (Albuquerque), 409–30.

Fuente, Beatríz de la

1977 *Los Hombres de Piedra: Escultura Olmeca* (Mexico).

1981 "Toward a Conception of Olmec Monumental Art," in *The Olmec and Their Neighbors: Essays in Memory of Matthew W. Stirling*, ed. Elizabeth P. Benson (Washington, D.C.).

1992 "Order and Nature in Olmec Art," in *The Ancient Americas: Art From Sacred Landscapes*, ed. Richard F. Townsend (Chicago), 121–33.

Fuente, Beatríz de la, and Nelly Gutiérrez Solana

1973 *Escultura Monumental Olmeca* (Mexico City).

Fuente, Beatríz de la, et al.

1992 *Mexico en el mundo de las colecionnes de arte 1: Mesoamerica* (Mexico City).

Furst, Jill Leslie

1978 *Codex Vindobonensis Mexicanus I: A Commentary* (Albany).

Furst, Peter T.

1967 *Selections from the Pre-Columbian Collection of Constance McCormick Fearing* (Santa Barbara, Cal.).

1968 "The Olmec Were-Jaguar Motif in the Light of Ethnographic Reality," in *Dumbarton Oaks Conference on the Olmec, October 28th and 29th, 1967*, ed. Elizabeth P. Benson (Washington, D.C.), 143–78.

1974 "Archaeological Evidence for Snuffing in Prehispanic Mesoamerica," *Botanical Museum Leaflets, Harvard University* 24 (1): 1–28.

1981 "Jaguar Baby or Toad Mother: A New Look at an Old Problem in Olmec Iconography," in *The Olmec and Their Neighbors: Essays in Memory of Matthew W. Stirling*, ed. Elizabeth P. Benson (Washington, D.C.), 149–62.

1991 "Crowns of Power: Bird and Feather Symbolism in Amazonian Shamanism," in *The Gift of Birds: Featherwork of Native South American Peoples*, ed. Ruben E. Reina and Kenneth M. Kensinger (Philadelphia), 91–109.

Garbe, Patricia Ann

1971 "The Olmec Jaguar Paw-Wing Motif: Correspondences in Associated Contexts," Master's thesis, University of Arizona.

Garber, James F., et al.

1987 "Jade Use in Portions of Mexico and Central America—A Summary," in *Precolumbian Jade: New Geological and Cultural Interpretations*, ed. Frederick W. Lange (Salt Lake City).

Gay, Carlo T. E.

1967 "Oldest Paintings in the New World," *Natural History* 76 (4): 28–35.

1971 *Chalcacingo* (Graz, Austria).

1972 *Xochipala: The Beginnings of Olmec Art* (Princeton, N.J.).

1973 "Olmec Hieroglyphic Writing," *Archaeology* 26 (4).

Girard, Rafael

1966 *Los Mayas: Su civilización, su historia, sus vinculaciones continentales* (Mexico City).

Goldman, Irving

1963 *The Cubeo, Indians of the Northwest Amazon* (Urbana, Ill.).

Goldwater, Robert, et. al

1969 *Art of Oceania, Africa, and the Americas from the Museum of Primitive Art* (New York).

Graham, John A.

1989 "Olmec Diffusion: A Sculptural View from Pacific Guatemala," in *Regional Perspectives on the Olmec*, ed. Robert J. Sharer and David C. Grove (Cambridge), 227–46.

Griffin, Gillett G.

1981 "Olmec Forms and Materials Found in Central Guerrero," in *The Olmec and Their Neighbors: Essays in Memory of Matthew W. Stirling*, ed. Elizabeth P. Benson (Washington, D.C.), 209–22.

Grim, John A.

1983 *The Shaman: Patterns of Religious Healing among the Ojibway Indians* (Norman, Okla.).

Grove, David C.

1968 "Chalcatzingo, Morelos, Mexico: A Reappraisal of the Olmec Rock Carvings," *American Antiquity* 33 (4): 486–91.

1970 "The Olmec Paintings of Oxtotitlan Cave, Guerrero, Mexico," in *Studies in Pre-Columbian Art and Archaeology*, no. 6 (Washington, D.C.), 1–32.

1973 "Olmec Altars and Myths," *Archaeology* 26: 128–35.

1981 "Olmec Monuments: Mutilation as a Clue to Meaning," in *The Olmec and Their Neighbors : Essays in Memory of Matthew W. Stirling*, ed. Elizabeth P. Benson (Washington, D.C.).

1984 *Chalcatzingo: Excavations on the Olmec Frontier* (New York and London).

1987a (ed.) *Ancient Chalcatzingo* (Austin, Tex.).

1987b "Ground Stone Artifacts," in *Ancient Chalcatzingo*, ed. David C. Grove (Austin, Tex.).

1987c "'Torches,' 'Knuckledusters,' and the Legitimization of Formative Period Rulership," *Mexicon* 9 (3): 60–65.

1989a "Olmec: What's in a Name?" in *Regional Perspectives on the Olmec*, ed. Robert J. Sharer and David C. Grove (Cambridge), 8–14.

1989b "Chalcatzingo and Its Olmec Connection," in *Regional Perspectives on the Olmec*, ed. Robert J. Sharer and David C. Grove (Cambridge), 122–47.

1992 "The Olmec Legacy: Updating Olmec Prehistory," *National Geographic Research and Exploration* 8 (2): 148–65.

1993 "'Olmec' Horizons in Formative Period Mesoamerica: Diffusion or Social Evolution?," in *Latin American Horizons*, ed. Donald S. Rice (Washington, D.C.), 83–112.

Grove, David C., and Jorge Angulo V.

1987 "Catalog and Description of the Monuments," in *Ancient Chalcatzingo*, ed. David C. Grove (Austin, Tex.).

Grove, David C., and Susan D. Gillespie

1992a "Ideology and Evolution at the Pre-State Level, Formative Period Mesoamerica," in *Ideology and Pre-Columbian Civilizations*, ed. Arthur A. Demarest and Geoffrey W. Conrad (Santa Fe), 15–36.

Grove, David C., and Ann Cyphers Guillén

1987 "The Excavations," in *Ancient Chalcatzingo*, ed. David C. Grove (Austin, Tex.).

Grove, David C., and Louise I. Paradis

1971 "An Olmec Stela from San Miguel Amuco, Guerrero," *American Antiquity* 36 (1): 95–102.

Grube, Nikolai

1992 "Classic Maya Dance: Evidence from Hieroglyphics and Iconography," *Ancient Mesoamerica* 3: 201–18.

Guillén, Ann Cyphers

1993a "Investigaciones Arqueológicas Recientes en San Lorenzo Tenochtitlán, Veracruz: 1990–1992," in *Anales de Antropológicas* (Mexico City).

1993b "From Stone to Symbols: Olmec Art in Social Context at San Lorenzo Tenochtitlan," paper delivered at Dumbarton Oaks, Washington, D.C., Oct. 10.

1994 "Three New Olmec Sculptures from Southern Veracruz," *Mexicon* 16: 30–32.

Hammond, Norman

1991 "Cultura Hermana: Reappraising the Olmec," *Quarterly Review of Archaeology* 9: 1–4.

Harbottle, Garman, and Phil C. Weigand

1992 "Turquoise in Pre-Columbian America," *Scientific American* 266: 78–85.

Heizer, Robert F.

1968 "New Observations on La Venta," in *Dumbarton Oaks Conference on the Olmec, October 28th and 29th, 1967*, ed. Elizabeth Benson (Washington, D.C.), 9–40.

Heizer, Robert F., John A. Graham, and Lewis K. Napton

1968 "The 1968 Investigations at La Venta," in *Contributions of the University of California Archaeological Research Facility*, no. 5 (Berkeley), 127–203.

Helms, Mary W.

1979 *Craft and the Kingly Ideal: Art, Trade and Power* (Austin, Tex.).

Hirth, Kenneth G.

1984 (ed.) *Trade and Exchange in Early Mesoamerica* (Albuquerque).

Hirth, Kenneth G., and Susan Grant Hirth

1993 "Ancient Currency: The Style and Use of Jade and Marble Carvings in Central Honduras," in *Pre-Columbian Jade: New Geological and Cultural Interpretations*, ed. Frederick W. Lange (Salt Lake City), 186–87.

Hissink, Karin, and Albert Hahn

1961 *Die Tacana: Ergebnisse der Frobenius-Expedition nach Bolivien 1952 bis 1954: Erzählungsgut*, vol. 1 (Stuttgart).

Houston, Stephen, and David Stuart

1989 "The *Way* Glyph: Evidence for 'Co-Essences' among the Classic Maya," in *Research Reports on Ancient Maya Writing*, no. 30 (Washington, D.C.).

1990 "T632 as *muyal*, 'Cloud'," in *Central Tennessean Notes in Maya Epigraphy*, no. 1, note circulated by authors.

Hugh-Jones, Stephen

1974 "Barasana Initiation: Male Initiation and Cosmology among the Barasana Indians of the Vaupés Area of Colombia," Ph.D. diss., Cambridge University.

Hurtado, E. Dávalos
1965   *Teme de Antropologia Fisica* (Mexico City).
Jansen, Maarten E. R. G. N.
1983   *Huisi Tacu, estudio interpretativo de un libro mixteca antiguo: Codex Vindobonensis Mexicanus I* (Amsterdam).
Jones, Julie
1969   *Pre-Columbian Art in New York: Selections from Private Collections* (New York).
Joralemon, Peter David
1971   "A Study of Olmec Iconography," in *Studies in Pre-Columbian Art and Archaeology,* no. 7 (Washington, D.C.), 35.
1976   "The Olmec Dragon: A Study in Pre-Columbian Iconography," in *Origins of Religious Art and Iconography in Preclassic Mesoamerica*, ed. Henry B. Nicholson (Los Angeles), 27–71.
1981   "The Old Woman and the Child: Themes in the Iconography of Preclassic Mesoamerica," in *The Olmec and Their Neighbors: Essays in Memory of Matthew W. Stirling*, ed. Elizabeth P. Benson (Washington, D.C.).
Jou, Tsung Hwa
1981   *The Tao of Tai-Chi Chuan: Way to Rejuvenation* (Warwick, N.Y.), 112–13, 141–42.
Joyce, Rosemary, et al.
1991   "Olmec Bloodletting: An Iconographic Study," in *Sixth Palenque Round Table, 1986,* ed. Virginia M. Fields (Norman, Okla.), 143–50.
Justeson, John S., and Terrence Kaufman
1993   "A Decipherment of Epi-Olmec Hieroglyphic Writing," *Science* 259 (5102): 1703–11.
Justeson, John S., and Peter Matthews
1990   "Evolutionary Trends in Mesoamerican Hieroglyphic Writing," *Visible Language* 24 (1).
Karsten, Rafael
1964   "Studies in the Religion of South American Indians East of the Andes," in *Societas Scientarium Fennica, Commentationes humanarum litterarum,* ed. Arne Runeberg and Michael Webster, vol. 29 (Helsinki).
Kelemen, Pál
1969   *Medieval American Art: Masterpieces of the New World Before Columbus*, 3d. ed. (New York).
Kitagawa, Joseph W.
1966   *Religion in Japanese History* (New York), 3–45.
Koch-Grünberg, Theodor
1909   *Zwei Jahre unter den Indianern: Reisen in Nordwest-Brasilien 1903/1905*, vol. 2 (Berlin).
Koontz, Rex
1993   "Aspects of Founding Central Places in Post-classic Mesoamerica," in *Cosmology and Natural Modeling Among Aboriginal American Peoples* (Austin, Tex.).
Krotser, Paula
1980   "Potters in the Land of the Olmec," in *In the Land of the Olmec: The People of the River*, vol. 2, ed. Michael D. Coe and Richard A. Diehl (Austin, Tex.).
Landa, Fray Diego de
1937   *Diego de Landa's Yucatan Before and After the Conquest*, trans. William Gates (New York), 76.
Lange, Frederick W.
1987   (ed.) *Precolumbian Jade: New Geological and Cultural Interpretations* (Salt Lake City).

Lauck, Rebecca Gonzalez
1988   "Proyecto arqueológica La Venta," *Arqueológica* 4:121–65.
1989   "Recientes investigaciones en La Venta, Tabasco," in *El Preclasico o formativo: avances y perspectivas*, ed. Martha Carmone Macías (Mexico), 81–90.
Lathrap, Donald W.
1971   "The Tropical Forest and the Cultural Context of Chavín," in *Dumbarton Oaks Conference on Chavín*, ed. Elizabeth P. Benson (Washington, D.C.), 73–100.
Layton, Robert
1981   *The Anthropology of Art* (New York).
Lennox, William Gordon, and Margaret A. Lennox
1960   *Epilepsy and Related Disorders*, vol. 1 (Boston and Toronto).
León-Portilla, Miguel
1963   *Aztec Thought and Culture* (Norman, Okla.).
1987   "The Ethnohistorical Record for the Huey Teocalli of Tenochtitlan," in *The Aztec Templo Mayor*, ed. Elizabeth Boone (Washington, D.C.).
Linduff, Kathryn M.
1974   *Ancient Art of Middle America* (Huntington, W. Va.).
Lines, Jorge
1942   "Dos nuevas Gemas en la arqueologia de Costa Rica," in *Proceedings of the Eighth American Scientific Congress: Anthropological Sciences*, no. 2: 117–222.
1964   *Costa Rica: Land of Exciting Archaeology* (San José, Costa Rica).
Linné, Sigvald
1956   *Tresures of Ancient Mexico,* trans. Albert Read (Stockholm), 50–51.
Lommel, Andreas
1967   *Shamanism, the Beginnings of Art* (London and New York).
Looper, Mathew G.
1994   "Observations on the Morphology of Sprouts in Olmec Art," in *Notes on Precolumbian Art, Writing, and Culture*, no. 58 (Austin, Tex.).
López-Austin, Alfredo
1988   *The Human Body and Ideology: Concepts of the Ancient Nahuas*, trans. Thelma Ortiz de Montellano and Bernard Ortiz de Montellano (Salt Lake City).
1993   "El Arbol cosmico en las tradición Mesoamericana," *iichiko intercultural*, no. 5: 47–66.
Lothrop, Samuel K.
1929   "Further Notes on Indian Ceremonies in Guatemala," *Indian Notes* 6: 1–25.
1964   *Treasures of Ancient America* (Cleveland).
Lothrop, Samuel K., and Gordon F. Ekholm
1975   "Pre-Columbian Objects," in *The Guennol Collection*, vol. 1., ed. Ida Ely Rubin (New York), 307.
Lothrop, Samuel K., et al.
1961   *Essays in Pre-Columbian Art and Archaeology* (Cambridge, Mass.).
Lothrop, Samuel K., William F. Foshag, and Joy Mahler
1957   *The Robert Woods Bliss Collection of Pre-Columbian Art* (London).
Lowe, Gareth W.
1989   "The Heartland Olmec: Evolution of Material Culture," in *Regional Perspectives on the Olmec*, ed. Robert J. Sharer and David C. Grove (Cambridge), 33–67.
Lumholtz, Carl
1900   *Symbolism of the Huichol Indians* (New York).

Macías, Martha Carmona
1989   (ed.) *El Preclasico o Fromativo: avances y perspectivas* (Mexico City).
McNear, Everett
1982   *High Culture in the Americas Before 1500* (Chicago).
MacNeish, Richard S.
1981   "Tehuacan's Accomplishments," in *Supplement to the Handbook of Middle American Indians: Archaeology*, ed. Jeremy A. Sabloff with the assistance of Patricia A. Andrews, vol. 1 (Austin, Tex.), 31–41.
MacNeish, Richard S., et al.
1972   *The Prehistory of The Tehuacan Valley Excavations and Reconnaissance*, vol. 5 (Austin, Tex.).
Marcus, Joyce
1989   "Zapotec Chiefdoms and the Nature of Formative Religions," in *Regional Perspectives on the Olmec*, ed. Robert J. Sharer and David C. Grove (Cambridge), 148–97.
Martin, Alastair
1975   "Pardon a Hunter," in *The Guennol Collection*, vol. 1, ed. Ida Ely Rubin (New York), *xv–xvii*.
Medellín-Zenil, Alfonso
1965   "La Escultura de las Limas," in *Boletín del Instituto Nacional de Antropología y Historia*, vol. 21.
1968   "El Dios Jaguar de San Martin," in *Boletín del Instituto Nacional de Antropología y Historia* 33: 9–16.
Meltzer, David J.
1993   "Coming to America," *Discover* 14 (10): 90–97.
The Merrin Gallery
1971   *Works of Art from Pre-Columbian Mexico and Guatemala* (New York).
Merry de Morales, Marcia
1987   "Chalcatzingo Burials as Indicators of Social Ranking," in *Ancient Chalcatzingo*, ed. David C. Grove (Austin, Tex.), 95–114.
Mesulam, M-Marsel
1981   "Dissociative States with Abnormal Temporal Lobe EEG: Multiple Personality and the Illusion of Possession," *Arch Neurology* 38.
The Metropolitan Museum of Art
1973   *Masterworks from the Museum of the American Indian Foundation* (New York).
Milbrath, Susan
1979   "A Study of Olmec Sculptural Chronology," in *Studies in Pre-Columbian Art and Archaeology*, no. 23 (Washington, D.C.).
Miller, Mary Ellen
1989   "The Ballgame," *Record of The Art Museum, Princeton University* 48 (2): 22–31.
1991   "Pre-Hispanic Jade," *Latin American Art* (Spring).
Miller, Mary Ellen, and Karl A. Taube
1993   *The Gods and Symbols of Ancient Mexico and the Maya: An Illustrated Dictionary of Mesoamerican Religion* (London and New York).
Milliken, William M.
1946   *Art of the Americas Picture Book Number Two* (Cleveland).
Monaghan, John
1989   "The Feathered Serpent in Oaxaca," *Expedition* 31: 12–18.
Moreno, Wigberto Jimenez
1966   "Mesoamerica before the Toltecs," in *Ancient Oaxaca: Discoveries in Mexican Archaeology and History*, ed. John Paddock (Stanford, Cal.).

Nicholson, Henry B.

1976   (ed.) *Origins of Religious Art and Iconography in Preclassic Mesoamerica* (Los Angeles).

Niederberger Betton, Christine

1987   *Paleopaysages et archeologie pre-urbaine du Bassin de Mexico*, 2 vols., bk. 2 (Mexico City).

Nimuendajú, Curt

1914   "Die Sagen von der Erschaffung und Vernichtung der Welt als Grundlage der Religion der Apapopúva-Guarani," *Zeitschrift für Ethnologie* 46: 284–403.

1948   "Tribes of the Lower and Middle Xingú River," in *Handbook of South American Indians: Archaeology of Southern Mesoamerica*, vol. 3, ed. Gordon R. Willey (Washington, D.C.), 213–43.

Norman, Garth V.

1976   *Izapa Sculpture: Text*, vols. 1 and 2, *Papers of the New World Archaeological Foundation*, no. 30 (Provo, Ut.).

Oakland, Amy

1982   "Teotihuacan: The Blood Complex at Atetelco," paper delivered at the seminar, "The Transition from Preclassic to Classic Times," University of Texas at Austin.

Ortiz, Ponciano

1975   "La cerámica de los Tuxtlas," professional thesis, University of Veracruz.

Ortiz, Ponciano, and María del Carmen Rodríguez

1989   "Proyecto Manatí 1989," *Arqueología* 1: 23–52.

1993   "Olmec Ceremonial Behavior Seen in the Offerings of El Manati," paper delivered at the Pre-Columbian Symposium at Dumbarton Oaks, Washington, D.C.

Ortiz, Ponciano, María del Carmen Rodríguez, and Paul Schmidt

1988   "El Proyecto Manatí, Temporada 1988: Informe Preliminar," *Arqueología* 3:141–54.

Park, Willard Z.

1938   "Shamanism in Western North America: A Study in Cultural Relationships," in *Northwestern University Studies in the Social Sciences*, no. 2 (Evanston and Chicago).

Parsons, Lee Allen

1980   *Pre-Columbian Art: The Morton D. May and The Saint Louis Art Museum Collections* (Saint Louis).

1986   "The Origins of Maya Art: Monumental Stone Sculpture of Kaminaljuyu, Guatemala, and the Southern Pacific Coast," in *Studies in Pre-Columbian Art and Archaeology*, no. 28 (Washington, D.C.).

Parsons, Lee Allen, John B. Carlson, and Peter David Joralemon

1988   *The Face of Ancient America: The Wally and Brenda Zollman Collection of Precolumbian Art* (Indianapolis).

Parsons, Mark

1982   "Three Thematic Complexes in the Art of Teotihuacan," paper delivered at a seminar, "The Transition from Preclassic to Classic Times," at the University of Texas at Austin.

Pasztory, Esther

1976   *The Murals of Tepantitla, Teotihuacan* (New York).

1982   "Shamanism and North American Indian Art," in *Native North American Art History: Selected Readings*, ed. Zena P. Mathews and Aldona Jonaitis (Palo Alto, Cal.), 7–30.

Peabody Museum and the William Hayes Fogg Art Museum, Harvard University

1940   *An Exhibition of Pre-Columbian Art* (Cambridge, Mass.).

Persinger, Michael A.

1983   "Religious and Mystical Experiences as Artifacts of Temporal Lobe Function: A General Hypothesis," *Perceptual and Motor Skills* 57: 1255–62.

Pickands, Martin

1986   "The Hero Myth in Maya Folklore," in *Symbol and Meaning Beyond the Closed Community: Essays in Mesoamerican Ideas*, ed. Gary H. Gossen (Albany, N.Y.), 101–24.

Pijoan, José

1946   *Arte Precolombiano, Mexicano, y Maya* (Madrid).

Piña Chán, Román

1958   *Tlatilco: A través de su cerámica* (Mexico City).

1977   *Quetzalcóatl: Serpiente emplumada* (Mexico City).

1989   *The Olmec: Mother Culture of Mesoamerica* (New York).

Piña Chán, Román, and Luis Covarrubias

1964   *El Pueblo del jaguar* (Mexico City).

Plog, Stephen

1976   "Measurement of Prehistoric Interaction between Communities," in *The Early Mesoamerican Village*, ed. Kent V. Flannery (New York), 255–72.

Pohorilenko, Anatole

1977   "On the Question of Olmec Deities," *Journal of New World Archaeology* 2 (1): 1–16.

1981   "The Olmec Style and Costa Rican Archaeology," in *The Olmec and Their Neighbors: Essays in Memory of Matthew W. Stirling*, ed. Elizabeth P. Benson (Washington, D.C.), 309–27.

Porter, Muriel Noé

1953   "Tlatilco and the Pre-Classic Cultures of the New World," in *Viking Fund Publications in Anthropology*, no. 19 (New York).

Powell, Jane

1960   *Ancient Art of the Americas* (New York).

Preuss, Konrad Theodor

1921   *Die Religion und Mythologie der Witoto. Textaufnahmen und Beobachtungen bei einem Indianerstamm in Kolumbien, Südamerika*, vol. 1 (Göttingen).

Price, Lorna

1988   *Masterpieces from the Los Angeles County Museum of Art* (Los Angeles).

Princeton University, The Art Museum

1977   *Record of The Art Museum, Princeton University* 36 (1).

1983   *Record of The Art Museum, Princeton University* 42 (1).

1986   *Selections from The Art Museum, Princeton University* (Princeton, N.J.).

1988   *Record of The Art Museum, Princeton University* 47 (1).

1989   *Record of The Art Museum, Princeton University* 48 (2).

1992   *Record of The Art Museum, Princeton University* 51 (1).

1993   *Record of The Art Museum, Princeton University* 52 (1).

1994   *Record of The Art Museum, Princeton University* 53 (1).

Pugh, Marion Stirling

1981   "An Intimate View of Archaeological Exploration," in *The Olmec and Their Neighbors: Essays in Memory of Matthew W. Stirling*, ed. Elizabeth P. Benson (Washington, D.C.), 1–15.

Pyne, Nanette

1976   "The Fire-Serpent and Were-Jaguar in Formative Oaxaca: A Contingency Table Analysis," in *The Early*

Mesoamerican Village, ed. Kent V. Flannery (New York), 273.

Quirarte, Jacinto

1976   "The Relationship of Izapan-Style Art to Olmec and Maya Art: A Review," in *Origins of Religious Art and Iconography in Preclassic Mesoamerica*, ed. Henry B. Nicholson (Los Angeles), 73–86.

1981   "Tricephalic Units in Olmec, Izapan-Style, and Maya Art," in *The Olmec and Their Neighbors: Essays in Memory of Matthew W. Stirling*, ed. Elizabeth P. Benson (Washington, D.C.), 289–308.

Rands, Robert L.

1965   "Jades of the Maya Lowlands," in *Handbook of Middle American Indians, Archaeology of Southern Mesoamerica*, vol. 3, ed. Gordon R. Willey (Austin, Tex.).

Reents-Budet, Dorie

1982   "Pre-classic Development in the Valley of Teotihuacan, and Teotihuacan and Maya Contacts as Evidenced in the Maya Iconographic Programs," paper delivered at the seminar, "The Transition from Preclassic to Classic Times," University of Texas at Austin.

Reichel-Dolmatoff, Gerardo

1961   "Anthropomorphic Figurines from Colombia, Their Magic and Art," in Samuel K. Lothrop, et al., *Essays in Pre-Columbian Art and Archaeology* (Cambridge, Mass.), 229–41.

1971   *Amazonian Cosmos* (Chicago).

1975   *The Shaman and the Jaguar: A Study of Narcotic Drugs among the Indians of Colombia* (Philadelphia).

1988   *Goldwork and Shamanism: An Iconographic Study of the Gold Museum* (Medellín, Colombia).

Reilly, F. Kent, III

1987   "The Ecological Origins of Olmec Symbols of Rulership," Master's thesis, University of Texas at Austin.

1989a   "The Shaman in Transformation Pose: A Study of the Theme of Rulership in Olmec Art," *Record of The Art Museum, Princeton University* 48 (2): 4–21.

1990   "Cosmos and Rulership: The Function of Olmec-Style Symbols in Formative Period Mesoamerica," *Visible Language* 24 (1): 12–37.

1991   "Olmec Iconographic Influences on the Symbols of Maya Rulership: An Examination of Possible Sources," in *Sixth Palenque Round Table, 1986*, ed. Virginia M. Fields (Norman, Okla.), 151–74.

1994a   "Visions to Another World: Art, Shamanism, and Political Power in Middle Formative Mesoamerica," Ph.D. diss., University of Texas at Austin.

1994b   "Enclosed Ritual Space and the Watery Underworld in Formative Period Architecture: New Observations on the Function of La Venta Complex A," in *Seventh Palenque Round Table, 1989*, ed. Merle Green Robertson (San Francisco).

1994c   "The Lazy S: Evidence for a Formative Period Iconographic Loan to Maya Hieroglyphic Writing," in *Seventh Palenque Round Table, 1989*, ed. Merle Green Robertson.

Robiscek, Francis

1983   "Of Olmec Babies and Were-Jaguars," *Mexicon* 5 (1): 7–19.

Roe, Peter G.

1982   *The Cosmic Zygote: Cosmology in the Amazon Basin* (New Brunswick, N.J.).

Roland, Alan

1989   *In Search of Self in India and Japan: Toward a Cross-Cultural Psychology* (Princeton, N.J.).

Roys, Ralph L.

1933   *The Book of Chilam Balam of Chumayel* (Washington, D.C.).

Rubin, Ida Ely

1975   (ed.) *The Guennol Collection* (New York).

Rueda, Hernando Gomez

1989   "Nuevas exploraciones en la region Olmeca; una aproxamación a los patrones de asentamiento," in *El Preclasico o formativo: avances y perspectivas*, ed. Martha Carmona Macías (Mexico City), 91–100.

1991   "Territorios y Asentamientos en la Region Olmeca: hacia un modelo de distribución de población," *Trace* 20: 60–67.

Rust, William F., III

1992   "New Ceremonial and Settlement Evidence at La Venta, and Its Relation to Preclassic Maya Cultures," in *New Theories of Ancient Maya*, ed. Elin C. Danien and Robert J. Sharer (Philadelphia), 123–29.

Rust, William F., III, and Barbara Leyden

1992   "Evidence of Maize Use at Early and Middle Preclassic La Venta Olmec Sites," in *Corn and Culture in the Prehistoric New World*, ed. Sissel Johannessen and Christine A Hastorf (Boulder, Col.), 181–201.

Rust, William F., III, and Robert J. Sharer

1988   "Olmec Settlement Data from La Venta, Tabasco, Mexico," *Science* 242: 102–4.

Sabloff, Jeremy A.

1981   (ed.) *Supplement to the Handbook of Middle American Indians, Archaeology*, vols. 1 and 2, with the assistance of Patricia A. Andrews (Austin, Tex.).

Sabloff, Jeremy A., and E. Wyllys Andrews, v

1986   (ed.) *Late Lowland Maya Civilization, Classic to Postclassic* (Albuquerque).

Sahagún, Fray Bernardino de

1950   *Florentine Codex: General History of the Things of New Spain*, trans. Arthur J. O. Anderson and Charles E. Dibble, pt. 11 (Santa Fe).

Sands, Harry (ed.)

1982   *Epilepsy: A Handbook for the Mental Health Professional* (New York).

Santley, Robert S.

1983   "Obsidian Trade and Teotihuacan Influence in Mesoamerica," in *Highland-Lowland Interaction in Mesoamerican: Interdisciplinary Approaches*, ed. Arthur G. Miller (Washington, D.C.), 69–124.

Saville, Marshall H.

1900   "A Votive Axe of Jadeite from Mexico," *Monumental Records* 1: 138–40.

Schaffer, Anne-Louise

1991   "The Maya 'Posture of Royal Ease,'" in *Sixth Palenque Round Table, 1986*, ed. Virginia M. Fields (Norman, Okla.), 203–16.

Schele, Linda

1992a   *Workbook for the XVIth Maya Hieroglyphic Workshop at Texas, with Commentaries on the Group of the Cross at Palenque* (Austin, Tex.).

1992b   "Sprouts and the Early Symbolism of Rulers in Mesoamerica," paper delivered at *Die Welt den Maya*, Hildesheim, Germany.

Schele, Linda, and David Freidel

1990   *A Forest of Kings: The Untold Story of the Ancient Maya* (New York).

Schele, Linda, David Freidel, and Joy Parker

1993   *Maya Cosmos: Three Thousand Years Down the Shaman's Path* (New York).

Schele, Linda, and Mary Ellen Miller

1986   *The Blood of Kings: Dynasty and Ritual in Maya Art* (Fort Worth).

Schele, Linda, David Stuart, and Nikolai Grube

1991   "A Commentary on the Inscriptions of Structure 10L-22A at Copan," in *Copán Note* 98 (Honduras).

Schnell, Anton

1989   "An Olmec Group of Sculptures at El Azuzul," *Mexicon* 11 (6): 106–07.

Schoenhals, Alvin, and Louise Schoenhals

1965   *Vocabulario Mixe de Totontepec* (Mexico City).

Schultze Jena, Leonhard

1933   *Leben, Glaube und Sprache de Quiché von Guatemala* (Jena, Germany).

Seler, Eduard E.

1923   *Gesammelte Abhandlungen zur Amerikanischen Sprach-und Alterthumskunde*, vol. 4 (Berlin).

Sharer, Robert J., and David C. Grove

1989   (eds.) *Regional Perspectives on the Olmec* (Cambridge).

Smith, Bradley

1968   *Mexico: A History in Art* (New York).

Sommerville, Maxwell

1889   *Engraved Gems: Their History and Place in Art* (Philadelphia).

Sotheby Parke Bernet, Inc.

1981   *The Bogousslavsky Collection of Pre-Colombian Art* (New York).

Soustelle, Georges

1959   *Trésors d'art précolombien* (Paris).

Soustelle, Jacques

1979   *Les Olmeques: La plus ancienne civilization du mexique* (Paris).

Spinden, Herbert J.

1947   "An Olmec Jewel," *Brooklyn Museum*, Bulletin 9 (1): 1–12.

1957   *Maya Art and Civilization* (Indian Hills, Col.).

Spratling, William

1964   *Escultura Precolombina de Guerrero* (Mexico City).

Stark, Barbara L.

1981   "The Rise of Sedentary Life," in *Supplement to the Handbook of Middle American Indians: Archaeology*, vol. 2, ed. Jeremy A. Sabloff, with the assistance of Patricia A. Andrews (Austin, Tex.), 345–72.

1986   "Origins of Food Production in the New World," in *American Archaeology, Past and Future, A Celebration of the Society for American Archaeology 1935–1985*, ed. David J. Meltzer, Don D. Fowler, and Jeremy A. Sabloff (Washington, D.C.), 277–321.

Stevenson, Matilda C.

1904   "The Zuni Indians: Their Mythology, Esoteric Fraternities, and Ceremonies," in *23rd Annual Report of the Bureau of American Ethnology for the Years 1901–1902* (Washington, D.C.).

Stirling, Matthew W.

1943   "Stone Monuments of Southern Mexico," in *Bureau of American Ethnology*, Bulletin 138.

1955   "Stone Monuments of the Río Chiquito, Veracruz, Mexico," in *Bureau of American Ethnology*, Bulletin 157, 1–23.

1965   "Monumental Sculpture of Southern Veracruz and Tabasco," in *Handbook of Middle American Indians: Archaeology of Southern Mesoamerica*, vol. 3, ed. Gordon R. Willey (Austin, Tex.), 716–38.

1966   "Aboriginal Jade Use in the New World," in *Proceedings of the 37th International Congress of Americanists*, vol. 4 (Buenos Aires), 22.

1968   "Early History of the Olmec Problem," in *Dumbarton Oaks Conference on the Olmec*, ed. Elizabeth P. Benson (Washington, D.C.), 1–8.

Stirling, Matthew W., and Marion Stirling

1942   "Finding Jewels of Jade in a Mexican Swamp," *National Geographic Magazine* 82 (5): 635–61.

Stocker, Terrence L., and Michael W. Spence

1973   "Trilobal Eccentrics at Teotihuacan and Tula," *American Antiquity* 38: 195–99.

Stone, Doris

1957   "The Archaeology of Central Southern Honduras," in *Papers of the Peabody Museum* 49, no. 3.

Stross, Brian

1989   "Olmec Vessel with a Crayfish Icon: An Early Rebus," in *Word and Image in Maya Culture*, ed. William F. Hanks and Donald S. Rice (Salt Lake City).

1991   "Mesoamerican Writing at the Crossroads: The Late Formative Period," *Visible Language* 29 (1): 38–61.

1992   "Maize and Blood," *Res* 22: 93.

Stuart, David

1984   "Blood Symbolism in Maya Iconography," in *Maya Iconography*, ed. Elizabeth P. Benson and Gillett G. Griffin (Princeton, N.J.), 175–221.

1987   "Ten Phonetic Syllables," in *Research Reports on Ancient Maya Writing*, no. 14 (Washington, D.C.).

1990   "A New Carved Panel from the Palenque Area," in *Research Reports on Ancient Maya Writing*, no. 32 (Washington, D.C.).

Tate, Carolyn E.

1992   *Yaxchilan: The Design of a Maya Ceremonial City* (Austin, Tex.).

1993   "The Shaman's Stance: Mind, Body, and Cosmos in Olmec Sculpture," paper delivered at the Eighth Palenque Round Table, 1993 (in press).

Taube, Karl A.

1984   "The Teotihuacán Spider Woman," *Journal of Latin American Lore* 9: 107–89.

1986   "The Teotihuacan Cave of Origin: The Iconography and Architecture of Emergence Mythology in Mesoamerica and the American Southwest," in *Res* 12: 51–83.

1989a   "Ritual Humor in Classic Maya Religion," in *World and Image in Maya Culture*, ed. William Hanks and Donald S. Rice, 351–82.

1989b   "*Itzam Cab Ain*: Caimans, Cosmology, and Calendrics in Postclassic Yucatan," in *Research Reports on Ancient Maya Writing*, no. 26 (Washington, D.C.).

1992a   "The Major Gods of Yucatán," in *Studies in Pre-Columbian Art and Archaeology*, no. 32 (Washington, D.C.), 17–27.

1992b   "The Temple of Quetzalcoatl and the Cult of Sacred War at Teotihuacan," *Res* 22: 53–87.

1995   "The Olmec Maize God: The Face of Corn in Formative and Late Preclassic Mesoamerica," paper delivered at the Thirteenth Annual Maya Weekend, Philadelphia.

Tedlock, Dennis
1985   *Popol Vuh: The Definitive Edition of the Mayan Book of the Dawn of Life and the Glories of God and Kings* (New York).

Temkin, Owsei
1970   *The Falling Sickness: A History of Epilepsy from the Greeks to the Beginnings of Modern Neurology*, 2d ed., rev. (Baltimore and London).

Thompson, J. Eric S.
1941   "Dating of Certain Inscriptions of Non-Maya Origin," in *Carnegie Institution of Washington: Theoretical Approaches to Problems,* vol. 1 (Washington, D.C.).
1970   *Maya History and Religion* (Norman, Okla.).

Thomson, Charlotte
1971   *Ancient Art of the Americas from New England Collections* (Boston).
1987   "Chalcatzingo Jade and Fine Stone Objects," in *Ancient Chalcatzingo*, ed. David C. Grove (Austin, Tex.), 295–304.

Tolstoy, Paul
1978   "Western Mesoamerica before A.D. 900," in *Chronologies in New World Archaeology*, ed. Royal Ervin Taylor and Clement W. Meighan (New York), 275–302.
1990   "Western Mesoamerica and the Olmec," in *Regional Perspectives on the Olmec*, ed. Robert J. Sharer and David C. Grove (Cambridge), 275–302.

Toro, Miguel Alvarez del
1982   *Los Reptiles de Chiapas,* 3d. ed. (Tuxtla Gutierrez), 211–12.

Townsend, Richard F.
1979   "State and Cosmos in the Arch of Tenochtitlan," in *Studies in Pre-Columbian Art and Archaeology,* no. 20 (Washington, D.C.).

1992   (ed.) *The Ancient Americas: Art From Sacred Landscapes* (Chicago).

Tozzer, Alfred M.
1941   "Landa's Relacion de las Cosas de Yucatan," in *Papers of the Peabody Museum of American Archaeology*, vol. 18 (Cambridge, Mass.).

Vaillant, George C.
1932   "A Pre-Columbian Jade," *Natural History* 32: 512–20, 556–58.

Vaillant, Susannah B., and George C. Vaillant
1934   "Excavations at Gualupita," in *Anthropological Papers of the American Museum of Natural History*, vol. 35, pt. 1 (New York).

Valadez, Susana Eger
1995   "Wolf Power and Inter-Species Communication," in *People of the Peyote: Huichol History, Religion and Survival*, ed. Stacy B. Schaefer and Peter T. Furst (Albuquerque).

Valdés, Juan Antonio
1989   "El Grupo H de Uaxactún: evidencias de un centro de poder durante el Preclásico Temprano," in *Memorias el Segunda Coloquio International de Mayistas,* vol. 1, (Mexico City), 603–24.

Van der Marck, Jan
1984   *In Quest of Excellence: Civic Pride, Patronage, Connoisseurship* (Miami).

Vásquez, Alfredo Barrera
1980   (ed.) *Diccionario Maya Cordemex: Maya-Español, Español-Maya* (Mérida).

Vega, Fray Francisco Nuñez de la
1988   "Constituciones diocesanas de obispado de Chiapa," in *Fuentes para el estudio de la cultura Maya*, no. 6 (Mexico City).

Vishnudevananda, Swami
1972   *The Complete Illustrated Book of Yoga* (New York).

Wadsworth Atheneum
1958   *Wadsworth Atheneum Handbook* (Hartford).

Walter, Heinz
1956   "Der Jaguar in der Vorstellungswelt der südamerikanischen Naturvölkern," Ph.D. diss., University of Hamburg.

Warman, Arturo, and Cristina Sanchez de Bonfil
1967   *Olmecas, Zapotecas, and Mixtecos* (Mexico City).

Weaver, Muriel Porter
1972   *The Aztecs, Maya and Their Predecessors* (New York).

Weiant, Clarence Wolsey
1943   "An Introduction to the Ceramics of Tres Zapotes, Mexico," in *Bureau of American Ethnology,* Bulletin 139.

Wilbert, Johannes
1972   "Tobacco and Shamanistic Ecstasy among the Warao Indians of Venezuela," in *Flesh of the Gods: The Ritual Use of Hallucinogens*, ed. Peter T. Furst (New York), 55–83.

Willey, Gordon R.
1965   (ed.) *Handbook of Middle American Indians, Archaeology of Southern Mesoamerica*, vol. 3 (Austin, Tex.)

Winning, Hasso von
1968   *Pre-Columbian Art of Mexico and Central America* (New York).

Zara, Louis
1969   *Jade* (New York).

Zengel, Marjorie Smith, et al.
1968   *The Art of Ancient and Modern Latin America* (New Orleans).

Zerries, Otto
1962   "Die Vorstellung vom Zweiten Ich und die Rolle der Harpyre in der Kultur der Naturvölker Süd Amerikas," trans. Peter T. Furst, *Anthropos* 57: 889–914.

Index

343